Why You Need This New Edition

See the Future of Group Communication Studies with *Working in Groups*, Fifth Edition

Since its first edition in 1997, *Working in Groups* has led the study of group communication by introducing new topics, new features, and new skills. The Fifth Edition of *Working in Groups* continues to innovate while retaining its intellectual rigor, practical focus, and commitment to engaging student learning.

New! A **full-color design** and **dynamic visual program** will help engage contemporary, visual learners.

New! **Original *Case Studies*** appear in every chapter, accompanied by case-related questions based on chapter content. A ***Critical Thinking about the Case Study*** feature at the end of each chapter revisits the case study and connects it to broader issues by asking critical thinking questions. Several of the case studies are also featured in the book's accompanying ***Video Scenarios***.

New! ***Theory in Groups* features** in every chapter—in addition to theory-rich chapter content—highlight key theories that illuminate how we behave and work in groups and why.

New! ***Groups in Balance* features** apply communication strategies to balancing the contradictory forces inherent in all group work.

An **unsurpassed treatment of virtual groups and technology**, including related ***Virtual Groups*** features in every chapter, helps students apply group theory, methods, and skills to the work of virtual groups.

An enhanced **civic engagement focus** provides revised examples, illustrations, photographs, and case studies that emphasize the role of groups in communities and civic associations.

A revised and expanded **group dialectics** approach—emphasizing the book's continuing theme of ***balance***—better explains how group members balance and negotiate the opposing, or ***dialectic***, tensions they encounter while working together to achieve a common goal.

An **expanded Group Diversity chapter** goes beyond culture and gender to include generational and religious dimensions.

Fifth Edition

Working in Groups

Communication Principles and Strategies

Isa N. Engleberg
Prince George's Community College

Dianna R. Wynn
Nash Community College

Allyn & Bacon

Boston • New York • San Francisco
Mexico City • Montreal • Toronto • London • Madrid • Munich • Paris
Hong Kong • Singapore • Tokyo • Cape Town • Sydney

Acquisitions Editor: Jeanne Zalesky
Series Editorial Assistant: Megan Lentz
Production Editor: Claudine Bellanton
Editorial Production Service: Publisher's Design and Production Service, Inc.
Manufacturing Buyer: JoAnne Sweeney
Electronic Composition: Publisher's Design and Production Service, Inc.
Interior Design: Ellen Pettengell
Photo Researcher: Katharine S. Cebik
Cover Administrator: Joel Gendron

For related titles and support materials, visit our online catalog at www.pearsonhighered.com.

Credits appear on page 384, which constitutes an extension of the copyright page.

Library of Congress Cataloging-in-Publication Data
Engleberg, Isa N.
Working in groups / Isa N. Engleberg, Dianna R. Wynn. — 5th ed.
p. cm.
Includes bibliographical references and index.
ISBN-13: 978-0-205-65882-4 (alk. paper)
ISBN-10: 0-205-65882-2 (alk. paper)
1. Group relations training. 2. Small groups 3. Communication in small groups.
I. Wynn, Dianna. II. Title.
HM1086.E53 2010
302'.14—dc22 2008056057

10 9 8 7 6 5 4 3 2 1 WEB 13 12 11 10 09

Allyn & Bacon
is an imprint of

www.pearsonhighered.com

ISBN 10: 0-205-65882-2
ISBN 13: 978-0-205-65882-4

Contents

2 Group Development 28

3 Group Membership 51

4 Group Diversity 76

5 Group Leadership 107

6 Group Motivation 137

7 Verbal and Nonverbal Communication in Groups 162

8 Listening in Groups 186

9 Conflict and Cohesion in Groups 210

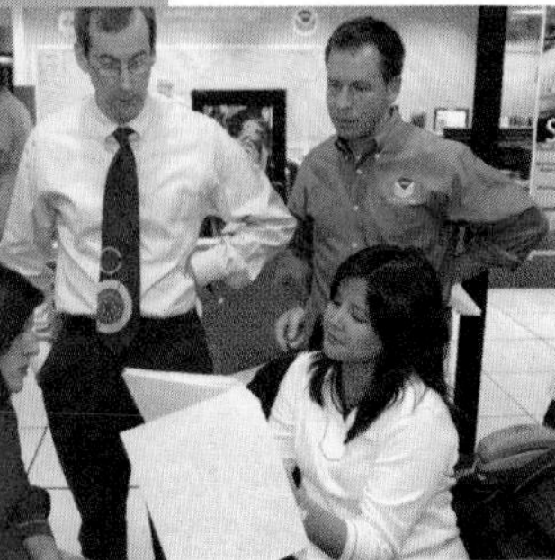

10 Structured and Creative Problem Solving in Groups 235

11 Critical Thinking and Argumentation in Groups 267

12 Planning and Conducting Meetings 292

13 *Making Presentations in Groups* 313

14 Technology and Virtual Groups 337

Glossary 365

Index 377

Web Chapter: Parliamentary Procedure 1

available at www.pearsonhighered.com

Preface

One central question has always guided our research and writing for *Working in Groups*:

What do college students enrolled in a group communication course *really* need to know?

We use two criteria to help us answer this question. First, we include both classic and current theories of group communication that focus on "how groups work." Second, we include practical information on group communication strategies and skills that emphasize "how to work in groups." These criteria help us select and balance the amount and types of theory and skills appropriate for a college course in group communication.

Unified Perspective: Balance and Group Dialectics

Beginning with the first edition of *Working in Groups*, we have used the concept of **balance** as a central metaphor. A group that reaches a decision or completes a task is not in balance if group members end up disliking or mistrusting one another. A group that relies on two or three members to do all the work is not in balance. Effective groups balance factors such as task and social functions, individual and group needs, and leadership and followership. Achieving balance requires an understanding of the contradictory forces that operate in all groups.

The previous edition of *Working in Groups* further developed the balance metaphor by introducing the concept of **group dialectics**—the interplay of opposing or contradictory forces inherent in group work. A dialectic approach examines how group members negotiate and resolve the tensions and pressures they encounter while working together to achieve a common goal. In this edition, we use contemporary theories and new research to enhance the nine group dialectics that characterize the delicate balance achieved by effective groups.

Group Dialectics

Individual Goals	◀▶	**Group Goals**
Conflict	◀▶	**Cohesion**
Conforming	◀▶	**Nonconforming**
Task Dimensions	◀▶	**Social Dimensions**
Homogeneous	◀▶	**Heterogeneous**
Leadership	◀▶	**Followership**
Structure	◀▶	**Spontaneity**
Engaged	◀▶	**Disengaged**
Open System	◀▶	**Closed System**

Comprehensive Topic Coverage

The fifth edition of *Working in Groups* strengthens the textbook's scholarship and applicability. Before reading further, flip through the detailed table of contents to get a feel for the depth and breadth of topic coverage. We include **classic and traditional group communication** subject matter, such as

- Group Development
- Member Diversity
- Group Climate
- Working in Virtual Groups
- Structured and Creative Decision Making and Problem Solving
- Group Norms and Roles
- Leadership Theories and Power
- Group Cohesiveness and Conflict
- Meetings and Agendas
- Oral Presentations in Groups

We also include **cutting-edge topics** such as

- Group Dialectics and Balance
- "Team Talk" Strategies and Skills
- Communication Apprehension in Groups
- Group Goal Setting
- Effective Argumentation in Groups
- Motivating and Rewarding Group Members
- Linking Listening Skills and Group Roles
- Leadership and Decision-Making Models

We also provide comprehensive coverage of relevant and somewhat unique topics. Detailed descriptions follow.

Group Diversity

Chapter 4, Group Diversity, addresses many different kinds of diversity—including traditional topics such as cultural, gender, and generational diversity, as well as religious diversity, personality types, and other factors that affect how diverse group members work with one another. Groups that know how to balance and benefit from member diversity have the power to create a collaborative climate that enhances group excellence and teamwork.

Communication Apprehension in Groups

Because so many people experience some level of communication apprehension, we devote significant attention in Chapter 3, Group Membership, to this topic and to member assertiveness in terms of how they affect group processes and member confidence—how they greatly impact members' productivity and satisfaction.

Technology in Groups

In addition to Chapter 14, Technology and Virtual Groups, *every* chapter in this edition includes a **Virtual Groups** feature. Both Chapter 14 and the in-chapter Virtual Groups features apply group theory, methods, and skills to the work of virtual groups.

We have updated and revised Chapter 14 in several ways. We have added research comparing the effectiveness of face-to-face (FTF) and computer-mediated communication (CMC) environments. In addition, we have enhanced our discussion of audioconferences, videoconferences, textconferences, electronic meeting systems, and the use of email, bulletin boards, blogs, and wikis to do group work. Most important, we provide clear guidelines for group member participation when using each of type of technology as well as criteria for deciding which technology best suits group and member needs and abilities.

Group Motivation

Chapter 6, Group Motivation, emphasizes that although effective communication is an absolute prerequisite for group success, it does not necessarily guarantee that the group will achieve a common goal or that the group experience will satisfy members' needs and expectations. In addition to effective goal setting (see Chapter 2, Group Development), member *motivation* is necessary to focus and fuel group performance.

Verbal and Nonverbal Behavior in Groups

Chapter 7, Verbal and Nonverbal Communication in Groups, addresses how these two essential factors affect group communication by focusing on the *roles of* and *relationship between* verbal and nonverbal communication. *Working in Groups* offers unique coverage on how the nature of *team talk* affects group effectiveness, as well as guidelines for using effective team talk to improve group productivity and member satisfaction. Moreover, we apply verbal and nonverbal communication concepts directly to *group* contexts and discuss the influence of culture on how we speak and behave.

Listening in Groups

An entire chapter is devoted to the unique challenge of listening in a group setting, including how to improve listening by capitalizing on the relationship between listening abilities and member roles. Chapter 8, Listening in Groups, links listening to group-specific topics such as note taking in meetings, self-listening during discussions, adapting to differences in members' listening styles, and listening in virtual groups. Two valuable applications are worthy of special mention: (1) How can group members enlist different types of listening (comprehensive, empathic, analytical, and appreciative) to achieve group goals? (2) How do members' listening abilities and types of listening skills relate to the wide variety of group roles?

Critical Thinking and Argumentation in Groups

We wrote Chapter 11, Critical Thinking and Argumentation in Groups, to help group members advance their own viewpoints and to analyze the viewpoints of others. Effective critical thinking and argumentation help a group understand and analyze ideas, persuade members, make informed and critical decisions, and achieve its goal.

Parliamentary Procedure

The vast majority of professional organizations, community associations, corporate boards, and government agencies specify in their constitution or bylaws that their groups must use parliamentary procedure to conduct official meetings. Most students belong to or will belong to groups that use parliamentary procedure to govern discussion and debate. Our Web Chapter, Parliamentary Procedure, explains why and how to learn the basic rules of this complex, highly principled, and proven decision-making system. For those not using the Web Chapter, we devote a brief section of Chapter 12, Planning and Conducting Meetings, to the basic principles of parliamentary procedure.

Pedagogical Features

The Fifth Edition of *Working in Groups* includes several features that link the theories of group communication (how groups work) with communication strategies and skills (how to work in groups). Five of these features are new: **Study Questions, Case Studies, Groups in Balance, Theory in Groups,** and **Critical Thinking about the Case Study**. In this edition we have also restored the end-of-chapter **Summary Study Guide** that appeared in earlier editions.

New Feature: Study Questions

Every chapter begins with a set of text-specific **Study Questions** paired with a chapter outline that links chapter headings to each question. The Study Questions and outline serve as a chapter preview.

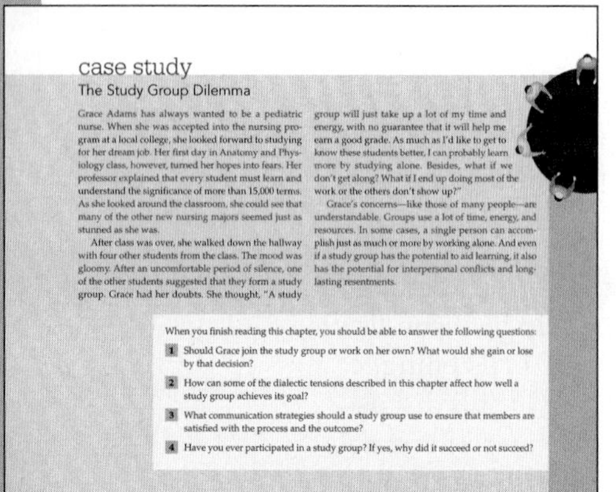

case study

The Study Group Dilemma

Grace Adams has always wanted to be a pediatric nurse. When she was accepted into the nursing program at a local college, she looked forward to studying for her dream job. Her first day in Anatomy and Physiology class, however, turned her hopes into fears. Her professor explained that every student must learn and understand the significance of more than 15,000 terms. As she looked around the classroom, she could see that many of the other new nursing majors seemed just as stunned as she was.

After class was over, she walked down the hallway with four other students from the class. The mood was gloomy. After an uncomfortable period of silence, one of the other students suggested that they form a study group. Grace had her doubts. She thought, "A study group will just take up a lot of my time and energy, with no guarantee that it will help me earn a good grade. As much as I'd like to get to know these students better, I can probably learn more by studying alone. Besides, what if we don't get along? What if I end up doing most of the work or the others don't show up?"

Grace's concerns—like those of many people—are understandable. Groups use a lot of time, energy, and resources. In some cases, a single person can accomplish just as much or more by working alone. And even if a study group has the potential to aid learning, it also has the potential for interpersonal conflicts and long-lasting resentments.

When you finish reading this chapter, you should be able to answer the following questions:

1. Should Grace join the study group or work on her own? What would she gain or lose by that decision?
2. How can some of the dialectic tensions described in this chapter affect how well a study group achieves its goal?
3. What communication strategies should a study group use to ensure that members are satisfied with the process and the outcome?
4. Have you ever participated in a study group? If yes, why did it succeed or not succeed?

New Feature: Case Studies and Critical-Thinking Questions

The Fifth Edition of *Working in Groups* provides a relevant **case study** near the beginning of every chapter, followed by questions students should be able to answer after reading the chapter. Our case studies tell stories about people working in groups who face the challenge of making decisions or solving problems. For three of the case studies, we use the situations portrayed in the *Working in Groups* Video Scenarios available upon request through your Pearson Allyn & Bacon sales representative. The case studies give students information but do not supply answers. Nor do they imply or lead to a single or correct answer. Rather, they ask students to apply what they learn in the chapter to select what they believe is an appropriate response. Each case study is revisited at the end of its chapter in **Critical Thinking about the Case Study**. After reading the chapter, students are asked to answer critical questions about the case study in relation to the chapter material.

Examples of **Case Studies**

The Study Group Dilemma: Is it worth the time, effort, and potential frustration to form and work with other students in a study group?

Monday Morning Blues: How do you cope with or help a group that meets every two weeks on Monday afternoons even when there's no reason to have a meeting?

The Leader in Sheep's Clothing: What do you do when the public face of your boss is gentle as a lamb, but his private demeanor is rough and ruthless?

How to Sink the Mayflower: When the powers-that-be are stacked against your committee and its important proposal, how do you win the day?

Sociology in Trouble: How can conflicts be resolved when faculty members in an academic department won't agree on courses for an upcoming semester?

Virtual Misunderstanding: If you can't meet with members face to face, how do you get everyone to work efficiently and effectively in a virtual group?

New Feature: Groups in Balance

The new **Groups in Balance** feature highlights group dialectics and the need to balance the contradictory forces inherent in all group work. The feature also examines the ways in which groups negotiate and resolve a variety of tensions.

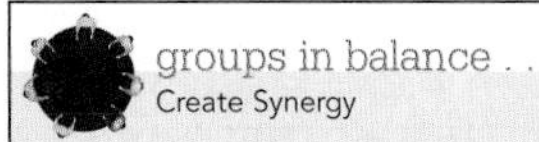

When three or more interdependent group members interact and work toward a common goal, they have the potential to create a synergistic system. **Synergy** is a term that describes the cooperative interaction of several factors that results in a combined effect greater than the total of all individual contributions. In other words, the whole is greater than the sum of its individual parts. The term *synergy* comes from the Greek word *synergos*, meaning "working together." Synergy does not occur when people work alone; it occurs only when people work together.

Effective groups are synergistic. Baseball teams without superstars have won the World Series. Companies whose executives earn modest salaries have surpassed those companies in which the CEOs are paid millions of dollars. Ordinary groups have achieved extraordinary results. Synergy occurs when the knowledge, talents, and dedication of group members merge into a force that surpasses anything group members could have produced without cooperative interaction.

Examples of **Groups in Balance Features**

Empower Members	Curb Compulsive Talkers
Let Members Save Face	Encourage Questions
Change Norms as Needed	Motivate Apathetic Members
Know When to Apologize	Avoid Analysis Paralysis

New Feature: Theory in Groups

Every chapter of *Working in Groups* includes significant theories and research that explain why and how we behave and work in groups. We also emphasize in Chapter 1 that theories, methods, and tools are inseparable components of effective groups. Throughout this edition, we use the new **Theory in Groups** feature to highlight particular theories that focus on why groups succeed or fail and how the strategies and skills in this book can enhance group effectiveness.

theory in groups
Systems Theory

Systems Theory, also known as the Systems Perspective, is not a single theory, but a group of theories that examine how interdependent factors affect one another. In communication studies, Systems Theory recognizes that "communication does not take place in isolation, but rather necessitates a communication system."[1] Although there are many approaches to studying systems, several characteristics emerge as common to most systems:[2]

- *Systems function in a particular environment in which they receive input and produce output.* A computer system relies on input in order to produce output.
- *System components are interdependent.* The contamination of one skin cell can lead to the contamination of many cells.
- *Systems have a purpose or goal.* The digestive system converts food into fuel for the body.
- *Systems are unpredictable.* There are usually multiple ways to achieve a goal in most systems. When a company is losing money, there are many options for solving the problem.
- *Systems try to maintain balance in their environment.* When an ecosystem is invaded by unwelcome intruders, native organisms may defend their territory or move to a less hostile environment in order to restore equilibrium and harmony.

[1]John A. Courtright, "Relational Communication: As Viewed from the Pragmatic Perspective," in *Explaining Communication: Contemporary Theories and Exemplars*, ed. Bryan B. Whaley and Wendy Samter (Mahwah, NJ: Lawrence Erlbaum Associates, 2007), p. 313.

[2]For additional information on systems theory, see Marianne Dainton and Elaine D. Zelley, *Applying Communication Theory for Professional Life* (Thousand Oaks, CA: Sage, 2005), pp. 51–54; Eric M. Eisenberg and H. L. Goodall, Jr., *Organizational Communication: Balancing Creativity and Constraint*, 4th ed. (Boston: Bedford/St. Martin's, 2004), pp. 92–116; Dominic A. Infante, Andrew S. Rancer, and Deanna F. Womack, *Building Communication Theory*, 4th ed. (Prospect Heights, IL: Waveland, 2003), pp. 66–74.

Examples of **Theory in Groups Features**

Systems Theory	Group Development Theories
Muted Group Theory	Emotional Intelligence
Functional Leadership Theory	Aristotle's Ethos
Expectancy-Value Theory of Motivation	Listening and Working Memory Theory

Ethics in Groups

Every chapter includes an **Ethics in Groups** feature that examines the many ethical issues that frequently arise when interdependent members interact to achieve a group goal.

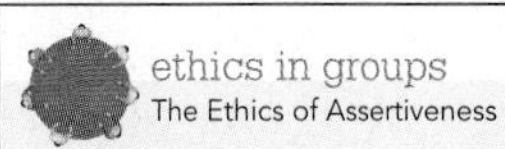

Psychologists Robert Alberti and Michael Emmons call attention to the fact that the principle of assertive action is embedded in our culture and even addressed in the U.S. Constitution.[1] Americans enjoy the constitutional rights of free speech, free press, and the right to peaceably assemble in the furtherance of asserting their convictions. Assertive communication is often culturally accepted, but in some instances it may also be an ethical expectation.

The National Communication Association's Credo for Ethical Communication calls for a commitment to the "courageous expression of personal conviction in pursuit of fairness and justice."[2] Ethical group members have an obligation to assert themselves, not only to pursue their own goals, but to prevent unjust or unethical group action. For instance, the members of a medical team must have the courage to speak up if they believe that a patient is being given the wrong medication. Whether your group is deciding how to trim a budget, determining the best candidate to hire, or developing a marketing campaign, each group member has the ethical responsibility to act assertively in expressing opposition to group decisions that are potentially unethical.

[1] Robert Alberti and Michael Emmons, *Your Perfect Right*, 8th ed. (Atascadero, CA: Impact, 2001), p. 222.

[2] The complete credo is available on the National Communication Association website at www.natcom.org/policies/External/EthicalComm.htm.

Examples of **Ethics in Groups Features**

The NCA Credo for Ethical Communication
The Ethics of Assertiveness
Leadership Integrity
Self-Centered Roles and Listening
The Morality of Creative Outcomes
Ethical Arguments in Groups
Using Power and Punishment
Ten Commandments for Computer Ethics

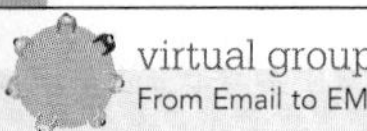

virtual groups
From Email to EMS

Instead of meeting face to face, many groups interact virtually. A **virtual group** uses technology to communicate synchronously and/or asynchronously, often across time, distance, and organizational boundaries. **Synchronous communication** occurs simultaneously and in real time. Audioconferences, videoconferences, textconferences, and electronic meeting systems (EMS) allow for synchronous interaction. **Asynchronous communication** is electronic communication that does not occur simultaneously or in real time. Messages sent via email, voice mail, and electronic bulletin boards are asynchronous.

In their analysis of virtual groups, Deborah Duarte and Nancy Snyder point out that because virtual communication has become the way in which many companies do business, "understanding how to work in or lead a virtual team is now a fundamental requirement for people in many organizations. . . . Organizations that do not use virtual teams effectively may be fighting an uphill battle in a global, competitive, and rapidly changing environment."[1] Jon Katzenbach and Douglas Smith further observe that "today, organizations are no longer confined to team efforts that assemble people from the same location or the same time zone. Indeed, small groups of people from two or more locations and time zones routinely convene for collaborative purposes."[2]

Virtual groups are complex. Members may come from different organizations, cultures, time zones, and geographic locations—not to mention that they interact via technology. As a result, virtual groups develop a different group dynamic from those meeting face to face.[3] Chapter 14, Technology and Virtual Groups, discusses the unique issues these groups face. In addition, every chapter provides advice on adapting to the virtual group environment.

[1]Deborah L. Duarte and Nancy Tennant Snyder, *Mastering Virtual Teams: Strategies, Tools, and Techniques That Succeed*, 3rd ed. (San Francisco: Jossey-Bass, 2006), p. 4.

[2]Jon R. Katzenbach and Douglas K. Smith, *The Discipline of Teams: A Mindbook-Workbook for Delivering Small Group Performance* (New York: John Wiley & Sons, 2001), p. 23.

[3]Susan B. Barnes, *Online Connections: Internet Interpersonal Relationships* (Cresskill, NJ: Hampton Press, 2001), p. 41.

Virtual Groups

In each chapter, the **Virtual Groups** feature guides readers in the use of technology to help achieve group goals in face-to-face settings as well as in virtual groups.

Examples of **Virtual Groups Features**

From Email to EMS
Cultural Diversity in Cyberspace
Developmental Tasks
Sharing Leadership Functions
Mediated Motivation
Think Critically about the Internet

summary study guide

Succeeding in Groups

- Working in groups is an inescapable part of life; most people spend a considerable amount of time and energy working in groups.
- Surveyed employers view group-related skills as more important than written communication skills, proficiency in the field of study, and computer skills.

Defining Group Communication

- Group communication is the interaction of three or more interdependent people working to achieve a common goal.
- Group interaction requires communication among group members who use verbal and nonverbal messages to generate meanings and establish relationships within a group context.
- The most significant factor separating successful groups from unsuccessful ones is having a clear understanding of the group's common goal.
- Public groups communicate to and for the benefit of an audience. Four types of public groups are panel discussions, symposiums, forums, and governance groups.
- Virtual groups rely on technology to communicate synchronously and/or asynchronously.

Advantages and Disadvantages of Working in Groups

- Six advantages of working in groups include improved performance, member satisfaction, learning, cultural sensitivity, creative thinking, and civic engagement.
- The disadvantages of working in groups include the amount of time, energy, and resources expended by groups and the interpersonal conflicts and people problems that may arise.
- Understanding and applying theories, methods, and tools are inseparable components in learning about the group communication process.

Summary Study Guide

At the end of every chapter, a **Summary Study Guide** reviews the major concepts covered in that chapter. Any reader able to explain and provide examples of the summary statements in each guide should have an excellent understanding of the chapter and its content.

group work It Was the Best of Groups; It Was the Worst of Groups

Directions: Think about two groups to which you now belong or have belonged. One should be the "best of groups," that is, a group that is or was highly successful and/or personally satisfying. The other should be the "worst of groups"—one that is or was unsuccessful, disappointing, and/or frustrating. Identify at least three characteristics that were unique to the best group and three that were unique to the worst group. Fill in the following table with your answer. If possible, identify five characteristics for each type of group.

THE BEST OF GROUPS	THE WORST OF GROUPS
Example: One member kept track of everyone's birthday. On the meeting day closest to our birthday, we got a card signed by everyone and shared a cake or cookies.	*Example:* The head of the group refused to explain his decisions. When we'd ask why we could or couldn't do something, he'd say, "Because I said so."
1.	
2.	
3.	
4.	
5.	

Group Work

The **Group Work** feature at the end of every chapter provides a group-based exercise designed to demonstrate, illustrate, or practice a principle covered in the chapter. In addition to including more class activities, the *Instructor's Manual* gives directions for expanding Group Work into interactive collaborative exercises.

Examples of **Group Work Features**

Classroom Norms
The Least-Preferred Co-Worker Scale
What Is Your Decision-Making Style?
Disrupting Disruptive Behavior
The Engagement Index
Practice Paraphrasing

Group Assessment

The end of every chapter includes a **Group Assessment** feature for evaluating student and group understanding of textbook concepts or mastery of skills. Other assessment instruments are provided in the *Instructor's Manual.*

Examples of **Group Assessment Features**

Group Diversity Awareness Questionnaire	Ross-DeWine Conflict Management Message Styles Inventory
Are You Ready to Lead?	Problem-Solving Competencies
Group Motivational Inventory	Post-Meeting Report (PMR) Form

group assessment Essential Group Elements

Directions: Group communication includes five basic elements: (1) group size, (2) interaction, (3) a common goal, (4) interdependence, and (5) working. Think about the groups you belong to or a group that has just formed in your class or at work. Answer the following questions to assess the extent to which your group contains the basic group elements. If you can answer *yes* to most of the questions, your group is likely to succeed.

Essential Elements of Group Communication

Group Size	**Yes**	**No**	**Sometimes**
1. Do group members communicate with one another directly?	☐	☐	☐
2. Does the group have enough people to achieve its goal?	☐	☐	☐
3. Can the group function effectively without forming subgroups?	☐	☐	☐
Interaction			
1. Do group members communicate with one another easily and frequently?	☐	☐	☐
2. Do members send, receive, and respond to messages in a way that enhances communication?	☐	☐	☐
Common Goal			
1. Does the group have a clear goal?	☐	☐	☐
2. Do members understand and support the group's goal?	☐	☐	☐
Interdependence			
1. Do members feel responsible for the group's actions?	☐	☐	☐
2. Do members understand their individual and group responsibilities?	☐	☐	☐
3. Do members believe that "we're all in this together"?	☐	☐	☐
Working			
1. Are members ready, willing, and able to participate as active group members?	☐	☐	☐
2. Do members give the time and energy needed to achieve the group's goal?	☐	☐	☐

Key Terms and Glossary

Key terms lists have been added to each chapter, and a large glossary at the back of the book includes every term or phrase defined in the textbook. Words, phrases, and the names of theories printed in **bold** are defined within chapters as well as in the glossary.

key terms

ad hoc committee 12
asynchronous communication 14
channel 8
civic group 12
committee 12
conflict ↔ cohesion 18
conforming ↔ nonconforming 18
context 9
dialectics 18
engaged ↔ disengaged 18
ethics 22
feedback 8
forum 13
governance group 13
group communication 4
Group Dialectics 17
heterogeneous group 20
homogeneous group 20
homogeneous ↔ heterogeneous 18
individual goals ↔ group goals 18
interaction 6
interdependence 7
leadership ↔ followership 18
learning group 12
member 8
method 17
noise 9
open system ↔ closed system 18
panel discussion 13
primary group 12
public group 11
Relational Dialectics Theory 19
self-help group 12
service group 12
social dimension 20
social group 12
standing committee 12
structure ↔
symposium 13
synchronous communication 14
synergy 11
system 10
Systems Theory 9
task dimension 20
task dimension ↔ social dimension 18
task force 12
theory 17
tool 17
virtual group 14
work group 11
work team 12

Glossary

abdicrat A group member whose need for control is not met; an abdicrat is submissive and avoids responsibility.

abstract words A word that refers to an idea or concept that cannot be perceived by your five senses.

accent The sound of one language imposed on another language.

Accommodation Conflict Style An approach to conflict in which a person gives in to other group members, even at the expense of his or her own goals.

Achievement Norm A norm that determines the quality and quantity of work expected from group members.

action item An item in the written minutes of a meeting that identifies the member responsible for an assigned task.

***ad hoc* committee** A committee that is formed for a specific purpose and disbands once it has completed its assignment or task.

***ad hominem* attack** The fallacy of making an irrele-

aggressor A group member who puts down other members to get what she or he wants (a self-centered role).

analysis paralysis A situation in which group members become so fixated on seeking more information and on analyzing an issue or problem that they are reluctant or unable to make a decision.

analytical listening A type of listening that focuses on evaluating and forming opinions about a message.

antecedent phase The first phase of new member socialization in which the newcomer's beliefs and attitudes, culture, traits, and prior experiences are identified.

anticipatory phase The second phase of new member socialization in which group members determine if a newcomer meets the group's expectations in terms of characteristics and motives.

apathy The indifference that occurs when members do not consider the group or its goal to be impor-

Working in Groups Video Scenarios

The *Working in Groups* Video Scenarios, available on DVD through your Pearson Allyn & Bacon representative, offer original case studies that highlight important group communication principles and strategies. Instructors can use these videos to supplement classroom lectures and discussions, as the basis for exam questions, or as cases for analysis in student papers. Video case studies include the following scenarios:

- *Planning a Playground.* A group of community residents meets for the first time to discuss raising funds for a neighborhood playground. (This case study is included in Chapter 2 as *Nice to Meet You, Too.*)
- *The Politics of Sociology.* Members of a college's sociology department discuss possible course offerings for the next semester. (This case study is included in Chapter 9 as *Sociology in Trouble.*)
- *Helping Annie.* A school nurse has called a meeting with a psychiatrist and a social worker to discuss the best treatment plan for Annie, a high school student with possible depression and an eating disorder.
- *Virtual Misunderstanding.* A project manager has organized a conference call with an offsite staff writer and designer to discuss a missed deadline for their sales brochure. (This case study is included in Chapter 14 as *Virtual Misunderstanding.*)

Supplements Package

Instructor's Manual

The *Instructor's Manual* is text-specific, comprehensive, easily used, *and* written by the textbook authors. The manual includes course information and sample syllabi, chapter-by-chapter classroom activities, and assignments with matched assessment instruments. Supplementing these items are a *Group Communication Resource Library* and discussion questions to accompany the *Working in Groups* Video Scenarios.

The *Instructor's Manual* includes the following resources:

- An introduction to group communication studies and pedagogy
- Sample syllabi
- Ready-to-use group assignments
- Ready-to-use assessment instruments
- Service Learning assignment and assessment instruments
- Chapter-by-chapter activities with accompanying teaching tips
- An instructor's resource library
- A guide to using the *Working in Groups* Video Scenarios

Test Bank

Also written by the textbook authors, the Test Bank contains multiple-choice, true/false, and essay questions for each chapter. Test questions are referenced by difficulty level to assist with question selection.

MyTest Computerized Test Bank

The printed test bank that accompanies this textbook is also available in a new electronic format. The user-friendly, Web-based interface enables instructors to view, edit, and add questions; transfer questions into tests; and print tests from any computer with Internet access. Search and sort features allow instructors to locate questions quickly and arrange them in their preferred order. Available online at www.pearsonmytest.com (access code required).

MyCommunicationKit

MyCommunicationKit is an electronic supplement that offers book-specific learning objectives, chapter summaries, flashcards, and practice tests as well as video clips and activities to aid student learning and comprehension. Also included in MyCommunicationKit are Research Navigator and Web links that give you access to powerful and reliable research material. Available at www.MyCommunicationKit.com (access code required).

Research Navigator

Pearson's Research Navigator is the easiest way for students to start a research assignment or research paper. This password-protected website provides extensive help with the research process and access to four exclusive databases of credible and reliable source material: the EBSCO Academic Journal and Abstract Database, "Best of the Web" Link Library, and *Financial Times* Article Archive and Company Financials. Available at www.ResearchNavigator.com (access code required).

A&B Small-Group Communication Video Library

This small-group communication collection presents video case studies of groups working in diverse contexts and highlights key concepts of communication, including group problem solving, leadership roles, diversity, power, conflict, virtual group communication, and more. Contact your Pearson Allyn & Bacon sales representative for details.

A&B Small-Group Communication Study Site

This website, prepared by Rita Rahio-Gilchrest of Winona State University, features small-group communication study materials, including flashcards and a complete set of practice tests (with multiple choice, true/false, and essay questions) for all major topics. Access this site at www.absmallgroups.com.

Acknowledgments

At the top of our list of acknowledgments and thank-yous is Karon Bowers, Editor-in-Chief for Communication Studies at Allyn & Bacon. Karon's professionalism, good will, and marketing savvy have made our experience with a new publisher secure and satisfying. We also thank our diligent and patient team of editors and directors: Jeanne Zalesky, acquisitions editor; Brenda Hadenfeldt, development editor; Claudine Bellanton, production editor; Denise Botelho, project manager; Suzan Czajkowski, marketing manager. We extend heartfelt thanks to Jerry Higgins, our always-dependable sales representative and loyal friend who correctly predicted that someday we'd become Allyn & Bacon authors.

In preparing the fifth edition of *Working in Groups,* we are particularly indebted to the students and faculty members who have shared their opinions and provided valuable suggestions and insights about the textbook. They are the measure of all things.

We are particularly grateful to the following conscientious reviewers, whose excellent suggestions and comments enriched this edition of *Working in Groups:*

Todd Allen, Geneva College
Diane Auten, Allan Hancock College
Susan S. Easton
Ann D. Fannin
Dennis S. Gouran, Penn State University
Heather L. Hill
Nancy Hoar, Western New England College
Bernadette Kapocias, Southwestern Oregon Community College
Roxane Sutherland, Clark College

Isa Engleberg and Dianna Wynn

About the Authors

Isa Engleberg, professor *emerita* at Prince George's Community College in Maryland, is a past president of the National Communication Association. In addition to writing five college textbooks in communication studies and publishing more than three dozen articles in academic journals, she earned the Outstanding Community College Educator Award from the National Communication Association and the President's Medal from Prince George's Community College for outstanding teaching, scholarship, and service. Her professional career spans appointments at all levels of higher education as well as teaching abroad.

Dianna Wynn is a professor at Nash Community College in North Carolina. Previously she taught at Midland College in Texas and Prince George's Community College in Maryland, where she was chosen by students as the Outstanding Teacher of the Year. She has co-authored two communication textbooks and written articles in academic journals. In addition to teaching, she has many years of experience as a trial consultant, assisting attorneys in developing effective communication strategies for the courtroom.

chapter 1

Introduction to Group Communication

chapter outline

Succeeding in Groups

Defining Group Communication
Three or More Members • Interaction • Common Goal • Interdependence • Working

The Nature of Group Communication
The Group Communication Process • Groups as Systems

Types of Groups

Advantages and Disadvantages of Working in Groups
Advantages • Disadvantages

Balance: The Guiding Principle of Group Work
Group Dialectics • Ethics and Group Communication

study questions

Why is learning to work in groups important?

What makes group communication different from interaction in crowds or gatherings of people?

What makes groups work?

How do groups differ in terms of their goals and membership?

In what ways do the advantages of working in groups outweigh the disadvantages?

How does a both/and approach help resolve dialectic tensions in groups?

Succeeding in Groups

The New York Giants were not supposed to win the 2008 Super Bowl. The New England Patriots—with an undefeated season—were supposed to win it all. But they didn't. When the Super Bowl dust settled and the triumphant Giants went home with their championship trophy, the sportscasters began to dissect the game. What had happened? The Patriots had super players, a megastar quarterback, a legendary coach, and a perfect season. Yet, with a 10–6 record, the Giants became the first wild card team to win a Super Bowl. The Giants also demonstrated the power of groups to engage the right combination of talent and willpower to overcome all odds.

The power of groups is not just a sports phenomenon. A few hours after hearing that he had won the 2003 Nobel Prize in Chemistry, Dr. Peter Agre stepped up to a microphone at the Johns Hopkins University School of Medicine and made a startling announcement: "I didn't do this work." Agre said that he didn't deserve all the credit for his discovery of aquaporins, proteins that regulate the flow of water in all living cells. The real work, he stressed, was done by the young researchers in his laboratory, who put in long hours each day. "I made the coffee and sharpened the pencils," he said.

Dr. Agre's colleagues were not misled by his humility: Even the researcher's scientific rivals agreed that he earned the honor. But Agre's remarks highlight an important point about group work. In an age when most scientific breakthroughs are the result of many people working together for many years, who should get the credit? Today's scientific discoveries are rarely made by lone geniuses locked in their laboratories. Rather, collaborative, cross-disciplinary research is much more common.[1]

Study groups, research groups, management teams, volunteer groups, sports teams, and everyday work groups are just what their names imply: organized groups or teams of people working together to achieve a shared goal. In all of these groups, "members work with one another to achieve their goals: they don't just get on with their jobs and leave other people to get on with theirs."[2]

With a 10–6 record, the 2008 New York Giants became the first wild card team to win a Super Bowl. How did the Giants exemplify the definition of group communication: the interaction of three or more interdependent members working to achieve a common goal?

case study

The Study Group Dilemma

Grace Adams has always wanted to be a pediatric nurse. When she was accepted into the nursing program at a local college, she looked forward to studying for her dream job. Her first day in Anatomy and Physiology class, however, turned her hopes into fears. Her professor explained that every student must learn and understand the significance of more than 15,000 terms. As she looked around the classroom, she could see that many of the other new nursing majors seemed just as stunned as she was.

After class was over, she walked down the hallway with four other students from the class. The mood was gloomy. After an uncomfortable period of silence, one of the other students suggested that they form a study group. Grace had her doubts. She thought, "A study group will just take up a lot of my time and energy, with no guarantee that it will help me earn a good grade. As much as I'd like to get to know these students better, I can probably learn more by studying alone. Besides, what if we don't get along? What if I end up doing most of the work or the others don't show up?"

Grace's concerns—like those of many people—are understandable. Groups use a lot of time, energy, and resources. In some cases, a single person can accomplish just as much or more by working alone. And even if a study group has the potential to aid learning, it also has the potential for interpersonal conflicts and long-lasting resentments.

When you finish reading this chapter, you should be able to answer the following questions:

1. Should Grace join the study group or work on her own? What would she gain or lose by that decision?
2. How can some of the dialectic tensions described in this chapter affect how well a study group achieves its goal?
3. What communication strategies should a study group use to ensure that members are satisfied with the process and the outcome?
4. Have you ever participated in a study group? If yes, why did it succeed or not succeed?

Groups communicate in a variety of settings and circumstances—at school and at work, with family members and with friends, and in highly diverse arenas ranging from sports and science to courtrooms and classrooms. Individual achievement was once the hallmark of personal success; today, success often depends on your ability to work in groups.

Working in groups may be the most important skill you learn in college. A study commissioned by the Association of American Colleges and Universities asked employers to rank essential learning outcomes for college graduates entering the workplace. In two major categories, Intellectual and Practical Skills and Personal and Social Responsibility, the top-ranked outcome was "teamwork skills and the ability to collaborate with others in diverse group settings." Recent graduates ranked the same learning outcomes as top priorities.[3] One business executive wrote that he looks for employees who "are good team people over anything else. I can teach the technical."[4]

A report by the National Association of Colleges and Employers also emphasizes the importance of group communication.[5] Oral communication, motivation,

teamwork, and leadership were the top-ranked skills. Employers viewed group-related skills as more important than written communication skills, proficiency in the field of study, and computer skills. A survey of personnel directors asked to identify the most important skills for successful group participation concluded that members of work groups must be able to

- listen effectively.
- understand their roles within the group.
- actively contribute to group problem solving.
- ask clear questions to obtain information.
- establish a professional rapport with other members.
- communicate effectively with members from different cultures.
- use language effectively.
- convey a professional image nonverbally.
- resolve group conflict.
- demonstrate leadership.[6]

Working in Groups has one overriding mission: To help you become a more effective, efficient, and ethical group member who can apply the theories, strategies, and skills needed to work in a variety of groups. We also emphasize that successful groups learn to balance the competing and contradictory forces that operate in all groups.

Defining Group Communication

When does a collection of people become a group? Do people talking in an elevator or discussing the weather at an airport constitute a group? Are the members of a church congregation listening to a sermon or fans cheering at a baseball game a group? Although the people in these examples may look like a group, they are not working for or with other members. Working in groups requires sustained and purposeful interaction.

Group communication is the interaction of three or more interdependent members working to achieve a common goal. We use the terms *group* and *team* interchangeably. Given our definition of group communication, groups (or teams) vary in their formality, structure, complexity, membership, and titles. Thus, a group of friends organizing a large annual block party can be just as diligent, structured, and productive as a corporate team organizing a stockholders' meeting. Rather than worrying about fine distinctions between groups and teams, we are more interested in explaining how to interact effectively with group members in order to achieve a common goal. So although we don't call a football team a football group or a group of family members a team (unless they're playing a sport or game together), we can say that all of these people are interdependent and interact in order to achieve a common goal. Now, let's break down the essential components of group communication (see Figure 1.1).

Three or More Members

A group consists of at least three members. The saying "two's company, three's a crowd" recognizes that a conversation between two people is quite different from a three-person discussion. When two people engage in a conversation, the interaction is limited to two possibilities: Jill communicates with Jack; Jack communicates with Jill. When a third person is added, the dynamics of the situation change. A third per-

Figure 1.1 Components of Group Communication

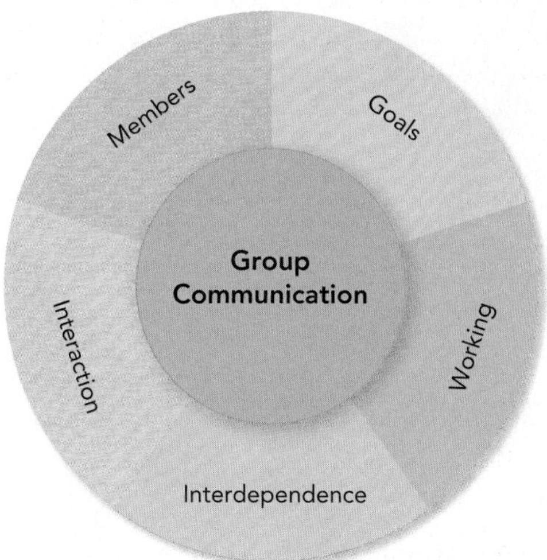

son can change a tie vote into a two-to-one decision. A third person can be the listener who judges and influences the content and style of the conversation. As the size of a group increases, the number of possible interactions (and potential misunderstandings) increases even faster. For example, a group with five members has the potential for 90 different types of interaction; a group with seven members has the potential for 966 different types of interaction.[7]

Although three is the minimum number of members needed for group communication, a maximum size is more difficult to recommend. In general, the ideal group size for a problem-solving discussion is five to seven members. To avoid ties in voting, an odd number of members is usually better than an even number. Groups with more than seven members tend to divide into subgroups. As groups grow larger, individual satisfaction with and commitment to the group often decrease.[8] Members may feel left out or inconsequential. On the other hand, groups with fewer than five members often lack the resources and diversity of opinions needed for effective problem solving.

A group size of five to seven members has proved ideal in many settings. For example, successful evangelical megachurches in the United States may have thousands of members in their congregations, but small groups are the key to their success. Church members are encouraged to create or join tightly knit groups of five to seven people who meet in a member's home to pray and support one another in times of need. Such groups are very personal, convenient, flexible, and supportive, and they cost nothing. Worshipers match their interests with those of other group members—new parents, retired accountants, mountain bike riders—and use their commonalities as the basis for religious discussions, member support, and volunteer projects. Thus, and ironically, successful megachurches boast large congregations that share a common belief system, but rely on the motivation and comfort of small groups to strengthen their religious faith.[9]

Obviously, many groups consist of more than seven members. Yet even a large group usually has a core of five to seven members who do more work and take on leadership functions. In groups with more than fifteen members, coordination and control become difficult. Members may not know one another or be able to communicate

Created in the early 1990s to help impoverished Jewish families in Argentina, groups of teenagers meet monthly as part of the Joint 13-17 Project designed to provide a social assistance network and a sense of belonging for members of the Jewish community. How would you describe this type of group in terms of its task and social dimensions? To what extent do these members demonstrate a group at work?

directly with other members. Discussion often requires elaborate rules and procedures in order to organize group tasks and control the flow of communication.

Interaction

Interaction requires communication among group members, who use verbal and nonverbal messages to generate meanings and establish relationships.[10] Communication allows members to share information and opinions, make decisions and solve problems, and develop interpersonal relationships. The way in which group members communicate does more than reveal group dynamics; it creates them.[11] Members learn which behaviors are appropriate and inappropriate, and which communication rules govern the interaction among members. Regardless of whether group members are meeting face to face or in cyberspace, group communication requires interaction.

Common Goal

Group members come together for a reason. Their collective reason or goal defines and unifies the group. A **goal** is the purpose or objective toward which group work is directed. The label—goal, objective, purpose, mission, assignment, or vision—doesn't matter. Without a common goal, groups would wonder: Why are we meeting? Why should we care or work hard? Where are we going?

Often a group's goal is assigned. For example, a marketing instructor may assign a semester-long project to a group of students so that members of the group can demonstrate their ability to develop a marketing campaign. A chemical company may assemble a group of employees from various departments and ask them to develop recommendations for safer storage of hazardous chemicals.

Some groups have the freedom to establish their own goals. A gathering of neighbors may meet to discuss ways to reduce crime in their neighborhood. Nursing students may form a study group to review course materials for an anatomy exam.

Whatever the circumstances, effective groups have a common goal and dedicate their efforts to the work needed to accomplish that goal.

The importance of a group's goal should not be underestimated. If there is one single factor that separates successful groups from unsuccessful ones, it is having a clear goal. Why? Because goals guide action, set standards for measuring success, provide a focus for resolving conflict, and motivate members.

Interdependence

Interdependence means that each group member is affected and influenced by the actions of other members. A successful interdependent group functions as a cohesive team in which every member is responsible for doing his or her part. The failure of a single group member can adversely affect the entire group. For example, if one student in a study group fails to read an assigned chapter, the entire group will be unprepared for questions related to the subject matter covered in that chapter. When a group strives to achieve a common goal, members exert influence on one another. Whether we like it or not, there are not many tasks that can be accomplished by a group without information, advice, support, and assistance from all interdependent members.

Working

Work is the physical or mental effort you use when trying to accomplish something. That "something" can be a social goal such as getting friends together for a surprise party, a family goal such as deciding jointly where to go on vacation, a work team goal such as planning training sessions for improving patient care, or a management goal in which members develop a strategic plan for their organization.

Thus, we chose *Working in Groups* as the title of this textbook to describe how members work with one another to achieve a common goal. *Working in Groups* is not about hard labor or exhausting effort. Rather, when we work effectively in groups, we join others in a productive and motivating experience in which members combine their talents and energy to achieve a worthy goal.

The Nature of Group Communication

Two important perspectives explain how groups work: (1) the basic process of human communication and (2) a systems approach to understanding groups. By examining these concepts, you will better understand the complex and contradictory nature of group communication. And once you know how groups work, you can focus on developing the effective strategies and skills essential for working in groups.

The Group Communication Process

Central to group communication is the notion of *interaction*. That is, members must communicate with one another as they work together toward achieving a common goal. Communication is complex when just two people interact, and the process becomes more complicated when additional people are involved. At its

Figure 1.2 The Group Communication Process

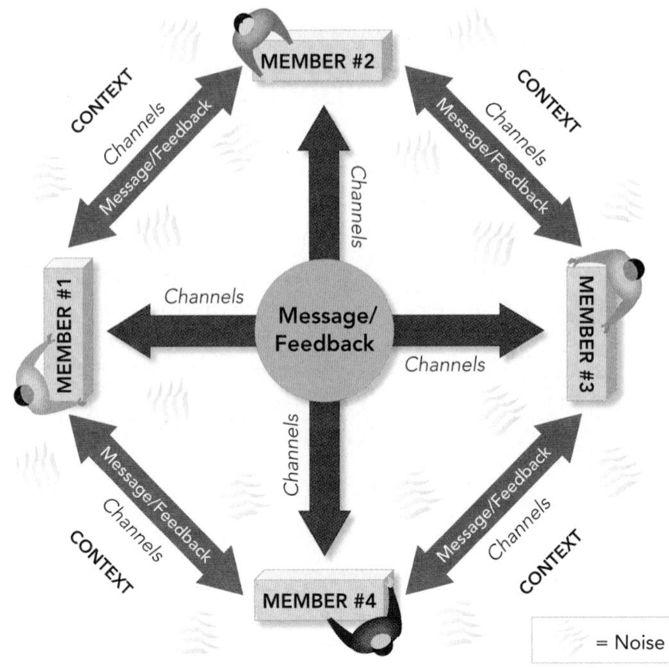

most fundamental level, the group communication process includes basic elements common to all forms of human communication (see also Figure 1.2):

Members
- Members are individuals whom other members recognize as belonging to the group.
- Members bring distinctive skills, knowledge, experiences, personality traits, cultural backgrounds, and points of view to a group.
- Members interact with one another by sending and receiving verbal and nonverbal messages.

Messages
- Messages consist of ideas, information, opinions, and/or feelings that generate meaning.
- *Example:* If you believe that your group has done an excellent job on a project, how can you communicate this to other members? You could thank members for a job well done, praise the group's commitment to excellence, send emails congratulating the group, or smile as you applaud the group's success.

Channels
- Channels are the media through which group members share messages.
- Members send and receive messages through one or more of their five senses: hearing, seeing, touching, smelling, and tasting.
- *Example:* You can email group members to thank them for their good work or bring a box of cookies to the next meeting to show your appreciation.

Feedback
- Feedback is the response or reaction to a message. By recognizing and adapting to feedback, you can assess how well others receive and interpret your messages.

- Feedback can be verbal or nonverbal. Group members may recognize that you appreciate their contributions when you nod, smile, or look attentive when they speak. They, in turn, may respond with a verbal message, such as "Thanks; I'm pretty proud of the way we pulled together on this project." Or they may respond by becoming more motivated and productive.

Context

- Context is the physical and psychological environment in which a group communicates.
- Context includes the type and size of the group, the group's purpose and history, the physical setting, the group's role and status in an organization, and the characteristics of and relationships among group members.
- *Example:* A newly formed study group meeting in the college cafeteria works in a different context from a well-established corporate marketing team holding a videoconference with international clients.

Noise

- Noise describes anything that interferes with or inhibits communication.
- Noise can be external—such as loud people in the hallway, an uncomfortable room, or a member walking in late to a meeting.
- Noise can be internal and psychological. Biases, distracting thoughts, fatigue, and hunger all affect how well you express your thoughts or interpret the messages of other group members.

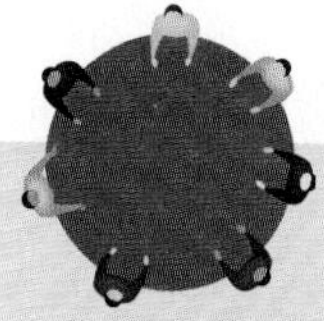

theory in groups

Systems Theory

Systems Theory, also known as the Systems Perspective, is not a single theory, but a group of theories that examine how interdependent factors affect one another. In communication studies, Systems Theory recognizes that "communication does not take place in isolation, but rather necessitates a communication system."[1] Although there are many approaches to studying systems, several characteristics emerge as common to most systems:[2]

- *Systems function in a particular environment in which they receive input and produce output.* A computer system relies on input in order to produce output.
- *System components are interdependent.* The contamination of one skin cell can lead to the contamination of many cells.
- *Systems have a purpose or goal.* The digestive system converts food into fuel for the body.
- *Systems are unpredictable.* There are usually multiple ways to achieve a goal in most systems. When a company is losing money, there are many options for solving the problem.
- *Systems try to maintain balance in their environment.* When an ecosystem is invaded by unwelcome intruders, native organisms may defend their territory or move to a less hostile environment in order to restore equilibrium and harmony.

[1]John A. Courtright, "Relational Communication: As Viewed from the Pragmatic Perspective," in *Explaining Communication: Contemporary Theories and Exemplars*, ed. Bryan B. Whaley and Wendy Samter (Mahwah, NJ: Lawrence Erlbaum Associates, 2007), p. 313.

[2]For additional information on systems theory, see Marianne Dainton and Elaine D. Zelley, *Applying Communication Theory for Professional Life* (Thousand Oaks, CA: Sage, 2005), pp. 51–54; Eric M. Eisenberg and H. L. Goodall, Jr., *Organizational Communication: Balancing Creativity and Constraint*, 4th ed. (Boston: Bedford/St. Martin's, 2004), pp. 92–116; Dominic A. Infante, Andrew S. Rancer, and Deanna F. Womack, *Building Communication Theory*, 4th ed. (Prospect Heights, IL: Waveland, 2003), pp. 66–74.

Groups as Systems

Every group we describe in this textbook is a system. By **system**, we mean a collection of interacting, interdependent elements working together to form a complex whole that adapts to a changing environment. Groups, however, are not the only systems in our lives. For example, in biology, we study the digestive system, the nervous system, and the immune system. We also know that when one part of a biological system fails, the consequences can be serious or even deadly. When a computer system crashes, we hope it will be up and running again without losing any data. We praise the democratic system of government and marvel at our solar system.

Groups are complex systems. The actions of individual members affect everyone in the group as well as the outcome of the group's efforts. Think about a recipe. Eggs, sugar, cream, and bourbon have very different and individual tastes, but when combined properly, the result is an irresistible and intoxicating eggnog. In groups, people are the major ingredients; in the right combination, they can produce a highly productive and satisfying experience.

Systems theory (see page 9) tells us a great deal about the nature of groups and helps prepare us for the unpredictable tensions that characterize the work of a group and its members. It also helps us understand the behavior of groups and their members:

- *Group members function in a particular environment in which they receive input and produce output.* A group receives members, instructions, information, and resources. It also makes decisions, solves problems, produces products, and implements programs that affect people within and outside the group.
- *Group members are interdependent.* If one member fails to cooperate or contribute, the entire group may suffer. If a group member suggests a creative solution to a problem, everyone benefits.
- *Groups and their members have a purpose or goals.* Without a goal, a group is little more than a collection of isolated individuals. Individual and group goals must complement one another in order for the group to function effectively and efficiently.
- *Groups and their members are unpredictable.* A group may unexpectedly come up with new ideas and new techniques. Group members may behave in unexpected ways that help or hinder the group's ability to achieve its common goal.
- *Groups and members attempt to balance complex and contradictory tensions.* Members may take time off to "play" when work becomes too intense. Group members may oppose a leader when they believe the issue is important to the group as a whole.

In addition to the general characteristics of systems, every system is part of a larger system. For example, if your instructor gives you a group assignment, your group is part of the class as a whole. If you are assigned to a group or department at work, your group is just one component of a larger organization. Your group's decisions and actions affect other groups in the same system. Furthermore, the decisions and actions of other groups—some within the same organization and some beyond that organization—affect how well and whether you and your group achieve a common goal.

groups in balance . . .
Create Synergy

When three or more interdependent group members interact and work toward a common goal, they have the potential to create a synergistic system. **Synergy** is a term that describes the cooperative interaction of several factors that results in a combined effect greater than the total of all individual contributions. In other words, the whole is greater than the sum of its individual parts. The term *synergy* comes from the Greek word *synergos,* meaning "working together." Synergy does not occur when people work alone; it occurs only when people work together.

Effective groups are synergistic. Baseball teams without superstars have won the World Series. Companies whose executives earn modest salaries have surpassed those companies in which the CEOs are paid millions of dollars. Ordinary groups have achieved extraordinary results. Synergy occurs when the knowledge, talents, and dedication of group members merge into a force that surpasses anything group members could have produced without cooperative interaction.

Types of Groups

Groups, like their individual members, have diverse characteristics and goals. Although a basketball team, a study group, a corporate board of directors, and a homecoming committee meet our definition of a group, each one has unique features and functions. At the same time, the theories, methods, and tools of group communication apply equally to every type of group.

We have sorted the most basic types of groups into eight categories: primary groups, social groups, self-help groups, learning groups, service groups, civic groups, work groups, and public groups (see Table 1.1 on page 12). These categories range from the most personal and informal types of groups to more formal types. You can identify each type of group by observing its setting (where and when the group meets) and its membership (who is in the group).

The eight types of groups in Table 1.1 are not absolute categories. Many types of groups overlap. A Girl Scout belongs to both a social group and a learning group, whereas the adults who run a troop or form the national association belong to both a service group and a work group.

The last two types of groups in Table 1.1—work groups and public groups—serve the interests of organizations and public audiences. Their goal may be as complex as reengineering a global corporation or as simple as reporting their progress at a weekly staff meeting. Given their importance and impact, let's look at these in more detail.

Work groups are responsible for achieving specific tasks or performing routine duties on behalf of a company, organization, association, agency, or institution. If you are employed, you probably belong to several work groups. You may be a member of a production team or a work crew. You may be part of a sales staff, service department, management group, or research team. Among the many types of work groups, two deserve special attention: committees and work teams. Table 1.2, also on page 12, describes these groups and provides examples.

A **public group** interacts in front of or for the benefit of the public. Although public groups may engage in information sharing, decision making, or problem solving, they are also concerned with making a positive impression on a public audience. Table 1.3 explains the types of public groups and provides examples.

Table 1.1 Basic Types of Groups

Type of Group	Overall Purpose	Examples
Primary Group	To provide members with affection, support, and a sense of belonging and confidence	Families, best friends
Social Group	To share common interests in a friendly setting or participate in social activities	Athletic teams, hobby groups, sororities and fraternities, peer groups
Self-Help Group	To offer support and encouragement to members who want or need help with personal problems	Therapy groups and programs such as Weight Watchers, Alcoholics Anonymous, Parents without Partners
Learning Group	To help members gain knowledge and develop skills	Classmates, study groups, book discussion groups, professional workshops, health and fitness classes
Service Group	To support worthy causes that help people *outside* the group	Kiwanis, Police Athletic League, charitable foundations
Civic Group	To support worthy causes that help people *within* the group	PTA, labor unions, veterans' groups, fire and police auxiliary groups, neighborhood and community associations
Work Group	To achieve specific tasks and routine duties on behalf of a business or organization	Committees, task forces, work teams, management teams
Public Group	To discuss important issues in front of or for the benefit of the public or key decision makers	Public panel discussions, symposiums, forums, and governance groups

Table 1.2 Types of Work Groups

<table>
<tr><td rowspan="4">Committees</td><td colspan="2">• are given a specific assignment by a larger group or by a person in a position of authority
• are most common in the work environment
• are often used by service groups to accomplish specific tasks</td></tr>
<tr><td>ad hoc committee
forms for a specific purpose and disbands once it has completed its assignment or task</td><td>Examples: An ad hoc committee could plan a high school reunion, organize a company's fund-raising campaign for a charity, or promote a community cleanup for a neighborhood.</td></tr>
<tr><td>standing committee
remains active in order to accomplish an ongoing task</td><td>Examples: Many businesses and organizations have ongoing social committees, membership committees, program committees, and finance committees.</td></tr>
<tr><td>task force
gathers information and makes recommendations regarding a specific issue or problem</td><td>Examples: A government task force could examine the health-care system or analyze the decline in a school system's test scores.</td></tr>
<tr><td>Work Teams</td><td colspan="2">• are given full responsibility and resources for their performance
• are relatively permanent groups
• do not take time from work to meet—they unite to work
Examples: A health-care team attends to a specific patient or group of patients. A research team takes on a specific research project. A legal team forms and works to defend or prosecute a specific case.</td></tr>
</table>

Table 1.3 Types of Public Groups

Panel Discussions	• involve several people who interact with one another on a common topic for the benefit of an audience • usually feature a moderator who tries to control the flow of communication • are designed to educate, influence, or entertain an audience *Examples:* Panel discussions are very common on television shows such as *Oprah.* Some present bizarre discussions, while more serious discussions are moderated on Sunday morning political shows and business programs such as *Wall Street Week* or *Face the Nation.*
Symposiums	• require each group member to present a short, uninterrupted speech on different aspects of a topic for the benefit of an audience • are unique because group members give speeches to an audience rather than interact with other group members *Example:* A local PTA may sponsor a drug symposium in which a physician, a psychologist, a police officer, and a former drug addict are given uninterrupted time to inform parents about the drug problem and to recommend strategies for prevention and treatment.
Forums	• provide an opportunity for audience members to comment, express concerns, or ask questions • need a strong moderator to make sure that audience members have an equal opportunity to speak *Examples:* Employees may ask questions after listening to a manager's plan for cutting expenses. Citizens may comment and ask candidates or elected officials at a town meeting.
Governance Groups	• make public policy decisions in public settings *Examples:* State legislatures, city and county councils, and the governing boards of public agencies and educational institutions must conduct their meetings in public. The U.S. Congress cannot deny the public access to congressional debates.

Advantages and Disadvantages of Working in Groups

If you are like most people, you have had to sit through long, boring meetings run by incompetent leaders. Perhaps you have lost patience with a group that couldn't accomplish a simple task that you could easily do all by yourself. In the end, however, the advantages of working in effective groups outweigh the potential disadvantages.

Advantages

Although participating in groups can be time-consuming and even aggravating, the advantages are significant. In general, groups perform better than individuals working alone do. When groups work effectively, members find the experience motivating and rewarding. Group members also learn a great deal, develop greater cultural understanding, enhance their creativity, and become more engaged in civic life.

virtual groups

From Email to EMS

Instead of meeting face to face, many groups interact virtually. A **virtual group** uses technology to communicate synchronously and/or asynchronously, often across time, distance, and organizational boundaries. **Synchronous communication** occurs simultaneously and in real time. Audioconferences, videoconferences, textconferences, and electronic meeting systems (EMS) allow for synchronous interaction. **Asynchronous communication** is electronic communication that does not occur simultaneously or in real time. Messages sent via email, voice mail, and electronic bulletin boards are asynchronous.

In their analysis of virtual groups, Deborah Duarte and Nancy Snyder point out that because virtual communication has become the way in which many companies do business, "understanding how to work in or lead a virtual team is now a fundamental requirement for people in many organizations. . . . Organizations that do not use virtual teams effectively may be fighting an uphill battle in a global, competitive, and rapidly changing environment."[1] Jon Katzenbach and Douglas Smith further observe that "today, organizations are no longer confined to team efforts that assemble people from the same location or the same time zone. Indeed, small groups of people from two or more locations and time zones routinely convene for collaborative purposes."[2]

Virtual groups are complex. Members may come from different organizations, cultures, time zones, and geographic locations—not to mention that they interact via technology. As a result, virtual groups develop a different group dynamic from those meeting face to face.[3] Chapter 14, Technology and Virtual Groups, discusses the unique issues these groups face. In addition, every chapter provides advice on adapting to the virtual group environment.

[1]Deborah L. Duarte and Nancy Tennant Snyder, *Mastering Virtual Teams: Strategies, Tools, and Techniques That Succeed*, 3rd ed. (San Francisco: Jossey-Bass, 2006), p. 4.

[2]Jon R. Katzenbach and Douglas K. Smith, *The Discipline of Teams: A Mindbook-Workbook for Delivering Small Group Performance* (New York: John Wiley & Sons, 2001), p. 23.

[3]Susan B. Barnes, *Online Connections: Internet Interpersonal Relationships* (Cresskill, NJ: Hampton Press, 2001), p. 41.

Advantages of Working in Groups

- *Superior Performance*
- *Greater Member Satisfaction*
- *More Learning*
- *Enhanced Cultural Understanding*
- *More Creativity*
- *Greater Civic Engagement*

Superior Performance. Groups make decisions and solve problems. They decide how businesses compete, how staff members work, how instructors teach, and how doctors attend to patients' needs. The reason so many groups are doing so much that affects our daily lives is fairly simple: Groups that share the workload can perform better and accomplish more than individuals working alone. As MIT management professor Peter Senge writes, "If you want something really creative done, you ask a team to do it—instead of sending one person off to do it on his or her own."[12]

Despite such impressive claims about group performance, there are exceptions. If the task is fairly simple and routine (write a memo, mail a letter, total the receipts), it may be easier for an individual working alone to accomplish the task. If one person knows the answer to a question, or if the task requires a specialized expert, then a single person may be better equipped to get the job done. However, when the task is complex and the answers are unclear, an effective group will perform better.

Greater Member Satisfaction. Even if groups didn't accomplish more than individuals working alone, many people would still join and work in groups. The social benefits can be just as important as task achievement. People belong to and work in

groups because groups give them the opportunity to make friends, socialize, receive peer support, and feel part of a unified and successful team. Not surprisingly, the more opportunities group members have to communicate with one another, the more satisfied they are with the group experience.

More Learning. An added advantage of working in groups is the amount of learning that occurs within an effective group. Groups can enhance learning by sharing collective information, stimulating critical thinking, challenging assumptions, and even raising standards of achievement. A review of 168 studies of college students comparing cooperative, group-based learning with traditional approaches indicates that collaborative learning promotes higher individual achievement in knowledge acquisition, retention, accuracy, creativity in problem solving, and higher-level reasoning.[13]

Working in groups gives us the opportunity to learn from and with other members. New members learn from veterans; amateurs learn from experts. Not only do members learn more about the topics they discuss, but they also learn more about how to work as a group.

Enhanced Cultural Understanding. In most groups, members differ in characteristics, life experiences, cultures, interests, and attitudes. Working effectively in groups requires that you understand, respect, and adapt to differences in members' skills, experiences, opinions, and behavior as well as differences in gender, age, race, nationality, ethnicity, religion, status, and worldviews. By recognizing, appreciating, and adapting to members' differences, you can become a more effective communicator in your group, and in your community, your studies, your work, and your travels within this country or throughout the world. Chapter 4, Group Diversity, provides a detailed examination of the ways in which member similarities and differences benefit groups.

More Creativity. Not only do groups perform better than individuals working alone, they can also generate more innovative ideas and creative solutions. Lee Towe, author of *Why Didn't I Think of That? Creativity in the Workplace,* writes that the "key to creativity is the mental flexibility required to mix thoughts from our many different experiences."[14] When you mix your thoughts with those of other group members, you increase the group's creative potential. Groups provide a creative multiplier effect by tapping more information, more brainpower, and more insights. Groups have "awesome superiority" when trying to unleash creativity and solve challenging problems.[15]

Greater Civic Engagement. The theories, methods, and tools you learn in a group communication course prepare you for effective participation in a democratic society. In recent years, many educational institutions have implemented service-learning programs as a way of connecting students to the community in which they live and work. Rather than confining the study of group communication to the classroom, service learning provides student groups the opportunity to use the strategies and skills they learn in class as they work together toward achieving a genuine, community-based goal.[16] Sara Chudnovsky Weintraub, an expert in service learning, claims that "service-learning projects [or any community-based group projects] help engage students in meaningful experiences that bridge the gap between theory and practice."[17]

Whether you participate in a service-learning group project, organize a neighborhood watch group, or are a member of a city task force, learning effective group communication skills will help you better engage in service to your community.

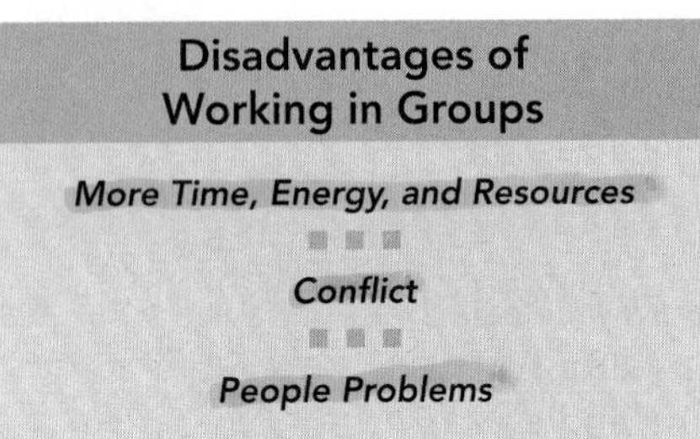

Disadvantages of Working in Groups
More Time, Energy, and Resources
Conflict
People Problems

Disadvantages

The advantages of working in groups occur when groups are working efficiently and effectively. The disadvantages are more likely to occur when working in a group is not the appropriate way to achieve a goal, when members do not work to their full potential, or when problems interfere with group members' willingness and ability to communicate. The most common complaints about working in groups concern the amount of time, energy, and resources expended by groups and the conflict and people problems that can arise.

More Time, Energy, and Resources. Working in groups costs time, energy, and resources. The 3M Corporation examined the many factors that affect the cost of meetings, including the hourly wages of group members, the wages of those who help prepare for meetings, the cost of materials used in meetings, and overhead costs. Here's its conclusion: The 3M Corporation spends a staggering $78.8 million annually for meetings.[18] A Microsoft survey concludes that nonproductive meetings, poor communication, and hazy group objectives gobble up two of every five workdays. In another study, workers report that they spend an average of 5.6 hours a week in meetings and rate 69 percent of those meetings as "ineffective."[19] We spend a lot of time in groups; if that time is wasted, we are throwing away valuable resources and effort.

Conflict. Very few people enjoy or seek out conflict. However, when group members work together to achieve a common goal, there is always the potential for disagreement. Unfortunately, those who disagree are often seen as aggressive and disruptive. As a result, some people will do almost anything to avoid conflict and confrontation. They may even avoid working in groups. Most researchers and writers contend that "in a good discussion, arguing our different viewpoints might lead to clarifying and reconciling them."[20] Yet because of apprehension about conflict, some people avoid meetings in which controversial issues are scheduled for discussion, or are unwilling to express their opinions.

People Problems. As much as we may want others to share our interests, viewpoints, and willingness to work, there is always the potential for individual group members to create problems. Like anyone else in our daily lives, group members can be stubborn, lazy, and even cruel. When deciding whether to work in a group, we often consider whether we want to spend time working with certain members of that group.

Members who lack confidence or are unprepared may have little to contribute. To avoid conflict or extra work, some members may go along with the group or play "follow the leader" rather than search for the best solution to a problem. Strong, domineering members can put so much pressure on others that dissent is stifled. Although no one wants to work with a group of unpleasant members, there may be circumstances in which people problems cannot be avoided. When this situation occurs, the disadvantages of group work can overwhelm the advantages.

Balance: The Guiding Principle of Group Work

At the heart of this book is a guiding principle that gives real-world significance to your experiences in and study of group communication: An ideal group succeeds because it achieves *balance*.

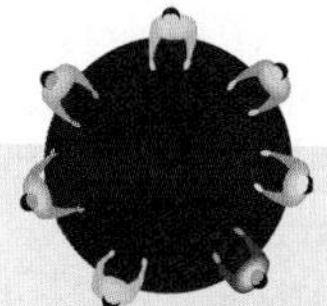

groups in balance . . .
Link Theories, Methods, and Tools

Management expert Peter Senge has successfully applied a systems perspective to managing organizations. Senge and his colleagues believe that theories, methods, and tools are inseparable components of effective organizations.[1] Throughout this textbook, we examine the theories, methods, and tools needed to promote and balance group productivity and member satisfaction.

- A **theory** is a statement that tries to explain or predict events and behavior. Group communication theories help us understand *what* is occurring in a group and *why* a group succeeds or fails.
- A **method** is a strategy, guideline, procedure, or technique for dealing with the issues and problems that arise in groups. Effective methods are based on theories. Without theories, you won't know why a particular method works in one situation and fails in another.
- A **tool** in the context of group work is a resource and skill that helps a group carry out or achieve its common goal. Communication skills are the most important tools available to group members. Like methods, tools are most effective when their use is based on theories.

Although a master carpenter can tell you what tool to use, you may have no idea how to use it or why it works. In our eagerness to solve problems or achieve a group's goal, we may grab easy-to-use tools that do not address the causes of a problem or help us achieve the goal. Using tools without an understanding of methods and theories can make the process of working in groups inefficient, ineffective, and frustrating for all members.

[1]Peter M. Senge et al., *The Fifth Discipline Fieldbook: Strategies and Tools for Building a Learning Organization* (New York: Doubleday, 1994), pp. 28–31.

Balance describes a state of equilibrium in which no significant factor dominates or interferes with other factors. In group communication, the group's common goal is the point on which members must balance many factors. A group that makes a decision or completes an assigned task is not in balance if group members end up hating one another. A group that relies on one or two members to do all the work is not in balance. Effective groups balance factors such as the group's task and social functions, individual and group needs, and the responsibilities of leadership and followership. Achieving balance requires an understanding of the interplay of the contradictory forces that operate in all groups.

Group Dialectics

You deal with competing options every day. Should you work or play? Should you spend or save? Should you eat a big bowl of ice cream or a fresh salad? These kinds of tensions are best resolved by taking a *both/and* approach rather than an *either/or* perspective. For example, if you're lucky, you may *both* have a job you love *and* enjoy it as much as play. If you *both* spend wisely *and* save more, you can look forward to a more secure financial future. If you eat *both* small portions of ice cream *and* fresh salads, the result is a more balanced diet. Even in close personal relationships, a couple may *both* cherish their time together *and* respect each other's need for time apart. As you will see, this *both/and* approach also applies to achieving balance in group interactions.

We define **Group Dialectics** as the contradictory tensions groups experience as they work toward a common goal. Effective groups engage in a cooperative effort to balance group dialectics through effective group communication strategies.

Successful groups learn to balance the competing and contradictory forces that operate in all groups. How does a cheerleading squad balance dialectic factors such as the squad's task and social functions, individual and group needs, the responsibilities of leadership and followership, and the homogeneous and heterogeneous characteristics of group members?

Although the word **dialectics** may be new to you, it captures the way in which successful groups balance competing pressures. It may help you to remember that the prefix *di-* means two, as in diagonal (joining two opposite points) or dialogue (a conversation between two people). Dialectics looks at two extremes or oppositions, as in work or play, similar or different.

Successful groups and group members balance dialectic tensions by using the *both/and* approach. For example, in some groups, you may *both* enjoy warm friendships with some members *and* effectively cope with members who are difficult. Your group may want *both* a stable, predictable process in some situations *and* the freedom to experiment and change in other circumstances. In Table 1.4 we present nine dialectic tensions that characterize the delicate balance needed by effective groups.[21]

Individual Goals and Group Goals. A group will not function well—or at all—if members focus entirely on their individual goals rather than on the group's common goal. When a group agrees upon a clear and important goal, members can pursue both group *and* individual goals, as long as their personal goals do not undermine the group goal. For example, if you join a group because you're interested in forming a romantic attachment with another member, you may strongly support the group or its goal, in part, because it will impress the object of your desires.

In the best of groups, your personal goals support the group's common goal. If you do not share the group's goal, you may become frustrated or try to undermine the group. In ideal groups, members negotiate their personal needs and interests to achieve a balance

Table 1.4 Group Dialectics

Group Dialectics	Balancing Group Dialectics
Individual Goals ↔ Group Goals	Members' personal goals are *balanced* with the group's common goal.
Conflict ↔ Cohesion	The value of constructive conflict is *balanced* with the need for unity and cohesiveness.
Conforming ↔ Nonconforming	A commitment to group norms and standards is *balanced* with a willingness to differ and change.
Task Dimensions ↔ Social Dimensions	The responsibility and motivation to complete tasks are *balanced* with promoting member relationships.
Homogeneous ↔ Heterogeneous	Member similarities are *balanced* with member differences in skills, roles, personal characteristics, and cultural perspectives.
Leadership ↔ Followership	Effective and ethical leadership is *balanced* with committed and responsible followership.
Structure ↔ Spontaneity	The need for structured procedures is *balanced* with the need for innovative and creative thinking.
Engaged ↔ Disengaged	Member energy and labor are *balanced* with the group's need for rest and renewal.
Open System ↔ Closed System	External support and recognition are *balanced* with internal group solidarity and rewards.

theory in groups
Relational Dialectics Theory

Communication scholars Leslie Baxter and Barbara Montgomery use the term *dialectics* to describe the complex and contradictory nature of relationships. Baxter and Montgomery's **Relational Dialectics Theory** claims that relationships are characterized by ongoing, dialectic tensions between the multiple contradictions, complexities, and changes in human experiences.[1] The following pairs of common folk proverbs illustrate such contradictory, dialectic tensions:

"Opposites attract" *but* "Birds of a feather flock together."

"Two's company; three's a crowd" *but* "The more, the merrier."[2]

Rather than trying to prove that one of these contradictory proverbs is truer than the other—an *either/or* response—relational dialectics takes a *both/and* approach. There are several ways to resolve relational dialectic tensions:

- You can choose one option in different situations and at different points in time. *Example:* Normally, group meetings follow a highly structured agenda. Because group members are having difficulty coming up with a good solution to a problem, they decide to set aside the agenda for thirty minutes so they can do some unstructured brainstorming.
- You can choose different options for different psychological contexts. *Example:* Joe normally goes with the flow and adheres to group norms about keeping conflict under control, but when one member personally embarrasses another, he feels compelled to speak out against this behavior in front of the entire group.
- You can choose one option and ignore the other. *Example:* Even though a group knows that two absent members would vote against a potential decision they're discussing, they go ahead and make the decision anyway.

Generally, choosing one option over another is the *least* effective way to resolve relational dialectics because you or someone else must "give up" or "lose" one option over another. Engaging both options to some degree is a better way.

[1]Leslie A. Baxter and Barbara M. Montgomery, *Relating: Dialogues and Dialectics* (New York: Guilford Press, 1996).

[2]Baxter and Montgomery, p. 3.

between the dialectic tension of being independent and being part of an interdependent group.

Conflict and Cohesion. Conflict is unavoidable in effective groups. How else can members express disagreements that may lead to better solutions? How else can groups ensure that ethical standards are upheld? Groups without constructive conflict are groups without the means to analyze the wisdom of their decisions. At the same time, groups also benefit from cohesion—the mutual attraction that holds the members of a group together. All for one and one for all! Cohesive groups are committed, unified, and willing to engage in conflict. Chapter 9, Conflict and Cohesion in Groups, examines the conflict-cohesiveness dialectic in detail.

Conforming and Nonconforming. Group norms (accepted standards of behavior) affect the quality and quantity of work by group members. Dialectic tensions can arise, however, when one or more members challenge the group's norms or achievement standards. When members question standards, methods, or norms, a group may benefit from reconsidering its position. Constructive criticism that also promotes a group's goal can contribute to group effectiveness. In Chapter 2, Group Development, we explore the ways in which group norms address the need for both conformity and nonconformity.

Task Dimensions and Social Dimensions. The best groups negotiate the task/social dialectic by balancing work with pleasure. A group's **task dimension** focuses on the job—the goal or product of group effort. The **social dimension** is concerned with people—the interpersonal relationships among group members. Thus, a group discussing a department's budget primarily focuses on its task. However, if, at the end of the meeting, the group surprises a member with a cake in celebration of her birthday, the group's focus shifts to the social dimension. More often, groups exhibit both task and social dimensions when they get the job done in a way that makes everyone feel socially accepted and valued. The task and social dimensions of a group "exert mutual and reciprocal influences on each other and are thus virtually inseparable in practice."[22]

When groups balance work and play, they are more productive. Think of how frustrating it is to work on a group task when members don't get along. Think of how disappointing it is to work with friends who don't take a task seriously or don't make significant contributions. While both teamwork and "social" work are essential to team success, getting the whole group to balance these two dialectics is extremely important. The old saying "All work and no play makes Jack [or Jill] a dull boy [or girl]" certainly applies to groups. On the other hand, all play and no work can make you unemployed.[23]

Homogeneous and Heterogeneous. The prefixes *homo* and *hetero* come from the Greek language. *Homo* means *same* or *similar; hetero* means *different.* Thus a **homogeneous group** is composed of members who are the same or very similar to one another and a **heterogeneous group** includes members who are different from one another. Not surprisingly, there is no such thing as a purely homogeneous group because no two members can be exactly the same. Certainly some groups are more homogeneous than heterogeneous. For example, the Black Caucus in the U.S. Congress will be more homogeneous than the Congress as a whole. The legal team representing a client will be more homogeneous in terms of education, income, professional experience, and lifestyle than the jury selected to hear the case. In Chapter 4, Group Diversity, we emphasize that every person on this earth—and thus every member of a group—is different. And that's a good thing. If every group member were exactly alike, the group would not achieve much more than one member working alone. At the same time, similarities assure members that they share some common characteristics, traits, and attitudes.

Leadership and Followership. Chapter 5, Group Leadership, examines the components and challenges of effective leadership. Here we only note that effective leadership is not a solo task—it requires loyal, competent, and responsible followers. Effective leaders have the confidence to put their egos aside and bring out the leadership in others.[24] When group members assume specific leadership functions, the group has achieved an optimum balance of leadership and followership.

Structure and Spontaneity. In Chapter 10, Structured and Creative Problem Solving in Groups, we quote group communication scholar Marshall Scott Poole, who notes that procedures are "the heart of group work [and] the most powerful tools we have to improve the conduct of meetings."[25] Structured procedures help groups balance participation, resolve conflicts, organize discussions, and empower members. If, however, a group becomes obsessed with rigid procedures, it misses out on the benefits of spontaneity and creativity. Whether it's just "thinking outside the box" or organizing a creative problem-solving session, groups can reap enormous benefits

by encouraging innovation and "what-if" thinking. Effective groups balance the need for structure with time for spontaneous and creative thinking.

Engaged and Disengaged. The engaged-disengaged dialectic has two dimensions—one related to the amount of activity; the other related to the level of commitment. Groups often experience two opposite types of activities: high-energy, nonstop action relieved by periods of relaxation and renewal. Effective groups understand that racing toward a distant finish line may only exhaust group members and leave some sitting on the sidelines. At the same time, low energy and inaction will accomplish nothing. Balancing the urge to run with the need for rest and renewal challenges most groups.

Sometimes, high-energy, nonstop action is unstoppable because group members are extremely motivated, personally committed, and appropriately rewarded for their work. Stopping to recharge or relax would only frustrate a group with pent-up energy. At the other end of the dialectic spectrum, groups that plod through problems with little enthusiasm may be unmotivated, uncaring, and unrewarded for their work. Asking them to pick up speed would only increase their resentment.

Open System and Closed System. Although all groups are systems, effective groups maintain a balance by moving between open or closed systems. When a group functions as an open system, it welcomes input from and interchange with its

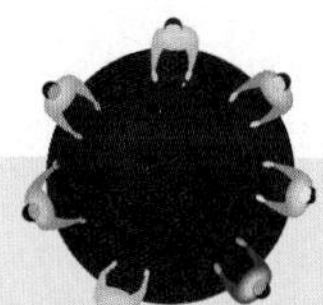

groups in balance . . .
Empower Members

When groups resolve dialectic tensions by using a *both/and* approach, they become empowered. Empowerment describes a shift in power and authority in a group so that members assume responsibility for their work. Rather than relying on a senior manager, boss, or designated leader to direct their work, empowered groups have the authority to make relevant decisions and carry out their work effectively.[1]

Group empowerment is a documented dimension of successful groups and teams. Not surprisingly, members of empowered groups feel powerful and able to control how the group works toward achieving its goal.[2] This powerful feeling comes from knowing that you and your group have the freedom and authority to resolve the inevitable dialectic tensions that arise.

Bradley L. Kirkman and Benson Rosen studied 122 teams in four organizations to learn whether empowerment affected group success. They concluded that empowered groups are more successful and generally share four characteristics:[3]

1. *Potency.* The group believes it has the power and ability to achieve its common goal.
2. *Meaningfulness.* The group believes that its common goal is important, valuable, and worthwhile.
3. *Autonomy.* The group is optimistic about achieving its goal because it has the freedom to make decisions and implement those decisions.
4. *Impact.* The group believes that its work produces significant benefits for other people and organizations.

Empowered groups enjoy a sense of excitement about their work. Members genuinely respect and like one another. They even look forward to working together in pursuit of a worthy common goal.

[1]Nicky Hayes, *Managing Teams: A Strategy for Success*, 2nd ed. (London: Thomson, 2002), p. 99.

[2]James M. Kouzes and Barry Z. Posner, *The Leadership Challenge*, 3rd ed. (San Francisco: Jossey-Bass, 2002), p. 282.

[3]Bradley L. Kirkman and Benson Rosen, "Beyond Self-Management: Antecedents and Consequences of Team Empowerment," *Academy of Management Journal* 42 (1999), pp. 58–74.

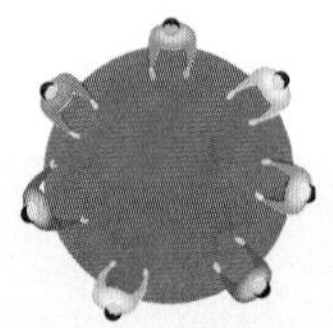

ethics in groups

The National Communication Association Credo for Ethical Communication

Questions of right and wrong arise whenever people communicate. Ethical communication is fundamental to responsible thinking, decision making, and the development of relationships and communities within and across contexts, cultures, channels, and media. Moreover, ethical communication enhances human worth and dignity by fostering truthfulness, fairness, responsibility, personal integrity, and respect for self and others. We believe that unethical communication threatens the well-being of individuals and the society in which we live. Therefore we, the members of the National Communication Association, endorse and are committed to practicing the following principles of ethical communication:

- We advocate truthfulness, accuracy, honesty, and reason as essential to the integrity of communication.
- We endorse freedom of expression, diversity of perspective, and tolerance of dissent to achieve the informed and responsible decision making fundamental to a civic society.
- We strive to understand and respect other communicators before evaluating and responding to their messages.
- We promote access to communication resources and opportunities as necessary to fulfill human potential and contribute to the well-being of families, communities, and society.
- We promote communication climates of caring and mutual understanding that respect the unique needs and characteristics of individual communicators.
- We condemn communication that degrades individuals and humanity through distortion, intimidation, coercion, and violence, and through the expression of intolerance and hatred.
- We are committed to the courageous expression of personal conviction in pursuit of fairness and justice.
- We advocate sharing information, opinions, and feelings when facing significant choices while also respecting privacy and confidentiality.
- We accept responsibility for the short- and long-term consequences of our own communication and expect the same of others.

environment. That input can be the opinions of nongroup members, information from outside research, or challenges from competing groups. When a group functions as a closed system, it guards its boundaries and discourages input or interaction with the outside. Depending on the situation, a group may open its boundaries and welcome input or close them to protect the group and its work. Effective groups understand that there are times when they must function as an open system and other times when they must close the door and work in private. For example, a hiring committee may function as an open system in order to recruit candidates and research their backgrounds. When they have finished this process, they meet privately and confidentially to evaluate the candidates and make a hiring recommendation.

Ethics and Group Communication

Ethics requires an understanding of whether behaviors meet agreed-upon standards of right and wrong.[26] Ethical questions—Are we doing the right thing? Is he dishonest? Is she tolerant of different viewpoints?—arise whenever we communicate because communication has consequences. What you say and do can help or hurt both group members and other people who are affected by the group's decisions and actions.

Sadly, the theories, methods, and tools in this textbook can be and have been used for less-than-ethical purposes. For example, a group member may support a good but inexperienced friend for an important job, only to suffer the consequences when the friend botches the job or fails to meet the group's expectations.

The National Communication Association (NCA) provides a credo for ethical communication.[27] In Latin, the word *credo* means "I believe." Thus, an ethics credo is a belief statement about what it means to be an ethical communicator. All of these ethical principles apply to working in groups. Ethical communication requires an understanding of the dialectic tensions that operate in all groups as well as a desire to communicate in a way that meets agreed-upon standards of right and wrong.

summary study guide

Succeeding in Groups

- Working in groups is an inescapable part of life; most people spend a considerable amount of time and energy working in groups.
- Surveyed employers view group-related skills as more important than written communication skills, proficiency in the field of study, and computer skills.

Defining Group Communication

- Group communication is the interaction of three or more interdependent people working to achieve a common goal.
- Group interaction requires communication among group members who use verbal and nonverbal messages to generate meanings and establish relationships within a group context.
- The most significant factor separating successful groups from unsuccessful ones is having a clear understanding of the group's common goal.

The Nature of Group Communication

- The basic elements of the group communication process are members, messages, channels, feedback, noise, and context.
- Effective groups are synergistic; they combine the best qualities and talents of all members into something that surpasses anything group members could have produced without cooperative interaction.
- Groups are complex systems in which the actions of individual members affect everyone in the group as well as the outcome of group work.

Types of Groups

- Groups can be sorted into eight categories: primary, social, self-help, learning, service, civic, work, and public groups.
- Public groups communicate to and for the benefit of an audience. Four types of public groups are panel discussions, symposiums, forums, and governance groups.
- Virtual groups rely on technology to communicate synchronously and/or asynchronously.

Advantages and Disadvantages of Working in Groups

- Six advantages of working in groups include improved performance, member satisfaction, learning, cultural sensitivity, creative thinking, and civic engagement.
- The disadvantages of working in groups include the amount of time, energy, and resources expended by groups and the interpersonal conflicts and people problems that may arise.
- Understanding and applying theories, methods, and tools are inseparable components in learning about the group communication process.

Balance: The Guiding Principle of Group Work

- Group dialectics represent the balance between competing and contradictory components of group work by taking a both/and approach to resolving such tensions.
- Engleberg and Wynn identify nine group dialectics: individual goals ↔ group goals; conflict ↔ cohesion; conforming ↔ nonconforming; task dimensions ↔ social dimensions; homogeneous ↔ heterogeneous; leadership ↔ followership; structure ↔ spontaneity; engaged ↔ disengaged; open system ↔ closed system.
- The National Communication Association (NCA) Credo for Ethical Communication sets forth guiding principles to assess how well communication behaviors meet agreed-upon standards of right and wrong.

key terms

ad hoc committee 12
asynchronous communication 14
channel 8
civic group 12
committee 12
conflict ↔ cohesion 18
conforming ↔ nonconforming 18
context 9
dialectics 18
engaged ↔ disengaged 18
ethics 22
feedback 8
forum 13
goal 6
governance group 13
group communication 4
Group Dialectics 17
heterogeneous group 20
homogeneous group 20
homogeneous ↔ heterogeneous 18
individual goals ↔ group goals 18
interaction 6
interdependence 7
leadership ↔ followership 18
learning group 12
member 8
message 8
method 17
noise 9
open system ↔ closed system 18
panel discussion 13
primary group 12
public group 11
Relational Dialectics Theory 19
self-help group 12
service group 12
social dimension 20
social group 12
standing committee 12
structure ↔ spontaneity 18
symposium 13
synchronous communication 14
synergy 11
system 10
Systems Theory 9
task dimension 20
task dimension ↔ social dimension 18
task force 12
theory 17
tool 17
virtual group 14
work group 11
work team 12

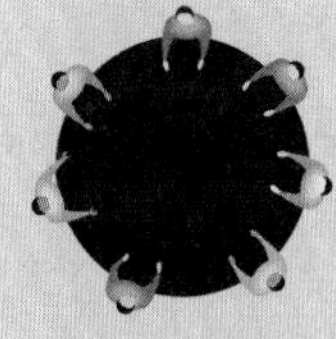

critical thinking about the case study

The Study Group Dilemma

1. Given Grace's concerns about spending a lot of her valuable time and energy in a study group, what would you say to encourage her to join?
2. What kind of *noise* is a study group likely to encounter?
3. Which dialectic tensions are most likely to affect how well Grace and her study group achieve their common goal?
4. Is it ethical for a study group to work together in order to improve their chances of earning a good grade in an Anatomy and Physiology course when other students in the class study alone? If yes, why? If not, why not?

group work It Was the Best of Groups; It Was the Worst of Groups

Directions: Think about two groups to which you now belong or have belonged. One should be the "best of groups," that is, a group that is or was highly successful and/or personally satisfying. The other should be the "worst of groups"—one that is or was unsuccessful, disappointing, and/or frustrating. Identify at least three characteristics that were unique to the best group and three that were unique to the worst group. Fill in the following table with your answer. If possible, identify five characteristics for each type of group.

THE BEST OF GROUPS	THE WORST OF GROUPS
Example: One member kept track of everyone's birthday. On the meeting day closest to our birthday, we got a card signed by everyone and shared a cake or cookies.	*Example:* The head of the group refused to explain his decisions. When we'd ask why we could or couldn't do something, he'd say, "Because I said so."
1.	
2.	
3.	
4.	
5.	

group assessment Essential Group Elements

Directions: Group communication includes five basic elements: (1) group size, (2) interaction, (3) a common goal, (4) interdependence, and (5) working. Think about the groups you belong to or a group that has just formed in your class or at work. Answer the following questions to assess the extent to which your group contains the basic group elements. If you can answer *yes* to most of the questions, your group is likely to succeed.

Essential Elements of Group Communication

Group Size	**Yes**	**No**	**Sometimes**
1. Do group members communicate with one another directly?	☐	☐	☐
2. Does the group have enough people to achieve its goal?	☐	☐	☐
3. Can the group function effectively without forming subgroups?	☐	☐	☐
Interaction			
1. Do group members communicate with one another easily and frequently?	☐	☐	☐
2. Do members send, receive, and respond to messages in a way that enhances communication?	☐	☐	☐
Common Goal			
1. Does the group have a clear goal?	☐	☐	☐
2. Do members understand and support the group's goal?	☐	☐	☐
Interdependence			
1. Do members feel responsible for the group's actions?	☐	☐	☐
2. Do members understand their individual and group responsibilities?	☐	☐	☐
3. Do members believe that "we're all in this together"?	☐	☐	☐
Working			
1. Are members ready, willing, and able to participate as active group members?	☐	☐	☐
2. Do members give the time and energy needed to achieve the group's goal?	☐	☐	☐

notes

1. Michael Stroh and Scott Shane, "Who Gets Credit Still a Nobel Issue," *The Sun*, October 12, 2003, p. A1.
2. Nicky Hayes, *Managing Teams: A Strategy for Success* (Oxford: Thomson, 2002), pp. 51–52.
3. Peter D. Hart Research Associates, *How Should Colleges Prepare Students to Succeed in Today's Global Economy?* (Washington, DC: Peter D. Hart Research Associates, December 28, 2006), p. 2. Also see Association of American Colleges

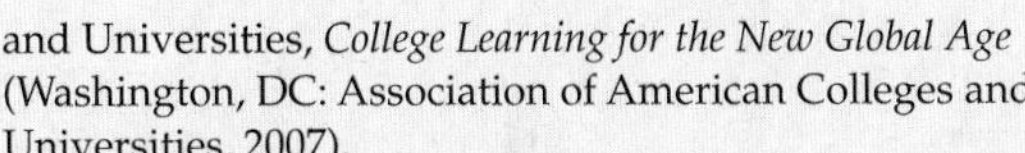

and Universities, *College Learning for the New Global Age* (Washington, DC: Association of American Colleges and Universities, 2007).

4. Peter D. Hart Research Associates, p. 7.
5. National Association of Colleges and Employers, *Special Report: Job Outlook '96* (Bethlehem, PA: NACE, November 1995).
6. Katherine W. Hawkins and Bryant P. Fillion, "Perceived Communication Needs for Work Groups," *Communication Research Reports* 16 (1999), pp. 171–172.
7. Rodney W. Napier and Matti K. Gershenfeld, *Groups: Theory and Experience,* 7th ed. (Boston: Houghton Mifflin, 2004), pp. 42–43.
8. Joseph A. Bonito and Andrea Hollingshead, "Participation in Small Groups," in *Communication Yearbook 20,* ed. Brant R. Burleson (Thousand Oaks, CA: Sage, 1997), p. 236.
9. Malcolm Gladwell, "The Cellular Church," *The New Yorker,* September 12, 2005, pp. 61–63.
10. Based on the Association for Communication Administration's 1995 Conference on Defining the Discipline statement that "the field of communication *focuses* on how people use verbal and nonverbal messages to generate meanings within and across various contexts, cultures, channels, and media." See *Spectra,* the newsletter of the National Communication Association, October 1995, p. 12.
11. Anne Donnellon, *Team Talk: The Power of Language in Team Dynamics* (Boston: Harvard Business School Press, 1996), p. 28.
12. Peter M. Senge et al., *The Fifth Discipline Fieldbook: Strategies and Tools for Building a Learning Organization* (New York: Doubleday, 1994), p. 51.
13. Quoted in David W. Johnson, R. T. Johnson, and K. A. Smith, "Cooperative Learning Returns to College," *Change,* July/August (1998), p. 31.
14. Lee Towe, *Why Didn't I Think of That? Creativity in the Workplace* (West Des Moines, IA: American Media, 1996), p. 8.
15. Donald J. Noone, *Creative Problem Solving,* 2nd ed. (Hauppauge, NY: Barron's, 1998), p. 132.
16. The National Communication Association (NCA) offers *Service-Learning and Communication: A Disciplinary Toolkit* on its website. This seventy-four-page document provides excellent information on how to develop a comprehensive service learning program. Go to www.natcom.org. The instructor's manual for this textbook includes a detailed Service Learning Assignment with an Assessment component prepared by Shirlee Levin, professor of speech communication, College of Southern Maryland.
17. Sara Chudnovsky Weintraub, "Constructing Communication Courses with Service-Learning Projects" (paper presented at the Eastern Communication Association Convention, Pittsburgh, April 27–30, 2000).
18. 3M Meeting Management Team with Jeannine Drew, *Mastering Meetings: Discovering the Hidden Potential of Effective Business Meetings* (New York: McGraw-Hill, 1994), p. 12.
19. *The Week,* Ap[illegible]
20. Warren Benn[illegible] *eyond Leadership: B*[illegible] n- bridge, MA: [illegible]
21. The first edit[illegible] al- ance metaph[illegible] up communicati[illegible] tion are an extensi[illegible] principle and are based on five major, contemporary sources: The dialectics of (1) autonomy and connectedness, (2) predictability and novelty, and (3) openness and closedness in Leslie A. Baxter and Barbara M. Montgomery, *Relating: Dialogues and Dialectics* (New York: Guilford Press, 1996); the dialectics of affect and instrumentality and judgment and acceptance in William K. Rawlins, *Friendship Matters: Communication, Dialectics, and the Life Course* (New York: Aldine De Gruyter, 1992); the dialectic of groups in Michael W. Kramer, "Toward a Communication Theory of Group Dialectics: An Ethnographic Study of a Community Theater Group," *Communication Monographs* 71 (2004): pp. 311–332; Larry A. Erbert et al., "Perceptions of Turning Points and Dialectical Interpretations in Organizational Team Development," *Small Group Research* 36 (2005), pp. 21–58; and Scott D. Johnson and Lynette M. Long, "Being a Part and Being Apart," in *New Directions in Group Communication,* ed. Lawrence Frey (Thousand Oaks, CA. Sage, 2002), pp. 25–41. Special thanks are extended to the faculty members participating in the group communication seminar at the 2005 NCA Hope Institute for Faculty Development at Luther College in Iowa. Participants helped consolidate dozens of group tensions into nine dialectics that closely resemble those presented in this textbook.
22. Donald G. Ellis and B. Aubrey Fisher, *Small Group Decision Making: Communication and the Group Process* (New York: McGraw-Hill, 1994), p. 51.
23. Harvey Robbins and Michael Finley, *The New Why Teams Don't Work: What Went Wrong and How to Make It Right* (Princeton, NJ: Peterson's/Pacesetter Books, 2000), pp. 27–29.
24. Carl E. Larson and Frank M. J. LaFasto, *Team Work: What Must Go Right/What Can Go Wrong* (Newbury Park, CA: Sage, 1989), p. 128.
25. Marshall Scott Poole, "Procedures for Managing Meetings: Social and Technical Innovation," in *Innovative Meeting Management,* ed. Richard A. Swanson and Bonnie Ogram Knapp (Austin, TX: 3M Meeting Management Institute, 1990), pp. 54–55.
26. Richard L. Johannesen, *Ethics in Human Communication,* 5th ed. (Prospect Heights, IL: Waveland, 2002), p. 1.
27. The NCA Credo for Ethical Communication was developed at the 1999 conference sponsored by the National Communication Association and facilitated by the authors of this textbook. The credo was adopted and endorsed by the Legislative Council of the National Communication Association in November 1999. www.natcom.org/aboutNCA/Policies/Platform.html.

chapter 2

Group Development

chapter outline

Group Development Stages

Forming Stage • Storming Stage • Norming Stage • Performing Stage • Adjourning Stage • Group Stages at Work

Group Goals

Goal Theory • Developing Group Goals • Hidden Agendas

Group Norms

Types of Norms • Conformity • Nonconformity

Characteristics of Effective Groups

study questions

- *How do groups evolve through a series of development stages?*
- *Why is a clear and elevated goal critical to successful group work?*
- *How do group norms affect group productivity and member interaction?*
- *What critical elements characterize highly successful groups?*

Group Development Stages

How do you behave when you attend the first meeting of a new group? Do you march into the room briskly, extend your hand to the first person you see, and say "Hi, I'm (your name)—Nice to meet you." Or, do you pause at the door, check things out as you move into the room, and look for a suitable moment to introduce yourself? Like many people, you may choose the second, more cautious entrance. Although you want to make a good first impression, you don't want to appear pushy and aggressive. If you recognize yourself in the first scenario, members may tell you later, "You scared me that first day" or "You behaved as if you were running for office." Welcome to the world of group development! In this chapter, we examine how groups form and evolve as they try to balance the complex and contradictory dialectic tensions inevitable in group work.

There are recognizable milestones in the lives of most groups. Like individuals, groups move through stages as they develop and mature. An "infant" group behaves differently than a group that has worked together for a long time and has matured into an "adult." A group's ability to "grow up" directly affects whether and how well its members work together to achieve a common goal.

More than one hundred theoretical models describe how a group moves through several "passages" during its lifetime.[1] In this chapter, we use **Tuckman's Group Development Stages** model because it is well recognized, easy to remember, and considered one of the most comprehensive models of group development relevant to all types of groups.[2]

In 1965, Bruce W. Tuckman, an educational psychologist, identified four discrete stages in the life cycle of groups—forming, storming, norming, and performing.[3] He and Mary Ann Jensen refined the model in 1977 by adding a fifth stage—adjourning[4] (see Table 2.1).

Forming Stage

When you join a group, you rarely know what to expect. Will everyone get along together and work hard? Will you make a good first impression? Will this be a positive experience or a nightmare? Most people enter a new group with caution.

During the initial **forming stage**, members carefully explore *both* their personal goals *and* the group's goal. They may be tentative and somewhat uncomfortable about working with a group of strangers or unfamiliar colleagues, and they try to understand their tasks and test personal relationships. Although little gets done during this orientation phase, members need this time to become acquainted with one another and to assess the group's goal. At this point in the group development process, "the most important job . . . is not to build a better rocket or debug . . . a new software product or double sales—it is to orient itself to itself."[5]

Table 2.1 Tuckman's Group Development Stages

Forming	Storming	Norming	Performing	Adjourning
Members are socially cautious and polite.	Members compete for status and openly disagree.	Members resolve status conflicts and establish norms.	Members assume appropriate roles and work productively.	Members disengage and relinquish responsibilities.

Primary Tension. Group communication scholar Ernest G. Bormann describes **primary tension** as the social unease and stiffness that accompanies the getting-acquainted stage in a new group.[6] Because most members of a new group want to create a good first impression, they tend to be overly polite with one another. Members don't interrupt one another, and there may be long, awkward pauses between comments. When members do speak, they often speak softly and avoid expressing strong opinions. Although laughter may occur, it is often strained, inappropriate, or uncomfortable. When the group starts its discussion, the topic may be small talk about sports, the weather, or a recent news event.

A group that experiences primary tension may talk less, provide little in the way of content, and be perceived as ineffective. Before a group can work efficiently and effectively, members should try to reduce primary tension. Usually, this initial tension decreases as members come to feel more comfortable with one another. In some groups, primary tension lasts for only a few minutes. In less fortunate groups, primary tension may continue for months. The group may fail to become a cohesive and productive team.

Resolving Primary Tension. In many groups, primary tension will disappear quickly and naturally as group members get to know one another and gain confidence. Other groups need direct intervention to relieve this early form of tension. Recognizing and discussing primary tension is one way of breaking its cycle. A perceptive member may purposely exhibit behavior that counteracts primary tension, such as talking in a strong voice, looking involved and energized, sticking to the group's topic, and expressing an opinion. Usually, with each group meeting, the amount of primary tension decreases. However, if primary tension remains, a group can stall and never get beyond the forming stage. Here are some suggestions for resolving primary tension:

- Be positive and energetic. Smile. Nod in agreement. Laugh. Exhibit enthusiasm.
- Be patient and open-minded, knowing that primary tension should decrease with time.
- Be prepared and informed before your first meeting so you can help the group focus on its task.

Storming Stage

After spending some time in the forming stage, group members realize that "being nice" to one another may not accomplish very much, particularly when there are real issues to address and problems to solve. As the group gradually moves from the forming stage to the storming stage, disagreements arise.

In the **storming stage**, groups confront the conflict ↔ cohesion dialectic and the leadership ↔ followership dialectic. Some members lose their patience with forming stage niceties while others begin competing with one another to determine their status and to establish group roles. During this stage, group members often become argumentative and emotional. As the group tries to get down to business, the most confident members begin to compete for both social acceptance and leadership. They openly disagree on issues of substance. However, it is still too early in the group's existence to predict the outcome of such competition.

Many groups try to skip this stage in order to avoid competition and conflict. However, storming is a necessary part of a group's development. Without it, a group may not resolve issues related to member roles, leadership responsibilities, and the group's goal. Conflict is also necessary to establish a climate in which members understand the value of disagreeing with one another.[7]

case study

Nice to Meet You, Too

A group of community volunteers meets for the first time to plan and raise funds for building a neighborhood playground.* Although Dave, Betty, Ray, Bill, and Aisha live in the same community, they don't know one another. They begin the meeting by introducing themselves. They all smile a lot, but communication seems a bit stiff and awkward. Betty's handshake connects to other members only at her fingertips, while Ray and Bill offer firm handshakes. As Aisha introduces herself, she giggles and runs a hand through her long hair. Dave sits at the head of the table and chairs the meeting.

Aisha has come to the meeting well prepared. She hesitantly raises her hand to speak and Dave recognizes her. She reports that, according to her research, a simple playground can range from $5,000 to $50,000. She suggests that $35,000 would be a good target budget. Bill starts to respond by saying, "Well, uh . . ." but when he sees that Ray has raised his hand, he concludes with "Go ahead." Ray says, "Oh, I was going to say—ah—I've looked it over a bit. $35,000 is—ah—I don't know—I guess that would be good, but I think we should stay as high as we can." Bill now responds with "Ah—I was thinking just the opposite—kind of—we should go lower—uh. . . ." Dave interrupts and suggests that they go with the $35,000 Aisha proposed, just to get started. Bill seems a bit annoyed with Dave's suggestion, but doesn't say anything.

Dave notes that regardless of the cost, they need to discuss ways of raising money for the playground. At this point Aisha begins taking notes. Betty says, "Well—it worked at our church—in the other city where I lived . . . we had great bake sales—twice a year." Ray politely tells Betty that a bake sale is a great idea, but that it may not raise enough funds. The rest of the group grimaces and ignores Betty's offer to run a bake sale. Aisha then asks if group members know anyone who works for a foundation that might donate some of the money. Betty reveals that she has a dear friend who is actively involved in a large, local foundation. The group sits up and pays a lot more attention to Betty. Ray even jokes that maybe the foundation can help with the bake sale, too. Everyone laughs.

Only three minutes of the meeting have gone by. The group has a lot more to discuss but members have slowly become better acquainted with one another and have a better feeling about how they will work together and get along.

*A short video of this group discussion is available through the publisher, Pearson/Allyn & Bacon. Watching the discussion adds important nonverbal perspectives to understanding group development.

When you finish reading this chapter, you should be able to answer the following questions:

1. What verbal and nonverbal behaviors demonstrated the forming stage of group development?
2. In your opinion, which members are most likely to compete for status and influence in the storming stage?
3. What strategies did group members use or should they have used to decrease primary tension?
4. What, if any, dialectic tensions will affect how well this group achieves its goal and how well members get along with one another?
5. What implicit norms emerged during the discussion and did these norms help the group move through the forming stage?

Secondary Tension. The frustrations and personality conflicts experienced by group members as they compete for acceptance and achievement within a group are the source of what Bormann calls **secondary tension.** Whereas primary tension arises from lack of confidence, secondary tension emerges when members have gained enough confidence to become assertive and even aggressive as they pursue positions of power and influence. Conflicts can result from disagreements over issues, conflicts in values, or an inability to deal with disruptive members. Regardless of the causes, a group cannot hope to achieve its common goal without managing secondary tension.

The signs of secondary tension are almost the direct opposite of those of primary tension. There is a high level of energy and agitation. The group is noisier, more dynamic, and physically active. Members speak in louder voices, interrupting and overlapping one another so that two or three people may be speaking at the same time. Members sit up straight, lean forward, or squirm in their seats. Everyone is alert and listening intently.

Resolving Secondary Tension. Members of successful groups develop ways to handle this phase in a group's development. Often, one or two members will joke about the tension. The resulting laughter is likely to ease the stress. Sometimes individual members will work outside the group setting to discuss the personal difficulties and anxieties of group members. Dealing with secondary tension can be difficult and even painful. However, if a group fails to resolve human relations problems, it will not become an effective and cohesive work group.

Most groups experience some form of primary and secondary tension during the forming and storming stages. In fact, a little bit of tension is a good thing. It can motivate a group toward action and increase a group's sensitivity to feedback. Most effective groups learn to balance the need for both conflict and cohesion. As group communication scholars Donald Ellis and Aubrey Fisher point out, "the successful and socially healthy group is not characterized by an absence of social tension, but by successful management of social tension."[8]

Norming Stage

During the forming and storming stages, groups lack balance. They are either too cautious or too confrontational. Once a group moves to the **norming stage**, members resolve these early tensions and learn to work as a cohesive team. They also develop methods for achieving group goals and establish norms and "rules of engagement." In addition, members feel more comfortable with one another and are willing to disagree and express opinions. The group is ready and even eager to begin working as a committed and unified team. Feelings of trust and clear goals emerge as members become more comfortable with one another and with agreed-upon group procedures. "Communication becomes more open and task oriented" as "members solidify positive working relationships with each other."[9] There is more order and direction during this third stage of group development. Members have begun to resolve a wide range of group dialectics, with special emphasis on norms (conforming ↔ nonconforming), task requirements (structure ↔ spontaneity), and adapting to member characteristics (homogeneous ↔ heterogeneous).

Performing Stage

When (and if) a group reaches the **performing stage**, members are fully engaged and eager to work. Roles and responsibilities are fluid; they adapt and change according to group needs and task requirements. In this stage, group identity, loyalty, and morale are generally high. When groups reach the performing stage, members focus their energies on both the task and social dimensions of group work as they make major decisions and solve critical problems.

Just about everyone shares in and supports a unified effort to achieve a common goal. Although disagreements occur, they are usually resolved intelligently and amicably. During this stage, "interaction patterns reflect virtually no tension; rather, the members are jovial, loud, boisterous, laughing, and verbally backslapping each other."[10]

Adjourning Stage

When a group reaches the **adjourning stage**, it has usually achieved its common goal and may begin to disband.[11] Groups end their work and their existence for many

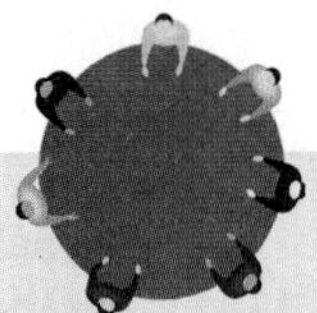

theory in groups
Group Development Theories

Group development research began in the early 1950s and continues on to this day. Many early theories—like Tuckman's Model—are linear, that is, they describe development stages as small changes that follow one another in a fixed path.[1] During the 1990s, researchers challenged this linear model, by theorizing that "groups alternate between periods of inertia and revolution triggered primarily by their members' awareness of time and deadlines.[2] In simpler terms, groups don't move through each successive stage systematically, or as though they are running a clearly marked obstacle course. Most groups work through a stage until circumstances motivate them to take on the necessary challenges of another stage. Factors such as "changes in membership, external demands, and changes in leadership" may slow development or push a group back to a previous stage.[3]

Group communication scholar Marshall Scott Poole suggests that the stages described in most theoretical models may be "ideal" steps but that groups often stray from the ideal.[4] For example, a very large group may be unable to get past initial development. If a group's goal is unclear, the result will be wasted time, member frustration, and unproductive work. If, however, members are cooperative, a group will move through the stages much more easily. Also, when group members have worked together before with successful outcomes, a group may skip or spend very little time in early stages.

[1]Artemis Chang, Julie Duck, and Prashant Bordia, "Understanding the Multidimensionality of Group Development," *Small Group Research* 37 (2006), pp. 327–50.

[2]K. L. Bettenhausen, "Five Years of Group Research: What We Have Learned and What Needs to Be Addressed," *Journal of Management* 17 (1991), p. 352.

[3]Susan A. Wheelan, *Creating Effective Teams: A Guide for Members and Leaders* (Thousand Oaks, CA: Sage, 1999), p. 29.

[4]Marshall Scott Poole and J. Roth, "Decision Making in Small Groups, V: Test of a Contingency Model," *Human Communication Research* 15 (1989), pp. 549–89. For more analysis of sequential group stage models, see Holly Arrow et al., "Time, Change, and Development: The Temporal Perspective on Groups," *Small Group Research* 35 (February 2004), pp. 73–105.

[5]Bruce W. Tuckman and Mary Ann C. Jensen, "Stages of Small Group Development Revisited," *Group and Organizational Studies* 2 (1977), pp. 419–27.

[6]B. Aubrey Fisher, "Decision Emergence: Phases in Group Decision Making," *Speech Monographs* 37 (1970), pp. 53–66.

[7]Susan A. Wheelan, *Creating Effective Teams* (Thousand Oaks, CA: Sage, 1999), pp. 23–36, 93–132.

[8]Yvonne M. Agazarian, "Phases of Development in the Systems-Centered Psychotherapy Group," *Small Group Research* 30 (1999), pp. 82–107.

Group Development Theories

Bruce Tuckman[5]	B. Aubrey Fisher[6]	Susan Wheelan[7]	Yvonne Agazarian[8]
Forming	Orientation	Dependency and Inclusion	Authority—Flight
Storming	Conflict	Counterdependency and Fight	Authority—Fight
Norming	Emergence	Trust and Structure	Intimacy
Performing	Reinforcing	Work and Productivity	Interdependent Work
Adjourning		Termination	

reasons. After achieving a goal or completing an assigned task, a group may have no reason to continue. In other cases, individual members may leave a group for personal or professional reasons or to search out and join another group. Individual rather than group goals become more prominent. When an entire group disbands, however, most members experience the stress and strain that comes with relinquishing group responsibilities. They also confront relational issues such as how to retain friendships with other members.[12] Generally, members are proud of what they've achieved, but they may feel a sense of loss when the group dissolves. When groups adjourn, the dialectic balance shifts from engagement to disengagement. Some writers describe this fifth stage as "mourning," recognizing the loss felt by group members.[13]

Group Stages at Work

Juries provide a useful example for understanding Tuckman's Group Development stages. Juries form when a group of unaquainted individuals are selected to deliberate and achieve a very specific goal—making a decision in a court case. The forming stage begins as soon as members enter the jury room. Jurors don't know one another, but they do know that the issues in the case will probably cause some conflict. Initial interaction is often awkward and polite. During the forming stage, members may exchange some personal information and engage in small talk rather than jump into a discussion of the case.

During the storming stage, jurors voice opinions about the case and challenge one another's positions with comments such as "I thought the defendant was telling the truth," "The defense attorney was too slick," or "Didn't you look at what their contract said?" During this stage, jurors form impressions of one another and look for procedures and rules to control conflict.

During the norming stage, the jury settles down and develops an orderly method for dealing with the issues. Norms might include listening respectfully to others, not interrupting one another, and voting in a certain order. At this point, the jury is ready to enter the performing stage.

During the performing stage, roles are clear. For example, the jury may rely on one juror who recalls witnesses' testimony accurately, another who is good at encouraging jurors to express and justify their positions, and a third who conscientiously reviews the documents presented in the courtroom. Members are comfortable with others and their personal differences. They are moving toward a consensus on the issues. In other words, they are doing their job—and, in most cases, doing it well. Finally, the jury reports its decision to the court and reaches the adjournment stage. After its decision has been recorded, the jury is dismissed, the group is disbanded, and court is adjourned.

Keep in mind that Tuckman's stages represent only one of the many theories that attempt to explain the process of group development. Although each theory uses different words to describe the process, the descriptions of group development in these theories are strikingly similar. Group development theories are useful for explaining how groups and their members behave at different points in their development and why.

Group Goals

An effective group has *both* a clear understanding of its goal *and* a belief that its goal is meaningful and worthwhile.[14] The Apollo Moon Project is a good example. Which goal is more motivating: "To be leaders in space exploration" or "To place a man on the moon by the end of the 1960s"? Fortunately, NASA adopted the second goal, and

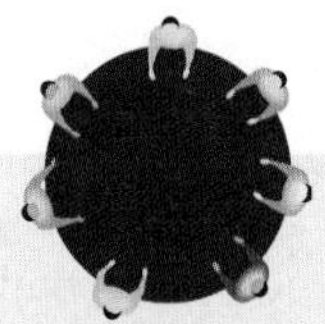

groups in balance . . .
Socialize Newcomers

Regardless of how many groups you belong to, you are a newcomer every time you join a group. Not surprisingly, your experiences in other groups affect how you adapt to and communicate with new group members. Understanding the socialization process can help you reduce the uncertainty that accompanies every new group experience.

The socialization process is important in groups because "positive socialization creates stronger commitments to confront and balance the multiple issues and tensions involved in participating in group activities."[1] Much like Tuckman did with his group development stages, Carolyn Anderson and her colleagues view socialization as a passage through five phases:

1. ***Antecedent phase.*** As a newcomer, you bring your beliefs and attitudes, culture, needs and motives, communication skills, personality traits, knowledge, and prior group experiences to a new group. These factors influence how well the group accepts you. If you bring factors the group needs and values, socialization will be faster and easier.
2. ***Anticipatory phase.*** Members of an established group have expectations about newcomers. They may look for someone with certain types of knowledge or communication skills. They may have heard that you share their beliefs and attitudes. Socialization is more likely to succeed if a group's expectations match your characteristics and motives.
3. ***Encounter phase.*** During the encounter phase, newcomers try to fit in. You can do this by adjusting to group expectations, assuming needed roles, communicating effectively, and finding an appropriate balance between your individual goals and the group's goals.
4. ***Assimilation phase.*** During this phase, newcomers become fully integrated into the group's culture. Established members and newcomers blend into a comfortable state of working together to achieve common goals.
5. ***Exit phase.*** Some groups, such as families, may never disband, although they change as new members join and others leave. Working groups manage this process by giving departing members a warm send-off and welcoming new members who take their place. Regardless of the reason (whether positive or negative), leaving an established group can be a difficult experience.[2]

Socialization in groups is a give-and-take process in which members and groups come together to satisfy needs and accomplish goals. During the socialization process, newcomers, established members, and the group as a whole adapt to one another. When socialization is successful, the group creates a unique culture and group structure, engages in relevant activities, and pursues individual and group goals.[3]

[1]The definition of socialization is based on Carolyn M. Anderson, Bruce L. Riddle, and Matthew M. Martin, "Socialization Process in Groups," in *The Handbook of Group Communication Theory and Research*, ed. Lawrence R. Frey; Dennis S. Gouran and Marshall Scott Poole, assoc. eds. (Thousand Oaks, CA: Sage, 1999), p. 155.

[2]Anderson, Riddle, and Martin, p. 139.

[3]Anderson, Riddle, and Martin, p. 142.

its simple words were both clear and inspiring.[15] In Carl Larson and Frank LaFasto's three-year study of characteristics that explain how and why effective groups develop, "a clear and elevated goal" was at the top of the list.[16] Any old goal is not enough.

Clear, elevated goals create a sense of excitement and even urgency. They challenge group members and give them the opportunity to excel—both as individuals and as a group. Here is how Larson and LaFasto describe what happens when groups work to achieve such goals:

> [Groups] lose their sense of time. They discover to their surprise that it's dark outside and they worked right through the supper hours. The rate of communication among team members increases dramatically, even to the point that individuals call each other at all hours of the night because they can't get something out of their minds. There is a sense of great excitement and feelings of elation whenever even minor progress is made toward the goal.[17]

Rescue teams, NASA astronauts, surgical teams, mountain climbers, and sports teams engage in challenging and strenuous activities as they work together to achieve a goal. What are the characteristics of an effective group goal?

Goal Theory

Edwin Locke and Gary Latham's **Goal Theory** examines the value of setting group goals and methods for accomplishing those goals. They conclude that groups function best when their goals (1) are specific, (2) are hard but realistic, (3) are accepted by members, (4) are used to evaluate performance, (5) are linked to feedback and rewards, (6) are set by members and groups, and (7) allow for member growth.[18]

Locke and Latham claim that effective goal setting does more than raise group productivity and improve work quality. It also clarifies group and members' expectations, increases satisfaction with individual and group performance, and enhances members' self-confidence, pride, and willingness to accept future challenges. Difficult or challenging goals can lead to greater effort and persistence than easy goals, assuming that a group accepts the difficult goals as worthwhile.[19]

Think of your own accomplishments. If you set out to earn a passing C in your courses, you may not work hard or feel proud of the results if you succeed. If, however, you strive for As, you will work harder, be proud of your work, and, if you succeed, enjoy the reward of achieving an enviable grade-point average.

Developing Group Goals

If your group is given what someone *else* thinks is a clear and elevated goal, group members may not be impressed or inspired. However, if your group develops its *own* goal, the motivation of members to achieve that goal is heightened.[20] This increase in motivation comes about because group-based goal setting produces a better match of member and group needs, a better understanding of the group actions needed to achieve the goal, and a better appreciation of how individual members can contribute to group action. Moreover, when group members set the group's goals, the process can create a more interdependent, cooperative, and cohesive environment in which to work.[21]

Group goals should be both specific and challenging. Specific goals lead to higher performance than do generalized goals. For example, telling a group to "do your best" in choosing someone for a job is a generalized goal. A specific goal would be: Review the candidates for the job, recommend three top candidates, and include a list of each top candidate's strengths and weaknesses.

Think of the difference between a specific, challenging class assignment and one that is vague and undemanding. "Be prepared to discuss the questions at the end of the chapter" doesn't give you much direction, whereas "Choose one of the discussion questions at the end of the chapter, outline your answer with references to textbook content, and turn in your outline on Monday" gives both clear and (ideally) thought-provoking directions.

Locke and Latham's Goal Theory goes beyond explaining why goals are important. They also recommend a step-by-step method for setting goals and achieving optimum results. Table 2.2 integrates Locke and Latham's key steps for setting goals in a group context.

Setting a specific, clear, and elevated goal benefits *every* group. You don't have to be a NASA scientist or a corporate executive to set impressive goals. Even if your only task is to participate in a graded classroom discussion, your group should take

Table 2.2 Setting Group Goals

Goal-Setting Steps	Goal-Setting Question	Sample Goals
1. Specify the nature of the task(s) to be accomplished in terms of outcomes and/or group actions or behaviors.	What do we want to accomplish?	• We will raise funds to support textbook scholarships for needy students. • We want to increase student attendance at college theatre productions.
2. Specify how group outcomes, action, or behavior will be measured.	How will we know we've achieved our goal?	• We will raise $10,000 to support 50 textbook scholarships of $200 each. • More than 1,500 students will attend each college theatre production this year.
3. Specify the performance standard for achieving the goal.	How well have we achieved our goal?	• We will raise $10,000 by July 1. • More than 90 percent of audience members who fill out a survey will rate the play as excellent or very good.
4. Specify the time span and deadlines for achieving subgoals and the overall group goal.	What tasks do we need to complete in order to achieve our goal by a specific date?	• We will develop a list of potential donors by May 1, cultivate and seek donations from the donors in May and June, and reach $10,000 by July 1. • We will work with the college PR office to promote the plays in the spring, ask professors to require students to see discipline-related plays, and seek free publicity from local media.
5. Specify the coordination requirements for goal achievement.	How will we coordinate the work and contributions of group members most efficiently and effectively?	• We will divide up the list of potential donors and expect each member to contact and seek donations from their contacts. • We will assign two members to work with the PR office, two to work with academic departments, and two to contact local media.

the time to develop a set of appropriate goals. For example, in many group communication classes, instructors require students to participate in a problem-solving discussion. The group usually chooses its topic, creates a discussion agenda, and demonstrates its preparation and group communication skills in class. This is nothing like "putting a man on the moon." Yet, even a classroom discussion can be more effective if the group establishes a clear, elevated goal, such as "Our group and every member will earn an A on this assignment." In order to achieve this goal, your group will have to do many things: Choose a meaningful discussion topic, prepare a useful agenda, research the topic thoroughly, make sure that every member is well prepared and ready to contribute, and demonstrate effective group communication skills during the discussion.

A clear, elevated goal does more than set your sights on an outcome; it helps your group decide how to get there. Regardless of the circumstances or the setting, your group will benefit by asking six questions about your goals:

1. *Clarity*. Is the goal clear, specific, and observable if achieved?
2. *Challenge*. Is the goal difficult, inspiring, and thought provoking?
3. *Commitment*. Do members see the goal as meaningful, realistic, and attainable? Are they dedicated to achieving the goal?
4. *Compatibility*. Can *both* group *and* individual goals be achieved?
5. *Cooperation*. Does the goal require cooperation among group members?
6. *Cost*. Does the group have adequate resources, such as time and materials, to achieve the goal?[22]

Routine goals can be boring. Clear and elevated goals can be powerful motivators. When President John F. Kennedy declared that the United States would put a man on the moon and bring him back safely, no one doubted the magnificence of the challenge, even if they doubted whether it could be achieved.

Hidden Agendas

Most groups know what they want and how they intend to go about achieving their goals. The same is true of group members. Many (if not most) members may have personal goals and preferred methods for achieving those goals. As long as a member's personal goals and work preferences support the group's goal, all is well. A **hidden agenda,** however, occurs when a member's private goal conflicts with the group's goals. Hidden agendas represent what people really want rather than what they say they want. When hidden agendas become more important than a group's stated agenda or goal, the result can be group frustration, unresolved conflict, and failure. Hidden agendas disrupt the flow of communication. Real issues and concerns may be buried while pseudoarguments dominate the discussion.

A student reported this incident in which a hidden agenda disrupted a group's deliberations:

> I was on a student government board that decides how college activities funds should be distributed to student clubs and intramural teams. About halfway through the process, I became aware that several members were active in intramural sports. By the time I noticed their pro-sports voting pattern, they'd gotten most of what they wanted. You wouldn't believe the bizarre reasons they came up with to cut academic clubs while fully supporting the budgets of athletic teams. What made me mad was that they didn't care about what most students wanted; they only wanted to make sure that *their* favorite teams were funded.

If unrecognized and unresolved during the forming stage, hidden agendas can permeate and infect *all* stages of group development. Effective groups deal with hidden agendas by recognizing them and trying to resolve them whenever they occur.

When a group member is hesitant to get involved with other members and the group process or if the group's progress is unusually slow, look for hidden agendas. A question such as "What seems to be hanging us up here?" may encourage members to reveal some of their private concerns. Recognizing the existence of hidden agendas may be sufficient to keep a group moving from stage to stage in its development.

Even when you recognize the existence of hidden agendas, some of them cannot and should not be shared because they may create an atmosphere of distrust. Not many people would want to deal with the following revelation during a group discussion: "I only joined this group because I have a crush on one of the members." Recognizing hidden agendas means knowing that some of them can and should be confronted, whereas others cannot and should not be shared with the group.

Groups can resolve the dialectic tensions caused by hidden agendas through early agreement on the group's goal and careful planning of the group's process. Sociologists Rodney Napier and Matti Gershenfeld suggest that discussing hidden agendas during the early stages of group development can counteract their blocking power.[23] Initial discussion could include some of the following questions:

- What are the group's goals?
- Does the leader have any personal concerns or goals that differ from these?
- Do any members have any personal concerns or goals that differ from these?
- What outcomes do members expect?

Discussing these questions openly can help a group recognize and respect the inevitability and function of hidden agendas. Hidden agendas do not necessarily cause problems or prevent a group from achieving its goal. Understanding them can help explain why members are or are not willing to participate fully in the work of a group.

Group Norms

One factor that influences a group's passage from the forming to the performing stage is the creation of norms. Communication scholar Patricia Andrews defines **norms** as "sets of expectations held by group members concerning what kinds of behaviors or opinions are acceptable or unacceptable, good or bad, right or wrong, appropriate or inappropriate."[24] Norms serve several important purposes to ensure positive and consistent interaction among group members. Group norms

- express the values of the group.
- help the group to function smoothly.
- define appropriate social behavior.
- help the group to survive.[25]

Norms are the group's rules. They affect how members behave, dress, speak, and work. For example, the norms for the members of a company's sales team might include meeting before lunch, applauding one another's successes, and wearing suits to work. Without norms, accomplishing group goals would be difficult. There would be no agreed-upon way to organize and perform work.

Some norms, however, can work against a group and its goals. If group norms place a premium on friendly and peaceful discussions, group members may be reluctant to voice disagreement or share bad news. If group norms permit members to arrive late and leave early, meetings may not have enough members to make important decisions. Norms that do not support a group's goal can prevent the group from succeeding.

Group norms are powerful predictors of group behavior. According to Nicky Hayes, a British psychologist, "Group norms are intangible and often difficult to express in words, but that doesn't mean that they are not real. People who belong to groups often try very hard to conform to their group's norms—because the price of failure may be exclusion from the group, or even ridicule."[26]

Types of Norms

There are two general types of group norms—explicit and implicit. Because **explicit norms** are put in writing or are stated verbally, they are easy to recognize. Explicit norms are often imposed on a group. The group leader may have the authority to determine rules. A large group or organization may have standard procedures that it expects everyone to follow. For example, the workers in a customer service department may be required to wear name badges. The staff may have recommended this rule, the supervisor may have ordered this "custom," or the company may have established a policy regarding employee identification.

Implicit norms are rarely discussed or openly communicated. As a result, they are not as easy to recognize. Generally, they evolve as members interact with one another. For example, it may take new group members several weeks to learn that meetings begin fifteen minutes later than scheduled. Even seating arrangements may be

governed by implicit norms. Group members often learn about an implicit norm when they violate one. Almost all of us have been unsettled when we walked into a classroom and discovered someone sitting at "our" desk. Although groups rarely discuss such rules, offending members soon sense that they have violated an implicit norm. Insensitive members may never "get it."

Regardless of whether norms are openly communicated or implicitly understood, they can be divided into four categories: interaction norms, procedural norms, status norms, and achievement norms (see Table 2.3). **Interaction norms** determine how group members communicate with one another and reveal what types of communication behavior are appropriate in a group. **Procedural norms** dictate how the group operates. Knowing these norms will help you adapt to the rules and procedures the group typically follows. **Status norms** identify the levels of influence among group members and help explain how status is determined. In this context, we define status as the degree of prestige, respect, or influence that a member holds. **Achievement norms** determine the quality and quantity of work expected from group members. They can help you make decisions about how much time and energy must be devoted to working with a particular group.

Conformity

Group norms function only to the extent that members conform to them. **Conformity** occurs when group members adopt attitudes and actions that a majority favors or that adhere to the group's social norms.[27] We learn the value of conformity at a young age. In the classroom, children learn that standing in line and raising their hands are expected behaviors. On the playground, children who refuse to play by the rules may find themselves playing alone.

Groups can exert enormous pressure to conform. Two classic (and disturbing) studies illustrate our tendency to conform to unreasonable norms.[28] During the 1960s, Stanley Milgram of Yale University designed a series of experiments to find out whether people would obey commands from a powerless stranger who tells them to inflict what seems to be considerable pain on another person. Subjects were told by the supposed experimenter to administer painful electric shocks to research associates if the associate answered a question incorrectly. In fact, *no* shock was given. The associates were trained to writhe in pain, scream, and pound on walls. Even though the

Table 2.3 Types of Norms

	Interaction Norms	Procedural Norms	Status Norms	Achievement Norms
Key Question	What communication behavior is appropriate?	How does the group operate and run meetings?	Who has power and control?	What are the group's standards?
Example of Implicit Norm	We tend to use the pronouns *we, us,* and *our* rather than *I, me,* and *my.*	Everyone turns off cell phones and other technologies during meetings.	The group leader always sits at the head of the table.	Everyone shows up on time or early for our scheduled meetings.
Example of Explicit Norm	The group leader is responsible for making sure that everyone gets a chance to speak.	We always get an agenda in advance and use it during our meetings.	When a group vote is tied, the leader casts the deciding vote.	All members must have full references for any reports or research they cite.

Group norms express group values, help groups function efficiently, and define appropriate social behavior. Why, as the authors of your textbook claim, does constructive nonconformity also help a group achieve its common goal?

subjects thought they were causing enormous pain, very few subjects refused to increase the shocks as directed by an experimenter. In this case, pressure from an authority figure outweighed individual judgment and morality.

In another famous study conducted in the early 1970s, Philip Zimbardo created a realistic-looking prison in a Stanford University basement in which student subjects were assigned to play the role of prison guard or prisoner for several days. Very quickly, the prison guards used their power and became increasingly abusive and cruel. After a brief period of rebellion, the prisoners became passive, demoralized, and depressed. Zimbardo halted the experiment because it was "out of control" and causing psychological and physical damage to the subjects.[29]

Although some group members may have reasons for ignoring or wanting to change norms, most groups pressure their members to conform. You are more likely to conform to norms when one or more of the following factors are present:

- You want to continue your membership in the group.
- You have a lower status than other group members and don't want to risk being seen as an upstart.
- You feel obligated to conform.
- You get along with and like working with the other group members.
- You may be punished for violating norms and/or rewarded for compliance.[30]

Nonconformity

Members decide whether they will or will not conform to group norms. **Nonconformity** occurs when a member does not meet the expectations of the group. Although conformity to norms is essential to the functioning of a group, nonconformity can, in some cases, improve group performance. For example, members may deviate from the group when they have legitimate concerns and alternative suggestions. **Constructive nonconformity** occurs when a member resists a norm while still working to promote a group goal.

There are times when constructive nonconformity is needed and valuable. Movies, television shows, and books have championed the holdout juror, the stubbornly honest politician, and the principled but disobedient soldier or crew member. Sometimes there is so much pressure for group members to conform that they need a deviant to shake up the process, to provide critical feedback, and to create doubt about what had been a confident but wrong decision. Nonconformity can serve a group well if it prevents members from ignoring important information or making a hasty decision. Effective groups balance the benefits of both conforming and nonconforming. The following statements are examples of constructive deviation:

- "I know we always ask the newest group member to take minutes during the meeting, but we may be losing the insight of an experienced member and skilled note taker by continuing this practice."
- "I can't attend any more meetings if they're going to last for three hours."

When a member voices constructive concerns or objections, other members will justify their positions, address important issues, and explore alternatives. Constructive nonconformity contributes to more effective group decisions and more creative solutions.[31] In contrast, **destructive nonconformity** occurs when a member resists conforming to norms without regard for the best interests of the group and its goal.

Nonconformity of either type provides a group with an opportunity to examine its norms. When members deviate, the group may have to discuss the value of a particular norm and subsequently choose to change it, clarify it, or continue to accept it. At the very least, nonconforming behavior helps members recognize and understand

ethics in groups
Ethical Group Norms

Group communication scholar Ernest G. Bormann contends that ethical dilemmas surface whenever groups face unavoidable dialectic tensions.[1] Group norms can present ethical dilemmas when they serve unethical purposes. In some groups, norms exclude people because of race, gender, age, or personal philosophy. When group norms restrict members' freedom of expression, an ethical member should object to the norm and try to change it. If all else fails, ethical members may publicly renounce the group or quit in protest.

A group and its members have ethical responsibilities. We offer some conclusions based on Bormann's advice and urge you to meet these standards as you interact with group members to achieve a common goal:[2]

- When you join a group, focus on the group's goals rather than your own.
- If someone asks you to do something unethical, object or decline the assignment—and make the rest of the group aware of the ethical issues and consequences.
- If a group adopts unethical norms, such as restricting the free flow of information or diversifying membership, take responsibility and push for changes to such restrictive norms.
- Promote a group climate in which all members can develop their full potential as individuals of worth and dignity.
- Build group cohesiveness, raise the status of others, volunteer to help the group, and release social tensions.
- As you become more knowledgeable about group communication, develop a well-thought-out code of ethics.

[1]Ernest G. Bormann, *Small Group Communication: Theory and Practice*, 3rd ed. (Edina, MN: Burgess, 1996), pp. 270–74.

[2]Bormann, pp. 286–88.

the norms of the group. For instance, if a member is reprimanded for criticizing an office policy, other members will learn that the boss should not be challenged. Some groups will attempt to correct deviating members or may change their norms as a result of constructive nonconformity.

While most groups can handle an occasional encounter with a renegade, dealing with highly disruptive members is another story. Fortunately, several strategies can help a group deal with a member whose disruptive behavior becomes destructive. The following methods begin with efforts to accommodate a disruptive member and escalate to a more permanent solution. A group can accept, confront, or even exclude the troublesome member.

Accept. In some cases, a group will accept and put up with disruptive nonconformity. Acceptance is not the same as approval; it involves learning to live with disruptive behavior. When the disruption is not critical to the group's ultimate success, or when the member's positive contributions far outweigh the inconvenience and annoyance of putting up with the behavior, a group may allow the disruptive behavior to continue. For example, a member who is always late for meetings but puts in more than her fair share of work may find her tardy behavior accepted as an unavoidable idiosyncrasy.

Confront. Another strategy for dealing with disruptive nonconformity is confrontation, particularly when a member's behavior is impossible to accept or ignore and when it threatens the success of a group and its members. At first, rather than singling out the disruptive member, you may address the entire group about the issue—talk generally about coming to meetings prepared and on time, not interrupting others while they're speaking, and criticizing ideas, not people. When, however, a member becomes "impossible," groups may confront the perpetrator in several ways. At first, members may direct a lot of attention to the wayward member in an attempt to reason with him or her. They may even talk about him or her during the course of the discussion: "Barry, it's distracting and disrupts our discussion when you answer your cell phone in meetings. Please turn it off." Although such attention can be intimidating and uncomfortable for the nonconforming member, it may not be sufficient to overcome the problem.

As an alternative to a public confrontation, there may be value in discussing the problem with the disruptive member outside the group setting. A frank and open conversation between the disruptive member and the leader or a trusted member of the group may uncover the causes of the problem as well as solutions for it. Some nonconforming members may not see their behavior as disruptive and, as a result, may not understand why the group is ignoring, confronting, or excluding them. Taking time to talk with a disruptive member in a nonthreatening setting can solve both a personal and a group problem.

Exclude. When all else fails, a group may exclude disruptive members. Exclusion can take several forms. During discussions, group members can turn away from problem members, ignore their comments, or refuse to make eye contact. Exclusion might mean assigning disruptive members to unimportant, solo tasks or ones that will drive them away. Finally, a group may be able to expel unwanted members and be rid of the troublemakers. Being asked to leave a group or being barred from participating is a humiliating experience that all but the most stubborn members would prefer to avoid.

Once, one of us had to ask a group member to leave a work group. For a variety of reasons, the person's behavior had become highly disruptive. Everyone was

frustrated and often angry. Attempts to accept the behavior were unsuccessful. On various occasions, members had confronted or talked with the disruptive person. The member's behavior did not improve. Instead, it became more hostile and problematic. The group decided to expel the member. Although the exclusion caused a great deal of anxiety for everyone, the result was astonishing. Within a few weeks, the group became much more cohesive and productive. The difficult decision was the right decision.

Rather than covering up for disrupters and noncontributors, effective groups deal with such members. As Jon Katzenback and Douglas Smith wrote in *The Discipline of Teams*, "Sometimes that requires replacing members, sometimes it requires punishing them, and sometimes it requires working with them. The real team does whatever it takes to eliminate disruptive behavior and ensure productive contributions from all of its members."[32]

Characteristics of Effective Groups

A major study by Carl E. Larson and Frank M. J. LaFasto asked one central question: What are the secrets of successful teams? To answer this question, Larson and LaFasto interviewed the leaders and members of various types of groups—from a McDonald's Chicken McNuggets team to the space shuttle *Challenger* investigation team, cardiac surgery teams and a Notre Dame championship football team. They discovered that the most effective groups share the following eight characteristics:[33]

- *A clear, elevated goal.* Members understand and embrace the group's common goal.
- *A results-driven structure.* Members select an appropriate structure or system for solving problems, creating something, or implementing well-defined plans.

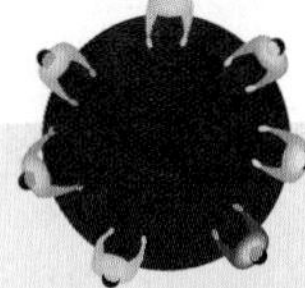

groups in balance . . .
Change Norms as Needed

When norms no longer meet the needs of a group or its members, new ones should be established. Some norms may be too rigid or too vague. Other norms may have outlived their usefulness. Finding an appropriate balance between old, rigid, or useless norms and creating new norms presents a challenge to every group. Effective groups learn how to change norms in order to prevent or curb recurring disruptions or problems. Norms can be difficult to change, especially when they are implicit or unspoken. Changes in group norms typically occur in the following ways:

- through contagious behavior, as in dress style and speech patterns
- through the suggestions or actions of high-status members
- through the suggestions or actions of highly confident members
- through the suggestions of consultants
- through group discussion and decision making (for explicit norms)
- through continued interaction (for implicit norms)[1]

Some members will resist changes in norms because change can be disruptive and threatening. However, norms that are no longer useful can impede a group's progress. The natural development of most groups requires changes in goals, membership, and norms.

[1]Rodney W. Napier and Matti K. Gershenfeld, *Groups: Theory and Experience*, 7th ed. (Boston: Houghton Mifflin, 2004), pp. 147–148.

- *Competent team members.* Members have the necessary technical, intellectual, and communication skills and the personal characteristics required to achieve excellence.
- *Unified commitment.* Members are loyal and dedicated to the group and its goal.
- *A collaborative climate.* Members work well together and create a climate that fosters honesty, openness, consistency, and respect for others.

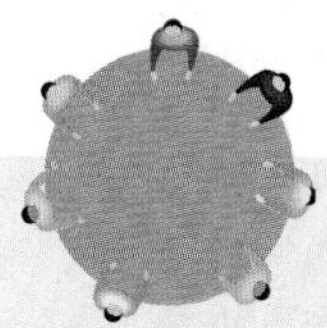

virtual groups
Developmental Tasks

Most group development theories assume that members interact face to face at the same time and in the same place. This assumption does not apply when describing development stages in virtual groups. Two developmental features of virtual groups require added attention:

- The planning, organization, and use of technology adds components to each stage of group development.
- Member technical expertise, attitudes about, and confidence with technology affects how groups move through group development stages.

During the forming stage of virtual groups, members experience many of the same tasks and tensions as those in face-to-face groups. In virtual groups, however, members begin to develop codes of virtual conduct, to review software and hardware requirements, and to answer questions about how technology will be used to achieve the group's goal.

During a virtual group's storming stage, members must deal with the added complication imposed by the virtual environment. In addition to expressing opinions and debating substantive issues, the group may have to address technical problems as well as different levels in member expertise. What should the group do if technical systems are not compatible or if some members are technically unskilled or apprehensive about using advanced technology? What is the best way to assign responsibilities, given the group's inability to meet face to face? Virtual groups must solve technical problems if they hope to address task-related issues.

In the norming stage, virtual groups will define members' roles, resolve conflicts, solve most technical problems, and accept the group's norms for interaction. They will be ready to focus on the task. They also will resolve issues related to differences in time, distance, technology, member cultures, and organizational environments. At this point, the group knows how to work virtually and effectively.

Once a virtual group reaches the performing stage, members engage in ongoing virtual interaction and encourage equal participation by all members. They have learned to address technical roadblocks and have become comfortable with the virtual media used by the group.

Finally, a group may rely on virtual communication to blunt the separation anxiety that comes with the adjourning stage. If a group has matured and performed well, members will be reluctant to give up their relationships with their colleagues. Even if a virtual group no longer operates in an official capacity, members may continue consulting with one another on other issues.

As is the case with face-to-face groups, virtual groups may skip one or more stages.[1] For example, experienced virtual groups may move directly to the performing stage when working on routine tasks or tasks that they have successfully completed many times before. Members know the rules and expectations and can concentrate on performing the task. On the other hand, virtual groups addressing new or unique problems, the redistribution of resources, or the addition of new members may have to devote more time and attention to the second and third stages.

Interestingly, many virtual groups hold face-to-face meetings at the beginning of a virtual team's life cycle, especially when members "do not know each other and the project or work is complex and requires a high degree of interaction. Face-to-face orientation meetings also help orient groups when the task is new and ambiguous."[2]

[1]Deborah L. Duarte and Nancy Tennant Snyder, *Mastering Virtual Teams: Strategies, Tools, and Techniques That Succeed,* 3rd ed. (San Francisco: Jossey-Bass, 2006), p. 104.

[2]Duarte and Snyder, p. 190.

- *Standards of excellence.* Members establish concrete standards for assessing group excellence and exert pressure on one another to achieve those standards.
- *External support and recognition.* Members are rewarded for excellence as a team and for behaving as a team.
- *Principled leadership.* Effective leaders suppress their own ego needs in favor of the group's goal by bringing out leadership in others and giving members the self-confidence to act and take responsibility.[35]

Think about the groups to which you have belonged. To what extent do Larson and LaFasto's characteristics describe the best of these groups? Did your group have standards for assessing excellence? Did the leader of your group put group goals ahead of ego-based goals? Were members consistently honest, open, and respectful of one another? Your answers to these questions say a great deal about what can go right and what can go wrong in groups as they move through the stages of group development.

summary study guide

Group Development Stages

- According to Tuckman and Jensen, there are five discrete stages in the life cycle of groups—forming, storming, norming, performing, and adjourning.
- During the forming stage, many groups experience primary tension, the social unease and stiffness that accompany the getting-acquainted stage in a new group.
- During the storming stage, secondary tensions often emerge when members gain enough confidence to become assertive and even aggressive as they pursue positions of power and influence.
- The process of socializing newcomers in a group moves through five phases: antecedent, anticipatory, encounter, assimilation, and exit.

Group Goals

- An effective group has *both* a clear understanding of its goal *and* a belief that its goal is meaningful and worthwhile.
- Locke and Latham's Goal Theory claims that groups function best when their goals are specific, challenging, accepted, used to evaluate performance, and promote member growth.
- Hidden agendas occur when a member's private goal conflicts with the group's goal.

Group Norms

- Norms are expectations held by group members concerning acceptable behavior; norms can be explicit or implicit.
- Norms can be classified as interaction, procedural, status, and achievement norms.
- Constructive nonconformity occurs when a member resists a norm while still working to promote a group goal. Destructive nonconformity occurs when a member resists conforming to norms without regard for the best interests of the group and its goal.
- When a member's disruptive behavior becomes intolerable or destructive a group can accept, confront, or even exclude the troublesome member.
- Effective groups find an appropriate balance between useless or counterproductive norms and creating new, useful norms.

Characteristics of Effective Groups

- Larson and LaFasto claim that the most effective groups share the following eight characteristics: a clear elevated goal, a results-driven structure, competent team members, unified commitment, a collaborative climate, standards of excellence, external support and recognition, and principled leadership.
- Two developmental features of virtual groups require special attention: (1) planning, organization, and use of technology and (2) member technical expertise, attitudes about, and confidence with technology.

key terms

achievement norm 40
adjourning stage 33
antecedent phase 35
anticipatory phase 35
assimilation phase 35
conformity 40
constructive nonconformity 41
destructive nonconformity 42
encounter phase 35
exit phase 35
explicit norm 39
forming stage 29
Goal Theory 36
hidden agenda 38
implicit norm 39
interaction norm 40
nonconformity 41
norm 39
norming stage 32
performing stage 32
primary tension 30
procedural norm 40
secondary tension 32
status norm 40
storming stage 30
Tuckman's Group Development Stages 29

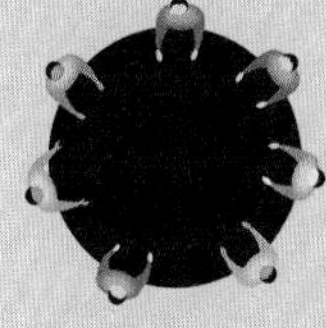

critical thinking about the case study

Nice to Meet You, Too

1 What verbal and nonverbal behaviors tell you that the group of community volunteers are meeting for the first time and negotiating the forming stage of group development?

2 Which of the members are most likely to compete for status and influence as the group eventually enters the storming stage of group development?

3 Briefly assess the communicative effectiveness of each group member—Dave, Betty, Ray, Bill, and Aisha—and how that member could become more *effective* in terms of helping the group achieve its goal.

4 Did the group use any strategies to reduce primary tensions? If yes, did the strategies succeed? If not, what strategies should they have used?

5 Which dialectic tensions are most likely to affect how well the community volunteer group achieves its goal?

6 What implicit norms emerged during the discussion and did these norms help the group move through the forming stage?

7 In the long run, do you believe this particular group has the potential to succeed as a highly effective group that will achieve its common goal? Why or why not?

group work Classroom Norms

Directions: List three implicit norms and three explicit norms that operate in one of your classes. When you have identified three of each type of norm, rank the norms in terms of their usefulness in ensuring quality instruction and effective learning.

EXPLICIT CLASSROOM NORMS	YOUR RANKING	IMPLICIT CLASSROOM NORMS	YOUR RANKING
Example: The syllabus states that no makeup work is allowed without a legitimate written excuse.		*Example:* When students come in late, they tiptoe to the closest available seat near the door.	
1.		**1.**	
2.		**2.**	
3.		**3.**	

Are there any additional norms needed in the class you are describing? If yes and you are willing to share your proposed norm with the members of this class, write it here:

____

____

____

group assessment How Good Is Your Goal?

Directions: For each of the following questions, circle "yes" or "no" to assess the goals of a group you belong to or belonged to in the past. Each time you circle a "no" response, consider how the goal or situation could have been improved.

1. Does the group have a goal?	Yes	No
2. Is the goal specific?	Yes	No
3. Do group members understand the goal?	Yes	No
4. Do group members believe the goal is worthwhile?	Yes	No
5. Is the goal achievable?	Yes	No
6. Are the resources available to achieve the goal?	Yes	No
7. Is the goal sufficiently challenging to group members?	Yes	No
8. Are all group members committed to the goal?	Yes	No
9. Do all group members understand their contribution to the goal?	Yes	No
10. Does the goal require group cooperation?	Yes	No
11. Does the group recognize any individual hidden agendas?	Yes	No
12. Has the group resolved any hidden agendas?	Yes	No
13. Will group members receive feedback about their progress toward the goal?	Yes	No
14. Is there a reward for achieving the group's goal?	Yes	No
15. When achieved, is the goal observable or measurable?	Yes	No

notes

1. Artemis Chang, Julie Duck, and Prashant Bordia, "Understanding the Multidimensionality of Group Development," *Small Group Research* 37 (2006), p. 329.
2. Ibid., pp. 331, 337–338.
3. Bruce W. Tuckman, "Developmental Sequence in Small Groups," *Psychological Bulletin* 63 (1965), pp. 384–399. Tuckman's 1965 article is reprinted in *Group Facilitation: A Research and Applications Journal* 3 (Spring 2001) and is available as a Word document at http://dennislearningcenter.osu.edu/references/Group%20DEV%20ARTICLE.doc. See also Mark K. Smith, "Bruce W. Tuckman—Forming, Storming, Norming, and Performing in Groups," *The*

Encyclopaedia of Informal Education, www.infed.org/thinkers/tuckman.htm, updated March 14, 2005; "Famous Models: Stages of Group Development" (Chimaera Consulting Limited), www.chimaeraconsulting.com/tuckman.htm, 2001. Retrieved March 10, 2008.

4. Bruce W. Tuckman and Mary Ann C. Jensen, "Stages of Small Group Development Revisited," *Group and Organizational Studies* 2 (1997), pp. 419–427.
5. Harvey Robbins and Michael Finley, *Why Teams Don't Work: What Goes Wrong and How to Make It Right* (Princeton, NJ: Peterson's/Pacesetter Books, 1995), p. 26.
6. Ernest G. Bormann, *Small Group Communication: Theory and Practice,* 3rd ed. (Edina, MN: Burgess, 1996), pp. 132–135, 181–183.
7. Susan A. Wheelan and Nancy Brewer Danganan, "The Relationship Between the Internal Dynamics of Student Affairs Leadership Teams and Campus Leaders' Perceptions of the Effectiveness of Student Affairs Divisions," *NASPA Journal* 40 (Spring 2003), p. 96.
8. Donald G. Ellis and B. Aubrey Fisher, *Small Group Decision Making: Communication and the Group Process,* 4th ed. (New York: McGraw-Hill, 1994), pp. 43–44.
9. Wheelan and Danganan, p. 27.
10. B. Aubrey Fisher, "Decision Emergence: Phases in Group Decision Making," *Speech Monographs,* 37 (1970), p. 160.
11. In 1997, Tuckman and Jensen proposed an updated model that includes a fifth stage: adjourning. Bruce W. Tuckman and Mary Ann C. Jensen, "Stages of Small Group Development Revisited," *Group and Organizational Studies* 2 (1977), pp. 419–427.
12. Carolyn M. Anderson, Bruce L. Riddle, and Matthew M. Martin, "Socialization Process in Groups," in *The Handbook of Group Communication Theory and Research,* ed. Lawrence R. Frey; Dennis S. Gouran and Marshall Scott Poole, assoc. eds. (Thousand Oaks, CA: Sage, 1999), p. 155.
13. www.chimaeraconsulting.com/tuckman.htm. Retrieved March 11, 2008.
14. Carl E. Larson and Frank M. J. LaFasto, *TeamWork: What Must Go Right/What Can Go Wrong* (Newbury Park, CA: Sage, 1989), p. 27.
15. Larson and LaFasto, p. 28.
16. Larson and LaFasto, p. 27–38.
17. Larson and LaFasto, p. 33.
18. Edwin A. Locke and Gary P. Latham, *Goal Setting: A Motivational Technique That Works!* (Englewood Cliffs, NJ: Prentice-Hall, 1984); also see Andrew J. DuBrin, *Leadership: Research Findings, Practice, and Skills,* 4th ed. (New York: Houghton Mifflin, 2004), pp. 297–298.
19. Locke and Latham, pp. 18–19.
20. David W. Johnson and Frank P. Johnson, *Joining Together: Group Theory and Group Skills,* 2nd ed. (Englewood Cliffs, NJ: Prentice Hall, 1982), p. 174.
21. Johnson and Johnson, p. 174.
22. Based on Locke and Latham, pp. 27–40; Johnson and Johnson, pp. 173–174.
23. Rodney W. Napier and Matti K. Gershenfeld, *Groups: Theory and Experience,* 7th ed. (Boston: Houghton Mifflin, 2004), p. 182.
24. Patricia H. Andrews, "Group Conformity," in *Small Group Communication: Theory and Practice,* 7th ed., ed. Robert S. Cathcart, Larry A. Samovar, and Linda D. Henman (Madison, WI: Brown & Benchmark, 1996), p. 185.
25. Nicky Hayes, *Managing Teams: A Strategy for Success* (London: Thomson, 2004), p. 31.
26. Hayes, p. 29.
27. Robert A. Baron, Donn Byrne, and Nyla R. Branscombe, *Social Psychology,* 11th ed. (Boston: Allyn & Bacon, 2006); Charles Pavitt and Ellen Curtis, *Small Group Discussion: A Theoretical Approach,* 2nd ed. (Scottsdale, AZ: Gorsuch, Scarisbrick, 1994), pp. 178, 339.
28. For detailed descriptions of these classic studies, see Sharon S. Brehm, Saul M. Kassin, and Steven Fein, *Social Psychology,* 6th ed. (Boston: Houghton Mifflin, 2005), pp. 250–255, 472–475. For a detailed description of Milgram's work, see Robert A. Baron, Donn Byrne, and Nyla R. Branscombe, *Social Psychology,* 11th ed. (Boston: Allyn & Bacon, 2006), pp. 364–369. Today, neither experiment would be conducted because an institution's research board must approve all research using human subjects to ensure that the study will not harm the subjects.
29. Philip Zimbardo describes the famous Stanford prison study and its consequences as well as how it foreshadowed the abusive actions of U.S. military guards at Abu Ghraib prison in Iraq. See Philip G. Zimbardo, "Revisiting the Stanford Prison Experiment: A Lesson in the Power of Situation," *The Chronicle of Higher Education,* March 30, 2007, pp. B6–B7.
30. Napier and Gershenfeld, pp. 137–140.
31. Carole A. Barbato, "An Integrated Model of Group Decision-Making" (paper presented at the meeting of the National Communication Association, Chicago, IL, November 1997), p. 19.
32. Jon R. Katzenbach and Douglas K. Smith, *The Discipline of Teams: A Mindbook-Workbook for Delivering Small Group Performance* (New York: Wiley, 2001), pp. 141–142.
33. Mark L. Knapp, "Introduction," in Carl E. Larson and Frank M. J. LaFasto, *TeamWork: What Must Go Right/What Can Go Wrong* (Thousand Oaks, CA: Sage, 1989), pp. 7–8.
34. Larson and LaFasto.

chapter 3

Group Membership

chapter outline

Followership

Member Needs

Maslow's Hierarchy of Needs • Schutz's Theory of Interpersonal Needs

Member Roles

Group Task Roles • Group Maintenance Roles • Self-Centered Roles

Member Confidence

Communication Apprehension • Strategies for Reducing Communication Apprehension • Strategies for Helping Apprehensive Members

Member Assertiveness

Balancing Passivity and Aggression • Assertiveness Skills

study questions

What types of competencies characterize highly effective group members?

How do groups satisfy members' needs?

Which group roles enhance or obstruct group effectiveness?

How does communication apprehension affect group competence and confidence?

How does assertiveness achieve a balance between passivity and aggressiveness?

Followership

Do you have the "right stuff" to be a group follower? But, you may wonder, who wants to be a follower? Well, for one thing, without followers, there would be no one for leaders to lead. In the United States we place great value on leaders, but rarely do we stop to understand or appreciate followers. Interestingly, the U.S. admiration of leaders is not shared by all cultures. In many countries, standing out from the crowd is considered arrogant. Loyal, hard-working followers are admired. As we see it, the full participation of followers is the engine that makes groups work effectively. When you belong to a group, your competence determines whether your group will achieve its common goal. It also affects how well your group negotiates the leadership ↔ followership dialectic, which balances effective and ethical leadership with loyal and responsible followership.

Belonging to a group is not the same as being a competent group member. Here, the engaged ↔ disengaged dialectic has two dimensions—one related to the amount of activity, the other related to the level of commitment. Disengaged members are neither active nor committed. They are quite content sitting on the sidelines and letting others do the work. They lack enthusiasm or the will to participate actively. Highly engaged members are active and energized by the group's common goal and the quality of member interaction.

In Chapter 2, Group Development, we presented the eight characteristics of effective groups identified in a major study by Larson and LaFasto. They concluded that competent members have the skills necessary to achieve the group's goal and "the personal characteristics required to achieve excellence while working well with others." They also conclude that effective groups look for the necessary balance of member skills.[1] In this chapter, we examine how groups meet member needs and how group roles, member confidence, and assertiveness influence group productivity and member satisfaction.

Member Needs

Most of us join groups because they satisfy personal needs. For example, some people join volunteer fire departments or participate in neighborhood watch programs to become involved in an activity they value. College students frequently join campus clubs and societies in order to be with or make new friends. Job applicants may decline an offer if they view members of the work team as unpleasant. In many cases, you may join a group to meet a need separate from the group's goal. For instance, a young attorney might join a local civic organization in an effort to meet prospective clients. A retiree may volunteer as a teacher's aide to feel productive and appreciated.[2] Please note that these examples do not constitute the hidden agendas we discuss in Chapter 2; members may openly admit their reasons for joining a group. Unlike hidden agendas, these motives may neither conflict with nor undermine the group's overall goal.

Two psychological theories—Maslow's Hierarchy of Needs and Schutz's theory of interpersonal behavior—have made significant contributions to understanding why we join, stay in, and leave groups.

Maslow's Hierarchy of Needs

Psychologist Abraham H. Maslow claims that as we move through life, some needs are more important than others. Basic survival needs must be satisfied before we can

case study

Taming Tony the Tiger

Anthony (Tony) Tigertino is a talkative, conscientious, hard-working, and assertive man who has always liked working in groups. In addition to being the member of a large family and group of friends, he enjoys playing Tuesday night basketball games on a neighborhood team and making Saturday morning food deliveries for Meals on Wheels. At work, Tony manages the sales and advertising department for a small business. For the last twenty years, his group experiences have been interesting and enjoyable.

However, in the last few years, he has sensed a change in his feelings and commitment to several groups. The members of his basketball team often miss games. They say they're too tired, too busy, or too injured to play. His solo drives to deliver Meals on Wheels have become lonely. On the job, he seems to have less time to complete more tasks and must work with several young and less experienced colleagues. Although they respect his expertise, he no longer gets a boost from their admiration for his work.

Tony understands that things have changed in twenty years. His family has grown up and he has less control over their lives. Some of his close friends have moved out of the neighborhood. Retirements have claimed several of his best coworkers. He also recognizes that his way of working may not be in sync with the job and the work styles of others. He can tell that some staff members don't like his insistence on establishing clear schedules and meeting all deadlines. He knows he becomes aggravated and critical when a basketball game is cancelled, a Meals on Wheels schedule is changed, or someone makes a last-minute request for an advertisement. He finds himself losing patience with his wife and kids when they change plans without telling him. To make matters worse, everyone knows when he's frustrated, but he doesn't know how to temper his reactions. A few times, he's lost his temper over small issues and then apologized for his behavior. Tony decides he needs to take a good look at himself and how he works in groups. He hopes that this kind of analysis will help him rediscover why he always enjoyed participating in many different types of groups—and how he can recapture his commitment to group work.

When you finish reading this chapter, you should be able to answer the following questions.

1. What needs motivate Tony's participation in groups?
2. How do Tony's roles affect his behavior as a group member?
3. How can Tony use his own confidence and expertise to help group members who experience communication apprehension?
4. What can Tony do to determine whether his interaction style has become more aggressive or passive than assertive?

fulfill higher psychological needs. That is, you will not spend time achieving personal success or meeting your emotional needs if you are cold, homeless, and hungry. **Maslow's Hierarchy of Needs** ranks critical needs in the following order: physiological, safety, belongingness, esteem, and self-actualization (see Figure 3.1).[3] In order to satisfy the higher needs for belongingness, esteem, and self-actualization, you must first satisfy basic physiological and safety needs.

Although Maslow's hierarchy describes individual needs, his theory also applies to the ways in which group membership satisfies such needs. At the most basic level, people join groups in order to survive; at the highest level, people join groups in order

Figure 3.1 Maslow's Hierarchy of Needs

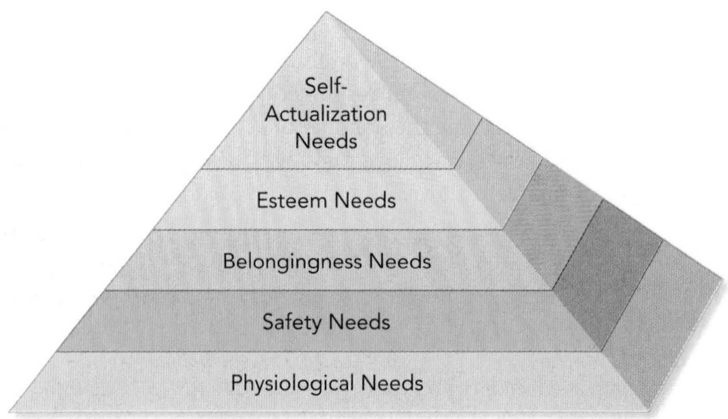

to reach their own full potential. Table 3.1 relates Maslow's Hierarchy of Needs to general examples of group needs and specifically to the ways in which group needs were met during the Hurricane Katrina disaster in 2005.

Schutz's Theory of Interpersonal Needs

William Schutz developed a theory of interpersonal behavior called the **Fundamental Interpersonal Relationship Orientation (FIRO)**.[4] Unlike Maslow's hierarchy of

Table 3.1 Applying Maslow's Hierarchy of Needs to Group Work

Maslow's Hierarchy of Needs	Satisfying Group Needs	Example: Hurricane Katrina
1. Physiological Needs: Water, Food, and Shelter	• Hunting clans need member cooperation to survive. • Farming families rely on members to survive.	• Victims banded together to share water, food, and shelter. • Groups of neighbors saved stranded families.
2. Safety Needs: Security and Protection	• Police forces and fire departments protect neighborhoods. • Unions protect members from unfair labor practices.	• Neighbors joined forces to protect homes and belongings. • Medical groups set up makeshift clinics to care for victims.
3. Belongingness Needs: Friendship and Love	• Teenage groups provide friendships and a sense of belonging. • Families provide affection and social support.	• Volunteer groups organized to find and reunite family members. • Relief workers provided counseling to victims.
4. Esteem Needs: Respect and Admiration	• Joining an exclusive club may earn a person admiration. • Leading a group may enhance a member's status.	• Unlikely heroes emerged to help victims. • Volunteer groups were publicly recognized for their rescue and rebuilding efforts.
5. Self-Actualization Needs: Fulfilling Your Personal Potential	• People find personal rewards in helping others. • Intellectual and creative needs become important.	• Boat owners from distant towns and states rallied to aid flood victims. • Volunteers took leave from families and jobs to search for and aid victims.

needs, FIRO concentrates on three *interpersonal* needs that most people share to some degree: the needs for inclusion, for control, and for affection (see Figure 3.2 on page 56). Schutz maintains that people join groups in order to satisfy one or more of these needs.

The Need for Inclusion. An **inclusion need** represents our desire to belong, to be involved, to be accepted. For some group members, the need for inclusion is strong—they want to fit in and be appreciated by other members. For other group members, the need for inclusion may be less important—they are quite content to work without significant involvement in the group. When a group meets a member's inclusion need, the result is what Schutz calls a **social member**—a person who enjoys working with people but is also comfortable working alone.

When inclusion needs are not met, members do not feel accepted; they do not fit in with the group and may engage in undersocial behavior or oversocial behavior. An **undersocial member** feels unworthy or undervalued by the group and may withdraw and become a loner. Because these people believe that no one values them, they avoid being hurt by trying not to be noticed. A quiet or unproductive member may be someone whose inclusion need is unmet. An **oversocial member** tries to attract attention to compensate for feelings of inadequacy. Such members seek companionship for all activities because they can't stand being alone. They try to impress other members with what and whom they know.

Dealing with undersocial and oversocial members requires group behavior that satisfies inclusion needs. Making new members feel welcome and veteran members feel valued requires a careful balance between the needs of the members and the needs of the group.

The Need for Control. **Control need** refers to whether we feel competent, confident, and free to make our own decisions. The need for control is often expressed by a member who wants to be the group's leader. For some members, the need for control is strong—they want to take charge of the group and influence members. For other group members, the need for control may be less important—they are quite content to be followers and let others lead. When a group meets a member's control need, the result is what Schutz calls a **democratic member**—a person who has no problems with power and control and who feels just as comfortable giving orders as taking them. Such members are often excellent leaders because they can exercise control when needed, but they put the group's goal ahead of their own needs.

Unmet control needs can result in the emergence of an abdicrat or an autocrat. Each type manifests control needs through opposite behaviors. An **abdicrat** may want control but be reluctant to pursue it. Abdicrats are often submissive members because they have no hope of having any control in the group. They may do what they are told and avoid responsibilities. The **autocrat** tries to take control by dominating the group. Autocrats may criticize other members and try to force their decisions on the group.

Dealing with abdicrats and autocrats requires granting members a sense of control appropriate to their needs. Giving members responsibility for and leadership of special projects or tasks may satisfy their need for control. For example, asking a member to chair a highly visible and important subcommittee may satisfy that person's control need.

The Need for Affection. An **affection need** reflects our desire to be liked by others.[5] Members with strong affection needs seek close friendships, intimate relationships, and expressions of warmth from others. As was the case with inclusion and

Figure 3.2 Schutz's Fundamental Interpersonal Relationship Orientation (FIRO) Theory

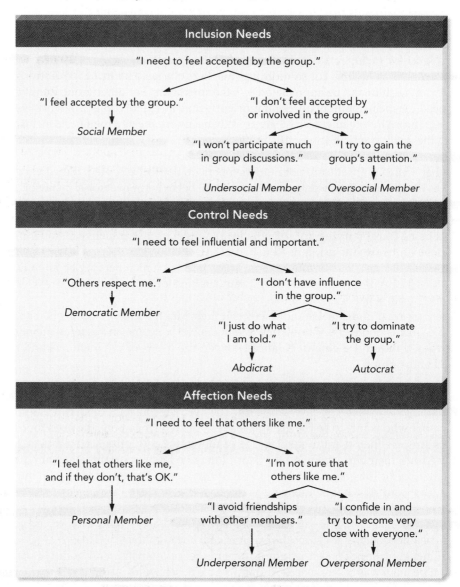

control, some group members have a high need for affection—they want to be liked and develop strong friendships with group members. For others, the need for affection may be less important—they don't need to be liked to be productive members of the group. When a group meets a member's affection need, the result is what Schutz calls a **personal member**—a person who has no emotional problems dealing with group members. While preferring to be liked, an ideal personal member is secure enough to function in a group where social interaction and affection are not high priorities.

When affection needs are not met, members do not feel liked; they become uncomfortable in the group setting. Reactions to this deficit fall into two categories: underpersonal behavior and overpersonal behavior. **Underpersonal members** believe no one likes them and may establish only superficial relationships with other members.

When pressed, they rarely share their honest feelings or opinions and may appear aloof and uninvolved. An **overpersonal member** tries to get close to everyone and seeks intimate friendships despite the disinterest of other members. Such members may be too talkative, too personal, and too confiding.

Dealing with underpersonal and overpersonal members requires expressions of fondness and friendliness to those who need affection. Expressing liking to new members and taking the time to communicate affection to long-standing members can take extra time but have the potential to convert unsatisfied participants into ideal personal members.

Applying FIRO Theory to Groups. Using Schutz's theory to improve a group's performance requires adapting to members' inclusion, control, and affection needs. For example, a member who seeks attention or tries to impress other members may have a strong inclusion need. This need can be satisfied by praising that member's good work. When members have strong control needs but are not capable enough or eligible to lead a group, there may be value in assigning them to head up a special project. Just as praising and rewarding effective group behavior can satisfy esteem needs, such reinforcement can help group members feel included, competent, and well liked.

There are, however, reasons to be cautious about using FIRO theory to explain and predict group behavior. Undersocial behavior may not reflect an unmet inclusion need; the member may be quite comfortable and happy working alone. Overpersonal behavior may not reflect an unmet affection need; such behavior may represent an enthusiastic effort to create a positive social climate for the group.

Member Roles

When a group member exhibits a unique set of skills or behavior patterns that serve specific functions within the group, that member has assumed a **role**.[6] For example, a group may rely on Portia to generate enthusiasm for the group's work and promote

Throughout history and in all cultures, people have joined and relied on groups to satisfy important needs. What kinds of needs are satisfied by public service groups such as firefighters, police officers, and emergency medical teams? What kinds of needs are satisfied by belonging to and working in such groups?

Figure 3.3 Group Role Categories

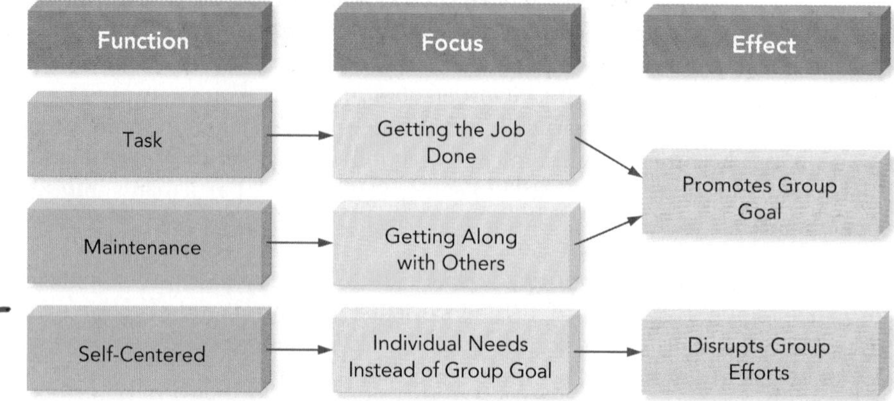

teamwork, whereas Will is best at reconciling disagreements, reducing tension, and calming anxious members. Portia's role is that of energizer; Will is the group's harmonizer. Both of these roles serve valuable group functions.

Depending on your characteristics, attitudes, and skills, you will probably assume one or more group roles. The members of successful groups know how to identify appropriate roles for themselves and how to work with the roles that other group members adopt.[7]

We have modified the original Benne and Sheats list of roles and Belbin's role categories (see *Theory in Groups: Team-Role Theory*) by combining functional behaviors we have observed in groups and roles identified by other writers and researchers.[8] The following sections divide twenty-five participant roles into three functional categories: group task roles, group maintenance roles, and self-centered roles (see Figure 3.3).

Group **task roles** affect a group's ability to achieve its common goal by focusing on behaviors that help get the job done. Group **maintenance roles** affect how group members get along with one another while pursuing a shared goal. They are concerned with building relationships and keeping the group cohesive and cooperative. **Self-centered roles** put individual needs ahead of the group's goal and other members' needs. In the following sections, each functional role is categorized, named, described, and illustrated with a statement that might be heard from a member assuming such a role.

Group Task Roles

1. **Initiator.** Proposes ideas and suggestions; provides direction for the group; gets the group started.
   "Let's begin by looking at the problem from the client's point of view."
2. **Information seeker.** Asks for needed facts and figures; requests explanations and clarification of ideas; makes the group aware of information gaps.
   "How can we decide on a policy for students with disabilities without knowing more about the new federal laws and regulations?"
3. **Coordinator-chairperson.** Clarifies goals; delegates tasks; facilitates meetings.
   "Beth and Karla—please review the study and give us a summary at our next meeting."

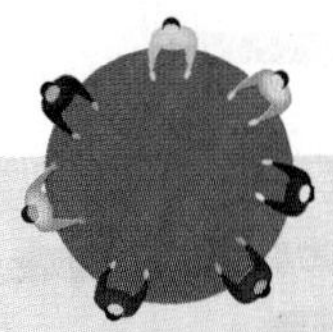

theory in groups
Team-Role Theory

Most group communication textbooks—including this one—rely on a classic 1948 essay by Kenneth D. Benne and Paul Sheats that identifies and describes the functional roles of group members.[1] Benne and Sheats's role classifications have several strengths. The roles apply to most groups regardless of their purpose or context. Rather than describing personality traits or overall interaction styles, the roles focus on how group members interact with one another. In addition, the roles are open—members can adopt whichever role appears to suit a particular moment or they can take on a permanent role.

There is, however, a role theory that identifies roles critical to group decision making in work settings. R. Meredith Belbin's **Team-Role Theory** recognizes that group members seek out certain roles, and that in highly effective groups, members perform the roles that are most natural to them.[2] In other words, members assume roles that are compatible with their personal characteristics and skills. As is the case with Benne and Sheats's roles, there are no such things as "pure" roles in Belbin's model. Most members assume a mix of roles depending on the needs of the group and its members. Belbin identifies nine roles:[3]

[1]Kenneth D. Benne and Paul Sheats, "Functional Roles of Group Members," *Journal of Social Issues* 4 (1948), pp. 41–49.

[2]See R. Meredith Belbin, *Management Teams* (London: Heinemann, 1981) and R. Meredith Belbin, *Team Roles at Work* (Oxford: Butterworth Heinemann, 1993).

[3]The table summarizes functions and characteristics from several sources: Belbin 1993, p. 22; Nicky Hayes, *Managing Teams: Strategies for Success* (London: Thomson, 2004), p. 47; http://chimaeraconsulting.com/belbin.htm. Retrieved December 8, 2008.

Belbin's Roles	Function	Characteristics
Coordinator/ Chairperson	Clarifies goals; helps allocate roles, responsibilities, and duties; articulates group conclusions	Calm, trusting, impartial, self-disciplined, mature, positive thinker, confident; decisive when necessary; may be seen as manipulative
Shaper	Seeks patterns in group work; pushes group toward agreement and decisions; challenges others	Energetic, high achiever, anxious, impatient, outgoing, argumentative, provocative, dynamic; can be abrasive
Innovator	Advances proposals and offers new and creative ideas; provides insights on courses of action	Creative, individualistic, serious and knowledgeable, unorthodox, intellectual; may disregard practical details and people
Resource Investigator	Explores opportunities, makes contacts, shares external information; negotiates with outsiders; responds well to challenges	Extroverted, curious, versatile, sociable, innovative, communicative, noisy and energetic; sometimes lazy
Monitor/ Evaluator	Analyzes problems and complex issues; monitors progress and prevents mistakes; assesses the contributions of others; sees all options; judges accurately	Sober, clever, discreet, detached, unemotional, prudent, not easily aroused; takes time to consider; rarely wrong; may appear cold
Implementer	Transforms talk and ideas into practical action; develops action plans for group members	Tough-minded, practical, tolerant, conscientious, conservative, methodical
Teamworker	Gives personal support and help to others; socially oriented and sensitive to others; resolves conflicts; calms the waters; serves as an in-group diplomat	Cooperative, sensitive, team-oriented, indecisive, deputy leader, gregarious, supportive; may sacrifice task for social goals; listens well
Completer/ Finisher	Emphasizes the need for meeting schedules, deadlines, and completing tasks; searches out errors	Perfectionist, persevering, conscientious, detail oriented, persistent, anxious; sometimes obnoxious
Specialist	Single-minded, self-starting, dedicated; provides unique or rare expertise and skills	Contributes in narrow area; dwells on technicalities; overlooks the "big picture"

4. **Information giver.** Provides the group with relevant information; researches, organizes, and presents needed information.
"I checked with our minority affairs officer, and she said . . ."
5. **Opinion seeker.** Asks for others' opinions; tests for group opinions and consensus; tries to discover what others believe or feel about an issue.
"Lyle, what do you think? Will it work?"
6. **Opinion giver.** States personal beliefs and interpretations; shares feelings; offers analysis and arguments.
"I don't agree that radio ads are the answer because they'll use up our entire promotional budget."
7. **Clarifier-summarizer.** Explains ideas and their consequences; reduces confusion; sums up group progress and conclusions.
"We've been trying to analyze this problem for the last hour. Let me see if I can list the three causes we've identified so far."
8. **Implementer-completer.** Develops action plans; establishes and follows schedules and deadlines.
"Here's a spread sheet with each of your names, the task you've been assigned, and the deadlines for each task."
9. **Evaluator-critic.** Assesses ideas, arguments, and suggestions; functions as the group's critical thinker; diagnoses task and procedural problems.
"I think we've forgotten something here. The building figures don't take into account monthly operating costs, such as utilities and maintenance."
10. **Energizer.** Motivates group members to do their best; helps create enthusiasm for the task and, if needed, a sense of urgency; serves as the group's "cheerleader."
"This is incredible! We may be the first department to come up with such a unique and workable solution to this problem."
11. **Procedural technician.** Assists with preparation for meetings, including suggesting agenda items, making room arrangements, and providing needed materials and equipment.
"Before our next meeting, let me know whether any of you will need a computer for PowerPoint or a flip chart."
12. **Recorder-secretary.** Keeps and provides accurate written records of a group's major ideas, suggestions, and decisions.
"Maggie, please repeat your two deadline dates so I can get them into the minutes."

Group Maintenance Roles

1. **Encourager-supporter.** Praises and agrees with group members; provides recognition and person-to-person encouragement; listens empathically.
"The information you found has been a big help. Thanks for taking all that time to find it."
2. **Harmonizer.** Helps resolve conflicts; mediates differences among group members; emphasizes teamwork and the importance of everyone getting along.
"I know we're starting to get on each other's nerves, but we're almost done. Let's put aside our differences and finish up."

3. **Compromiser.** Offers suggestions that minimize differences; helps the group reach consensus; searches for solutions that are acceptable to everyone.
   "It looks as though no one is going to agree on this one. Maybe we can improve the old system rather than trying to come up with a brand new way of doing it."
4. **Tension releaser.** Alleviates tension with friendly humor; breaks the ice and cools hot tempers; monitors tension levels and tries to relax the group.
   "Can Karen and I arm wrestle to decide who gets the assignment?"
5. **Gatekeeper.** Monitors participation; encourages quiet members to speak and talkative members to stop speaking; tries to control the flow of communication.
   "I think we've heard from everyone except Sophie, and I know she has strong feelings on this issue."
6. **Observer-interpreter.** Explains what others are trying to say; monitors and interprets feelings and nonverbal communication; expresses group feelings; paraphrases other members.
   "I sense that you two are not really disagreeing. Tell me if I'm wrong, but I think that both of you are saying that we should . . ."
7. **Teamworker-follower.** Supports the group and its members; accepts others' ideas and assignments; serves as an attentive audience member.
   "That's fine with me. Just tell me when it's due."

Self-Centered Roles

1. **Aggressor.** Puts down members to get what he or she wants; is sarcastic toward and critical of others; may take credit for someone else's work or idea.
   "It's a good thing I had time to rewrite our report. There were so many mistakes in it, we would have been embarrassed by it."
2. **Blocker.** Stands in the way of progress; presents negative, disagreeable, and uncompromising positions; uses delaying tactics to derail an idea or proposal.
   "There's no way I'm signing off on this idea if you insist on putting Gabriel in charge of the project."
3. **Dominator.** Prevents others from participating; asserts authority and tries to manipulate others; interrupts others and monopolizes discussion.
   "That's crazy, Wanda. Right off the top of my head I can think of at least four major reasons why we can't do it your way. The first reason is . . ."
4. **Recognition seeker.** Boasts about personal accomplishments; tries to impress others and become the center of attention; pouts or disrupts the discussion if not getting enough attention.
   "As the only person here to have ever won the company's prestigious top achiever award, I personally suggest that . . ."
5. **Clown.** Injects inappropriate humor or commentary into the group; seems more interested in goofing off than in working; distracts the group.
   "Listen—I've been working on this outrageous impersonation of the boss. I've even got his funny walk down."
6. **Deserter.** Withdraws from the group; appears "above it all" and bored or annoyed with the discussion; remains aloof or stops contributing.
   "I'm leaving now because I have to go to an important meeting."

7. **Confessor.** Seeks emotional support from the group; shares very personal feelings and problems with members; uses the group for emotional support rather than contributing to the group's goal.
   "I had an argument with my boyfriend yesterday. I could really use some advice. Let me start at the beginning."
8. **Special interest pleader.** Speaks on behalf of an outside group or a personal interest; tries to influence group members to support nongroup interests.
   "Let's hire my brother-in-law to cater our annual dinner. We'd get better food than the usual rubber chicken."

Depending on your group's goal, the nature of its task, and the attitudes or abilities of other members, you could function in several different roles. If you know the most about the discussion topic, your primary function might be that of information giver. If two members strongly disagree about an important issue, you might help your group by functioning as a harmonizer. Moreover, when some group members perform critical task and maintenance roles effectively, they are more likely to become leaders.[9]

Group members must be "very clear about their roles," but they also must avoid the temptation of establishing inflexible roles.[10] Instead, seek balance. Call on group members' multiple talents.[11] In the best of all possible groups, all the task and maintenance functions should be available as strategies to mobilize a group toward achieving its goal.

Member Confidence

Confident groups are more likely to succeed. They cope with unexpected events, problematic behavior, and challenging assignments effectively because their members have a positive, "can do" attitude. Fostering group and member confidence is much more than the power of positive thinking—it helps groups commit to ambitious goals and believe in their ability to succeed.[12] Larson and LaFasto link member competence to confidence by noting that when members' strong skills combine with a desire to contribute and an abiity to collaborate, "the observable outcome is an elevated sense of confidence among team members."[13]

Communication Apprehension

Communication scholars have investigated the anxieties that people feel when they must speak to others in a variety of contexts. The result is a large body of research that has important implications for working in groups.

Communication scholar James McCroskey defines **communication apprehension** as "an individual's level of fear or anxiety associated with either real or anticipated communication with another person or persons."[14] About 20 percent of the U.S. population experience very high levels of communication apprehension. About 75 to 85 percent experience apprehension when faced with the prospect of making a presentation.[15] However, communication apprehension includes more than public speaking anxiety; it also encompasses fear of speaking in conversations, meetings, or group settings.

There are different levels of communication apprehension, depending on several factors, such as the personality of the speaker, the nature of the listeners, and the char-

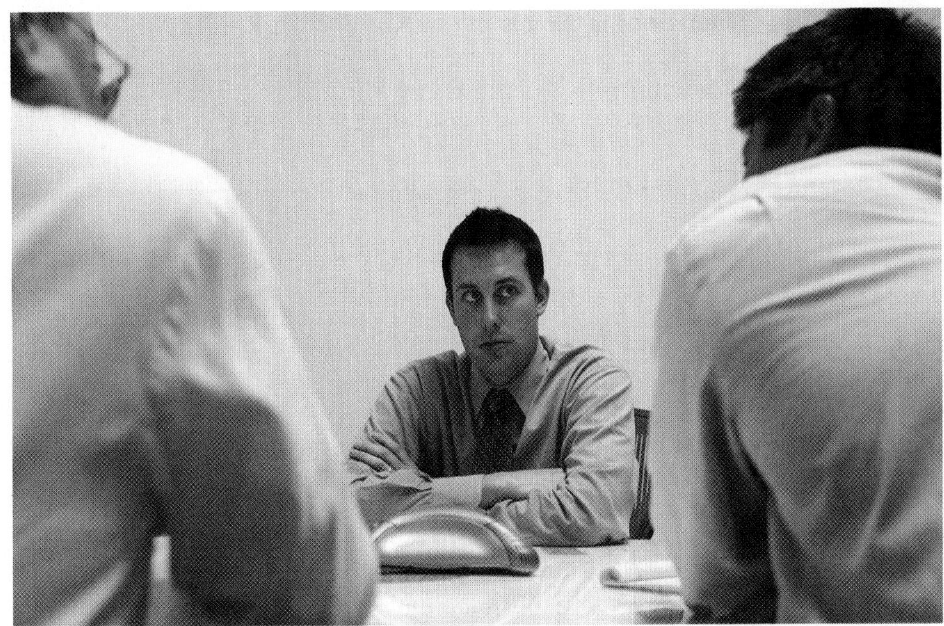

Communication apprehension can have a significant effect on group effectiveness because highly apprehensive members may be reluctant to participate in group discussions. What can you do to help members feel more confident about communicating in groups?

acteristics of the occasion or setting. For example, talking at a weekly staff meeting may be easy, but defending a department's actions at a meeting of company executives may generate high levels of anxiety.

James McCroskey and Virginia Richmond write that "it is not an exaggeration to suggest that CA [communication apprehension] may be the single most important factor in predicting communication behavior in a small group."[16] Consequently, it is not surprising that highly apprehensive people may avoid group communication or

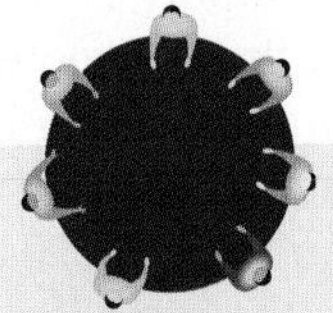

groups in balance . . .

Adapt to High and Low Apprehensives

At the end of this chapter, you'll find a self-test called the Personal Report of Communication Apprehension, or PRCA. You might want to complete this questionnaire and follow the scoring instructions before reading the rest of this section. Your PRCA scores, particularly those related to groups and meetings, will help you understand how communication apprehension can affect your participation in group discussions. Effective groups learn to *both* support members who experience high levels of communication apprehension *and* tactfully curb low apprehensives who may talk too much or are oblivious to how other members feel about speaking.

The Personal Report of Communication Apprehension instrument is the best available measure of trait-like communication apprehension; that is, it measures relatively enduring, personality-type orientations toward a given mode of communication across a wide variety of contexts.[1] In other words, your PRCA score is a relatively permanent trait that is unlikely to change significantly unless there is some type of effective intervention or training.

[1]Virginia P. Richmond and James C. McCroskey, *Communication: Apprehension, Avoidance, and Effectiveness*, 4th ed. (Scottsdale, AZ: Gorsuch, Scarisbrick, 1995), p. 43.

Table 3.2 Communication Apprehension in Groups

Members with High Apprehension May . . .	Members with Low Apprehension May . . .
• avoid group participation • talk less often • agree with others rather than voice disagreement • smile and giggle inappropriately • fidget • use awkward phrases as fillers, such as "well," "uh," "you know" • have difficulty following a discussion	• initiate discussions • speak more often • assert themselves and their beliefs • become group leaders • strategically choose when to speak and when to remain silent • appear more confident • dominate a discussion or talk compulsively

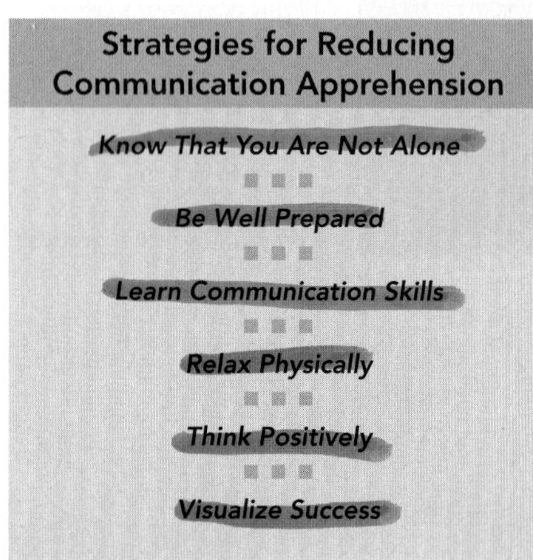

sit quietly in a group if they must be present.[17] Interestingly, both low and high apprehensives seem to have an innate ability to figure out where to sit in a small-group setting in order to either facilitate or avoid communication. For example, highly apprehensive group members with a low willingness to communicate often choose seats that inhibit communication and denote low status and power.[18] Table 3.2 lists some of the basic characteristics of low and high apprehensives in groups.

Strategies for Reducing Communication Apprehension
Know That You Are Not Alone
Be Well Prepared
Learn Communication Skills
Relax Physically
Think Positively
Visualize Success

Strategies for Reducing Communication Apprehension

If your PRCA score classifies you as an apprehensive speaker or if you believe that your level of anxiety associated with talking in groups is unusually high, there are several effective strategies to help you reduce your level of fear.

Know That You Are Not Alone. Everyone has experienced communication apprehension in certain settings. According to Richmond and McCroskey, "almost 95 percent of the population reports being scared about communicating with a person or group at some point in their lives."[19] If you dread the thought of communicating in a group or public setting, you are one of millions of people who feel the same way. Such feelings are normal. As you listen to other group members, don't assume that it is easy for them to talk. Several of them are probably experiencing the same level of fear and anxiety that you are.

Be Well Prepared. Although you cannot totally eliminate communication apprehension, you can and should be well prepared for every group discussion. Many successful group members who also experience high levels of communication apprehension spend extra time making sure that they are well prepared to participate in a scheduled discussion. Well-prepared members know more about the topic and have a clear idea of the positions they support. As a result, they are more confident when they are asked to participate. Being well prepared will not completely eliminate anxiety, but it can reduce a member's fear of being at a loss for relevant ideas and information when asked to contribute to the group discussion.

Learn Communication Skills. If you wanted to improve your tennis game, you would try to improve specific skills—perhaps your serve, your return, or your back-

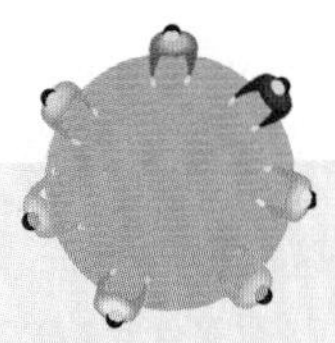

virtual groups
Confidence with Technology

When groups use audioconferences or videoconferences, or participate in online or computer-mediated discussions, members' confidence may erode or improve, depending on the electronic medium and the personal preferences of members. In a videoconference, for example, members who experience high levels of communication apprehension may find themselves more nervous because they are "on television." Every word and movement is captured for all to see and hear.

When a conference moves online, two different kinds of anxiety come into play. The first is writing apprehension.[1] Because online interaction depends on *written* words, poor writers and those who experience writing apprehension find themselves anxious about and preoccupied with the task of writing rather than being focused on the group's goal.

Computer anxiety—a condition affecting as many as 55 percent of all Americans—can complicate matters even further when members have negative attitudes about computers or express doubts about their technological skills. Fortunately, researchers have found that the more experience people have with computers, the less anxious they are.[2] The solution? Help anxious group members acquire and master computer skills, and their anxieties are likely to decrease.

There is, however, a flip side to the confidence coin when it's applied to online conferences and computer-mediated discussions. Some people are *more* confident when communicating via computer. A theory called **hyperpersonal communication** explains why some group members express themselves more competently and confidently in mediated settings than they do in face-to-face discussions.[3]

First, consider how you feel when communicating online. You have greater control over how you present yourself. An added confidence booster is the fact that your written message is separate from your appearance, your gender and race, your status, and your accent or dialect. None of these nonverbal factors is displayed in your message unless you choose to include remarks about them.

A second reason some participants prefer online communication is that other group members may overestimate the qualities of a member's online conversation. We tend to like cooperative and responsive online partners, and there's nothing comparable to being liked to boost one's confidence.

A third reason is that the online channel allows members to take the time to construct suitable replies. For example, depending on how soon you have been asked to reply to a question, you can consult a report or do research and sound like an expert.

Finally, online communication usually provides feedback that lets you know whether your message was received and interpreted as you intended. Confirming feedback reinforces confidence.[4]

[1]Andrew F. Wood and Matthew J. Smith, *Online Communication: Linking Technology, Identity, and Culture* (Mahwah, NJ: Erlbaum, 2001), p. 15. For more information about writing apprehension, see Virginia P. Richmond and James C. McCroskey, *Communication: Apprehension, Avoidance, and Effectiveness*, 4th ed. (Scottsdale, AZ: Gorsuch, Scarisbrick, 1995).

[2]Craig R. Scott and Steven C. Rockwell, "The Effect of Communication, Writing, and Technology Apprehension on Likelihood to Use New Communication Technologies," *Communication Education* 46 (1997), pp. 29–43.

[3]Wood and Smith, p. 80.

[4]Andrew F. Wood and Matthew J. Smith, *Online Communication: Linking Technology, Identity, and Culture*, 2nd ed. (Mahwah, NJ: Erlbaum, 2005), pp. 88–90.

hand shot. The same is true about communicating in groups. There are specific and learnable communication skills that can help you improve your ability to participate in groups. These skills are described throughout this textbook. Learning skills related to becoming sensitive to feedback, following a group's agenda, or serving as an effective group leader and participant can give you the tools you need to succeed in a group discussion. Improving your communication skills will not erase communication apprehension, but it can reduce your level of anxiety. So instead of telling yourself, "I can't participate; I'm not a skilled communicator," try telling yourself, "I'm learning."[20]

Relax Physically. One reason we experience communication apprehension is that our bodies feel tense. Our hearts beat faster, our hands shake, and we're short of breath. This response is a natural one and may reflect excitement and eagerness as much as anxiety and fear. By learning to relax your body, you may also reduce your level of communication apprehension. For example, break the word *relax* into two syllables: *re* and *lax*. Inhale slowly through your nose while saying the sound *re* ("ree") silently to yourself. Then breathe out slowly while thinking of the sound *lax* ("laks"). Inhale and exhale three or four times while thinking, "Reee-laaax." By the time you finish, your pulse should be slower, and, hopefully, you will also feel calmer.[21] Applying relaxation and meditation techniques can be the first step in reducing communication apprehension.

Think Positively. You may be able to reduce apprehension by changing the way you *think* about communicating. Rather than thinking, "They won't listen to me," try thinking, "Because I'm so well prepared, I'll make a valuable contribution." **Cognitive restructuring** assumes that communication anxiety is caused by worrisome, irrational, and nonproductive thoughts about speaking to and with others (cognitions) that need modifying (restructuring).[22] Researchers who study emotions contend that thinking happy or sad thoughts can make you *feel* happy or sad.[23] So think positively and feel confident! Next time you feel anxious, tell yourself these positive statements: "My ideas are important." "I am well prepared." "Nervousness just gives me extra energy."[24]

Visualize Success. Closely related to cognitive restructuring is **visualization,** a technique that encourages you to think positively about communicating in groups. Many professional athletes use visualization to improve their performance. They are told to find a quiet place where they can relax and visualize themselves competing and winning.[25] You can do the same thing. Take time—*before* you meet with your group—to visualize yourself communicating effectively. Mentally practice the skills you need in order to succeed while also building a positive image of your effectiveness. When you can visualize or imagine yourself succeeding in a group and you can maintain a relaxed state at the same time, you will have broken your fearful response to communicating in groups.

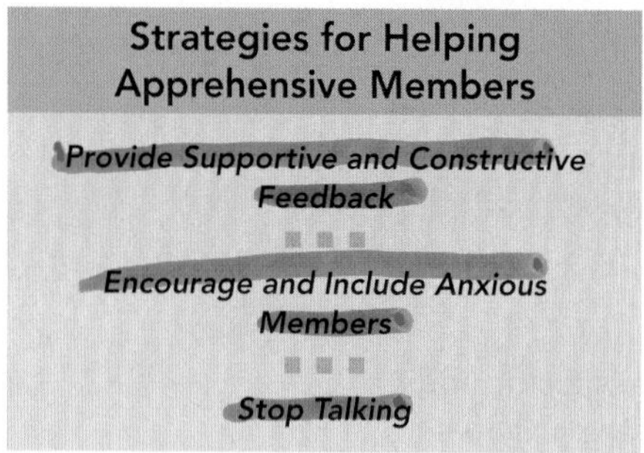

Strategies for Helping Apprehensive Members

If your PRCA score classifies you as a low apprehensive, you may be able to help group members whose anxieties hinder their ability to participate effectively in a group discussion. Four strategies may help reduce other members' level of communication apprehension:

Provide Supportive and Constructive Feedback. All group members work more effectively when they know how to give and accept supportive feedback. Supportive feedback also boosts members' confidence and reduces communication apprehension. When apprehensive group members speak, smile and nod, listen patiently, and don't interrupt or let other members interrupt them.

There are times, however, when feedback must address a problem. Here, you should provide constructive feedback as you describe your own feelings, thoughts, and wants: "I'm a little frustrated with this discussion (feeling), because we seem to be avoiding the real issue (thought). Let's talk about what's really hanging us up

(want)."[26] Expressing feedback constructively can increase your own credibility and other members' confidence, while also moving the group forward. Use the following guidelines to provide supportive and constructive feedback that enhances members' confidence, facilitates interpersonal understanding, and improves discussion:

- Focus on the behavior (rather than on the person).
- Describe the behavior (rather than judge it).
- Provide observations (rather than assumptions).
- Choose an appropriate time and place to contribute feedback (rather than ignoring the circumstances).
- Give supportive feedback to help others (rather than to meet your own needs).[27]

Encourage and Include Anxious Members. Patience and understanding alone may not be enough to encourage a member who is too frightened to join in a discussion. If you are a low apprehensive, try to include your nervous colleagues. Quiet members often have important information and good ideas. Encouraging anxious members to speak up contributes to the group's overall success.[28] There are, however, both effective and counterproductive ways to include someone. Confronting a reluctant speaker with a direct challenge, such as "Why in the world do you disagree with the rest of us?" is not very helpful. Asking a question that you know the apprehensive person is able to answer and taking turns speaking are much more effective ways to include all members.

Stop Talking. Finally, the most obvious thing you can do to help those who have difficulty participating is to stop talking. If you know that other members have difficulty entering the discussion or interrupting someone who is speaking, try to curb your own comments so that others have a chance to contribute. Keep a careful eye on less-than-confident participants. Often you will see members take a breath as though they want to speak, only to be stifled by your continued comments or by the comments of others. When that happens, conclude your remarks and turn to the person who was trying to contribute in order to give that person an opportunity to speak.

Member Assertiveness

Assertiveness—speaking up and acting in your own best interests without denying the rights and interests of others[29]—has the potential to enhance the confidence and effectiveness of a group and its members. When expressed appropriately, assertive communication can also raise your level of confidence and reduce communication apprehension.

Assertiveness seeks balance between passivity and aggression, and it applies to both groups and their members in task and social interactions. Assertive group members have the confidence to stand up for themselves while interacting with others to achieve a group goal. Assertive group members tend to:

- appear confident, honest, open, and cooperative.
- volunteer their ideas and opinions.
- ask and answer questions without fear or hostility.
- stand up for their beliefs, even when others disagree.
- express their feelings openly.
- respect and defend the rights and opinions of other group members.

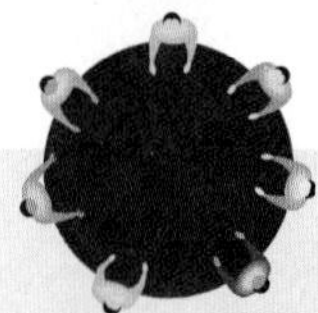

groups in balance . . .
Curb Compulsive Talkers

Group members who talk too much can be just as much of a problem as members who don't speak. Compulsive talkers tend to dominate a discussion, speak more frequently than others, feel less inhibited, and experience lower levels of communication apprehension.[1] Compulsive talkers focus on expressing their own ideas and fail to listen to what others have to say. Unfortunately, compulsive talkers are often unaware that their behavior is a problem. If you answer *yes* to several of the following questions, you may be a compulsive talker.[2]

- Do you speak significantly more than other group members?
- Do you direct the course of a group's discussion?
- Do you immediately take charge of a group?
- Do you forcefully express opinions on even minor issues?
- Do you speak for long periods of time without pausing?

A compulsive talker can frustrate group members who never get a chance to express or respond to ideas during a discussion. One way to rein in a compulsive talker is to set ground rules or time limits for discussion. For example, "In order for us all to have a say, let's limit our comments on this issue to two minutes each." In other instances, it may simply be necessary to interrupt: "Sean, I appreciate your comments, but I would like to hear what others have to say on the matter."

[1]Robert N. Bostrom and Nancy Grant Harrington, "An Exploratory Investigation of Characteristics of Compulsive Talkers," *Communication Education* 48 (1999), pp. 73–80.

[2]Bostrom and Harrington, p. 76.

Assertive members may choose to behave passively when an issue is unimportant or when the cost of getting their way is too high to achieve any benefits. In other situations, assertive members may express themselves aggressively when an issue is very important and the benefits of achieving a particular goal outweigh the cost of interpersonal conflict.

Balancing Passivity and Aggression

Passivity has a different effect on a group. Passive group members often lack confidence. They are reluctant to express their opinions and feelings, may experience high levels of communication apprehension, fear criticism from others, and do what they're told to do, even when they disagree with or dislike the order. Passive group members are rarely satisfied with their group experiences because they feel powerless and put-upon.

With **aggressiveness**, on the other hand, members act in their own self-interest at the expense of others. They are critical, insensitive, combative, and even abusive. They get what they want by taking over or by bullying other members into submission. As a consequence, they are often disliked and disrespected. In many cases, aggressive members behave this way because their needs are not met or they don't know how to express themselves assertively.

In some cases, passivity and aggression combine to create a third type of behavior—**passive-aggressive**. Passive-aggressives rarely exhibit aggressive behavior, even though they have little or no respect for the rights of others. They also may appear confident rather than passive because they speak up and contribute. However, beneath the façade of effective participation lies an insecure member. Passive-aggressives often get their way by undermining other members behind their backs,

ethics in groups
The Ethics of Assertiveness

Psychologists Robert Alberti and Michael Emmons call attention to the fact that the principle of assertive action is embedded in our culture and even addressed in the U.S. Constitution.[1] Americans enjoy the constitutional rights of free speech, free press, and the right to peaceably assemble in the furtherance of asserting their convictions. Assertive communication is often culturally accepted, but in some instances it may also be an ethical expectation.

The National Communication Association's Credo for Ethical Communication calls for a commitment to the "courageous expression of personal conviction in pursuit of fairness and justice."[2] Ethical group members have an obligation to assert themselves, not only to pursue their own goals, but to prevent unjust or unethical group action. For instance, the members of a medical team must have the courage to speak up if they believe that a patient is being given the wrong medication. Whether your group is deciding how to trim a budget, determining the best candidate to hire, or developing a marketing campaign, each group member has the ethical responsibility to act assertively in expressing opposition to group decisions that are potentially unethical.

[1]Robert Alberti and Michael Emmons, *Your Perfect Right,* 8th ed. (Atascadero, CA: Impact, 2001), p. 222.

[2]The complete credo is available on the National Communication Association website at www.natcom.org/policies/External/EthicalComm.htm.

by behaving cooperatively but rarely following through with promised contributions, and by appearing to agree while privately planning an opposite action.

Assertive members are trusted because they do not violate the rights and interests of others. Instead, they establish strong interpersonal relationships with other group members. Assertive members speak up and help a group make decisions and solve problems. They enjoy working in groups and take great satisfaction in achieving a group goal.

The graph pictured in Figure 3.4 demonstrates how group or member assertiveness represents a balance between passivity and aggression.[30] Group or member effectiveness increases as you move from passivity to assertiveness and then decreases as you move beyond assertiveness into aggressiveness.

Figure 3.4 Group Effectiveness and Member Assertiveness

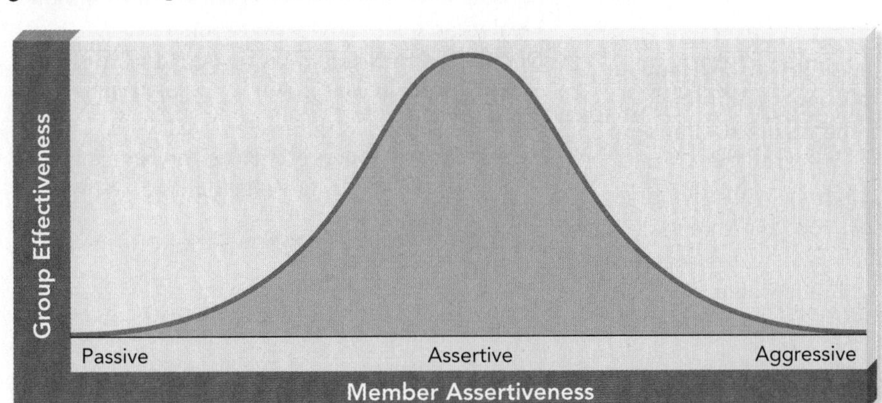

Assertiveness Skills

Regardless of how assertive you are, you can always improve your assertiveness skills. Building assertiveness skills incrementally can help you and your group increase in confidence while reducing social tensions. The following list includes both simple and complex skills for enhancing your assertiveness:

- Devote a significant amount of time to preparing for meetings.
- Enlist an assertive colleague who will make sure that you are recognized and given time to speak at meetings.
- Express your opinions clearly. Don't talk around the issue or ramble.
- Establish and maintain direct eye contact with individual group members.
- Assume an assertive body posture. Your body should be alert and focused in the direction of other speakers.
- Express your feelings as well as your thoughts. If you let group members see your emotions, your recommendations may be taken more seriously.
- Speak expressively—use volume, pitch, and rate to help your statements stand out.

groups in balance . . .
Know When to Say *No*

One of the most basic but difficult assertiveness skills is having the ability and confidence to say *no.* Randy Paterson, author of *The Assertiveness Workbook,* puts it this way: "If you cannot say *no,* you are not in charge of your own life."[1] Why, then, do so many people believe that if someone asks them to do something, they have to do it? Paterson offers several reasons:

- They won't accept my *no* and will expect me to do it anyway.
- They won't accept or like *me* if I say *no.*
- Given our relationship, I don't have the right or the courage to say *no.*[2]

Think of it this way: If someone said, "Can I have your car?" you'd say *no,* wouldn't you? What about "Would you write the group's paper and put everyone's name on it?" or "Can the group meet at your house on Sunday?"

Certainly there's nothing wrong with saying *yes* when the request is reasonable and you want to do it or to help someone. But what if you want to say *no*? Fortunately, there are several communication strategies and skills you can use to say *no*:

- Use assertive body posture. If you say *no* with your words, but signal *maybe* with your body, people will believe that you can be persuaded to do what they want.
- Wait for the question. Don't say *yes* or *no* until you hear a request. For example, if someone says, "I can't ask the group to stay late and help me," don't say, "I'll do it for you."
- Decide on your wording. Use a clear statement, such as "No, I'm not willing to do that," rather than "Gee, I'm not sure . . . maybe another time."
- Don't apologize or make an excuse when it isn't necessary. Avoid statements such as "I'm sorry but I really can't . . ." or "I wish I could but . . ."
- Don't ask permission to say *no.* Avoid saying, "Would it be okay if I didn't . . . ?" or "Will you be upset if I say *no?*"
- Accept the consequences. Just as you have the right to say *no,* others have the right not to like it.[3]

[1]Randy J. Paterson, *The Assertiveness Workbook* (Oakland, CA: New Harbinger, 2000), p. 149.

[2]Paterson, p. 150.

[3]Paterson, pp. 151–153.

Memorizing a list of skills for enhancing your assertiveness is not the same thing as becoming more assertive. As is the case with many communication skills, you must choose the strategy that suits your purpose. In some cases, a simple statement may serve your needs. In other cases, you will have to describe a situation, share your feelings, and state your intentions.[31]

Assertive group members reap many rewards. Generally, they are more satisfied with and proud of the work they do in groups. They are also more likely to become group leaders. Because assertive members respect the rights of others, they are well liked. There is much to be gained from exhibiting assertive behavior in groups, and first among those benefits is increased confidence.

summary study guide

Followership

- The full participation of followers is the engine that makes groups work effectively.
- Competent members have the skills necessary to achieve the group's goal and the personal characteristics required to achieve excellence while working well with others.

Member Needs

- Maslow's Hierarchy of needs identifies five needs—physiological, safety, belongingness, esteem, and self-actualization—all of which may be satisfied by working in groups.
- Schutz's FIRO Theory identifies three interpersonal needs (inclusion, control, and affection) that affect member behavior and group effectiveness.
- Whereas a social member's inclusion needs are met, undersocial or oversocial behavior may indicate that a member's inclusion needs are not met.
- Whereas a democratic member's control needs are met, control needs may not be met when members behave as abdicrats or autocrats.
- Whereas personal member's affection needs are met, underpersonal or overpersonal behavior may indicate that a member's affection needs are not met.

Member Roles

- When a group member exhibits a unique set of skills or behavior patterns that serve specific functions within the group, that member has assumed a role.
- Group task roles include: initiator, information seeker, coordinator-chairperson, information giver, opinion seeker, opinion giver, clarifier-summarizer, implementer-completer, evaluator-critic, energizer, procedural technician, and recorder-secretary.
- Group maintenance roles include: encourager-supporter, harmonizer, compromiser, tension releaser, gatekeeper, observer-interpreter, and teamworker-follower.
- Self-centered group roles include: aggressor, blocker, dominator, recognition seeker, clown, deserter, confessor, and special interest pleader.

Member Confidence

- James McCroskey defines communication apprehension as an individual's level of fear or anxiety associated with either real or anticipated communication with another person or persons.
- The following strategies can help you reduce your level of communication apprehension: recognize that you are not alone, be well prepared, learn communication skills, relax physically, think positively (cognitive restructuring), and use visualization techniques.
- You can help members reduce their level of apprehension in several ways: provide supportive and constructive feedback, encourage and include anxious members, and stop talking.

Member Assertiveness

- Assertiveness—speaking up and acting in your own best interests without denying the rights and interests of others—has the potential to enhance the confidence and effectiveness of a group and its members.
- Effective assertiveness seeks a balance between passivity and aggression.

key terms

abdicrat 55
affection need 55
aggressiveness 68
aggressor 61
assertiveness 67
autocrat 55
belongingness need 54
blocker 61
clarifier-summarizer 60
clown 61
cognitive restructuring 66
communication apprehension 62
completer/finisher 59
compromiser 61
confessor 62
control need 55
coordinator-chairperson 58, 59
democratic member 55
deserter 61
dominator 61
encourager-supporter 60
energizer 60
esteem need 54
evaluator-critic 60
Fundamental Interpersonal Relationship Orientation (FIRO) 54
gatekeeper 61
harmonizer 60
hyperpersonal communication 65
implementer-completer 59, 60
inclusion need 55
information giver 60
information seeker 58
initiator 58
innovator 59
maintenance role 58
Maslow's Hierarchy of Needs 53
monitor/evaluator 59
observer-interpreter 61
opinion giver 60
opinion seeker 60
overpersonal member 57
oversocial member 55
passive-aggressive 68
passivity 68
personal member 56
physiological need 54
procedural technician 60
recognition seeker 61
recorder-secretary 60
resource investigator 59
role 57
safety need 54
self-actualization need 54
self-centered role 58
shaper 59
social member 55
special interest pleader 62
specialist 59
task role 58
Team-Role Theory 59
teamworker 59
teamworker-follower 61
tension releaser 61
underpersonal member 56
undersocial member 55
visualization 66

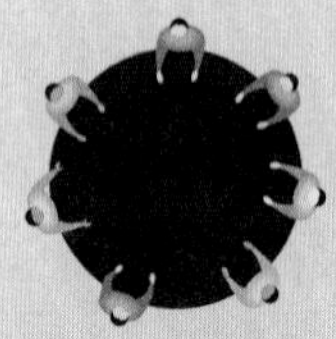

critical thinking about the case study

Taming Tony the Tiger

1. What needs motivate Tony's participation in groups? To what extent are those needs met in his current job?
2. What roles does Tony assume in his group and how do these roles affect his attitude and behavior as a group member?
3. Is Tony dissatisfied because his needs and roles have changed or are the needs and roles of new group members the reason he is depressed and frustrated? Justify your answer.
4. Tony is eager to use his expertise and years of experience to help group members overcome communication apprehension. What strategies should he use?
5. How can Tony balance his interaction style and become more assertive than aggressive?
6. Which dialectic tensions help explain the problems Tony is experiencing as he works in groups?

group work Meeting Member Needs

Directions: Review the five human needs identified by Abraham Maslow. Consider the ways in which a group might help fulfill each need. Identify two group examples for each need and fill in the following table with your answers.

MASLOW'S HIERARCHY OF NEEDS	EXAMPLE #1	EXAMPLE #2
Physiological Needs: Water, Food, and Shelter		
Safety Needs: Security and Protection	*Example*: Neighbors form a neighborhood watch group to deter street crime and promote community safety.	
Belongingness Needs: Friendship and Love		
Esteem Needs: Respect and Admiration		
Self-Actualization: Fulfilling Your Personal Potential	*Example*: As president of a professional association, you focus on helping the executive committee work efficiently, effectively, and ethically.	

group assessment Personal Report of Communication Apprehension (PRCA-24)

Directions: This instrument is composed of twenty-four statements concerning feelings about communication with other people. Please indicate the degree to which each statement applies to you by marking whether you (1) strongly agree, (2) agree, (3) are undecided, (4) disagree, or (5) strongly disagree. Work quickly; record your first impression.

_____ 1. I dislike participating in group discussions.
_____ 2. Generally, I am comfortable while participating in group discussions.
_____ 3. I am tense and nervous while participating in group discussions.
_____ 4. I like to get involved in group discussions.
_____ 5. Engaging in a group discussion with new people makes me tense and nervous.
_____ 6. I am calm and relaxed while participating in a group discussion.
_____ 7. Generally, I am nervous when I have to participate in a meeting.
_____ 8. Usually I am calm and relaxed while participating in a meeting.
_____ 9. I am very calm and relaxed when I am called on to express an opinion at a meeting.
_____ 10. I am afraid to express myself at meetings.
_____ 11. Communicating at meetings usually makes me feel uncomfortable.
_____ 12. I am very relaxed when answering questions at a meeting.
_____ 13. While participating in a conversation with a new acquaintance, I feel very nervous.
_____ 14. I have no fear of speaking up in conversations.
_____ 15. Ordinarily I am very tense and nervous in conversations.
_____ 16. Ordinarily I am very calm and relaxed in conversations.
_____ 17. While conversing with a new acquaintance, I feel very relaxed.
_____ 18. I'm afraid to speak up in conversations.
_____ 19. I have no fear of giving a speech.
_____ 20. Certain parts of my body feel very tense and rigid while I am giving a speech.
_____ 21. I feel relaxed while giving a speech.
_____ 22. My thoughts become confused and jumbled when I am giving a speech.
_____ 23. I face the prospect of giving a speech with confidence.
_____ 24. While giving a speech, I get so nervous that I forget facts I really know.

Scoring: The PRCA permits computation of one total score and four subscores. The subscores are related to communication apprehension in each of four common communication contexts: group discussions, meetings, interpersonal conversations, and public speaking. To compute your scores, merely add or subtract your scores for each item as indicated here.

To obtain your total score for the PRCA, simply add your four subscores together. Your score should be between 24 and 120. If your score is below 24 or above 120, you have made a mistake in computing the score. Scores for each of the four contexts (groups, meetings, interpersonal conversations, and public speaking) can range from a low of 6 to a high of 30. Any score above 18 indicates some degree of apprehension. If your score is above 18 for the public speaking context, you are like the overwhelming majority of Americans.

Scoring Formula

Group Discussions: 18 + scores for items 2, 4, and 6; minus scores for items 1, 3, and 5.
Meetings: 18 + scores for items 8, 9, and 12; minus scores for items 7, 10, and 11.
Interpersonal Conversations: 18 + scores for items 14, 16, and 17; minus scores for items 13, 15, and 18.
Public Speaking: 18 + scores for items 19, 21, and 23; minus scores for items 20, 22, and 24.

Subscores

_____ Group Discussions
_____ Meetings
_____ Interpersonal Conversations
_____ Public Speaking

Norms for PRCA-24:

	Mean	Standard Deviation
Total Score	65.5	15.3
Group	15.4	4.8
Meetings	16.4	4.8
Interpersonal	14.5	4.2
Public Speaking	19.3	5.1

Source: PRCA-24 reprinted with permission from the author. See James C. McCroskey, *An Introduction to Rhetorical Communication*, 6th ed. (Englewood Cliffs, NJ: Prentice-Hall, 1993), p. 37.

notes

1. Carl E. Larson and Frank M. J. LaFasto, *TeamWork: What Must Go Right/What Can Go Wrong* (Newbury Park, CA: Sage, 1989), p. 62.
2. Rodney W. Napier and Matti K. Gershenfeld, *Groups: Theory and Experience*, 7th ed. (Boston: Houghton Mifflin, 2004), pp. 72–74.
3. Abraham H. Maslow, *Motivation and Personality* (New York: Harper & Row, 1954).
4. Will Schutz, *The Human Element: Productivity, Self-Esteem, and the Bottom Line* (San Francisco: Jossey-Bass, 1994).
5. In his more recent works, Schutz uses the term *openness* instead of *affection*. However, we find that students understand the third need better when we use Schutz's original term—*affection*.
6. Scott D. Johnson and Lynette M. Long, "Being a Part of Being Apart: Dialectics and Group Communication," in *New Directions in Group Communication*, ed. Lawrence R. Frey (Thousand Oaks, CA: Sage, 2002), p. 35.
7. Jeanne M. Plas, *Person-Centered Leadership: An American Approach to Participator Management* (Thousand Oaks, CA: Sage, 2000), p. 88.
8. Kenneth D. Benne and Paul Sheats, "Functional Roles of Group Members," *Journal of Social Issues* 4 (1948), pp. 41–49.
9. Michael Z. Hackman and Craig E. Johnson, *Leadership: A Communication Perspective*, 4th ed. (Long Grove, IL: Waveland, 2004), p. 82.
10. Jon R. Katzenbach and Douglas K. Smith, *The Discipline of Teams: A Mindbook-Workbook for Delivering Small Group Performance* (New York: Wiley, 2000), pp. 20, 138.
11. Katzenbach and Smith, p. 138.
12. James M. Kouzes and Barry Z. Posner, *The Leadership Challenge*, 3rd ed. (San Francisco: Jossey-Bass, 2002), p. 296. Also see the discussion of a leader's role in building group confidence in Frank M. J. LaFasto and Carl Larson, *When Teams Work Best* (Thousand Oaks, CA: Sage, 2001), pp. 121–130.
13. Larson and LaFasto, p. 71.
14. Virginia P. Richmond and James C. McCroskey, *Communication: Apprehension, Avoidance, and Effectiveness*, 4th ed. (Scottsdale, AZ: Gorsuch, Scarisbrick, 1995), p. 41.
15. Michael T. Motley, *Overcoming Your Fear of Public Speaking: A Proven Method* (Boston: Houghton Mifflin, 1997), p. 3; Virginia P. Richmond and James C. McCroskey, *Communication: Apprehension, Avoidance, and Effectiveness*, 5th ed. (Boston: Allyn & Bacon/Longman, 1998).
16. James C. McCroskey and Virginia P. Richmond, "Communication Apprehension and Small Group Communication," in *Small Group Communication: A Reader*, 6th ed., ed. Robert S. Cathcart and Larry A. Samovar (Dubuque, IA: Wm. C. Brown, 1992), p. 368. Also see Beth Bonniwell Haslett and Jenn Ruebush, "What Differences Do Individual Differences in Groups Make?" in *The Handbook of Group Communication Theory and Research*, ed. Lawrence R. Frey; Dennis S. Gouran and Marshall Scott Poole, assoc. eds. (Thousand Oaks, CA: Sage, 1999), p. 124.
17. Richmond and McCroskey, 4th ed., p. 57.
18. Richmond and McCroskey, 4th ed., p. 58.
19. Richmond and McCroskey, 4th ed., p. 46.
20. Diane Dreher, *The Tao of Personal Leadership* (New York: HarperCollins, 1996), p. 75.
21. Isa N. Engleberg and John A. Daly, *Presentations in Everyday Life: Strategies for Effective Speaking*, 3rd ed. (Boston: Pearson/Allyn & Bacon, 2009), p. 32.
22. Karen Kangas Dwyer, *Conquer Your Speech Anxiety*, 2nd ed. (Belmont, CA: Thomson Wadsworth, 2005), pp. 72–94; Richmond and McCroskey, 4th ed., pp. 102–105.
23. See Chapter 2, "Listening to the Cries and Whispers of the Articulate Body," in Randolph R. Cornelius, *The Science of Emotions: Research and Tradition in the Psychology of Emotions* (Upper Saddle River, NJ: Prentice-Hall, 1996).
24. Delaine Fragnoli, "Fear of Lying," *Bicycling* 38 (1997), pp. 46–47.
25. Joe Ayres, Tim Hopf, and Debbie M. Ayres, "An Examination of Whether Imaging Ability Enhances the Effectiveness of an Intervention Designed to Reduce Speech Anxiety," *Communication Education* 43 (1994), pp. 252–258; Joe Ayres, Brian Heuett, and Debbie A. Sonandre, "Testing a Refinement in an Intervention for Communication Apprehension," *Communication Reports* 11 (1998), pp. 73–84.
26. Ron Short, *A Special Kind of Leadership: The Key to Learning Organizations* (Seattle, WA: The Leadership Group, 1991), pp. 17, 26.
27. Sam R. Lloyd, *Leading Teams: The Skills for Success* (West Des Moines, IA: American Media, 1996), p. 57.
28. Joseph A. Bonito and Andrea B. Hollingshead, "Participation in Small Groups," in *Communicating Yearbook*, 20, ed. Brant R. Burleson (Thousand Oaks, CA: Sage, 1997), p. 249.
29. A more detailed definition and explanation of assertiveness can be found in Robert E. Alberti and Michael L. Emmons, *Your Perfect Right: Assertiveness and Equality in Your Life and Personal Relationships*, 8th ed. (Atascadero, CA: Impact, 2001).
30. Joshua D. Guilar, *The Interpersonal Communication Skills Workshop* (New York: AMACOM, 2001), p. 70.
31. Counseling and Mental Health Center, University of Texas at Austin, *Learning to Be Assertive*, http://www.utexas.edu/student/cmhc/booklets/assert/assertive.html, updated 10/10/02.

chapter 4

Group Diversity

chapter outline

Heterogeneous Groups

Barriers to Understanding Others
Ethnocentrism • Stereotyping • Prejudice • Discrimination

Personality Dimensions
The Big Five Personality Traits • The Myers-Briggs Type Indicator® • Adjusting to Personality Traits in Groups

Cultural Dimensions
Individualism–Collectivism • Power Distance • Uncertainty Avoidance • Masculine–Feminine Values • High Context–Low Context • Monochronic Time–Polychronic Time

Gender Dimensions

Generational Dimensions

Religious Dimensions

Balancing Group Diversity

study questions

- *How does the homogeneous ↔ heterogeneous dialectic affect group effectiveness?*
- *What barriers prevent group members from understanding, respecting, and adapting to member diversity?*
- *How do members' personality traits affect group productivity and member satisfaction?*
- *In what ways do cultural differences affect both group productivity and member satisfaction?*
- *How do gender differences affect both group productivity and member satisfaction?*
- *How does the interaction of different age groups affect both group productivity and member satisfaction?*
- *How do members' religious beliefs affect both group productivity and member satisfaction?*
- *What communication strategies can help members understand, respect, and adapt to group diversity?*

Heterogeneous Groups

Once upon a time, the majority of U.S. doctors, lawyers, professors, elected officials, and corporate executives had two things in common: They were white and male. They also worked with other white males very much like themselves. Today the world of work is very different. Corporations, institutions, work sites, and neighborhoods are multicultural communities: A forty-year-old female from India, Chile, or Germany might be an orderly, a manager, a nurse, a doctor, a clerk, or a hospital's chief executive officer. Learning to communicate effectively in the global village that characterizes life in the twenty-first century is challenging, particularly when you must collaborate with other people in diverse group settings.

Every person on this earth—and thus every member of a group—is different. Even identical twins have different experiences as well as different characteristics, abilities, and beliefs. Think about the many ways in which you differ from others by asking the following questions:

- Where did you grow up, and how did that influence who you are now?
- What aspects of your culture do you most appreciate and are you not likely to give up?[1]
- Which of your physical characteristics do you like or dislike?
- What are your interpersonal, intellectual, and physical skills?
- When you have free time from work or studies, what do you like to do?
- What are your dominant personality traits?

Your answers to these questions reflect who you are and how you differ from other group members. These differences are not trivial. Your and your group's success depends, in large part, on your ability to handle the inevitable dialectic tensions that arise in diverse groups.

In Chapter 1, we discuss a study commissioned by the Association of American Colleges and Universities that asked employers to rank critical learning outcomes for college graduates entering the workplace. The number one outcome was "teamwork skills and the ability to collaborate with others in diverse group settings." Recent graduates ranked the same learning outcome as their top priority.[2] Note that the top choice was *not* "teamwork skills" alone. The survey respondents were loud and clear about the need for teamwork skills that also include the abililty to work with others in *diverse* groups. Understanding, respecting, and adapting to diverse members and group settings are absolute necessities.

According to the 2000 Census, the "face" of the United States has changed signficantly from that known by previous generations. During the 1990s, the Hispanic population increased 58 percent and the Asian population increased 48 percent. Between 1990 and 2000, more than thirteen million people immigrated to the United States, the largest immigration number in a ten-year span in the country's history.[3]

In 2000, 75 percent of the U.S. population was classified as white. By 2006, the percent of whites had decreased to 56.6 percent.[4] Today, more than half the people living in California are nonwhite, as are the majority of big-city dwellers. Soon after the middle of this century, white Americans will become one of the many minority groups living in the United States.[5] In other words, there will be no majority culture. In many group settings, members will interact with classmates and colleagues from cultures different from their own.

Before embarking on the study of group diversity, we need to define the term *culture*. **Culture** is "a learned set of shared interpretations about beliefs, values, and norms which affect the behaviors of a relatively large group of people."[6] Within most

cultures, there are also groups of people—members of **co-cultures**—who coexist within the mainstream society, yet remain connected to one another through their cultural heritage.[7] In the United States, Native American tribes are co-cultures, as are African Americans, Hispanic/Latino Americans, Asian Americans, Arab Americans, Irish Americans, and members of large and small religious groups. Given our broad definition of culture, a Nebraska rancher and a Boston professor can have very different cultural perspectives, as would a native Brazilian, an Indonesian Muslim, and a member of the Chippewa tribe.

Now let's compare the notion of culture to what we see as a broader concept: *diversity*. Diversity describes more than a person's country of origin, skin color, or ethnic heritage. When discussing group communication, we use the term *diversity* in its most general sense—the quality of being different. In just about every group, you will work with members whose physical characteristics, status, traits, and attitudes are different from yours. These distinctive characteristics include age, occupation, physical ability, marital status, personality preferences, and much more.

The homogeneous ↔ heterogeneous dialectic is directly applicable to the study of group member diversity. As we note in Chapter 1, the prefix *homo* comes from the Greek language and means "same" or "similar"; *hetero* means "different." Thus, a homogeneous group is composed of members who are the same or similar, and a heterogeneous group is composed of members who are not the same. And remember, there is no such thing as a purely homogeneous group because no two members can be *exactly* the same. Diversity exists in all groups.

As the member of a group, you join a diverse collection of people. Although you may share similar backgrounds, interests, and talents with the other members, you rely on differences to establish your unique identity and value to the group. James Surowiecki, author of *The Wisdom of Crowds*, explains that member diversity helps groups make better decisions because it "adds perspectives that would otherwise be absent and because it takes away . . . some of the destructive characteristics" of poor group decision making.[8] James G. Marsh, an organizational theorist, contends that groups that are too much alike find it harder to keep learning because each member is bringing less and less new information to the table.[9] Lee Gardenswartz and Anita Rowe, authors of *Diverse Teams at Work*, note that "individual differences and uniqueness make every group diverse . . . . [In addition to race], gender, ethnicity, variations in age, education level, parental status, geographic location, sexual orientation, and work experience are a few of the many ways in which people can be different."[10]

Figure 4.1 on page 80 displays the three layers of diversity within every group member.[11] Your core personality—which permeates all the other layers—is at the center and represents your unique ways of experiencing, interpreting, and behaving in the world around you. The next layer represents internal dimensions over which you have no control. For example, you cannot change your race, age, or ethnicity. You may try to look younger or mask an accent, but you cannot change the number of years you have lived, the ethnicity of your parents, or your place of birth.

The third and outer layer represents societal and experiential factors such as religion, marital status, income, and educational background. Although you may be able to change these dimensions by converting to another religion, by getting married or divorced, or by enhancing your income and educational background, your "new" external dimensions will affect how you see yourself and how others see you.

Not only do these three layers of diversity distinguish you from others, but they also form the screen through which you see yourself and those around you. In this chapter, we examine how elements in all three diversity layers affect your interaction in groups as well as overall group productivity and member satisfaction.

case study
No Offense Intended

The local arts council is proud of the diversity on its governing board. The president is a male from Barbados who chairs the chemistry department at a nearby liberal arts college. The vice president is a black female who retired from the local school system after forty years of teaching high school music classes. The treasurer is a young black man with a master's degree in finance, appointed to the board by the county executive to oversee grants distribution. The secretary is a white gay male who has supported local arts programs for many years as a donor. The fifth member of the board is a white Jewish woman with a degree in theatre. The sixth member is a poet whose Japanese father and Chilean mother immigrated to the United States from Chile twenty years ago. You are the seventh member of the board.

During a long and heated discussion about the procedures for applying, screening, and awarding grant funds to artists and arts organizations, the exasperated treasurer announces, "Look, we've got to draft and implement a final solution to deal with the funding question." The Jewish woman gasps audibly. The secretary pauses in midsentence as he records the minutes of the meeting. Silence reigns. The treasurer breaks the silence with "What's wrong?" The poet responds, "Don't you know the meaning of the *final solution*?" Then the Jewish woman says, "Please don't use the phrase *final solution*. You phrased your sentence almost exactly the way Hitler described his plan for exterminating the Jews." Another awkward silence. Would you break the silence and say something? If yes, what would you say? If no, why would you be reluctant to contribute?

When you finish reading this chapter, you should be able to answer the following questions:

1. How much should you know about the diverse characteristics and cultures of other group members?
2. Which dimensions of diversity are most likely to influence how well group members work together?
3. What communication strategies enhance a group's willingness and ability to understand, respect, and adapt to the many layers of diversity among its members?
4. Did you find the phrase "to draft and implement a final solution to deal with the funding question" objectionable? Why or why not?

Barriers to Understanding Others

Barriers to Working in Diverse Groups

Ethnocentrism

Stereotyping

Prejudice

Discrimination

Effective group members develop strategies and skills for interacting with others from diverse backgrounds. Yet simply *learning* about other cultures and the differences among group members will not make you a more effective group member. You must also avoid four obstacles that prevent groups from interacting productively and achieving their goals: ethnocentrism, stereotyping, prejudice, and discrimination.

Ethnocentrism

Ethnocentrism is a belief that your culture is superior to others. Ethnocentrism is not just about patriotism or pride; it is a mistaken belief that your culture is a superior

Figure 4.1 Three Layers of Diversity

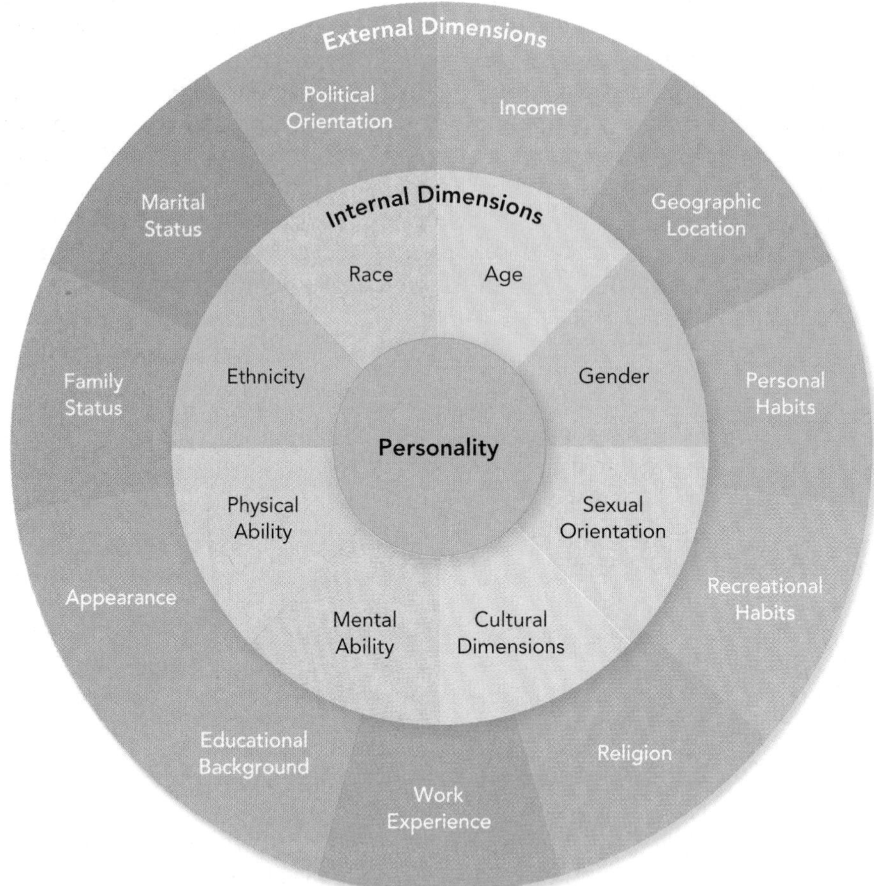

culture, with special rights and privileges that are or should be denied to others. An ethnocentric communicator believes the following:

- My culture should be the role model for other cultures.
- People would be happier if they lived like people in my culture.
- Most other cultures are backward when compared with my culture.

Ethnocentric group members offend others when they imply that they represent a superior culture with superior values. For example, have you ever been insulted by someone who implies that her religious beliefs are "true," whereas yours are not? Have you been disrespected by someone who believes that his traditions, language, or music preferences are "better" than yours? If so, you have seen ethnocentrism in action. Group members with ethnocentric attitudes can derail group progress before it begins.

Stereotyping

A **stereotype** is a generalization about a group of people that oversimplifies their characteristics. When we stereotype others, we rely on exaggerated beliefs to make judgments about a group of people. Unfortunately, stereotyping usually attributes

negative traits to an entire group when, in reality, only a few people in that group may possess those traits. A study of college students found that, even in the 1990s, African Americans were stereotyped as lazy and loud, and Jews were described as shrewd and intelligent.

In addition to negative stereotypes, we may hold positive ones, such as "Asian students excel in math and science" or "Females are more compassionate than males." While positive stereotypes may not seem harmful, they can lead to unfair judgments. Stereotyping other group members does more than derail progress; it prevents members from contributing their best skills and may create long-lasting resentment and anger. For example, groups often ask or appoint a female to chair a social committee or take notes because "women are better at that."

Prejudice

Stereotyping leads to **prejudices**—"negative attitudes about other people that are based on faulty and inflexible stereotypes."[12] Prejudices about an individual or cultural group often arise when we have little or no direct experience with that person or group. The word *prejudice* has two parts: *pre*, meaning "before," and *judice*, as in *judge*. When you believe or express a prejudice, you are making a judgment about someone before you have taken time to get to know that person and see whether your opinions and feelings are justified.

Although prejudices can be positive—"He must be brilliant if he went to Yale"—most prejudices are negative. Statements such as "He can't be brilliant if he only has a community college degree," "I don't want a person with disabilities working on our group project," and "I'm not voting for a pregnant woman to lead this group" are all examples of prejudices based on stereotypes. Such prejudices have several characteristics:

- They rarely are based on extensive direct experience and firsthand knowledge.
- They result in irrational feelings or dislike and even hatred for certain groups.
- They justify a readiness to behave in negative and unjust ways toward members of the group.[13]

Discrimination

Discrimination describes how we act out and express prejudice. When we discriminate, we exclude groups of people from opportunities granted to others: employment, promotion, housing, political expression, and equal rights.

Sadly, discrimination comes in many forms: racial, ethnic, religious, and gender discrimination; sexual harassment; discrimination based on sexual orientation, disability, or age; and discrimination against people from different social classes and political ideologies. Discrimination has no place in groups.

Personality Dimensions

How would you answer the following question: Do members' personalities affect group productivity and member satisfaction? Anyone who has ever worked in a group knows the answer: Of course they do. Each of us has a unique way of interacting with others. Depending on the circumstances, these traits can help or hinder a group's interaction and progress toward a common goal.[14] Understanding personality theories helps a group balance its collection of diverse temperaments, traits, and talents.

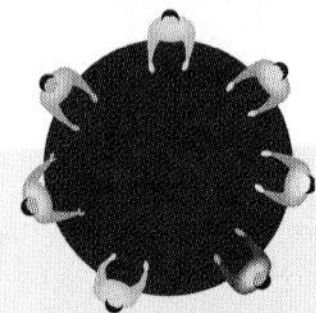

groups in balance . . .

Seek Intellectual Diversity

Let's assume that you belong to a group in which members boast a higher-than-average IQ. You're eager and ready to roll because your group is so brilliant! Not so fast. Smart groups do not always make smart decisions.

Member diversity improves group performance and member satisfaction in many ways—even in terms of how well a group makes "smart" decisions. Scott Page, a political scientist at the University of Michigan, studies groups and problem solving. He concludes that

> On the group level, intelligence alone is not enough, because intelligence alone cannot guarantee you different perspectives on a problem. . . . Grouping only smart people together doesn't work that well because the smart people (whatever that means) tend to resemble each other in what they can do. . . . Adding in a few people who know less, but have different skills, actually improves the group's performance.[1]

Think about the many intelligent people on a U.S. president's staff—and then consider some of the poor decisions made within the White House; for example, the U.S. invasion of Cuba, Watergate, and the war in Iraq. Then think about the well-educated, intelligent people who run U.S. corporations and consider some of their poor decisions—from useless or defective consumer products to crooked officers. In Chapter 9, Conflict and Cohesion in Groups, we examine Irving Janis's concept of *groupthink*, a phenomenon that describes the deterioration of group effectiveness that results from in-group pressure. As you will see, it takes a lot more than collective intelligence to avoid poor decision making.

[1]James Surowiecki, *The Wisdom of Crowds: Why the Many Are Smarter Than the Few and How Collective Wisdom Shapes Business, Economics, Societies, and Nations* (New York: Doubleday, 2004), p. 30.

The Big Five Personality Traits

Most psychologists use the **Big Five Personality Traits** to describe five factors that, together, describe a personality. Like many of the group dimensions discussed in this textbook, personality traits have a dialectic perspective as well. Consider the five personality traits and their opposites in Table 4.1.[15]

Group researchers who study the Big Five Personality Traits offer several conclusions that are not surprising. The first is that certain traits can predict group performance. For example, high levels of agreeableness and emotional stability in groups are associated with group cohesiveness while conscientiousness is associated with task performance. After all, who would choose or want to work with members who were unkind, neurotic, or careless?[16]

The Myers-Briggs Type Indicator®

In addition to the Big Five Personality Traits, a second personality theory demonstrates why and how group members react to group tasks and social interactions in different ways. The **Myers-Briggs Type Indicator (MBTI)** developed by Katharine C. Briggs and her daughter, Isabel Briggs Myers,[17] looks at the different ways in which "people *prefer* to use their minds, specifically, the way they perceive and the way they make judgments."[18] Thousands of corporations, including most Fortune 100 companies, use the Myers-Briggs Type Indicator "to identify job applicants whose skills match those of their top performers," and "to develop communication skills and promote teamwork among current employees."[19]

Table 4.1 The Big Five Personality Traits

Big Five Personality Traits	Characteristics of The Big Five Personality Traits	Opposite Personality Trait
Extraversion	Outgoing, talkative, sociable, assertive, active	Introversion
Agreeableness	Cooperative, friendly, courteous, flexible, trusting, good-natured, forgiving, soft-hearted, tolerant	Disagreeableness
Conscientiousness	Self-disciplined, organized, careful, thorough, responsible, hard-working, achievement oriented, persevering	Carelessness
Emotional Stability	Calm, poised, secure	Neuroticism
Openness to Experience	Imaginative, curious, broadminded, intelligent, original, artistically sensitive	Closed to Experience

According to the MBTI, all of us have preferences of thought and behavior that fall into four categories, with two opposite preferences in each category. As you read about the following categories, ask yourself which preferences best describe the reasons you choose one way of reacting or behaving over another.[20]

Extrovert–Introvert. These two traits relate to where you like to focus your attention. An **extrovert**[21] focuses outward; an **introvert** focuses inward. Notice how the differences between extroverts and introverts represent dialectic traits:

Extrovert	**Introvert**
Outgoing, sociable, expressive	Reserved, private, contained
Enjoys groups and discussions	Prefers one-to-one interactions
Talks first, then thinks	Thinks first, then talks
Does many things at once	Focuses on one thing at a time
Thinks out loud	Thinks to himself or herself
May dominate discussion	May speak less in discussion
Gets energy from being with others	Needs time alone to reenergize

Whereas an extrovert usually likes working in groups and on committees, an introvert may prefer a solo assignment. Introverts need more time to think before they speak or act. A group may miss good ideas and needed analysis if it rushes into solutions proposed by enthusiastic extroverts.

Misunderstandings between extroverts and introverts are common in groups. "Extroverts complain that introverts don't speak up at the right time in meetings. Introverts criticize extroverts for talking too much and not listening well."[22] Effective groups balance the needs of both personality types by accommodating the differences in communication style and tapping the best ideas from all members.

Sensor–Intuitive. These two traits focus on how you look at the world around you. A **sensor** sees the trees; sensors like facts and details. An **intuitive** sees the forest;

groups in balance . . .
Value Introverts

In *The Introvert Advantage: How to Thrive in an Extrovert World*, psychologist Marti Olsen Laney discusses the many pitfalls awaiting introverts in group settings. She writes, "introverts are often surprised when they are not valued for their considerable contributions" to a group, in part because they don't speak up. They also "find it hard to both absorb all the information *and* formulate an opinion about it. They need time away from meetings to sift and sort data." Some introverts can become "brainlocked" because they can't find the right words to express their meaning.[1] Given the inherent challenges facing introverts in group settings, Laney offers a list of strategies for letting other group members know that they are present, interested, and involved in a group and its work:

- Don't schedule too many meetings on the same day.
- Say hello and smile when you enter a room.
- Take notes to help you focus your thoughts and avoid becoming overloaded with information.
- Use nonverbal signals like nodding your head, smiling, and eye contact to let others know that you are paying attention.
- Say *something*. Ask a question, or restate what someone else has said.
- Let people know that you will continue to think about the topic and get back to them with a reaction.
- Email or jot a note to other group members to ask for and provide feedback about issues discussed in a meeting.[2]

[1]Marti Olsen Laney, *The Introvert Advantage: How to Thrive in an Extrovert World* (New York: Workman, 2002), pp. 190, 191–92.

[2]Laney, pp. 193–94.

intuitives prefer the big picture. Notice how the differences between sensors and intuitives reflect dialectic perspectives:

Sensor	**Intuitive**
Focuses on details	Focuses on the big picture
Prefers one task at a time	Likes juggling many tasks
Practical and realistic	Theoretical
Likes concrete information	Likes abstract information
Likes facts	Gets bored with facts and details
Trusts experience	Trusts inspiration and intuition
Values common sense	Values creativity and innovation
Likes rules	Likes to bend or break rules

Sensors and intuitives often see things quite differently. Sensors focus on rules, systematic explanations, and facts, whereas intuitives focus on outwitting the rules, supplying theoretical explanations, and ignoring details.[23] Communication between sensors and intuitives can be difficult "because they see things so differently, and each believes that his or her information is more accurate, valid, and real."[24]

Groups need both kinds of members in order to function effectively and efficiently. For example, "in the construction business it's important to have the 'big picture' people who can see the conceptual side of a project and know when major changes are necessary. This viewpoint needs to be balanced by people who are at the job site supervising the very detail-oriented portions of the work. Both are necessary members of a good project team."[25]

Thinker–Feeler. These two traits explain how you go about making decisions. The **thinker** is task oriented and logical. Thinkers take pride in their ability to think objec-

tively and logically. They often enjoy arguing and making difficult decisions; they want to get the job done, even if the cost is bad feelings among some group members. The **feeler** is a people-oriented member who seeks group harmony. Feelers want everyone to get along. They will spend time and effort helping other members. Notice how the differences between thinkers and feelers reflect dialectic perspectives:

Thinker	**Feeler**
Task oriented	People oriented
Objective, firm, analytical	Subjective, humane, appreciative
Enjoys arguing	Finds arguing disruptive
Prefers businesslike meetings	Prefers social interchange in meetings
Values competence, reason	Values relationships, harmony, and justice
Direct and firm minded	Tactful and tenderhearted
Thinks with the head	Thinks with the heart

When thinkers and feelers work together in groups, there is a potential for misunderstanding. Thinkers may appear unemotional and aggressive. Feelers may annoy others by "wasting" time with social chitchat. Thinkers should try to modify their criticism of others—what is intended as good advice may seem cruel to others. Feelers should learn not to take criticism so personally and to speak up if they feel they're being treated unfairly.[26] When thinkers and feelers appreciate their differences as decision makers, they can form an unbeatable team. While the thinkers make decisions and move the group forward, feelers make sure that the group is working harmoniously.

Judger–Perceiver. The last two traits focus on how you deal with the outer world and its problems. The **judger** is highly structured and well organized. Judgers plan ahead, follow lengthy "to do" lists, and like closure. They are very punctual and can become impatient with people who show up late or waste time. The **perceiver** likes open-endedness; being on time is less important than being flexible and adaptable. Perceivers are risk takers who are willing to try new options. However, they often procrastinate and end up in a frenzy to complete a task on time. Consider how the following dialectical differences can affect group interaction:

Judger	**Perceiver**
Values organization and structure	Values flexibility and spontaneity
In control and definite	Goes with the flow
Likes deadlines	Dislikes deadlines
Work now/play later	Play now/work later
Needs standards and expectations	Feels constrained by rules, takes risks
Adjusts schedules to complete work	Works at the last minute
Punctual	

Judgers and perceivers often have difficulty working together. To a judger, a perceiver may appear scatterbrained. To a perceiver, a judger may appear rigid and controlling. Whereas judgers come prepared to make decisions and solve problems, perceivers "aren't comfortable with things being 'decided'; [they] want to reopen, discuss, rework, argue for the sake of arguing."[27] As difficult as it is for them, judgers should try to stop "doing" and take time to relax with others. Perceivers should try to respect deadlines and keep the promises that they make to judgers.

Adjusting to Personality Traits in Groups

Most groups benefit when there is an appropriate mix and balance of personality traits. A group without judgers or members who possess the conscientiousness trait may miss important deadlines and fail to achieve its goal. A group that lacks members who are open to experience will fail to develop innovative approaches or seek creative solutions. A group without a sensor can overlook important details or critical flaws in a proposal. Although it is tempting to choose members who are just like you, your group will perform better with representatives of every type. According to Otto Kroeger and Janet Thuesen, in an ideal group, "we would have a smattering of Extroverts, Introverts, Sensors, Intuitives, Thinkers, Feelers, Judgers, and Perceivers—and we would put them together in such a way that they would not only understand their differences but could also draw upon them."[28]

Cultural Dimensions

We owe a great deal to a social psychologist and an anthropologist for identifying several significant dimensions of culture. Dutch social psychologist Geert Hofstede's groundbreaking research on cultural dimensions has transformed our understanding of culture and diversity. He defines an **intercultural dimension** as "an aspect of a culture that can be measured relative to other cultures."[29] Here are four of Hofstede's dimensions: individualism–collectivism, power distance, uncertainty avoidance, and masculine–feminine values. Anthropologist Edward T. Hall adds two more dimensions: high-context and low-context cultures and monochronic-polychronic time.[30] Table 4.2 provides an overview of these six cultural dimensions and how they can be used to recognize and adapt to group member diversity.

Individualism–Collectivism

According to Hofstede and many contemporary researchers, most of us in the United States accept **individualism** as a cultural value. As a whole, we believe that the individual is important, that independence is worth pursuing, that personal achievement should be rewarded, and that individual uniqueness is an important value.[31] In the United States, an "I" orientation prevails. However, most cultures do not put as much value on individualism. As much as 70 percent of the world's population regards *inter*dependence or **collectivism** as a more important value.[32] In these cultures, "we" is much more important than "I." The following behaviors are characteristic of collectivist cultures:

- There is greater emphasis on the views, needs, and goals of the group than on the individual's views, needs, and goals.
- Social norms and duties are defined by the group rather than by the individual's personal pleasure or personal benefits.
- Beliefs shared with the group are more important than beliefs that distinguish an individual from the group.
- There is greater readiness to cooperate with group members.[33]

At first, a collectivist perspective may appear ideally suited for group work. Yet, the opinions of individualistic members help a group recognize and adapt to a variety of useful perspectives.

Be careful not to stereotype *all* Americans as individualistic just because the United States ranks first among individualistic cultures. Many Americans are not highly

Table 4.2 Cultural Dimensions of Group Members

Cultural Dimension	Definition and Example	Group Member Behavior	Recommended Adaptations
Individualism–Collectivism	Prefer to act independently or interdependently. *Individualism*: Value individual achievement and freedom. **United States, Australia, Canada** *Collectivism:* Emphasize group identity. **Asian and Latin American countries**	**Individualistic** members will work alone and seek credit for their own work; collectivist members will work in groups and try to help each other. **Collectivist** members may prefer face-to-face discussions instead of virtual discussion.	Encourage collectivism. Make sure that individualistic members understand that they are part of a larger group that needs their input and participation to achieve a shared goal.
Power Distance	Extent of equity or status among members. *High Power:* Inequity between high- and low-status members. **Mexico, India, Singapore** *Low Power:* Equity and interdependence among group members. **Israel, New Zealand, Denmark**	**High-power-distance** members try to take charge and make decisions; **low-power-distance** members seek consultation and consensus.	Establish clear norms for member behavior. To what extent will members participate in decision making? How will specific tasks be assigned? How and by whom will members be evaluated? Who will serve as leader(s)?
Uncertainty Avoidance	Extent of comfort in uncertain situations *High Uncertainty:* Prefer rules, plans, and routines. **Japan, Belgium, Greece** *Low Uncertainty:* Comfortable with ambiguity and unpredictability. **Jamaica, Hong Kong**	**High-uncertainty** members require structured tasks and spend more time on details; **low-uncertainty** members want less structure and can work independently with little supervision.	Provide clear instructions to the high-uncertainty members while giving low-uncertainty members opportunities to function unaided.
Masculinity–Femininity	Concern for self and success versus a focus on caring and sharing. *Masculine:* Assertive, decisive, dominant. **Japan, Venezuela, Italy** *Feminine:* Nurturing, cooperative. **Sweden, Norway, Denmark**	**Masculine-oriented** members focus on the task and personal success; **feminine-oriented** members focus on member relations and respect for others.	Balance masculine and feminine values in order to achieve task and social goals. Do not forgo action in order to achieve total cooperation and consensus.
High Context–Low Context	Directness of communication in specific circumstances. *High Context:* Messages are implied and context-sensitive. **Japan, China, Greece, Mexico** *Low Context:* Messages are explicit, factual, and objective. **England, United States, Germany**	**High-context** members consider background, nonverbal cues, and interpersonal history when communicating; **low-context** members want facts and clear, direct, explicit communication.	Give high-context members time to review information and react; demonstrate the value of going beyond "just facts" to low-context members.
Monochronic–Polychronic	How people organize and value time. *Monochronic:* Adhere to plans, schedules, and deadlines because time is valuable. **North America and Northern European.** *Polychronic:* Not obsessed with promptness or schedules because time is not highly valued. **Kenya, Argentina, African American**	**Monochronic** members focus on one task at a time and work hard to meet deadlines; **polychronic** members are frequently late, do many things at once, are easily distracted and tolerant of interruptions.	Encourage monochronic members to take responsibility for time-sensitive tasks while accepting that polychronic members will vary promptness based on the nature and importance of a situation or relationship.

individualistic. For example, African Americans often share the characteristics of collectivist societies, as do Mexican Americans and other Hispanic/Latino co-cultures. Even so, the predominant U.S. focus on individual achievement and personal rewards can make interaction with group members from collectivist cultures quite difficult. Group members from these cultures may view a highly individualistic communication style and behavior as selfish, arrogant, antagonistic, power-hungry, ruthless, and impatient.

Power Distance

Can you walk into your boss's office unannounced or do you have to navigate your way through an army of secretaries and administrative assistants? Is it easy to make a personal appointment with the president of your college or university? Does our society truly believe in the sentiments expressed in the U.S. Declaration of Independence that all people "are created equal"? These are the questions addressed in Hofstede's power distance dimension. **Power distance** refers to the physical and psychological distance between those who have power and those who do not have power in relationships, institutions, and organizations. It also represents "the extent to which the less powerful person in society accepts inequality in power and considers it normal."[34]

In cultures with **high power distance**, individuals accept major differences in power as normal, assuming that all people are *not* created equal. In a high-power-distance culture, you dare not challenge authority. Parents, for example, may have total control over their children, and men may have total control over the women in their family. The government, corporate officers, and religious or legal authorities dictate the rules of behavior and have the power to enforce them.

In cultures with **low power distance**, power distinctions are minimized: Supervisors work with subordinates; professors work with students; elected officials work with constituents. Despite the fact that the United States claims to be the greatest democracy on earth and an equal opportunity society, Hofstede ranks the United States sixteenth on the list of low-power-distance cultures—after countries such as Finland, Switzerland, Great Britain, Germany, Costa Rica, Australia, the Netherlands, and Canada.[35]

Power distance has enormous implications for groups, particularly given the strong correlation between collectivism and high power distance and between individualism and low power distance. If you are individualistic and are strongly encouraged to express your own opinion, you are more willing to challenge group members and leaders. If, on the other hand, your culture is collectivist and your personal opinion is subordinate to the welfare of others, you are less likely to challenge the collective authority of a group or its leader.

Uncertainty Avoidance

How well do you handle unexpected events? Do you feel more comfortable if your life is orderly and predictable? Hofstede defines **uncertainty avoidance** as the extent to which people within a culture are nervous in situations they perceive as unstructured, unclear, or unpredictable. If uncertainty makes them nervous, they avoid these situations by maintaining strict codes of behavior and a belief in absolute truths.[36]

In cultures with **high uncertainty avoidance**, members "feel threatened by uncertainty or unknown situations. This feeling is expressed through nervous stress and in a need for predictability: a need for written and unwritten rules."[37] Hofstede puts it

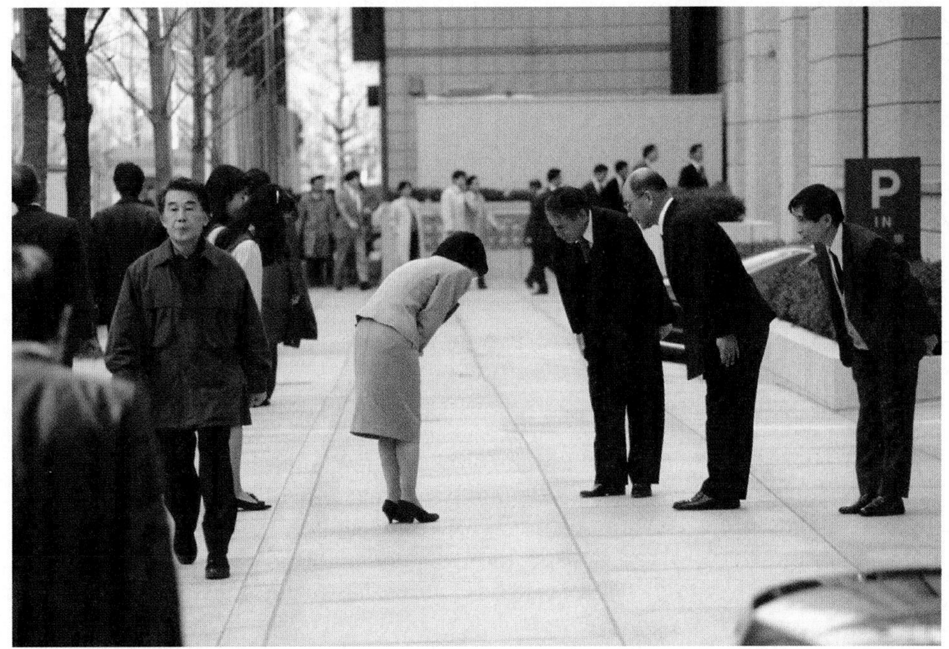

Power distance refers to the physical and psychological distance between those who have power and those who do not have power in relationships, institutions, and organizations. How do the Japanese people in this photograph demonstrate the power distance dimension in their culture?

this way: "What is different, is dangerous."[38] Cultures with **low uncertainty avoidance** accept change as part of life, tolerate nonconformity, take risks, and view rules and regulations as restricting. Members of low-uncertainty-avoidance cultures "tend to live day to day. . . . Conflict and competition are natural, dissent is acceptable, deviance is not threatening, and individual achievement is regarded as beneficial."[39]

The United States is eleventh on the list of countries that feel comfortable with uncertainty. More highly ranked countries include Malaysia, India, and the Philippines. Imagine the communication challenge you face if you are comfortable with change and ambiguity, but work with group members who want to avoid uncertainty. While you are willing to take risks, other members find your attitude unreasonable and even threatening. At the same time, you may see the other member as rigid, uncompromising, and fearful to break or bend rules.

Masculine–Feminine Values

Hofstede uses the terms *masculine* and *feminine* to describe whether a culture values masculine or feminine traits. These traits describe a societal perspective, not individual men or women.

In **masculine societies**, men are supposed to be assertive, tough, and focused on material success, whereas women are supposed to be more modest, tender, and concerned with the quality of life. In **feminine societies**, gender roles overlap: *Both* men *and* women are modest, tender, and concerned with the quality of life.[40]

Hofstede ranks the United States as fifteenth in terms of masculine values, but less masculine than Australia, New Zealand, and Greece.[41] Masculine societies admire and value personal success, competition, assertiveness, and strength. Unselfishness and nurturing is often seen as a weakness or "women's work." Although women have come a long way from the rigid roles of past centuries, they have miles to go before achieving genuine equality in a masculine-oriented culture.

Think of the challenges groups face when there is a mix of masculine and feminine values. Members with masculine perspectives may compete for leadership positions

and exhibit highly assertive behavior. Members with more feminine values may be highly effective and supportive but never achieve a real voice or influence in the group. Later in this chapter, we take a closer look at the ways in which men and women view group work as well as how they participate.

High Context–Low Context

All communication occurs in a **context**, a physical and psychosocial environment. Anthropologist Edward T. Hall sees context as the information that surrounds an event and clarifies its meaning.[42] He claims that context in and of itself may hold more meaning than the actual words in a message. As with Hofstede's dimensions, we can place cultures on a continuum from high context to low context.

In a **high-context culture**, people are not dependent on words to express their meaning. Gestures, silence, and facial expressions as well as the relationships among communicators have meaning. In high-context cultures, meaning is also conveyed through status (age, gender, education, family background, title, and affiliations) and through an individual's informal network of friends and associates.[43]

In a **low-context culture**, people are more dependent on language to express what they mean. As members of a low-context culture, North Americans tend to speak more, speak louder, and speak more rapidly than people from a high-context culture. We "speak up," "spell it out," "tell it like it is," and "speak our mind." Table 4.3 contrasts the characteristics of high- and low-context cultures.

High-context communication is a common characteristic in collectivist cultures where members share similar attitudes, beliefs, and values. As a result, spoken communication can be indirect and implied because everyone *gets* the meaning by understanding the context, the person's nonverbal behavior, and the significance of the communicator's relationships with others. Notice how the following sayings capture the nature of high-context communication:

Seeing is better than hearing. (Nigeria)
Once you preach, the point is gone. (Zen phrase)

Group members from high- and low-context cultures express and interpret messages differently. For example, suppose everyone knows that Allison and Philip have a close personal relationship. During a group discussion, Allison scowls every time Philip expresses his opinion or makes a suggestion. However, when asked whether she agrees with Philip, she says yes. Group members with high-context perspectives would pay more attention to Allison's nonverbal behavior and decide that she may be angry with Philip and disapproves of his ideas, whereas members with low-context perspectives may only hear the "yes" and assume that Allison and Philip are in total agreement.

Table 4.3 Characteristics of High- and Low-Context Cultures

High-Context Characteristics	Low-Context Characteristics
Rely on nonverbal meanings	Rely on verbal meanings
Reserved reactions	Reactions on the surface
Strong in-group bonds	Flexible group membership
High level of group commitment	Low level of group commitment

Monochronic Time–Polychronic Time

Edward Hall classifies time as a form of communication. He claims that cultures organize time in one of two ways: either monochronic or polychronic.[44] In **monochronic time (M time)**, events are scheduled as separate items—one thing at a time. M-time people like to concentrate on one job before moving to another and may become irritated when someone in a meeting brings up a personal topic unrelated to the purpose of the meeting.

In **polychronic time (P time)**, schedules are less important and are frequently broken. People in polychronic cultures are not slaves to time and are easily distracted and tolerant of interruptions. P-time people are frequently late for appointments or may not show up at all.[45] If you are a P-time person, you probably like thinking about and doing several tasks at one time, and feel comfortable holding two or three conversations at the same time. In polychronic-time cultures—such as the Spanish-speaking cultures in Spain and Latin America—relationships are far more important than schedules. "Appointments will be quickly broken, schedules readily set aside, and deadlines unmet without guilt or apology when friends or family members require attention."[46]

When monochronic- and polychronic-time people interact in groups, the results can be frustrating. Hall notes that monochronic members become distressed by how polychronic people treat schedules. For P-time people, schedules and commitments, particularly plans for the future, are not firm, and even important plans may change right up to the last minute.[47]

If you are an M-time person, you can try to modify and relax your obsession with time and scheduling when working with P-time members. If you are a P-time person, you can do your best to respect and adapt to monochronic members' need for careful scheduling and promptness.

Gender Dimensions

In the context of cultural dimensions, Hofstede's phrases *masculine values* and *feminine values* describe a societal perspective, rather than individual men or women. Individual gender differences, however, can affect group productivity and member satisfaction. As you read this section, keep in mind that Hofstede ranks the United States as a more masculine-oriented culture—one in which men are assertive, tough, and focused on material success, whereas women are supposed to be more modest, tender, and concerned with the quality of life.

John Gray's popular book *Men Are from Mars, Women Are from Venus* describes enormous psychological differences between men and women. His book has sold more than thirty million copies and has been translated into forty languages.[48] Deborah Tannen's *You Just Don't Understand: Women and Men in Conversation* claims that boys and girls grow up in what are essentially different cultures, making talk between men and women a cross-cultural experience. Whereas men seek status and independence, women seek connection and interdependence.[49] Unfortunately, books like these have perpetuated stereotypes that cause harm in numerous realms, including women's opportunities in the workplace, couple conflict and communication, and self-esteem problems among adolescents.[50] They also hamper groups seeking to achieve a common goal.

Researchers who carefully examine studies of male and female differences claim that men and women are alike on most—but not all—psychological variables.[51] In

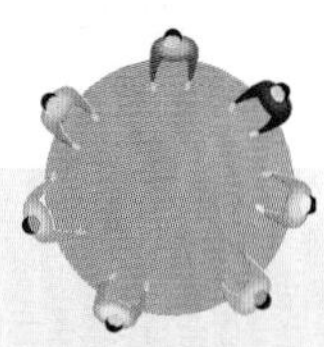

virtual groups
Cultural Diversity in Cyberspace

In their book *Mastering Virtual Teams*, Deborah Duarte and Nancy Snyder use Hofstede's dimensions and Hall's research on context to explain how culture affects the way we use communication technology.[1] We have expanded Duarte and Snyder's discussion to additional dimensions.

- *Individualism–collectivism.* Members from collectivist cultures may prefer face-to-face interactions, whereas individualistic communicators may like having the screen to themselves as they present their ideas and opinions.
- *Power distance.* Members from high-power-distance cultures may communicate more freely when technologies are asynchronous (do *not* occur in real time) and when they allow anonymous input. In other words, when asynchronous technology conceals power relationships, members from high-power-distance cultures may be more willing to challenge others.
- *Uncertainty avoidance.* Members from cultures with high uncertainty avoidance may be slower to adopt technology. They may also prefer technology that produces permanent records of discussions and decisions.
- *Masculinity–femininity.* Members from cultures with more feminine values may use technology as a way of encouraging, supporting, and motivating others while members from cultures with more masculine values may see such nurturing behavior as a waste of precious meeting time.
- *High context–low context.* People from high-context cultures may prefer more information-rich technologies (such as videoconferences), as well as those that offer the feeling of social presence. People from low-context cultures may prefer more asynchronous communication.
- *Monochronic–polychronic.* Monochronic members may become frustrated by polychronic members who are late to join a teleconference. Polychronic members may become distracted during an online meeting and interrupt the group to discuss unrelated issues.

[1]Deborah L. Duarte and Nancy Tennant Snyder, *Mastering Virtual Teams*, 3rd ed. (San Francisco: Jossey-Bass, 2006), pp. 60–61, 118–119.

other words, males and females are much more similar than different. Men are not from Mars; women are not from Venus. In fact, we're all from Earth.

Despite the strength of such research, many people still believe there are significant psychological differences between men and women. These beliefs are learned perceptions based on outdated assumptions, traditional family roles, and the influence of various media. In cartoons, books, and films, knights in shining armor still save maidens in distress. Handsome heroes still sweep ravishing young women off their feet. And Mom still knows the best detergents for cleaning auto grease off Dad's pants. As a result, both women and men may accept such invalid gender-based differences.

Research in group communication finds that some female members feel undervalued or even invisible when working with male group members. William Sonnenschein, a diversity consultant and university professor, often hears working women complain that when they say something in a meeting, no one responds, yet a few minutes later a man makes the same suggestion and is praised for the quality of his input.[52]

Clearly, women and men share frustrations and confusion about how to act in mixed company. Such unresolved dialectic tensions between men and women can prevent a group from working collaboratively to achieve a common goal. Group members should consider any differences between female and male members as differences in personality preferences even though, in Myers-Briggs terms, many men classify themselves as thinkers and many women see themselves as feelers. Here's

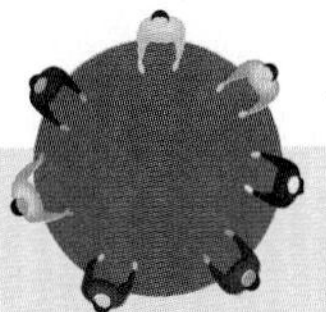

theory in groups

Muted Group Theory

Cheris Kramarae's **Muted Group Theory** explains "how power imbalance affects communication." She claims "that the English language is primarily a *man*-made means of communication." As a result, women (as well as the poor and other minorities) must struggle to participate and be heard. When they are not heard, there is an imbalance between the powerful and the less powerful.[1] In other words, those with power in a society "mute" the voices of less powerful groups.

The following three assumptions in Muted Group Theory explain how women's voices are subdued or silenced in many cultures:

- Women have been led to perceive the world differently than men because of traditional divisions of labor. *Examples*: Homemaker versus breadwinner, nurse versus doctor.
- Men's dominance limits women's freedom of expression. *Examples*: Women in the United States only gained the right to vote in 1920. The "glass ceiling" prevents women from achieving professional advancement.
- Women must transform their thinking and behavior in order to fully participate in society. *Example*: Women have become more politically active and even militant to make sure that sexual harassment, date and marital rape, and spouse abuse are seen as serious crimes against women rather than practices that may be excused or tolerated.[2]

Muted Group Theory has direct relevance to the ways in which men and women communicate in groups. Kramarae claims that women (and other minority groups) are not actually muted, "but that they do not control language and speech in the same way men do."[3]

[1]Marianne Dainton and Elaine D. Zelley, *Applying Communication Theory for Professional Life* (Thousand Oaks, CA: Sage, 2005), p. 97.

[2]Cheris Kramarae, *Women and Men Speaking: Frameworks for Analysis* (Rowley, MA: Newbury House, 1981). For summaries and analysis of Kramarae's perspective and assumptions, see Richard West and Lynn H. Turner, *Introducing Communication Theory*, 2nd ed. (Boston: McGraw-Hill, 2004), pp. 477–78. See also Katherine Miller, *Communication Theories: Perspectives, Processes, and Contexts* (Boston: McGraw-Hill, 2002), p. 292.

[3]Interview with Cheris Kramarae in Katherine Miller, *Communication Theories: Perspectives, Processes, and Contexts* (Boston: McGraw Hill, 2002), p. 294.

some additional advice for adapting to both thinkers (frequently men) and feelers (frequently women) in group settings:

Thinkers (men):

- Don't use sarcasm or tell women they're illogical.
- Don't tell women they're too sensitive or too emotional.
- Listen to what women say, but unless they ask for advice, don't try to solve their problems for them.
- Let women know that you appreciate their warmth, understanding, and compassion.

Feelers (women):

- Don't expect or force men to talk about or display their emotions.
- Ask men what they think, rather than what they feel.
- Express your disagreements with men without worrying about being unkind or starting an argument.
- Let men know that you appreciate their insightful analysis and their ability to remain calm and detached.[53]

Are all men thinkers and all women feelers? No. Are some men more sympathetic, gentle hearted, tactful, and emotional than some women? Yes. Unfortunately,

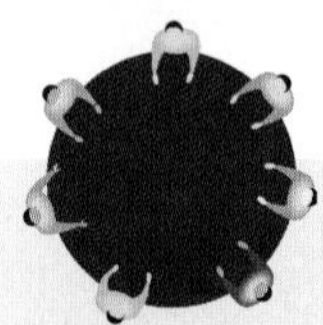

groups in balance . . .
Give Men and Women Equal Time

Who talks more—men or women? Many people believe that women talk more than men do. Yet, most women experience just the opposite, particularly when they're working in groups. Social scientists Rodney Napier and Matti Gershenfeld explain how this myth evolved and why just the opposite is true:

> Throughout history, women have been punished for talking too much or in the wrong way. In colonial America, there were a variety of physical punishments: women were strapped to dunking stools and held under water; they had to wear signs declaring their misconduct in public; they were gagged and silenced with a cleft stick applied to their tongues. . . . Yet study after study shows that it is men who talk more—at meetings, in mixed-group discussions held in classrooms where girls or young women sit next to boys or young men. . . . And not only did men speak for a longer time, but the women's longest turns were shorter than the men's shortest turns."[1]

A recent study of college students found that the number of words uttered by males and females were virtually the same. Men actually "yakked slightly more than women, especially when interacting with spouses or strangers and when the topic was non-personal." Women talked more with classmates, with parents and children, and situations where the topic of conversation required disclosure of feelings.[2]

[1]Rodney W. Napier and Matti K. Gershenfeld, *Groups: Theory and Experience*, 7th ed. (Boston: Houghton Mifflin, 2004), p. 29.

[2]David Brown, "Stereotypes of Quiet Men, Chatty Women Not Sound Science," *The Washington Post*, July 6, 2007, p. A2. See also Donald G. McNeill, Jr. "Yada, Yada, Yada. Him? Or Her?" *The New York Times*, July 6, 2007, p. A13.

assertive, thinking women may be viewed as unfeminine, while caring, feeling men may be dismissed as effeminate. Both labels are absurd and counterproductive to the work of good groups.

Generational Dimensions

Given the amazing advances in technology and improvements in health care, we have more intergenerational communication than ever before. Just think about the ways in which different generations use language. For example, to people from an older generation, the term *communication skills* means writing and speaking abilities, but it may mean email and text messaging to a young college student.[54]

The mixing of generations in family groups, communities, college classrooms, and work settings adds diversity *and* potential difficulties to the challenge of communicating in groups. Of all the generational mixes, the interaction of Baby Boomers with Generation Xers and Millennials may create problems. When a young worker says, "Why should you care what I wear if I do my job?" the Baby Boomer may explain that "Dressing appropriately is part of your job." When a Millennial says, "You're threatened by us because we can use technology," the Baby Boomer may say, "Who do you think invented the technology?"[55]

Let's take a closer look at one set of intergenerational differences—how Baby Boomers and Generation Xers can learn to interact more effectively.[56] Many of these strategies also apply to the interaction of Baby Boomers and Millennials.

groups in balance . . .

Adapt to Generational Differences

Once upon a time, we classified people based on their age by putting them into one of two categories: old and young. Today—probably because of marketing and advertising research—we catalogue, grade, and pigeonhole people of different ages based on their potential as buyers and voters. Labeling any group allows members to identify with their contemporaries and to view other generations with some level of suspicion and even disapproval. After all, how can "they" be as good and as smart as "we" are? What follows is an unofficial list of generational descriptions based on broad generalizations:[1]

- *Traditionalists or the Builder Generation, born 1900 to 1945.* Two world wars and the Great Depression taught this generation how to live within limited means. Traditionalists are loyal, hardworking, financially conservative, and faithful to institutions.
- *Baby Boomers or the Boomer Generation, born 1946 to 1964.* This generation grew up with television and experienced the Vietnam War. Many of them bravely challenged the status quo and are responsible for many of the civil rights and opportunities we now take for granted. As a whole, this generation is politically adept when it comes to navigating political minefields in the workplace. Its members often believe they are always right and are willing to work hard to get what they want. The term *workaholic* was coined to describe Baby Boomers.
- *Generation Xers or the X Generation, born 1965 to 1980.* Generation Xers are technologically savvy in the era of video games and personal computers. Because they witnessed skyrocketing divorce rates; employment layoffs; and challenges to the presidency, organized religion, and big corporations, they are often skeptical and distrustful of institutions. Generation Xers believe that work isn't the most important thing in their lives.
- *Millennials, the Net Generation, Generation Yers, or Nexters, born 1981 to 1999.* Many Millennials are still in school or just graduating from college. This generation grew up with cell phones, pagers, and personal computers. Generally, they're confident and have high self-esteem. They're collaborators and favor teamwork, having functioned in groups in school, organized sports, and extracurricular activities from a very young age. They take on many activities at once and like keeping their career options open.

[1]Mayo Clinic, "Workplace Generation Gap: Understand Differences Among Colleagues," Special to CNN.com, http://www.cnn.com/HEALTH/library/WL/00045.html, July 6, 2005.

If you belong to Generation X and work in groups with Baby Boomers, you should

- Show respect to Baby Boomers and acknowledge that you have less experience than the Baby Boomers and can learn from them.
- Communicate face to face rather than relying totally on email or text messages. Many Baby Boomers prefer speaking with someone face to face.
- Learn to play the political game. Baby Boomers are often diplomatic and can help Generation Xers navigate politically charged group environments.
- Learn the corporate history and culture. Nothing bothers Baby Boomers more than a new employee who wants to change things, with seemingly no thought given to what's gone on before.

As a Baby Boomer working with Generation Xers, you should

- Get to the point. State your objectives clearly when communicating with Generation Xers.
- Avoid micromanaging Generation Xers, who need autonomy.

- Get over the notion of dues paying. Although Baby Boomers may have worked sixty hours a week to get ahead, don't expect members of younger generations to do the same. Generation Xers—who value a healthy work–life balance—rarely spend that many hours at work, and they're getting ahead anyway.
- Lighten up. Remind yourself that it's OK for work to be fun. Generation Xers tend to think that Baby Boomers are too intense and set in their ways.

In general, the need to feel part of a group or team is a common value among Baby Boomers but is less important to Generation Xers and Millennials. Whereas many Baby Boomers see group work as being more like a football game in which all members act together according to a plan, the younger generations see group work as more like a relay race: "I'll give it all I've got—when and where I'm supposed to."[57]

Not surprisingly, the American Association of Retired People points to research studies showing that older adults are better at solving problems, more flexible in their strategies, and better able to keep their cool during a crisis than are younger people. They also tend to bounce back from a bad mood more quickly. As one neurobiologist notes, in the old days, you called it wisdom.[58] Of course, in the not too distant future, young people will be older (and hopefully just as wise), and researchers will probably make the same claims about them.

Religious Dimensions

In his book *Religious Literacy*, Stephen Prothero notes that Americans are a very religious people: 90 percent of adults in the United States believe in God, 80 percent say that religion is important to them personally, and more than 70 percent report praying daily.[59] Yet these same Americans know very little about their *own* religion, let

Religious leaders in Warren, Michigan, hold hands and pray during a rally for racial unity held by a faith-based community organizing group, MOSES (Metropolitan Organizing Strategy Enabling Strength). How can members' religious beliefs affect both group productivity and member satisfaction?

alone the religions of others. Prothero shares the following results from several of his surveys:[60]

- Only 50 percent of American adults can name even one of the four Gospels.
- Most Americans cannot name the first book of the Hebrew Bible.
- Ten percent of Americans believe that Joan of Arc was Noah's wife.

Regardless of whether you are a Catholic, Mormon, Jew, Muslim, Buddhist, Baptist, Hindu, Sikh, Jainist, or atheist, "you must remember that people feel strongly about their religion, and that differences between religious beliefs and practices do matter."[61] For example, the Oriya Brahmans of India consider it shameful and shocking if a husband and wife eat a meal together. The French government bans religious attire in public schools, including headscarves for Muslim girls, Christian crosses, and skullcaps.[62]

Although a group's goal may have nothing to do with religion, members should be sensitive to the diverse religious beliefs of others. Lee Gardenswartz and Anita

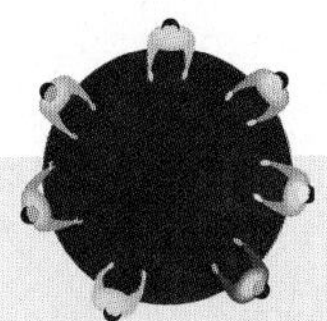

groups in balance . . .

Promote Religious Literacy

There are more than four thousand religions in the world. Like most of us, you may be familiar only with the "big" religions and a few "obscure" faiths. Yet, as Stephen Prothero explains, many of us are illiterate about our own and others' religions. He defines **religious literacy** as "the ability to understand and use the religious terms, symbols, images, beliefs, practices, scripture, heroes, themes, and stories that are employed in American public life."[1]

The following true/false items test your knowledge about a few of the world's major religions.[2]

T = True F = False ? = I Don't Know

1. T F ? Muslims believe in Islam and the Islamic way of life.
2. T F ? Judaism is an older religion than Buddhism.
3. T F ? Islam is a monotheistic religion (belief in one God) just like Christianity and Judaism.
4. T F ? A Christian Scientist believes that disease is a delusion of the carnal mind that can be cured by prayer.
5. T F ? Jews fast during Yom Kippur; Muslims fast during Ramadan.
6. T F ? Jesus Christ was Jewish.
7. T F ? Roman Catholics throughout the world outnumber all other Christians combined.
8. T F ? Sunni Muslims compose about 90 percent of all adherents to Islam.
9. T F ? Hindus believe in the idea of reincarnation.
10. T F ? The Ten Commandments form the basis of Jewish laws.
11. T F ? Mormonism is a Christian faith founded in the United States.
12. T F ? Protestant reformer Martin Luther labeled the beliefs of Muslims, Jews, and Roman Catholics as false.
13. T F ? One-third of the world's population is Christian.
14. T F ? One-fifth of the world's population is Muslim.
15. T F ? Hinduism is the oldest of the world's major religions, dating back more than 3,000 years.

Answers: All the above statements are true.

[1]Stephen Prothero, *Religious Literacy: What Every American Needs to Know—and Doesn't* (New York: HarperSanFrancisco, 2007), p. 11. See also Prothero, pp. 27–28, 235–239.

[2]Questions are based on three sources: Robert Pollock, *The Everything World's Religions Book* (Avon, MA: Adams Media, 2002); Leo Rosen (ed.), *Religions of America: Fragment of Faith in an Age of Crisis* (New York: Touchstone, 1975); *Encyclopedia Britannica Almanac 2004* (Chicago: Encyclopedia Britannica, 2003).

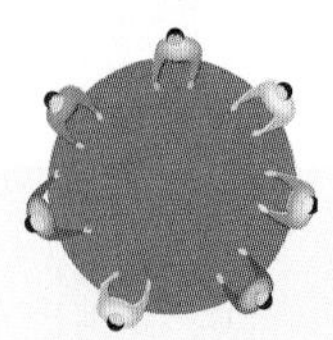

ethics in groups

The Golden Rule May *Not* Apply in Diverse Groups

The well-known Golden Rule—"Do unto others as you would have them do unto you"—may not work in groups with diverse members. Intercultural communication scholars Judith Martin and Thomas Nakayama note that "ethical principles are often culture-bound, and intercultural conflicts arise from varying notions of what constitutes ethical behavior."[1] For example, someone from an individualistic culture may see self-serving ambition as appropriate and ethical behavior—after all, that's how you get ahead. In collectivist cultures, however, the same behavior may be seen as unethical, because the member is not putting group interests ahead of personal interests.

Ethical group members learn about cultural differences—the differences between their own culture and those of others. Martin and Nakayama recommend three strategies:[2]

1. *Practice self-reflection.* When you learn about other cultures, you also learn more about your own intercultural beliefs—and your prejudices. For example, you may believe that arranged marriage is unethical because it denies individuals the right to choose a spouse that they love. If, however, you meet someone who is in a successful arranged marriage, you may discover that there are some advantages, including a much lower divorce rate compared with traditional romantic marriages.
2. *Interact with others.* Ethical group members learn about others by interacting with them and talking about differences. Although you can read about differences in white and black perspectives or western European and Asian values, talking about such differences can help you understand group members as individuals rather than as stereotypical representatives of a different culture.
3. *Listen to others' voices.* Listening to the experiences of others has the power to transform your understanding of cultures and realize how their voices may be stifled. When, for example, Catholic priests from Spain established missions in what is now Texas, they imposed conditions on native people who sought the food, water, shelter, protection, and medical care offered in those missions. Native people had to give up their language and learn Spanish, change many of their customs and dress, and convert to Catholicism. Whether you believe the Catholic priests were ethical or unethical depends, in large part, on how you view the value of diversity and the sanctity of diverse cultures. Ethical group members should listen carefully to different voices as a way of integrating the contributions and perspectives of all members into the group process.

[1]Judith N. Martin and Thomas K. Nakayama, *Experiencing Intercultural Communication*, 2nd ed. (New York: McGraw-Hill, 2005), p. 18.

[2]Martin and Nakayama, pp. 20–22.

Rowe provide several examples. Seventh-day Adventists and observant Jews celebrate the Sabbath on Saturdays. These members may resent being asked or refuse to do group work on a Saturday. A Muslim group member who prays five times a day may want to be excused from meetings at worship times. Non-Christians and atheists may resent using group time for other members' religious holiday celebrations.[63] Groups can avoid such problems by asking and answering the following questions:

- How do the needs, attitudes, and practices of group members' religions affect our work?
- What adaptations should we make so we don't exclude members because of religious practices or beliefs?[64]

Balancing Group Diversity

As an effective group member you should try to understand, respect, and adapt to the personality, cultural, gender, generational, and religious differences that shape every group. William Sonnenschein writes that "we can be equal and still acknowledge our differences. . . . Embracing differences does not mean that all differences are acceptable. . . . Yet, we need to discover those differences, acknowledge their existence, and learn how to best utilize whichever ones we can to create a good team."[65] Some behaviors and values are detrimental to a group and must be resolved. At the same time, we must understand, respect, and adapt to differences that can make a group more effective. Groups that learn how to balance and benefit from the diversity within the group have the power to create a collaborative climate. This kind of climate is the essence of group excellence and teamwork.[66]

summary study guide

Heterogeneous Groups

- A homogeneous group is composed of members who are the same or similar, and a heterogeneous group is composed of members who are not the same. Diversity exists in all groups.
- Within most cultures there are co-cultures—groups who coexist within mainstream society, yet remain connected to their own cultural heritage.
- Diversity describes more than nationality, skin color, or ethnicity. It includes age, gender, occupation, physical ability, personality preferences, religion, marital or parental status, work experience, and much more.

Barriers to Understanding Others

- Ethnocentric group members offend others by implying that they represent a superior culture with superior values.
- Stereotypes are generalizations about a group of people that oversimplify their characteristics; when we stereotype others, we rely on exaggerated and often negative beliefs to make judgments about a group of people.
- Prejudices are negative attitudes based on faulty or inflexible stereotypes rather than getting to know someone before drawing a conclusion.
- Discrimination wrongly excludes groups of people from opportunities granted to others.

Personality Dimensions

- The Big Five Personality Traits—extraversion, agreeableness, conscientiousness, emotional stability, and openness to experience—represent factors that, taken together, describe someone's personality.
- High levels of agreeableness and emotional stability in groups are associated with group cohesiveness while conscientiousness is associated with task performance.
- The Myers-Briggs Type Indicator® looks at the different ways in which people *prefer* to use their minds—specifically, the way they perceive and the way they make judgments. It also helps explain how group members see, think, and make decisions about their group, its goals, and the world around them.
- Myers-Briggs categorizes personality traits in four categories with opposite preferences: extrovert or introvert; sensor or intuitive; thinker or feeler; judger or perceiver.

Cultural Dimensions

- As much as 70 percent of the world's population regards collectivism, or interdependence, as more important than individualism.
- High-power-distance cultures accept differences in power as normal, whereas low-power-distance cultures prefer to minimize power distinctions.
- High-uncertainty-avoidance cultures feel more threatened in situations they perceive as unstructured, unclear, or unpredictable, whereas low-uncertainty-avoidance cultures are more comfortable accepting change, taking risks, and tolerating nonconformity.
- In masculine societies, men are supposed to be assertive and tough while women are expected to be more modest and tender. In feminine societies, gender roles overlap.

- In high-context cultures, members are not dependent on words to express their meaning. Gestures, silence, and facial expressions as well as the relationships among communicators generate meaning. Low-context cultures depend more on language for meaning.
- In monochronic-time cultures, events are scheduled as separate items and deadlines are emphasized. In polychronic-time cultures, schedules are less important and many tasks are done at once.

Gender Dimensions

- Group members should monitor and, if necessary, adapt to differences in the ways in which men and women interpret events and express their opinions.
- Muted Group Theory explains that those with power in a society "mute" the voices of less powerful groups. As a result, women (as well as the poor and other minorities) must struggle to participate and be heard.

Generational Dimensions

- Given the advances in health care, we engage in more intergenerational communication than ever before.
- Generational mixes of Traditionalists, Baby Boomers, Generation Xers, and Millennials present special challenges when working in groups.

Religious Dimensions

- Most people living in the United States know very little about their own religion and much less about other religions.
- Religious literacy is the ability to understand and use the religious terms, symbols, images, beliefs, practices, scripture, heroes, themes, and stories that are employed in American public life.

Balancing Group Diversity

- Effective groups understand, respect, and adapt to the personality, cultural, gender, generational, and religious differences among group members.
- Groups need to discover the differences among members, acknowledge their existence, and learn how to best utilize whichever ones we can to create a good team.

key terms

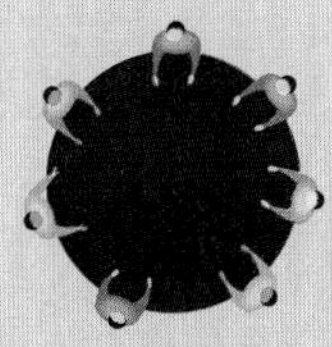

critical thinking about the case study

No Offense Intended

1. How does the diversity of the arts council's governing board help or hinder the group's ability to achieve its goals?
2. Which dialectic tensions are most likely to affect communication among the governing board's members? Why?
3. Which dimensions of diversity are most likely to affect the board members' interactions? What strategies will help the board members enhance their abilities to understand, respect, and adapt to these dimensions?
4. Did generational differences influence these group members' interpretation of the phrase "final solution"? Why or why not?
5. As a member of the governing board, how would you respond to the use of the phrase "final solution" and the resulting awkward silence in the group?
6. Using Martin and Nakayama's three ethics strategies, describe how the arts council can enhance cultural understanding among its members.

group work Identifying Cultural Dialectics

Directions: This textbook identifies six dialectical dimensions that also explain many cultural differences. The twenty statements listed here represent a group member's attitude or behavior. Match each statement with the appropriate cultural dimension or dimensions. Use the blank space before each statement and place the appropriate letter (A through F) in that space to indicate which dimension best explains the cultural perspective of the member. In some cases, more than one answer may be appropriate.

Cultural Dimensions

A. Individualism–Collectivism
B. High Power–Low Power Distance
C. Uncertainty Avoidance–Uncertainty Acceptance
D. Masculine–Feminine
E. High Context–Low Context
F. Polychronic–Monochronic

_____ 1. When a member of my group wins a prize, I feel proud.
_____ 2. I function best in a group when I can organize my responsibilities and put them on a schedule.
_____ 3. I prefer a leader who makes decisions promptly, communicates them to the group, and expects us to carry out the task.
_____ 4. I rely on a member's nonverbal behavior to tell me what he or she is really thinking.
_____ 5. I am good at figuring out what other members think about me and my ideas.
_____ 6. Groups don't function effectively if members are emotional and sensitive.
_____ 7. I am confident in my ability to predict how other group members will behave.
_____ 8. I enjoy "doing my own thing" in a group.
_____ 9. I prefer working in groups in which members are appreciative, curious, forgiving, kind, and understanding.
_____ 10. I become frustrated when someone in a meeting brings up a personal topic that is unrelated to the purpose of the meeting.
_____ 11. Group norms should be followed—even when I disagree with them.
_____ 12. Groups don't function effectively when members are aggressive, hardheaded, and opinionated.
_____ 13. My satisfaction in a group depends very much on the feelings of other members.
_____ 14. I don't like to focus my attention on only one thing at a time because I may be missing something important or interesting.
_____ 15. I prefer a leader who calls a meeting when an important issue comes up, gives us the problem to discuss, and seeks a group decision.
_____ 16. I can sit with another group member, not say anything, and still be comfortable.
_____ 17. I find silence awkward in conversations and group discussions.
_____ 18. I like to be clear and accurate when I speak to other group members.
_____ 19. I like doing several tasks at one time.
_____ 20. I like working in groups where I can compete with other members.

group assessment Group Diversity Awareness Questionnaire[1]

Directions: Think of a group to which you belong or have belonged in the recent past. Use the following responses to indicate how well you can answer diversity questions about that group. When you've completed the questionnaire, examine the ways in which your answers reflect your level of awareness about group diversity issues.

Yes = I am sure I know the answer.
No = I do not know the answer.
Maybe = I think I know the answer to all or part of the question.

DIVERSITY DIMENSION	CAN YOU ANSWER THESE QUESTIONS?	YES	NO	MAYBE
Age	What is the age range in our group and how does it affect the group?			
Gender	Do men and women in our group have equal opportunities to interact with one another?			
Sexual Orientation	How open are group members about their sexual identity? Are members comfortable interacting with members of a different sexual orientation?			
Physical Ability	How well do we deal with the physical challenges of any group members?			
Ethnicity	Do group members know about each other's ethnic backgrounds?			
Race	How well does our group acknowledge and deal with racial differences?			
Religion	How well does our group understand, respect, and adapt to members' religious practices and beliefs?			
Marital Status	Are there different assumptions and differences in treatment based on members' marital status?			
Parental Status	What assumptions, if any, do we make about members who are parents or not parents?			
Political Affiliation	In what ways, if any, do members' political affiliations or preferences affect group work and member morale?			

DIVERSITY DIMENSION	CAN YOU ANSWER THESE QUESTIONS?	YES	NO	MAYBE
Income	How do differences in income show themselves and affect group relationships and productivity?			
Experience	What kinds of expertise and group experiences do members bring to this group? To what extent do we value or disregard group members' experiences?			

[1]Questions based on examples in Lee Gardenswartz and Anita Rowe, *Diverse Teams at Work: Capitalizing on the Power of Diversity* (New York: McGraw-Hill, 1997), pp. 37–53.

notes

1. William Sonnenschein, *The Diversity Toolkit* (Chicago: Contemporary Books, 1997), p. 101.
2. Peter D. Hart Research Associates, *How Should Colleges Prepare Students to Succeed in Today's Global Economy?* (Washington, DC: Peter D. Hart Research Associates, December 28, 2006), p. 2. Also see Association of American Colleges and Universities, *College Learning for the New Global Age* (Washington, DC: Association of American Colleges and Universities, 2007).
3. The statistics and their interpretation in this section come from two sources: *Encyclopedia Britannica Almanac 2004* (Chicago: Britannica Almanac, 2003), pp. 770–775; United States Census Bureau, Census 2000, www.census.gov/population.
4. "The 300 Millionth Footprint on U.S. Soil," *The New York Times*, October 8, 2006, p. WK 2. Sources: U.S. Census Bureau; National Center for Education Statistics; Social Security Administration.
5. U.S. Census Bureau. www.census.gov/population.
6. Myron W. Lustig and Jolene Koester, *Intercultural Competence: Interpersonal Communication across Cultures*, 5th ed. (New York: Longman, 2006), p. 25.
7. Intercultural authors use a variety of terms (*co-cultures*, *microcultures*) to describe the cultural groups that coexist within a larger culture. Using either of these terms is preferable to using the older, somewhat derogatory term *subcultures*. The combined co-cultures living in the United States will, by midcentury, make up the majority population.
8. James Surowiecki, *The Wisdom of Crowds: Why the Many Are Smarter Than the Few and How Collective Wisdom Shapes Business, Economics, Societies, and Nations* (New York: Doubleday, 2004), p. 29.
9. Quoted in Surowiecki, p. 31.
10. Lee Gardenswartz and Anita Rowe, *Diverse Teams at Work: Capitalizing on the Power of Diversity* (New York: McGraw-Hill, 1994), p. 18.
11. Diversity layers based on Gardenswartz and Rowe, 31–80. Primary source: Marilyn Loden and Judy R. Rosener, *Workforce America!* (New York: McGraw-Hill, 1990).
12. Lustig and Koester, p. 151.
13. Myron W. Lustig and Jolene Koester, *Intercultural Competence: Interpersonal Communication across Cultures*, 4th ed. (New York: Longman, 2003), p. 153.
14. Gardenswartz and Rowe, pp. 34–35.
15. Miranda A. G. Peeters, et al., "The Big Five Personality Traits and Individual Satisfaction with Teams," *Small Group Research* 37 (2006), pp. 190–191.
16. Andrea B. Hollingshead, et al., "A Look at Groups from the Functional Perspective," in *Theories of Small Groups: Interdisciplinary Perspectives*, ed. Marshall Scott Poole and Andrea B. Hollingshead (Thousand Oaks, CA: Sage, 2005), pp. 40–41.
17. Hundreds of books and articles have been written about the Myers-Briggs Type Indicator®. The material in this chapter is based on Isa N. Engleberg's background and experience as a certified Myers-Briggs Type Indicator® trainer and a synthesis of materials from several MBTI resources: Isabel Briggs Myers (Revised by Linda K. Kirby and Katharine D. Myers), *Introduction to Type*, 7th ed. (Palo Alto, CA: Consulting Psychologists, 1998); Isabel Briggs Myers with Peter B. Myers, *Gifts Differing: Tenth Anniversary Edition* (Palo Alto, CA: Consulting Psychologists, 1990); Otto Kroeger and Janet M. Thuesen, *Type Talk* (New York: Delacorte, 1988); Otto Kroeger and Janet M. Thuesen, *Type Talk at Work: How the 16 Personality Types Determine Your Success on the Job* (New York: Delta/Tilden Press, 1992); David Keirsey, *Please Understand Me II* (Del Mar, CA:

Prometheus Nemesis, 1998); Sandra K. Hirsh, *Introduction to Type and Teams* (Palo Alto, CA: Consulting Psychologists, 1992); Larry Demarest, *Looking at Type in the Workplace* (Gainesville, FL: Center for Applications of Psychological Type, 1997). A modified Myers-Briggs instrument in the *Instructor's Manual* will help students identify their personality type.

18. Myers with Myers, p. 1.
19. Annie Murphy Paul, *The Cult of Personality* (New York: Free Press, 2004), pp. 125–127.
20. The Myers-Briggs Type Indicator® is for licensed use only by qualified professionals whose qualifications are on file and have been accepted by Consulting Psychologists Press, Inc.
21. The Myers-Briggs Type Indicator® (MBTI) uses the word *extravert*—with an *a* in the middle of the word—to describe this personality preference rather than *extrovert*. Some dictionaries and psychology textbooks use *extrovert* to note the alliterative similarities between *introvert* and *extrovert*. *Working in Groups* uses the term *extrovert*, but here acknowledges the MBTI preference for *extravert*.
22. Robert E. Levasseur, *Breakthrough Business Meetings: Shared Leadership in Action* (Holbrook, MA: Bob Adams, 1994), p. 79.
23. J. M. Jaffe, "Of Different Minds," *Association Management* 37 (1985), pp. 120–124.
24. Renee Baron, *What Type Am I?* (New York: Penguin, 1998), pp. 20–21.
25. Carl E. Larson and Frank M. J. LaFasto, *TeamWork: What Must Go Right/What Can Go Wrong* (Newbury Park, CA: Sage, 1989), p. 63.
26. Baron, pp. 29–30.
27. Kroeger and Thuesen, *Type Talk*, p. 80.
28. Kroeger and Thuesen, *Type Talk*, p. 114.
29. Geert Hofstede, *Cultures and Organizations: Software of the Mind* (New York: McGraw-Hill, 1997), p. 14. Also see Geert Hofstede, *Culture's Consequences*, 2nd ed. (Thousand Oaks, CA: Sage, 2001), p. 29. Hofstede identifies a fifth dimension: long-term versus short-term orientation, which relates to the choice of focus for people's efforts—either the future or the present. Cultures in Asia rank at the top of the list on long-term orientation, whereas those with a shorter-term orientation include English-speaking countries as well as Zimbabwe, Philippines, Nigeria, and Pakistan. We have not included this fifth dimension in the textbook because fewer cultures have been thoroughly studied on this dimension.
30. See Edward T. Hall, *The Silent Language* (Greenwich, CT: Fawcett, 1959); Edward T. Hall, *Beyond Culture* (New York: Anchor, 1976); Edward T. Hall, *The Dance of Life: The Other Dimension of Time* (New York: Doubleday, 1983); Edward T. Hall and M. R. Hall, *Understanding Cultural Differences: Germans, French and Americans* (Yarmouth, ME: Intercultural Press, 1990).
31. Harry C. Triandis, *Individualism and Collectivism* (Boulder, CO: Westview, 1995).
32. Harry C. Triandis, "The Self and Social Behavior in Different Cultural Contexts," *Psychological Review* 96 (1994), pp. 506–520. Also see Triandis, *Individualism and Collectivism*.
33. Harry C. Triandis, "The Cross-Cultural Studies of Individualism and Collectivism," in *Cross-Cultural Perspectives*, ed. J. J. Berman (Lincoln, University of Nebraska Press, 1990), p. 52.
34. Geert Hofstede, "The Cultural Relativity of the Quality of Life Concept," in *Cultural Communication and Conflict: Readings in Intercultural Relations*, 2nd ed., ed. Gary R. Weaver (Boston: Pearson, 2000), p. 139.
35. Hofstede, *Culture's Consequences*, quoted in Larry A. Samovar and Richard Porter, *Communication Between Cultures*, 5th ed. (Belmont, CA: Wadsworth, 2004), p. 65.
36. Hofstede, *Cultures and Organizations*, p. 113.
37. Hofstede, *Cultures and Organizations*.
38. Hofstede, *Cultures and Organizations*, p. 119.
39. Hofstede, *Cultures and Organizations*, p. 118.
40. Hofstede, *Cultures and Organizations*, p. 84.
41. Hofstede, *Cultures and Organizations*.
42. Hall and Hall, p. 6.
43. Dean Allen Foster, *Bargaining across Borders* (New York: McGraw-Hill, 1992), p. 280.
44. Edward T. Hall, *The Dance of Life*, p. 42.
45. James W. Neuliep, *Intercultural Communication: A Contextual Approach*, 2nd ed. (Boston: Houghton Mifflin, 2003), pp. 132–33.
46. Lustig and Koester, *Intercultural Competence*, 5th ed., p. 226.
47. Edward T. Hall, "Monochronic and Polychronic Time," in *Intercultural Communication: A Reader*, 10th ed., ed. Larry A. Samovar and Richard E. Porter (Belmont, CA: Wadsworth, 2002), p. 263.
48. John Gray, *Men Are from Mars, Women Are from Venus* (New York: HarperCollins, 2005). Also see www.marsvenus.com. Retrieved June 18, 2008.
49. Deborah Tannen, *You Just Don't Understand: Women and Men in Conversation* (New York: Morrow, 1990).
50. Janet Shibley Hyde, "The Gender Similarities Hypothesis," *American Psychologist* 60 (2005), p. 590, as quoted in Deborah Cameron, *The Myth of Mars and Venus* (Oxford: Oxford, 2007), pp. 41–44.
51. Cameron, p. 43.
52. Sonnenschein, pp. 19–20.
53. Baron, p. 28.
54. Dennis Kersten, "Today's Generations Face New Communication Gaps," www.usatoday.com/money/jobcenter/workplace/communication/2002-11-15-communication-gap_x.htm, posted 11/15/2002, 10:03 a.m.
55. T. J. Wilhera, "Millenials Large and in Charge: Tech-Savvy Generation Taking Over," *Denver Post*, June 6, 2008, www.denverpost.com/opinion/ci_9494738; John Davidson, "We Invented the World You Live in, Kid," *Denver Post*, June 13, 2008, www.denverpost.com/search/ci_9570975.
56. Mayo Clinic, "Workplace Generation Gap: Understand Differences among Colleagues," special to CNN.com,

www.cnn.com/HEALTH/library/WL/00045.html, July 6, 2005.

57. David Stauffer, "Motivating Across Generations," in Harvard Business School Press, *Teams That Click* (Boston: Harvard Business School, 2004), p. 119.
58. Kelly Griffin, "You're Wiser Now," *The AARP Magazine*, September/October 2005, p. 77.
59. Stephen Prothero, *Religious Literacy: What Every American Needs to Know—and Doesn't* (New York: HarperSanFrancisco, 2007), p. 23.
60. Prothero, p. 30.
61. J. Richard Hoel, Jr. "Developing Intercultural Competence," in *Intercultural Communication with Readings*, ed. Pamela J. Cooper, Carolyn Calloway-Thomas, and Cheri J. Simonds (Boston: Allyn & Bacon, 2007), p. 305.
62. Hoel.
63. Gardenswartz and Rowe, p. 46.
64. Gardenswartz and Rowe.
65. Sonnenschein, p. 100.
66. Larson and LaFasto, p. 94.

chapter 5

Group Leadership

chapter outline

What Is Leadership?

Leadership and Power

Types of Power • The Power of Power

Becoming a Leader

Designated Leaders • Emergent Leaders • Strategies for Becoming a Leader

Leadership Theories

Trait Leadership Theory • Styles Leadership Theory • Situational Leadership Theory • Transformational Leadership Theory

The 5M Model of Leadership Effectiveness

Model Leadership Behavior • Motivate Members • Manage Group Process • Make Decisions • Mentor Members

Diversity and Leadership

Gender and Leadership • Cultural Diversity and Leadership

study questions

How do the concepts of leadership and leader differ?

How do leaders use different types of power?

What strategies should I use to become a leader?

How does understanding and applying theories improve leadership?

What communication strategies and skills characterize effective group leadership?

How does diversity affect both leaders and group members?

What Is Leadership?

If you use the word *leadership* to search Amazon.com, you will discover more than 250,000 books on that subject. And if you review the first 250 offerings, you'll see that most of them are written by highly respected scholars and well-regarded business leaders. Some unusual exceptions, however, demonstrate the popularity of leadership as a subject. Here are just a few:

Popular Trade Books on Leadership

Leadership Secrets from Harry Potter	*The Leadership Secrets of Santa Claus*
Leadership Secrets of the Rogue Warrior	*Leadership Secrets of Attila the Hun*
Moses on Leadership	*Jesus on Leadership*
Make It So: Leadership Lessons from Star Trek the Next Generation	*Shakespeare on Management: Leadership Lessons for Today's Management*

Apparently, everyone has something to say about leadership. You do, too. You have observed leaders at work, voted for leaders at school and in public elections, and probably led a group at some point in your life. That group could have been a sports team, a study group, a work team, or a group of children left in your charge.

All groups need leadership. Without leadership, a group may be nothing more than a collection of individuals, lacking the coordination and motivation to achieve a common goal. Quite simply, "there are no successful groups without leaders. . . . Leaders lead because groups demand it and rely on leaders to satisfy needs."[1]

A leader and leadership are not the same thing. **Leadership** is the ability to make strategic decisions and use communication effectively to mobilize group members toward achieving a common goal. *Leader* is the title given to a person; *leadership* refers to the actions a leader takes to help group members achieve a common goal. Even groups without official leaders may rely on several members to perform leadership functions.

Another way to understand the nature of leadership is to contrast it with the functions of management. Whereas managers concentrate on getting an assigned job done, leaders focus on the ultimate direction and goal of the group. Note how the employee in the following situation describes the difference between a manager and a leader:

> Lee is the manager of our department, so he's technically our leader. He always follows procedures and meets deadlines for paperwork, so I guess he's a good manager. But we don't get much guidance from him. I think that managing and leading are somehow different. Allison supervises the other department. She seems to inspire her workers. They're more motivated and innovative, and they work closely with one another. We do our job, but they seem to be on a mission. I've always thought that working for Allison would be more rewarding and enjoyable.

Ronald Heifetz, director of the Leadership Education Project at Harvard's School of Government, describes the dialectic tensions inherent in leadership as an adaptive challenge. The leader, he writes, must create a balance between the tensions required to motivate change and the need to avoid overwhelming followers.[2] Effective leaders walk a well-chosen path between *both* fostering interdependence *and* encouraging self-reliance, between *both* welcoming disagreement *and* building cohesion, and between *both* imposing structure *and* promoting spontaneity.

case study

The Leader in Sheep's Clothing

The Peoples Project is a nonprofit organization with the mission of serving displaced families within their local communities. If a homeless family qualifies for help, the Project moves them into a local Peoples Project apartment. Every family receives job counseling, skills training, child care, and assistance in looking for a permanent home.

For twenty years, the Peoples Project was directed by Bill Blessing, one of its founders. When Mr. Blessing announced his retirement, the board of trustees hired an energetic and experienced director named Will Dupree. From his first day at work, Mr. Dupree jumped right into the job. He met with the residents of Peoples Project housing to listen to their needs and complaints. He scheduled meetings with community leaders and politicians to solidify their support. He delivered an eloquent speech at a local church that assists the Peoples Project. And when a fire left three families without shelter, he rolled up his sleeves and spent two days helping them move into Peoples Project housing. The board was thrilled. The community was delighted with the new charismatic leader. Families served by the organization viewed Mr. Dupree as a friend, not just a leader.

Meanwhile, back at the Peoples Project headquarters, the mood was quite different. During his first week on the job, Dupree called a meeting of the senior staff, most of whom had been working for the Peoples Project for many years. He told them that to the outside community, he would always be responsive, caring, and empowering. Behind closed doors at the Peoples Project, he would be a tough, uncompromising director. "I don't want to be your friend," he said. "You will meet all deadlines, take on some of my work when I'm out in the field, and do so without complaining. I will put in 150 percent, so the least you can do is 110 percent." Within a few days, they learned that Dupree was a man of his word. One afternoon at 4:30, he marched into a senior staff member's office and said, "I need a report on how the proposed zoning legislation will affect our buildings and those we're trying to buy. I need it by noon tomorrow." The staff member worked past midnight to write the report. The next morning she came in early to make revisions. By noon the report was sitting on the director's desk. A day later, she asked the director what he thought of the report. His response was "Oh, I've been busy—haven't read it yet." As incidents like these increased, the senior staff became frustrated and wary of their new director. His popularity outside headquarters was high so they didn't think they could do anything. But when Dupree started to have "favorites" among the staff, several veteran employees decided that retirement or looking for work elsewhere was a better and healthier option.

The senior staff's frustration was becoming a serious problem. Even though the Peoples Project had never been more successful, staff members were at a breaking point. At the same time, their commitment and loyalty to the organization and its mission was strong. No one knew what to do or how to respond to the new leader.

When you finish reading this chapter, you should be able to answer the following questions.

1 What kind of power is Will Dupree using and is it appropriate for the organization and its staff?

2 What kinds of challenges do designated leaders face and how should they handle them?

3 How would you apply one or more leadership theories to analyze the problems developing at the Peoples Project?

4 How does Will Dupree measure up to the 5M Model of Leadership Effectiveness?

5 What could senior staff do to address the problems they have working for Dupree?

Leadership and Power

You cannot fully understand the dynamics of leadership unless you also understand the dynamics of power. In the context of group communication, **power** is the ability or authority to influence and motivate others. Leadership experts Warren Bennis and Bruce Nanus claim that power is "the quality without which leaders cannot lead."[3] In the hands of a just and wise leader, power is a positive force; in the hands of an unjust and foolish leader, power corrupts and destroys.

Types of Power

Many researchers study power and its relationship to group leadership. Here, we combine the work of two sets of researchers. John French and Bertram Raven classify power into five categories: reward power, coercive power, legitimate power, expert power, and referent power. Psychologists Gary Yukl and Cecilia Fable add three additional types of power: information power, persuasive power, and charisma. Yukl and Fable note that if you combine French and Raven's five categories with their three categories, you end up with two basic types of power,[4] which we've named *position power* and *personal power.* **Position power** depends on a member's job or status within an organization. **Personal power** stems from a member's individual characteristics. Table 5.1 lists the eight types of power in each of these two categories.

The Power of Power

What kind of power is best? The answer depends on many factors, including the situation or organization, member characteristics, and the group's goal. For example, reward power works best in groups where the leader controls something members value. It is less effective when the so-called rewards are insignificant or trivial.

Research examining French and Raven's five categories of power concludes that reward power, legitimate power, and coercive power are the least effective. "They either have no influence or a negative influence both on how people act at work and on job satisfaction. Expert and referent power tend to produce positive outcomes."[5]

In the extreme, highly coercive leaders can range from the "abusive tyrant, who bawls out and humiliates people, to the manipulative sociopath. Such leaders have

Table 5.1 Types of Power in Groups

Position Power: Comes with the Position		Personal Power: Comes from Personal Characteristics	
Legitimate Power: relies on a job title or duty	"I have the duty and authority to lead."	**Expert Power:** relies on expertise and credentials	"I have the knowledge and skills we need."
Reward Power: controls and gives out resources valued by members	"I can reward you."	**Referent Power:** relies on members' opinion of and experience with the leader	"I've earned your respect and trust."
Coercive Power: controls and deals out sanctions and punishments	"I can punish you."	**Persuasive Power:** relies on effective communication skills	"I know how to persuade and encourage others."
Informational Power: controls and transmits information and sources	"I have the information you need."	**Charismatic Power:** relies on leader's character, competence, and vitality	"I have the energy, will, and passion to make things happen."

an emotional impact a bit like the 'dementors' in the Harry Potter series, who 'drain peace, hope, and happiness out of the air around them.' At their worst, leaders who rely on coercive power have no idea how destructive they are—or they simply don't care."[6] On the other hand, coercive power can be "effective when those subject to this form of power are aware of expectations and are warned in advance about the penalties for failure to comply. Leaders using coercive power must consistently carry out threatened punishments."[7]

Contrast coercive power with referent power. Referent power is the personal power or influence held by people we like, admire, and respect. Referent power, as a form of personal power, is influential because it is recognized and conferred by the group rather than by an outside source.

In most groups, a leader employs several kinds of power, depending on the needs of the group and the situation. Some leaders may have the power to reward, coerce, and persuade as well as having legitimate, expert, informational, referent, and charismatic power. In other groups, a leader may depend entirely on one type of power. The more power a leader has, the more carefully the use of that power must be balanced with the needs of the group. If you exert too much power, your group may lose its energy and enthusiasm. If you don't exert enough power, your group may flounder and fail.

Becoming a Leader

Anyone can become a leader. Abraham Lincoln and Harry S. Truman rose from humble beginnings and hardship to become U.S. presidents. Corporate executives have worked their way up from the sales force and the secretarial pool to become chief executive officers. Condoleezza Rice, the great-grandchild of slaves, was born in segregated Birmingham, Alabama, and became a U.S. Secretary of State. The path to a leadership position can be as easy as being in the right place at the right time or being the only person willing to take on a difficult job. Becoming the leader of a group primarily occurs in one of two ways: being chosen to lead or naturally emerging as a leader.

Designated Leaders

A **designated leader** is selected by group members or by an outside authority. You may be hired for a job that gives you authority over others. You may be promoted or elected to a leadership position. You may be assigned to chair a special work team or subcommittee. In all these cases, the selection of the leader depends on an election or an appointment.

Sometimes, less-than-deserving people are appointed or elected to powerful positions. Voters, service groups, and work groups often elect a compromise candidate or appoint a politically connected group member as a leader, and neither practice is any guarantee of leadership ability. Is it possible, then, for a designated leader to be an effective leader? Of course it is, particularly when a leader's abilities match the needs of the group and its goal.

Designated leaders face unique challenges. When a newly appointed leader enters a well-established group, there can be a long and difficult period of adjustment for everyone. One student described this difficult process as follows:

> For five summers, I worked as a counselor at a county day camp for underprivileged children. Harry was our boss, and all of us liked him. We worked hard for Harry

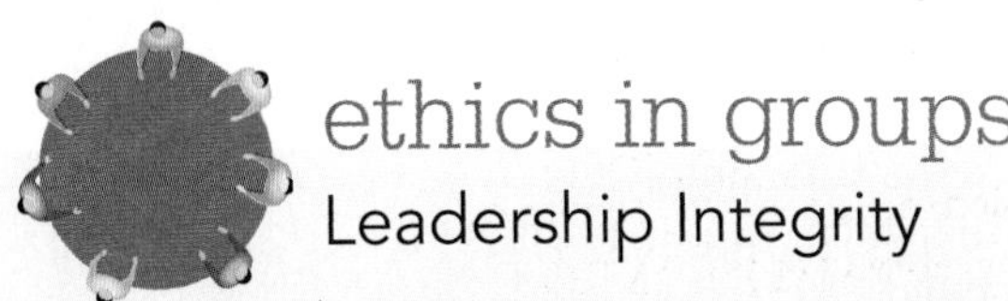

ethics in groups
Leadership Integrity

In his book on leadership, Andrew DuBrin makes the case that ethical leaders do "the *right* thing as perceived by a consensus of *reasonable* people."[1] Doing the right thing requires honesty, trustworthiness, and integrity. Leaders with integrity honor their commitments and their promises. They practice what they preach, regardless of emotional or social pressure. For example, if a good friend in your group asks to chair a committee, and you've promised the position to someone with better skills, you should keep your promise even if it upsets your friend.[2]

Unethical leadership has enormous consequences, regardless of whether it affects a small study group or a global corporation. Unethical behavior has bankrupted companies, led to thousands of layoffs, and exposed the unrestrained spending of self-centered corporate executives.[3]

The Center for Business Ethics at Bentley College poses six questions to help you decide whether your leadership behaviors are ethical or unethical:[4]

- *Is it right?* Do you conform to universally accepted principles of rightness and wrongness, such as "thou shalt not steal"?
- *Is it fair?* Would you overlook a competent person in order to promote a less competent relative or friend?
- *Who gets hurt?* Do you try to do the greatest good for the greatest number of people?
- *Would you be comfortable if the details of your decisions or actions were made public in the media or through email?* What would you tell your child or a young relative to do in similar circumstances?
- *How does it smell?* If a reasonable person with good common sense were to look at your decision or action, would it "smell" suspicious or bad to that person? Would it seem wrong?

Leadership can become an ego trip—or, even worse, a power trip. Bennis and Goldsmith describe leadership as a three-legged stool—ambition, competence, and integrity—that must remain in balance if the leader is to be a constructive force rather than a destructive force, interested only in achieving her or his own goals.[5]

[1]Andrew J. DuBrin, *Leadership: Research Findings, Practice, and Skills,* 4th ed. (New York: Houghton Mifflin, 2004), p. 168.

[2]DuBrin, p. 168.

[3]DuBrin, pp. 175–176.

[4]Kris Maher, "Wanted: Ethical Employer," *Wall Street Journal,* July 9, 2002, p. B1, as quoted in DuBrin, pp. 172–173.

[5]Warren Bennis and Joan Goldsmith, *Learning to Lead: A Workbook on Becoming a Leader,* Updated Edition (Cambridge, MA: Perseus, 1997), p. 3.

> because we knew he'd look the other way if we showed up late or left early on a Friday. As long as the kids were safe and supervised, he didn't bother us. But when Harry was promoted into management at the county government office, we got Frank. The first few weeks were awful. Frank would dock us if we were late. No one could leave early. He demanded that we come up with more activities for the kids. Weekend pool parties were banned. He even made us attend a counselors' meeting every morning, rather than once every couple of weeks. But, in the end, most of us had to admit that Frank was a better director. The camp did more for the kids, and that was the point.

Both Harry and Frank were leaders with legitimate power, but the kinds of power available to them made them different. Because Harry had earned the admiration and respect of the staff, he could rely on referent power. Frank, however, had to use coercive power to establish order and authority.

When group members elect or appoint a leader from within a group, the problems can be as difficult as those faced by a leader from outside the group. If the person who once worked next to you becomes your boss, the adjustment can be problematic.

Here, a business executive describes how difficult it was when she was promoted to vice president:

> When I was promoted, I became responsible for making decisions that affected my colleagues, many of whom were close friends. I was given the authority to approve projects, recommend salary increases, and grant promotions. Colleagues who had always been open and honest with me were more cautious and careful about what they said. I had to deny requests from people I cared about, while approving requests from colleagues with whom I often disagreed. Even though I was the same person, I was treated differently, and, as a result, I behaved differently.

Being plucked from a group in order to lead it can present problems because it changes the nature of your relationship with the other members of the group. Even though the members know you well, you still must earn their trust and respect as a leader. Here are three suggestions:

- Involve the group in decision making as much as possible.
- Discuss ground rules for interactions with friends while assuring them of your continued friendship.
- Openly and honestly address leadership concerns with group members and seek their help in resolving potential problems.[8]

Emergent Leaders

Very often, the most effective leadership occurs when a leader emerges from a group rather than being promoted, elected, or appointed. The leaders of many political, religious, and community organizations emerge. An **emergent leader** gradually achieves leadership by interacting with group members and contributing to the achievement of the group's goal. Leaders who emerge from within a group do not have to spend time learning about the group, its goals, and its norms. They also have some assurance that the group wants them to be its leader rather than having to accept their leadership because an election or an outside authority says it must.

Strategies for Becoming a Leader

Although there is no method of guaranteeing that you'll emerge or be designated as a group's leader, certain strategies can improve your chances. All of these strategies require a balanced approach that takes advantage of opportunities without abusing the privilege of leadership.

Strategies for Becoming a Leader

Talk Early and Often (and Listen)

Know More (and Share It)

Offer Your Opinion (and Welcome Disagreement)

Talk Early and Often (and Listen). Research shows that the person who speaks first and most often is more likely to emerge as the group's leader.[9] The number of contributions is even more important than the quality of those contributions.

The quality of your contributions becomes more significant after you become a leader. The link between participation and leadership "is the most consistent finding in small group leadership research. Participation demonstrates both your motivation to lead and your commitment to the group."[10] Although talking early and often does not guarantee you a leadership position, failure to talk will keep you from being considered as a leader. Yet, don't overdo it. If you talk too much, members may think that you are not interested in or willing to listen to their contributions. While it is important to talk, it is just as important to demonstrate your willingness and ability to listen.

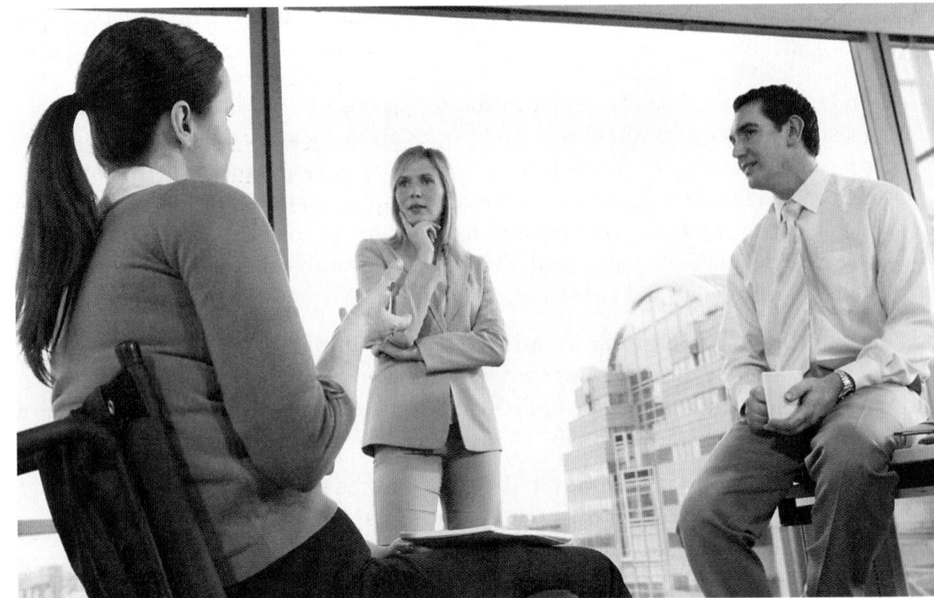

Research shows that the person who speaks first and most often is more likely to emerge as the group's leader. What, then, is the leader's role and responsibilities as a listener?

Know More (and Share It). Leaders often emerge or are appointed because they are seen as experts—people who know more about an important topic. Even if a potential leader is simply able to explain ideas and information more clearly than other group members, that person may be perceived as knowing more.

Groups need well-informed leaders, but they do not need know-it-alls. Know-it-alls see their own comments as most important; leaders value everyone's contributions. Members who want to become leaders understand that they must demonstrate their expertise without intimidating other group members.

Offer Your Opinion (and Welcome Disagreement). When groups have difficulty making decisions or solving problems, they appreciate someone who offers good ideas and informed opinions. Members often emerge as leaders when they help a group out of some difficulty. Offering ideas and opinions, however, is not the same as having those ideas accepted. Because your opinions may conflict with those of other group members, use caution when discussing these differences. Criticizing the ideas and opinions of others risks causing resentment and defensiveness. Bullying your way into a leadership position can backfire. If you are unwilling to compromise or to listen to alternatives, the group may not want to follow you. Effective leaders welcome constructive disagreement and discourage hostile confrontations. "They do not suppress conflict, they rise and face it."[11]

The strategies for *becoming* a leader are not necessarily the strategies needed for successful leadership. Although you may talk a lot, demonstrate superior knowledge, and assert your personal opinions in order to *become* a leader, you may find that the dialectic opposites—listening rather than talking, relying on the knowledge of others, and seeking a wide range of opinions—are equally necessary to *succeed* as a leader.

Leadership Theories

In a review of group leadership theories and research, Charles Pavitt notes, "The literature on group leadership is staggering. . . . I would estimate that close to 8,000

relevant studies have been published [about leadership]."[12] In *Leadership,* Warren Bennis and Bruce Nanus point out that "no clear and unequivocal understanding exists as to what distinguishes leaders from non-leaders, and perhaps more important, what distinguishes effective leaders from ineffective leaders."[13]

Despite inconclusive results from thousands of research studies, you can learn a great deal from several leadership theories. This chapter examines four theoretical approaches to leadership (see Figure 5.1).[14] These theories are closely connected and build on the ideas of their predecessors.[15]

Trait Leadership Theory

Leadership scholars refer to the Trait Theory as the "Great Man" theory. This theory stands on an assumption many people now reject—that leaders are born, not made. **Trait Leadership Theory** identifies and prescribes individual characteristics and behaviors needed for effective leadership.

Think of the leaders you admire. What traits do they have? In his book *Leadership,* Andrew DuBrin identifies several personality traits that contribute to successful leadership: self-confidence, humility, trustworthiness, high tolerance of frustration, warmth, humor, enthusiasm, extroversion, assertiveness, emotional stability, adaptability, farsightedness, and openness to new experiences.[16] However, just because you have most of these traits does not mean that you will be a great leader. Personality traits alone are not enough to guarantee effective leadership. For example, if you lack expertise or knowledge about the group task, basic intelligence, and the necessary technical or work skills, personality traits will not be enough to lead a group successfully.

Although most of us would gladly follow a leader with the qualities described by DuBrin, many effective leaders only exhibit a few of these traits. Harriet Tubman, an illiterate runaway slave, did little talking but led hundreds of people from bondage in the South to freedom in the North. Bill Gates, an introverted computer geek, became one of the richest men on earth as head of Microsoft, a company that all but dictates how we use personal computers.

According to proponents of the Myers-Briggs Type Indicator®, the personality measure that we discuss in Chapter 4, Group Diversity, a set of traits characterizes "life's natural leaders." These "extroverted thinkers" (the ENTJ type) use reasoning

Figure 5.1 Leadership Theories

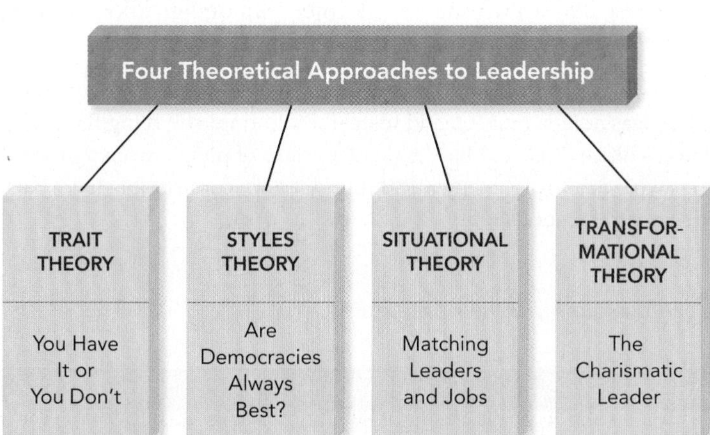

ability to control and direct those around them.[17] They are usually enthusiastic, decisive, confident, organized, logical, and argumentative. They love to lead and can be excellent communicators. However, although they often assume or win leadership positions, extroverted thinkers may not necessarily be effective leaders because they may intimidate or overpower others. They also may be insensitive to the personal feelings and needs of group members. Although many extroverted thinkers become leaders, they may need a less intense, more balanced approach in order to be effective leaders.

Styles Leadership Theory

As a way of expanding the trait approach to the study of leadership, researchers reexamined the traits they had identified. Rather than look for individual leadership traits, they developed the **Styles Leadership Theory**—a collection of specific behaviors or styles that could be identified and *learned.* Actors work in different styles—tough or gentle, comic or tragic. Even sports teams differ in style; the South American soccer teams are known for their speed and grace, the European teams for their technical skill and aggressiveness. Different styles are attributed to leaders, too. Early attempts to describe different leadership styles yielded three categories as shown in Figure 5.2: autocratic, democratic, and laissez-faire.[18]

Autocratic Leaders. The **autocratic leader** seeks power and authority by controlling the direction and outcome of group work. You can recognize an autocrat by looking for the following behaviors:

- Tries to control direction and outcome.
- Makes many of the group's decisions.
- Expects followers to obey orders.
- Takes responsibility and credit for group work and results.
- Often uses reward and coercive power.

There are costs to using the autocratic style. By exerting too much control, autocratic leaders may lower group morale and sacrifice long-term productivity. Many autocratic leaders defend their actions by arguing that the group can't get the job done without the strict control of the leader.

Dr. Sandy Faber, a world-renowned astronomer, wrote about her experience as the leader of a group of six astronomers who developed a new theory about the expansion of the universe. An unfortunate back injury made her take a new look at her leadership style:

> My usual style would have been to take center stage . . . and control the process. My back problem was at its worst . . . and instead I found myself lying flat on a portable cot in Donald's office. It is very hard to lead a group of people from a prone position. My energies were at a low ebb anyway. I found it very comfortable to lie back and avoid taking central responsibility.

Figure 5.2 The Leadership Style Continuum

> It was the best thing that could have happened to us. The resultant power vacuum allowed each of us to quietly find our own best way to contribute. This lesson has stood me in good stead since. I now think that in small groups of able and motivated individuals, giving orders or setting up a well-defined hierarchy may generate more friction than it is designed to cure. If a good spirit of teamwork prevails, team leadership can be quite diffuse.[19]

Although many people assume that democratic leadership is always best, an autocratic style may be more effective under certain circumstances. During a serious crisis, there may not be enough time to discuss issues or consider the wishes of all members and a group may be thankful when a leader takes control of the situation.

Democratic Leaders. A **democratic leader** promotes the interests of group members and practices social equality. As their name implies, democratic leaders behave quite differently than autocratic leaders. A democratic leader:

- shares decision making with the group.
- helps plan and implement a course of action.
- focuses on *both* the task *and* group morale.
- gives the group credit for success.
- relies on referent and expert power to motivate members.
- promotes collaboration, manages conflict, and listens effectively.

There are, however, potential costs to democratic leadership. Democratic leaders may sacrifice productivity by avoiding direct leadership. By failing to take charge in a crisis or to curb a discussion when final decisions are needed, democratic leaders may be perceived as weak or indecisive by their followers.

In groups with democratic leadership, members are often more satisfied with the group experience, more loyal to the leader, and more productive in the long run. Whereas members often fear or distrust an autocratic leader, they usually enjoy working with a democratic leader. Not surprisingly, groups led by democratic leaders exhibit lower levels of stress and conflict along with higher levels of innovation and creative problem solving.[20]

Laissez-Faire Leaders. *Laissez-faire* is a French phrase that means "to let people do as they choose." A **laissez-faire leader** lets the group take charge of all decisions and actions. In mature and highly productive groups, a laissez-faire leader may be a perfect match for the group. Such a laid-back leadership style can generate a climate in which open communication is encouraged and rewarded. Unfortunately, laissez-faire leaders do little or nothing to help a group when it needs decisive leadership. Laissez-faire leaders may have legitimate power, but they hesitate or fail to exert any influence on group members and group work.

Situational Leadership Theory

Situational Leadership Theory claims that effective leaders use different leadership styles and strategies depending on the situation. Most of us do this in our daily interactions with other people. We try to be extra patient with nervous colleagues on their first few days at a new job. We check up on some group members more than others because we know they'll forget meeting times and deadlines.[21] We adapt based on what we know about other people and how they work. Situational Leadership Theory gives us the tools we need to become more effective leaders once we

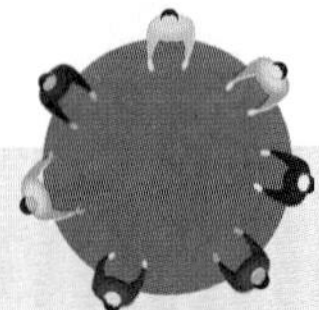

theory in groups
Functional Leadership Theory

Functional Leadership Theory is actually a group of theories that explore questions such as "What is the ideal group size?" How does conflict management affect group productivity and member satisfaction? In other words, functional perspectives try "to understand the factors and processes that help and hurt the quality of group performance."[1]

One of those factors studied by functional theorists and researchers is group leadership. According to **Functional Leadership Theory,** a capable group member often assumes leadership functions when necessary. The functional approach focuses on what a leader *does* rather than on who a leader *is*. Even more significant, the functional approach does not assume that leadership is the sole responsibility of the leader. Instead, it assumes that anyone in a group can and should help the group achieve its goal. Leadership is a job, not a person.

Although a functional approach shifts leadership responsibilities to anyone capable of performing them, this does not mean that leadership is unnecessary. Just the opposite may be true. If one member is better at motivating others, while another member excels at keeping the group on track, the group may be better off with each member's assuming of those leadership functions. Rather than relying on a leader's natural traits, style, or motivation, the functional approach concentrates on what a leader says and does in a group situation.[2]

[1] Andrea B. Hollingshead et al., "A Look at Groups from the Functional Perspective," in *Theories of Small Groups: Interdisciplinary Perspectives*, ed. Marshall Scott Poole and Andrea B. Hollingshead (Thousand Oaks, CA: Sage, 2005), p. 22.

[2] For more on functional leadership theory, see Michael Z. Hackman and Craig E. Johnson, *Leadership: A Communication Perspective*, 4th ed. (Long Grove, IL: Waveland Press, 2004), pp. 79–83; Andrea B. Hollingshead et al., "A Look at Groups from the Functional Perspective," in *Theories of Small Groups: Interdisciplinary Perspectives*, ed. Marshall Scott Poole and Andrea B. Hollingshead (Thousand Oaks, CA: Sage, 2005), pp. 21–62.

have carefully analyzed ourselves, our group, and the circumstances in which we work together.

Fiedler's Contingency Model of Leadership Effectiveness. One of the most influential theories of situational leadership was developed by managerial expert Fred Fiedler. His **Contingency Model of Leadership Effectiveness** contends that effective leadership occurs only when there is an ideal match between the leader's style and the group's work situation.[22] Fiedler characterizes leaders as being either task motivated or relationship motivated. Notice the dialectic tensions between these two leadership styles in Table 5.2.

Table 5.2 Task- and Relationship-Motivated Leaders

Type of Leader	Leader Motivation	Leader Behavior
Task-Motivated Leader	Gets the job done even at the cost of getting along with other members.	• May ignore group morale • May confront disruptive members • May appear efficient and strong • May do the work of other members because they're not satisfied with the quality or quantity
Relationship-Motivated Leader	Gets along with other members even at the cost of getting the job done.	• May ignore task requirements • May tolerate disruptive members • May appear inefficient and weak • May do the work of other members to avoid asking them to do more

Fiedler acknowledges that a small group of leaders are *both* task motivated *and* relationship oriented. Maintaining this delicate balance, however, is difficult given that most leaders are motivated by one style more than the other. At the same time, enlightened leaders recognize the leadership style they prefer and try to compensate by adopting the opposite style when it best serves the group and its members.

Once you have determined your leadership style, the next step is to analyze how your style matches the group's situation. According to Fiedler, every situation has three important dimensions: leader–member relations, task structure, and power.

- *Leader–member relations:* Because **leader–member relations** can be positive, neutral, or negative, they affect the way a leader goes about mobilizing a group toward its goal. Are group members friendly and loyal to the leader and the rest of the group? Are they cooperative and supportive? Do they accept or resist the leader?
- *Task structure:* The second situational factor requires leaders to analyze the structure of the task. **Task structure** ranges from disorganized and chaotic to highly organized and rule driven. Are the goals and the task clear? Is there an accepted procedure or set of steps for achieving the goal? Are there well-established standards for measuring success?
- *Power:* The third situational factor is power, the ability or authority to influence and motivate others. Is the source of that power an outside authority, or has the leader earned it from the group? What differences would the use of reward, coercive, legitimate, expert, referent, informational, persuasive, and charismatic power have on the group?

Fiedler's research suggests that there are ideal matches between leadership style and group situations. As depicted in Figure 5.3, task-motivated leaders perform best in extremes—such as when the situation is highly controlled or when it is almost out of control. These leaders shine when there are good leader–member relationships, a clear task, and a lot of power. They also do well in stressful leadership jobs where there may be poor leader–member relationships, an unclear and unstructured task,

Figure 5.3 Contingency Model of Leadership Effectiveness

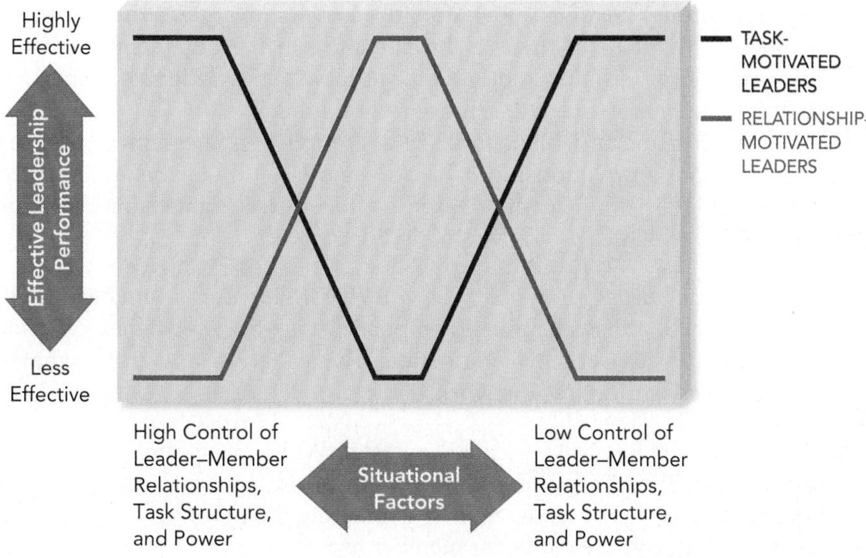

and little power. Task-motivated leaders do well in extreme situations because their primary motivation is to take charge and get the job done.

Relationship-motivated leaders are most effective when there is a mix of conditions. They may have a structured task but an uncooperative group of followers. Rather than taking charge and getting the job done at all costs, the relationship-motivated leader uses diplomacy and works with group members to improve leader–member relationships. If there are good leader–member relationships but an unstructured task, the relationship-motivated leader may rely on the resources of the group to develop a plan of action. Whereas a task-motivated leader might find these situations frustrating, a relationship-motivated leader will be quite comfortable.

According to Fielder's Contingency Model of Leadership, when you know your leadership style and understand the situation in which you must lead, you can begin to predict how successful you will be as a leader. Of course, you cannot always choose when and where you will lead. You may find yourself assigned or elected to a leadership situation that does not match your leadership style. In such a case, rather than trying to change your leadership style, you may find it easier to change the situation in which you are leading. For example, if leader–member relationships are poor, you may decide that your first task is to gain the group's trust and support. You can schedule time to listen to members' problems or take nonmeeting time to get to know key individuals in the group.

If your task is highly unstructured, you can exert your leadership by providing structure or by dividing the task into smaller, easier-to-achieve subunits. On the other hand, you may find yourself in a leadership situation where the task is so highly structured that there is almost no need for leadership. The group knows exactly what to do. Rather than allowing the group to become bored, ask for or introduce new and less structured tasks to challenge the group.

Finally, you may be able to modify the amount of power you have. If you are reluctant to use coercive power, or if you don't have enough legitimate power, you can earn referent and charismatic power by demonstrating your leadership ability. If you have a great deal of power and run the risk of intimidating group members, you may want to delegate some of your duties and power.

Hersey-Blanchard's Situational Leadership® Model. Paul Hersey and Kenneth H. Blanchard's **Situational Leadership Model** links leadership style to the readiness of group members.[23] **Member readiness** is the extent to which group members are willing (confident, committed, and motivated) and able (knowledgable, expert, and skilled) to work together in order to achieve a common goal.

According to Hersey and Blanchard, as a group's readiness increases, leaders should rely more on relationship behaviors and less on task behavior. Here is a summary of guidelines for leaders based on the Hersey-Blanchard Situational Leadership model, which is also illustrated in Figure 5.4:[24]

Situation 1. Low Readiness—The Telling Stage. When followers are unable, unwilling, or insecure, the leader should emphasize task-oriented behavior while being very directive and even autocratic. The leader *tells* the group what to do and closely supervises the work.

Situation 2. Moderate Readiness—The Selling Stage. When group members are unable but willing or confident, the leader should focus on being more relationship oriented. The leader *sells* by explaining the rationale for decisions and providing opportunities for member input.

Figure 5.4 Hersey-Blanchard's Situational Model

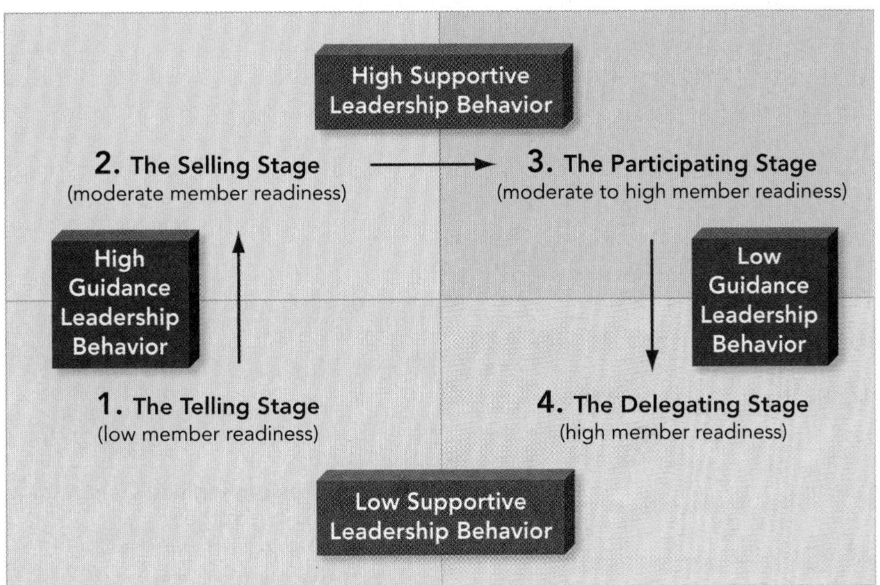

Situation 3. Moderate to High Readiness—The Participating Stage. When group members are able but unwilling or insecure, the leader should provide a high degree of relationship-oriented behavior. The leader *participates* by sharing ideas, facilitating decision making, and motivating members.

Situation 4. High Readiness—The Delegating Stage. When group members are able as well as being willing and confident, they are self-sufficient and competent. The leader *delegates* by granting group members independence and trust.

Now think back to Chapter 2, Group Development, and Tuckman's stages: forming, storming, norming, and performing. You should see a close relationship between Hersey and Blanchard's four types of leader behavior and Tuckman's first four stages of group development. As a group moves from the forming stage to storming, norming, and performing stages, members also increase their readiness, that is, their ability, willingness, and confidence. Whereas a group in the forming stage needs more guidance and direction from a leader, a group in the performing stage shares a common vision and can function with little or no interference from a leader. In this case, an effective leader provides help and may delegate responsibilities and oversee a task or project.

In Figure 5.5 on page 122, we have augmented the Hersey-Blanchard model to demonstrate how Tuckman's four stages of group development effectively match telling, selling, participating, and delegating leadership tasks.[25]

Transformational Leadership Theory

In the late 1970s, researchers took a more sophisticated look at a special set of leadership traits. What qualities, they asked, are common to those leaders who change the world in which they live—leaders such as Abraham Lincoln, Martin Luther King Jr., Mohandas Gandhi, and the "giants" of corporate industry? This investigation resulted in the development of **Transformational Leadership Theory,** which looks

Figure 5.5 Connecting Group Development and Leadership Stages

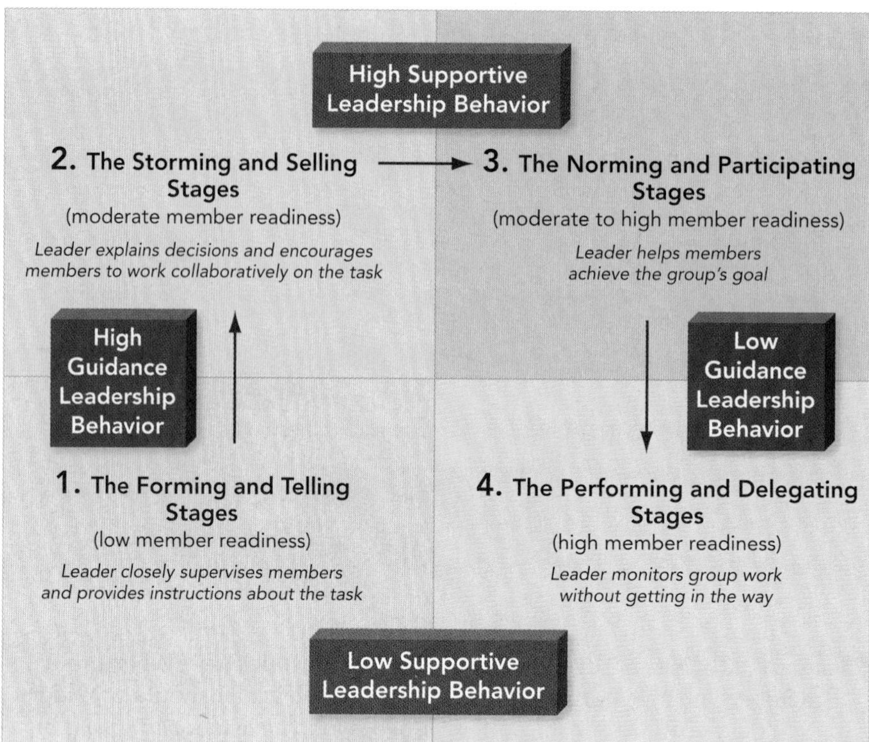

at what leaders accomplish rather than at their personal characteristics or their relationship with group members. Transformational leaders do exactly what the word *transform* implies—they bring about major, positive changes by moving group members beyond their self-interests for the good of the group and its goal.[26] Transformational leaders inspire members "to become highly committed to the leader's mission, to make significant personal sacrifices in the interests of the mission, and to perform above and beyond the call of duty."[27]

Transformational leaders are doers—they convert goals into action. With a clear and compelling goal, trust and openness among group members, confidence, optimism, and purposeful action, a leader can transform a group into a remarkable and productive team of colleagues.[28] A review of transformational leadership research identifies six attributes that transformational leaders often possess.[29]

- *Charismatic.* Leaders present a combination of agreeableness and extroversion while earning the respect, confidence, and loyalty of group members. Charismatic leaders possess "a positive and compelling quality . . . that makes many others want to be led by him or her."[30]
- *Visionary.* Leaders communicate a set of values that guide and motivate group members and that help members go beyond their individual self-interests to look at the "big picture" and how their work contributes to a worthy and inspiring goal.
- *Supportive.* Leaders encourage the personal development of members, provide clear directions and focus, and help members fulfill their personal and professional needs.

- *Empowering.* Leaders involve members in decision making and help members focus on a quest for self-fulfillment, rather than on minor satisfactions.
- *Innovative.* Leaders encourage innovation and creativity, and help members understand the need for change, both emotionally and intellectually.
- *Modeling.* Leaders provide a model of member effectiveness and build a climate of mutual trust between the leader and group members.

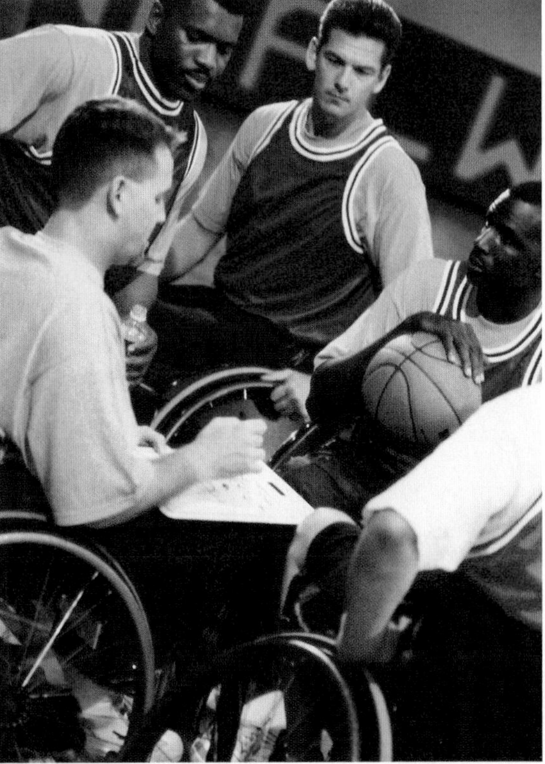

Transformational leaders do exactly what the word *transform* implies—they bring about major, positive changes by moving group members beyond their self-interests for the good of the group and its goal. What leadership strategies enable an athletic team coach or captain to transform individual players into a highly cohesive and successful team?

The 5M Model of Leadership Effectiveness

Given the millions of words about leadership published by scholars, management gurus, and popular press writers, you may have difficulty sorting out the "dos and don'ts" of effective leadership. To help you understand and balance the contributions made by these various approaches, we offer an integrated model of leadership effectiveness that focuses on specific communication strategies and skills.

The **5M Model of Leadership Effectiveness,** shown in Figure 5.6, divides leadership tasks into five interdependent leadership functions: (1) **m**odel leadership behavior, (2) **m**otivate members, (3) **m**anage the group process, (4) **m**ake decisions, and (5) **m**entor members. These strategies incorporate the features of several theories and provide a set of behaviors characteristic of effective leadership.[31]

Figure 5.6 The 5M Model of Leadership Effectiveness

Model Leadership Behavior

Model leaders project an image of confidence, competence, trustworthiness, and optimism. Leadership expert Martin Chemers refers to this function as *image management* and notes that when "image management is particularly successful, the leader may be described as charismatic."[32] Yet no matter how much you may *want* to be a model leader, only your followers can grant you that honor. We recommend the following strategies for modeling effective leadership:

1. Publicly champion your group and its goals. In addition to praising group members directly, praise them to others outside the group.
2. Speak and listen effectively and confidently.
3. Behave consistently and assertively. Think about how you would want to be treated and make sure that you follow your own golden rule.
4. Demonstrate competence and trustworthiness. Roll up your sleeves and take on difficult tasks. Stick with the task and the group until the goal is achieved.

Motivate Members

Motivating leaders guide, develop, support, defend, and inspire group members. They develop relationships that "match the personal needs and expectations of followers."[33] In Chapter 6, Group Motivation, we focus on how both group members and leaders can enlist the power of motivation to create an optimal group experience. Four leadership skills are central to motivating members:

1. Secure members' commitment to the group's shared goal. Even if it takes extra time and effort, make sure members genuinely support a clear and elevated goal.
2. Appropriately reward the group and its members. You can be firm as long as you are fair in recognizing and rewarding outstanding group work.
3. Help solve interpersonal problems and conflicts. Use the conflict resolution skills described in this textbook to resolve conflicts constructively.
4. Adapt tasks and assignments to members' abilities and expectations. Don't try to fit the "square peg" member into a "round hole" role. Use group members' talents to enhance group productivity and members' satisfaction.

Manage Group Process

From the perspective of group survival, managing group process may be the most important function of leadership.[34] If a group is disorganized, lacks sufficient information to solve problems, or is unable to make important decisions when they are called for, the group cannot be effective. Four leadership skills can enhance this important function:

1. Organize and fully prepare for group meetings and work sessions. In some cases, you may take more time to prepare for a meeting as to lead one.
2. Understand and adapt to members' strengths and weaknesses. Capitalize on member strengths and help shore up member weaknesses.
3. Help solve task-related and procedural problems. When a group is working productively, help them organize their task and adjust timetables. Secure necessary resources.

4. Monitor and intervene to improve group performance. If you see a problem developing, intervene and assist members before it becomes a crisis.

Make Decisions

A leader's willingness and ability to make appropriate, timely, and responsible decisions characterizes effective leadership. Too often we hear disgruntled group members talk about their leader's inability to make critical decisions. A high school teacher described this fatal leadership flaw as follows:

> Everyone agrees that our principal is a "nice guy" who wants everyone to like him. He doesn't want to "rock the boat" or "make waves." As a result, he doesn't make decisions or take decisive action when it's most needed. He listens patiently to a request or to both sides of a dispute, but that's all he does. Our school comes to a standstill because he won't "bite the bullet." The teachers have lost respect for him, students and their parents know that they'll get what they want if they yell loudly enough or long enough, and the superintendent has to intervene to fix the mess that results.

When you assume a leadership role, you must accept that some of your decisions may be unpopular, and some may even turn out to be wrong. But you still have to make them. In *The New Why Teams Don't Work,* Harvey Robbins and Michael Finley contend that it's often better for a group leader to make a bad decision than to make no decision at all, "For if you are seen as chronically indecisive, people won't let you lead them."[35] One company executive also noted that as much as you may value collaborative consensus, "sometimes you just need to make a decision."[36] The following strategies can help you determine when and how to intervene and make a decision.

1. Make sure that everyone shares information needed to make a quality decision.
2. If appropriate, discuss your pending decision and solicit feedback from members. As long as members don't interpret your out-loud thinking as an "order," you and your group will benefit by sharing ideas and options.
3. Listen to members' opinions, arguments, and suggestions. When you listen effectively, you may discover that the group only needs a little help to make a decision or solve a problem.
4. Explain the rationale for the decision you intend to make. When you are about to make a decision, let your group know. Not only will they be prepared for the outcome, they may help you make a better decision.

Mentor Members

Most successful people tell stories about significant mentors who helped them mature and move ahead. The word *mentor* comes from Ancient Greece. In Homer's *Odyssey,* Mentor was the tutor and advisor to the hero Odysseus's son, Telemachus. Thus the word *mentor* has come to mean a wise and trusted counselor who is usually older and more experienced than the *mentee*—that is, the person being mentored.

Good leaders are very busy people, particularly if they model leadership, motivate members, manage group process, and make decisions. Great leaders find the time and energy to mentor others. They know that good mentoring does more than teach someone how to do a job—it also motivates that person to set high standards, seek advice when needed, and develop the skills needed to become an excellent leader.

In his book *Great Leadership,* Anthony Bell urges would-be leaders to find a mentor because a good "mentor will challenge you to ask (and answer) the tough questions."[37] Yet it's difficult to find a good mentor if the leaders around you don't want or know how to mentor. The following strategies can help you decide when and how to mentor group members.

1. *Be ready and willing to mentor every group member.* Although you cannot be a full-time mentor for everyone, you should be open to requests for advice. Eventually, you may develop a close relationship with a few mentees who share your vision.
2. *Encourage and invite others to lead.* Look for situations in which group members can assume leadership responsibilities. Ask them to chair a meeting, take full responsibility for a group project, or implement a group's decision. And make sure they know you're there as backup.
3. *Inspire optimism.* When problems or setbacks occur, do not blame the group or its members. Instead, convert the situation into a teachable moment and make sure members learn to accept personal responsibility for a problem and its consequences.[38]

You cannot spend all of your time mentoring others. Nor should you delve into members' personal problems. Effective mentors create appropriate balance and boundaries. They know when to intervene and when to back off. A mentor is neither a psychiatric counselor nor a group member's best friend. At some point, even the best mentors must let their mentees succeed or fail on their own.

Diversity and Leadership

For most of the twentieth century, leadership studies concentrated on the traits, styles, and functions of white male leaders. Today, successful organizations and groups must understand, respect, and adapt to diverse leaders if they hope to tap the potential of their members. However, even under the best of circumstances, negative stereotypes still hamper the ability of women and culturally diverse members to lead.

Gender and Leadership

In the early studies of leadership, there was an unwritten but additional prerequisite for becoming a leader: Be a man. Even today, despite the achievements of exceptional women leaders, some people still question the ability of women to serve in leadership positions.

In a summary of the research on leadership and gender, Susan Shimanoff and Mercilee Jenkins conclude that "women are still less likely to be preselected as leaders, and the same leadership behavior is often evaluated more positively when attributed to a male than a female."[39] In other words, even when women talk early and often, are well prepared and always present at meetings, and offer valuable ideas, a man who has done the same things is more likely to emerge as leader. After examining the research on gender and leadership, Rodney Napier and Matti Gershenfeld conclude, "even though male and female leaders may act the same, there is a tendency for women to be perceived more negatively or to have to act differently to gain leadership."[40]

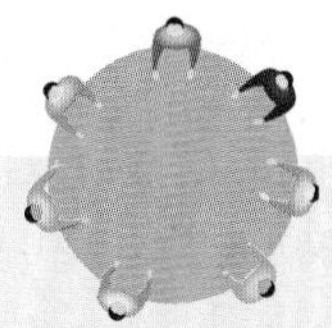

virtual groups
Sharing Leadership Functions

Leadership is pervasive and necessary in successful virtual groups. But, according to Jessica Lipnack and Jeffrey Stamps, the authors of *Virtual Groups*, "each member of a virtual team must adopt a leadership perspective."[1] Why? Consider the added responsibilities required of someone who leads a virtual group—be it a teleconference, an email discussion, or an intercontinental videoconference.

When participants live in different cities or time zones, arranging a virtual meeting can be more difficult than calling a regular meeting in a conference room down the hall. In order to prepare members for a virtual meeting:

- Someone must develop and send a detailed agenda to all members well in advance.
- Someone must make sure that the technology required for the conference is up and running.
- Someone must lead the discussion in which participants may neither see nor hear one another in real time.

As functional theory suggests, effective virtual groups manage these added tasks by sharing leadership roles rather than by assuming that one superhuman leader can handle all of these complex challenges.

The 5M Model of Leadership Effectiveness also applies to the unique responsibilities of a virtual group leader. When virtual groups first "meet," they often depend on a leader to model appropriate behavior. The leader must demonstrate effective participant behavior for other virtual group members. Motivating a virtual group can be more difficult than motivating participants in a face-to-face discussion. Unmotivated members may ignore messages or respond infrequently. When this happens, a group is vulnerable to miscommunication, poor quality of work, missed deadlines, lack of cohesion, inefficiencies, and disaffected team members.

A virtual group leader also has additional managerial duties. For example, members may need training in the use of specialized software. Making decisions in a virtual group can be difficult when group members are not communicating in real time. In virtual groups, the leader may be responsible for determining when the virtual group will "meet," the rules of interaction, and the criteria for group decision making. Finally, leaders can mentor members who are apprehensive about interacting with group members in a virtual environment or members who lack the technical skills needed to "keep up" with the group.

[1]Jessica Lipnack and Jeffrey Stamps, *Virtual Teams*, 3rd ed. (New York: Wiley, 2006), p. 218.

Unfortunately, such negative perceptions can make it difficult for women to assume and succeed in leadership positions. If their behavior is similar to that of male leaders, they are perceived as unfeminine. If they act "like a lady," they are viewed as weak or ineffective. One professional woman described this dilemma as follows:

> I was thrilled when my boss evaluated me as "articulate, hard-working, mature in her judgment, and a skillful diplomat." What disturbed me were some of the evaluations from those I supervise or work with as colleagues. Although they had a lot of good things to say, a few of them described me as "pushy," "brusque," "impatient," "a disregard for social niceties," and "hard-driving." What am I supposed to do? My boss thinks I'm energetic and creative, while other people see the same behavior as pushy and aggressive.

The preference for male leaders may come down to a fear of or an unwillingness to adjust to different kinds of leaders. Because many people have worked with or for male leaders, they may feel uncomfortable when the leadership shifts to a woman. Even though extensive research indicates that there are only slight differences

between men and women leaders, stereotypical, negative expectations persist. These expectations make it more difficult for women to gain, hold, and succeed in leadership positions.[41] Our best advice is that instead of asking whether a female leader is different from a male leader, it is more important to ask whether she is an effective leader.

Cultural Diversity and Leadership

The ways in which a leader models leadership behavior, motivates group members, manages group process, makes decisions, and mentors members may not match the cultural dimensions of all group members. If, as a leader, you model leadership behavior by strongly and publicly advocating group goals, you may upset members from high-context cultures who would be less direct. Your way of modeling leadership behavior may not reflect *their* view of a model leader. For example, people from Western cultures (the United States, Canada, and Europe) assume that group members are motivated by personal achievement and status. However, when group mem-

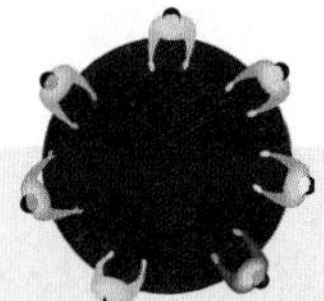

groups in balance . . .
Rely on the Two Sides of Leadership

In *Leadership without Easy Answers,* Ronald Heifetz describes effective leaders as people who walk a razor's edge (ouch!). He offers this example: If you challenge group members too quickly with too much, they will resist your leadership and resent the chaos your expectations create for them. If you challenge members too slowly with too little, they will blame *you* for their lack of motivation and progress. Heifetz claims that effective leaders stay balanced on the edge by adapting to the group, its members, and changing situations.[1]

Jim Collins, author of *Good to Great,* suggests a gentler approach to leadership that seeks a balance of professional will and personal humility—a tough challenge for most leaders. Collins contends that unless you are willing to keep your ego in check for the sake of the group's goal and its well-being, you are not "made" for this kind of leadership. "For these people, work will always be first and foremost about what they *get*—fame, fortune, adulation, power, whatever—and not what they *build,* create, and contribute."[2] Here is our summary of Collins's "two sides" of leadership:[3]

Professional Will	Personal Humility
Creates superb results in achieving a clear goal	Acts modest, never boastful; shuns public glorification
Does what needs to be done to achieve the goal	Acts with quiet, calm determination; relies on inspiring stands and motivational strategies
Sets high standards for achieving the goal	Channels ambition into achieving the group's goal; sets up worthy successors
Apportions responsibility for succeeding or failing objectively and fairly	Gives credit for success to other people, not to self

[1] Ron Heifetz, *Leadership without Easy Answers* (Cambridge, MA: The Belknap Press of Harvard University Press, 1994), pp. 126–127.

[2] Jim Collins, *Good to Great: Why Some Companies Make the Leap . . . and Others Don't* (New York: HarperBusiness, 2001), p. 36.

[3] Collins.

bers' cultural backgrounds are more collectivist, the same motivational strategies may not work. A collectivist member may act out of loyalty to the leader and the group rather than for personal achievement or material gain.[42]

Managing group process in a group composed of culturally diverse members can be difficult. Members from uncertainty-avoidance cultures will want more structure and instruction from a leader. If your leadership style is more feminine (nurturing, collaborative, caring), you may find yourself fighting a losing leadership battle with members who are more competitive, independent, and aggressive. Your feminine leadership style may be interpreted as weakness or indecision.

The decision-making style of a leader may not match that of a culturally diverse group. If members come from a low-power-distance culture, they will not welcome an authoritarian leader who takes control of all decision making. Conversely, a leader who prefers a more democratic approach to decision making may frustrate members who come from high-power-distance cultures, in which leaders make most decisions with little input from group members.

Negative stereotypes about leaders from minority groups are prevalent, and such members have more difficulty moving up the leadership ladder.[43] Balancing the needs of culturally diverse group members may be difficult, but the ability to do so is essential to providing effective leadership.

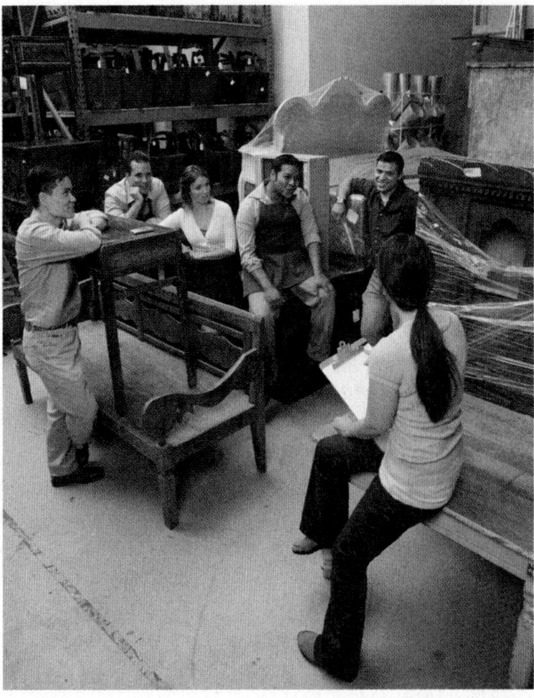

Researchers conclude that women are less likely to be selected as leaders and that the same leadership behavior is often evaluated more positively when attributed to a male than a female. What, then, should female group members do to ensure their selection and success as leaders?

summary study guide

What Is Leadership?

- Leadership is the ability to make strategic decisions and use communication effectively to mobilize group members toward achieving a common goal.
- Successful leaders effectively manage many dialectic tensions, especially the dialectics of individual goals ↔ group goals, conflict ↔ cohesion, and structure ↔ spontaneity.

Leadership and Power

- Power associated with the position of leadership can be categorized into legitimate power, reward power, coercive power, and informational power.
- Power associated with the personal characteristics of the leader can be categorized into expert power, referent power, persuasive power, and charismatic power.
- An effective leader usually uses several kinds of power depending on the needs of the group and the situation.

Becoming a Leader

- Designated leaders are selected by group members or by an outside authority. Effective designated leaders involve members in decision making, discuss ground rules for interaction, and openly address leadership concerns.
- Emergent leaders gradually achieve leadership by interacting with group members and contributing to the group's goal. Emergent leaders are already familiar with the group, its goals, and its norms.
- Strategies for becoming a leader include talking early and often, knowing more, and offering opinions. At

the same time, aspiring leaders should listen to others, share information, and welcome disagreement.

Leadership Theories

- Trait Leadership Theory identifies and prescribes individual characteristics and behaviors needed for effective leadership. However, personality traits alone do not guarantee effective leadership.
- Styles Leadership Theory describes a collection of specific behaviors that can be categorized into autocratic leadership, democratic leadership, or laissez-faire leadership styles.
- Functional Leadership Theory focuses on what leaders *do* rather than who leaders are, and it assumes that any group member can and should engage in leadership behaviors that help the group achieve its goal.
- Fiedler's Contingency Model of Leadership Effectiveness seeks an ideal fit between a leader's style (task or relationship motivated) and three dimensions of the group's situation (leader-member relations, task structure, and leadership power).
- The Situational Leadership Model links leadership style to member readiness and ability. The more willing and able a group is to work together, the more a leader should rely on relationship behaviors and less on task behaviors.
- Transformational Leadership Theory describes how a leader can bring about major, positive changes by moving group members beyond self-interests to work for the good of the group's goal. Transformational leaders are often charismatic, visionary, supportive, empowering, innovative, and models of effective behavior.

The 5M Model of Leadership Effectiveness

- The 5M Model of Leadership Effectiveness is an integrated model of leadership that focuses on specific communication strategies and skills by incorporating the features of several leadership theories.
- The 5M Model of Leadership Effectiveness divides leadership tasks into five interdependent functions: (1) **M**odel leadership behavior, (2) **M**otivate members, (3) **M**anage group process, (4) **M**ake decisions, and (5) **M**entor members.

Diversity and Leadership

- In general, women are less likely to be selected as leaders, and the same leadership behavior is often evaluated more positively when attributed to a man rather than a woman.
- Negative stereotypes about leaders from minority groups make it more difficult for these members to gain leadership positions.
- Diversity in leadership requires an understanding of, respect for, and adaptation to different cultural dimensions and behaviors.

key terms

autocratic leader 116
charismatic power 110
coercive power 110
Contingency Model of Leadership Effectiveness 118
democratic leader 117
designated leader 111
emergent leader 113
expert power 110
5M Model of Leadership Effectiveness 123
Functional Leadership Theory 118
Hersey-Blanchard Situational Leadership® Model 120
informational power 110
laissez-faire leader 117
leader–member relations 119
leadership 108
legitimate power 110
member readiness 120
personal power 110
persuasive power 110
position power 110
power 110
referent power 110
relationship-motivated leader 118
reward power 110
Situational Leadership Model 120
Situational Leadership Theory 117
Styles Leadership Theory 116
task-motivated leader 118
task structure 119
Trait Leadership Theory 115
Transformational Leadership Theory 121

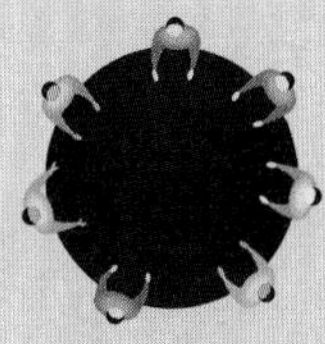

critical thinking about the case study

The Leader in Sheep's Clothing

1. What types of leadership power is Mr. Dupree using? Is his use of power effective in this group? Why or why not?
2. As a designated leader who was not a member of the original group, how could Mr. Dupree adapt his leadership more effectively to the existing staff?
3. To what extent does Mr. Dupree demonstrate the attributes of a transformational leader?
4. According to Fiedler's Contingency Model of Leadership Effectiveness, is Mr. Dupree a task-motivated or relationship-motivated leader? How well does his leadership style match the group's situational dimensions?
5. Which dialectic tensions are most likely to affect how well Mr. Dupree and the staff work together to achieve the Peoples Project's goals?
6. Given that many staff members are currently unhappy working for Mr. Dupree, what strategies could the staff use to improve the group's situation?

group work The Least-Preferred-Coworker Scale

Directions: All of us have worked better with some people than with others. Think of the one person in your life with whom you have worked least well, a person who might have caused you difficulty in doing a job or completing a task. This person may be someone with whom you have worked recently or someone you have known in the past. This person must be the single individual with whom you have had the most difficulty getting a job done, the person with whom you would least want to work.

On the scale below, describe this person by circling the number that best represents your perception of this person. There are no right or wrong answers. Do not omit any items, and circle a number for each item only once.

Pleasant	8	7	6	5	4	3	2	1	Unpleasant
Friendly	8	7	6	5	4	3	2	1	Unfriendly
Rejecting	1	2	3	4	5	6	7	8	Accepting
Tense	1	2	3	4	5	6	7	8	Relaxed
Distant	1	2	3	4	5	6	7	8	Close
Cold	1	2	3	4	5	6	7	8	Warm
Supportive	8	7	6	5	4	3	2	1	Hostile
Boring	1	2	3	4	5	6	7	8	Interesting
Quarrelsome	1	2	3	4	5	6	7	8	Harmonious
Gloomy	1	2	3	4	5	6	7	8	Cheerful
Open	8	7	6	5	4	3	2	1	Guarded
Backbiting	1	2	3	4	5	6	7	8	Loyal
Untrustworthy	1	2	3	4	5	6	7	8	Trustworthy
Considerate	8	7	6	5	4	3	2	1	Inconsiderate
Nasty	1	2	3	4	5	6	7	8	Nice
Agreeable	8	7	6	5	4	3	2	1	Disagreeable
Insincere	1	2	3	4	5	6	7	8	Sincere
Kind	8	7	6	5	4	3	2	1	Unkind

Scoring: Obtain your Least-Preferred-Coworker (LPC) score by adding up the numbers you circled on the scale. Your score should be between 18 and 144.

Relationship-Motivated Leader. If your score is 73 or above, you derive satisfaction from good relationships with group members. You are most successful when a situation has just enough uncertainty to challenge you: moderate leader–member relationships, moderate task structure, and moderate power.

Task-Motivated Leader. If your score is 64 or below, you derive satisfaction from getting things done. You are most successful when a situation has clear guidelines or no guidelines at all: excellent or poor leader–member relationships, highly structured or unstructured tasks, and high or low power.

Relationship- and Task-Motivated Leader. If your score is between 65 and 72, you may be flexible enough to function in both leadership styles.

Source: Fred E. Fiedler and Martin M. Chemers, *Improving Leadership Effectiveness: The Leader Match Concept*, 2nd ed. (New York: Wiley, 1984), pp. 17–42.

group assessment Are You Ready to Lead?

Directions: Indicate the extent to which you agree with each of the following statements, using the following scale: (1) strongly disagree; (2) disagree; (3) neutral or undecided; (4) agree; (5) strongly agree.

LEADERSHIP READINESS STATEMENTS					
1. I enjoy having people count on me for ideas and suggestions.	1	2	3	4	5
2. It would be accurate to say that I have inspired other people.	1	2	3	4	5
3. It's a good practice to ask people provocative questions about their work.	1	2	3	4	5
4. It's easy for me to compliment others.	1	2	3	4	5
5. I like to cheer people up even when my own spirits are down.	1	2	3	4	5
6. What my group accomplishes is more important than my personal glory.	1	2	3	4	5
7. Many people imitate my ideas.	1	2	3	4	5
8. Building team spirit is important to me.	1	2	3	4	5
9. I would enjoy coaching other members of the group.	1	2	3	4	5
10. It is important to me to recognize others for their accomplishments.	1	2	3	4	5
11. I would enjoy entertaining visitors to my group even if it interfered with my completing a report.	1	2	3	4	5
12. It would be fun to represent my group at an outside gathering.	1	2	3	4	5
13. The problems of my teammates are my problems.	1	2	3	4	5
14. Resolving conflict is an activity that I enjoy.	1	2	3	4	5

15. I would cooperate with another group with which my group works even if I disagreed with the position taken by its members.	1	2	3	4	5
16. I am an idea generator on the job.	1	2	3	4	5
17. It's fun for me to bargain whenever I have the opportunity.	1	2	3	4	5
18. Group members listen to me when I speak.	1	2	3	4	5
19. People have asked me to assume the leadership of an activity several times in my life.	1	2	3	4	5
20. I've always been a convincing person.	1	2	3	4	5

Scoring and Interpretation: Calculate your total score by adding the numbers circled. A tentative interpretation of the scoring is as follows:

90–100	high readiness for the leadership role
60–89	moderate readiness for the leadership role
40–59	some uneasiness with the leadership role
39 or less	low readiness for the leadership role

If you are already a successful leader and you scored low on this questionnaire, ignore your score. If you scored surprisingly low and you are not yet a leader or are currently performing poorly as a leader, study the statements carefully. Consider changing your attitude or your behavior so that you can legitimately answer more of the statements with a 4 or a 5.

Source: Andrew J. DuBrin, *Leadership: Research Findings, Practice, and Skills* 4th ed. (New York: Houghton Mifflin, 2004), pp. 13–14. *Note:* We have changed a few words to keep the language consistent with the terminology in this textbook.

notes

1. Robert S. Cathcart and Larry A. Samovar, "Group Leadership: Theories and Principles," in *Small Group Communication: A Reader,* 6th ed., ed. Robert S. Cathcart and Larry A. Samovar (Dubuque, IA: Wm. C. Brown, 1992), p. 364.
2. Ron Heifetz, *Leadership without Easy Answers* (Cambridge, MA: The Belknap Press of Harvard University Press, 1994), pp. 126–128, 228.
3. Warren Bennis and Bruce Nanus, *Leaders: The Strategies for Taking Charge* (New York: HarperPerennial, 1985), p. 15.
4. Gary A. Yukl and Cecilia M. Falbe, "Importance of Different Power Sources in Downward and Lateral Relations," *Journal of Applied Psychology* 76 (1991), pp. 416–423.
5. Nicky Hayes, *Managing Teams: A Strategy for Success* (London: Thomson, 2004), p. 96.
6. Daniel Goleman, Richard Boyatzis, and Annie McKee, *Primal Leadership: Learning to Lead with Emotional Intelligence* (Boston: Harvard Business School Press, 2002), p. 23.
7. Michael Z. Hackman and Craig E. Johnson, *Leadership: A Communication Perspective,* 4th ed. (Prospect Heights, IL: Waveland, 2004), p. 127.
8. Sam R. Lloyd, *Leading Teams: The Skills for Success* (West Des Moines, IA: American Media, 1996), p. 13.
9. Edwin P. Hollander, *Leadership Dynamics: A Practical Guide to Effective Relationships* (New York: Macmillan, 1978), p. 53.

10. Hackman and Johnson, p. 191.
11. Jorge Correia Jesuino, "Leadership: Micro-macro Links," in *Understanding Group Behavior,* vol. 2, ed. Erich H. White and James H. Davis (Mahwah, NJ: Lawrence Erlbaum Associates, 1996), pp. 93, 119.
12. Charles Pavitt, "Theorizing about the Group Communication-Leadership Relationships, " in *The Handbook of Group Communication Research,* ed. Lawrence R. Frey; Dennis S. Gouran and Marshall Scott Poole, associate eds. (Thousand Oaks, CA: Sage, 1999), p. 313.
13. Bennis and Nanus, p. 4.
14. In group communication studies, four theoretical approaches to leadership dominate group communication textbooks and many research efforts: (1) Trait Theory, (2) Styles Theory, (3) Situational/Contingency Theory, and (4) Functional Theory Approach. Additional approaches to leadership studies and theory include (5) The Emergent Approach, (6) The Transformational and Charismatic Leader Approach, (7) The Servant Leader Approach, (8) The Mediational Leadership Approach, (9) The Coaching Leader Approach, and many more. Most of these perspectives are not so much *theories* as models that describe leadership but do not explain, predict, or teach us how to lead. At the same time, every theory offers insights into the nature of leadership.
15. Lucy E. Garrick, "Leadership: Theory Evolution and the Development of Inter-Personal Leadership," Pacific Northwest Organization Development Network, 2004 (Copyright 2004, Lucy Garrick, North Shore Group, LLC, Seattle, WA).
16. Andrew J. DuBrin, *Leadership: Research Findings, Practice, and Skills,* 4th ed. (New York: Houghton Mifflin, 2004), pp. 51–53.
17. Otto Kroeger with Janet M. Thuesen, *Type Talk at Work: How the 16 Personality Types Determine Your Success on the Job* (New York: Dell, 1992), p. 385.
18. Kurt Lewin, Ron Lippit, and R. K. White, "Patterns of Aggressive Behaviour in Experimentally Created Social Climates," *Journal of Social Psychology,* 10 (1939), pp. 271–299.
19. Alan Dressler, *Voyage to the Great Attractor: Exploring Intergalactic Space* (New York: Alfred A. Knopf, 1994), pp. 193–194.
20. Jesuino, p. 99.
21. *Famous Models: Situational Leadership,* http://chimaera consulting.com/sitleader.htm. Retrieved March 10, 2008.
22. Fred E. Fiedler and Martin M. Chemers, *Improving Leadership Effectiveness: The Leader Match Concept,* 2nd ed. (New York: Wiley, 1984). In addition to Fiedler's Contingency Model of Leadership Effectiveness, several other situational theories offer valuable insights into the ways in which leaders must find a match between their styles and the needs of their group. See Chapter 4 in Martin M. Chemers, *An Integrative Theory of Leadership* (Mahwah, NJ: Erlbaum, 1994), for a discussion and analysis of the following theories: House's Path-Goal Directive, Vroom and Yetton's Normative Decision Theory, and Hersey and Blanchard's Situational Leadership.
23. DuBrin, p. 144.
24. Paul Hersey and Ken Blanchard, *Management of Organizational Behavior: Utilizing Human Resources,* 6th ed. (Upper Saddle River, NJ: Prentice-Hall, 1992).
25. www.businessballs.com/tuckmanformingstormingnorming performing.htm. Retrieved March 17, 2008.
26. Based on DuBrin, p. 80.
27. Martin M. Chemers and R. Ayman (eds.), *Leadership Theory and Research: Perspectives and Directions* (San Diego: Academic Press, 1993), p. 82.
28. Warren Bennis and Joan Goldsmith, *Learning to Lead: A Workbook on Becoming a Leader,* updated ed. (Cambridge, MA: Perseus, 1997), p. xvi.
29. Sally A. Carless, Alexander J. Wearing, and Leon Mann, "A Short Measure of Transformational Leadership," *Journal of Business Psychology* (Spring 2000), pp. 389–405. Also see DuBrin, pp. 80–82.
30. DuBrin, p. 64.
31. The 5M Model of Effective Leadership draws, in part, on Martin M. Chemers's integrative theory of leadership that identifies three functional aspects of leadership: image management, relationship development, and resource utilization. We have added a fourth and fifth function—decision making and mentoring members—and have integrated a stronger communication perspective into Chemers's view of leadership as a multifaceted process. See Martin M. Chemers, *An Integrative Theory of Leadership* (Mahwah, NJ: Lawrence Erlbaum Associates, 1997), pp. 151–173.
32. Chemers, p. 154.
33. Chemers, p. 155.
34. Chemers, p. 160.
35. Harvey A. Robbins and Michael Finley, *The New Why Teams Don't Work: What Goes Wrong and How to Make It Right* (San Francisco: Berrett-Koehler, 2000), p. 107.
36. Evan Rosen, *The Culture of Collaboration: Maximizing Time, Talent and Tools to Create Value in the Global Economy* (San Francisco: Red Ape, 2007), p. 37.
37. Anthony Bell, *Great Leadership: What It Is and What It Takes in a Complex World* (Mountain View, CA: Davies-Black, 2006), p. 67.
38. James M. Kouzes and Barry Z. Posner, *Credibility: How Leaders Gain and Lose It, Why People Demand It* (San Francisco: Jossey-Bass, 1993), pp. 230–231.
39. Susan B. Shimanoff and Mercilee M. Jenkins, "Leadership and Gender: Challenging Assumptions and Recognizing Resources," in *Small Group Communication: Theory and Practice,* 7th ed., ed. Robert S. Cathcart, Larry A. Samovar, and Linda D. Henman (Madison, WI: Brown & Benchmark, 1996), p. 327.
40. Rodney Napier and Matti Gershenfeld, *Groups: Theory and Experience,* 7th ed. (Boston: Houghton Mifflin, 2004), p. 347.
41. Chemers, p. 150.
42. Chemers, p. 126.
43. Martin M. Chemers and Susan E. Murphy, *Leadership for Diversity in Groups and Organizations: Perspectives on a Changing Workplace* (Newbury Park, CA: Sage, 1995).

chapter 6

Group Motivation

chapter outline

study questions

How does motivation enhance both group productivity and member satisfaction?

How do members' needs, personalities, and cultural characteristics affect motivation?

What factors enhance group motivation?

How does assessment and feedback affect motivation?

How should a group balance motivational rewards and punishment as a motivational tool?

The Role of Motivation

Once upon a time—but not all that long ago—workers worked and bosses bossed. The Traditionalist generation and many Baby Boomers began their careers in organizations that used a military model of management. The boss sat at the top of a hierarchy and expected everyone "below" him (most often the boss was a "him") to follow orders. As we note in Chapter 4, Group Diversity, today's Generation Xers and Millennials are neither interested in nor comfortable with working in work groups that resemble those of the Traditionalists and Baby Boomers.

Kenneth Thomas, in his book *Intrinsic Motivation at Work,* notes that "it was only in 1991 that the word *empowerment* began appearing in the *Business Periodicals Index.*"[1] The words *subordinate* and *employee* have given way to *associate* (and *cast member* at Disney resorts). Working in groups today requires carrots, not sticks, to motivate members. In this chapter we examine the nature of motivation as well as appropriate strategies and skills that can transform blind obedience into enlightened commitment.

The word *motivate* comes from a French word, *motif,* which means "causing to move." Thus, if you motivate someone, you give that person a reason to act. **Group motivation** provides the inspiration, incentives, and reasons that move group members to work together to achieve a common goal. Without motivation, we may know what we need to do and even how to do it, but we lack the will and energy to do it. Motivation is the power that moves us to work in groups.

Have you and your group ever been totally caught up in what you were doing, wholly focused on it, and also able to perform at a very high level with ease?[2] If your answer is *yes,* you have had an **optimal group experience.** When groups provide optimal experiences, members are highly committed and inspired. Creative thinking comes easily and working on the task is pleasurable. Hard work is energizing rather than exhausting. Some group members find the optimal experience so pleasurable that they'd rather do group work than relax or socialize.[3]

In order to achieve this optimal level of motivation, you and your group must negotiate several dialectic tensions. First, you must have a worthy goal that motivates *both* individual members *and* the group as a whole. You must balance *both* task *and* social dimensions by encouraging members to complete tasks and by promoting strong interpersonal relationships. You must *both* support and reward member engagement *and* accommodate members who need to disengage by pausing, recharging, and relaxing.

In Chapter 5, Group Leadership, we identify the ability to motivate as a basic competency in the 5M Model of Leadership Effectiveness. One motivator, however, is not enough—motivation is every member's responsibility. In this chapter, we recommend a variety of communication strategies and skills to help motivate members and create an optimal group experience for everyone in your group.

Member Motivation

What motivates *you* to work in groups? Will the same things that motivate you also motivate other group members? If there were universal motivators, group motivation would be easy. You could list all the motivators that work for you and then apply them to others. Unfortunately, that's exactly what some leaders and group members do. And it doesn't work. What works is a concerted effort to match motivators to members' needs, personality types, and cultural characteristics.

case study

Veni, Vidi, Vici

The newspaper headline read: "Study Finds Many Patients Dissatisfied with Hospitals."[1] When the federal government conducted its first national survey of hospital patients, the results were demoralizing and frightening. Former patients complained about arrogant doctors, crabby nurses, and dirty, noisy hospital rooms.

For Bendigo County Hospital, the results were shocking. Patients wrote that they would not recommend the hospital to friends and relatives. The hospital's board of trustees appointed a Quality Care Task Force to investigate the problem and make recommendations for improving patient care. The task force included two staff physicians, the head of nursing and a surgical nurse, an X-ray technician representing the allied health staff, and one member from the housekeeping department. The board also appointed Faith Fulbright, the hospital's vice president for administration, to chair the task force.

The very first meeting of the task force did not go well. The staff physicians angrily condemned the study because they certainly gave *every* patient high-quality care. The nurses objected to the assumption that they were not responsive to patients. The X-ray technician said she always received high evaluation scores from her supervisor. The member from housekeeping complained that the staff was overwhelmed with cleaning up the messes everyone else made. Faith Fulbright realized the task force members didn't want to be there and didn't want to acknowledge the problem.

Before the second meeting, Faith distributed the complete survey results and highlighted the most significant findings at their hospital—both positive and negative. She emailed the members, asking each one to read the report and identify two issues that deserved attention. At the beginning of the second meeting, she said, "You have enormous clout and influence. Our report will affect everyone in this hospital. So let's do it, and do it right. If we don't, the administration may decide to bypass the staff and implement their own solutions." Although her task force colleagues were still unhappy about serving, they did acknowledge that their input could have major consequences. For the rest of the meeting, they grudgingly put aside their personal concerns and discussed the survey results.

By the third meeting, Faith had sorted the issues provided by task force members. She reworded several issues to make them less critical and accusatory. She also added a few issues that no one had identified but were of paramount importance to hospital administrators. Faith began the meeting by praising the task force for its good work. She then posted each major issue on separate flip charts arranged around the room. Task force members spent time at each flip chart discussing and then recording ways to address the problem. By the end of the meeting, everyone could see progress on each issue. Before adjourning that day, one of the doctors apologized to the group for being so negative at the first meeting. The other members had fun teasing the doctor about not being "perfect."

As the task force continued meeting, Faith made sure she emailed all members to thank them for their input and to provide an agenda for the upcoming meeting. In the case of the surgical nurse and staff members, she sent emails to their supervisors praising their good work. By their fifth and last meeting, the task force unanimously agreed on a list of recommended actions for addressing each issue. To celebrate their success, the doctors brought in a tray of sandwiches. The nurses and staff members chipped in for three bottles of fake champagne and a cake decorated with a bizarre collection of hospital supplies. Faith handed out "medals" to every member, on which Julius Caesar's famous words were printed: *Veni, Vidi, Vici,* roughly translated as "We came, we saw, we conquered!"

When you finish reading this chapter, you should be able to answer the following questions.

[1]Robert Pear, "Study Finds Many Patients Dissatisfied with Hospitals," *The New York Times,* March 29, 2008, p. A13.

1. Why were employees annoyed and reluctant to serve on the task force?
2. To what extent, if any, did the task force meet any of the members' personal needs?
3. What strategies did Faith Fulbright use to enhance member motivation and effort?
4. To what extent, if any, did her assessments and feedback affect group motivation?

Motivating by Meeting Member Needs

In Chapter 3, Group Membership, we describe two psychological theories—Maslow's Hierarchy of Needs and Schutz's Fundamental Interpersonal Relationship Orientation (FIRO). These theories explain the various reasons we join, stay in, and leave groups. These theories also suggest ways of motivating group members.

Maslow's Hierarchy of Needs. The same needs that motivate us to join groups can also motivate us to achieve our group's common goal. In terms of group member motivation, we can divide Maslow's five needs into two categories: satisfiers and motivators.

Satisfiers (also called *deficiency needs*) include Maslow's most basic needs—physiological and safety needs. Many groups and the people who create those groups have the power to satisfy members' material needs—money for food and shelter, job security, health-care and life insurance benefits, and opportunities to advance in a career that will earn them more money. Money can satisfy deficiency needs, but it will not necessarily motivate a group or its members to work harder or better.

Motivators (also called *fulfillment needs*) include Maslow's higher-level needs—belongingness, esteem, and self-actualization needs. Group communication scholar Ernest Bormann describes how groups satisfy members' belongingness needs:

> The group furnishes refuge from loneliness. It provides members with friends and enemies, either within their own or within competing groups. Members gain a sense of belonging from the group. They learn to know other people and to find that they like and respect others.[4]

Groups also satisfy some members' esteem needs. However, when esteem needs are not satisfied, members may feel inconsequential and lack self-worth.[5] Psychologist Douglas Bernstein and his colleagues describe people with high achievement needs as follows:

> They actively seek success, take risks when necessary, and are intensely satisfied with success. But if they feel they have tried their best, people with high achievement motivation are not too upset by failure. . . . They select tasks with clear outcomes, and they prefer feedback from a harsh but competent critic rather than from one who is friendlier but less competent.[6]

Some members may not have high achievement needs; instead, they focus on meeting the needs of others. For example, in collectivist cultures, success and member satisfaction come from group work, not from individual achievement. Ernest Bormann maintains that working in groups can satisfy "the desire to do a good job, to make a contribution to other people, to feel that life has meaning over and above the satisfying of [basic] needs. If members do important and difficult tasks and see opportunities for additional training and competence, they can gratify some of their desire for self-actualization."[7] Figure 6.1 presents a view of Maslow's Hierarchy of Needs that illustrates the connection between need satisfaction and group motivation.

Schutz's Theory of Interpersonal Needs. Schutz's theory does more than explain why members participate in groups. It also describes the tools needed to motivate members.[8] As we explain in Chapter 3, Schutz identifies three interpersonal needs that affect why we join and work in groups.

- *Need for inclusion:* the need to belong and be accepted
- *Need for control:* the need to take charge, direct, and have power
- *Need for affection:* the need to feel liked and have close personal relationships

Figure 6.1 Maslow's Hierarchy of Needs and Group Motivators

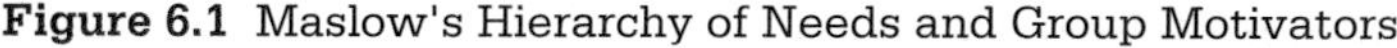

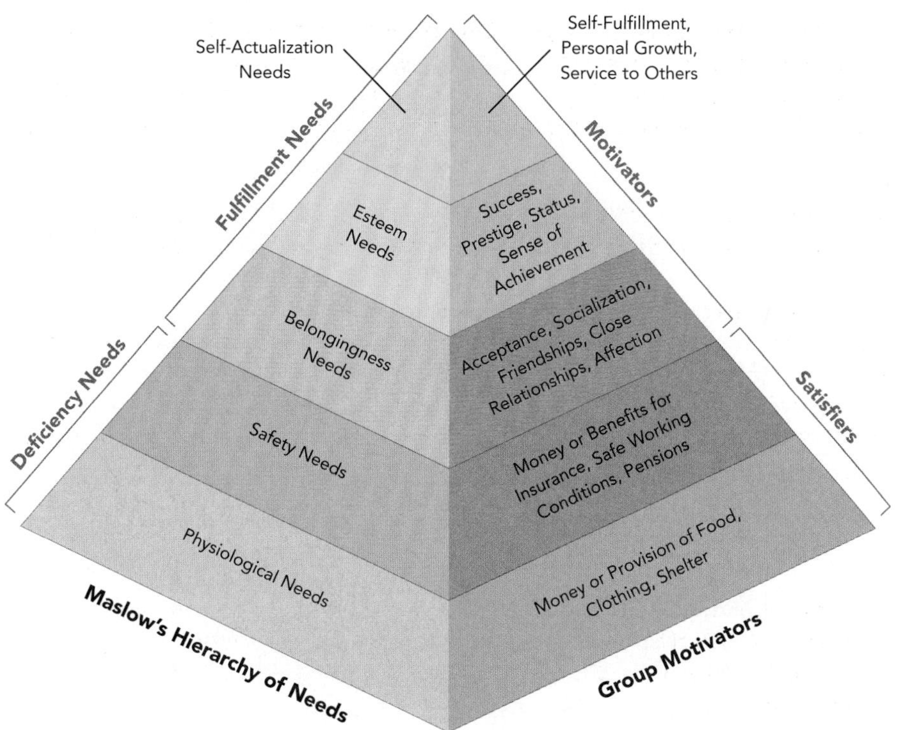

Certainly, a group can satisfy these interpersonal needs. Just belonging to a group can satisfy inclusion needs. Groups can provide leadership opportunities that satisfy control needs. Developing friendships within a group can satisfy affection needs.

Schutz's theory also suggests ways to motivate group members. If you know that some group members have unmet inclusion needs, invite them to participate more actively. Tell them how valuable they are to the group. If some members have strong affection needs, spend time with them in nonwork settings. Be open with these members, and listen carefully when they talk. If you do, they will feel well liked and highly motivated. If some members have high control needs, you don't have to appoint or elect them as leaders to satisfy those needs. Encourage them to chair a committee or volunteer for special assignments in which they have full control over their work.

Motivating Diverse Personality Types

As we indicate in Chapter 4, Group Diversity, the Myers-Briggs Type Indicator contends that every person has preferences of thought and behavior that fit into four categories, each with opposite preferences: extrovert–introvert, sensor–intuitive, thinker–feeler, and judger–perceiver. Each type responds to different motivators. Understanding the different personality types in a group can help you choose the most appropriate motivational strategies. Table 6.1 provides a brief look at the many ways in which different personality types call for different approaches to motivation.[9]

You can motivate both extroverts and introverts by providing all group members with meeting agendas well in advance. Introverts need the time to prepare materials and develop their thoughts before a meeting. Extroverts may need time to collect information that supports their already formed ideas.

Table 6.1 Personality Types and Member Motivation

Personality Type	Type-Based Beliefs about Groups	Type-Based Motivational Strategies
Extrovert	Groups get work done and create useful relationships.	• Encourage interaction. • Allow time for "talking out" ideas. • Provide frequent feedback.
Introvert	Groups can waste time, make decisions too quickly, and create more work.	• Set clear and valued goals. • Provide thinking time before and during discussions. • Provide opportunities to speak.
Sensor	Groups need to gather and use facts but often get bogged down in vague and unrealistic discussions.	• Set realistic goals. • Keep meetings short and relevant. • Request real, practical information.
Intuitive	Groups uncover possibilities and can make inspired decisions.	• Develop an engaging goal. • Encourage visioning and creativity. • Encourage brainstorming.
Thinker	Groups must test ideas and possible solutions if they want to make good decisions.	• Focus on task dispassionately. • Encourage debate on substantive issues. • Encourage logical decision making.
Feeler	Groups provide opportunities for cooperation and growth.	• Discuss impact of decisions on people. • Encourage cooperation and harmony. • Recognize members' contributions.
Judger	Groups get the task done when they're structured and task-focused.	• Encourage closure on issues. • Provide an agenda and deadlines. • Set standards and expectations.
Perceiver	Groups examine possibilities during the discussion process.	• Focus on a variety of alternatives. • Keep the time frame open. • Let a decision gradually emerge from discussion.

Sensors are motivated by the opportunity to share information and observations. Intuitives want group members to give serious consideration to their creative, big-picture ideas. During a discussion, give sensors uninterrupted time to present their information and conclusions. Then let the intuitives "loose" to use that information as a springboard for new ideas and innovative solutions.

Motivating thinkers and feelers requires a balance between task and social dimensions. Group members should thank thinkers for their analyses but also remind them that purely logical decisions may adversely affect real people. Feelers need time to discuss personal perspectives, but they should remember that disagreements can help a group reach good, people-focused decisions.

Motivating judgers and perceivers requires patience, skill, and balance. Judgers may see perceivers as flaky and undisciplined. Perceivers may see their judging colleagues as rigid and intolerant. Neither type deserves such harsh labels. Both types will take their responsibilities seriously and get the job done. You can motivate judgers by assuring them that the group will make a decision that includes a detailed implementation plan. You can motivate perceivers by assuring them that the group will take time to reconsider decisions and make midcourse adjustments if needed.

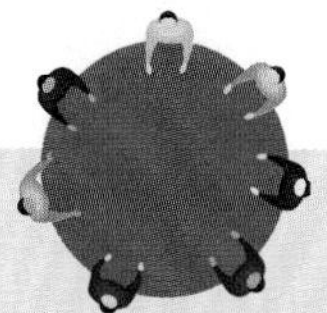

theory in groups

Expectancy-Value Theory of Motivation

Expectancy-Value Theory claims that motivation results from a combination of two factors: (1) the value of the goal to individual members and (2) the likelihood or expectation of obtaining the goal.[1] Thus, even when a goal is highly valued (becoming a famous rock star, inventing the next computer operating system, captaining a spaceship), you may not be highly motivated to pursue that goal if your chance of reaching it is very small. If a group has a shared goal that everyone values, and if the chances of achieving that goal are good, group motivation should provide the level of commitment and energy needed to achieve it.

Expectancy-Value Theory claims that motivation is a function of three perceptions: expectancy, instrumentality, and valence.

- *Expectancy:* the probability that effort will produce a desired outcome (If our class group works hard and plans well, we will do a good job on this assignment.)
- *Instrumentality:* whether achieving a desired result will result in a reward or benefit (If we do a good job on this assignment, we'll earn an A in this course.)
- *Valence:* the value you place on the reward (Do we care whether we get an A? Is it worth the effort?)

If any of these three perceptions is missing, motivation will also be missing. For example, even if your group works hard and believes that their hard work will earn them an A, a majority of members may not think that earning an A is worth the effort—and, thus, will not be motivated to put in the work necessary to get a good grade.[2]

The following guidelines can help you use Expectancy-Value Theory principles to motivate group members:

- Make sure members understand and accept a realistic, but challenging, group goal.
- Make sure rewards are attainable and are sufficient to motivate group members.
- Recognize individual differences or preferences. For example, whereas a risky or complex assignment might motivate one group member, another may prefer routine tasks. In collectivist cultures, recognizing someone in front of the group could be inappropriate and embarrassing.[3]

[1]See Herbert L. Petri, *Motivation: Theory, Research, and Applications,* 4th ed. (Pacific Grove, GA: Brooks/Cole, 1996), pp. 245–54; Martin Fishbein and Icek Ajzen, *Belief, Intention, and Behavior* (Reading, MA: Addison-Wesley, 1975); Julien B. Rotter, "Generalized Expectancies for Internal Versus External Control of Reinforcement," *Psychological Monographs* 80 (1966), pp. 1–28.

[2]Fishbein and Ajzen; Rotter, 1–28; Petri, pp. 245–254. See also "Expectancy Theory," *Quick MBA,* available at www.quickmba.com/mgmt/expectancy-theory.

[3]Andrew J. DuBrin, *Leadership: Research Findings, Practice, and Skills,* 4th ed. (New York: Houghton Mifflin, 2004), pp. 293–296.

Group Motivation

In addition to motivating individual group members, there are theories, methods, and tools for motivating groups as a whole. In *Intrinsic Motivation at Work,* Kenneth Thomas describes four categories of motivators needed to energize and reinforce an entire group (see also Figure 6.2 on page 145).

- A **sense of meaningfulness**—the shared feeling that the group is pursuing a worthy task
- A **sense of choice**—the shared feeling that the group has the power and ability to make decisions about how to organize and do its job
- A **sense of competence**—the shared feeling that your group is doing good, high-quality work on a task
- A **sense of progress**—the shared feeling that the group is accomplishing something[10]

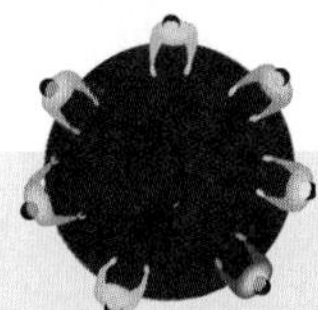

groups in balance . . .
Motivate Culturally Diverse Members

In Chapter 4, Group Diversity, we describe six cultural dimensions, each of which has implications for group members' motivation. Here we suggest ways to balance and adapt motivational strategies to culturally diverse members.

- *Individualism–collectivism.* Individualistic members may need and seek public recognition and praise for personal achievement. Members with a collectivist perspective may be embarrassed by public praise and prefer being honored as a member of an outstanding group.
- *High power distance–low power distance.* Members from high-power-distance cultures value recognition by a leader and take pride in following instructions accurately and efficiently. Members from low-power-distance cultures prefer compliments from other group members and enjoy working in a more independent and collaborative environment.
- *High uncertainty avoidance–low uncertainty avoidance.* Members who avoid uncertainty and change are motivated when a group follows tried-and-true ways of doing things. Something that is new and different may frighten and even *de*motivate them. Members with low uncertainty avoidance view uncertainty and change as stimulating and energizing. What is new and different is motivating.[1]
- *Masculine–feminine.* Members—both male and female—who hold masculine values are motivated by competitive goals, opportunities for leadership, and tasks that require assertive behavior. Members with more feminine values may be extremely effective and supportive of group goals but have difficulty achieving a respected voice or influence in the group. Such members are motivated by taking on group maintenance roles, such as encourager-supporter, harmonizer, compromiser, or tension releaser.
- *High context–low context.* Group members from high-context cultures do not need to *hear* someone praise their work—they are highly skilled at detecting admiration and approval because they are more sensitive to nonverbal cues. Members from low-context cultures often complain that they never receive praise or rewards when, in fact, other members respect them and value their contributions. Low-context members need to hear words of praise and receive tangible rewards.
- *Monochronic–polychronic.* Members from monochronic cultures are motivated in groups that concentrate their energies on a specific task and that meet deadlines. Members from polychronic cultures often find the single-mindedness of monochronic members stifling rather than motivating. Giving polychronic members the opportunity to work on multiple tasks with flexible deadlines can motivate them to work more effectively.

[1]Lee Gardenswartz and Anita Rowe, *Diverse Teams at Work: Capitalizing on the Power of Diversity* (New York: McGraw-Hill, 1994), p. 133.

A Sense of Meaningfulness

Groups are more motivated when they work toward meaningful and achievable goals. During this process, members need feedback that tells them whether their efforts are contributing to the group's goal.[11] In short, and as Expectancy-Value Theory suggests (see Theory in Groups box, "Expectancy-Value Theory of Motivation" on page 143), highly motivated groups believe that the job is worth doing and that they are capable of getting it done.[12]

Whether your group is setting out to climb Mt. Everest, planning a homecoming rally, or establishing a new product line, you should have a clear and elevated goal supported by every member of the group. History teaches us that groups will expend enormous amounts of energy to pursue worthy goals. People have guarded secrets,

Figure 6.2 Thomas's Intrinsic Motivators in Action

endured hardships, and fought and died for causes when they believed that those causes were worthwhile. You can help promote a sense of meaningfulness in your group by

- expressing enthusiasm, and not being cynical about the group's work.
- learning what motivates you as an individual and what motivates the other members of your group.
- understanding what the group is capable of accomplishing and discussing those capabilities with your group.
- volunteering for group tasks that interest you.

A sense of meaningfulness is especially important in volunteer groups. Here's what one student wrote after participating in a service-learning project with members of his class:

> This project went well because the cause was such a great one; everyone was willing to work equally hard on it, despite their busy schedules. There were a few times when some were more motivated than others were, but when it came time to actually collect the canned foods, our group jelled so solidly that it became one of the great experiences that some only dream about. We felt purposeful and became satisfied with each other and with ourselves; we were extremely proud of our group and individual efforts.

A Sense of Choice

In addition to sharing a worthy goal, motivated groups develop a plan for getting to that goal. They engage in critical thinking and choose agreed-upon strategies for achieving their goal. Every member knows what she or he is expected to do. Members communicate frequently in an effort to share information, discuss issues, and

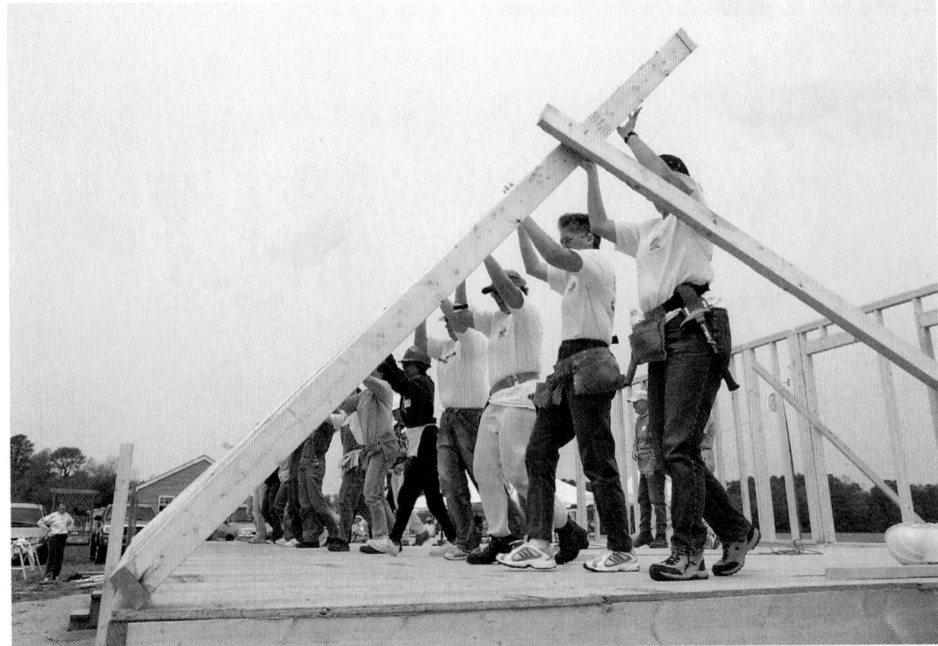

Group members are more motivated when they work toward meaningful and achievable goals. What specific strategies can help promote a sense of meaningfulness in various types of groups?

make decisions.[13] Highly motivated teams choose appropriate strategies for achieving worthwhile and attainable goals. You can help promote a sense of choice by

- letting members make decisions about how the group does its work
- demonstrating that the group can exercise authority responsibly
- accepting the inevitability of making mistakes when exploring innovative approaches.
- seeking and taking advantage of new opportunities

When group members have the power to make decisions, they are motivated by a greater sense of personal control and responsibility.

A Sense of Competence

Motivated groups need more than a clear goal and strategies for achieving that goal. They also need competent group members who are ready, willing, and able to perform the tasks necessary to achieve their common goal. For example, if group work and discussions are disorganized, someone will step in as a facilitator, procedural technician, or gatekeeper. If enthusiasm fades, someone will assume the role of energizer or encourager-supporter. If conflict erodes motivation, someone will function as a harmonizer, compromiser, or tension releaser.

Group members who cannot perform the tasks and roles required by the group may feel overwhelmed and defeated before they begin. You can help promote a sense of competence in your group by

- providing constructive feedback to group members and listening to their feedback.
- recognizing rather than minimizing the value of your skills.
- complimenting other group members' abilities and achievements.
- setting high standards for yourself and others.

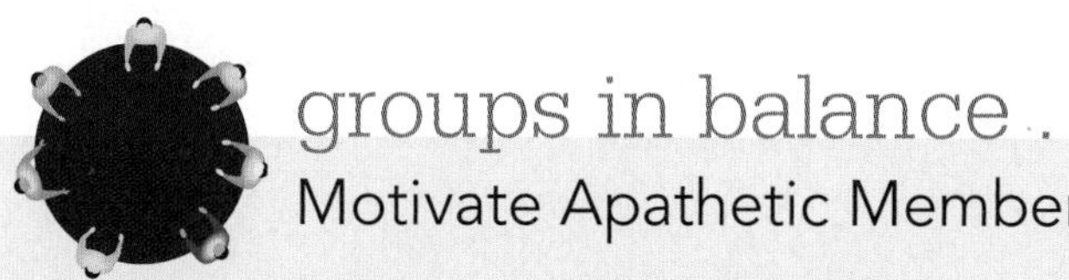

groups in balance . . .
Motivate Apathetic Members

Member apathy can derail a *both/and* approach to the engaged ↔ disengaged dialectic. **Apathy**—the most visible symptom of an unmotivated group—is the indifference that occurs when members do not consider the group or its goal important, interesting, or inspiring. Group motivators—meaningfulness, choice, competence, and progress—are minimal or missing. As Expectancy-Value Theory predicts, members exhibit signs of apathy when the group does not meet their personal needs and expectations. You can lose your motivation if your ideas are blocked or the group takes too much time with what seem to be meaningless tasks. If it appears that your group cannot reach its goal or that it requires too much time and energy, you may disengage rather than tackle a seemingly impossible task.

Dealing with group or member apathy depends on correctly diagnosing its cause. If a group's goal does not meet members' expectations, ask yourself questions such as: Does the goal meet member and group needs? Is it meaningful, inspiring, visionary? Is there a reasonable plan for achieving the goal? Is the group capable of achieving it?

Sometimes members are unsure of how they can contribute. Assigning specific responsibilities to members based on their needs, interests, and skills can increase their commitment to and involvement in the group. Apathetic members may not necessarily be uninterested or lazy; they may be intimidated or frustrated. Help them by finding something that they are ready, willing, and able to do.

Sometimes confronting apathy head-on is the only way to deal with apathetic members or groups. Bring up the issue and talk about it. For example, asking an entire group why it seems bogged down or talking privately with an apathetic member can uncover causes and generate solutions.

Group members create a sense of competence by recognizing and praising one another's abilities and contributions. Groups that feel confident about the value of their abilities will be motivated to put their skills to work.

A Sense of Progress

"How are we doing?" is an important question for all groups. It's difficult for members to stay motivated throughout the life of a group if they have no idea whether the group is making progress toward its goal. A well-chosen, structured goal should be measurable. Motivated groups "create good, objective measurements that people can relate to their specific behavior."[14] In the upcoming section on assessment and feedback, we offer several ways of measuring group effectiveness and progress.

You and your group can provide a sense of progress by

- developing a group method of tracking and measuring progress.
- looking for collaborative ways to resolve group difficulties.
- monitoring and, if needed, finding ways to sustain group motivation at various points in the work process.
- recognizing and celebrating group accomplishments.

Assessment and Feedback

How do you know whether your group is *both* motivated *and* making progress? At times, a highly motivated group may do a job enthusiastically but still not achieve its goal. Groups need regular assessment and constructive feedback to determine whether they are doing good work and making progress.

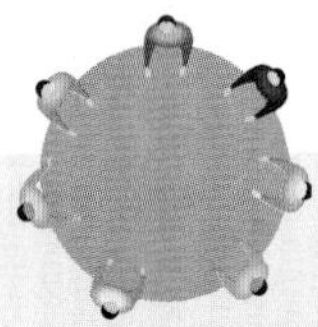

virtual groups
Mediated Motivation

Motivating "real" groups is complicated and challenging. Motivating virtual groups adds new dialectic tensions to an already complicated challenge. Whereas technically skilled group members may thrive in virtual groups, members new to virtual interaction may struggle with new technologies, new behaviors, and new work relationships. Whereas some group members communicate more confidently and effectively in virtual groups, others are intimidated or use it as an easy way to avoid participating. For example, in an audioconference, you can engage a speakerphone and do other work while half-listening to a less-than-exciting discussion. By making an occasional supportive comment, you may sound as though you're involved in the interaction, even though your attention is a million miles away. In computer-mediated discussions—whether synchronous or asynchronous—you can ignore comments made by other group members, withhold your own comments, or not respond at all. When other group members aren't physically present and able to look at you, you may find it easy to disengage and disappear.

Here are several methods and tools designed to make working in virtual groups a more rewarding and motivating experience:[1]

- If possible, schedule a face-to-face orientation meeting with all members of the virtual group—even if it means spending time and money. Use the orientation meeting to agree on or to clarify the group's goal, to develop mutual respect and trust, to explain how and when to use technology, to agree on norms for interaction, and to build motivation.
- Provide a detailed agenda well in advance of a scheduled virtual meeting, along with any resources and online documents needed to prepare for the meeting.
- Make a special effort to adapt to members' needs, personality preferences, and cultural differences. Consider questions such as: Do members who prefer to focus on facts become lost in wide-ranging online discussions? Do members have enough time to think about information before they must comment or make decisions? Make sure that everyone contributes. Go "around the room" virtually. Ask each person to comment or express an opinion. Assign specific tasks and/or roles to group members to stimulate interaction and motivation.
- Use technology such as group editing, collaborative writing, bulletin boards, and online voting to obtain "buy-in" from everyone.
- Structure the meeting so that members can come in and out of it according to their need to obtain information or offer input. Don't make members endure prolonged discussions that have little or nothing to do with their interests or talents.

[1]Deborah L. Duarte and Nancy Tennant T. Snyder, *Mastering Virtual Teams: Strategies, Tools, and Techniques That Succeed*, 3rd ed. (San Francisco: Jossey-Bass, 2006), pp. 170–172.

The Role of Assessment

Assessment is a mechanism for monitoring group progress and a way of determining whether a group has achieved its goals. Rather than viewing assessment negatively as an evaluation system designed to determine or withhold group rewards, use assessment to answer questions about how well the group is doing and how it can improve its performance.

Regardless of whether you belong to a group of community volunteers or the management team in a multinational corporation, assessment serves a variety of purposes:[15]

- to motivate work performance
- to inform members about their job performance
- to clarify the job to be done
- to encourage increased competence and growth

- to enhance and improve communication
- to correct problems
- to encourage responsibility

Throughout this textbook, we include assessment instruments at the end of every chapter. Many of these instruments measure variables related to group motivation. Table 6.2 summarizes selected instruments that assess various aspects of group motivation.

Assessment instruments can help determine how well a group is progressing toward its goal and whether interpersonal or procedural problems are impeding its effectiveness. Using assessment instruments, however, is not the only way in which a group can determine whether it is making progress. Face-to-face discussions about a group's progress can be just as effective.

The Role of Feedback

In *Encouraging the Heart,* James Kouzes and Barry Posner note, "Goals without feedback, and feedback without goals, have little effect on motivation."[16] Feedback "requires us to get close to people, show that we care about them, and demonstrate that we are interested in others."[17]

Feedback can motivate or discourage a group, depending on whether it is controlling or informational. **Controlling feedback** tells people what to do, whereas

Table 6.2 Group Assessment Instruments

Chapter	Instrument	Motivational Assessment
Chapter 1: Introduction to Group Communication	Essential Group Elements (p. 26)	Assesses whether a group embodies the five basic elements needed to work in groups.
Chapter 2: Group Development	How Good Is Your Goal? (p. 49)	Assesses the extent to which a group has a worthwhile and achievable goal.
Chapter 4: Group Diversity	Group Diversity Awareness Questionnaire (p. 103)	Assesses the group's willingness and ability to understand, respect, and adapt to cultural differences.
Chapter 5: Group Leadership	Are You Ready to Lead? (p. 134)	Assesses whether a member is motivated to become a group leader.
Chapter 6: Group Motivation	The Engagement Index *and* the Group Motivation Inventory (pp. 159, 160)	Assesses members' level of engagement and their motivation level in a current or previous group.
Chapter 8: Listening in Groups	Student Listening Inventory (p. 207)	Assesses member attitudes (their *motivation* to listen) as well as their knowledge and skills.
Chapter 9: Conflict and Cohesion in Groups	Ross-DeWine Conflict Management Message Style Instrument (p. 231)	Assesses whether group members are motivated to help the group resolve substantive conflict.
Chapter 11: Critical Thinking and Argumentation in Groups	Argumentativeness Scale (p. 290)	Assesses whether group members enjoy and are motivated to engage in argumentation.

informational feedback tells people how they are doing. Although both forms of feedback can be positive or negative, informational feedback works much better.[18] For example, a manager who reminds group members that their performance evaluations will affect their job security is providing controlling feedback. In effect, the manager is saying, "If you don't do better, you may lose your job." You can also word controlling feedback in positive terms: "If you continue to make such good progress, you may earn a bonus." Even so, controlling feedback, whether negative or positive, imposes a leader's or outside authority's will on the group instead of tapping factors that intrinsically motivate group members.

Informational feedback is any feedback that tells a group how well it's doing and to what extent it's achieving the group's goal.[19] Whereas controlling feedback emphasizes the power to reward or punish performance, informational feedback focuses on the group's work and how that work contributes to group success.

"It" Statements. You can provide constructive, informational feedback by avoiding "you" statements, which imply "you messed up" or "you failed." Instead, provide feedback using "it" statements. "You" statements suggest a personal opinion about a person or the members of a group, while "it" statements talk about how the group is working and progressing, not about how members are doing or what you feel about them.[20] Which of the following statements would you rather hear: "You're way behind schedule," or "It looks as though we will miss our deadline"? The following guidelines can help you use "it" statements to provide informational feedback.

- "It" statements avoid using the word *you* when describing individual or group behavior.
- "It" statements focus on the task rather than on individual group members.
- "It" statements are based on objective information about the group's work.
- "It" statements answer the question "How is *it* going?" rather than "How am *I* doing?"[21]

Reprimands. Sometimes positive and informational feedback fails to motivate group members or to correct a problem. Rather than punishing a group or individual members, consider using a reprimand. **Reprimands** are not punishments; they are a form of feedback that identifies work-related problems or deficiencies. Think of it this way: A reprimand is similar to a driver's warning ticket. Before reprimanding a group member or a group as a whole, make sure that you can answer the following questions:[22]

- Are you certain that you have all the facts concerning the situation?
- Has the group or member been reprimanded previously for the same problem?
- Are group members aware of the rules or standards that have been violated?
- Will the reprimand benefit the group or be counterproductive?
- Were other groups or group members involved in the incident?
- Was the infraction intentional, an honest mistake, or a matter beyond the member's or group's control?
- Was this a personal problem or a group-based problem?

Depending on how you answer these questions, you may discover that a reprimand is not necessary or that it only represents the first step toward correcting a serious problem. If a reprimand is appropriate, make sure that you follow the guidelines for constructive feedback.

Your comments should be informational and should be phrased as "it" statements rather than as "you" statements. Most important of all, the reprimand must be fair

and impersonal. Regardless of the infraction, you should make it perfectly clear that the reprimand involves something a member *did,* not who the member *is.*

Rewards

A **reward** is something you give or get for excellent service, outstanding achievements, or worthy behavior. Groups and their members receive rewards when they contribute and progress toward achieving their common goal. Certainly, the *prospect* of receiving a reward can motivate individual group members and the group as a whole. However, in many cases, motivation may have little or nothing to do with rewards.

Extrinsic and Intrinsic Rewards

Why do you go to work? One obvious answer is that you work to earn money. The money you earn allows you to live comfortably and securely. If you earn a lot of money, you can enjoy a luxurious life. There's a second answer to this question, though. Many of us work because we like what we do, get satisfaction from our accomplishments, and enjoy the company and friendship of colleagues.

Extrinsic Rewards. **Extrinsic rewards** come from the "external environment in which we live."[23] They include the money we earn and the benefits and perks that come with a job. Most extrinsic rewards don't come from groups; they are doled out by supervisors. Money and work benefits are extrinsic rewards that satisfy our most basic needs—physiological and safety needs. Depending on the size of the extrinsic rewards, they also can satisfy esteem needs. Extrinsic rewards, however, do not

Firefighter John Horican is congratulated by his co-workers after receiving an award during the Fire Department of New York's Medal Day ceremony held at City Hall. What kinds of needs do such extrinsic rewards satisfy? How well do extrinsic rewards motivate groups to work together in pursuit of a common goal?

The Lady Tigers at Greenfield High School, Illinois, celebrate their win for the regional championship. What intrinsic rewards motivate team members to work for victory or achieve a common goal?

motivate groups to work together in pursuit of a common goal. They do not appeal to members' passions, nor do they demand much of members' collective intelligence and expertise.[24]

Intrinsic Rewards. In the opinion of many researchers and human relations experts, we put too much emphasis on extrinsic rewards and not enough emphasis on their counterpart—intrinsic rewards. R. Brayton Bowen gives us a broad definition of intrinsic rewards. An **intrinsic reward,** he writes, is "anything that is satisfying and energizing in itself."[25] Completing a challenging project can provide intrinsic rewards. So can participating in a retreat with respected colleagues or representing your organization at a professional or public event. In most groups, intrinsic rewards have more power than do extrinsic rewards.

Researchers studying employee effectiveness emphasize the power of intrinsic rewards. One survey examining employee turnover found that the chief reason people give for leaving a job has nothing to do with salaries and benefits. When asked why they are leaving, the need for praise and recognition rises to the top. Employees rate "the ability to recognize and acknowledge the contributions of others as the skill their managers need to develop."[26] In *Recognizing and Rewarding Employees,* Bowen describes motivation as an "inside" job—no one can make you do something against your will. The decision to act is yours. Bowen also notes, "You can't buy motivation. It has to come from within."[27]

How, then, do you reward an individual or a group? It's not a simple process or decision. Rewards must be attractive to group members.[28] Thus, a person who receives a bonus of $500 when she is expecting $5,000 may greet the reward with disgust. A person rewarded with the prestigious assignment of chairing a major work team may not be grateful if the group is composed of incompetent or disagreeable members. Given that most of us enjoy receiving rewards and sincere appreciation from others, groups face the challenge of finding the right rewards and reward system for the right reasons.[29]

Rewards are meaningless and even resented if "who you know" is more important in determining them than the quantity and quality of the work you do. Rewards are just as meaningless and resented when everyone receives the same rewards—both those who deserve them and those who don't. Rewards should be associated with worthy behavior and should be determined fairly or they will fail to motivate groups and their members.

Objective Rewards

Groups or leaders with "the power" to reward should consider four criteria when developing a reward system for their groups: The rewards should be fair, equitable, competitive, and appropriate.[30]

Fair. The reward should be fair; more work and more risk deserve more rewards. Someone who exerts little effort and takes few risks should not get the same reward

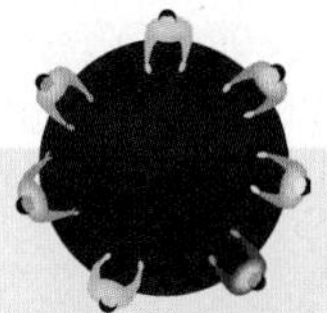

groups in balance . . .
Use Power to Reward

Power is the ability or authority to influence and motivate others. In Chapter 5, Group Leadership, we discuss the various types of a leader's power: reward, coercive, legitimate, expert, referent, informational, persuasive, and charismatic. A leader may use one or more of these types of power to motivate a group to complete a goal.

A leader may reward members for their good work or punish them for not performing well. However, leaders who rely on rewards to motivate group members may be in for a rude awakening. The group, not the leader, must see the reward as appropriate and worthwhile.

A leader with legitimate power can order groups to perform tasks but may not be able to count on members to accept those tasks with dedication and enthusiasm. Leaders with referent, expert, informational, persuasive, or charismatic power are more likely to motivate their members. In these cases, the leader is either a role model or an expert who has earned the admiration of group members. When leaders use coercive power to punish, discipline, demote, or dismiss group members, groups may do nothing more than "stay out of trouble."

as more productive and inventive members. Because many leaders and groups do not want to disappoint or upset group members, they may give the same rewards to everyone when, in fact, only a few members did most of the work responsible for the group's success. Fairness requires us to give rewards to those who have earned them.

Equitable. The reward system should be equitable. This does not mean giving the same rewards to everyone. Being equitable means giving everyone an equal opportunity to earn rewards. If the group's leader is the only one who receives a reward for the group's performance, members will lose their motivation. If each member does not have an equal opportunity to earn rewards, group morale may deteriorate. The group may become less productive or, even worse, counterproductive.

Competitive. The rewards should be competitive and similar to the rewards given to others who do the same kind of work; intergroup competition should be fair and based on objective standards. If your group achieves the same goal as another group, the reward should be the same. If the group next door earns an all-expenses-paid vacation to a fancy resort, and your group gets a $50 Wal-Mart coupon, the reward system will not work.

Appropriate. The rewards should be appropriate for the achievement. A simple thank-you note for a job well done may be an appropriate reward for a simple task. A thank-you note will not work if the task was complex, difficult, stressful, and critical to the success of a company or organization. Think of it this way: What potential reward would you offer as a pre-task motivator: "If you finish this eighteen-month project on time, I'll send you a thank-you note," or "If you finish this eighteen-month project on time, I'll make sure that each of you receives a bonus that equals 10 percent of your salary"?

Effective Rewards

Rewards range from taking the time to shake a colleague's hand to offering valuable stock options. The list of potential rewards is almost endless, given the many

An intergenerational, multi-ethnic group of men and women pose with their Proclamation award for participating in Easter Seals Intergenerational Day in Miami, Florida. What are the benefits, rewards, and motivational factors that lead us to join together with others in order to achieve a worthy goal? How effectively do group versus individual rewards affect member motivation?

different ways in which you can compensate or show your appreciation to fellow group members.[31]

Here, we've divided rewards into two forms: personal recognition and material compensation. No matter what rewards you use, make sure that they are meaningful and appropriate for the individual or group that you are rewarding.

Personal Recognition. Most of us crave recognition for a job well done. Unfortunately, few of us receive the encouragement we need. One study found that about 40 percent of North American workers report that they *never* receive recognition for outstanding individual performance.[32]

Individual members and groups as a whole want and need recognition. The following suggestions are only a few of the many ways to reward a team and its members:

- letters of praise, thanks, and recognition
- public recognition at a major event or meeting
- individual and group awards for achievement
- public display of a group's product or accomplishment
- video or newsletter articles about the group and its achievements
- giveaway rewards such as team T-shirts, pen sets, or achievement pins
- public signs or a prize for group achievement, such as "Team of the Month," "Most Valuable Team Member," or "Best Team Spirit"
- recognition parties, luncheons, and dinners
- time or days off

All of these suggestions celebrate individual and group achievements. In their book *Corporate Celebration,* Terrence Deal and M. K. Key argue that "celebration is an integral element of culture, and . . . provides the symbolic adhesive that welds a community together.[33] In one study, researchers found that high-performing groups frequently hosted celebratory events to express recognition and appreciation.[34]

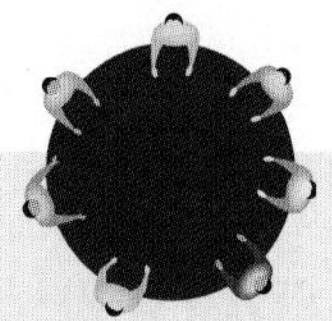

groups in balance . . .
Reward Members with Affection

What quality separates highly effective, best-performing leaders from less effective leaders? A study conducted by the Center for Creative Leadership found that a high score on Schutz's affection scale was the *only* factor differentiating top managers from those rated as least effective. "Contrary to the myth of the coldhearted boss who cares very little about people's feelings, the highest-performing managers show more warmth and fondness toward others than do the bottom 25 percent."[1]

James Kouzes and Barry Posner put it this way: We all really do want to be loved.[2] Very few of us doubt the importance of this need in our most personal relationships. Then why should we doubt it with regard to our relationships in groups? When we believe that our colleagues like us, we feel better about ourselves. We also look forward to working with people who like us. Sharing affection with other group members is not about hugging, dating, or intimacy. Sharing your affection involves a willingness to be open with other group members—to share your feelings with them. At the same time, we recognize that expressing affection must be balanced with recognizing task-focused work. Rewards that appeal to both the head and the heart can make a significant contribution to group motivation and productivity.

[1]James M. Kouzes and Barry Z. Posner, *Encouraging the Heart: A Leader's Guide to Rewarding and Recognizing Others* (San Francisco: Jossey-Bass, 1999), p. 9.

[2]Kouzes and Posner, p. 11.

Take time to celebrate. It's fun, and it can help motivate your group to new heights of achievement.

Material Compensation. In the world of work, most employers primarily rely on extrinsic rewards. These rewards take the form of material compensation for a job well done. Some of these rewards are costly, whereas others need only limited resources to implement. Here are some examples:

- salary bonuses and promotions
- larger and better-equipped offices
- paid attendance at professional seminars and meetings
- funds for special supplies, software, books, subscriptions, or professional memberships
- a group "retreat" devoted to anything but work
- office parties with award presentations
- lunch or dinner with staff and spouses
- mini-bonuses for reaching interim milestones
- tickets to theater and sporting events
- laptop computers, cell phones, BlackBerries

Many companies offer special perks to high-achieving individuals and teams. Such a "perk buffet"[35] might include a company car, an exclusive club membership, child care, a reserved parking place, box seats at a sporting event, or educational tuition and scholarships.

Always keep in mind that a group member's needs have a significant impact on the extent to which material rewards can motivate that person's behavior. For example, a new parent may value free child care more than membership in a country club. An individual may feel that working with friends is more important than working in a highly competitive, work-obsessed group.

The Role of Punishment

So far, we have not discussed the use of punishment as a motivational tool—and for a good reason: Punishment does not motivate. In fact, it *de*motivates. If the threat and use of punishment were effective ways to motivate people to behave properly and to do their jobs, our prison population would be low, students would never break rules, and parents would merely threaten punishment to transform unruly kids into perfect angels.

Punishment—subjecting a member to a penalty or negative consequences—is the opposite of motivation. When groups and their members are punished (denied advancement, recognition, resources, perks, and so on), they may spend more energy complaining, getting even, pursuing outside interests, or even sabotaging the work of others. The world's great animal trainers use positive reinforcement, not whippings and denials. Our human colleagues deserve the same humane treatment. There are some situations, however, in which a group member's behavior—despite multiple constructive feedback sessions and reprimands—is so disruptive or nonproductive that the group would be much better off without that person.

When a group or a member breaks a significant rule or law, do not overlook or minimize the problem. In such cases, the exclusion of a member from the group may be the "punishment that fits the crime." For example, John Sortino, the founder of the Vermont Teddy Bear Company, posts only three rules, but they are strictly enforced: No stealing, no lying, and all employees must follow the laws prohibiting discrimination, sexual harassment, and so forth. If a worker breaks one of these rules, that person is out of a job.[36]

ethics in groups
Using Power and Punishment

The decision to punish a group member has ethical consequences. Punishing a member is unethical if used to suppress differences of opinion or penalize opponents. A group behaves unethically if it refuses to listen to, understand, and respect other members before judging and punishing them. Ethical groups promote a communication climate of caring and mutual understanding that respects the unique needs and characteristics of individuals rather than punishing or excluding members who are different or disagreeable.

If you and your group decide that someone deserves to be punished, the punishment should be predictable (everyone should know the rules/expectations), immediate (applied as soon as possible after notice of the violation), consistent (applied equally to all), and impersonal.[1] The following guidelines may help you apply these four standards:

1. Make sure that everyone has the same understanding of the rules. Don't punish someone who is unaware of the group's norms and policies.
2. Make sure that the rules apply to everyone and are enforced equally.
3. Make sure that a policy is in place for dealing with those who violate the rules. Don't make up a policy and assign punishments as you go along.
4. Make sure that you enforce all the rules—all the time. To do less may damage your respect among group members.[2]

[1]Michael Ramundo with Susan Shelly, *The Complete Idiot's Guide to Motivating People* (Indianapolis, IN: Alpha Books, 2000), p. 187.

[2]Ramundo, p. 183.

When our students worked as interns at Walt Disney World, they had to follow three no-exceptions rules: (1) You cannot miss more than a specified number of mandatory training sessions, (2) a person of the opposite sex may not be in your Disney apartment after a specified hour at night, and (3) you may not use illegal drugs. An intern breaking any of these rules would be sent home immediately.

The three rules at the Vermont Teddy Bear Company and at Walt Disney World set expectations and standards, but they do not motivate. All workers know that crossing these lines of behavior will result in the ultimate punishment: immediate dismissal.

summary study guide

The Role of Motivation

- Group motivation provides the inspiration, incentives, and reasons that move group members to work together to achieve a common goal.
- To achieve an optimal group experience, the group must balance many dialectic tensions, especially the task dimension ↔ social dimension and engaged ↔ disengaged dialectics.

Member Motivation

- Groups are more motivated when individual member needs are also met by working with the group.
- In terms of understanding group motivation, Maslow's five needs can be divided into satisfiers (physiological and safety needs) and motivators (belongingness, esteem, and self-actualization needs).
- Schutz's Theory of Interpersonal Needs suggests that members are motivated to work toward the group's goal when their individual needs for inclusion, control, and affection are satisfied.
- Expectancy-Value Theory claims that motivation results from (1) the value of the goal to individual members and (2) the likelihood or expectation of obtaining the goal.
- Each of the four Myers-Briggs personality type categories responds to different motivators. Understanding different personality types can help you choose the most effective motivational strategies.

Group Motivation

- Members are motivated when they have a sense of meaningfulness—a shared feeling that the group's goal is a worthy task.
- Motivated groups have a sense of choice, or the feeling that they have the power and ability to make decisions about how to organize and accomplish the group's task.
- Members must feel a sense of competence—the belief that the group is doing quality work—to stay motivated toward the group's goal.
- Members remain motivated as long as they have a sense of progress.

Assessment and Feedback

- Assessment answers questions about how well the group is doing and how it can improve.
- Controlling feedback tells members what to do, whereas informational feedback tells people how they are doing. Informational feedback is more likely to motivate.
- Constructive informational feedback uses "it" statements rather than "you" statements, which often imply fault.
- Reprimands should be fair, impersonal, and in the form of constructive informational feedback.

Rewards

- Extrinsic rewards such as pay and benefits rarely motivate members to work together in pursuit of a common goal, whereas an intrinsic reward (anything that is satisfying in itself) motivates. The satisfaction of achieving a challenging and worthwhile goal is often a strong intrinsic motivator.
- Effective rewards must meet four objective criteria. Rewards must be fair, equitable, competitive, and appropriate.
- Rewards often take one of two forms—personal recognition (awards or letters of praise) or material compensation (such as a bonus or bigger office).
- The threat of punishment for failing to accomplish the group's goal rarely motivates members. Punishment should be reserved for members who continuously violate critical rules or expectations.

key terms

apathy 147
assessment 148
controlling feedback 149
Expectancy-Value Theory 143
extrinsic reward 151
group motivation 138
informational feedback 150
intrinsic reward 152
motivators 140
optimal group experience 138
punishment 156
reprimand 150
reward 151
satisfiers 140
sense of choice 143
sense of competence 143
sense of meaningfulness 143
sense of progress 143

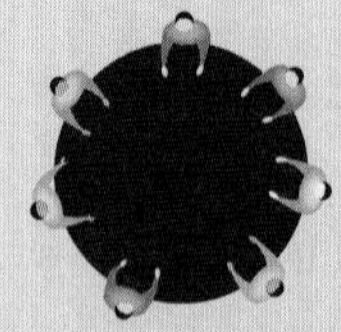

critical thinking about the case study

Veni, Vidi, Vici

1. Was Faith able to motivate members to work collectively toward achieving the group's goal? Why or why not?
2. To what extent were task force members motivated by a sense of meaningfulness, a sense of choice, a sense of competence, and a sense of progress?
3. How, if at all, did extrinsic rewards motivate task force members?
4. How well did Faith use the power to reward as a group motivator? Were these rewards fair, equitable, competitive, and appropriate?
5. How did Faith describe the potential negative consequences if the task force did not develop recommendations for improving patient care? To what extent were group members motivated to achieve the task force's goal in order to avoid a negative outcome?
6. To what extent would the threat of punishment have increased task force motivation?
7. Which dialectic tensions were most evident in the hospital task force?

group work The Engagement Index

Directions: Write in the number that best describes how often you use each of the following behaviors when working in groups.

1 = Almost never 2 = Seldom 3 = Sometimes 4 = Usually 5 = Almost always

Item	Your Score	Behavior
1.	_______	I personally congratulate and thank members for a job well done.
2.	_______	I express a positive outlook even when times are tough.
3.	_______	I pay more attention to the positive things members do than the negative ones.
4.	_______	I get to know, at a personal level, the group members with whom I work.
5.	_______	I spend time listening to the needs, interests, and concerns of other group members.
6.	_______	I carefully watch members' nonverbal behavior to understand what they mean and how they feel.
7.	_______	I express high expectations about what our group can accomplish.
8.	_______	I work to set high standards that motivate us to do better in the future than we are doing now.
9.	_______	I celebrate member and group accomplishments.
10.	_______	I find ways to make our work enjoyable and fun.
	_______	TOTAL (Add together all your rating numbers)

Score Interpretation

40–50: You are a great motivator. Group members like working with you. They feel appreciated and good about the contributions they're making.

30–39: You're doing well as a motivator. Group members are generally happy working with you, but you may feel as though you could do more to motivate and encourage them. Try to overcome your uneasiness about praising and helping others.

20–29: You understand the need for motivation but may not know how or feel uncomfortable doing it. Try to pay more attention to member achievements and recognize them in some way. Begin with small gestures until you feel comfortable celebrating and inspiring others more enthusiastically.

10–19: Your score may not really be this low. Perhaps you should give yourself more credit for supporting other group members—even if it's in small ways. Try to understand how important encouragement is to other people. Maybe you can team up with another member to plan ways of recognizing and appreciating others. Rather than intimidating or trying to control others, try kindness and encouragement instead.

Source: This instrument is a modified version of "The Encouragement Index" in James M. Kouzes and Barry Z. Posner, *Encouraging the Heart: A Leader's Guide to Rewarding and Recognizing Others* (San Francisco: Jossey-Bass, 1999), pp. 35–37. For score interpretation, pp. 38–41.

group assessment Group Motivation Inventory

Directions: This instrument assesses the motivation level of a group of which you are currently a member or in which you have worked in the past. Use the following scale to assign a number to each statement:

5 = strongly agree   4 = agree   3 = neutral   2 = disagree   1 = strongly disagree

_____ 1. I work very hard in my group.
_____ 2. I work harder in this group than I do in most other groups.
_____ 3. Other members work very hard in this group.
_____ 4. I am willing to spend extra time on group projects.
_____ 5. I try to attend all group meetings.
_____ 6. Other members regularly attend group meetings.
_____ 7. I often lose track of time when I'm working in this group.
_____ 8. Group members don't seem to mind working long hours on our project.
_____ 9. When I am working with this group, I am focused on our work.
_____ 10. I look forward to working with the members of my group.
_____ 11. I enjoy working with group members.
_____ 12. Group members enjoy working with one another.
_____ 13. I am doing an excellent job in my group.
_____ 14. I am doing better work in this group than I have done in other groups.
_____ 15. The other members are making excellent contributions to this group.
_____ 16. I am willing to do whatever this group needs in order to achieve our goal.
_____ 17. I trust the members of my group.
_____ 18. The other group members are willing to take on extra work.
_____ 19. I am proud of the work my group is doing.
_____ 20. I understand the importance of our group's work.
_____ 21. Everyone is committed to successfully achieving our goal.
_____ 22. I am proud of the contributions I have made to this group.
_____ 23. This group appreciates my work.
_____ 24. I am proud to be a member of this group.
_____ 25. This group really works well together.

Scoring and Interpretation: Add your ratings for all the statements.

Score Ranges	Interpretation	Questions for Analyzing Group Motivation
Below 75	Low Motivation	Does the group support a clear and elevated goal? Is the task too difficult or complex? Are member expectations unclear or unreasonable? Do some members make it difficult for others to participate? Are some members doing most of the interesting work, while others do routine assignments? Do some members feel left out or ignored?
75–99	Moderate Motivation	
Above 99	High Motivation	

Source: The Team Motivation Inventory acknowledges the contributions of other inventories, including the JML Inventory in Alexander Hiam, *Motivating and Rewarding Employees: New and Better Ways to Inspire Your People* (Holbrook, MA: Adams Media, 1999), and the Encouragement Index in James M. Kouzes and Barry Z. Posner, *Encouraging the Heart: A Leader's Guide to Rewarding and Recognizing Others* (San Francisco: Jossey-Bass, 1999).

notes

1. Kenneth W. Thomas, *Intrinsic Motivation at Work* (San Francisco: Berrett-Koehler, 2000), p. 3.
2. Alexander Hiam, *Motivating and Rewarding Employees: New and Better Ways to Inspire Your People* (Holbrook, MA: Adams Streetwise, 1999), p. 17.
3. Hiam, p. 17.
4. Ernest G. Bormann, *Small Group Communication: Theory and Practice* (Edina, MN: Burgess International Group, 1996), p. 86.
5. Herbert L. Petri, *Motivation: Theory, Research, and Applications*, 4th ed. (Pacific Grove, CA: Brooks/Cole, 1996), p. 320.
6. Douglas A. Bernstein et al., *Psychology* (Boston: Houghton Mifflin, 2001), p. 378.
7. Bormann, 90. See also Petri, pp. 321–328.
8. See Will Schutz, *The Human Element* (San Francisco: Jossey-Bass, 1994).
9. The following resources were used to develop the table of personality type motivators: Larry Damerest, *Looking at Type in the Workplace* (Gainesville, FL: Center for Applications of Psychological Type, 1997); Jean M. Kummerow, Nancy J. Barger, and Linda K. Kirby, *Work Types* (New York: Warner Books, 1997).
10. Thomas, p. 44.
11. Hiam, p. 152.
12. Eric Klinger, *Meaning and Void: Inner Experiences and the Incentives in People's Lives* (Minneapolis: University of Minnesota Press, 1997). Klinger provides a discussion of *meaningfulness* as a motivator. He claims that people pursue objects, events, and experiences that are emotionally important for them. However, individuals are not necessarily willing to work to obtain everything that has incentive value when the time and effort needed to obtain the goal are more than the individual is willing or able to expend.
13. Carl E. Larson and Frank M. LaFasto, *Team Work: What Must Go Right/What Can Go Wrong* (Newbury Park, CA: Sage, 1989), pp. 39–58.
14. Michael Ramundo with Susan Shelly, *The Complete Idiot's Guide to Motivating People* (Indianapolis, IN: Alpha Books, 2000), p. 86.
15. Deborah Harrington-Mackin, *The Team Building Tool Kit* (New York: AMACOM, 1994), pp. 118–119.
16. James M. Kouzes and Barry Z. Posner, *Encouraging the Heart: A Leader's Guide to Rewarding and Recognizing Others* (San Francisco: Jossey-Bass, 1999), pp. 54–55.
17. Kouzes and Posner, p. 59.
18. Hiam, p. 170.
19. Hiam, p. 178.
20. Hiam, p. 183.
21. Hiam, p. 183.
22. Based on strategies in Ramundo.
23. R. Brayton Bowen, *Recognizing and Rewarding Employees* (New York: McGraw-Hill, 2000), p. 179.
24. See Thomas, pp. 6–7.
25. Bowen, p. 163.
26. Kouzes and Posner, p. 13.
27. Bowen, p. 30.
28. Bormann, pp. 83–84.
29. Daniel Goleman, "In New Research, Optimism Emerges as the Key to a Successful Life," *New York Times*, December 24, 1991, p. 81.
30. For a discussion of reward criteria, see Bowen, p. 29; Bob Nelson and Dean R. Spitzer, *The 1001 Rewards and Recognition Fieldbook: The Complete Guide* (New York: Workman, 2003).
31. Many books offer long lists and numerous examples of rewards. See Bob Nelson and Dean Spitzer, *The 1001 Rewards and Recognition Fieldbook* (New York: Workman, 2003) and Bowen.
32. Kouzes and Posner, p. 4.
33. Terrence E. Deal and M. K. Key, *Corporate Celebration: Play, Purpose, and Profit at Work* (San Francisco: Berrett-Koehler, 1998), p. 11.
34. Quoted in Kouzes and Posner, p. 114, from M. O. James et al., "Performing Well: The Impact of Rituals, Celebrations, and Networks of Support" (paper presented at the Western Academy of Management Conference, California).
35. Hiam, pp. 245–247.
36. Ramundo, p. 182.

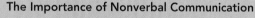

chapter 7

Verbal and Nonverbal Communication in Groups

chapter outline

Two Essential Tools

Language and Meaning

Denotation and Connotation • Levels of Meaning

Team Talk

The Dimensions of Team Talk • Use "I," "You," and "We" Language

Language Challenges

Language Difficulties • Language Differences

The Importance of Nonverbal Communication

Nonverbal Behavior

Personal Appearance • Facial Expression and Eye Contact • Vocal Expression • Physical Expression

The Nonverbal Environment

Arrangement of Space • Perceptions of Personal Space

Nonverbal Communication and Culture

Creating a Supportive Communication Climate

study questions

- *What is the relationship between verbal and nonverbal communication?*
- *Why do the meanings of words differ from person to person?*
- *How does team talk help groups achieve their goals?*
- *How can groups overcome language-based challenges?*
- *Why is nonverbal communication important in groups?*
- *In what ways does nonverbal behavior affect group effectiveness?*
- *How does the arrangement and use of space affect group effectiveness?*
- *How do diverse cultures use nonverbal cues differently?*
- *How can you resolve the dialectic tensions that affect group climate?*

Two Essential Tools

Every group member uses verbal and nonverbal communication to create messages that generate meaning. **Verbal communication** focuses on how you use words and language. Communication may be "face to face, fax to fax, over the phone, or through electronic mail, but regardless of the channel used, groups do their work through language."[1] Without language, you cannot have a group discussion; you cannot follow an agenda, take minutes, read a report, or interact effectively with other group members. Linguists Victoria Fromkin and Robert Rodman note, "Whatever else people do when they come together—whether they play, fight, make love, or make automobiles, they talk. We live in a world of language."[2]

The other essential communication tool, nonverbal communication, is just as important as language. **Nonverbal communication** refers to message components other than words that generate meaning. Without the nonverbal component, it would be difficult to interpret the meaning of spoken language. Tone of voice, directness of eye contact, and physical proximity of group members can reveal at least as much about their thoughts and feelings as the words they speak. Some researchers claim that we convey as much as two-thirds of our meaning through nonverbal behavior.[3] Generally, group members use words to express the content of a message and use nonverbal behavior to express the emotional element of a message.[4]

In dialectic terms, effective group members rely on *both* verbal *and* nonverbal communication to generate meaning in *both* homogeneous *and* heterogeneous groups. For example, as you know from Chapter 4, Group Diversity, people in high-context cultures put more emphasis on nonverbal codes and interpersonal relationships to generate and interpret meaning. In low-context cultures, most people rely on words to generate and interpret the meaning of a message. For example, African American and Latino members may be more sensitive to nonverbal components, whereas European Americans may rely on and trust a member's words.[5]

Language and Meaning

Your ability to use language helps to determine the extent to which you successfully express your ideas and influence the actions of other group members. Several basic principles of language address the complex relationship between words and meaning.

Denotation and Connotation

When communicating in groups, you will encounter different meanings for and reactions to words, depending on the type of group, its goal, its history of interaction, and the background and experience of its members. The multiple meanings of words fall into two categories: denotation and connotation.

Denotation refers to the objective, dictionary-based meaning of a word. However, words usually have more than one definition. For example, the *minutes* taken in a meeting are not the same as the *minutes* it may take to get a meeting started. **Connotation** refers to the personal feelings connected to the meaning of a word. Semanticist S. I. Hayakawa refers to connotation as "the aura of feelings, pleasant or unpleasant, that surround practically all words."[6] We evaluate the extent to which we like or dislike the thing or idea that the word represents.

Connotation is more likely than denotation to influence how you respond to words. For example, the denotative meaning or dictionary definition of a *meeting* is "an assembly or gathering of people, as for a business, social, or religious purpose."[7]

However, the word *meeting* can connote hours of wasted time to some members or the best way to solve a complex problem to others. When the word *meeting* comes to mean a dreaded event at which people argue over trivial issues, you are letting the word influence your feelings about the event it symbolizes.

Levels of Meaning

Group members can minimize the misinterpretation of words by recognizing the ways in which different levels of meaning affect communication. The more abstract your language is, for instance, the more likely group members will interpret its meaning other than the way you intended. **Abstract words** refer to ideas or concepts you cannot see or touch. Words such as *fairness, freedom,* and *love* do not have the same meaning for everyone. Reliance on abstract words increases the chances of misunderstanding. **Concrete words** refer to specific things that you perceive with your senses—things you can see, hear, touch, smell, or taste. Concrete words narrow the number of possible meanings and decrease the likelihood of misinterpretation.

Avoid using overly abstract words when working in groups. Use words that refer directly to observable objects, people, or behavior. For example, saying, "Greg's behavior was disruptive" could imply many things. Did he yell at a group member, use profanity, or refuse to participate? Saying, "Greg arrived fifteen minutes late to the meeting" is descriptive. Clarifying what you mean by using concrete words helps prevent misunderstandings.

Team Talk

Team Talk, by sociologist Anne Donnellon, examines the power of language in team dynamics. Donnellon uses the term **team talk** to describe the language that group members should use as they work together. Not only does team talk enable group members to share information and express opinions, but analysis of team talk also "reveals where the team is coming from and where it is headed. More importantly, talk is a tool for changing a team's destination" and achieving success.[8] Team talk is the means we use to achieve group goals, the stimulus we use to build group relationships, and the evidence we use to assess group work.

The Dimensions of Team Talk

Group members should listen carefully for words, sentences, and patterns of speech used repeatedly during discussions. By listening to one another talk and analyzing how the group uses language, group members can discover how the group's language fosters or inhibits success. Table 7.1 illustrates six dimensions of team talk and provides examples of successful and unsuccessful language use.

Language is more than the verbal medium through which groups communicate. Language also "creates thoughts, feelings, and behavior in team members which affect the way the team uses power, manages conflict, and negotiates."[9] Once group members analyze the nature of team talk, they can take steps to modify the way they interact and work with one another. The following suggestions can help produce a stronger and more cooperative group by using team talk:

- Use the pronouns *we, us,* and *our* when referring to the group and its work.
- Express shared rather than individual needs: "We need to . . ." rather than "I want . . ."

- If you are in a position of power, refrain from talking and interrupting more than others and asking more questions than others.
- Speak in a specific and active voice: "I haven't finished the report due next week" rather than an abstract and passive voice "The task hasn't been completed."
- Ask group members to address you by your first name or nickname.
- Encourage group members to express disagreement and listen patiently to dissenters.
- Ask more "what if" questions and make fewer "we can't do it" statements.
- When in doubt, rephrase or ask questions about what someone else has said to ensure understanding.

Table 7.1 The Dimensions of Team Talk

Team Talk Dimensions	Successful Examples	Unsuccessful Examples
1. ***Identification*** **by using plural pronouns.** Members use plural pronouns rather than singular ones when talking about the group and its work.	"Let's keep working on this until we're ready for lunch." "We've finished this in record time."	"I don't think you should quit until you've finished." "I'm pleased the discussion took so little time."
2. ***Interdependence*** **by using collective language.** Members use language that acknowledges shared needs, solicits opinions, and expresses the need for cooperation.	"If we can develop a plan, our work will be much easier to schedule. What do you all think?" "Wouldn't it be great if we submitted a plan based on total group consensus?"	"Fred and I can develop this plan without input from the group. I'll tell the boss that the two of us will do it on our own." "If there's no agreement here, the group must vote."
3. ***Minimal Power Differentiation*** **by using considerate language.** Members talk to one another on equal terms.	"Sorry. My other meeting ran overtime. Is there a way I can catch up?" "Fred, could you tell me more about that? Thanks."	"Stop and tell me what's happened so far." "I don't like this. If you can't do it, we'll have to assign this to someone else."
4. ***Social Equality*** **by using casual, informal language.** Members use casual language, nicknames, slang. Members express empathy and liking and avoid titles.	"What's up, Doc?" "Fred, try to find out where Bob stands on this." "Hey, guys!"	"The secretary should review our progress thus far." "Mr. Nunez, contact Dr. Ford after the meeting." "Ladies and gentlemen. . . ."
5. ***Conflict Management*** **by using collaborative language.** Members express interest in solving problems and use a nonthreatening tone and nonjudgmental language. Members paraphrase others.	"What do you need to know from us to do this?" "Could we back up and look at this from a different angle?"	"How many of you think that Fred is right?" "We're not getting anywhere, so I'll take it up with Dr. Ford after the meeting."
6. ***Negotiation*** **by using exploratory language.** Members ask "what if" questions, propose objective criteria for solutions, and summarize areas of agreement.	"What if we wrote up a justification for the cost?" "Does this meet our standard?" "What else can we do to make this work?"	"We've always done it this way." "Why? Because I just don't like it, that's why." "What's it going to take to get you to change your mind?"

Based on Anne Donnellon, *Team Talk: The Power of Language in Team Dynamics* (Boston, Harvard Business School, 1996), pp. 31–33. We have added qualifying phrases to Donnellon's categories to aid comprehension and recall.

case study

How to Sink the Mayflower

The minute Joan Archer walked into the conference room, she knew she'd have a fight on her hands. Administrators from each state college were finding seats along the sides of a long conference table. Sitting at the far end of the table was Dr. Barton Mayflower III, a representative from the state Board of Higher Education and the person most likely to cause problems. He had the large picture windows at his back to make sure the sun was not shining in his eyes.

Joan looked at the table. There were empty seats along the sides, but no one had chosen the seat at the other end of the table. Realizing that she had to be seen and heard by everyone at this meeting, she planted her attaché case in front of the unoccupied end seat. She tossed her jacket over the back of the chair.

The group was meeting to discuss and recommend a policy for accepting college credits from students transferring from one state college to another. As chair of the committee charged with drafting a policy, Joan had written most of the document herself. Given the difficulty of scheduling face-to-face meetings, the five-person committee had interacted only through conference calls and email. Two of the members made almost no contributions. The other two had faithfully read her draft and suggested changes. Fortunately, everyone on the committee had endorsed the draft policy and had asked Joan to present it at the statewide meeting.

Although no one officially chaired these meetings, Barton Mayflower called the meeting to order. As usual, he wore a well-cut dark suit with a starched white shirt and silk tie. His gray hair was meticulously groomed and his shoes were shined. The delegates had always deferred to his leadership and guidance. Without looking at Joan or addressing her by name, he used his "I'm in charge" voice and asked that the chair of the policy committee present her report.

Joan stood. She put a stack of neatly stapled reports in front of her, made eye contact with group members around the table, and smiled. Although the sun was in her eyes, the group could see her quite well without straining their eyes. She began her presentation with these words:

"Beth, Michael, Walter, Grace, and I are pleased to share this report with you. If nothing else, we can now involve all of you in making this policy stronger and better. We spent a lot of time working on this policy in phone conferences and by emailing each other. All of us fully endorse this policy—the vote was unanimous. Now we have something to share with all of you. The committee has asked me to present the report on their behalf. I think you'll see that we've addressed your concerns and come up with a plan that will help our students move from one college to another while ensuring that we maintain high academic standards. And please remember that if we don't come up with an acceptable policy, the state legislature will write it for us—and that's the last thing any of us want. Right? Right!"

As she spoke, Joan could see the four committee members basking in her praise. Barton Mayflower scowled. He could see that the rest of the delegates were buying into the policy even though Joan hadn't begun to describe its content. Much to his chagrin, no one saw his annoyance because they were looking at and listening to Joan.

When you finish reading this chapter, you should be able to answer the following questions.

1 How did Joan use the seating arrangement to her advantage?

2 Why was the group willing to let Barton Mayflower III call the meeting to order and begin the discussion?

3 In what ways did Joan use the principles of team talk to address the group?

4 How did Joan's physical behavior enhance her credibility and competence?

5 What might have told Barton Mayflower that the rest of "the delegates were buying into the policy"?

Use "I," "You," and "We" Language

When you use the word *I*, you take responsibility for your own feelings and actions: *I* feel great; *I* am a straight-A student; *I* am worried about the team's work on this project. Some people avoid using the word *I* because they think they're showing off, being selfish, or bragging. Other people use the word *I* too much and appear self-centered or oblivious to those around them.

Unfortunately, some people avoid "I" language when it is most important. Instead, they shift responsibility from themselves to others by using the word *you.* "You" language can be used to express judgments about others. When the judgments are positive—"You did a great job" or "You look marvelous!"—there's rarely a problem. When *you* is used to accuse, blame, or criticize, you can arouse defensiveness, anger, and even revenge. Consider the following statements: "You make me angry." "You drive too fast." Sometimes, the word *you* is implied, as in "Stop telling me what to do" and "What a stupid thing to do."

Successful teams use the plural pronouns *we* and *you* when talking to one another.[10] Plural pronouns are inclusive. They announce that the group depends on everyone rather than on a single member. Plural pronouns also share credit for team achievements.[11] Members say *we, us,* and *our* when talking about the group and its work. When members say *you,* they are usually addressing the whole group.

At the famous Mayo Clinic in Minnesota, where collaboration is the norm, "you usually find that people very uncomfortably or rarely use the singular word *I*. . . . So it's always what *we,* rather than *I,* will do."[12]

Language Challenges

Every language on earth is a system: an interrelated collection of words and rules used to construct messages that generate meaning. All languages have grammatical rules to explain how words should be arranged, modified, and punctuated. Although words have great power, they also pose challenges. As Mark Twain, the great American humorist, observed, "The difference between the almost right words and the right words is really a large matter—'tis the difference between the lightening bug and the lightening."[13]

Language Difficulties

Group members can avoid many misunderstandings by overcoming language-based barriers to communication. Among the most common language difficulties are bypassing, offensive language, and jargon.

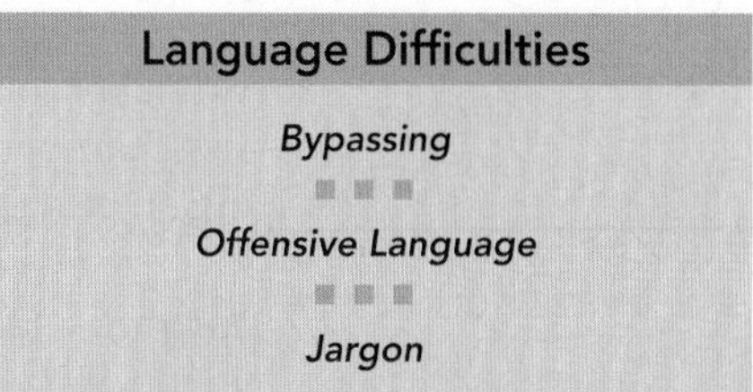

Bypassing. When group members use different meanings for the same words and phrases, they run the risk of **bypassing,** a form of miscommunication that occurs when people "miss each other with their meanings."[14] An entire group project may falter or fail if there are differences in the interpretation of a single word or phrase. Note the problems created by the following example of bypassing:

> At a routine staff meeting, a vice president tells her managers, "Survey the members of your department to find out whether they are satisfied with the new email system." During the following week, the vice president receives a copy of a memo from one

manager requesting that everyone in his department fill out a two-page questionnaire about the email system. The vice president telephones the manager and asks, "What's this questionnaire all about?" The manager replies, "I thought you said I have to survey everyone in my department."

What the vice president had in mind was for the manager to informally ask staff members for their initial impressions rather than ask for a detailed analysis of the new system. Although the manager heard the vice president's words, the communicators "missed" each other's meaning.

"Communicators who habitually look for meanings in the people using words, rather than in the words themselves, are much less prone to bypass or to be bypassed."[15] In other words, it's not what words mean but what group members mean when they use words.

Offensive Language. **Offensive language** demeans, inappropriately excludes, or stereotypes people. For example, sexist language may alienate and offend both male and female group members. Referring to women as "girls" implies that women are childlike and not capable of adult thought and responsibilities. Refer to female group members as "girls" only if you also refer to male members as "boys." Avoid words that specify the gender of individuals in particular roles or occupations. Instead, use words that refer to both men and women. For example, instead of referring to the *chairman,* use the term *chair* or *chairperson.*

Poorly chosen words can perpetuate discrimination. Avoid language that stereotypes people based on their culture, race, religion, or lifestyle.[16] Words such as *nigger, trailer trash,* and *faggot* are offensive and demeaning. Is it okay to use such words if none of your group members would be targeted by them? Absolutely not! This type of language can offend and alienate everyone in the group. A member of an insurance investigation team recounted the following experience:

> We were meeting to discuss ways to recognize fraudulent claims. At one point, another member said, "I'm working on a claim now involving a carload of wetbacks." I couldn't believe he used that term. He obviously didn't know that my husband is Latino. I was insulted. Other group members were offended, too.

Two problems occur when you label someone or accept a label that you hear or see. First, you reduce an entire person to a label—black doctor, dumb blonde, deaf cousin, or rich uncle. Second, labels can affect your perceptions of or relationship with that person. For example, if you label a person as inconsiderate, you may question the motives behind an act of kindness: "I wonder what prompted her to do that?" When you label someone as near perfect, you may go to great lengths to justify or explain less-than-perfect behavior: "Tiger Woods is still the best player in golf; he's just having an off year."

Jargon. **Jargon** is the specialized or technical language of a profession. Groups use jargon as "verbal shorthand that allows members to communicate with each other clearly, efficiently, and quickly."[17] In some groups, the ability to use jargon properly is a sign of team membership. In other groups, jargon can make ideas difficult to understand and, in some cases, can conceal the truth. Members who are unfamiliar with a group's jargon are easily intimidated and frustrated. Consider the experience of the vice president of a large corporation:

> When I first joined the company, I had to learn the lingo of the various groups in which I worked. I remember attending my first CMG meeting (I didn't even know what that

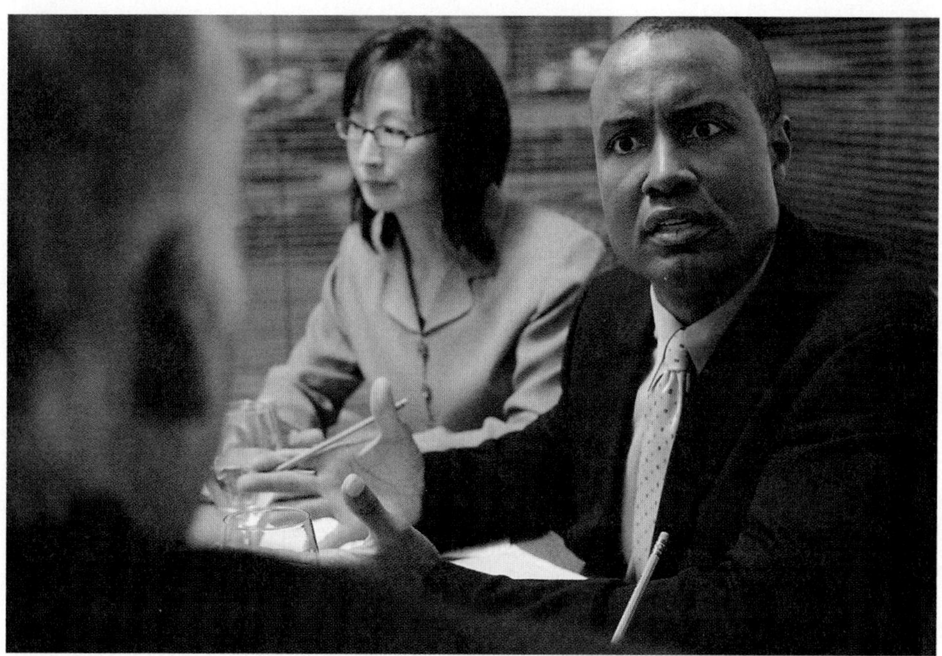

Every group member relies on verbal and nonverbal messages to generate meaning. What message is this group member sending to another group member?

meant at the time) and listening to people talk about red files and green files. Do we color-code files? No. Rather, the terms red file and green file refer to different pricing structures for our products. I also discovered that the same term might be used differently from one group to another. For instance, in some meetings IP refers to Internet provider. As an attorney, I use the term to refer to intellectual property. I'm now familiar with the language of our company, but I know how confusing it can be when you're new to the team.

Some people use jargon to impress others with their specialized knowledge. Such tactics usually fail to inform others and often result in misunderstandings and resentment. Use jargon only when you are sure that all the members of your group will understand it and that it's absolutely necessary. If some of the jargon or technical terms of a field are important, take the time to explain those words to new members.

Language Differences

Most groups include diverse members who influence how we use and listen to language. Although there is nothing right or wrong about the different ways in which people use language, these differences can create misunderstandings among group members.

Language and Gender. In Chapter 4, Group Diversity, we explain that gender-based cultures account for differences in perspectives and communication styles. All group members should monitor and adapt to the different ways in which women and men may express their opinions.

As we also note in Chapter 4, some researchers claim that men and women use language quite differently.[18] Rather than stereotyping men and women, we see these differences as tendencies rather than characteristics. For example, women tend to use language to maintain relationships and cooperate with others. Many women speak tentatively. Their speech is more likely to contain qualifiers and tag questions. A

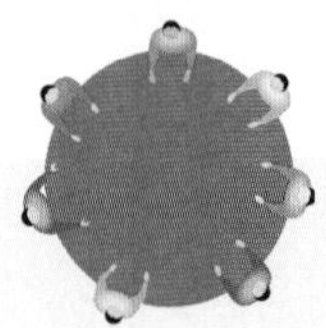

ethics in groups

Sticks and Stones May Break Your Bones, But Words Can Hurt Forever

When under assault by abusive language, group members can become discouraged, withdrawn, and isolated or can be provoked into shouting matches with their attacker. Abusive language has the "immediate result of spoiling relationships (and productivity based on such relationships), and the long-term effect of ruining morale, teamwork, and loyalty."[1] Some characteristics of verbal abuse:

- *Tone of voice:* Harsh, sarcastic, angry, or belittling
- *Content:* Sexual references, racial slurs, cruel comments about someone's appearance
- *Language choice:* Foul or obscene words
- *Nonverbal cues:* Insulting facial expressions, gross gestures, threatening movements
- *Speaking volume:* Loud, screaming voice or hissed messages.[2]

Ethical communicators *both* take responsibility for what they say *and* take action when others use abusive language. Here we offer several techniques for avoiding, interrupting, challenging, and stopping verbal abuse:

1. *Express your objections.* At the first sign of verbal abuse, calmly explain that you feel abused, but you are willing to continue the discussion if the language becomes less inflammatory.
2. *Ask for repetition.* Ask the person to repeat what he or she has just said, as in "Please repeat that. I want to make sure I heard what you said."
3. *Step back.* When someone is verbally abusive, step back four or five steps, as if to say that you want to talk about the problem, but you won't put up with yelling and insults. If the abuse continues, walk away.
4. *Quote the law.* When a discussion becomes abusive, quote the law or group norms: "That kind of language is illegal in the workplace" or "That word violates company policies."
5. *Take a time out.* Say "time out" when a discussion becomes uncomfortable or abusive. Follow that with "Let's take a minute to calm down before we continue."
6. *Practice what you preach.* If you take action against others, make sure that you avoid all forms of verbal abuse:
   - Do not raise your voice.
   - Do not swear.
   - Do not call members insulting names.
   - Do not use sarcasm to wound others.
7. *Listen.* Listen more than you speak when you're upset, particularly if you're so mad that you're afraid of what you might say. As you listen, try to calm down physically and mentally.[3]

[1]Thomas J. Housel, "Foreword," in Arthur H. Bell, *You Can't Talk to Me That Way!* (Franklin Lakes, NJ: Career Press, 2005), p. 11.

[2]Based on Arthur H. Bell, *You Can't Talk to Me That Way!* (Franklin Lakes, NJ: Career Press, 2005), pp. 24–25.

[3]Based on Bell, pp. 192–200.

qualifier is a word that conveys uncertainty, such as *maybe* and *perhaps.* Tag questions are questions connected to a statement. For instance, "It may be time to move on to our next point, don't you think so?" is a tentative statement with a tag question. This style does not necessarily represent a lack of confidence. Instead, it can be a cooperative approach that encourages others to respond.

Men tend to use language to assert their ideas and compete with others. Men are less likely to express themselves tentatively. Male speech is generally more direct and forceful. One style of communication is no better than another. The two are simply different. Effective group members use elements from both male and female approaches to language.

Language and Culture. For most groups, a single language is the medium of interaction, even though members from different backgrounds, generations, and geo-

graphic areas may speak the same language quite differently. A **dialect** is a variation in vocabulary, pronunciation, syntax, and style that distinguishes speakers from different ethnic groups, geographic areas, and social classes. In the United States, there are Southern dialects, New England dialects, and Brooklyn dialects, among others, and a whole range of foreign accents.

In the United States, Standard American English is the most commonly accepted dialect spoken by as much as 60 percent of the U.S. population. If, however, you enjoy "pizzer" and "beah" instead of pizza and beer, you may be from Massachusetts. If you say, "Ah nevah go theyuh," you could be from Alabama or parts of Texas. Unfortunately, studies repeatedly find that "accented speech and dialects provoke stereotyped reactions in listeners so that the speakers are usually perceived as having less status, prestige, and overall competence."[19] Moreover, people with Appalachian dialects and "those who speak Black Standard English are sometimes unfairly assumed to be less reliable, less intelligent, and of lower status than those who speak General American Speech."[20] The implications of such research are clear: Group members who do not use Standard American English in business and academic settings may be viewed as less articulate or less competent.

Because dialects have the potential to influence the perceptions of group members, speakers may engage in codeswitching as a way to avoid negative stereotypes related to language. **Codeswitching** refers to the ability to change from the dialect of your own cultural setting and adopt the language of the majority in particular situations. In other words, the dialect you speak at home may not be the best way to communicate in a business meeting.

African Americans often switch their linguistic codes depending on the context. They may speak one way among white people or in business settings (Standard English) and quite differently at home (Black English). Linguist John McWhorter notes that many middle-class African Americans typically speak both Black English and Standard English, switching constantly between the two, often in the same sentence.[21]

Communication scholar Carley Dodd concludes that: "(1) people judge others by their speech, (2) upward mobility and social aspirations influence whether people

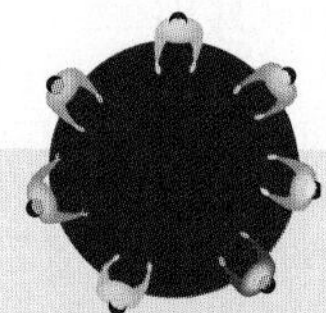

groups in balance . . .
Distinguish Accents from Dialects

Accents and dialects are not the same thing. An **accent** is the sound of one language imposed on another. For example, some Asian speakers have difficulty producing the "r" and "v" sounds in English. Dialects differ from accents in that they represent regional and cultural differences within the same language. What people call a Southern accent is really a Southern dialect.[1]

Linguists have identified eighteen regional dialects of American English. For example, a carbonated soft drink is called *soda* in the Northeast; *pop* in the inland and Northwest; *tonic* in eastern New England; and *soda pop* in parts of southern West Virginia, eastern Kentucky, western Carolina, and eastern Tennessee.[2]

Dialects may also have a distinctive sound. Northeast dialects, for example, range from the unique sound of New York City residents to the loss of "r" sounds in New England (in words such as *park, car, Harvard,* and *yard*). Southern dialects are also marked by the loss of the "r" sound as well as by distinctive phrases such as *y'all.*

[1] Isa Engleberg and John Daly, *Presentations in Everyday Life,* 3rd ed. (Boston: Pearson/Allyn & Bacon, 2009), pp. 328–329; William O'Grady et al., *Contemporary Linguistics,* 5th ed. (Boston: Bedford/St. Martin's, 2005), pp. 627, 635.

[2] Ethel C. Glenn, Phillip J. Glenn, and Sandra Forman, *Your Voice and Articulation,* 4th ed. (Boston: Allyn & Bacon, 1998), p. 10.

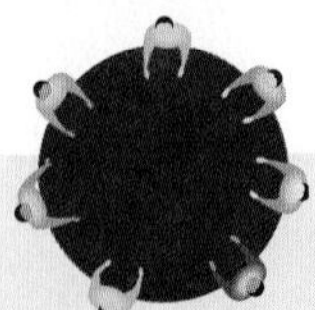

groups in balance . . .
Speak "Silently"

The well-known phrase "silence is golden" may be based on a Swiss saying, "Sprechen ist silbern, Schweigen ist golden," which means "speech is silver; silence is golden." This metaphor suggests that while speech is important, silence may be even more significant. The power of silence is recognized and embraced in many cultures:

- Those who know do not speak. Those who speak do not know. (*Tao Te Ching*)
- Silence is also speech. (African proverb)
- Silence is a friend who will not betray. (Confucius)

Understanding the communicative value of silence is important for several reasons. We use silence to communicate many things: to establish interpersonal distance, to put our thoughts together, to show respect for another person, or to modify others' behaviors.[1] When you work in groups, your silence may communicate a lot more than speech. If you are a talkative extrovert, silence gives you time to think and gives introverts a chance to speak. If someone's nasty tone during a heated discussion bothers you, silence can communicate your unwillingness to join the fray. Silence can also signal agreement, particularly when a group has talked an issue to death. Your silence says, "We've said it all, now let's vote or move on to another issue." Finally, remember that members from collectivist cultures assign great meaning to silence. "Listening" to their silence can tell you more than any words.

[1] Virginia P. Richmond and James C. McCroskey, *Nonverbal Behavior in Interpersonal Relationships*, 5th ed. (Boston: Allyn & Bacon, 2004), p. 103.

change their speech to the accepted norms, (3) general American speech is most accepted by the majority of the American culture, and (4) people should be aware of these prejudices and attempt to look beyond the surface."[22] Thus, you should try to understand, respect, and adapt to the dialects you hear in group communication contexts.

The Importance of Nonverbal Communication

Nonverbal communication refers to the behavioral elements of messages other than the actual words spoken. Your appearance, posture, and facial expressions also send messages. Research suggests that nonverbal behavior accounts for between 60 and 70 percent of all meaning.[23] That is, people base their understanding of what you mean not only on what you say, but also on how you use nonverbal cues.

Group communication researcher Robert Cathcart and his colleagues note that "groups provide a rich source of nonverbal messages because so many behaviors occur simultaneously."[24] Using and interpreting nonverbal behavior are critical to effective communication in groups. Unfortunately, we often put more thought into choosing the best words than into selecting the most appropriate behavior for conveying our ideas.

Nonverbal Behavior

Group members send messages through their personal appearance as well as through their facial, vocal, and physical expression. When all of these nonverbal elements are combined, they add enormous complexity and subtlety to group interaction.

Personal Appearance

When group members meet for the first time, they know very little about one another beyond what they see. Physical appearance influences first impressions. Based on others' physical appearance, we draw conclusions about their education, success, moral character, social position, and trustworthiness.[25] For better or worse, we tend to see attractive people as friendlier and as more credible than those who are less attractive. One study found that good-looking people tend to make more money and get promoted more often than those with average looks.[26]

Even the clothes you wear send messages to other group members. Nonverbal communication scholar Peter Andersen maintains that "effective small group members should view clothes and hair styles as an important silent statement made to the group. Dress that is appropriate is perhaps most important."[27] Casual attire is more acceptable in informal groups, whereas a professional appearance is expected in business settings and important group presentations. Your appearance should communicate that you respect the group and take its work seriously.

Facial Expression and Eye Contact

Your face can produce more than a thousand different expressions.[28] Facial expressions allow listeners to contribute continuously to an ongoing group discussion.[29] The facial expressions of group members let you know if they are interested in, agree with, or understand what you have said. Generally, women tend to be more facially expressive, while men are more likely to limit the amount of emotion they reveal. Good listening includes looking at a speaker's facial expressions in order to comprehend the full message.

Of all your facial features, your eyes are the most revealing. Generally, North Americans perceive eye contact as an indicator of attitude. Lack of eye contact is frequently perceived as signifying rudeness, indifference, nervousness, or dishonesty. However, perceptions about eye contact vary in different cultures. For example, "direct eye contact is a taboo or an insult in many Asian cultures."[30]

Eye contact influences interaction in groups. A seating arrangement that allows group members to face one another and establish eye contact helps maintain interaction. Eye contact also tells others when you want to speak. Returning eye contact to a group leader indicates that you are ready to respond, whereas avoiding eye contact is perceived as an attempt to avoid interaction.

Vocal Expression

Vocal expression is the *way* you say a word rather than the word itself. Some important vocal characteristics are pitch, volume, rate, and word stress. Variations in these elements can result in different messages. For example, a group may find it difficult or unpleasant to listen to a member with a monotone voice. A loud voice can imply anger, excitement, or dominance. Group members speaking quietly may signal that information is confidential. Also, a group may be bored by or stop listening to a member who speaks too slowly. A speaking rate that is too fast makes it difficult to understand the message. Adjust your volume and rate to the group setting and type of activity.

When pitch, volume, and rate are combined, they can be used to vary the stress you give to a word or phrase. **Word stress** refers to the "degree of prominence given to a syllable within a word or a word within a phrase or sentence."[31] Notice the differences in meaning as you stress the italicized words in the following three sentences:

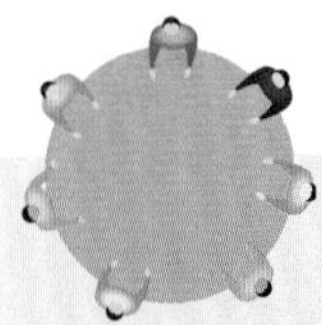

virtual groups

Expressing Emotions Online

When groups meet face to face, members can listen to other members' tone of voice and can observe their nonverbal behavior. However, most virtual groups rely on technologies that don't allow the members to hear or see one another. Participants can't see the facial expressions, head nods, gestures, or posture of other group members.

As a result, early users of computer-mediated communication developed emoticons to function in place of nonverbal cues. An **emoticon** is the use of ordinary typographical characters to convey a nonverbal expression. For example, ☺, :-), ;-), :-(, and :-D are commonly used emoticons that convey smiles, winks, frowns, or laughing.

In theory, emoticons serve as substitutes for nonverbal behavior. However, research suggests that emoticons have little or no effect on the interpretation of a typed message.[1] Thus, virtual group members are more likely to rely on your words than on your emoticons when interpreting the intention of your message.

In their book *Rules of the Net,* Thomas Mandel and Gerard Van der Leun offer the following suggestion: "Nothing—especially the symbols on the top row of your keyboard—can substitute for a clear idea simply expressed. Avoid :-) and all associated emoticons as you would avoid clichés—for example, like the plague."[2]

Generally, we advise you to avoid emoticons. However, if using emoticons is a norm within your group, ☺ away.

[1]Joseph B. Walther and K. P. D'Addario, "The Impacts of Emoticons on Message Interpretation in Computer-Mediated Communication" (paper presented at the meeting of the International Communication Association, Washington, DC, May 2001).

[2]Thomas Mandel and Gerard Van der Leun, *Rules of the Net: Online Operating Instructions for Human Beings* (New York: Hyperion, 1996), p. 92.

Is *that* the report you want me to read? Is that the report you want *me* to read? Is that the report you want me to *read?* Although the same words are used in all three sentences, the meaning of each question is quite different.

Physical Expression

Kinesics is the study of body movement and physical expression**.** Gestures are one of the most animated forms of kinesics. They can emphasize or stress parts of a message, reveal discomfort with the group situation, or convey a message without the use of words. For example, Jeff points to his watch to let the chairperson know that they will soon run out of time. At the end of a discussion, a thumbs-up gesture from group members signals that they are satisfied with the group's progress. Many people have difficulty expressing their thoughts without using gestures. Why else would we gesture when we are speaking on the phone? Research suggests that gesturing helps ease the mental effort when communication is difficult.[32]

Even your posture can convey moods and emotions. For example, if you slouch back in your chair, others may interpret your posture as lack of interest or dislike for the group. On the other hand, sitting upright and leaning forward communicate interest and are signs of attentive listening. Research links gestures and body movement to perceptions of leadership. Group members who lean forward, maintain eye contract, gesture often, smile, and assume a relaxed posture are more likely to emerge as group leaders and to be viewed as attractive by other group members.[33]

One of the most potent forms of physical expression is touch. Touch can convey a wide range of meanings. In groups, members often use touch to express encouragement, support, or happiness. Peter Andersen points out that "touch in a small group may establish greater teamwork, solidarity, or sharing."[34]

Some group members, however, are more comfortable with touch than others. At one end of a continuum are touch avoiders; at the other end are touch approachers. Misunderstandings can occur between these two kinds of people. Approachers may view avoiders as cold and unfriendly; avoiders may perceive approachers as invasive and rude. It is important to remember that gender and culture influence touch avoidance. Women are more likely to avoid opposite-sex touch, whereas men often avoid same-sex touch. In particular, Far Eastern women exhibit more touch avoidance than people from other cultures.[35] We suggest a balanced approach to touching others. Make sure you know the members of your group very well before hugging them or putting your arm around their shoulder. A handshake is usually the safest option.

The Nonverbal Environment

Nonverbal communication extends beyond the behavior of group members; it also includes the group's environment. Two important aspects of a group's nonverbal environment are the arrangement of space and perceptions of personal space.

Arrangement of Space

Seating arrangements can affect group interaction in significant ways. Arrangements that physically separate group members make group interaction difficult. For example, the traditional classroom arrangement of rows facing the teacher promotes interaction between the students and the teacher, but it does not encourage communication among the students. Arrangements that bring people closer together and permit direct eye contact among all members promote group interaction. Group members arranged in a circle or around a table can more easily interact with one another.

Your choice of seating position in groups has a direct effect on interaction and influence.[36] A number of studies have demonstrated that group members prefer corner-to-corner or side-by-side seating for cooperative activities. Such an arrangement allows them to be close enough to share materials. Members who anticipate competition or disagreement often choose seats across from each other.

A member's seating position often reflects the person's official position and amount of power. Group leaders are more likely to choose or be assigned a seat at the head of a table. Task-oriented leaders are attracted to the head of a table, while the middle position at the side of a table attracts more socially oriented leaders—members who are more concerned about group relationships and encouraging everyone to participate.[37] These two locations put the leader in a position to see and be seen by everyone in the group. Choosing one of the centrally located positions as depicted in Figure 7.1 on page 176 also makes it easier for a member to gain speaking opportunities.

Even the arrangement of a room or the shape of a conference table sends a message to group members. A long, rectangular table gives a group's leader a special place of prominence at its head. A round table allows all members to sit in equally important positions. The Paris peace talks that helped end the war in Vietnam bogged down for eight months until delegates from South Vietnam, the National Liberation Front, and the United States agreed to a round table as the setting for negotiation. When the leaders of Bosnia, Croatia, and Serbia met at Wright-Patterson Air Force Base in Ohio, the United States made sure that each party had equal seating space around a modest but perfectly round table. The arrangement of space is not a trivial matter when the success of a group is so consequential.

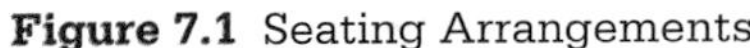

Figure 7.1 Seating Arrangements

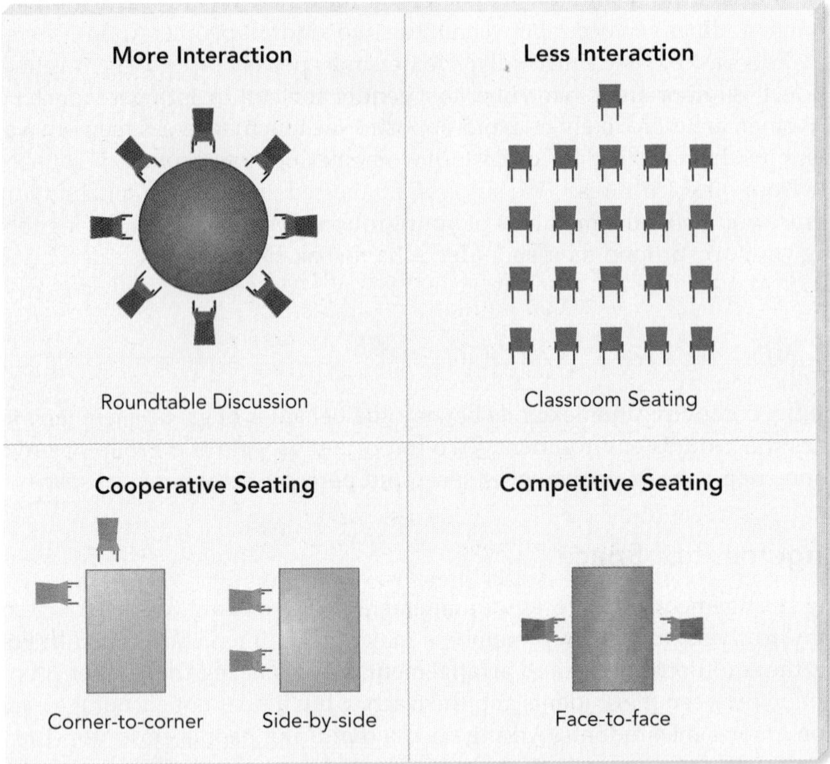

In addition to seating arrangement, the décor of a room can have a direct influence on a group and its work. A New England advertising agency learned this lesson the hard way when a fistfight broke out during a focus group session.[38] Facilitators reported that regardless of the discussion topic, no one ever seemed happy in the room. Participants were grumpy, negative, and resistant to new ideas. The company discovered that the problem was the room itself: It was cramped, stifling, and forbidding—a cross between a hospital room and a police interrogation room. The solution: a total redesign and redecoration. The company expanded the room and gave it long, gently curved walls. Soft, indirect light filtered in through curved windows. Participants could choose to sit in armchairs or on small couches surrounding circular coffee tables. The results were better than expected. There were no more fistfights. Instead, focus group participants became much more cooperative and positive.

Perceptions of Personal Space

Groups and their members may function quite differently depending on how they perceive the space and people around them. **Proxemics** refers to the study of how we perceive and use personal space. Within groups, two important proxemic variables are territoriality and interpersonal space.

Territoriality. **Territoriality** is the sense of personal ownership we attach to a particular space. For instance, in most classrooms, students sit in the same place every day. If you have ever walked into a classroom and found another person in *your* seat,

you may have felt that your territory had been violated. Objects acting as territorial markers often designate ownership of space. Placing a coat or books on a chair lets others know that that space is taken. As a group develops, members often establish their individual territories. They may sit in the same place near the same people during every meeting. Individuals who fail to respect the territory of others are violating an important group norm.

Seating arrangements can affect group interaction in significant ways. For example, arrangements that bring people closer together and permit direct eye contact among all members promote group interaction. How does the seating arrangement in this photo enhance or inhibit member interaction?

Interpersonal Space. **Interpersonal space** is an invisible, psychological "bubble" surrounding each person that expands or shrinks depending on the communicators and the context. Anthropologist Edward T. Hall identifies four zones of interaction used by most North Americans (see Figure 7.2).[39]

- **Intimate distance** ranges from touching to approximately eighteen inches apart. Close friends, some family members, and lovers use this very private zone. Peter Andersen notes that "at such close distances group members will feel inhibited from interacting and will make an attempt to restore their personal space bubble by moving back even if that means leaving the group."[40]
- **Personal distance** ranges from about eighteen inches to four feet apart. The typical distance is an arm's length away. We use this zone for conversations with friends and acquaintances. Members of most well-established groups interact with one another at this distance. They feel close enough to engage in discussion but far enough away to be comfortable.
- **Social distance** encompasses a range of four to eight feet apart. We usually interact with new acquaintances and strangers in this zone. Groups in which members use the outer limits of this zone will find it difficult to maintain interaction.
- **Public distance** extends beyond eight feet. Speakers use this distance for lectures and presentations. Groups are unlikely to use this zone unless they are making a presentation to a larger audience.

Figure 7.2 Zones of Personal Space

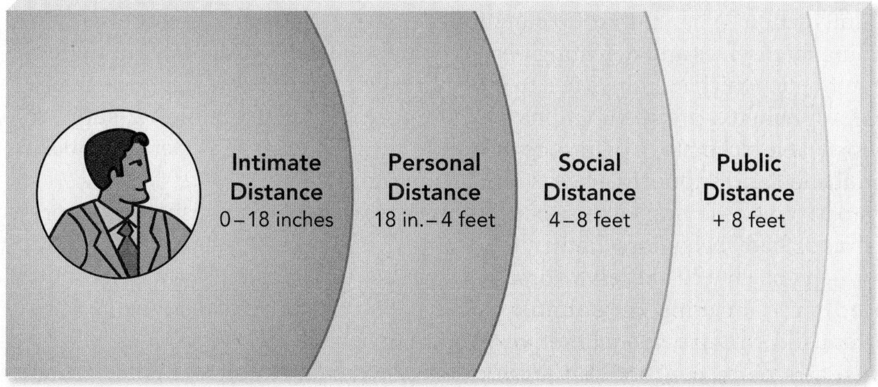

Nonverbal Communication and Culture

When we interact with group members from different cultural backgrounds, interpreting their nonverbal behavior may be as difficult as translating an unfamiliar foreign language. The multiple meanings of nonverbal communication in other cultures can be illustrated by focusing on two elements: personal space and eye contact. Research on personal space indicates that most Latin Americans, Arabs, and Greeks require less distance between people than North Americans do. Cultural differences also are evident when measuring the amount and directness of eye contact. If, for example, a white supervisor reprimands a young black male, the employee may respond by looking downward rather than looking at the supervisor. In some cases, the employee's response may anger the supervisor and be interpreted as inattention or defiance. Intercultural researchers report that "members of certain segments of black culture reportedly cast their eyes downward as a sign of respect; in white cultures, however, members expect direct eye contact as a sign of listening and showing respect for authority."[41]

There is a danger, however, of stereotyping people from different backgrounds and cultures on the basis of their nonverbal behavior. Latino, Arab, and Greek group members may not be comfortable with less personal space than a North American. Young black males may look directly at a white supervisor with respect. When interpreting nonverbal behavior, try to understand, respect, and adapt to individual differences rather than assuming that all people from a particular culture behave alike.

If you are unsure about the appropriate way to respond nonverbally, ask. Too often, we find out about the nonverbal rules of another culture only after we have broken them.

Creating a Supportive Communication Climate

Our use of and reaction to language and nonverbal communication establishes a unique group atmosphere or climate. Specifically, a group's **climate** is the degree to which group members feel comfortable interacting. In some groups, the climate is warm and supportive. Members like and trust one another as they work toward a common goal. In chillier group climates, defensiveness and tension pollute the atmosphere. Members may feel threatened by and suspicious of one another.

In 1961, Sociologist Jack Gibb identified six pairs of communication behavior that influence whether a group's climate is defensive or supportive.[42] A **defensive climate** triggers our instinct to protect ourselves when we are being physically or verbally attacked by someone. Even though such reactions are natural, they hinder productive group interaction. When the group climate is defensive, members devote attention to defending themselves and defeating perceived opponents. A **supportive climate** creates a setting in which members feel free to share their opinions and feelings. Synergy occurs only when a group functions in a supportive climate. Table 7.2 shows the behaviors of each climate in pairs, one the opposite of the other, with defensive behaviors on the left and supportive behaviors on the right.

Try to avoid classifying Gibb's six pairs of supportive and defensive behaviors as "good" and "bad" behaviors. Rather, they represent dialectic tensions. There may be times when you should express yourself in evaluative, controlling, strategic, neutral, superior, or certain terms. For example, you may behave strategically when you have important and strong personal motives. You may behave with certainty when your expertise is well recognized and a critical decision must be made. And you may

Table 7.2 Gibb's Defensive and Supportive Group Climates

Defensive Behaviors	Supportive Behaviors
1. **Evaluation.** Judges another person's behavior. Makes critical statements. *Examples:* "Why did you insult Sharon like that? Explain yourself!" "What you did was terrible."	1. **Description.** Describes another person's behavior. Makes understanding statements. Uses more *I* and *we* language. *Examples:* "When we heard what you said to Sharon, we were really embarrassed for her." "I'm sorry you did that."
2. **Control.** Imposes your solution on someone else. Seeks control of the situation. *Examples:* "Give me that report and I'll make it better." "Since I'm paying for the vacation, we're going to the resort I like rather than the spa you like."	2. **Problem Orientation.** Seeks a mutually agreeable solution. *Examples:* "Okay. Let's see what we can do to get that report finished to specifications." "Let's talk and figure out how both of us can enjoy our vacation."
3. **Strategy.** Manipulates others. Hides hidden agendas or personal motives. *Examples:* "Frankie's going to Florida over spring break." "Remember when I helped you rearrange your office?"	3. **Spontaneity.** Makes straightforward, direct, open, honest, and helpful comments. *Examples:* "I'd like to go to Florida with Frankie over spring break." "Would you help me move some heavy boxes?"
4. **Neutrality.** Appears withdrawn, detached, and indifferent. Won't take sides. *Examples:* "You can't win them all." "Life's a gamble." "It doesn't matter to me." "Whatever."	4. **Empathy.** Accepts and understands another person's feelings. *Examples:* "I can't believe she did that. No wonder you're upset." "It sounds as though you're having a hard time deciding."
5. **Superiority.** Implies that you and your opinions are better than others. Promotes resentment and jealousy. *Examples:* "Hey—I've done this a million times—let me have it. I'll finish in no time." "Is this the best you could do?"	5. **Equality.** Suggests that everyone can make a useful contribution. *Examples:* "If you don't mind, I'd like to explain how I've handled this before. It may help." "Let's tackle this problem together."
6. **Certainty.** Believes that your opinion is the only correct one. Refuses to consider the ideas and opinions of others. Takes inflexible positions. *Examples:* "I can't see any other way of doing this that makes sense." "There's no point in discussing this any further."	6. **Provisionalism.** Offers ideas and accepts suggestions from others. *Examples:* "We have a lot of options here—which one makes the most sense?" "I feel strongly about this, but I would like to hear what you think."

respond neutrally when the issue is of little consequence to you or others. Gibb's categories offer both a strategy and a set of skills for developing a supportive communication climate that fosters openness and social awareness.

Take one more look at Gibb's six pairs of communication behavior in Table 7.2. Every one can be expressed verbally and nonverbally. If you or your group ignores the nonverbal components of Gibb's communication behaviors, you may miss the most important part of a message. Here are two sketches depicting the nonverbal differences between defensive and support behavior:

- Defensive: She rolls her eyes or audibly sighs when other members make suggestions. She often intimidates others by standing and looking down at them or by interrupting them when they speak. If group members need help, she looks the other way or concentrates on her own work. Everything about her—the way she walks, dresses, stands, and speaks—conveys her conviction that she is right and better than other group members.
- Supportive: He always listens carefully to other members and speaks kindly even when he disagrees. He avoids bragging about his own accomplishments

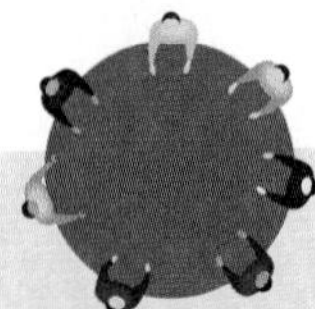

theory in groups

Nonverbal Immediacy and Group Climate

Jack Gibb's contribution to group communication illuminates the dialectic tensions between defensive and supportive communication. A supportive climate, however, requires more than the right intentions and words. It also requires appropriate nonverbal communication.

Groups in supportive climates also show evidence of **nonverbal immediacy**—behaviors that indicate greater physical closeness to or liking of others. Based on research by nonverbal communication researcher Albert Mehrabian, the following cluster of nonverbal behaviors generate positive interactions:[1]

- more leaning forward
- more physical closeness to others
- more eye contact
- more openness of arms and body
- more direct body orientation
- more touching
- more relaxed posture
- more positive facial and vocal expressions
- more laughing and smiling

The concept of nonverbal immediacy applies directly to group interaction. When group members are physically comfortable with one another, they work in a more supportive climate. Just think of the opposite behaviors and you'll see why members become more defensive in the absence of immediacy behaviors. Rather than leaning forward and closer in an open position, nonimmediate members lean back, sit farther away, and cross their arms or hunch over. Rather than facing members directly and establishing eye contact, nonimmediate members sit sideways and rarely make eye contact. Rather than smiling at others, nonimmediate members have no expression or even scowl. If you find yourself leaning back, sitting in a rigid posture, or looking at everything but the members of your group during a discussion, it may be time to change your nonverbal behavior to mannerisms and actions that communicate greater physical closeness to or liking of others. Once you take on a more relaxed posture and smile, you may even find yourself enjoying the group experience and the company of members.

[1] Mark L. Knapp and Judith A. Hall, *Nonverbal Communication in Human Interaction* (Belmont, CA: Thomson/Wadsworth, 2006), pp. 414–15.

but is quick to praise the group and its efforts. When other members need help, he stops what he's doing to listen and, if possible, helps them. He smiles, leans forward, nods his head, maintains eye contact, and is physically close to others. Most members like and respect him, largely because he radiates honesty, warmth, and openness.

summary study guide

Two Essential Tools

- Whereas verbal communication focuses on how you use words and language, nonverbal communication refers to message components other than words that generate meaning.
- In dialectic terms, effective group members rely on *both* verbal *and* nonverbal communication to generate meaning. When verbal and nonverbal messages contradict one another, a group can become confused and defensive.

Language and Meaning

- Denotation refers to the objective, dictionary-based meaning of a word. However, words usually have more than one definition.
- Connotation refers to the personal feelings connected to the meaning of a word.
- Words vary on a continuum from specific, understandable concrete words to less tangible, abstract words.

Team Talk

- Team talk is the means used to achieve group goals, the stimulus to build group relationships, and the evidence used to assess group work.
- When group members use team talk effectively, they use plural pronouns as well as collective, considerate, casual, collaborative, and exploratory language.

Language Challenges

- Avoiding bypassing and offensive language and minimizing jargon can improve group understanding.
- Some women use a more tentative language style, whereas men's language tends to be more direct and to the point.
- General American Speech is the most commonly accepted form of language in the United States.
- Codeswitching refers to the ability to change from the dialect of your own cultural setting and adopt the language of the majority in particular situations.

The Importance of Nonverbal Communication

- Nonverbal communication conveys as much or more meaning than do words.
- As much as two-thirds of all meaning may be derived from nonverbal behavior.

Nonverbal Behavior

- Group members send messages through their personal appearance as well as through their facial, vocal, and physical expressions.
- The directness and length of eye contact significantly influences group interaction.
- Vocal characteristics include pitch, volume, rate, and word stress.
- Research suggests that emoticons have little or no effect on the interpretation of a typed email message.
- Physical expression includes gestures, posture, and touch.

The Nonverbal Environment

- Group seating arrangements can promote or discourage communication. Leaders tend to sit in centrally located positions.
- Territoriality refers to a sense of ownership of a particular space.
- Proxemics refers to the study of how we perceive and use personal space, particularly in terms of the four zones of interaction: intimate, personal, social, and public.

Nonverbal Communication and Culture

- Two significant cultural differences include the dimensions of a culture's personal space and the appropriateness of sustained eye contact.
- When interpreting nonverbal behavior, try to understand, respect, and adapt to individual differences rather than assuming that all people from a particular culture behave alike.

Creating a Supportive Communication Climate

- Whereas a defensive climate triggers our instinct to protect ourselves when we are being physically or verbally attacked by someone, a supportive climate creates a setting in which members feel free to share their opinions and feelings.
- Jack Gibb matches defensive and supportive characteristics: evaluation and description, control and problem orientation, strategy and spontaneity, neutrality and empathy, superiority and equality, certainty and provisionalism.
- Defensive and supportive communication can be expressed verbally and nonverbally.
- When group members engage in nonverbal immediacy behavior, they do *more* of the following behaviors: leaning forward, eye contact, openness of arms and body, touching, relaxed posture, positive facial and vocal expressions, and laughing and smiling.

key terms

critical thinking about the case study

How to Sink the Mayflower

1. How did Joan Archer know when she walked into the conference room that she'd have a fight on her hands if she didn't do something to prevent it?
2. Do you believe that sitting at the head or foot of a table gives a group member more status and power? Why or why not?
3. How effectively did Joan use team talk to engage her audience and win them over to her side?
4. How did Joan's physical behavior enhance her credibility?
5. What signs did Barton Mayflower notice that told him he had little hope of derailing Joan and her committee?
6. What dialectic tensions were evident in the conference room and how were they resolved?

group work Getting Emotional about Nonverbal Cues

Directions: The following table lists seven types of nonverbal cues in the left column. Four types of emotions you will encounter in groups are listed across the top row. As in the example for *warmth,* indicate the kind of nonverbal behavior you or others often use to express these feelings to one another. Be prepared to share your results with group members or the entire class in order to identify nonverbal cues that typically portray specific emotions.

TYPES OF NONVERBAL CUES				
NONVERBAL BEHAVIOR AND EMOTIONS	*EXAMPLE:* WARMTH	HAPPINESS	ANGER	BOREDOM
Facial Cues	Smiling, Calm, Interested			
Eye Contact	Direct			
Vocal Cues	Soft, Expressive			
Touch	Gentle, Reassuring			
Gestures and Body Movement	Open, Slow, Welcoming			
Distance	Close, Intimate, Personal			
Posture	Leaning in, Relaxed			

group assessment Auditing Team Talk

Directions: Circle the term that best describes the extent to which the members of your group engage in productive team talk.

When your group communicates . . .

1. Do members use plural pronouns rather than singular ones?	Very often	Sometimes	Rarely
2. Do members use language that acknowledges shared needs?	Very often	Sometimes	Rarely
3. Do members solicit opinions and express the need for cooperation?	Very often	Sometimes	Rarely
4. Do members talk to one another on equal terms?	Very often	Sometimes	Rarely
5. Do members use casual language, nicknames, slang?	Very often	Sometimes	Rarely
6. Do members express empathy and liking?	Very often	Sometimes	Rarely
7. Do members express interest in solving problems?	Very often	Sometimes	Rarely
8. Do members use a nonthreatening tone and nonjudgmental language?	Very often	Sometimes	Rarely
9. Do members paraphrase one another?	Very often	Sometimes	Rarely
10. Do members ask "what if" questions?	Very often	Sometimes	Rarely
11. Do members propose objective criteria for solutions?	Very often	Sometimes	Rarely
12. Do members summarize areas of agreement?	Very often	Sometimes	Rarely

Scoring: Analyze your group's team talk by looking at the number of times you circled *Very often*, *Sometimes*, and *Rarely*. The more times you circled *Very often*, the more likely it is that your group engages in productive team talk. The more times you circled *Rarely*, the more likely it is that talk inhibits the progress and success of your group. To get a more accurate assessment of team talk for your entire group, everyone should complete the questionnaire and share their responses. Is there a consistent response to each question? If there are significant disagreements on several questions, the members of your group may benefit from a discussion about the nature of their team talk.

notes

1. Anne Donnellon, *Team Talk: The Power of Language in Team Dynamics* (Boston: Harvard Business School, 1996), p. 6.
2. Victoria Fromkin and Robert Rodman, *An Introduction to Language*, 6th ed. (Ft. Worth, TX: Harcourt Brace, 1998), p. 3.
3. Mark Hickson III, Don W. Stacks, and Nina-Jo Moore, *Nonverbal Communication: Studies and Applications*, 4th ed. (Los Angeles: Roxbury, 2004), p. 7.
4. Virginia P. Richmond and James C. McCroskey, *Nonverbal Behavior in Interpersonal Relations*, 5th ed. (Boston: Allyn & Bacon, 2004), p. 5.
5. Myron W. Lustig and Jolene Koester, *Intercultural Competence: Interpersonal Communication across Cultures*, 5th ed. (Boston: Allyn & Bacon, 2006), pp. 110, 111.
6. S. I. Hayakawa and Alan R. Hayakawa, *Language and Thought in Action*, 5th ed. (San Diego, CA: Harcourt Brace Jovanovich, 1990), p. 43.
7. *The American Heritage Dictionary of the English Language*, 4th ed. (Boston: Houghton Mifflin, 2000), p. 1093.
8. Donnellon, p. 25.
9. Donnellon, p. 25.
10. Donnellon, p. 33.
11. Donnellon, pp. 40–41.
12. Evan Rosen, *The Culture of Collaboration: Maximizing Time, Talent and Tools to Create Value in the Global Economy* (San Francisco: Red Ape, 2007), p. 204.
13. Mark Twain, "Letter to George Bainton, October 15, 1888," www.twainquotes.com/lightning.html.
14. William V. Haney, *Communication and Interpersonal Relations: Text and Cases*, 6th ed. (Homewood, IL: Irwin, 1992), p. 269.
15. Haney, p. 290.
16. Vivian Cook, *Inside Language* (London: Arnold, 1997), p. 244.
17. William Lutz, *Doublespeak* (New York: HarperPerennial, 1990), p. 3.
18. Deborah Tannen, *You Just Don't Understand: Women and Men in Conversation* (New York: William Morrow, 1990).
19. Lustig and Koester, p. 200.
20. Lustig and Koester, p. 199.
21. John McWhorter, *Word on the Street: Debunking the Myth of a "Pure" Standard English* (Cambridge, MA: Perseus, 1998), p. 143.
22. Carley H. Dodd, *Dynamics of Intercultural Communication*, 4th ed. (Madison, WI: Brown & Benchmark, 1995), p. 151.
23. See Mark Hickson, III, Don W. Stacks, and Nina-Jo Moore, *Nonverbal Communication: Studies and Applications*, 4th ed. (Los Angeles: Roxbury Publishing, 2004), p. 7; Albert Mehrabian, *Silent Messages: Implicit Communication of Emotions and Attitudes*, 2nd ed. (Belmont, CA: Wadsworth, 1981), p. 77.
24. Robert S. Cathcart, Larry A. Samovar, and Linda D. Henman, *Small Group Communication: Theory and Practice*, 7th ed. (Madison, WI: Brown & Benchmark, 1996), p. 236.
25. Hickson, Stacks, and Moore, p. 189.
26. From The Federal Reserve Bank of St. Louis, *The Regional Economist*, April 2005, quoted in "Good Looks Can Mean Good Pay, Study Says," *The Sun*, April 28, 2005, p. D1.
27. Peter A. Andersen, "Nonverbal Communication in the Small Group," in *Small Group Communication: A Reader*, 6th ed., ed. Robert S. Cathcart and Larry A. Samovar (Dubuque, IA: Wm. C. Brown, 1992), p. 273.
28. Martin S. Remland, *Nonverbal Communication in Everyday Life* (Boston: Houghton Mifflin, 2000), p. 169.
29. Nicole Chovil, "Measuring Conversational Facial Displays," in *The Sourcebook of Nonverbal Measures: Going Beyond Words*, ed. Valerie Manusov (Mahwah, NJ: Lawrence Erlbaum, 2005), p. 174.
30. Guo-Ming Chen and William J. Starosta, *Foundations of Intercultural Communication* (Boston: Allyn & Bacon, 1998), p. 91.
31. Lyle V. Mayer, *Fundamentals of Voice and Diction*, 13th ed. (Madison, WI: Brown & Benchmark, 2004), p. 229.
32. Sharon Begley, "Gesturing as You Talk Can Help You Take a Load Off Your Mind," *Wall Street Journal*, November 14, 2003.
33. Sandra M. Ketrow, "Nonverbal Aspects of Group Communication," in *The Handbook of Group Communication Theory and Research*, ed. Lawrence R. Frey; Dennis S. Gouran and Marshall Scott Poole, assoc. eds. (Thousand Oaks, CA: Sage, 1999), p. 255.
34. Andersen, p. 267.
35. Peter A. Andersen, "The Touch Avoidance Measure," in *The Sourcebook of Nonverbal Measures: Going beyond Words*, ed. Valerie Manusov (Mahwah, NJ: Lawrence Erlbaum, 2005), p. 62.
36. See Judith K. Burgoon, "Spatial Relationships in Small Groups," in *Small Group Communication: Theory and Practice*, 8th ed., ed. Randy Y. Hirokawa, Robert S. Cathcart, Larry A. Samovar, and Linda D. Henman (Los Angeles: Roxbury, 2003), pp. 85–96.
37. Mark L. Knapp and Judith A. Hall, *Nonverbal Communication in Human Interaction*, 4th ed. (Fort Worth, TX: Harcourt Brace, 1997), p. 177.
38. Jeffrey Krasner, "Fistfights and Feng Shui," *Boston Globe*, July 21, 2001, pp. C1–C2.
39. Edward T. Hall, *The Hidden Dimension* (New York: Doubleday, 1982).
40. Andersen 1992, p. 269.
41. Dodd, p. 160.
42. Jack R. Gibb, "Defensive Communication," *Journal of Communication* 2 (1961), pp. 141–148. Also see Jack R. Gibb, "Defensive Communication," in *Small Group Communication: A Reader*, 2nd ed., ed. Robert S. Cathcart and Larry A. Samovar (Dubuque, IA: Wm. C. Brown, 1974), pp. 327–33.

chapter 8

Listening in Groups

chapter outline

study questions

How should you balance speaking and listening in groups?

How do different types of listening affect group communication?

What is the relationship between member roles and listening?

What basic principles and skills help improve listening?

How should I handle the listening challenges related to diversity, note taking, and self-monitoring?

The Challenge of Listening in Groups

Do you listen attentively and responsibly when you work in groups? Most students answer this question with a resounding "Yes!" or "Of course." Nevertheless, most students—like most people—overestimate their listening ability. Here are some questions to help you rethink your answer:

- Do you review your notes or the agenda before the beginning of a meeting?
- Do you make yourself listen even when the topic or members' comments are boring?
- Do you listen objectively even if you don't agree with or like what someone says?
- Do you ask questions if you don't understand or if you need clarification?
- Do you make eye contact with group members during a discussion?
- Can you summarize the main points of a discussion at its completion?

If you answered with an honest *yes* to all or most of the questions, you are probably an effective listener and valued group member. If you answered *no* or *only sometimes,* you have a lot to learn about listening. Accordingly, we devote this entire chapter to the challenge of listening in the hopes of enhancing your awareness of and improving your abilities in this essential group communication skill.[1]

Listening is more difficult in groups than in almost any other communication situation. There are multiple speakers, perspectives, and goals. You *both* listen *and* respond quickly to unexpected news, unusual ideas, and conflicting points of view. Instead of concentrating on what *one* person says and does, you must pay attention to *everyone's* reactions. In a group discussion, a short daydream or a side conversation can result in missed information, misinterpreted instructions, or inappropriate reactions. Complicating matters is the fact that the social pressure to listen is not as strong in groups as it would be in a two-person conversation. If one group member doesn't listen or respond, others usually will. Consequently, group members may not listen well because they count on others to listen for them.[2]

The Nature of Listening

Listening is the ability to understand, analyze, respect, and appropriately respond to the meaning of another person's spoken and nonverbal messages. At first, listening may appear to be as easy and natural as breathing. In fact, nothing could be further from the truth. Although most of us can *hear,* we often fail to *listen* to what others say. Hearing requires only physical ability; listening requires complex thinking ability. People who are hearing impaired may be better listeners than those who can hear the faintest sound.

Listening is our number-one communication activity. A study of college students found that listening occupies more than half of their communicating time.[3] In the corporate world, studies estimate that managers may devote more than 60 percent of their workday to listening to others.[4] Chief executives may spend as much as 75 percent of their communicating time listening.[5] Although percentages vary from study to study, Figure 8.1 on page 189 shows how most of us divide up our daily communicating time.

Despite the enormous amount of time we spend listening, most of us are not very good listeners. In fact, we tend to think we're better listeners than we really are. Several studies report that immediately after listening to a short talk, most of us cannot accurately report 50 percent of what was said. Without training, we listen at only 25 percent efficiency.[6] And, of that 25 percent, most of what we remember is a distorted or inaccurate recollection.[7]

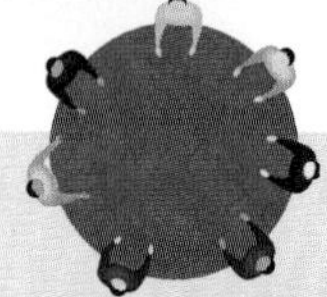

theory in groups

Listening and Working Memory Theory

Our definition of listening describes what effective listeners *do:* they understand, analyze, respect, and appropriately respond to another person's spoken and nonverbal messages. This definition, however, does not explain how the listening process works. Listening—just like speaking, reading, and writing—is a complex process that goes beyond "you speak, I listen."

Early studies of listening focused on **short-term memory,** the content a person remembers immediately after listening to a series of numbers, words, sentences, or paragraphs. Psychologist Samuel Wood and colleagues note that this kind of "short-term memory has a very limited capacity—about seven (plus or minus two) different items or bits of information at one time. This is just enough for phone numbers and ordinary zip codes."[1] We use something more complex than short-term memory to engage in effective listening.

Early listening research relied on tests similar to those used for reading comprehension. Much like a reading comprehension test, in which you read a passage and answer questions about it, test takers answered questions after listening to a series of audio passages. This kind of listening is important and relevant when you're listening to a public speech, a classroom lecture, or a recorded book. However, it is not the kind of listening you must do in groups.

Listening researcher Laura Janusik explains that in conversations, listening is a transaction. "Message reception is not enough; the listener must respond. Thus, the goals and processes are unique in conversational listening, as interpersonal communication requires one simultaneously to be a sender and receiver."[2] Janusik's insight also applies to the way group members listen to one another. During a group discussion, members' remarks are connected and responsive to what other members say.

Working Memory Theory recognizes that listening involves more than the ability to tap your short-term memory. Listening engages your **working memory.** Psychologists define working memory as "the memory subsystem we use when we try to understand information, remember it, or use it to solve a problem or communicate with someone."[3] Janusik describes working memory as "a dual-task system involving processing and storage functions. The processing function is synonymous with attention, and the storage function is synonymous with memory. Attention is allocated, and resources not used for attention are available for storage."[4] Your working memory does more than store what you've heard, it allows you to shift what you've heard and understood "from and into long-term memory" as a way to create new meanings.[5] Another metaphor for this is mental juggling. In other words, how many items can you hold and respond to in a conversation with other people?

Group members with more working memory capacity understand what other members mean, analyze complex issues and discussion threads as they develop, track relevant and irrelevant interactions, and develop appropriate responses. As we note in the opening of this chapter, listening is more difficult in groups than in almost any other communication situation. Engaging your working memory is a complex process when talking to one person. It becomes a huge challenge when communicating with several group members, as you must both listen and be able to respond, on the spot, to multiple ideas and views you can't anticipate.

[1]Samuel E. Wood, Ellen Green Wood, and Denise Boyd, *The World of Psychology*, 6th ed. (Boston: Pearson/Allyn & Bacon, 2008), p. 199.

[2]Laura Ann Janusik, "Building Listening Theory: The Validation of the Conversational Listening Span," *Communication Studies* 58 (2007), p. 140. See also Laura Ann Janusik, "Researching Listening from the Inside Out: The Relationship between Conversational Listening Span and Perceived Communicative Competence" (doctoral dissertation, 2004). *UMI Proquest: Digital Dissertations*. Available at www.lib.umi .com/dissertations.

[3]Wood, Wood, and Boyd, p. 200.

[4]Janusik, "Building Listening Theory," p. 142.

[5]Janusik, p. 142.

Surveys of business leaders often point to listening as the communication skill most lacking in new employees. When asked how many high school graduates have good listening skills, the answer was only 19 percent.[8] A study of Fortune 500 company training managers concludes that "poor listening performance is ranked as a serious problem during meetings, performance appraisals, and superior-subordinate communication."[9]

Figure 8.1 Time Spent Communicating

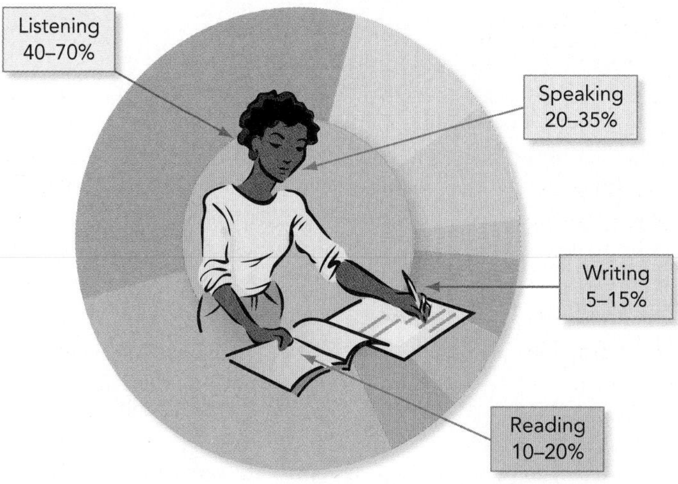

The Dialectics of Listening

Speaking and listening are two sides of a single coin, twin competencies that rely on and reflect each other. Thus, the dialectics of speaking and listening affect how members become and succeed as leaders. As discussed in Chapter 5, Group Leadership, the member who speaks first and most often is more likely to emerge as the group's leader.[10] The number of contributions is even more important than the quality of those contributions. On the other hand, once a person becomes a leader, listening is more important in determining that person's success. Effective leaders engage in listening more than talking and in asking more than telling.[11]

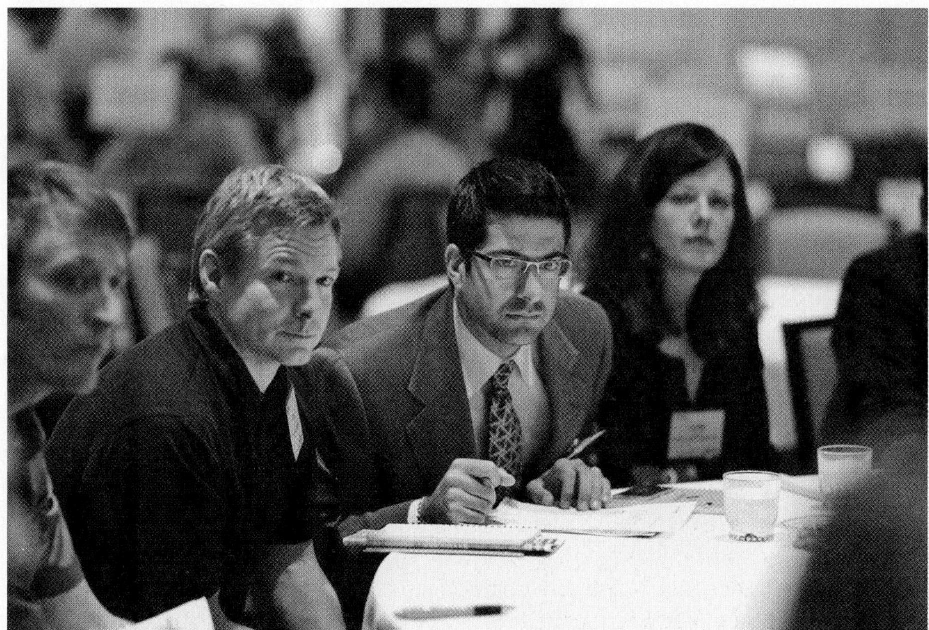

Businesspeople at Convio's annual summit collaborate to further business relationships with their best customers. What nonverbal communication cues reveal that group members are genuinely interested and involved in the discussion?

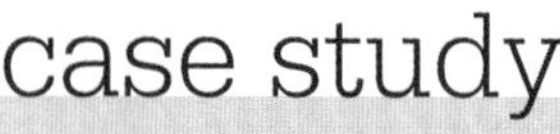

case study

A Message for Michael

Michael Mahwah is the newest member of the humanities department at a small college. Although new to teaching, he worked several years as a freelance writer. His department welcomed him with open arms. Almost immediately, everyone could see that he worked hard, that his students respected and liked him, and that he cheerfully volunteered for committee work.

At faculty meetings, Michael contributed good ideas and demonstrated a positive attitude. In many respects, he was the perfect faculty member. Except for one thing: Michael didn't listen. At first his colleagues made excuses because he was new. Soon they realized that for all his talents and positive outlook, he was missing something.

When faculty members talked to Michael at meetings, he behaved as though he was a great listener. He looked at the person speaking, nodded his head, and didn't interrupt. Yet, something in his eyes said, "I'm not *really* listening to you." One colleague decided to test this notion. When discussing course requirements, he inserted some nonsense phrases by saying, "All liberal arts majors will be required to take intermediate algebra, flower arranging, and a basic communication course." Michael nodded his head. "At the same time, we will give students more options in the humanities so they can take a theatre course, a welding course, or an art history course." Again, Michael nodded his head. Pretty soon the faculty began to giggle, but Michael didn't seem to notice. He just smiled along with everyone else.

Rather than confronting Michael, his colleagues began asking him to respond to what others said during discussions. Finally, Michael caught on. The risk of having nothing to say made him pay more attention. Faculty members thought they'd solved the problem. Instead, they'd created a new one. Michael was so intent on listening *and* responding, he soon had an opinion about everything. Even worse, his way of expressing his opinion occasionally hurt people's feelings. Many of his responses were just blunt: "Here's a much better way to do that." A few, however, were harsh: "Rachel, that's just dumb." Now he seemed incapable of "listening" to everyone's negative nonverbal reactions to his statements. Michael's honeymoon at the college was over.

Michael soon realized that something was wrong. His colleagues were less friendly. They stopped asking him to join committees or after-work get-togethers. He decided to have a talk with the department chair. He made an appointment, arrived promptly, and began by saying, "I am thrilled to have this job. But I don't think the other faculty members like or respect me. Maybe I'm just imagining it—I'm not good at picking up on this sort of thing. Please, just tell me what I'm doing wrong or whether I'm imagining things." The department head realized she had to phrase her response with care. What she was about to say could affect Michael's future and the department's well-being.

When you finish reading this chapter, you should be able to answer the following questions.

1. How does effective and ineffective listening affect a group's ability to interact effectively and achieve group goals?
2. What types of listening are essential to group work and which types does Michael need to improve?
3. How would you help members like Michael realize that their blunt and often cruel responses upset others?
4. Which listening principles and strategies would improve Michael's listening abilities?
5. If you were head of the department, how would you paraphrase Michael's request for help and advice?

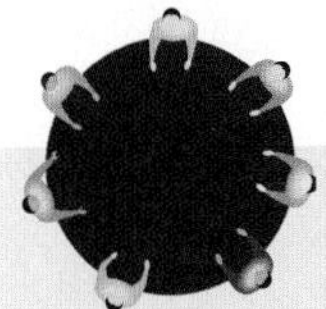

groups in balance . . .
Always *Want* to Listen

Stephen R. Covey, the author of *The 7 Habits of Highly Effective People,* provides a definition of *habit* that also describes effective communication. In Covey's opinion, a habit requires knowledge, skills, and desire. Knowledge plays a role similar to that of methods and theories by describing *what* to do and *why* to do it. Skills represent *how* to do it. And, most important, you must have the desire to communicate effectively and ethically. In order to make something a habit, you have to have all three. Effective listening relies as much on your attitude (*wanting* to do it) as on your knowledge and skills. Covey uses the challenges of listening to illustrate the three components of an effective habit:

1. *Knowledge.* I may be ineffective in my interaction with my work associates, my spouse, or my children because I constantly tell them what I think, but I never really listen to them. Unless I understand principles of human interaction, I may not even *know* I need to listen.
2. *Skills.* Even if I do know that to interact effectively with others, I really need to listen to them, I may not have the skill. I may not know how to really listen deeply to another human being.
3. *Desire.* But knowing I need to listen and knowing how to listen is not enough. Unless I *want* to listen, unless I have the desire, it won't be a habit in my life.[1]

The best listeners are motivated to listen; they let go of what's on their mind long enough to hear what's on the other person's mind. An appropriate listening attitude does not mean that you know exactly what another person thinks or feels. Instead, it is a genuine willingness and openness to listen and discover.[2]

[1]Stephen R. Covey, *The 7 Habits of Highly Effective People* (New York: Simon and Schuster, 1989), p. 48.

[2]Michael P. Nichols, *The Lost Art of Listening* (New York: Guilford, 1995), pp. 42, 43.

You will spend the vast majority of your time in groups listening to others. Even during a half-hour meeting of five people, it is unlikely that any member will talk more than a total of ten minutes—unless that member wants to be accused of monopolizing the discussion. Unfortunately, many of us place more emphasis on the roles and responsibilities of group members who talk rather than on those who listen. "This unbalanced emphasis, especially as it actually affects persons in real discussions, could be an important cause of the problems that speaking is supposed to cure."[12] In other words, if you only focus on what you intend to say in a group discussion, you can't give your full attention to what others say.

Types of Listening

Effective group members use different types of listening to advance group goals. For example, if your group is discussing a controversial proposal, you may engage analytical listening skills. If you're celebrating a group member's birthday, you may put aside analytical listening to enjoy the festivities. Researchers have identified several types of listening, each of which calls upon unique listening skills.

Types of Listening

Discriminative Listening

Comprehensive Listening

Empathic Listening

Analytical Listening

Appreciative Listening

Discriminative Listening

In Chapter 4, Group Diversity, we define discrimination as the way in which people act out and express prejudice. The meaning of

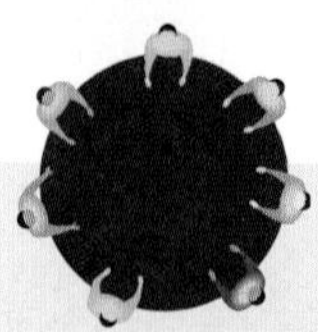

groups in balance . . .

Ask Questions to Enhance Comprehension

Asking good questions can enhance listening comprehension.[1] Here are a few listening strategies that can help you become a more effective group member:

1. *Have a plan.* Make sure you have a clear and appropriate goal. If you don't know your purpose, your question may be misunderstood or worthless.
2. *Keep the questions simple.* Ask one question at a time and make sure it's relevant to the discussion.
3. *Ask nonthreatening questions.* Avoid questions that begin with "Why didn't you . . . ?" or "How could you . . . ?" because they can create a defensive climate in responders.
4. *Ask permission.* If a topic is sensitive, explain why you are asking the question and ask permission before continuing. "You say you're fearful about sharing this report with Tom. Would you mind helping me understand why you're so apprehensive?"
5. *Avoid biased or manipulative questions.* Tricking someone into giving you the answer you want can destroy trust. There's a big difference between "Why did we miss the deadline?" and "Who screwed up?"
6. *Wait for the answer.* In addition to asking good questions, respond appropriately. After you ask a question, give other members time to think and then wait for the answer.

[1]Based on Tony Alessandra and Phil Hunsaker, *Communicating at Work* (New York: Fireside, 1993), pp. 76–77.

discriminative listening is very different. In fact, the primary definition of *discriminate* is "to make a clear distinction; distinguish," as in "Can you discriminate among the different sounds of orchestra instruments?"[13] Thus, **discriminative listening** is the ability "to distinguish auditory and/or visual stimuli."[14]

Discriminative listening answers this question: Do I hear accurately? At its simplest level, it involves the ability to make clear, aural distinctions among the sounds and words in a language. Discriminative listeners also notice nonverbal behavior, such as a smile, a groan, or the shrug of a shoulder.

Discriminative listening comes first among the five types of listening because it forms the basis for the other four. If you cannot hear the difference between an on-key and an off-key note, you may not be able to listen appreciatively to a singer. If you cannot hear or recognize the distress in a person's voice, you may not be able to listen empathically.

Comprehensive Listening

Comprehensive listening in a group discussion answers this question: What do group members mean? **Comprehensive listening** focuses on accurately understanding the meaning of group members' spoken and nonverbal messages. If you don't understand what a person means, how can you respond in a reasonable way? For example, an after-class discussion might begin as follows: "Let's have a party on the last day of class," says Geneva. A comprehensive listener may wonder whether Geneva means that (1) we should have a party instead of an exam, (2) we should ask the instructor whether we can have a party, or (3) we should have a party after class. Misinterpreting the meaning of Geneva's comment could result in an inappropriate response.

Answering the following questions can help you focus on several strategies for effective comprehensive listening:

- Do you understand the words spoken by other group members?
- Can you accurately identify the main ideas and evidence used to support a group member's claim?
- Does the message confirm what you already know or believe?

Empathic Listening

Empathic listening in a group discussion answers this question: How do group members feel? **Empathic listening** goes beyond comprehending what a person means; it focuses on understanding a member's situation, feelings, or motives. Can you see the situation through the other member's eyes? How would you feel in a similar situation?

By not listening for feelings, you may overlook the most important part of a message. Even if you understand every word a person says, you can still miss anger, enthusiasm, or frustration in a group member's voice. As an empathic listener, you don't have to agree with or feel the same way as other group members, but you do have to try to understand the type and intensity of feelings that those members are experiencing. For example, the after-class discussion might continue as follows: "A class party would be a waste of time!" exclaims Kim. An empathic listener may wonder whether Kim means that (1) she has more important things to do during exam week, (2) she doesn't think the class or the instructor deserves a party, or (3) she doesn't want to attend such a party.

Empathic listening is difficult, but it also is "the pinnacle of listening" because it demands "fine skill and exquisite tuning into another's mood and feeling."[15] You can improve your empathic listening ability by using one or more of the following strategies:

- Monitor your feedback. Are you showing interest and concern? Do your vocal tone, gestures, and posture communicate friendliness and trust?
- Avoid evaluative reactions.
- Focus on the speaker, not on yourself. Avoid talking about your own experiences and feelings.[16]

Analytical Listening

Analytical listening answers this question: What's my opinion? **Analytical listening** focuses on evaluating and forming appropriate opinions about a message. It requires critical thinking and analysis. Once you comprehend and empathize with group members, you may ask yourself whether you think they are right or wrong, logical or illogical. Analytical listeners understand why they accept or reject another member's ideas and suggestions.

Russell makes the following proposal: "Suppose we chip in and give Professor Hawkins a gift at the party?" An analytical listener might think that (1) the instructor could misinterpret the gift, (2) some class members won't want to contribute, or (3) there isn't enough time to collect money and buy an appropriate gift.

Recognizing that another group member is trying to persuade—rather than merely inform—is the first step in improving your analytical listening. The following strategies can help you improve this critical listening skill:[17]

- Learn to recognize persuasive strategies. Is the group member appealing to your emotions and/or to your critical thinking ability?
- Evaluate the quality of arguments and evidence. Are conclusions valid and based on logical reasoning?
- Recognize any changes in your beliefs or attitudes. Have you changed your original position? Why or why not?

Appreciative Listening

Appreciative listening answers this question: Do I like or value what another member has said? **Appreciative listening** focuses on the *way* group members think and speak—the way they choose and use words; their ability to inject appropriate humor, argue persuasively, or demonstrate understanding. For example, if a group is struggling with the wording of a recommendation, appreciative listening can help identify the statement that best expresses the central idea and spirit of the proposal. When we are pleased to hear a member find the right words to calm a frustrated member or energize an apathetic group, we are listening appreciatively. Appreciative listening skills help us enjoy and acknowledge good talk in groups.

"Well," suggests Paul, "why not buy a thank-you card, ask class members to sign it, and present it to Mr. Hawkins at the party?" An appreciative listener might think, (1) Paul always comes up with the best ideas, (2) a well-selected card may express our appreciation better than we could, or (3) I will thank Paul for making a suggestion that doesn't obligate anyone to contribute to or attend the party.

In *Perceptive Listening,* Florence Wolff and Nadine Marsnik note that "listeners often devote a great part of their day to appreciative listening, but often without a conscious plan."[18] We listen appreciatively to a favorite radio station or CD. We appreciate a spellbinding or funny story. But when we are asked to listen to something new or challenging, we're often hard-pressed to listen appreciatively. Here are some suggestions for improving this type of listening:

- Set aside time for appreciative listening. For example, don't scan a magazine article or watch television when listening to a friend's story or problem.
- Welcome opportunities to hear something new or challenging.
- Pay attention to the clarity and eloquence of a member's words and nonverbal behavior.

Group Roles and Listening

No one is a perfect listener. For that reason, you should not expect every group member to be a perfect discriminative, comprehensive, empathic, analytical, and appreciative listener. One way to assess and improve the listening behavior of a group as a whole is to understand the relationship between listening abilities and member roles.

Task Roles and Listening

Members who assume important task roles are often good comprehensive and analytical listeners. For example, clarifier-summarizers use comprehensive listening to accurately explain ideas and summarize group conclusions. Evaluator-critics are usually effective analytical listeners who assess information and recommendations as well as the validity of arguments. An effective recorder-secretary, however, must be a comprehensive listener when taking minutes. If several group members effectively assume most of the traditional task roles, the group, as a whole, is likely to be good at comprehensive and analytical listening.

Maintenance Roles and Listening

Maintenance roles affect how well a group gets along. They focus on building relationships and maintaining a friendly atmosphere. Members who assume important

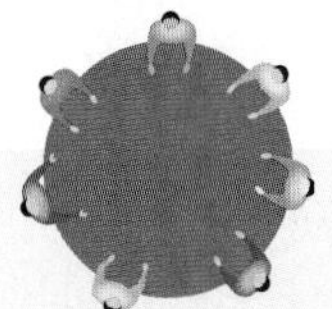

ethics in groups
Self-Centered Roles and Listening

As you know from Chapter 2, Group Development, self-centered roles emerge when members put their own needs ahead of the group's goal and other members' needs. Although members who assume self-centered roles may be excellent comprehensive and analytical listeners, their goals may be counterproductive and unethical. For example, aggressors and dominators may be analytical listeners who expose the weaknesses in others' comments in order to get their own way. Blockers may be good listeners who purposely ignore what they hear or poor listeners who are incapable of comprehending or appreciating the comments of others. Recognition seekers, confessors, and special interest pleaders may be so preoccupied with their own needs that they are unable to listen to anyone else in the group.

Unethical listening can take other forms that serve self-centered goals:

- listening behavior that shows no respect for the opinions of others.
- listening for the purpose of criticizing the ideas of others.
- listening for personal information that can be used to humiliate or criticize others.
- faking listening in order to curry favor with high-status members.

Ethical listening is as important as ethical speaking, particularly because we spend most of our communicating time listening. Alexander Solzhenitsyn, a winner of the Nobel Prize in literature, lamented that "many hasty, immature, superficial, and misleading judgments are expressed every day . . . without any verification."[1] Ethical listeners have a responsibility to understand, analyze, and respond appropriately to messages that have personal, professional, political, and moral consequences for themselves and others.

[1]Alexander Solzhenitsyn, "A World Split Apart," *Vital Speeches*, (September 1978), p. 680.

maintenance roles are often good empathic and appreciative listeners. Encourager-supporters and observer-interpreters use comprehensive, empathic, and appreciative listening to explain how others feel and what others are trying to say. Harmonizers and tension releasers are often empathic listeners who understand when and how to resolve conflicts, mediate differences, and relax the group. If several group members effectively assume most maintenance roles, the group, as a whole, is likely to be good at empathic and appreciative listening.

Leadership Functions and Listening

Researchers describe strong links between listening skills and successful leadership.[19] Not surprisingly, good leaders are good listeners. They know when and how to use comprehensive, empathic, analytical, and appreciative listening. Effective leaders are also proactive listeners. They don't wait to clear up misunderstandings; they make sure that every group member comprehends what is being said. They don't wait for disputes to escalate into destructive conflict; they intervene at the slightest hint of hostility. Proactive leaders try to find out what members think and feel by asking them rather than by guessing what is on their minds.

Leaders who are good listeners do not fake attention, pretend to comprehend, or ignore other group members. They work as hard as they can to understand accurately what members are saying and how their comments affect the group and its goals. In the words of a successful aerospace leader: "The worst failing is a team leader who's a nonlistener. A guy who doesn't listen to his people—and that doesn't

mean listening to them and doing whatever the hell he wants to do—can make a lot of mistakes."[20]

Improving Listening

Two major listening principles balance the need for comprehensive and analytical listening with the need for empathic and appreciative listening: (1) use your extra thought speed, and (2) apply the golden listening rule. Once group members understand and apply these principles, they can work to improve specific listening methods and skills.

Use Your Extra Thought Speed

Most people talk at about 125 to 150 words per minute. There is good evidence that if thoughts were measured in words per minute, most of us can think at three to four times the rate at which we speak.[21] Thus, we have about four hundred extra words of spare thinking time during every minute a person is talking to us.

Thought speed is the speed (in words per minute) at which most people can think compared to the speed at which others can speak. Listening researcher Ralph Nichols asks the obvious question: "What do we do with our excess thinking time while someone is speaking?"[22] Poor listeners use their extra thought speed to daydream, engage in side conversations, take unnecessary notes, or plan how to confront the speaker. Good listeners—and effective group members—use their extra thought speed productively to:

- enhance comprehensive and analytical listening.
- identify and summarize key ideas.
- interpret the meaning of nonverbal behavior.
- analyze arguments.
- assess the relevance of a member's comments.

Apply the Golden Listening Rule

The **golden listening rule** is easy to remember: Listen to others as you would have them listen to you. Unfortunately, this rule can be difficult to follow. It asks you to suspend your own needs in order to listen to someone else's.

The golden listening rule is not so much a "rule" as it is a positive listening attitude. If you aren't motivated to listen, you won't listen. If you aren't willing to stop talking, you won't listen. The following six positive listening attitudes have six negative counterparts:[23]

Positive Listening Attitudes	Negative Listening Attitudes
Interested	Uninterested
Responsible	Irresponsible
Group-centered	Self-centered
Patient	Impatient
Equal	Superior
Open-minded	Closed-minded

virtual groups

Listening Online

Effective listening in virtual groups requires adapting to a different medium. In a sophisticated videoconference, this adaptation is relatively easy—you can see and hear group members sitting at a conference table in another place almost as clearly as you can see and hear colleagues sitting next to you. Your primary technical concern is making sure that your microphone is on or off at appropriate times. In an email discussion, however, you can neither see nor hear participants, but you still must "listen" to their messages.

Ironically, it may be easier to "listen" to group members in a virtual meeting than in a face-to-face setting. In a face-to-face discussion, you hear what members say and respond immediately. Members can see you grimace, smile, or roll your eyes. In an email discussion—whether synchronous or asynchronous—you have more time to listen to others and can control the content and style of your responses.

For example, you can reread what someone has written to make sure that you comprehend the message. In a virtual discussion, time also allows you to use several listening styles. Because you have more than the few seconds given to a listener in a face-to-face discussion, you can interpret and analyze a message, determine the content and tone of your response, and choose appropriate words.

The downside is that it is easier to fake attention in electronic meetings. You can pretend to participate online by occasionally typing a comment. During a teleconference, you can stop listening and work on other tasks, checking in and responding with an "I agree" or "Good job" to feign participation. Although you can fake listening in a face-to-face discussion, your physical presence makes it difficult to "be elsewhere."

Listening Strategies

Although using your extra thought speed and applying the golden listening rule are critical listening goals, how to achieve them may not be obvious. Several strategies can improve your listening ability and help you apply the two basic principles of effective listening.

Listening Strategies

Listen for Big Ideas

Overcome Distractions

"Listen" to Nonverbal Behavior

Listen before You Leap

Help Your Group Listen

Listen for Big Ideas. Good listeners use their extra thought speed to identify a speaker's overall purpose. Poor listeners listen for and remember isolated facts rather than identifying big ideas. Sometimes listening for big ideas can be difficult when a speaker's message lacks a clear structure or a person's voice lacks expressiveness. In a group setting, good listeners interrupt a member and politely ask, "Could you help me out and summarize your point in a couple of sentences?" Although you may want to blame poor speakers when you can't comprehend their message, good listeners cut through irrelevant material to identify the most important ideas.

Overcome Distractions. Distractions can take many forms in a group discussion.[24] Loud and annoying noises, uncomfortable room temperature and seating, frequent interruptions, or distracting décor and outside activities are environmental distractions. Distractions also occur when members speak too softly, too rapidly, or too slowly; when someone speaks in a monotone or with an unfamiliar accent; or when a member has unusual or annoying mannerisms. It is difficult to listen when

someone is fidgeting, doodling, tapping a pencil, or openly reading or writing something unrelated to the discussion.

When a distraction is environmental, you can get up and shut the door, open the window, or turn on more lights. When another member's behavior is distracting, you can try to minimize or stop the disruption. If members speak too softly, have side conversations, or use unreadable visual aids, a conscientious listener will ask a member to speak up, postpone their side conversations, or move closer to a visual.

"Listen" to Nonverbal Behavior. Speakers may not communicate all their meaning through words. Often you can understand others by observing their nonverbal behavior. A change in vocal tone or volume may be another way of saying, "Listen up—this is very important." A person's sustained eye contact may be a way of saying, "I'm talking to you!" Facial expressions can reveal whether a thought is painful, joyous, exciting, serious, or boring. Even gestures can express an excitement that words cannot convey.

It is, however, easy to misinterpret nonverbal behavior. Effective listeners verbally confirm their interpretation of someone's nonverbal communication. A question as simple as "Do your nods indicate a *yes* vote?" can ensure that everyone is on the same nonverbal wavelength. If, as research indicates, more than half of a speaker's meaning is conveyed nonverbally,[25] we miss a lot of important information if we fail to "listen" to nonverbal behavior.

Correctly interpreting nonverbal responses can tell you as much as or more than spoken words. The nonverbal reactions of listeners (head nods, smiles, frowns, eye contact, and gestures) can also help you adjust what you say when you are speaking. Even the nonverbal setting of a group discussion can communicate a wealth of meaning about the status, power, and respect given to group members.

Listen before You Leap. One of the most often-quoted pieces of listening advice from Ralph Nichols's writings is, "We must always withhold evaluation until our comprehension is complete."[26] This counsels listeners to make sure that they understand a speaker before they respond.

When we become angry, friends may sometimes tell us to "count to ten" before reacting. This is also good advice when we listen. Counting to ten, however, implies more than withholding evaluation until comprehension is complete. You may comprehend a speaker perfectly but be infuriated or offended by what you hear. If an insensitive leader says, "One of you girls take minutes," it may take a count to twenty to collect your thoughts before you can respond to this sexist comment in a professional manner. If a group member tells an offensive joke, you may have a double reaction—anger at the speaker and disappointment with those who laughed. Listening before you leap gives you time to adjust your reaction in a way that will help rather than disrupt a group discussion.

Help Your Group Listen. In effective groups, members help one another listen. The most effective listeners may become the group's translators, explaining what other members mean and interpreting their responses. One way to help a group listen is to do periodic group listening checks that ask for a confirmation of comprehension. By asking, "What is everyone's understanding of . . . ?" or "Am I right in saying that all of us agree to . . . ?" you are making sure that everyone understands and is responding to the same message.

You also can help a group listen when group members disagree or argue. When members are emotional, their thoughts often focus on responding to the "opposition"

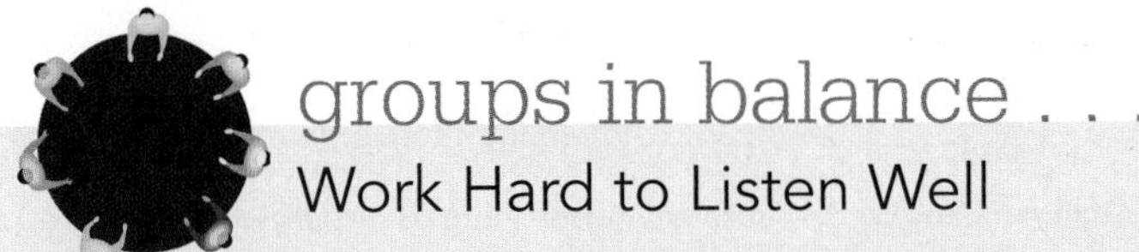

groups in balance . . .
Work Hard to Listen Well

Effective listening is hard work and requires a great deal more than keeping quiet and recognizing individual words. Researchers note that "active listeners register an increase in blood pressure, a higher pulse rate, and even more perspiration. [Active listening] means concentrating on the other person rather than on yourself. As a result, a lot of people just don't do it."[1]

Listening requires the kind of preparation and concentration required of attorneys trying a case, psychologists counseling a client, and physicians seeking a diagnosis based on patients' reported symptoms. Intensive listening can be an exhausting experience. If you are not willing to work at listening, you will not be a good listener.

[1]Tony Alessandra and Phil Hunsaker, *Communicating at Work* (New York: Fireside, 1993), p. 55.

rather than applying the golden listening rule. You can help a group resolve such conflicts by summarizing different positions in accurate and neutral terms.

Try to keep good listening habits at the forefront of the group's attention. Remind members how important it is for everyone to improve her or his listening behavior. Such reminders can have powerful consequences. In fact, some experts claim that 50 percent of our potential improvement in listening can come from simply realizing that we have poor listening habits and are capable of listening much better.[27]

The Art of Paraphrasing

Paraphrasing (also called *reflective listening* or *mirror responses*) is the ability to restate what people say in a way that indicates you understand them. When you paraphrase, you go beyond the words you hear to understand the feelings and underlying meanings that accompany the words. Too often, we jump to conclusions and incorrectly assume that we know what a speaker means and feels.

Paraphrasing is a form of feedback—a listening check—that asks, "Am I right—is this what you mean?" Paraphrasing is not repeating what a person says; it requires finding *new* words to describe what you have heard. In addition, a paraphrase usually includes a request for confirmation.

Use paraphrasing to

- ensure comprehension before evaluation.
- reassure others that you want to understand them.
- clear up confusion and ask for clarification.
- summarize lengthy comments.
- help others uncover thoughts and feelings.
- provide a safe and supportive communication climate.
- help others reach their own conclusions.[28]

If you want to clarify someone's meaning, you might say, "When you said you were not going to the conference, did you mean that you want one of us to go instead?" If you want to make sure that you understand a person's feelings, you might say, "I know you said you approve, but I sense that you're not happy with the outcome—am I way off?" If you are summarizing someone's comments, you might say, "What you seem to be saying is that it's not the best time to change this policy, right?"

Table 8.1 Types of Paraphrasing

Type of Paraphrase	Effective Paraphrase Technique	Example of an Ineffective Paraphrase
Paraphrase Content	Find new words to express the same meaning. Paraphrase, don't parrot. *Example:* "What I'm hearing is that you've tried to figure out why you're often late but can't. Is that what you're saying?"	Susan: "I never seem to get anywhere on time, and I don't know why." You: "Ah, so you don't know why you never seem to get anywhere on time?" Susan: "Yeah, that's what I just said."
Paraphrase Depth	Match the emotions to the speaker's meaning. Avoid responding lightly to a serious problem and vice versa. *Example:* "When you say that people are angry, you sound as though it's become serious enough to put your job at risk or damage your relationships with your boss and coworkers?"	Susan: "People, including my boss, bug me about being late, and sometimes I can tell that they're pretty angry." You: "In other words, you worry that other people are upset by your lateness."
Paraphrase Meaning	Do not add unintended meaning or complete the person's sentence. *Example:* "Let me make sure I understand what you'don't know.' Is it that you don't know why you're always late or that you don't know how to manage your time?"	Susan: "I really don't know . . ."* You: ". . . how to manage your time?" (*Susan would have finished with "what to do.")
Paraphrase Language	Use simple language to ensure accuracy. *Example:* "It sounds as though being late has become a big problem at work and you're looking for ways to fix it. Right?"	Susan: "I never seem to get anywhere on time, and I don't know why." You: "Ahh, your importunate perplexities about punctuality are inextricably linked." Susan: "Huh?"

Paraphrasing is difficult. Not only are you putting aside your own interests and opinions, but you are also finding *new* words that best match someone else's meaning. Table 8.1 shows how phrasing of a paraphrase can vary in four critical ways: content, depth, meaning, and language.[29]

Paraphrasing says, "I want to hear what you have to say, and I want to understand what you mean." If you paraphrase accurately, the other person will appreciate your understanding and support. And if you don't get the paraphrase right, your feedback provides another opportunity for the speaker to explain.[30]

Special Listening Challenges

Effective listening is more than practicing a series of skills. Special challenges arise as you try to adjust your listening behaviors to member differences, to the task of taking useful notes, and to the ultimate challenge of monitoring your own listening.

Listening to Differences

Just as group members differ in their backgrounds, perceptions, and values, people differ in the ways they listen. In a group setting, different listening abilities and styles can be an asset. For instance, if you have difficulty analyzing an argument, another group member can take on the role of analytical listener. If members only focus on words rather than the emotions expressed nonverbally, appoint yourself as the group's empathic listener.

Gender Differences. Listening behavior may also differ between male and female members. Men, for example, may put more focus on the content of a message when they listen, whereas women focus on the relationships among speakers.[31] In other words, men tend to listen comprehensively and analytically, whereas women are more likely to listen empathically and appreciatively. If "males tend to hear the facts while females are more aware of the mood of the communication," a group is fortunate to have both kinds of listeners contributing to the group process.[32]

Personality Differences. Differences in personalities may also affect the way members listen. The Myers-Briggs Type Indicator predicts that introverts will be better comprehensive listeners than extroverts, who are eager to speak out—even when they haven't understood what others have said. Sensing members may listen for facts and figures, while intuitives listen for key ideas and overarching themes. Thinking members are often effective analytical listeners, whereas feeling members are more likely to be effective empathic listeners. Judging listeners may drive the group to reach a decision, while perceivers take the time to appreciate what they hear without leaping to immediate conclusions.[33]

Cultural Differences. Cultural differences have significant effects on the ways in which group members listen and respond to one another. One study concludes that international students see U.S. students as less willing and less patient listeners than students from African, Asian, South American, or European cultures.[34] Intercultural communication scholars Myron Lustig and Jolene Koester explain these differences in perceived listening behavior by noting that English is a speaker-responsible language in which the speaker structures the message and relies primarily upon words to provide meaning. In Japanese, however, which is a listener-responsible language, speakers indirectly indicate what they want the listener to know. The listener must rely on nonverbal communication and an understanding of the relationship between the speaker and the listener to interpret meaning.[35] Thus, English-speaking listeners may believe that Japanese speakers are leaving out important information; Japanese listeners may think that English speakers are overexplaining or talking down to them. Such misunderstandings and perceived discourtesies are the result of speaking and listening differences rather than of substantive disagreement.

Taking Notes in Groups

If most of us listen at only 25 percent efficiency, why not take notes during a discussion to make sure we remember? Why not write down the important ideas and facts? Taking notes makes a great deal of sense, but only when it is done correctly.

The inclination to take notes is understandable. After all, that's what we do in a classroom when an instructor lectures. However, if you are like most listeners, only one-fourth of what you hear will end up in your notes. Even if it were possible for you to copy down every word uttered in a group discussion, your notes would be missing the nonverbal cues that often tell you more about what a person means and feels. And if you spend all your time taking notes, when will you put aside your pen and participate? Ralph Nichols summarized the dilemma of balancing note taking and listening when he concluded that "there is some evidence to indicate that the volume of notes taken and their value to the taker are inversely related."[36] Thus, the challenge for a group member is this: How do I obtain brief, meaningful records of a group discussion? Several methods can help, depending upon your needs and your role in the group.

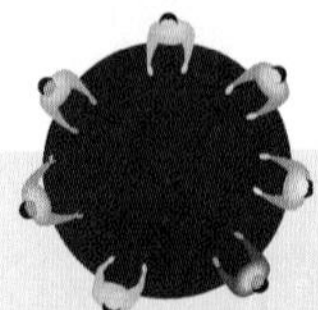

groups in balance . . .

Learn the Art of High-Context Listening

In Chapter 4, Group Diversity, we explore the high-context–low-context cultural dimension and note that someone from a high-context culture goes well beyond a person's words to interpret meaning. High-context communicators also pay close attention to nonverbal cues when they listen. Interestingly, the Chinese symbol for listening includes characters for eyes, ears, and heart.

For the Chinese "it is impossible to listen . . . without using the eyes because you need to look for nonverbal communication. You certainly must listen with ears" because Chinese is a tonal language in which intonation determines meaning. "Finally, you listen with your heart because" you must sense the "emotional undertones expressed by the speaker." In Korean, there is a word, *nunchi,* that means that you communicate through your eyes. "Koreans believe that the environment supplies most of the information that we seek, so there is little need to speak."[1]

[1]Elizabeth A. Tuleja, *Intercultural Communication for Business* (Mason, OH: Thomson Higher Education, 2005), p. 43.

If a member takes minutes, you can rely on the official record of the meeting. But here, too, there are potential problems. What if the recorder is a poor listener? What if you need the notes immediately and can't wait for the official minutes to be distributed and approved? Suppose you want more personalized meeting notes that also record your assignments? In such cases, minutes may not be enough.

Flexibility is the key to taking useful and personalized meeting notes. Good listeners adjust their note-taking system to a group's agenda or impose a note-taking pattern on a disorganized discussion. In some cases, margin notes on an agenda may be sufficient. If you attend a lot of meetings, you may find it helpful to use a brief form—such as the one in Figure 8.2—to record key details, information, and actions.

Self-Listening in Groups

As important as it is to listen to the other members of your group, it is just as important to listen to yourself. Poor self-listening is often the cause of communication breakdowns. Rebecca Shafir, author of *The Zen of Listening,* maintains that "if we could hear our words . . . through the ears of our listeners, we would be appalled at the overgeneralizations, the inaccuracies, and the insensitive, negative comments we make about ourselves and others."[37] If you can monitor, understand, and modify the effects of what you say, you can become a more effective group member. Two strategies can enhance your ability to listen to yourself. The first is to translate feedback into useful information about the way you speak and listen so that you can answer questions such as these:

- Do members listen to me, or do I seem to be talking to a blank wall?
- Do members seem to understand what I am saying, or do frequent questions and confusion follow my remarks?
- Do I feel my voice rising and my heart racing when I address a controversial issue or an argumentative member?

Figure 8.2 Sample Form for Meeting Notes

Meeting Notes

Group:	Goal/Topic:
Date and Time:	Place:
Members Attending:	
Members Absent:	
Vital Information	
1.	
2.	
3.	
Decisions Reached	
1.	
2.	
3.	
Personal To-Do List	Date Due
1.	
2.	
3.	
Date/Time/Place of Next Meeting:	

When you listen to yourself, "Whatever you have to say needs only to pass the simple test of teamwork: Are you saying something that is germane to the team as a whole—to its objectives, to its overriding vision, to the tasks it has set out for itself? . . . If not, fix your message so that it is direct, relevant, and respectful of others."[38]

A second way to listen to yourself is to become aware of your internal thought processes. This strategy recognizes that, in a group discussion, what you *want* to say may not be what you *should* say. Consider the following hypothetical situation:

> A college hires a professional facilitator to work with a student government council charged with rewriting the council's constitution and bylaws. Right from the start, the student government president and the facilitator do not hit it off. The situation has become so bad that the rest of the council is paralyzed. Nothing gets done because everyone spends valuable meeting time watching the president and facilitator fight over every issue on the group's agenda.

If you were a member of this group, what would you say or do to help resolve such a problem? A lot depends on how well you listen to others and to yourself, how efficiently you use your extra thought speed, and how fairly you apply the golden listening rule. Seven questions may help you assess your internal thought processes:

1. *What do I want to say?* "I wish you two would stop acting like babies. We're sick and tired of your bickering."

2. *What are the consequences of saying what I want to say?* Both of them will become angry or hurt, and what is left of group morale and cohesiveness could fall apart.
3. *Have I listened comprehensively?* What is each side trying to say? Is the president saying that the facilitator has no right to impose her will on the group? Is the facilitator saying that the president doesn't respect her as an expert?
4. *Have I listened analytically?* Is either side right or wrong? Both the president and the facilitator have legitimate complaints, but their arguments are becoming personal rather than substantive.
5. *Have I listened empathically?* How would I feel if someone treated me this way? I'd probably be just as angry.
6. *Have I listened appreciatively?* Do the president and the facilitator have positive contributions to make? The president should be commended for how well he has led our group. The facilitator should be thanked for sharing useful resources and helping us understand the scope of our assignment.
7. *So, what* should *I say?* I should speak on behalf of the group and tell the president and the facilitator how much we value both of them, but that the group, as a whole, is distressed by the conflict between them. I should ask whether there is something we can do to resolve the problem.

Taking the time to ask a series of self-listening questions can help you develop an appropriate and useful response. Analyzing your own thought processes lets you employ different types of listening to come up with a useful response that can help resolve a group problem.

summary study guide

The Challenge of Listening in Groups

- Listening is the ability to understand, analyze, respect, and appropriately respond to the meaning of another person's spoken and nonverbal messages.
- Although listening is our number-one communication activity, most people cannot accurately report 50 percent of what they hear after listening to a short talk.
- You can resolve the tensions characteristic of listening dialectics if you pay full attention to what members say before deciding what you want to say in response.
- Effective listening relies as much on your attitude (*wanting* to do it) as on your knowledge and skills.

Types of Listening

- There are five types of listening, each of which calls on unique listening skills: discriminative, comprehensive, empathic, analytical, and appreciative listening.
- Ask members good questions to enhance listening comprehension.

Group Roles and Listening

- Members who assume and excel at task roles are often good comprehensive and analytical listeners.
- Members who assume and excel at maintenance roles are often good empathic and appreciative listeners.
- Members who assume self-centered roles may be excellent listeners who use their listening to block, monopolize, or dominate discussions, whereas recognition seekers, confessors, and special-interest pleaders may be poor listeners because they are preoccupied with their own needs.

Improving Listening

- Use your extra thought speed (the fact that you think faster than you speak) by summarizing main ideas, interpreting nonverbal behavior, analyzing arguments, and assessing the relevance of member comments.
- When applying the golden listening rule, listen to others as you would have them listen to you.
- The following five listening strategies can improve how well you listen in groups: (1) listen for big ideas, (2) overcome distractions, (3) "listen" to nonverbal behavior, (4) listen before you leap, and (5) help the group listen.

- Paraphrasing is the ability to restate what people say in a way that indicates that you understand them and the feelings that underlie their meaning.

Special Listening Challenges

- Differences in listening skills, gender, personality types, and culture can enhance or diminish a group's ability to listen.
- Taking brief, meaningful notes during meetings can improve your ability to follow and remember what was said and decided.
- Self-listening helps you monitor and understand the effects of what you say during a group discussion.

key terms

analytical listening 193
appreciative listening 194
comprehensive listening 192
discriminative listening 192
empathic listening 193
golden listening rule 196
listening 187
paraphrasing 199
short-term memory 188
thought speed 196
working memory 188
Working Memory Theory 188

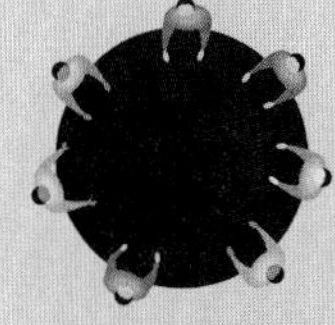

critical thinking about the case study

A Message for Michael

1. Given that Michael is a poor listener, why and how do you think Michael was able to make such a good impression on faculty members and students when he first started working at the college?
2. To what extent could the nature of the faculty meetings have affected Michael's lack of attention and comprehension to the matters being discussed?
3. Which three listener skills would help Michael the most in improving his listening ability?
4. If you were the head of the humanities department, what would you say to Michael that could help him?
5. Which dialectic tensions most likely affected faculty interaction and productivity during the meetings Michael attended? Why?

group work Practice Paraphrasing

Directions: Read the four statements made by group members and write the response you would make that best paraphrases their meaning. As a guide, we recommend that you include at least three components in your paraphrase:

- State your interest in understanding the other person, such as "I sense that . . ." or "If I understand you correctly, you . . ." or "It sounds as if you . . ."
- Identify the other person's emotion or feeling, but make sure you find alternatives to the words the person uses. For example, if a person says, "I'm angry," you will need to decide whether this means that the person is annoyed, irritated, disgusted, or furious. Try to find a word that matches the person's meaning and emotion.
- Describe the situation, event, or facts using alternative words.

Sample Situation and Paraphrase:

Group Member: I get really annoyed when André yells at one of us during a meeting.

Paraphrase: <u>You're saying you get very upset with André when he shouts at you or another group member. Am I right?</u>

1. **Group Member:** I have the worst luck with computers. Every single one I've ever used has problems. Just when the warranty runs out, something goes wrong and I have to spend a lot to get it fixed. The computer I have now has crashed twice, and I lost all of my documents. Maybe it's me—I mean maybe I'm doing something wrong. Why me? I must be cursed or something.

   Paraphrase: ______________________________

   ____

   ____

2. **Group Member:** I hope Anita doesn't react too strongly to Chris and Manuel's concerns about the scope of our project at today's meeting. She can be very emotional when she feels strongly about something she really believes in.

   Paraphrase: ______________________________

   ____

   ____

3. **Group Member:** I dislike saying *no* to anyone in our group who asks for help, but then I have to rush or stay up late to get my own work done. I want to help, but I also want to do my own job—and do it well.

   Paraphrase: ______________________________

   ____

   ____

4. **Group Member:** How on earth are we going to get an A on this assignment if we can't even find time to meet?

   Paraphrase: ______________________________

   ____

   ____

Source: Recommendations based on the Listener's Summarization Model in Madelyn Burley-Allen, *Listening: The Forgotten Skill,* 2nd ed. (New York: Wiley, 1995), p. 132.

group assessment Student Listening Inventory

Directions: This inventory should help identify your listening strengths and weaknesses within the context of a college classroom. Remember that "speaker" can mean the instructor or another student. Use the following numbers to indicate how often you engage in these listening behaviors:

1 = Almost never 2 = Not often 3 = Sometimes 4 = More often than not 5 = Almost always

LISTENING BEHAVIOR	1	2	3	4	5
1. When someone is speaking to me, I purposely block out distractions such as side conversations and personal problems.					
2. I am comfortable asking questions when I don't understand something a speaker has said.					
3. When a speaker uses words I don't know, I jot them down and look them up later.					
4. I assess a speaker's credibility while listening.					
5. I paraphrase and/or summarize a speaker's main ideas in my head as I listen.					
6. I concentrate on a speaker's main ideas rather than the specific details.					
7. I try to understand people who speak indirectly as well as I understand those who speak directly.					
8. Before reaching a conclusion, I try to confirm with the speaker my understanding of his or her message.					
9. I concentrate on understanding a speaker's message when she or he is explaining a complex idea.					
10. When listening, I devote my full attention to a speaker's message.					
11. When listening to someone from another culture, I factor in my knowledge of cultural differences to interpret meaning.					
12. I watch a speaker's facial expressions and body language for additional information about the speaker's meaning.					
13. I encourage speakers by providing positive nonverbal feedback—nods, eye contact, vocalized agreement.					
14. When others are speaking to me, I establish eye contact and stop doing other nonrelated tasks.					
15. I avoid tuning out speakers when I disagree with or dislike their message.					

LISTENING BEHAVIOR	1	2	3	4	5
16. When I have an emotional response to a speaker or the message, I try to set aside my feelings and continue listening to the message.					
17. I try to match my nonverbal responses to my verbal responses.					
18. When someone begins speaking, I focus my attention on the message.					
19. I try to understand how past experiences influence the ways in which I interpret a message.					
20. I attempt to eliminate outside interruptions and distractions.					
21. When I listen, I look at the speaker, maintain some eye contact, and focus on the message.					
22. I avoid tuning out messages that are complex, complicated, and challenging.					
23. I try to understand the other person's point of view when it is different from mine.					
24. I try to be nonjudgmental and noncritical when I listen.					
25. As appropriate, I self-disclose a similar amount of personal information as the other person shares with me.					

Scoring: Add up your scores for all of the questions. Use the following general guidelines to assess how well you think you listen. Please note that your score only represents your personal *perceptions* about your listening behavior and skills.

Score	Interpretation
0–62	You perceive yourself to be a poor classroom listener. Attention to all of the items on the inventory could improve your listening effectiveness.
63–86	You perceive yourself to be an adequate listener in the classroom. Paying attention to some types of listening could improve your overall listening effectiveness.
87–111	You perceive yourself to be a good listener in the classroom, but could still improve your listening skills.
112–125	You perceive yourself to be an outstanding listener in the classroom.

Source: Andrew Wolvin and Laura Janusik, "Janusik/Wolvin Student Listening Inventory," in *Communicating: A Social and Career Focus*, 9th ed., ed. Roy M. Berko, Andrew D. Wolvin, and Darlyn R. Wolvin (Boston: Houghton Mifflin, 2004), 129–131.

Note: We have modified several questions in this inventory to ensure clarity and facilitate scoring.

notes

1. Isa N. Engleberg and Dianna R. Wynn, *Instructor's Manual for The Challenge of Communicating: Guiding Principles and Practices* (Boston: Pearson/Allyn & Bacon, 2008), pp. 90–91. Based on The Listen to Learn Survey in Margarete Imhoff, "What Makes a Good Listener? Listening Behavior in Instructional Settings," *International Journal of Listening* 12 (1998), pp. 81–105.
2. Patrice Johnson and Kittie Watson, "Managing Interpersonal and Team Conflict: Listening Strategies," in *Listening in Everyday Life: A Personal and Professional Approach*, 2nd ed., ed. Michael Purdy and Deborah Borisoff (Lanham, MD: University Press, 1997), pp. 121–32; also see Katherine W. Hawkins and Bryant P. Fillion, "Perceived Communication Skill Needs for Workgroups," *Communication Research Reports* 16 (1997), p. 168.
3. Larry L. Barker et al., "An Investigation of Proportional Time Spent in Various Communication Activities by College Students," *Journal of Applied Communication Research* 8 (1980), pp. 101–09.
4. Andrew D. Wolvin and Carolyn G. Coakley, *Listening*, 5th ed. (Madison, WI: Brown and Benchmark, 1996), p. 15.
5. Michael Purdy, "The Listener Wins"; available at http://featuredreports.monster.com/listen/overview.
6. Ralph G. Nichols, "Listening Is a 10-Part Skill," *Nation's Business* 75 (September 1987), p. 40.
7. S. S. Benoit and J. W. Lee, "Listening: It Can Be Taught," *Journal of Education for Business* 63 (1986), pp. 229–32.
8. Donald Carstensen, vice president for education services at ACT, quoted in Michael Purdy, "The Listener Wins"; available at http://featuredreports.monster.com/listen/overview. Also see http://www.act.org/workkeys/assess/listen/levels.html for information about ACT's listening assessment criteria.
9. Florence I. Wolff and Nadine C. Marsnik, *Perceptive Listening*, 2nd ed. (Fort Worth, TX: Harcourt Brace Jovanovich, 1992), pp. 9–16.
10. Edwin P. Hollander, *Leadership Dynamics: A Practical Guide to Effective Relationships* (New York: Macmillan, 1978), p. 53.
11. Fran Rees, *How to Lead Work Teams*, 2nd ed. (San Francisco: Jossey-Bass, 2001), p. 41.
12. Charles M. Kelly, "Empathetic Listening," in *Small Group Communication: A Reader*, 2nd ed., ed. Robert S. Cathcart and Larry A. Samovar (Dubuque, IA: Wm. C. Brown, 1974), p. 340.
13. *The American Heritage Dictionary of the English Language*, 4th ed. (Boston: Houghton Mifflin, 2000), p. 517.
14. Wolvin and Coakley, p. 158.
15. Based on Wolff and Marsnik, p. 100.
16. Wolff and Marsnik, pp. 101–02.
17. Based on Wolff and Marsnik, pp. 94–95.
18. Wolff and Marsnik, p. 97.
19. Hawkins and Fillion, p. 172.
20. Carl E. Larson and Frank M. J. LaFasto, *TeamWork: What Must Go Right/What Can Go Wrong* (Newbury Park, CA: Sage, 1989), p. 90.
21. Ralph Nichols, p. 40.
22. Ralph Nichols, p. 40.
23. Wolvin and Coakley, pp. 135–38.
24. Madelyn Burley-Allen, *Listening: The Forgotten Skill*, 2nd ed. (New York: Wiley, 1995), pp. 68–70.
25. See Peter A. Andersen, *Nonverbal Communication: Forms and Functions* (Mountain View, CA: Mayfield, 1999), pp. 1–2.
26. Ralph G. Nichols, "Do We Know How to Listen? Practical Helps in a Modern Age," *Speech Teacher* 10 (1961), p. 121.
27. David Stauffer, "Yo, Listen Up: A Brief Hearing on the Most Neglected Communication Skill," *Harvard Management Update* 3 (July 1998), p. 11.
28. Adapted from Wolvin and Coakley, p. 299.
29. David W. Johnson's Questionnaire on Listening and Response Alternatives in *Reaching Out: Interpersonal Effectiveness and Self-Actualization*, 7th ed. (Boston: Allyn & Bacon, 2000), pp. 234–39.
30. Michael P. Nichols, *The Lost Art of Listening* (New York: Guilford, 1995), p. 126.
31. Deborah Tannen, *You Just Don't Understand: Women and Men in Conversation* (New York: William Morrow, 1990), pp. 149–51.
32. Melanie Booth-Butterfield, "She Hears . . . He Hears: What They Hear and Why," *Personnel Journal* 44 (1984), p. 39.
33. See Chapter 4 for a discussion of the Myers-Briggs Type Indicator.
34. Wolvin and Coakley, p. 125.
35. Myron W. Lustig and Jolene Koester, *Intercultural Competencies: Interpersonal Communication across Cultures*, 5th ed. (New York: HarperCollins, 2006), pp. 238–39.
36. Ralph G. Nichols, "Listening Is a 10-Part Skill," p. 40.
37. Rebecca Z. Shafir, *The Zen of Listening: Mindful Communication in the Age of Distraction* (Wheaton, IL: Quest Books, 2003), p. 18.
38. Harvey Robbins and Michael Finley, *The New Why Teams Don't Work: What Went Wrong and How to Make It Right* (Princeton, NJ: Peterson's/Pacesetter Books, 1995), p. 142.

chapter 9

Conflict and Cohesion in Groups

chapter outline

study questions

What are the primary sources of conflict in groups?

What communication strategies promote constructive conflict and reduce destructive conflict in groups?

Under what circumstances are the five conflict styles productive or counterproductive in groups?

How do different conflict management strategies address the needs of groups in conflict?

How do members' cultural and gender differences affect their responses to conflict?

What communication strategies enhance group cohesion and prevent groupthink?

Conflict in Groups

Many people mistakenly believe that good groups never have conflicts. On the contrary, conflict is unavoidable in all good groups. Rarely do conscientious group members work together for any length of time without expressing differences and disagreeing. Yet many of us go out of our way to avoid or suppress conflict. Too often, we believe that effective groups "are characterized by chumminess. Many effective teams look more like battlegrounds. . . . Teams with vastly competent members embrace conflict as the price of synergy and set good idea against good idea to arrive at the best idea."[1]

Communication scholars William Wilmot and Joyce Hocker describe conflict management as "a delicate balancing act, like that of a tightrope walker, or a rock climber who must find just the right handholds."[2] Without balance, conflict can devastate group productivity and morale.

Effective groups balance the conflict ↔ cohesion dialectic. In fact, group members with different perspectives can promote critical thinking and creative problem solving. On the other hand, "too many differences, or one difference that is so strong it dominates group resources, can overwhelm the group" and its ability to achieve the group's goal.[3]

The word *conflict* is frequently associated with fighting, anger, and hostility. Conflict does not have to involve negative emotions. When treated as an expression of legitimate differences, conflict can improve group problem solving, promote cohesiveness, increase group knowledge, enhance creativity, and promote the group's goal.[4]

We define **conflict** as the disagreement and disharmony that occur in groups when members express differences regarding group goals; member ideas, behavior, and roles; or group procedures and norms. This definition reflects three types of conflict: substantive, affective, and procedural (see Figure 9.1).[5]

Substantive Conflict

Substantive conflict occurs when members disagree about issues, ideas, decisions, actions, or goals. For example, when members of a student government council try to answer the question, "Should student activities fees be raised?" their conflict is substantive because it focuses on the group's goal of serving students' cocurricular needs.

Figure 9.1 Sources of Group Conflict

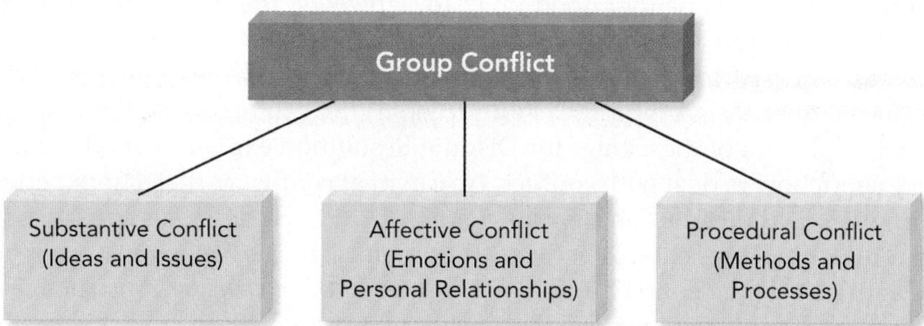

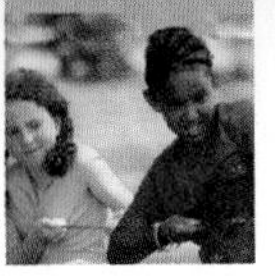

When a group cannot negotiate a *both/and* approach to the individual goal ↔ group goal dialectic, hidden agendas emerge. As we note in Chapter 2, Group Development, when members' hidden agendas become more important than a group's stated goal, the result can be group frustration, unresolved conflict, and failure. Dean Barnlund and Franklyn Haiman, two pioneers in the study of group communication, described hidden agendas as arising when "there are a significant number of private motives, either conscious or unconscious, lurking beneath the surface and influencing the course of the discussion in subtle, indirect ways."[6] Conflicts become serious problems when the members' hidden goals conflict and interfere with the group's goal.

Affective Conflict

Affective conflict is the result of interpersonal disagreements, differences in personalities and communication styles, and members' conflicting core values and beliefs. Affective conflict also occurs when members do not feel appreciated, feel threatened by the group, or struggle for power. Affective conflict is more difficult to resolve than substantive conflict because it involves people's feelings and the way members relate to one another.

Substantive and affective conflict may occur at the same time. For example, Dee advocates an increase in student fees to fund more activities. Charles disagrees; he suggests using existing funds more efficiently rather than placing a larger financial burden on students. At this point, the conflict is substantive; it focuses on issues. However, when Charles rolls his eyes and says to Dee, "Only a fool believes higher fees are the answer," not only does Dee disagree with Charles on the issues, she is also hurt and angry. The conflict has gone beyond substance; it has become personal as well.

Procedural Conflict

Procedural conflict is disagreement among group members about the method or process the group uses in its attempt to accomplish a goal. Some group members may want to begin by suggesting solutions to a problem, whereas others may want to gather information first. Some members may want to vote using secret ballots; others may want a show of hands.

Procedural conflicts sometimes arise when groups have difficulty resolving substantive or affective conflict. Rather than facing the issues, they rely on procedures such as moving to the next topic or taking a vote to get them through.[7]

Constructive and Destructive Conflict

All groups, no matter how conscientious or well mannered, experience conflict. In and of itself, conflict is neither good nor bad. However, the way in which a group deals with conflict can be either constructive or destructive.

Constructive conflict results when group members express disagreement in ways that value everyone's contributions and promotes the group's goal. Kenneth Cloke and Joan Goldsmith of the Center for Dispute Resolution explain that all of us have a choice about how to deal with conflict. We can treat conflict as dialectic experiences "that imprison us or lead us on a journey, as a battle that embitters us or as an opportunity for learning. Our choices between these contrasting attitudes and approaches will shape the way the conflict unfolds."[8] Groups in balance view constructive conflict as an opportunity to improve the quality of work necessary to achieve a common goal.

case study

Sociology in Trouble*

Five faculty members in a college's sociology department meet to discuss the course offerings for the next semester.

Steve, the department chair, thanks the group for the great brainstorming session they just completed. He then asks the tired faculty to address an important issue: Which courses should they eliminate and which new courses should they add to the curriculum? "We need," he says, "to balance the integrity of our department and our offerings with the need to bring in more students and the need to have a strong curriculum." Although faculty members nod their heads, they don't seem to have much enthusiasm for the task.

Trevor emphasizes, "We don't want enrollment to dictate—you know—what our offerings . . . ." Before he finishes his sentence, Helen interrupts. "Here we go, here we go. Trevor, you need to look at the enrollment numbers!" The group senses that Trevor seems more interested in preserving his own low-enrollment courses than developing new ones that attract more students. The faculty has dealt with this issue before. Should they allow faculty members to protect their smaller courses or should they cut these courses? Should they offer more popular courses to improve their numbers even it if means cutting time-honored sociology courses?

Art interrupts the interaction by telling everyone that he has an exciting idea for a new course, the Sociology of Time. He explains that the course would look at time as a commodity that people use for various sociological purposes. The group has mixed reactions. Trevor questions whether the course is rigorous enough and worthy of a separate course on its own. Georgia just nods her head at everything group members say. Helen supports Art's proposed new course. Steve reminds everyone they have to eliminate, not just add, courses. The group suggests cutting Trevor's Culture of Consumerism course. He strongly opposes this move. Helen raises her voice and declares that the enrollment numbers speak for themselves. Finally Georgia says, "We can do this without an argument happening." Helen accuses Trevor of living in the past. At this point, the chair intervenes again and tells the faculty they need to look at the bigger goal, not individual courses.

The lines of conflict are drawn. Whereas Art wants his course on the Sociology of Time approved, Trevor opposes it on academic grounds. He also doesn't want the department to cut his Culture of Consumerism course. The chair again reminds everyone that if they add new courses to attract more students, they must cut existing courses. Helen seems very aggravated—maybe she's heard all these arguments before, maybe she has a grudge against Trevor for something he did in the past, maybe she wants to stay in the department chair's favor, or maybe she's just tired. Georgia seems drained by all the agitation and only wants it to stop.

When you finish reading this chapter, you should be able to answer the following questions.

1. In what ways was the conflict constructive or destructive in this group?
2. What types of conflict styles were evident in the group and how did these styles affect the discussion?
3. What conflict management strategies or options would you have used to minimize or resolve the conflict in this group?
4. To what extent did differences in member demographic characteristics or personalities influence group interaction?
5. What steps could faculty members or their chair have taken to foster group cohesiveness?

*A short video of this group discussion is available through the publisher, Pearson/Allyn & Bacon. Watching the discussion provides a dramatization of how conflict affects group productivity and morale.

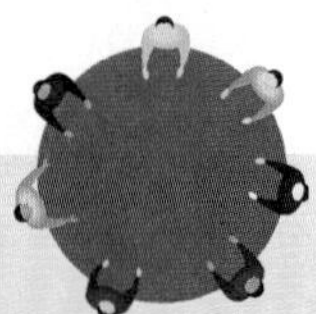

theory in groups

Attribution Theory and Member Motives

When you make an attribution about a group member's behavior, you are speculating (making attributions) about the causes of that behavior. For example, suppose Tyree says, "I propose we meet Thursday at 3:30 rather than Monday at 10:00 a.m." You may attribute his statement to one of several motives:

1. He acted that way because he knows only Melinda can't attend at that hour. What's he got against Melinda? That's mean, self-centered, and heartless.
2. He acted that way because he knows only Melinda can't attend at that hour. That was an ingenious way of getting rid of a highly disruptive member who causes most of our problems. He's very clever, group centered, and goal focused.
3. He acted that way because he knows only Melinda can't attend at the hour. That's certainly better than the 10 a.m. hour when three members can't attend. He's found the best option for the most members.

Attribution Theory claims that we make judgments about people's motives and characteristics that go beyond what we see and hear. Even though we know that we shouldn't make snap judgments about others, we often attribute negative motives or blame others rather than considering alternative explanations. "It's Melinda's fault we didn't finish the project on time" or "How could we expect to finish when three members couldn't attend the 10 a.m. meetings?"

Attribution Theory is the brainchild of psychologist Fritz Heider, who applied it to all kinds of human interaction.[1] Subsequent research used attribution theory to examine group conflict. Here, for example, are three attributions that could prompt anger among group members:

- What other members do seems to constrain what I want to do.
- What other members do seems intended to harm me or others.
- What other members do seems abnormal or illegitimate.[2]

All these attributions may be erroneous when, in fact, members are not trying to restrain a member, do harm, or behave illegitimately. One of the most significant types of attribution error is "a tendency to attribute negative consequences to external situational forces and positive consequences to our own behavior."[3] In other words, if your group has problems, it's their fault, not yours. At the same time, other group members may be thinking, if we're having problems, it's not our fault, it's your fault. Because attribution errors occur all the time, group members should watch out for and openly discuss them when they arise.

[1]Fritz Heider, *The Psychology of Interpersonal Relations* (New York: Wiley, 1958).

[2]Dudley D. Cann and Ruth Anna Abigail, *Managing Conflict through Communication*, 3rd ed. (Boston: Pearson/Allyn & Bacon, 2007), pp. 138–139.

[3]Joseph P. Folger, Marshall Scott Poole, and Randall K. Stutman, *Working through Conflict: Strategies for Relationships, Groups, and Organizations* (Boston: Pearson/Allyn & Bacon, 2005), p. 62.

Destructive conflict results when groups engage in behaviors that create hostility and prevent groups from achieving their goal. Complaining, personal insults, conflict avoidance, and loud arguments or threats contribute to destructive conflict.[9] The quality of group decision making deteriorates when members are inflexible and not open to other views. Destructive conflict has the potential to disable a group permanently. Table 9.1 characterizes the differences between destructive and constructive conflict.

Groups that promote constructive conflict abide by the following principles:[10]

- Disagreement does not result in punishment. "I'm not afraid of being fired if I disagree with powerful members."
- Members work with one another to achieve a mutually satisfying resolution of conflict. "We can work this out. After all, we're all after the same thing."

Table 9.1 Constructive and Destructive Conflict

Constructive Conflict	Destructive Conflict
Focus on issues	Personal attacks
Respect for others	Insults
Supportiveness	Defensiveness
Flexibility	Inflexibility
Cooperation	Competition
Commitment to conflict management	Conflict avoidance

- Lower-status group members are free to disagree with higher-status members. "I know she's the CEO, but I think there are some disadvantages to the approach she suggests."
- The group has an agreed-upon approach for conflict resolution and decision making. "Our group lets every member speak, so I know my ideas will be heard."

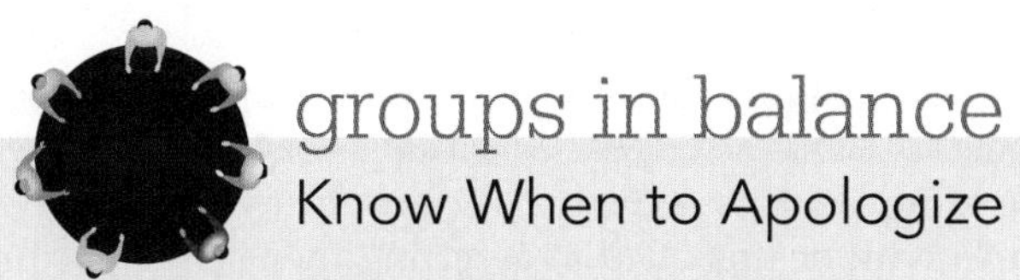

groups in balance . . .
Know When to Apologize

An apology can go a long way toward diffusing tension and opening the door to constructive conflict resolution. It may even deter lawsuits. Studies indicate that 73 percent of complainants will accept a settlement offer when a full apology is given. When there is no apology, only 52 percent are willing to accept a settlement and avoid going to court.[1]

In spite of the importance and simplicity of an apology, we often find it difficult to say, "I'm sorry." When you apologize, you take responsibility for your behavior and the consequences of your actions. Although you may feel you've lost some pride, a willingness to own up to your actions can earn the respect of other group members and help build trust. Here are some suggestions for making an effective apology:[2]

- *Take responsibility for your actions with "I" statements.* "I failed to put all the group members' names on the final report."
- *Clearly identify the behavior that was wrong.* "Everyone provided valuable input and should have been acknowledged."
- *Acknowledge how others might feel.* "I understand that most of you are probably annoyed with me."
- *Acknowledge that you could have acted differently.* "I should have asked the group about this first."
- *Express regret.* "I'm angry with myself for not thinking ahead."
- *Follow through on any promises to correct the situation.* "I'll send an email out tomorrow acknowledging that your names should have been included on the report."
- *Request, but don't demand, forgiveness.* "This group is important to me. I hope you will forgive me."

[1]"Full Apologies Deter Lawsuits, New Studies Find," *Newswise* (University of Nebraska), www.newswise.com/articles/view/500630/?sc=wire. Retrieved May 8, 2008.

[2]Kenneth Cloke and Joan Goldsmith, *Resolving Conflicts at Work: A Complete Guide for Everyone on the Job* (New York: Jossey-Bass, 2000), pp. 109–110; "When and How to Apologize," University of Nebraska Cooperative Extension and the Nebraska Health and Human Services System, http://extension.unl.edu/welfare/apology.htm.

- Members can disagree and still respect one another. "The group may not like my idea, but members would never personally attack me for expressing my opinion."

Conflict Styles

Research indicates that all of us have individual conflict styles we tend to use regardless of the situation.[11] Whereas some people will move heaven and earth to avoid conflict of any kind, others enjoy the competitive atmosphere and the exultation of "winning." Successful groups use various conflict styles to respond to different types and levels of conflict.

There are five traditional conflict styles: avoidance, accommodation, competition, compromise, and collaboration.[12] These styles reflect a dialectic tension between seeking *personal* goals and working cooperatively to achieve the *group's* goal. For example, if you are motivated to achieve your own goals, you may use a more competitive conflict style. If you are dedicated to achieving the group's goals, you may use a more accommodating or collaborative conflict style. Kenneth Thomas, whose research with Ralph Kilmann identified the five conflict styles illustrated in Figure 9.2, acknowledges the dialectic nature of these dimensions. "They are *not* opposites," he writes. Collaborating, for example, is *both* assertive *and* cooperative.[13]

Avoidance Conflict Style

Members use an **avoidance conflict style** when they are unable or unwilling to accomplish their own goals or contribute to achieving the group's goal. In some cases, members who care about the group and its goals may adopt the avoidance style because they are uncomfortable with or unskilled at asserting themselves. Group members who use this style may change the subject, avoid bringing up a controversial issue, and even deny that a conflict exists. Avoiding conflict in groups is usually counterproductive because it fails to address a problem and can increase group tensions. Ignoring or avoiding conflict does not make it go away.

Figure 9.2 Conflict Styles

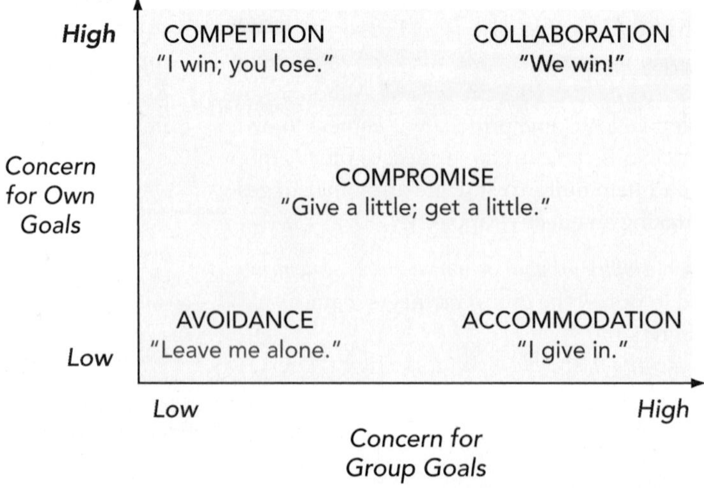

However, in some circumstances, avoiding conflict can be appropriate, specifically when:

- the issue is not that important to you.
- you need time to collect your thoughts or control your emotions.
- other group members are addressing the problem effectively.
- the consequences of confrontation are too risky.

Accommodation Conflict Style

Group members using the **accommodation conflict style** give in to other members at the expense of their own goals. Accommodators have a genuine desire to get along with other members. They believe that giving in to others serves the needs of the group, even when the group could benefit from further discussion. A group member who always approaches conflict by accommodating others may be perceived as less powerful and less influential.

The accommodation style can be appropriate when:

- the issue is very important to others but is not very important to you.
- it is more important to preserve group harmony than to resolve the issue.
- you realize you are wrong or you have changed your mind.
- you are unlikely to succeed in persuading the group to adopt your position.

Competition Conflict Style

The **competition conflict style** occurs when group members are more concerned with their own goals than the group. Competitive members want to win; they argue that their ideas are superior to alternatives suggested by others. When used inappropriately, the competitive style generates hostility, ridicule, and personal attacks against

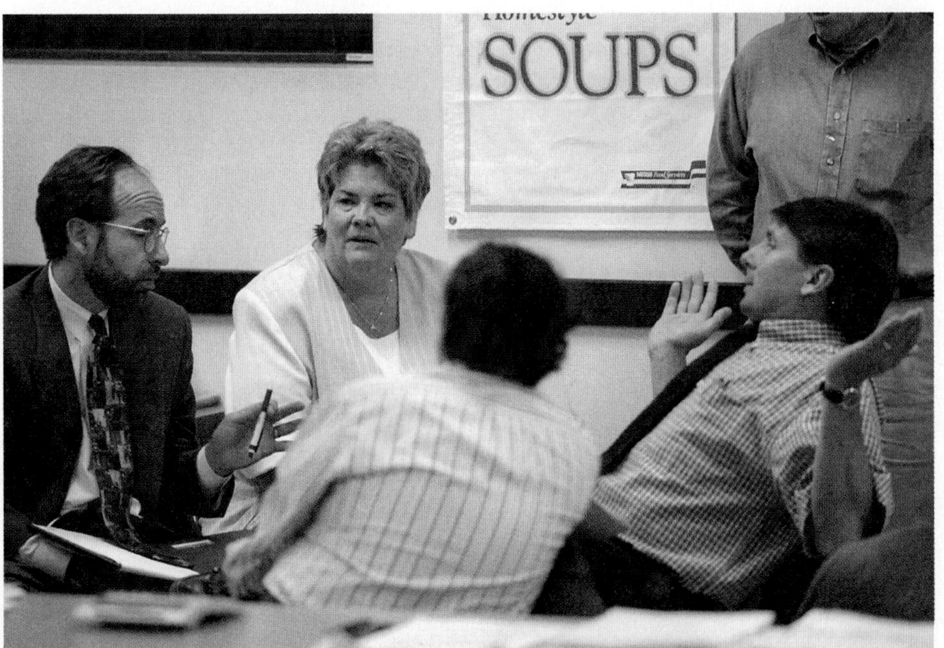

Elected officials in Amsterdam, New York, negotiate with other municipalities to bring water service from one town to another. Given that successful groups use various conflict styles to respond to different types and levels of conflict, which style or styles does this group seem to be using: avoidance, accommodation, competition, compromise, and/or collaboration?

group members. Approaching conflict competitively tends to divide group members into winners and losers. Ultimately, this may damage the relationships among group members.

In certain group situations, however, the competitive approach may be appropriate, such as when:

- you have strong beliefs about an important issue.
- the group must act immediately on an urgent issue or in an emergency.
- the consequences of the group's decision may be very serious or harmful.
- you believe that the group may be acting unethically or illegally.

Compromise Conflict Style

The **compromise conflict style** is a middle ground approach that involves conceding some goals in order to achieve others. When group members compromise, they accept some losses in exchange for gaining something they want. Group members who approach conflict through compromise argue that it is a fair method of resolving problems, since everyone loses equally. "However, when each person gives up something in order to meet the others halfway, the result is only partial satisfaction for all concerned. Commitment to solutions will be questionable."[14]

The compromise approach works best when:

- other methods of resolving the conflict are not working.
- the members have reached an impasse and are no longer progressing toward a reasonable solution.
- the group does not have enough time to explore more creative solutions.

Collaboration Conflict Style

The **collaboration conflict style** searches for new solutions that will achieve *both* the individual goals of group members *and* the goals of the group. Instead of arguing over who is right or wrong, the collaborative group seeks creative solutions that satisfy everyone's interests and needs.[15] Collaboration promotes synergy and resolves the dialectic tension between competition and cooperation. It also "involves trying to find an 'integrative' (or win-win) solution" that enables the group to make progress toward achieving its common goal.[16]

There are, however, two drawbacks to the collaborative approach. First, collaboration requires a lot of the group's time and energy, and some issues may not be important enough to justify this. Second, in order for collaboration to be successful, all group members must participate fully. Avoiders and accommodators can prevent a group from truly collaborating.

Groups should approach conflict resolution collaboratively when:

- they want a solution that will satisfy all group members.
- they need new and creative ideas.
- they need a commitment to the final decision from every group member.
- they have enough time to commit to creative problem solving.

Choosing a Conflict Style

While individuals may be predisposed to a particular conflict style, effective group members choose the style that is most appropriate for a particular group in a partic-

ular situation. As situations change, so may the approach. Consider the following example of a jury:

> During the first hour of deliberation, the jury engaged in a heated debate over a controversial, yet central, issue in the case. Tony was conspicuously silent throughout this discussion. Jury members asked his opinion several times. Each time, he indicated that he agreed with the arguments that Pam presented. On a later issue, Tony became a central participant. He argued vehemently that one of the defendants was not guilty. He said, "I'm just not going to give in here. It's not right for the man to go to jail over this." Eventually, one of the jurors suggested that Tony reexamine a document presented as evidence of the defendant's guilt. Tony was quiet for a few minutes and carefully reviewed the document for himself. He then looked up at the group and said, "Well, this changes everything for me. I guess he really was a part of the conspiracy."

Tony used several approaches to deal with conflict in the group. First, he avoided it altogether. He simply had nothing to add to the discussion. Tony then became competitive when he thought that a person might be unjustly imprisoned. However, he became accommodating when a review of the evidence convinced him that he had been wrong.

When selecting a conflict style, consider the following questions:

- How important is the issue to you?
- How important is the issue to other members?
- How important is it to maintain positive relationships within the group?

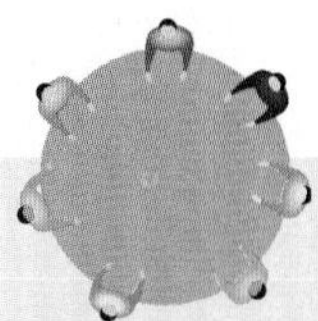

virtual groups
Conflict in Cyberspace

Conflicts in virtual groups arise for a variety of reasons and are difficult to resolve. In *The Argument Culture,* Deborah Tannen points out that "the potential for misunderstandings and mishaps with electronic communication expands in proportion to the potential for positive exchanges."[1] Have you ever received emails that were not intended for you and you found disturbing to read? Have you ever fired off an angry email, only to regret it later? The efficiency of email makes it easy to forward messages without reading them carefully, reply while you're still angry, and send a message to many people without knowing if each will interpret it the same way.

The time, distance, and possible anonymity that separate members of virtual groups can increase conflict. Unfortunately, some group members feel less obligated to behave politely when the interaction isn't face to face. As a result, virtual groups tend to communicate more negative and insulting messages than face-to-face groups do.[2] However, just because someone can't challenge or reprimand you in person is no reason to abandon civil behavior. Susan Barnes, author of *Online Connections,* notes that "challenging comments can quickly turn professional working adults into 'textual mud slingers.' Curt email messages are rapidly thrown back and forth."[3]

Some technologies are better suited for dealing with conflict than others.[4] Using audio-only (e.g., telephone) or data-only (e.g., email) technology is a poor way to deal with conflict. Videoconferencing works slightly better. However, major conflicts are best resolved face to face.

[1]Deborah Tannen, *The Argument Culture: Moving from Debate to Dialogue* (New York: Random House, 1998), p. 242.

[2]Deborah L. Duarte and Nancy Tennant Snyder, *Mastering Virtual Teams: Strategies, Tools, and Techniques That Succeed,* 3rd ed. (San Francisco: Jossey-Bass, 2006), p. 161.

[3]Susan B. Barnes, *Online Connections: Internet Interpersonal Relationships* (Cresskill, NJ: Hampton Press, 2001), p. 46.

[4]Duarte and Snyder, p. 26.

Figure 9.3 Approaches to Conflict Management

4Rs Method (Analyze the Conflict)
Choose Appropriate Approach to Conflict
We need the help of a third party.
We should express concerns and suggest a solution.
We should bargain to settle differences.
We need a third party to facilitate the discussion.
We need a third party to decide for us.
A–E–I–O–U Model
Negotiation
Mediation
Arbitration

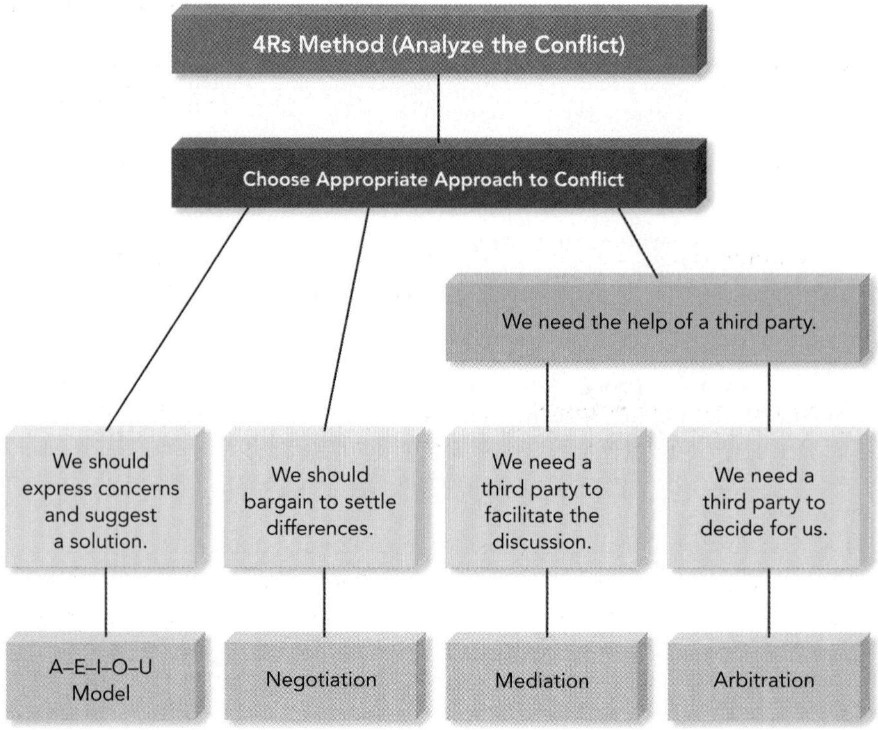

- How much time does the group have to address the issue?
- How fully do group members trust one another?[17]

Answers to these questions can suggest whether a particular conflict style is appropriate or inappropriate in a particular situation. For instance, if group members do not trust one another, the compromising style would be less appropriate. If the issue is very important to everyone, and the group has plenty of time to discuss it, collaboration is ideal. Effective groups do not rely on one conflict style. Rather, they balance their choice of conflict style with the needs of the group.

Conflict Management Strategies

Appropriate conflict styles help resolve disagreements. Sometimes, however, a group must set aside the substantive, affective, or procedural issues under discussion and address the causes of the conflict directly. In short, groups need a strategy for analyzing and resolving the conflict (see Figure 9.3).

The 4Rs Method

In order to choose an appropriate conflict management strategy, you must understand your group's conflict. We suggest using the **4Rs Method** to analyze the conflict before selecting a method for resolving the conflict. Each of the four steps requires group members to address several critical questions:

- **Reasons.** What are the reasons for or causes of the conflict? Are the causes substantive, affective, and/or procedural? Do other members agree with your assessment of the reasons for the conflict?
- **Reactions.** How are group members reacting to one another? Are the reactions constructive or destructive in nature? Can members adopt behaviors that are more constructive?
- **Results.** What are the consequences of the group's approach to the conflict? Is the conflict serious enough to jeopardize the group's goal and members' morale?
- **Resolution.** What are the available methods for resolving the conflict? Which method best matches the nature of the group and its conflict?

The A-E-I-O-U Model

Jerry Wisinski's **A-E-I-O-U Model** focuses on collaboration and what he calls *positive intentionality,* the assumption that other people are not trying to cause conflict.[18] Suppose your group is working on an important project that is behind schedule, and group members are blaming one another. The five steps in the A-E-I-O-U model can give you a constructive approach to managing this conflict:[19]

- *A—Assume that the other members mean well.* In this first step, you must believe that other group members want to resolve the conflict. You could express this as "I know that all of us want this project to succeed." If you sense that some people are not willing to cooperate or have hidden agendas, your group should spend time making sure that everyone is committed to resolving the conflict.
- *E—Express your feelings.* You can help your group interpret your reactions by expressing your feelings: "Like most of you, I'm frustrated because it seems we're not putting in the work that's needed." In addition, as you listen to others express their feelings, paraphrase what they've said to ensure that you and others understand their concerns.
- *I—Identify what you would like to have happen.* If you say, "I'd like to be assured that all of you are as concerned about the success of this project as I am, and that you've been thinking about how we can make sure the work gets done on time," the group can focus on solving the problem. As you listen to others, try to determine whether group members are close to or far from agreement.
- *O—Outcomes you expect are made clear.* Discuss the potential outcomes of member behavior: "I sincerely believe that if we don't work late for the next couple of days, we won't finish this project on time."
- *U—Understanding on a mutual basis is achieved.* Recognize that group members may need more time to reach a mutual understanding: "Could we try staying late for the next few days to get ahead of the game? What do you think?" A group will frequently reject an initial suggestion but then develop a more satisfactory solution.

Negotiation in Groups

Negotiation is a process of bargaining in order to settle differences or reach solutions. Normally, negotiation takes the form of compromise, with group members conceding some issues in order to achieve agreement on other points. Group members will be more willing to bargain if they believe that they will be no worse off and might even be better off by the end of the negotiation process.

Table 9.2 Elements of Principled Negotiation

Elements	Principles
People	**Separate the people from the problem.** Do not blame or accuse members. Rather, find a way of working together to resolve the problem and restore balance. You won't eliminate conflicts by ignoring or expelling members who disagree, but you can resolve or reduce the conflicts among them.
Interests	**Focus on interests, not positions.** Look for common needs and interests, not a position or specific point of disagreement. When members stake out positions, they feel obligated to defend them. Focusing on common interests directs members to looking for solutions rather than personal success.
Options	**Generate a variety of possible solutions for mutual gain.** Consider multiple options before deciding what to do. Be creative, flexible, and open to alternatives. Make sure that the group's common goal is specific, realistic, and achievable as well as clear and elevated.
Criteria	**Establish fair and objective criteria for evaluating and choosing a solution or course of action.** When a group seeks fair standards for resolving a conflict or choosing an option, they have an agreed-upon basis for making decisions.

Roger Fisher, William Ury, and Bruce Patton of the Harvard Negotiation Project offer a process for resolving conflict known as **principled negotiation.**[20] Four elements characterize this negotiation process: people, interests, options, and criteria. Keep in mind that principled negotiation is not a set of skills, but a process for resolving conflict.[21] Table 9.2 summarizes the four elements of principled negotiation.

When group members focus on defending their positions, the result is winners and losers. When the members focus on group interests, options, and fair criteria, the entire group wins. However, even principled negotiation can become deadlocked when members fail to recognize or appreciate the needs of others and are unwilling to make concessions. The following strategies can help break a deadlock:[22]

- Limit the scope of the problem by dividing it into manageable parts.
- Minimize defensive behavior by having members explain or paraphrase the other side's position.
- Summarize areas of agreement to promote cooperation.
- Take a break to relieve group tensions.
- Ask for more information to avoid inaccurate assumptions.

Clearly, group members must balance a variety of needs during negotiation.[23] They must be willing to cooperate with others while attempting to meet as many of their own needs as possible. They must openly communicate what they are willing to concede, yet not sacrifice more than is necessary. Finally, members must balance the need to gain their own short-term goals against the benefits of mutually desirable long-term conflict resolution.

Third-Party Intervention

Sometimes group conflicts are so intense and potentially destructive, members turn to a third party for help. **Third-party intervention** occurs when a group seeks the services of an impartial outsider who has no direct connections to the group, but has

the skills needed to analyze the conflict and help resolve it. Here we focus on two kinds of third-party interventions: mediation and arbitration.

Mediation. **Mediation** is "facilitated negotiation [that] employs the services of impartial third parties only for the purpose of guiding, coaching, and encouraging the disputants through negotiation to successful resolution and agreement."[24] Mediation is an appropriate approach to conflict resolution when group members cannot resolve the conflict by themselves and when everyone concerned is willing to participate in the process and abide by the final settlement. If members cannot agree to these terms, then mediation is not a good option.

When a group uses mediation, there are two basic requirements: an impartial mediator and a well-planned mediation session. The group must choose an impartial mediator who is not involved in the conflict. When a conflict involves all members of the group, a mediator from outside the group may be the best option. A group leader or member should act as mediator *only* when *not* involved in the conflict. Mediators do not take sides in the dispute. Instead, they guide the group through the process and facilitate negotiation.

Effective mediators follow a well-established series of steps:[25]

- *Introduction.* Explain the mediation process and create a supportive climate by offering encouragement and asking for questions prior to beginning.
- *Storytelling.* Allow each member to speak without interruption. Use members' stories to identify issues and establish commonalities. Summarize each group member's perspective.
- *Agenda building.* List the issues for negotiation and frame the goals of the session.
- *Negotiation and problem solving.* Guide the group members toward possible solutions.
- *Testing agreement.* After agreeing on a resolution to the conflict, discuss ways to implement the solution. Write a clear, unambiguous, and comprehensive agreement. Group members should sign the agreement.
- *Closure.* Praise the group and provide copies of the agreement to all members. If possible, lead a discussion on ways in which the group can resolve future conflicts.[26]

Effective mediators establish rapport with disputing group members through empathic listening.[27] They listen to each member's concerns, acknowledge the legitimacy of those concerns, and assure members that they will try to help everyone discover a solution that meets their needs.[28]

Arbitration. Groups often seek mediation when all other methods of resolving a conflict have failed. If mediation does not work, a group may seek arbitration. **Arbitration**, like mediation, involves a third party. After considering all sides, the agreed-upon arbitrator decides how to resolve the conflict. The arbitrator may choose one person's solution or may develop a solution the group has not considered. Whatever the final decision, group members are obligated to accept and implement the solution, no matter what they think about it.

When turning to an arbitrator, group members "have acknowledged that their own decision-making powers are insufficient to resolve the dispute. Their function, therefore, is to present their side of the case as fully and as capably as possible so that fairness and justice can 29evail."[29] Despite the hope for a just outcome, professional

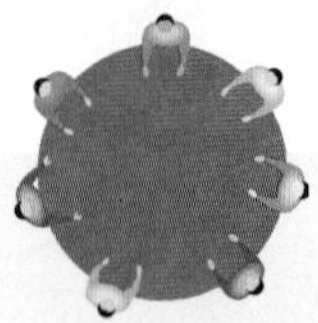

ethics in groups
Ethical Conflict Resolution

Ethical conflict resolution respects differences, uses power positively, encourages collaboration, seeks constructive change, and promotes positive relationships. Mediation experts Stephen Littlejohn and Kathy Domenici suggest the following strategies for resolving conflict constructively and ethically:[1]

- Speak to be understood rather than to win.
- Focus on your own perspective rather than criticizing others' behavior.
- Speak in ways that are respectful rather then attacking or threatening another.
- Recognize that there are many perspectives rather than polarizing a dispute into only two points of view.
- Recognize the complexities of an issue rather than oversimplifying it.
- Explore ideas in new ways.

Ethical and constructive conflict resolution does not guarantee that you will get what you want, nor does it preclude that possibility. Practicing ethical conflict resolution promotes respectful communication that encourages members to seek solutions that satisfy everyone involved.

[1]Stephen W. Littlejohn and Kathy Domenici, *Engaging Communication in Conflict: Systematic Practice* (Thousand Oaks, CA: Sage, 2001), pp. 44–45.

arbitrators understand that their decisions may not please everyone in a group. Yet, for groups that cannot solve problems on their own or with the help of a mediator, arbitration may be the only way to resolve a conflict.

Conflict and Member Diversity

Conflict becomes more complex in diverse groups. Differences in cultural and gender perspectives may result in misunderstandings, prejudices, and unintentionally offensive behavior. Organizations and companies that fail to understand, respect, and adapt to such differences are likely to have more strikes and lawsuits, low morale among workers, less productivity, and a higher turnover of employees.[30]

Cultural Responses to Conflict

The cultural values of individual members greatly influence the degree to which they feel comfortable with conflict and how it is resolved. Members from cultures that value conformity are less likely to express disagreement than those from cultures that place a higher value on individualism. While people from Japanese, German, Mexican, and Brazilian cultures value group conformity, those from Swedish and French cultures are generally more comfortable expressing differences.[31] In addition, Chinese group members may feel uncomfortable with adversarial approaches to conflict.[32] Also, remember that cultural differences may be regional rather than international. For example, Franco-Canadians are often more cooperative during the negotiation of conflict, while Anglo-Canadians are slower to agree to a resolution.[33]

Gender Responses to Conflict

Groups must be sensitive to the ways in which gender differences influence conflict. In general, women are more likely to avoid conflict or to leave a group when there is

continuous conflict.[34] In addition, women are more likely to address conflict privately rather than in front of the entire group.[35] Men and women can learn from each other's perspectives as they work through a group's conflict.

Studies show that men and women from similar cultures do not differ significantly in terms of the conflict strategies and styles they use. However, men and women do differ in terms of their expected focus and behavior in conflicts. Men tend to focus on substantive issues, while women tend to focus on the relationships among members. As a result, women tend to cooperate more than men under ideal conditions. At the same time, women may compete more forcefully in reaction to what they perceive as betrayal or underhanded behavior by others.[36]

Group Cohesion

Resolving conflict in groups does not guarantee success, nor does it ensure that group members will work together toward a common goal. Working in groups requires group **cohesion,** the mutual attraction that holds the members of a group together. Cohesive groups feel committed and unified; members develop a sense of teamwork and pride in the group. A cohesive group has:

- high levels of interaction.
- a friendly and supportive communication climate.
- a desire to conform to group expectations.
- the use of creative and productive approaches to achieving goals.
- satisfied members.[37]

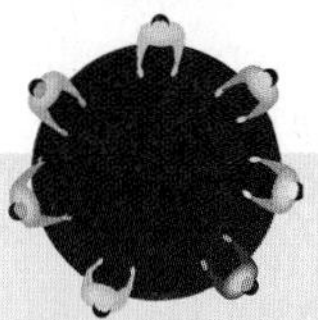

groups in balance . . .
Let Members Save Face

Collectivist cultures place a high value on "face." From a cultural perspective, **face** is the positive image you wish to create or preserve. Cultures that place a great deal of value on "saving face" discourage personal attacks and outcomes in which one person "loses." Keep in mind the following collectivist perspectives about conflict and face:[1]

- Conflict operates within the context of relationships and the need to preserve "face."
- Conflict resolution requires that "face" issues be mutually managed before discussing other issues.
- Conflict resolution succeeds when both parties save "face" and claim that they have "won."

In Chapter 4, Group Diversity, we note that the individualism–collectivism cultural dimension strongly influences how group members communicate. Not surprisingly, this dialectic also explains how members define and respond to conflict. For example, collectivist members may merge substantive and affective concerns, making conflict more personal. "To shout and scream publicly, thus displaying the conflict to others, threatens everyone's face to such an extreme degree that such behavior is usually avoided at all costs." In individualistic cultures, group members may express their anger about an issue and then joke and socialize with others once the disagreement is over. "It is almost as if once the conflict is resolved, it is completely forgotten."[2]

[1]William R. Cupach and Daniel J. Canary, *Competencies in Interpersonal Conflict* (New York: McGraw-Hill, 1997), p. 133.
[2]Myron W. Lustig and Jolene Koester, *Intercultural Competence: Interpersonal Communication across Cultures* (Boston: Pearson/Allyn & Bacon, 2006), pp. 283–94. Lustig and Koester summarize research by Stella Ting-Toomey and John G. Oetzel, *Managing Interpersonal Conflict Effectively* (Thousand Oaks, CA: Sage, 2002).

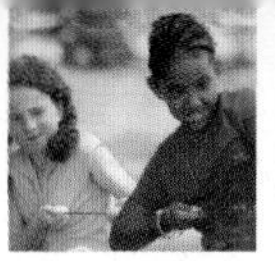

Group cohesion is the mutual attraction that holds the members of a group together, helps members feel committed and unified, and develops a sense of teamwork and pride in the group. How have these Shriners in the Beardstown, Illinois, 30th Annual Fall Festival established their group's identity and traditions as a way to demonstrate and enhance their cohesion?

Enhancing Group Cohesion

Four general strategies for developing group cohesion are to establish a group identity and traditions, emphasize teamwork, recognize and reward participation, and respect group members.[38]

- **Establish a group identity and traditions.** Refer to the group by using terms such as *we* and *our* instead of *I* and *my*. Some groups create more obvious signs of identity, such as a group name, logo, or motto. Many groups develop rituals and ceremonies to reinforce their traditions.
- **Emphasize teamwork.** Cohesive group members believe that their combined contributions are essential to group success. Group members feel responsibility for and take pride in both the work that they do and the work of other members. Rather than individual members taking credit for success, a cohesive group will emphasize the group's accomplishments.
- **Recognize and reward contributions.** Some group members become so involved in their own work, they don't praise others for their contributions. Other members are quick to criticize others. Cohesive groups establish a supportive climate. Many groups reward individual efforts and initiative with celebrations, letters of appreciation, certificates, and gifts.
- **Respect group members.** When there are strong interpersonal relationships in a group, members become more sensitive to one another's needs. Treating members with respect, showing concern for their personal needs, and appreciating diversity promotes a feeling of acceptance.

Groupthink

Groupthink is a term that describes the deterioration of group effectiveness "and moral judgment that results from in-group pressure."[39] Group pressure that produces too much conformity can have disastrous effects. The homogeneous ↔ heterogeneous dialectic discussed in Chapters 1 and 4 is particularly important when dealing with groupthink. The more members have in common, the more cohesive they may become. They also run the risk of being "more insulated from outside opinions, and therefore more convinced that the group's judgment on important issues must be right."[40]

Symptoms of Groupthink. Irving Janis, a Yale University researcher, developed the theory of groupthink after recognizing patterns in what he terms "policymaking fiascoes." He suggests that groupthink is a significant factor in several major policy decisions, including the Bay of Pigs invasion of Cuba, the escalation of the Vietnam war, and the Watergate burglary and cover-up.[41] Groupthink may also have contributed to the explosion of the space shuttle *Challenger*[42] and the U.S. decision to invade Iraq. After analyzing many of these policy decisions, Janis identified eight symptoms of groupthink.[43] Table 9.3 illustrates the symptoms and expressions of groupthink.

Preventing Groupthink. The best way to deal with groupthink is to prevent it from happening in the first place. The following list provides practical ways to minimize the potential of groupthink.[44] Choose the methods that are most appropriate for your group.

- Ask each member to serve in the role of critical evaluator.
- If possible, have more than one group member work on the same problem independently.
- Discuss the group's progress with someone outside the group. Report that feedback to the entire group.
- Periodically invite an expert to join your meeting and encourage constructive criticism.
- Discuss the potential negative consequences of any decision or action.
- Follow a formal decision-making procedure that encourages expression of disagreement and evaluation of ideas.

Table 9.3 Groupthink

Groupthink Symptoms	Expressions of Groupthink
Invulnerability: Is overly confident; willing to take big risks.	"We're right. We've done this many times, and nothing's gone wrong."
Rationalization: Makes excuses; discounts warnings.	"What does Lewis know? He's been here only three weeks."
Morality: Ignores ethical and moral consequences.	"Sometimes the end justifies the means."
Stereotyping Outsiders: Considers opposition too weak and stupid to make real trouble.	"Let's not worry about the subcommittee—they can't even get their own act together."
Self-Censorship: Doubts his or her own reservations; unwilling to disagree or dissent.	"I guess there's no harm in going along with the group—I'm the only one who disagrees."
Pressure on Dissent: Pressures members to agree.	"Why are you trying to hold this up? You'll ruin the project."
Illusion of Unanimity: Believes everyone agrees.	"Hearing no objections, the motion passes."
Mindguarding: Shields members from adverse information or opposition.	"Rhea wanted to come to this meeting, but I told her that wasn't necessary."

- Ask questions, offer reasons for positions, and demand justifications from others.
- Before finalizing the decision, give members a second chance to express doubts.

In the short term, groupthink decisions are easier. The group finishes early and doesn't have to deal with conflict. However, such decisions are often misguided and may result in serious harm. Spending the time and energy to work through differences will result in better decisions without sacrificing group cohesiveness. As James Surowiecki notes in *The Wisdom of Crowds,* "Diversity and independence are important because the best collective decisions are the product of disagreement and contest, not consensus or compromise.[45]

summary study guide

Conflict in Groups

- Conflict is the disagreement and disharmony that occurs in groups when members express differences regarding group goals, member behavior and roles, and group procedures.
- Substantive conflict occurs when members disagree about issues, ideas, decisions, actions, or goals.
- Affective conflict is the result of interpersonal disagreements, differences in personalities and communication styles, and members' conflicting core values and beliefs.
- Procedural conflict is disagreement among group members about the method or process the group uses in its attempt to accomplish a goal.

Constructive and Destructive Conflict

- Constructive conflict results when group members express disagreements in ways that value everyone's contributions and promote the group's goals.
- Destructive conflict results when group members engage in behaviors that create hostility and prevent the group from achieving its goals.

Conflict Styles

- All of the five conflict styles—avoidance, accommodation, competition, compromise, and collaboration—reflect the individual goals ↔ group goals dialectic tension.
- Effective groups choose conflict styles appropriate for their members and the particular situation. As the situation changes, so may a group's conflict style.

Conflict Management Strategies

- Before reacting to conflict, use the 4Rs Method to consider reasons for the conflict, reactions of members, results of the conflict, and resolution approaches.
- The A-E-I-O-U Model is a technique for expressing your concerns and proposing alternatives in a supportive and constructive manner.
- Principled negotiation involves separating the problem from attitudes about members, focusing on common issues, generating a variety of options, and establishing fair criteria.
- Mediation uses an impartial third party to guide a group through conflict resolution. Mediation is appropriate when members are unable resolve the conflict themselves.
- Arbitration is similar to mediation in that it involves an impartial third party to resolve group conflict. Unlike mediation, an arbitrator can dictate a final decision to the group.

Conflict and Member Diversity

- The cultural values of individual group members influence the degree to which they feel comfortable with conflict and how it is resolved.
- Men and women from similar cultures do not differ significantly in terms of conflict strategies and styles. However, men and women may differ in terms of their expectations and behavior in conflict situations.

Group Cohesion

- Groups can promote cohesion by establishing a group identity and tradition, stressing teamwork, recognizing and rewarding contributions, and respecting individual members' needs.
- Groupthink occurs when a group fails to sufficiently evaluate its decision in order to achieve a consensus.

Highly cohesive groups have a greater risk of succumbing to groupthink.

- Strategies for preventing groupthink include asking a member to serve as a critical evaluator, assigning more than one person to work independently on a problem, discussing group progress with someone outside the group, inviting an expert to a meeting, discussing negative consequences, following formal decision-making procedures, asking questions, and encouraging members to express their doubts.

key terms

accommodation conflict style 217
A-E-I-O-U Model 221
affective conflict 212
arbitration 223
Attribution Theory 214
avoidance conflict style 216
cohesion 225
collaboration conflict style 218
competition conflict style 217
compromise conflict style 218
conflict 211
constructive conflict 212
destructive conflict 214
face 225
4Rs Method 220
groupthink 226
mediation 223
negotiation 221
principled negotiation 222
procedural conflict 212
substantive conflict 211
third-party intervention 222

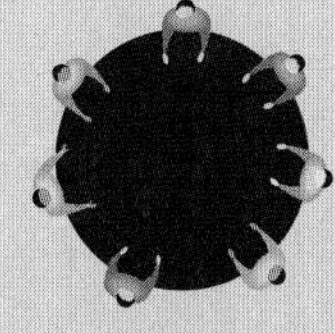

critical thinking about the case study

Sociology in Trouble

1. What types of conflict are evident in the sociology department's discussion? Explain your choices with an example.
2. To what extent is the sociology faculty's conflict constructive or destructive? How effectively does Steve, the department chair, encourage the group to engage in more constructive conflict?
3. What are the individual conflict styles of Steve, Trevor, Helen, Georgia, and Art? How could the group move toward a more collaborative group conflict style?
4. Which conflict management strategy or strategies would effectively resolve the sociology department's conflict in this situation? Why?
5. To what extent do group members' responses to conflict reflect diversity factors such as gender, culture, ethnicity, seniority, and age?
6. Based on this meeting, how cohesive does the sociology department appear? What strategies could the group use to enhance group cohesion within the department?
7. Which dialectic tensions are most evident in this group and what could be done to achieve a *both/and* resolution to these tensions?

group work "I Wish I'd . . . ." Conflict Awareness Log

Directions: Recall two memorable conflict situations in which you withheld your feelings, were less than open or truthful about your reactions, or now regret the way you behaved. Fill out the following table. In column 1, briefly describe the incident. In column 2, write down the reason(s) you behaved this way (e.g., what you feared would happen if you were more open or truthful). In column 3, describe what you wish you'd said or done.

INCIDENT	HOW DID YOU BEHAVE?	I WISH I HAD . . .
Example: Our group was preparing a customer service training presentation. I agreed to take the lead on preparing the team's PowerPoint slides, but Jim submitted an entire PowerPoint show to the group two days before my deadline for getting a draft of the slides to the group.	I was angry with Jim for hijacking my portion of the group's project. His PowerPoint slides were no better than what I had prepared. I said nothing and just let Jim take over that part of the task. I felt unappreciated and didn't want to contribute to any other group projects.	I wish I had spoken up and suggested that Jim work with me on the PowerPoint slides. I think I could have made a greater contribution to the group if I hadn't given in to the situation or become so angry.
Incident #1:		
Incident #2:		

group assessment Ross-DeWine Conflict Management Message Style Instrument

Directions: Below you will read questions and statements made by people in conflict situations. Consider each message separately, and decide how closely this message resembles what you might say in a similar situation. The language may not be exactly the way you would say it, but consider what these questions and statements mean rather than how you would say them. There are no right or wrong answers, nor are these messages designed to trick you. Answer in terms of the responses you actually make, not what you think you *should* say. Give each message a 1 to 5 rating on the answer sheet provided according to the following scale. Mark one answer only.

In conflict situations, I . . .

1	2	3	4	5
never say things like this	rarely say things like this	sometimes say things like this	often say things like this	usually say things like this

_____ 1. "Can't you see how foolish you're being with that thinking?"

_____ 2. "How can I make you feel happy again?"

_____ 3. "I'm really bothered by some things that are happening here; can we talk about these?"

_____ 4. "I really don't have any more to say on this . . . (silence)."

_____ 5. "What possible solutions can we come up with?"

_____ 6. "I'm really sorry that your feelings are hurt—maybe you're right."

_____ 7. "Let's talk this thing out and see how we can deal with this hassle."

_____ 8. "Shut up! You are wrong! I don't want to hear any more of what you have to say."

_____ 9. "It is your fault if I fail at this, and don't you ever expect any help from me when you're on the spot."

_____ 10. "You can't do (say) that to me—it's either my way or forget it."

_____ 11. "Let's try finding an answer that will give us both some of what we want."

_____ 12. "This is something we have to work out; we're always arguing about it."

_____ 13. "Whatever makes you feel happiest is OK by me."

_____ 14. "Let's just leave well enough alone."

_____ 15. "That's OK . . . it wasn't important anyway. . . . You feeling OK now?"

_____ 16. "If you're not going to cooperate, I'll just go to someone who will."

_____ 17. "I think we need to try to understand the problem."

_____ 18. "You might as well accept my decision; you can't do anything about it anyway."

Scoring Instructions: Next to each item, list the rating (from 1 to 5) that you gave that item. Enter the resulting score in the space provided.

	SELF Items	ISSUE Items	OTHER Items
	1. _____	3. _____	2. _____
	8. _____	5. _____	4. _____
	9. _____	7. _____	6. _____
	10. _____	11. _____	13. _____
	16. _____	12. _____	14. _____
	18. _____	17. _____	15. _____
Your Total Score	_____	_____	_____
Average Score	(13.17)	(24.26)	(21.00)

Score Interpretation: The average scores (indicated in parentheses) are what most people expect to receive on each item. Scores higher or lower than these means indicate a higher or lower use of this message style than would usually be expected.

All of us may use any one of these three styles in different settings and under different circumstances. However, we tend to have a predominant style in the messages we generally express during conflict situations.

Items	Item Descriptions
SELF Items → Your score: _________	You focus on your personal interests in conflict situations. Your primary concern is resolving the conflict by getting others to accept your personal view. This is a "win" approach to conflict resolution.
ISSUE Items → Your score: _________	You emphasize the substance of the problem. You have an overriding concern with the content of the conflict rather than winning or maintaining the personal relationship.
OTHER Items → Your score: _________	You want to maintain relationships, even at the cost of resolving conflict. You do not focus on either conflict issues or self-interests. You would rather ignore the problem to maintain a good relationship with others.

Source: Sue DeWine, *The Consultant's Craft: Improving Organizational Communication* (New York: St. Martin's, 1994), pp. 268–272; Rosanna Ross and Sue DeWine, "Communication Messages in Conflict: A Message-Focused Instrument to Assess Conflict Management Styles," *Management Communication Quarterly* 1 (1988), pp. 389–413.

notes

1. Jim Billington, "The Three Essentials of an Effective Team," *Harvard Management Update* 2 (January 1997), p. 3.
2. William W. Wilmot and Joyce L. Hocker, *Interpersonal Conflict,* 7th ed. (Boston: McGraw-Hill, 2007), p. 45.
3. John O. Burtis and Paul D. Turman, *Group Communication Pitfalls: Overcoming Barriers to an Effective Group Experience* (Thousand Oaks, CA: Sage, 2006), p. 127.
4. Peg Pickering, *How to Manage Conflict: Turn All Conflicts into Win-Win Outcomes,* 3rd ed. (Franklin Lakes, NJ: Career Press, 2000), p. 3.
5. Linda L. Putnam, "Conflict in Group Decision-Making," in *Communication and Group Decision-Making,* ed. Randy Y. Hirokawa and Marshall Scott Poole (Beverly Hills, CA: Sage, 1986), pp. 175–196. Also see Joseph P. Folger, Marshall Scott Poole, and Randall K. Stutman, *Working through Conflict,* 5th ed. (Boston: Allyn & Bacon, 2005), pp. 19–20.
6. Dean C. Barnlund and Franklyn S. Haiman, *The Dynamics of Discussion* (Boston: Houghton Mifflin, 1960), p. 39.
7. Putnam, p. 185.
8. Kenneth Cloke and Joan Goldsmith, *Resolving Conflicts at Work: A Complete Guide for Everyone on the Job* (San Francisco: Jossey-Bass, 2000), p. 23.
9. Ronald T. Potter-Efron, *Work Rage: Preventing Anger and Resolving Conflict on the Job* (New York: Barnes & Noble Books, 2000), pp. 22–23.
10. Based on Stephen W. Littlejohn and Kathy Domenici, *Engaging Communication in Conflict: Systematic Practice* (Thousand Oaks, CA: Sage, 2001), pp. 94–103.
11. Folger, Poole, and Stutman, p. 213.
12. See Kenneth W. Thomas and Ralph H. Kilmann, "Developing a Forced-Choice Measure of Conflict-Handling Behavior: The MODE Instrument," *Educational and Psychological Measurement* 37 (1977), pp. 390–95; see also Pickering, pp. 35–41. Whereas Thomas and Kilmann classify conflict styles as avoidance, accommodation, competition, compromise, and collaboration, other researchers use different terms for similar categories, e.g., competing, avoiding, accommodating, compromising, and problem solving, as in Robert R. Blake and Jane S. Mouton, *The Managerial Grid* (Houston: Gulf, 1964).
13. Kenneth W. Thomas, *Intrinsic Motivation at Work: Building Energy and Commitment* (San Francisco: Berret-Koehler, 2000), p. 94.
14. Littlejohn and Domenici, p. 181.
15. Gary Harper, *The Joy of Conflict Resolution: Transforming Victims, Villains, and Heroes in the Workplace and at Home* (Gabriola Island, Canada: New Society, 2004), p. 121.
16. Thomas, p. 94.
17. Folger, Poole, and Stutman, pp. 229–231.
18. Jerry Wisinski, *Resolving Conflicts on the Job* (New York: American Management Association, 1993), p. 27.
19. Wisinski, pp. 28–30.
20. Roger Fisher, William Ury, and Bruce Patton, *Getting to Yes: Negotiating Agreement without Giving In* (Boston: Houghton Mifflin, 1991), p. 15.
21. Wilmot and Hocker, p. 258.
22. Myra Warren Isenhart and Michael Spangle, *Collaborative Approaches to Resolving Conflict* (Thousand Oaks, CA: Sage, 2000), p. 58.
23. Jeffrey Z. Rubin, "Negotiation: An Introduction to Some Issues and Themes," in *Small Group Communication: A Reader,* 6th ed., ed. Robert S. Cathcart and Larry A. Samovar (Dubuque, IA: Wm. C. Brown, 1992), pp. 415–23.
24. William D. Kimsey, Rex M. Fuller, and Bruce C. McKinney, *Mediation and Conflict Management: General Mediation Manual* (Harrisonburg, VA: James Madison University Center for Mediation), p. 21.
25. Suzanne McCorkle and Melanie J. Reese, *Mediation Theory and Practice* (Boston: Allyn & Bacon, 2005), pp. 20–32; Bruce C. McKinney, William D. Kimsey, and Rex M. Fuller, *Mediator Communication Competencies: Interpersonal Communication and Alternative Dispute Resolution,* 4th ed. (Edina, MN: Burgess, 1995), pp. 67–98.
26. Dean Tjosvold and Evert van de Vliert, "Applying Cooperative and Competitive Conflict to Mediation," *Mediation Quarterly* 11 (1994), pp. 303–311.
27. Stephen B. Goldberg, "The Secrets of Successful Mediators," *Negotiation Journal* 3 (July 2005), p. 369.
28. Goldberg, p. 372.
29. John W. Keltner, *The Management of Struggle: Elements of Dispute Resolution through Negotiation, Mediation, and Arbitration* (Cresskill, NJ: Hampton, 1994), p. 168.
30. Bren Ortega Murphy, "Promoting Dialogue in Culturally Diverse Workplace Environments," in *Innovation in Group Facilitation: Applications in Natural Settings,* ed. Lawrence R. Frey (Cresskill, NJ: Hampton, 1995), pp. 77–93.
31. Myron W. Lustig and Laura L. Cassotta, "Comparing Group Communication across Cultures: Leadership, Conformity, and Discussion Processes," in *Small Group Communication: Theory and Practice,* 7th ed., ed. Robert S. Cathcart, Larry A. Samovar, and Linda D. Henman (Madison, WI: Brown & Benchmark, 1996), pp. 316–326.
32. Russell Copranzano, Herman Aguinis, Marshall Schminke, and Dina L. Denham, "Disputant Reactions to Managerial Conflict Resolution Tactics: A Comparison Among Argentina, the Dominican Republic, Mexico, and the United States," *Group and Organization Management* 24 (1999), p. 131.
33. Laura E. Drake, "The Culture–Negotiation Link: Integrative and Distributive Bargaining Through an Intercultural Communication Lens," *Human Communication Research* 27 (2001), p. 321.
34. William W. Wilmot and Joyce L. Hocker, *Interpersonal Conflict,* 6th ed. (New York: McGraw-Hill, 2001), p. 31.
35. Deborah Tannen, *The Argument Culture: Moving from Debate to Dialogue* (New York: Random House, 1998), p. 196.
36. Folger, Poole, and Stutman, p. 235.
37. Marvin E. Shaw, "Group Composition and Group Cohesiveness," in *Small Group Communication: A Reader,* 6th ed., ed. Robert S. Cathcart and Larry A. Samovar (Dubuque, IA: Wm. C. Brown, 1992), pp. 214–220.

38. Based on Ernest G. Bormann and Nancy Bormann, *Effective Small Group Communication,* 6th ed. (Edina, MN: Burgess, 1996), pp. 137–139.
39. Irving L. Janis, *Groupthink: Psychological Studies of Policy Decisions and Fiascoes,* 2nd ed. (Boston: Houghton Mifflin, 1982), p. 9.
40. James Surowiecki, *The Wisdom of Crowds: Why the Many Are Smarter Than the Few and How Collective Wisdom Shapes Business, Economies, Societies, and Nations* (New York: Doubleday, 2004), pp. 36–37.
41. Janis, pp. 174–175.
42. Gregory Moorhead, Richard Ference, and Christopher P. Neck, "Group Decision Fiascos Continue: Space Shuttle *Challenger* and a Groupthink Framework," *Human Relations,* 44, pp. 539–50, reprinted in *Small Group Communication: Theory and Practice,* 7th ed., ed. Robert S. Cathcart, Larry A. Samovar, and Linda D. Henman (Dubuque, IA: Brown & Benchmark, 1991), pp. 161–170. For a different perspective, see Diane Vaughan, *The Challenger Launch Decision: Risk Technology, Culture, and Deviance at NASA* (Chicago: University of Chicago, 1996).
43. Janis, pp. 174–175.
44. See Janis; R. J. W. Cline, "Groupthink and the Watergate Cover-Up: The Illusion of Unanimity," in *Group Communication in Context: Studies of Natural Groups,* ed. Lawrence R. Frey (Hillsdale, NJ: Erlbaum, 1994), pp. 199–223; 3M Meeting Management Team, *Mastering Meetings: Discovering the Hidden Potential of Effective Business Meetings* (New York: McGraw-Hill, 1994), p. 58.
45. Surowiecki, p. xix.

chapter 10

Structured and Creative Problem Solving in Groups

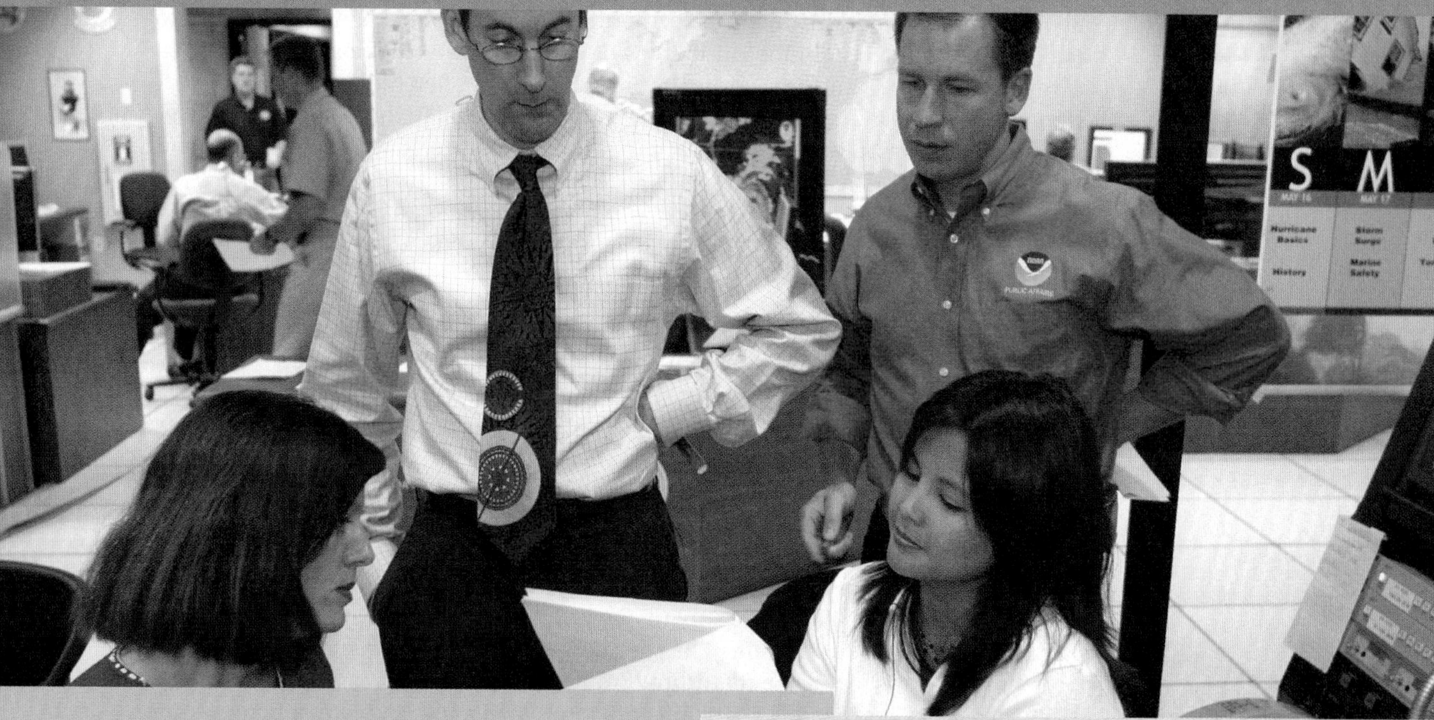

chapter outline

Group Decision Making

Decision Making and Problem Solving • Decision-Making Methods • Decision-Making Questions • Decision-Making Styles

Structured Problem Solving

The Standard Agenda • The Functional Perspective • The Single Question Format

Creative Problem Solving

Brainstorming • Nominal Group Technique (NGT) • Decreasing Options Technique (DOT) • Enhancing Group Creativity

Problem-Solving Realities

Politics • Preexisting Preferences • Power

study questions

- *How do decision-making methods and styles reflect dialectic tensions?*
- *What do the Standard Agenda, Functional Perspective, and Single Question Format have in common?*
- *What techniques enhance creative decision making and problem solving?*
- *In what ways do politics, preexisting preferences, and power affect group problem solving?*

Group Decision Making

What do you do when you have to make an important decision? Do you ponder several options and select the most reasonable one? Do you rely on your instincts and do what *feels* right? Or do you ask other people's advice and go with the majority? Now think about what groups must do when they make collective decisions. Should they use logic, instincts, majority rule, or other methods? As hard as it is to make a *personal* decision, the difficulties of *group* decision making are multiplied many times. At the same time, group decision making is often more effective and satisfying than decisions made by individuals working alone. In this chapter, we examine the many ways in which groups approach the challenge of making decisions and solving problems.

Decision Making and Problem Solving

Decision making and *problem solving* are not the same (see Table 10.1). **Decision making** refers to the "passing of judgment on an issue under consideration" and "the act of reaching a conclusion or making up one's mind."[1] Group decision making results in a position, opinion, judgment, or action. Most groups make decisions but may not solve problems. For example, hiring committees, juries, and families make decisions. Which applicant is best? Is the accused guilty? Whom should we invite to the wedding? Management expert Peter Drucker explains, "A decision is a judgment. It is a choice between alternatives."[2]

Problem solving is a more complex process in which groups analyze a problem and develop a plan of action for solving the problem or reducing its harmful effects. For example, if student enrollment has declined significantly, a college faces a serious problem that can jeopardize its future. Problem solving requires a group to make many decisions. Fortunately, there are decision-making and problem-solving procedures that can help a group "make up its mind."

There are many reasons to trust group decision making and problem solving. Sheer numbers enable a group to generate more ideas than a single person working alone. Even more important, a group is better equipped to find rational and workable solutions to complex problems. As a rule, group decision making generates more ideas and information, tests and validates more arguments, and produces better solutions to complex problems.[3]

Table 10.1 Decision Making and Problem Solving

Decision Making	A *judgment:* The group chooses an alternative. • Guilty or not guilty • Hire or not hire • Spend or save	Asks *who, what, where,* and *when.* • Whom should we invite? • What should we discuss? • Where should we meet? • When should we meet?
Problem Solving	A *process:* The group develops a plan. • Analyze the problem • Develop options • Debate pros and cons • Select and implement a solution	Asks *why* and *how.* • Why doesn't our promotional campaign attract students? • How should we publicize the college's new programs?

case study

No More Horsing Around

A group of horseback-riding stable owners in the county meets to develop a joint plan for attracting more customers, particularly in light of the recent economic downturn. Three group members own prestigious private stables that board and train horses for their owners. Four members own open-to-the public stables that rent horses by the hour and offer riding lessons. Sally—who owns one of the public stables—agrees to chair their meetings.

All seven group members are competent, hardworking, and interested in increasing business at their stables. At the first meeting, the group agrees to seek consensus when making decisions; *all* members have to be satisfied with every decision. They also talk about the need for a promotional campaign to increase their business.

At the second meeting, Sally works diligently to encourage equal participation by everyone in the group. Within a short time, however, things are not going well. The three members who own private stables are very forceful and insistent. Perhaps because these members are wealthy and highly respected among horse professionals, the rest of the group lets them do most of the talking. The tension is that the private and public stable owners see the problem quite differently. The private owners want to place full-color ads in specialized horse publications while the public owners are more interested in getting free publicity about their stables and in funding a few small ads in public outlets. Even though they constitute a majority, the public stable owners resent the unspoken power and influence of the other three members.

In an attempt to broaden the scope of the discussion, Sally distributes a list of questions she believes the group should talk about and answer:

- How serious is our decline in business?
- Why do we have fewer customers?
- How have stables in other counties responded to the problem?
- What limitations do we face in addressing this problem (financial, lack of public relations expertise)?
- What should we do?

The three private stable owners jump to the last question. One of them says, "We know the answers to these questions. We need a good PR campaign. So let's stop talking about other things and decide how to do this—as soon as possible." Rhett, the owner of a public stable, responds quickly with, "Whoa, there. The last thing I want to do is spend a lot of money on fancy-pants ads that none of my customers will see."

Sally interrupts and beseeches the group to slow down before deciding what to do. She tries to include everyone in the discussion by turning the meeting into a brainstorming session. Sally explains brainstorming "rules" and asks the group to think creatively about ways to increase business. If nothing else, the brainstorming session succeeds in reducing tensions between the two factions.

When you finish reading this chapter, you should be able to answer the following questions.

1 Was choosing consensus as the decision-making method appropriate for this group? Why or why not?

2 How would you word the question that the group should try to answer?

3 How well did the group select and use a structured problem-solving procedure?

4 How well did the group choose and use a creative problem-solving method?

5 How did politics, preexisting preferences, and/or power affect the group's ability to make decisions and solve problems?

In Chapter 1, we introduce the structure ↔ spontaneity dialectic by noting that structured procedures help groups balance participation, resolve conflicts, organize discussions, and empower members. They also help groups solve problems. However, if a group becomes obsessed with procedures, it loses the benefits of spontaneity and creativity. Whether "thinking outside the box" or organizing a creative problem-solving session, groups can reap enormous benefits by encouraging innovation and "what if" thinking. Group communication scholar Marshall Scott Poole notes:

> To be effective, a group must maintain a golden mean, a balance between independent, creative thinking and structured, coordinated work. Too much independence may shatter group cohesion and encourage members to sacrifice group goals to their individual needs. . . . Too much structured work . . . is likely to regiment group thinking and stifle novel ideas.[4]

Decision-Making Methods

Voting

Consensus Seeking

Authority Rule

Decision-Making Methods

There are many ways to make group decisions. You can let the majority have its way, reach a decision that everyone can live with, or leave the final decision to someone else. These decision-making methods translate into voting, consensus seeking, and letting a leader or outside authority make the decision. Effective groups match the strengths of each method to the needs and purpose of the group and its task.

Voting. Voting is the easiest and most obvious way to make a group decision. No other method is more efficient and decisive. Sometimes, though, voting is not the best way to make important decisions. When a group votes, some members win, but others lose.

A **majority vote** requires that more than half the members vote in favor of a proposal. When a group makes a major decision, there may not be enough support to implement the decision if only 51 percent of the members agree on it. The 49 percent who lose may resent working on a project they dislike. Some groups use a two-thirds vote rather than majority rule. In a **two-thirds vote,** at least twice as many group members must vote for a proposal as vote against it. A two-thirds vote ensures that a significant number of group members support the decision.

Voting works best when:

- a group is pressed for time.
- the issue is not highly controversial.
- a group is too large to use any other decision-making method.
- there is no other way to break a deadlock.
- a group's constitution or rules require voting on certain types of decisions.

Consensus Seeking. Because voting has built-in disadvantages, many groups rely on consensus to make decisions. A group reaches **consensus** when *every* group member agrees to support a decision or action. A consensus decision is one "that all members have a part in shaping and that all find at least minimally acceptable as a means of accomplishing some mutual goal."[5]

When reached, consensus can unite and energize a group. Not only does consensus avoid a disruptive win/lose vote, but it also presents a united front to outsiders. Table 10.2 lists guidelines for seeking consensus.

Table 10.2 Consensus Guidelines

Guidelines	Strategies
Listen carefully to other members and consider their information and points of view.	• Try to be logical rather than emotional. • Don't be stubborn and argue only for your own position.
Don't change your mind in order to avoid conflict or reach a quick decision.	• Don't give in, especially if you have a crucial piece of information to share. • Don't agree to a decision or solution you can't possibly support.
Avoid "easy" ways of reaching a decision.	• Avoid techniques such as flipping a coin, letting the majority rule, or trading one decision for another.
If the group is deadlocked, work hard to find the next best alternative that is acceptable to everyone.	• Make sure that members not only agree but also will be committed to the final decision.
Get everyone involved in the discussion.	• Engage even the quietest member, who may have key information or suggestions that can help the group make a better decision.
Welcome differences of opinion.	• Remind the group that disagreement is natural and can expose the group to a wide range of information and opinions.

Consensus does not work well for all groups. Imagine how difficult it would be to achieve genuine consensus if a leader had so much power that group members were unwilling to express their honest opinions. Consensus seeking works best in groups where members have equal status or in groups that create a climate in which everyone feels comfortable expressing their views.

Authority Rule. Sometimes groups use **authority rule**, in which a single person or an executive group within or outside the group makes the final decision. For this method, groups gather information for and recommend decisions to another person or a larger group. For example, an association's nominating committee may consider potential candidates and recommend a slate of officers to the association. A hiring committee may screen dozens of job applications and submit a top-three list to the person making the hiring decision.

Authority rule can have detrimental effects on a group. If a leader or an outside authority ignores or reverses group recommendations, members may become demoralized, resentful, and nonproductive on future assignments. Even within a group, a strong leader or authority figure may use the group and its members to give the appearance of collaborative decision making. The group thus becomes a "rubber stamp" and surrenders its will to authority rule.

Decision-Making Questions

Decision-making and problem-solving groups need a clear goal. One strategy is to word the group's goal as a question for the group to answer. A question focuses group

groups in balance . . .
Avoid the Hazards of Consensus

Many groups fall short of achieving their common goal because they believe the group *must* reach consensus on *all* decisions. The problem of false consensus haunts every decision-making group. **False consensus** occurs when members reluctantly give in to group pressures or an external authority. Rather than achieving consensus, the group has agreed to a decision masquerading as consensus.[1]

In addition, the all-or-nothing approach to consensus "gives each member veto power over the progress of the whole group." In order to avoid an impasse, members may "give up and give in" or seek a flawed compromise. When this happens, the group will fall short of success as "it mindlessly pursues 100% agreement."[2]

In *The Discipline of Teams,* John Katzenbach and Douglas Smith observe that members who pursue complete consensus often act as though disagreement and conflict are bad for the group. Nothing, they claim, could be further from the reality of effective group performance. "Without disagreement, teams rarely generate the best, most creative solutions to the challenges at hand. They compromise . . . rather than developing a solution that incorporates the best of two or more opposing views. . . . The challenge for teams is to learn from disagreement and find energy in constructive conflict, not get ruined by it."[3]

[1]Donald G. Ellis and B. Aubrey Fisher, *Small Group Decision Making: Communication and the Group Process,* 4th ed. (New York: McGraw-Hill, 1994), p. 142.

[2]John R. Katzenbach and Douglas K. Smith, *The Discipline of Teams* (New York: Wiley, 2001), p. 112.

[3]Katzenbach and Smith, p. 113.

Types of Decision-Making Questions

- *Questions of Fact*
- *Questions of Conjecture*
- *Questions of Value*
- *Questions of Policy*

members on seeking a specific and realistic answer. Choosing a question of fact, conjecture, value, or policy can help your group clarify what members need to know and do in order to make a good decision or solve a problem.

Questions of Fact. A **question of fact** asks whether something is true or false, whether an event did or did not happen, or whether something caused this or that. Did product sales decrease last year? The answer to this question is either *yes* or *no.* A question such as "What was the decrease in sales?" requires a more detailed answer, with possible subquestions about the sales of particular products or product sales in different regions. When a group confronts a question of fact, it must seek and scrutinize the best information available.

Questions of Conjecture. A **question of conjecture** asks whether something will or will not happen. Will sales increase next quarter? Will there be layoffs? Unlike a question of fact, only the future holds the answer to this type of question. Instead of focusing on what *is,* the group does its best to predict the future. If a group waits until the future arrives, it may be too late to make a good decision or solve a problem. Groups should seek reputable facts, expert opinions, and valid data to answer questions of conjecture.[6]

Questions of Value. A **question of value** asks whether something is worthwhile: Is it good or bad; right or wrong; moral or immoral; best, average, or worst? Questions of value are difficult to discuss because the answers depend on the attitudes, beliefs, and values of group members. In many cases, the answer to a question of value may be, "It depends." Is a community college a better place to begin higher education than

a prestigious university? The answer to this question depends on a student's finances, professional goals, academic achievement record, work and family situation, and beliefs about the quality of education at each type of institution.

Questions of Policy. A **question of policy** asks how to address a problem. How can we improve customer service? Which candidate should we support as president of the student government association? How can we ensure that our school system maintains a culturally diverse teaching staff? Policy questions often require answers to subquestions of fact, conjecture, and value.

Decision-Making Styles

The way you make decisions may be very different from other group members. In Chapter 4, Group Diversity, we identify two Myers-Briggs traits—thinking and feeling—that focus on how we make decisions. Thinkers, for example, are task-oriented members who use logic when making decisions. Feelers are people-oriented members who want everyone to get along, even if it means compromising to avoid interpersonal problems. When thinkers and feelers work together, misunderstandings can occur. However, when thinkers and feelers appreciate their differences as decision makers, they form an unbeatable team. Thinkers make decisions and move the group forward while feelers make sure the group is working harmoniously.

In *Decision Making Style,* Suzanne Scott and Reginald Bruce take a detailed look at various decision-making styles.[7] They describe five styles, all of which have the potential to improve or impair group decision making:

- **Rational Decision Maker.** "I've carefully considered all the issues." Rational decision makers carefully weigh information and options before making a decision. They use logical reasoning to reach and justify their conclusions. However, they must be careful not to analyze a problem so long that they never make a decision.
- **Intuitive Decision Maker.** "It just feels like the right thing to do." Intuitive decision makers make decisions based on instincts and feelings. They may not always be able to articulate specific reasons for decisions but know that their decisions "feel" right.

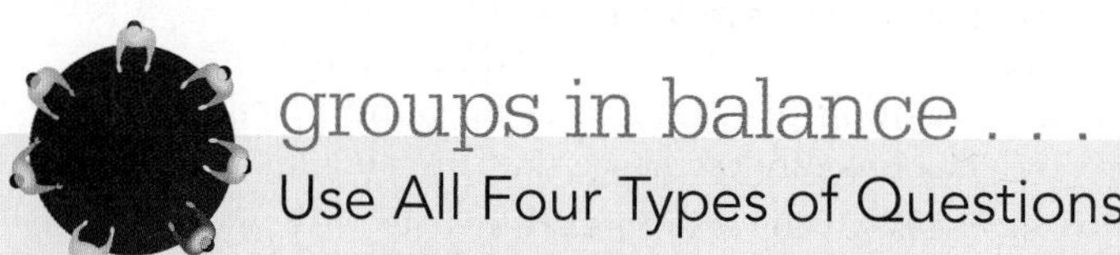

groups in balance . . .
Use All Four Types of Questions

Questions of fact, conjecture, value, and policy are not isolated inquiries. Within a group discussion, all four types of questions may arise. For example, if your family were trying to plan a summer vacation while saving money for a new car, you might start with questions of fact and conjecture: "How much do we usually spend on a summer vacation?" "How much money will we have in savings for a new car next year?" Then the discussion could move to questions of value: "How much do we value the time and place where our family vacations?" "How important is it that we buy a new car this year?" Finally, you would conclude with a question of policy: "How can we both take a summer vacation and save money for a new car?" In many cases, a group must address all four types of questions to make a rational decision or solve a complex problem.

- **Dependent Decision Maker.** "If you think it's okay, then I'll do it." Dependent decision makers seek the advice and opinions of others before making a decision. They feel uncomfortable making decisions that others may disapprove of or oppose. They may even make a decision they aren't happy with just to please others.
- **Avoidant Decision Maker.** "I just can't deal with this right now." Avoidant decision makers feel uncomfortable making decisions. As a result, they may not think about a problem at all or will make a final decision at the very last minute.
- **Spontaneous Decision Maker.** "Let's do it now and worry about the consequences later." Spontaneous decision makers are impulsive and make quick decisions on the spur of the moment. They often make decisions they later regret.

Consider the ways in which different decision-making styles could impair group decision making. For example, what would happen if half of the group were rational decision makers and the other half were intuitive decision makers? Also, consider the potential pitfalls of having only one type of decision-making style in a group, such as dependent or avoidant decision makers. Differences in decision-making styles require the same understanding, respect, and adaptation appropriate for other types of member diversity.

Structured Problem Solving

Group communication scholar Marshall Scott Poole identifies structured procedures as "the heart of group work [and] the most powerful tools we have" for improving the quality of group work.[8] Even a simple procedure such as constructing and following a short agenda enhances meeting productivity. Time and effort spent on developing and using a well-planned, structured procedure can reap the following benefits:

- *Balanced participation.* Procedures can minimize the impact of powerful leaders or members by making it difficult for them to dominate a group's discussion.
- *Conflict resolution.* Procedures often incorporate guidelines for managing conflict, resolving disagreements, and building genuine consensus.
- *Organization.* Procedures require members to follow a clear organizational pattern and focus on the same thing at the same time. Procedures also ensure that group members do not skip or ignore major discussion items.
- *Group empowerment.* Procedures provide a sense of control. "This happens when members know they have followed a procedure well, managed conflict successfully, given all members an equal opportunity to participate, and as a result have made a good decision."[9]

There is no "best" structured procedure to ensure effective problem solving in groups. As a group gains experience and successfully solves problems, members learn that some methods work better than others and some need modification to suit the group's needs. In this chapter, we present three well-established methods: the Standard Agenda, the Functional Perspective, and the Single Question Format (see Figure 10.1).

To appreciate the similarities and differences among these procedures, let's follow a hypothetical example that illustrates how the various steps apply to group problem solving.

Figure 10.1 Structured Problem-Solving Procedures

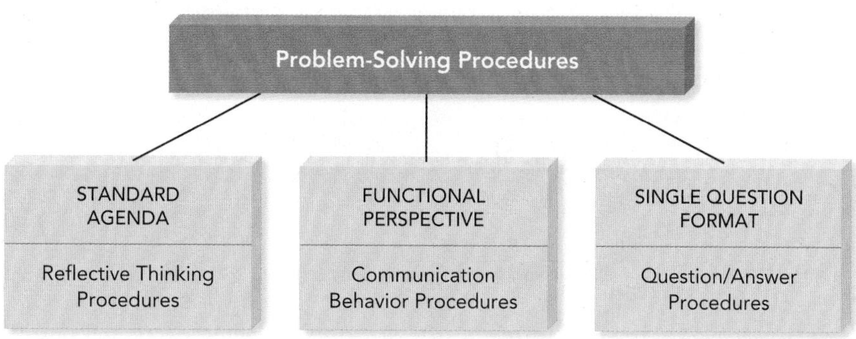

Fallingstar State College

For three consecutive years, Fallingstar State College has experienced declining enrollment and no increase in funding from the state. In order to balance the budget, the college has had to raise tuition every year. There are no prospects for more state funding in the near future. Even with significant tuition increases, overall college revenue is down. The college's planning council, composed of representative vice presidents, deans, faculty members, staff employees, and students, has been charged with answering the following question: Given the severe budget constraints and declining enrollment, how can the college preserve high-quality instruction and student services?

Although the Fallingstar example does not offer many details, it can help demonstrate the ways in which a group may use several of the most common structured procedures to solve problems.

The Standard Agenda

The founding father of problem-solving procedures is John Dewey, a U.S. philosopher and educator. In 1910, Dewey wrote *How We Think,* in which he described a set of practical steps that a rational person should follow when solving a problem.[10] These guidelines are known as the **Reflective Thinking Process.** Dewey's approach begins with a focus on understanding the problem and then moves on to a systematic consideration of possible solutions. The **Standard Agenda** incorporates the major steps in Dewey's process[11] (see Figure 10.2).

Task Clarification. During this initial phase, a group makes sure that everyone understands the task or assignment. For example, Fallingstar State College's planning council could dedicate the beginning of its first meeting to reviewing the council's goal and deadlines as well as the need to produce written recommendations. During this phase, group members ask questions about their roles and responsibilities in the problem-solving process.

Problem Identification. Overlooking this second step can send a group in the wrong direction. In the case of Fallingstar State College, there may be several different ways to define the college's problem. Is the problem declining enrollment? Some group members may consider this an advantage rather than a disadvantage because having fewer students can result in smaller classes, more individualized instruction,

Figure 10.2 The Standard Agenda

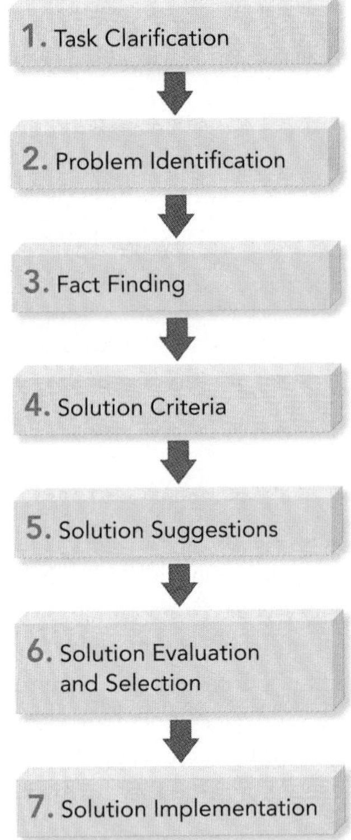

less chaos at registration, and easier parking. Is the problem a lack of money? Although lack of money seems to be a universal problem, an inefficiently run college could find that it in fact has enough money if it enhances productivity and becomes more businesslike.

The group should word the problem as an agreed-upon question. Whether this is a question of fact, conjecture, value, or policy determines the focus and direction of the discussion. The question, "Given the severe budget constraints and declining enrollment, how can the college preserve high-quality instruction and student services?" is a question of policy that also requires answering questions of fact, value, and conjecture.

Fact Finding. During the fact-finding step, group members have several obligations reflected in the following questions of fact and value: What are the facts of the situation? What additional information or expert opinions do we need? How serious or widespread is the problem? What are the causes of the problem? What prevents us from solving the problem? These questions require investigations of facts, conclusions about causes and effects, and value judgments about the seriousness of the problem.

Fallingstar State College's planning council could look at the rate of enrollment decline and future enrollment projections, the anticipated budgets for future years, the efficiency of existing services, the projected impact of inflation, estimated salary increases, predictable maintenance costs, and the likely causes of declining enrollment. It could take months to investigate these questions, and even then, there may not be clear answers to all of them. Failure to search for such answers, however, is much more hazardous than not trying to find them.

groups in balance . . .
Avoid Analysis Paralysis

We offer a word of caution about the fact-finding phase recommended in most problem-solving procedures. Sometimes, highly conscientious groups become immobilized by **analysis paralysis**, a fixation on seeking more information, more analysis, and more meetings without significant results. Psychologist Edward De Bono put it this way: "The usual approach to problem solving is to identify and remove the cause of the problem. Sometimes this is not possible because the cause cannot be found, because there are too many causes, or because the cause is human nature and cannot be removed. In such cases we are usually paralyzed."[1]

In the case of Fallingstar State College, the planning council could collect dozens of reports and identify ten possible causes of declining enrollment but still be unable to verify or settle on the most important reasons. Rather than spending months arguing about the issue or giving up on finding the correct answer, a group may have to move on and begin its search for solutions.

[1]Edward De Bono, *New Thinking for the New Millennium* (New York: Viking, 1999), quoted in Darrell Mann, "Analysis Paralysis: When Root Cause Analysis Isn't the Way," *The TRIZ-Journal*, 2006, www.triz-journal.com. Retrieved April 21, 2008.

Solution Criteria. **Solution criteria** are standards a group establishes for its solution to meet. In a review of group procedures, Susan Jarboe describes solution criteria as member ideas about what a solution should accomplish.[12] For example, the Fallingstar planning council recognizes the need for an *affordable* method for both increasing enrollment *and* preserving high-quality instruction and student services. Here are some general criteria to consider:

- Will the solution work—is it reasonable and realistic?
- Do we have the resources (money, equipment, personnel) to implement the solution?
- Do we have enough time to implement the solution?
- Does the solution reflect and protect our values?[13]

Criteria should reflect a realistic understanding of *solution limitations,* which may include financial, political, and legal restrictions. For the college planning council, criteria could include affordability, acceptance of the solution by all subgroups (administrators, faculty, staff, and students), a commitment to using fair and open procedures to assess existing programs, and considerations of the political and legal consequences of proposed actions.

Solution Suggestions. At this point in a group's deliberations, some solutions may be obvious. Even so, the group should concentrate on suggesting as many solutions as possible. Having spent time understanding the task, identifying the problem, analyzing its consequences and causes, and establishing solution criteria, members should be able to offer numerous solutions. Later in this chapter, we describe a technique called *brainstorming* that can help a group generate creative options.

Suggestions from the college's planning council could include a wide range of options: raise tuition, embark on a new promotional campaign, seek additional grants and corporate donations, freeze raises and promotions, require additional teaching by faculty, increase class size, reduce the number of administrators and staff, eliminate expensive programs and services, lobby the state for more funds, and charge students fees for special services. This list could double or triple, depending on the creativity and resourcefulness of the group.

Solution Evaluation and Selection. This stage of the Standard Agenda may be the most difficult and controversial. Here, group members discuss the pros and cons of each suggestion in light of their agreed-upon solution criteria. Questions of conjecture arise as the group considers the possible consequences of each option. Discussion may become heated, and disagreements may grow fierce. In some groups, members may be so tired or frustrated by the time they get to this phase that they have a tendency to jump to conclusions. If group members have been conscientious in analyzing the problem and establishing criteria for solutions, however, they will reject some solutions quickly, while others will swiftly rise to the top of the list.

The college's planning council may hear students argue against increased tuition, whereas faculty members predict a decline in instructional quality if they are required to teach more or larger classes. Administrators and staff may cringe at freezing salaries, whereas faculty may support reductions in administrative staff. In this phase, a group should remember its solution criteria and use them to evaluate the strengths and weaknesses of each suggested solution. At the end of this stage, a group selects one or more solutions.

Solution Implementation. Having made a difficult decision, a group faces one more challenge: How should we implement our solution? Is our group responsible for implementation or do we delegate implementation to someone else? For all the time a group spends trying to solve a problem, it may take even more time to organize and implement the solution. If the planning council wants a new promotional campaign to attract students, the campaign must be well planned and affordable to achieve its goal. If the college wants to enhance fund-raising efforts, a group or office must have the authority and resources to seek such funds. Brilliant solutions can fail if no one takes responsibility or has the authority to implement them.

Your textbook describes three structured procedures to solve problems (the Standard Agenda, the Functional Perspective, and the Single Question Format). Which procedure would you recommend to this group as it makes critical decisions about what to include in the next edition of the school newspaper?

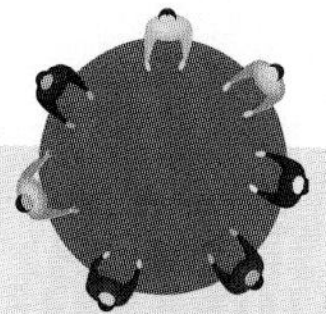

theory in groups

The Function of the Functional Perspective

In Chapter 5, Group Leadership, we describe functional theory as a group of theories that try "to understand the factors and processes that help and hurt the quality of group performance."[1] In addition to looking at how factors such as leadership, group size, and conflict management affect group productivity, functional theory also examines how communication affects group decision making and problem solving. Functional theorists ask: Why do some groups make better decisions than others?

Group communication scholars Dennis Gouran and Randy Hirokawa identified a set of "critical functions" that explain and predict how well a group will make decisions and solve problems.[2] Their **Functional Perspective** claims that "communication is the instrument by which members or groups, with varying degrees of success, reach decisions and generate solutions to problems."[3] Effective communication, they contend, is more important than the order in which groups perform these functions. If, however, groups stray too far from an agenda, the quality of the group's decision may suffer.

As was the case with the Standard Agenda, the origin of the Functional Perspective is John Dewey's Reflective Thinking Process. A second major source is sociologist Robert Bales's study of problem-solving groups. Bales claimed that groups strive for equilibrium (or a balance) in satisfying the demands of both task and social dimensions that enable members to perform as a unit.[4]

[1]Andrea B. Hollingshead, et al., "A Look at Groups from the Functional Perspective" in *Theories of Small Groups: Interdisciplinary Perspectives,* ed. Marshall Scott Poole and Andrea B. Hollingshead (Thousand Oaks, CA: Sage, 2005), p. 22.

[2]Dennis S. Gouran and Randy Hirokawa, "The Role of Communication in Decision-Making Groups: A Functional Perspective," in *Communications in Transition: Issues and Debate in Current Research,* ed. Mary S. Mander (New York: Praeger, 1983), pp. 168–185; Dennis S. Gouran and Randy Hirokawa, "Functional Theory and Communication in Decision-Making and Problem-Solving Groups; An Expanded View," in *Communication and Group Decision Making,* 2nd ed., ed. Randy Y. Hirokawa and Marshall Scott Poole (Thousand Oaks, CA: Sage, 1996), pp. 55–80.

[3]See Randy Y. Hirokawa and Roger Pace, "A Descriptive Investigation of the Possible Communication-Based Reasons for Effective and Ineffective Group Decision Making," *Communication Monographs,* 50 (1983), pp. 363–79; Randy Y. Hirokawa and Dirk Scheerhorn, "Communication and Faulty Group Decision-Making," in *Communication and Group Decision-Making,* ed. Randy Y. Hirokawa and Marshall Scott Poole (Beverly Hills, CA: Sage, 1986), pp. 63–80; Gouran and Hirokawa, "Functional Theory and Communication in Decision-Making and Problem-Solving Groups."

[4]Gouran and Hirokawa, "Functional Theory and Communication in Decision-Making and Problem-Solving Groups," p. 28.

The Functional Perspective

The Functional Perspective and the Standard Agenda have a great deal in common. Both focus on the importance of understanding a problem and its related issues as well as developing effective solution criteria as a basis for solving the problem. The Functional Perspective, however, has three unique qualities that distinguish it from the Standard Agenda model. By focusing on preparation, competence, and communication functions, a group enhances its ability to make sound decisions when seeking the best solution to a problem.

The Preparation Function. The Functional Perspective includes a unique preparation function that should occur *before* a group begins the problem-solving process. According to Dennis Gouran and Randy Hirokawa, certain conditions must exist for a group to make good decisions and to select appropriate solutions for problems. Before a group engages in specific problem-solving tasks, members should prepare for the process by:

- agreeing to make the best possible decision.
- identifying the resources necessary for making such a decision.

Figure 10.3 Functional Task Requirements

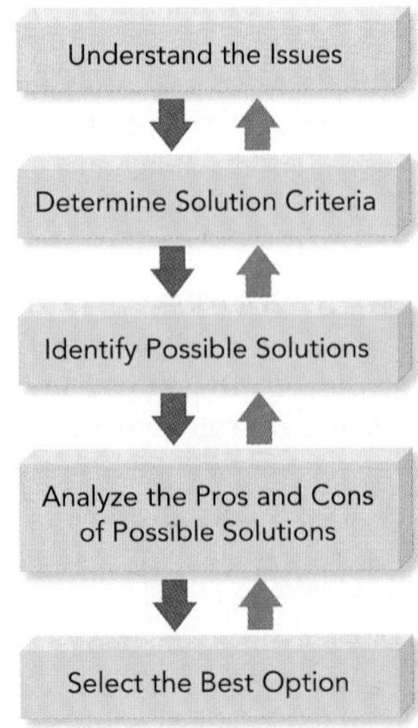

- recognizing possible obstacles to decision making and problem solving.
- specifying the procedures and ground rules the group will follow.[14]

These prerequisites ensure that the group is ready, willing, and able to tackle the issue. The first task—agreeing to make the best possible decision—is not sufficient to ensure success. Group members also must make sure that they have identified the sources of information they will need, the limits or constraints on their ability to make a decision, and the appropriate decision-making or problem-solving procedure. Hirokawa emphasizes that "the ability of a group to gather and retain a wide range of information is the single most important determinant of high-quality decision making."[15]

The Competence Function. The Functional Perspective emphasizes that the competent performance of each function is more important than the Standard Agenda's focus on following problem-solving steps in a specific order. When members are prepared to tackle an issue, the group should address five fundamental task requirements that constitute the heart of functional theory. Rather than completing each step in order, the group makes sure that each step is completed *competently,* regardless of the order. Figure 10.3 depicts the functional task requirements with two-way arrows that show a more flexible approach to addressing each function.

1. *Understand the Issues.* This function combines the second and third steps in the Standard Agenda—problem identification and fact finding. Functional competence ensures that the group accurately defines the problem and identifies the real causes of the problem. For example, if the Fallingstar planning council mistakenly decides that the decrease in enrollment is caused by higher tuition, it may be ignoring other factors such as competition from other colleges, the state of the economy and its effect on students' ability to find jobs, or even a public perception that the college does not offer high-quality instruction.

2. *Determine Solution Criteria.* This function is similar to the solution criteria step in the Standard Agenda. Functional competence ensures that this process is both open and guided by the group's clear and elevated goal. For example, if everyone on the Fallingstar planning council agrees that employee sacrifices are inevitable, they have cleared the road for a wider range of possible actions.
3. *Identify Possible Solutions.* Similar to the solution suggestions step in the Standard Agenda, functional competence ensures that the group uses its rational and rigorous standards to produce a wider range of solutions.
4. *Analyze the Pros and Cons of Possible Solutions.* The fourth function is the group's ability to analyze and discuss the positive and negative features of suggested solutions. Functional competence avoids breakdowns at this stage in the problem-solving process because group members go beyond the more obvious positive and negative attributes of certain attractive choices. As a result, the group has confidence in its assessment of each solution's strengths and weaknesses.
5. *Select the Best Option.* Although there may be several good options at this point, functional competence enhances group confidence that its choice reflects a comprehensive understanding and analysis of the issues and solutions based on clear solution criteria.

The Communication Function. The Functional Perspective emphasizes members' critical thinking and communication skills as prerequisites for understanding and discussing the pros and the cons of each solution. Among the many communication functions essential to effective problem solving, four functions stand out as critical to group success:

1. Members are well-prepared, skilled, critical thinkers and effective communicators who know how to generate strong arguments and analyze the validity of arguments made by other members.
2. Members establish and use agreed-upon criteria to evaluate possible solutions and, as a result, have a better basis for selecting the best solution.
3. Members base their arguments on valid facts and justified inferences, analyze and (if necessary) refute arguments made by other group members, and as a result, increase the group's chances of generating and selecting the best solution.
4. Members with leadership skills foster a supportive communication environment and push the group toward making a high-quality decision.[16]

The Single Question Format

The **Single Question Format** is a seemingly simple problem-solving procedure that approximates the way successful problem solvers and decision makers naturally think.[17] Its five steps, shown in Figure 10.4, provide a sharp focus on an agreed-upon question that, if thoroughly analyzed and responsibly answered, should provide the solution to a problem.[18]

Identify the Problem. What is the *single* question, the answer to which is all that the group needs to know in order to accomplish its agreed-upon goal? Although reaching agreement on the single question may take many hours, the investment is essential.[19] For example, Fallingstar State College's planning council decides to address this question: How can we increase enrollment and preserve high-quality

Figure 10.4 The Single Question Format

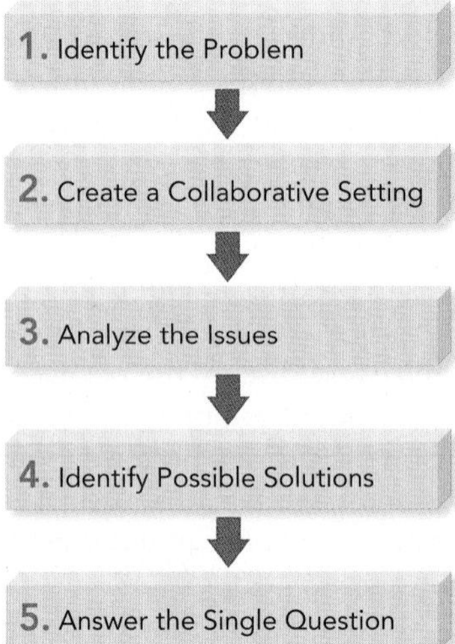

instruction and student services? In a business setting, a single question might be: How should we eliminate $4 million of annual expenses without damaging the company or its customer relationships? At home, you could ask: Given limited funds, how can we take a vacation and purchase another car?

Create a Collaborative Setting. This second step is absent from most other problem-solving procedures. Here, you ask your group to agree on a set of norms by generating a list of "we will" statements designed to foster open discussion and participation. For example:

- We will listen to *all* points of view.
- We will ask for facts as well as opinions.
- We will be tough on issues but not on one another.
- We will put aside personal agendas.

In addition to the "we will" list, identify assumptions and biases that may influence the discussion. Ask the group: Have past approaches worked, or do we need a new approach? Do we *really* understand the problem, or do we need to take a fresh look at the situation? Are we ignoring some approaches because of personal or political biases?

In the case of the Fallingstar planning council, members may decide not to use the names of specific administrators when describing failed programs. Rather than assuming that the college recruitment office "ain't broke, so why fix it?" they may decide that there is room for improvement in all offices. When a group such as the Fallingstar planning council examines volatile issues such as tuition increases, staff reductions, and increased workloads, members will understandably want to protect their personal interests. If the group fails to create a collaborative setting for such discussion, the process could deteriorate into destructive conflict and flawed decision making.

Analyze the Issues. The third step requires a group to identify and analyze relevant subquestions such as these:

- What issues should we address in order to answer our single question?
- Do we have accurate and relevant facts about each issue?
- Given what we know, what is the best or most reasonable response to each issue?

Completing this step helps a group "avoid arriving at a solution too early, before understanding the critical components of the problem."[20] This step is similar to the second and third steps in the Standard Agenda (problem identification and fact finding) and "understand the issue" in the Functional Perspective.

Analyzing issues differs by focusing on critical thinking rather describing. Fallingstar council members must do more than share facts about the rate of enrollment decline and future enrollment projections or anticipated budgets. They must determine whether the facts and suggested causes are valid.

Identify Possible Solutions. This step asks a group to suggest two or three reasonable solutions to the overall single question *and* to discuss the advantages and disadvantages of each solution, much like similar steps in the Standard Agenda and Functional Perspective. This is a crucial step in which strong opinions and disagreements may arise. By listing advantages and disadvantages, however, a group may be able to *see* that the advantages for one solution far outweigh the disadvantages.

A Fallingstar vice president might suggest efficiency moves such as increasing class size as well as a more aggressive marketing plan. A student might recommend an organized protest at the state capitol in support of more funding. In the Single Question Format, the group would consider the advantages and disadvantages of every reasonable solution and determine the extent to which each suggestion could or should be part of an ideal solution that answers its single question. A simple table helps group members generate the pros and cons for each option.

Possible Solution	Advantages	Disadvantages
Raising tuition	1. Increases college resources.	1. Spurs protests by angry students.
	2. Creates the perception of quality—you get what you pay for.	2. Causes students to leave for less expensive colleges.
	3. Provides additional funds for scholarships to financially needy students.	3. Leads to erroneous beliefs that the college can now fund expensive new projects.

Answer the Single Question. After analyzing the pros and cons of each potential solution, the group selects "the best solution to the problem based on a clear, shared understanding of all the relevant issues. This clarity, in turn, allows a group to proceed with sufficient confidence to their final decision and commit to it."[21]

Although the Single Question Format shares many characteristics with the Standard Agenda and Functional Perspective, two features make it both different and highly effective. First, it sharply focuses on goal clarity (a prerequisite for any work group) and issue analysis. Second, it cultivates a supportive group climate that helps members identify, raise, and resolve many interpersonal and procedural problems that can affect group success.

Table 10.3 Summary of Structured Problem-Solving Procedures

Standard Agenda	Functional Perspective	Single Question Format
1. Task Clarification 2. Problem Identification 3. Fact Finding 4. Solution Criteria 5. Solution Suggestions 6. Solution Evaluation and Selection 7. Solution Implementation	• Understand the Issues • Determine Solution Criteria • Identify Possible Solutions • Analyze the Pros and Cons of Possible Solutions • Select the Best Option	1. Identify the Problem as a Single Question 2. Create a Collaborative Setting a. Agree on Discussion Norms b. Identify Assumptions and Biases 3. Identify and Analyze the Issues 4. Identify Possible Solutions 5. Answer the Single Question

Table 10.3 summarizes the main features of the three structured problem-solving procedures discussed in this chapter.

Creative Problem Solving

Curiosity and creativity fuel all *great* groups. These qualities allow groups to "identify significant problems and find creative, boundary-bursting solutions rather than simplistic ones."[22] Effective group leaders understand the near-magical quality that creativity can inject into the group process. When, for example, Walt Disney "asked his artists to push the envelope of animation, he told them 'If you can dream it, you can do it.' He believed that, and, as a result, they did too."[23]

Creativity has two components: (1) the nonjudgmental process of searching for, separating, and connecting unrelated ideas and elements and (2) combining these elements into new ideas.[24]

Encouraging and rewarding creativity can be as important to problem solving as following any of the structured procedures described in this chapter. For example, one of us once chaired a meeting in which the injection of creativity broke through a problem-solving logjam:

> I was chairing a meeting of graphic artists, copywriters, and public relations staff members at the college. Our assignment was to write and design a commemorative booklet for the college's fortieth anniversary. On the conference table sat a dozen such booklets from other colleges. The group had reviewed all the samples and come up with a list of common features. The problem was this: We had limited funds to print the booklet, so we had to confine ourselves to twenty-four pages. Very quickly, the process bogged down. An uncomfortable silence settled over the group. At this point, I asked, "If you hadn't seen any of these model booklets, what would you write and design to commemorate our anniversary?" The response was immediate and energizing: "You mean we can come up with something new and different?" The answer was *yes*. The result: A new sense of excitement and eagerness permeated the group. The "model" booklets were swept off the table. Highly creative, out-of-the-box alternatives materialized.

When groups engage in creative problem solving, members share new connections and unusual possibilities. Although it is impossible to describe the creative process in precise terms (it wouldn't be all that creative if we could), we can outline the basic stages of the process in groups. Usually, there are four stages:

- *Investigation.* Group members gather information and attempt to understand the nature and causes of a problem.

- *Imagination.* Group members engage in free thinking by removing procedural and mental roadblocks. The group generates and discusses new and unusual ideas.
- *Incubation.* The group allows a period of time in which imaginative ideas can percolate and recombine in new ways. During this stage, the group may take a break or focus on another topic or issue.
- *Insight.* The "Aha!" moment occurs and a new approach or solution emerges. Group members recognize the breakthrough moment and may build upon or improve the idea.

For group members with strong control needs, creative problem solving may seem to divert energy from dealing with the problem. Despite these concerns, creative thinking in groups is well worth the effort and the laughter. Group members trained in creative problem solving participate more, criticize one another less, support new ideas more, exhibit humor, and produce ideas that are more worthwhile.[25] John Kao, the academic director of the Managing Innovations program at Stanford University, compares balancing creativity and structured group process to tending the flames of a fire. "The spark needs air, breathing room, and freedom to ignite. But let the air blow too freely, and the spark will go out. Close all the doors and windows, and you will stifle it."[26]

As is the case with structured problem solving, there are many creative problem-solving methods. Again, there is no "best" technique. Fortunately, there are effective procedures for making decision making and problem solving more effective by harnessing group ingenuity and creativity (see Figure 10.5).

Brainstorming

In 1953, Alex Osborn introduced the concept of brainstorming in his book *Applied Imagination.*[27] **Brainstorming** is a technique for generating as many ideas as possible in a short period of time. When a group wants to identify the causes of or solutions to a problem, brainstorming can increase the number and creativity of responses. Brainstorming is fairly simple and widely used. In fact, more than 70 percent of businesspeople use brainstorming in their organizations.[28] Unfortunately, many groups do not use brainstorming effectively.

Brainstorming is based on two key principles: (1) deferring judgment improves the quality of input, and (2) the quantity of ideas and output breeds quality. The idea that quantity breeds quality comes from the notion that the first ideas we come up with are usually the most obvious, and that truly creative ideas will come only after

Figure 10.5 Creative Problem-Solving Methods

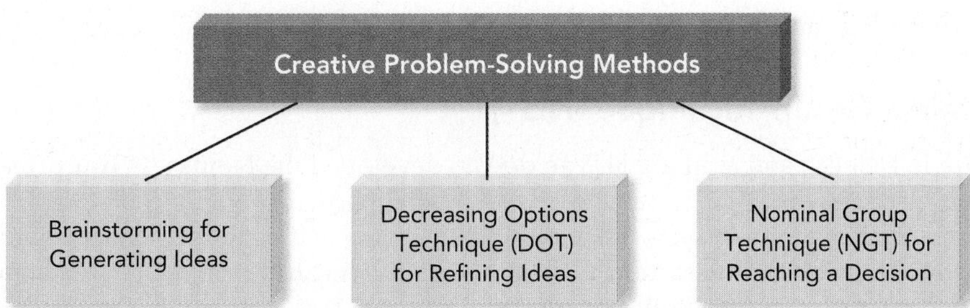

Figure 10.6 Brainstorming Guidelines

1. Sharpen the Focus
   - Start with a clear statement of the problem.
   - Give members a few minutes to think about possible ideas before brainstorming begins.
2. For All to See
   - Assign someone to write down the group's ideas.
   - Post the ideas where everyone can see them.
3. Number the Ideas
   - Numbering can motivate a group, e.g., "Let's try to get 100 ideas."
   - Numbering makes it easier to jump back and forth among ideas.
4. Encourage Creativity
   - Wild and crazy ideas are welcome.
   - Quantity is more important than quality.
5. All Input, No Putdown
   - Don't analyze, oppose, or praise another member's ideas.
   - Don't discuss, defend, clarify, or comment on your own suggestions.
   - Keep the ideas coming.
   - Ideas are evaluated only after brainstorming is over.
6. Build and Jump
   - Build on or modify ideas offered by others.
   - Combine two or more ideas into a new idea.
   - It's okay to jump back to an earlier idea or forward to a completely different line of thinking.

we have gotten the obvious suggestions out.[29] The guidelines in Figure 10.6 explain the nature and rules of brainstorming.

However, brainstorming may be counterproductive under certain circumstances.[30] For example, the comments of a powerful member or "the boss" may influence and limit the direction of ideas. In an effort to be more democratic, some groups have members speak in turn. But this approach prevents the group from building momentum and results in fewer ideas. Finally, some members try to write down all the group's ideas. Those members end up being so focused on note taking that they rarely contribute ideas. Instead, one person should record and post all the ideas contributed by the group members.

Although brainstorming is popular, its effectiveness depends on the nature of the group and its members. If a group is self-conscious and sensitive to implied criticism, brainstorming can fail. If a group is comfortable with such a freewheeling process, brainstorming can enhance creativity and produce many worthwhile ideas.

Nominal Group Technique (NGT)

Andre L. Delbecq and Andrew H. Van de Ven developed the **Nominal Group Technique**, also known as NGT, as a way of maximizing participation in problem-solving and program-planning groups while minimizing some of the interpersonal problems associated with group interaction.[31] The term *nominal* means "existing in name only." Thus, a nominal group is a collection of people who, at first, work individually rather

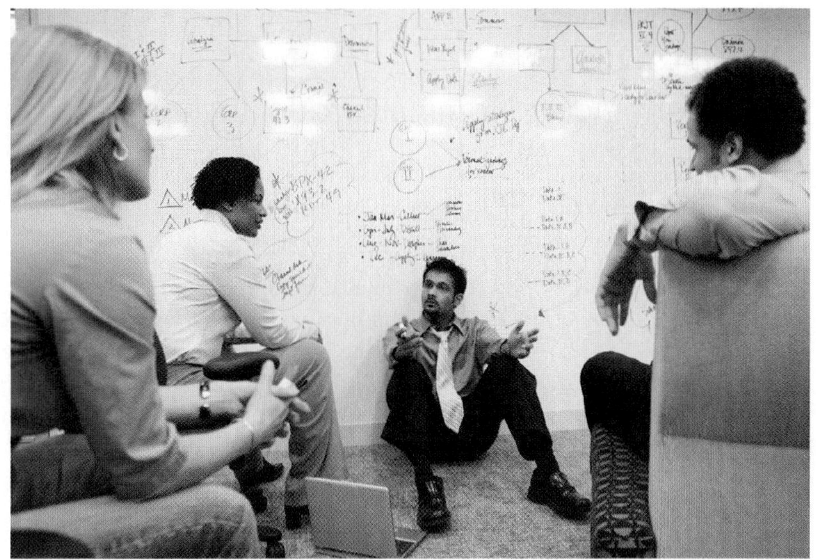

Brainstorming is based on two key principles: (1) deferring judgment improves the quality of input, and (2) the quantity of ideas and output breeds quality. How does this photograph illustrate a group's use of these principles?

than collectively. NGT combines aspects of silent voting with limited discussion to help a group build consensus and arrive at a decision.[32]

There are two separate phases in a Nominal Group Technique session: an idea generation phase and an evaluation/voting phase. During the idea generation phase, seven to ten individuals sit around a table in full view of one another.

Phase 1: Idea Generation

1. Each member writes his or her ideas on a piece of paper.
2. At the end of five to ten minutes, a structured sharing of ideas takes place. Each member, in turn, presents one idea from his or her private list.
3. A recorder writes the ideas on a flip chart (or posts ideas using computer projections) in full view of other members. There is no discussion at this point—only the recording of members' ideas.
4. Round-robin listing continues until all members have no further ideas to share.[33]

Returning to the case of the college planning council, members could use the Nominal Group Technique to generate a list of possible causes of declining enrollment or a list of possible solutions. The listing of ideas in an NGT session is different from brainstorming because members work alone to generate ideas.

During the second, evaluative phase of a Nominal Group Technique session, the group discusses each recorded idea and then votes to create a rank order of items.

Phase 2: Idea Evaluation and Voting

1. Members discuss each idea before independent voting.
2. Members may clarify or state their support or nonsupport for each listed item.
3. Members vote by ranking or rating ideas privately, in writing.
4. The group decision is the mathematically pooled outcome of the individual votes.[34]

Nominal Group Technique works particularly well when individual judgments and expertise are valued. Groups use NGT to rank job applicants, to determine which of many possible solutions receives the most support, to establish budget priorities,

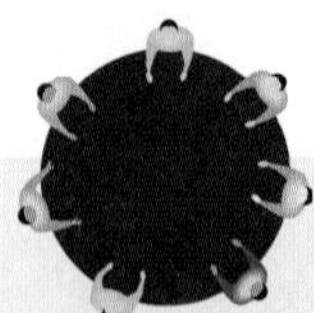

groups in balance . . .
Select Brainstorming or Nominal Group Technique Wisely

Several researchers investigating the relative usefulness of brainstorming and Nominal Group Technique conclude that Nominal Group Technique often works better than brainstorming for generating ideas that are both numerous and creative. There are several possible reasons for this conclusion.[1]

- Waiting for a turn to speak in a brainstorming group (rather than writing down ideas in advance) may disrupt the thinking of group members and slow the production of ideas.
- Group members who fear negative evaluation from others may withhold good ideas even though the brainstorming group has been told to defer judgment.
- Some members may loaf or "free ride" and let others do all the thinking and talking.
- Members who make more contributions to a brainstorming session often earn higher status, which may discourage others from speaking.

Nominal Group Technique avoids most of these problems because members have time to think and write during the idea-generating process. Brainstorming can avoid these problems when group members use networked computers programmed with groupware to generate a master list of ideas simultaneously *and* anonymously.[2]

[1]Craig E. Johnson and Michael Z. Hackman, *Creative Communication: Principles and Applications* (Prospect Heights, IL: Waveland, 1995), pp. 129–30.

[2]Johnson and Hackman., p. 131.

and to reach consensus on the causes of a problem. The highly structured NGT process guarantees equal participation during the idea generation phase and provides opportunities for discussion and critical evaluation in the second phase. NGT can also be useful when dealing with a sensitive or controversial topic on which contrary opinions or a myriad of details could paralyze the discussion.[35]

An NGT session requires a great deal of time and a skilled moderator to make it work efficiently and effectively. Given NGT's highly structured format, it is difficult to adjust or modify suggested items, and this may frustrate group members who prefer spontaneous interaction. At the same time, NGT can curb members who dominate or block the ideas and comments of others.

Decreasing Options Technique (DOT) Steps

Generate Ideas

Post the Ideas

Sort the Ideas

Dot the Ideas

Decreasing Options Technique (DOT)

The **Decreasing Options Technique (DOT)** is a decision-making tool that helps groups reduce and refine a large number of suggestions into a manageable number of ideas. As professional facilitators, we have used this technique to assist small and large groups facing a variety of decision-making tasks. We have enlisted the DOT strategy to write an identity statement for an academic discipline, to create an ethics credo for a professional association, to draft a vision statement for a college, and to create an academic curriculum for an emerging profession. The DOT method works best when a group must process a multitude of ideas and options.

- ***Generate Ideas.*** On an individual basis, group members generate and record ideas related to the topic under discussion. Ideas can be single words or full-sentence suggestions. For example, when creating an ethics credo at a National Communication Association conference, participants contributed

words such as *honesty, respect,* and *truth* for inclusion.[36] You can ask group members to generate and submit ideas before the group meets or ask them to contribute their ideas during a meeting. Each idea should be written on a separate sheet of paper in large, easy-to-read letters—only one idea per page.

- ***Post the Ideas.*** Post the separate sheets of paper on the walls of the group's meeting room. If members submit their ideas in advance, you can post the pages before the meeting begins. When members generate ideas during a meeting, post the results only after all members have finished writing their ideas.
- ***Sort the Ideas.*** Not surprisingly, many group members will contribute similar or overlapping ideas. When this happens, sort the ideas and post similar ideas close to one another. For example, when facilitating the development of a college's vision statement, phrases like *academic excellence, quality education,* and *high-quality instruction* were posted near one another. Once everyone is comfortable with the sorted ideas, give a title to each grouping. For example, in the vision statement session, the term *quality education* was used as an umbrella phrase for nearly a dozen similar concepts.
- ***Dot the Ideas.*** At this point, members face the difficult task of deciding which ideas are most important: Which concepts *must* be included in our association's ethics credo? Which units are essential in the new curriculum? Which actions will increase enrollment at Fallingstar State College? The final step requires all participants to "dot" their preferred ideas. Give every member a limited number of colored sticker dots. For example, after giving ten dots to each member of the vision statement group, we instructed them to choose the most important concepts from among the twenty-five phrases posted on the walls. After everyone has finished walking around the room and posting dots, the most important ideas are usually very apparent. Some ideas will be covered with dots; others will be speckled with only three or four; some will remain blank. After a brief review of the outcome, the group can eliminate

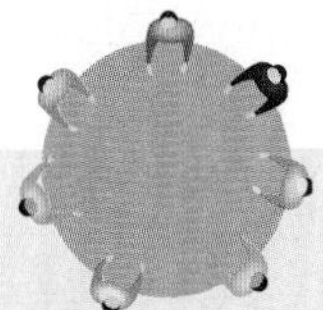

virtual groups

Adapting Decision-Making and Problem-Solving Methods

The group decision-making and problem-solving methods in this chapter were originally designed for face-to-face meetings. These methods also work well in virtual groups. Additionally, specialized computer software, or groupware, can facilitate group collaboration, decision making, and problem solving.

Researchers suggest that different types of technology are not equally well suited to all types of group interaction.[1] For example, if your group is engaged in brainstorming, using groupware that incorporates audio, video, and text will be more effective than using email. If a virtual group has to make a decision, a videoconference will be more useful than an electronic bulletin board. Group experts John Katzenbach and Douglas Smith remind us that "whenever teams gather through groupware to advance, they need to recognize and adjust to key differences between face-to-face and groupware interactions."[2] They also caution against approaching every virtual meeting in the same way. Group problem-solving and decision-making tasks require more opportunity for interaction than, for instance, information sharing or presentations. A virtual group should select the technology that is best suited to its problem-solving method.

[1]Deborah L. Duarte and Nancy Tennant Snyder, *Mastering Virtual Teams,* 3rd ed. (San Francisco: Jossey-Bass, 2006), p. 168.

[2]John R. Katzenbach and Douglas K. Smith, *The Discipline of Teams: A Mindbook-Workbook for Delivering Small Group Performance* (New York: Wiley, 2001), p. 167.

some ideas, decide whether marginal ideas should be included, and end up with a limited and manageable number of options to consider and discuss.

When a group generates dozens of ideas, members use valuable meeting time to discuss each idea, regardless of its merit or relevance. The DOT method reduces the quantity of ideas to a manageable number. Often DOT is a preface to an extended discussion of key ideas and suggestions. Consider using DOT when

- The group is so large that open discussion of individual ideas is unworkable or too time consuming.
- The group has generated a significant number of competing ideas.
- The group wants to ensure equal opportunities for input by all members.
- The group wants to restrain dominant members from exerting too much influence.
- The group does not have enough time to discuss multiple or controversial ideas.

Although the examples we have used to describe the DOT process focus on face-to-face interaction, DOT also works very well in virtual settings. Instead of writing ideas on sheets of paper, posting them on walls, and dotting preferences, a virtual group can follow the same steps by using networked software designed for interactive group work.

Enhancing Group Creativity

Given the benefits of creative problem solving, we recommend four strategies for enhancing group creativity, regardless of the chosen method: (1) control judgment, (2) encourage innovation, (3) ask *"what if,"* and (4) use metaphors.

Control Judgment. Almost nothing inhibits group creativity as much as negative responses to new ideas and innovative solutions. "That won't work." "We've tried that." "That's bizarre." Sometimes a bizarre idea can evolve into a creative solution. "Keeping the process open and avoiding premature closure are crucially important. Because creative work is exploratory in nature, it deserves suspension of belief in the early stages."[37]

Encourage Innovation. In his book on creativity in the workplace, Lee Towe presents four sources of action that guide us through how we solve problems.[38]

Inertia	We've done it before.
Instruction	Someone showed us how to do it.
Imitation	We've seen how it's done.
Innovation	We have developed a new way to do it.

These sources of action also apply to group problem solving. Remember the group trying to design the commemorative booklet for the college's anniversary? Until their creativity was released, they were bogged down in inertia, instruction, and imitation. Encouraging group members to be innovative and imaginative sparked the group's creative powers.

Ask "What If." Group members are often reluctant to think creatively because they have preconceived notions about what to do. Asking *"what if"* can set aside these

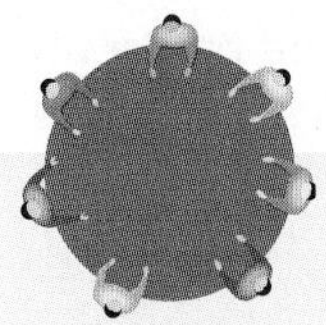

ethics in groups
The Morality of Creative Outcomes

In *Organizing Genius: The Secrets of Creative Collaboration,* Warren Bennis and Patricia Ward Biederman warn that "Creative collaboration is so powerful a phenomenon that it inevitably raises moral issues."[1] John Rawls, a contemporary ethicist, urges us to examine the consequences of group creativity. He believes fairness is an important consideration in creative problem solving.[2] For example, creative groups need to ask if their creative innovations have the potential to help or hurt others. Should political consulting firms help the wealthiest or the worthiest candidates? What are the consequences when corporate executives find creative ways to "cook the books" and collect millions of unearned dollars?

Many of the creative geniuses who collaborated to create and test the atomic bomb have subsequently struggled to deal with the consequences of their work. Dr. Richard Feynman, who later won a Nobel Prize in physics, was one of the scientists who created the atomic bomb. He recalls that the group became so caught up in the frenzy and excitement of creating the bomb that they didn't stop to think about the consequences. However, when a colleague of Feynman's said, "It's a terrible thing that we made," he realized that they had unleashed the greatest terror on earth.[3]

[1]Warren Bennis and Patricia Ward Biederman, *Organizing Genius: The Secrets of Creative Collaboration* (Reading, MA: Addison-Wesley, 1997), p. 216.

[2]John Rawls, *A Theory of Justice* (Cambridge, MA: Harvard University Press, 1971).

[3]James Gleick, *Genius: The Life and Science of Richard Feynman* (New York: Vintage, 1992), p. 208.

constraints. John Kao suggests that there are two types of knowledge. The first is raw knowledge—facts, information, and data. The second type of knowledge is insight, or the "Aha!" It is "a response to the *what ifs* and *if only we coulds.*"[39]

Here are some questions that the commemorative booklet committee could have asked: What if we had a million dollars to design and print the commemorative booklet; what would we do? What if we had one hundred pages to work with? What if we could hire a famous author to write the copy—what would the booklet say? Group members could consider one more "what if" scenario: What if we do nothing?[40] In other words, what are the consequences, if any, if we don't produce a commemorative booklet?

Use Metaphors. The answers to many problems already exist. It's just that they are hiding in other areas of our lives.[41] You can find these hiding places in common metaphors. Metaphors can help group members explain, understand, guide, and direct their creative thinking in ways they would not have thought of otherwise.[42] For example, the metaphor of an emergency room could help redesign the registration process at some colleges. Students who don't need help can register online or over the telephone. Those who need help meet a kind of "triage nurse," a college advisor who can answer simple questions, direct them to a clerk for processing, or send them to a private room where they can receive "intensive care" from a "specialist" counselor. The beauty of metaphors is that they force group members to look at a problem in new and creative ways.

Problem-Solving Realities

Although procedures give us powerful problem-solving tools, several other factors affect the outcome of group decisions and solutions. We would be remiss if we did not

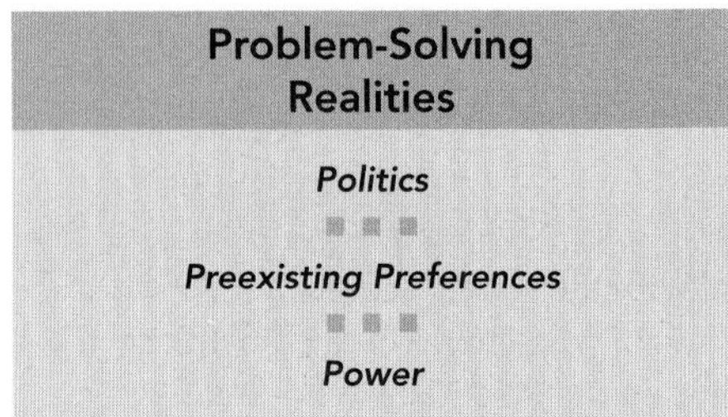

acknowledge that politics, preexisting preferences, and power often infiltrate the group process. Group "decision making in the real world is often messy."[43]

Politics

In organizational settings, almost all decisions have a political component. Regardless of the procedures, many group members come to meetings with hidden agendas and political interests. For example, a member who wants to get ahead may be reluctant to oppose an idea supported by the boss. Another member who knows why a plan won't work may remain silent in order to make sure that the person responsible for implementing the plan fails. Although most conscientious and ethical group members do not engage in such deceptive behavior, it would be naïve to assume that all members care equally about achieving the group's common goal. Meetings can become a political arena in which individuals and special-interest groups are dedicated to meeting their own needs. Fortunately, the use of clear procedures can minimize the influence of such members.

Preexisting Preferences

An intelligent group member is rarely a blank slate who walks into a meeting uninformed or unconcerned about the topic or issue to be discussed. Well before it's time for a decision, most of us have powerful preexisting preferences that affect how we vote. Psychologists report that we often resist or dismiss "information that doesn't mesh with our preconceived belief[s]." Not surprisingly, when we hear or read something that supports our preferences, we view it as valid and persuasive. When we encounter something that challenges our beliefs, we often view it as flawed.[44] In his book *True Enough,* Farhad Manjoo writes that in addition to holding different opinions, "we're also holding different facts" which distorts our "perceptions about what is 'real' and what isn't."[45] For example, in a 2004 survey of 928 studies about climate change published in prestigious scientific journals, "not a single one disagreed" with the view that humans contribute significantly to global warming. Why then do polls show that only 41 percent of Americans believe there is strong evidence that humans are changing the Earth's climate?[46] Preconceived preferences take a long time to change.

Fortunately, a combination of open discussions, clear goals, and the use of procedures can moderate these preferences, particularly when members analyze them logically and fairly. Even when members have preexisting preferences, procedures that require a pro-and-con discussion of each option help members understand the nature and causes of a problem.

Power

The power of individual group members can have a significant effect on whether a group achieves its goals. It is no secret that powerful people influence group decisions. They affect how and whether other members participate as well as whose ideas and suggestions get serious consideration. Highly influential members can convince a group "to accept invalid facts and assumptions, introduce poor ideas and suggestions, lead the group to misinterpret information presented to them, or lead the group off on tangents and irrelevant discussion."[47] In short, one powerful but misguided member can be responsible for the poor quality of a group's decision.

summary study guide

Group Decision Making

- Whereas decision making results in a judgment or a choice from among alternatives, problem solving is a complex process in which groups analyze a problem and agree to a plan that will solve or reduce the negative effects of the problem.
- Decision making and problem solving in groups generates more ideas and produces better solutions than can individuals working alone.
- Three ways in which groups can make a final decision—each of which has strengths and weaknesses—are voting, consensus seeking, and authority rule.
- A consensus decision is one that all members have a part in shaping and that all find at least minimally acceptable. Groups should be wary of false consensus, which occurs when members reluctantly give in to group pressures or an external authority.
- There are four types of discussion questions: questions of fact, conjecture, value, and policy. Some discussions require answers to all four types of questions.
- Differences in rational, intuitive, dependent, avoidant, and spontaneous decision-making styles can cause conflict and tension in groups.

Structured Problem Solving

- The Standard Agenda includes the following steps: task clarification, problem identification, fact finding, solution criteria and limitations, solution suggestions, solution evaluation and selection, and solution implementation.
- The Functional Perspective works best when the members of a decision-making or problem-solving group are committed to (1) making the best possible decision by understanding the task and its requirements, (2) seeking and relying on the best possible information and resources, and (3) having the critical thinking and communication skills needed for effective decision making or problem solving.
- The Single Question Format focuses a group on an agreed-upon question that requires group members to focus their attention on answering the question. Two features make the Single Question Format different and effective: (1) it focuses on goal clarity and issue analysis, and (2) it cultivates a supportive group climate.

Creative Problem Solving

- Creative problem solving in groups includes four stages: investigation, imagination, incubation, and insight.
- Brainstorming asks group members to generate as many ideas a possible in a short period of time without criticism or analysis.
- Nominal Group Technique (NGT) is a two-phase process in which individual members engage in fact finding and idea generation on their own, followed by an analytical discussion of ideas and, as a result, decision making.
- The Decreased Options Technique (DOT) is a method that helps groups reduce and refine a large number of ideas into more manageable categories.
- Virtual groups must carefully match the decision-making or problem-solving method to the appropriate technology.
- Regardless of the method, groups can enhance creativity by controlling judgment, encouraging innovation, asking "what if," and using creative metaphors.

Problem-Solving Realities

- Politics in a group manifest themselves in hidden agendas and special interests.
- Open discussion and clear procedures can diminish the impact of preexisting preferences.
- Differences in power affect how and whether group members participate, whose ideas get serious thought, how decisions are made, and which solutions are chosen.

key terms

analysis paralysis 245
authority rule 239
avoidant decision maker 242
brainstorming 253
consensus 238
creativity 252
decision making 236
Decreasing Options Technique (DOT) 256
dependent decision maker 242
false consensus 240
Functional Perspective 247
intuitive decision maker 241
majority vote 238
Nominal Group Technique (NGT) 254
problem solving 236
question of conjecture 240
question of fact 240
question of policy 241
question of value 240
rational decision maker 241
Reflective Thinking Process 243
Single Question Format 249
solution criteria 245
spontaneous decision maker 242
Standard Agenda 243
two-thirds vote 238

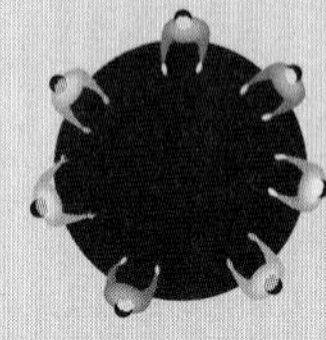

critical thinking about the case study
No More Horsing Around

1. How would you word the question that the group is trying to answer?
2. Is consensus seeking an appropriate method for developing a joint plan that will attract more customers? Why or why not?
3. How would you describe the differences between the private and public stable owners? Which, if any, of the group dialectic tensions are likely to affect the group's ability to achieve its goal?
4. What creative methods did the group use and were they effective? Would other problem-solving methods have been more effective? Why or why not?
5. Evaluate the relevance and usefulness of the agenda questions Sally proposed.
6. To what extent, if any, did politics, preexisting preferences, and power affect the group's ability to work together in pursuit of a common goal?
7. In your opinion, what one thing is most likely to prevent the group from achieving its goal? Explain your choice.

group work What Is Your Decision-Making Style?

Directions: For each of the following statements, indicate the degree to which you agree or disagree by placing a checkmark under a number on the following scale:

1 = Strongly disagree 2 = Disagree 3 = Undecided 4 = Agree 5 = Strongly agree

There are no right or wrong answers. Respond to the statements as honestly as you can. Think carefully before choosing option 3 (undecided)—it may suggest you cannot make decisions.

Scoring: To determine your score in each category, add the total of your responses to specific items for each type of

DECISION-MAKING STATEMENTS	1	2	3	4	5
1. When I have to make an important decision, I usually seek the opinions of others.					
2. I tend to put off decisions on issues that make me uncomfortable or that are unpleasant.					
3. I make decisions in a logical and systematic way.					
4. When making a decision, I usually trust my feelings or gut instincts.					
5. When making a decision, I generally consider the advantages and disadvantages of many alternatives.					
6. I often avoid making important decisions until I absolutely have to.					
7. I often make impulsive decisions.					
8. When making a decision, I rely on my instincts.					
9. It is easier for me to make important decisions when I know others approve or support them.					
10. I make decisions very quickly.					

decision making. Your higher scores identify your preferred decision-making styles.

Answers to items 3 and 5 = _____ (Rational Decision Maker)

Answers to items 4 and 8 = _____ (Intuitive Decision Maker)

Answers to items 1 and 9 = _____ (Dependent Decision Maker)

Answers to items 2 and 6 = _____ (Avoidant Decision Maker)

Answers to items 7 and 10 = _____ (Spontaneous Decision Maker)

Sources: www.uc.ie/careers/CMS/decision/student_skills_decision_styleex.html; www.acu.edu/campusoffices/ocad/students/exploration/assess/decision.html, updated August 24, 2005; and Suzanne Scott and Reginald Bruce, "Decision Making Style: The Development of a New Measure," *Educational and Psychological Measurement* 55 (1995), pp. 818–831.

group assessment Problem-Solving Competencies

Directions: Use this instrument to evaluate the performance of individual group members who participate in problem-solving discussions. There are five competencies related to accomplishing the group's task and three competencies dealing with conflict, climate, and interaction. Rate individual members and the group as a whole on each item in order to assess how well an observed group solves problems and makes important decisions.

1 = Superior 2 = Satisfactory 3 = Unsatisfactory

PROBLEM-SOLVING COMPETENCIES	1	2	3
Defines and analyzes the problem. Appropriately clarifies, defines, and analyzes the problem confronting the group.			
Identifies solution criteria. Appropriately participates in identifying criteria for assessing the quality of the group's outcome.			
Generates solutions. Appropriately identifies potential solutions or options.			
Evaluates solutions. Appropriately evaluates the potential solutions and options.			
Focuses on the task. Stays focused on the task, issue, or agenda item under discussion.			
Manages conflict. Encourages constructive disagreements and appropriately manages nonproductive conflict.			
Maintains a collaborative climate. Appropriately supports other group members.			
Communicates effectively. Interacts effectively and encourages other members to participate.			

notes

1. *The American Heritage Dictionary of the English Language*, 4th ed. (Boston: Houghton Mifflin, 2000), p. 484.
2. Peter R. Drucker, *The Effective Executive* (New York: HarperBusiness, 1967), p. 143.
3. See Charles Pavitt and Ellen Curtis, *Small Group Discussion: A Theoretical Approach*, 2nd ed. (Scottsdale, AZ: Gorsuch, Scarisbrick, 1994), pp. 25–52; Robert S. Cathcart, Larry A. Samovar, and Linda D. Henman, *Small Group Communication: Theory and Practice*, 7th ed. (Madison, WI: Brown & Benchmark, 1996), pp. 102–03; Donald G. Ellis and B. Aubrey Fisher, *Small Group Decision Making: Communication and the Group Process*, 4th ed. (New York: McGraw-Hill, 1994), pp. 17–18.

4. Marshall Scott Poole, "Procedures for Managing Meetings: Social and Technological Innovation," in *Innovative Meeting Management*, ed. Richard A. Swanson and Bonnie Ogram Knapp (Austin, TX: 3M Meeting Management Institute, 1990), pp. 73–74.
5. Julia T. Wood, "Alternative Methods of Group Decision Making," in *Small Group Communication: A Reader*, 6th ed., ed. Robert S. Cathcart and Larry A. Samovar (Dubuque, IA: Wm. C. Brown, 1992), p. 159.
6. Dennis S. Gouran, "Effective Versus Ineffective Group Decision Making," in *Managing Group Life: Communicating in Decision-Making Groups*, ed. Lawrence R. Frey and J. Kevin Barge (Boston: Houghton Mifflin, 1997), p. 139.
7. Suzanne G. Scott and Reginald A. Bruce, "Decision Making Style: The Development of a New Measure." *Educational and Psychological Measurement* 55 (1995), pp. 818–831.
8. Poole, pp. 54–55.
9. Pavitt and Curtis, p. 432.
10. John Dewey, *How We Think* (Boston: Heath, 1910).
11. Based on Kathryn Sue Young et al., *Group Discussion: A Practical Guide to Participation and Leadership*, 3rd ed. (Prospect Heights, IL: Waveland, 2001).
12. Susan Jarboe, "Procedures for Enhancing Group Decision Making," in *Communication and Group Decision Making*, 2nd ed., ed. Randy Y. Hirokawa and Marshall Scott Poole (Thousand Oaks: Sage, 1996), p. 357.
13. Jarboe, p. 358.
14. Dennis S. Gouran and Randy Y. Hirokawa, "Functional Theory and Communication in Decision-Making and Problem-Solving Groups," *Communication and Group Decision Making*, 2nd ed., ed. Randy Y. Hirokawa and Marshall Scott Poole (Thousand Oaks CA: Sage, 1996), p. 76.
15. Randy Y. Hirokawa, "Communication and Group Decision-Making Efficacy," in *Small Group Communication: Theory and Practice*, 7th ed., ed. Robert S. Cathcart, Larry A. Samovar, and Linda D. Henman (Madison, WI: Brown & Benchmark, 1996), p. 108.
16. Randy Hirokawa and Roger Pace, "A Descriptive Investigation of Possible Communication-Based Reasons for Effective and Ineffective Group Decision Making," *Communication Monographs*, 50 (December 1983), pp. 363–67.
17. Frank LaFasto and Carl Larson, *When Teams Work Best* (Thousand Oaks, CA: Sage, 2001), pp. 84–85.
18. LaFasto and Larson, p. 85.
19. LaFasto and Larson, p. 88.
20. LaFasto and Larson, pp. 89–90.
21. LaFasto and Larson, p. 90.
22. Warren Bennis and Patricia Ward Biederman, *Organizing Genius: The Secrets of Creative Collaboration* (Reading, MA: Addison-Wesley, 1997), p. 17.
23. Bennis and Biederman, p. 20.
24. Based on Lee Towe, *Why Didn't I Think of That?* (West Des Moines, IA: American Media, 1996), p. 7.
25. Roger L. Firestein, "Effects of Creative Problem-Solving Training on Communication Behaviors in Small Groups," *Small Group Research* 21 (1990), pp. 507–521.
26. John Kao, *Jamming: The Art and Discipline of Business Creativity* (New York: HarperBusiness, 1997), p. 17.
27. Alex F. Osborn, *Applied Imagination*, rev. ed. (New York: Scribner's, 1957).
28. Tom Kelley with Jonathan Littman, *The Art of Innovation: Lessons in Creativity from IDEO, America's Leading Design Firm* (New York: Currency, 2001), p. 55.
29. Some of the brainstorming guidelines are based on Kelley and Littman, pp. 56–59.
30. 3M Meeting Management Team with Jeannine Drew, *Mastering Meetings: Discovering the Hidden Potential of Effective Business Meetings* (New York: McGraw-Hill, 1994), p. 59.
31. Andre L. Delbecq, Andrew H. Van de Ven, and David H. Gustafson, *Group Techniques for Program Planning* (Glenview, IL: Scott, Foresman, 1975).
32. P. Keith Kelly, *Team Decision-Making Techniques* (Irvine, CA: Richard Chang Associates, 1994), p. 29.
33. Delbecq et al., p. 8.
34. Delbecq et al., p. 8.
35. Kelly, p. 29.
36. See Kenneth E. Andersen, "Developments in Communication Ethics: The Ethics Commission, Code of Professional Responsibilities, and Credo for Ethical Communication," *Journal of the Association for Communication Administration*, 29 (2000), pp. 131–44. The Credo for Ethical Communication is also posted on the National Communication Association's website, www.natcom.org.
37. Kao, p. 87.
38. Towe, p. 14.
39. Kao, p. 8.
40. Donald J. Noone, *Creative Problem Solving*, 2nd ed. (New York: Barron's, 1998), p. 60.
41. Towe, p. 77.
42. Noone, p. 93.
43. Dirk Scheerhorn, Patricia Geist, and Jean-Claude Teboul, "Beyond Decision Making in Decision-Making Groups: Implications for the Study of Group Communication," in *Group Communication in Context: Studies of Natural Groups*, ed. Lawrence R. Frey (Hillsdale, NJ: Erlbaum, 1994), p. 256.
44. See also Nicholas D. Kristoff, "Divided We Fall," *New York Times* (April 17, 2008), p. A27.
45. Frahad Manjoo, *True Enough: Learning to Live in a Post-Fact Society* (NY: John Wiley & Sons, 2008) (2008), p. 2.
46. Manjoo, p. 23.
47. Hirokawa and Pace, p. 379.

chapter 11

Critical Thinking and Argumentation in Groups

chapter outline

Critical Thinking and Argumentation
Arguments and Argumentation • The Value of Argumentation in Groups • Argumentativeness

Structuring Arguments
Claim, Evidence, and Warrant • Backing, Reservation, and Qualifier • Applying the Toulmin Model

Supporting Arguments
Types of Evidence • Tests of Evidence

Presenting Arguments
State Your Claim • Support Your Claim • Provide Reasons • Summarize Your Argument

Refuting Arguments
Listen to the Argument • State the Opposing Claim • Preview Your Objections • Assess the Evidence • Assess the Reasoning • Summarize Your Refutation

Adapting to Argumentation Styles
Gender Differences • Cultural Differences • Argumentation and Emotional Intelligence

study questions

- *How do critical thinking and argumentation differ from criticism and arguing?*
- *What are the six components of an effective argument?*
- *What are the characteristics of valid evidence?*
- *How do you present a clear, valid, and persuasive argument?*
- *How can you demonstrate that an argument is invalid?*
- *How should you demonstrate to differences in argumentation styles?*

Critical Thinking and Argumentation

Do you *like* being criticized? Do you *enjoy* arguing? Our guess is that most people would answer *no* to both questions. So why in the world do we include a chapter titled "Critical Thinking and Argumentation"? Is it because effective group members learn to endure criticism and arguments for the sake of the group's goal? Of course not. Critical thinking is not about criticizing and argumentation is not about fighting. After many years of teaching, coaching, and consulting, we have learned that effective group members excel as critical thinkers and know how to engage in constructive argumentation.

Critical thinking is the kind of thinking you use when you analyze what you read, see, or hear in order to arrive at a justified conclusion or decision. Critical thinking is a conscious process that always results in an outcome—a personal conclusion or opinion as well as group decisions and actions. It also results in productive argumentation among group members seeking to achieve a common goal.

Group communication scholars have no doubts about the role of skilled argumentation in effective group decision making.[1] Critical thinking and effective argumentation help group members develop, present, and defend their own viewpoints as well as objectively listen to and analyze the views of others. In a review of research on critical thinking in groups, D. Christopher Kayes concludes that critical thinking is more important than ever for groups dealing with a complex and changing world as they coordinate a diverse set of goals, roles, and intellectual challenges.[2]

Arguments and Argumentation

Many people think an argument is a hostile confrontation between two or more combatants. In communication studies, an argument is something much less threatening. An **argument** is a claim supported by evidence and reasons for accepting it. An argument is more than an opinion, such as "I think the Latino Heritage Club should be given more funds next year." An argument is an idea or opinion *supported* by evidence and reasoning: "The Latino Heritage Club should be given more funds next year because it has doubled in size and cannot provide the same number or quality of programs without more funds." When viewed this way, an argument does not necessarily involve conflict or disagreement. **Argumentation,** then, is the way in which group members use critical thinking to advocate proposals, examine competing ideas, and influence one another.

Unlike when two people argue, groups engage in unique kinds of argumentation. For example, once a group makes a decision based on listening to and analyzing arguments from its members, the argument is over. A decision signals the end of argumentation and the beginning of implementation or the discussion of a new issue. In addition, when an entire group argues—rather than only two people—there are more questions and challenges, which force "the group's argument into more complex realms of reasoning, challenging members to reevaluate" arguments "in light of new evidence."[3]

Effective arguers balance their personal desire to win an argument with the group's need to solve a problem or make a decision. As communication scholars Josina Makau and Debian Marty put it, argumentation in groups should be cooperative rather than competitive. They define **cooperative argumentation** as "a process of reasoned interaction . . . intended to help participants and audiences make the best assessments or the best decisions in any given situation."[4] Cooperative arguers focus on the group's shared goal of solving a problem or making the best decision.

case study

Slicing the Pie

At Gorgias College, the Student Finance Board is responsible for distributing funds to campus clubs and organizations. Board members include the president, vice president, and treasurer of student government, four members from active student groups, two faculty members, and the college's comptroller. The director of student activities chairs the meeting but has no voting power. However, he does provide data and background information about how previous boards made these decisions.

The board meets throughout the academic year to consider funding requests. Clubs usually request more money than is available. Board members read funding requests and listen to presentations by club members who argue that their organization should receive the funding they requested. Then, board members share their opinions and, in many cases, argue for or against proposed funding levels for particular organizations. After a period of discussion and debate, the group makes its final decision—even though it knows that some clubs and advisors will argue that the decision was unfair or unjust.

This year, the student members on the Student Finance Board come from the Philosophy Club, the Latino Heritage Club, the Intramural Sports Council, and the Drama Society. The group has $500,000 to distribute and requests for $875,000. Clearly, many groups will receive less than they requested.

Patrice, president of the student government, proposes that the board should begin with a blank slate. That is, they won't guarantee clubs the same budgets received in past years. Instead, they should use four criteria to decide how much each club should get: (1) the number of members, (2) the quality of their written funding request, (3) the value of their activities to students and others, and (4) their cost-effectiveness.

Several board members respond immediately. Wendell, a faculty member who is also the Nursing Club advisor, objects by saying, "Many clubs depend on getting what they've had in the past. Their numbers, as well as the quality and quantity of their activities, have not changed—so why should their funding change?"

Patrice responds, "Well, their funding may not change at all. It might even go up." Charlie, a member of the Philosophy Club, answers, "But that doesn't respond to Wendell's argument. For example, the Debating Society doesn't have many members, but their activities boost the college's reputation. So should we give them less?"

"The answer to your question, Charlie, is yes," says Mark, a member of the Intramural Sports Council. "Thirty times as many students participate in intramurals and we get only ten times as much as the debate team." Charlie quickly adds, "And the intercollegiate sports teams get more money than all the other clubs combined. Let's look at the quality of each program, its value to the college, and how much it costs. Remember when college Republicans invited Rush Limbaugh to speak on campus? Remember how much that cost?" The director of college activities gently interrupts and suggests that the group pause and listen to a couple of stories about how previous boards dealt with such problems in the past. Patrice—who's been silent as long as she can stand—interrupts the director: "The past is the problem. Some groups got more than they deserved and others got much less than they needed to survive."

Caesar, from the Latin Heritage Club, sighs audibly and shakes his head. "Look, that's fine for clubs that have been around for years. But the Latin Heritage Club is new. We don't have many members right now—but we will if we have the funds to get the word out to potential members. We don't have a track record—but we will if we have the funds to sponsor activities. We're not even sure we wrote the funding proposal correctly. As I see it, Patrice's criteria will only make sure we get nothing." The Drama Society member nods her head, but adds, "And then there are the thousands of people who come to our theatre productions—how do you count them?"

Finally the college's comptroller calls for order. "I'm appointed to this board by the college to make sure that our decisions are justifiable and legal. Let's stop bickering about the clubs we do and don't

(*continued*)

support. Instead, we need an orderly way of letting you make your arguments clearly and fairly. OK?"

When you finish reading this chapter, you should be able to answer the following questions.

1. To what extent did the arguments in this case study reflect effective critical thinking?
2. Which of the arguments included a claim, evidence, and warrant?
3. What kinds of evidence did the board members use in their arguments?
4. What fallacies of argument, if any, did board members use?
5. How well did the board adapt to different argumentative styles?

They recognize that the group learns and knows more if there is an open exchange of ideas. Those who disagree are resources, not rivals. Although cooperative arguers want to win arguments, they do not want to do so at the expense of the group goal and member relationships.

Argumentation in Groups

Promotes Understanding

Promotes Critical Thinking

Avoids Groupthink

Improves Group Decision Making

The Value of Argumentation in Groups

Effective argumentation helps groups understand and analyze ideas, influence members, and make informed decisions. Thus, the quantity and quality of argumentation is a significant factor in determining whether a group achieves its goal.

Promotes Understanding. Group members use argumentation to express various viewpoints in various ways. Some argue logically; others, emotionally. Some argue on behalf of what's best for the group; others argue for personal gain. For example, as a member of the Student Finance Board, Charlie argues in favor of funding the Philosophy Club because he is a club member. A faculty member may support the Philosophy Club request because it visibly highlights the academic goals of the humanities division. Both members support the same position but for different reasons. Understanding how other group members reason and feel about issues can help you adapt your arguments.

Promotes Critical Thinking. Effective argumentation helps group members analyze issues and critically examine ideas. When you present your position on an issue, another member may challenge your claims and ask you to justify your position. Your response requires skilled argumentation supported by strong evidence and sound reasoning. The process of argumentation may even cause you to rethink your own positions and beliefs. Argumentation in groups goes hand-in-hand with critical thinking.

Avoids Groupthink. As Chapter 9, Conflict and Cohesion in Groups, notes, groupthink occurs when, because of efforts to discourage conflict and maintain cohesion, a group makes flawed decisions. On the other hand, "unlike groups that engage in

groupthink, groups trained to employ cooperative argumentation are able to form constructive forms of cohesion."[5] Constructive and cooperative argumentation encourages the critical examination of opposing ideas without impairing group cohesion. Groups can avoid groupthink when members think critically, ask questions, offer reasons for their positions, and seek justifications from others.

Improves Group Decision Making. Argumentation helps group members examine the consequences of a potential action before making a final decision. Errors in reasoning are exposed, and weaknesses in evidence are uncovered. Argumentation can also improve group decision making because, unlike one-on-one argumentation, several members may work together to develop the same argument. In this "tag team" situation, like-minded members build on the arguments presented by others by providing additional evidence or reasons to support a particular position. The result is a single comprehensive argument constructed cooperatively by a subgroup. Tag-team arguing also produces "perceptions of unity and support for the subgroup's preferred option."[6] Although there is strong evidence that argumentation improves group decision making,[7] this conclusion relies on the assumption that group members know how to develop and use arguments effectively.

Argumentativeness

Chapter 3, Group Membership, introduces the concept of communication apprehension to explain why some group members lack confidence in their ability to interact in a group. Similarly, we may also vary in how comfortable we feel arguing—a characteristic called **argumentativeness,** or the willingness to argue controversial issues with others.[8] Argumentativeness is constructive when it does not promote aggression and hostility. The responsible argumentative member focuses on issues and avoids personal attacks.

At the end of this chapter is a self-test called the Argumentativeness Scale that will help identify your level of argumentativeness. You might want to complete the questionnaire and calculate your results before continuing with this chapter.

A group member's level of argumentativeness provides some insight into how that member will approach a discussion. Group members with lower levels of argumentativeness generally avoid conflict. As a result, other group members may view them not only as nonconfrontational, but also as unskilled in argumentation and less influential in group decision making. Highly argumentative group members enjoy the intellectual challenge of a good argument. They defend their positions confidently and challenge the arguments of others with skill. Groups usually view their most argumentative members as skilled communicators with high credibility and influence. Argumentative members often become group leaders. On the other hand, they are less likely to accept other members' arguments and may become inflexible and overly talkative.

Argumentative members are influential in group decision making. In fact, argumentative group members create more arguments on *both* sides of a position.[9] When the number of choices a group can consider expands, the group is less likely to reach a biased decision or succumb to groupthink.

Structuring Arguments

Stephen Toulmin, an English philosopher, believes that real-world arguments are less formal and more complex than those described in philosophy and logic textbooks. He

compares an argument to a living organism, with its own anatomical structure and specific physiological functions.[10] The **Toulmin Model of Argument** provides a way of building strong arguments and refuting the arguments of others.

Before you can build or refute an argument, you need to understand the components of a complete argument. In his layout of an argument, Toulmin identifies six components: claim, evidence, warrant, backing, reservation, and qualifier.[11] The first three are essential in all arguments; the second three help clarify the nature and power of an argument.

Claim, Evidence, and Warrant

The **claim** is the conclusion or position you advocate. **Evidence** describes the facts, statistics, opinions, examples, and other materials you use to support your claim. For example, the statement "My group will do well on our class project" is a claim. The evidence for this claim might be the fact that during the first meeting, all members of the group said that they would work hard on the project. Evidence answers a challenger's questions: "What makes you say that?" or "What do you have to go on?"

A **warrant** answers the question "How did you get there?"[12] The definition of the word *warrant* may help you understand this concept. A warrant can mean "justification for an action or belief," as in "Under the circumstances, the actions were warranted."[13] In argumentation, warrants explain how the evidence supports and proves a claim. For example, a warrant might state that when group members are willing to work hard, a successful outcome is usually the result.

Warrants authorize or confirm the validity of a conclusion and give you the right to make your claim. Here's an example of an unwarranted argument: Girlfriend says to boyfriend, "You saw me walking to my car with your friend Dale, and you jumped to the conclusion that we were seeing each other behind your back. That inference is *unwarranted*!" In this argument, the evidence (she walked to her car with Dale) is insufficient to make the claim (she's seeing Dale behind her boyfriend's back) because the warrant is unreasonable (if a woman talks to a man, she must be dating him or having an affair with him).[14]

Figure 11.1 illustrates the relationship among these three components of the Toulmin Model. The argument in Figure 11.1 would sound like this: "All group members say they will work hard. Because hard work usually results in success, the group will do well on the class project." The combined evidence, claim, and warrant make up the "basic T" of the Toulmin Model.

Figure 11.1 "Basic T" of the Toulmin Model

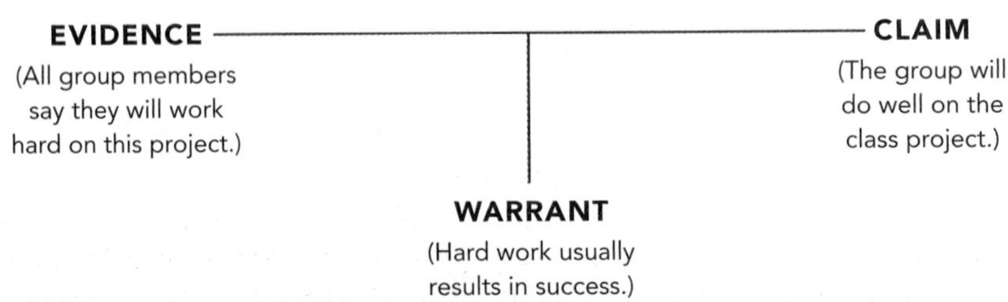
EVIDENCE
(All group members say they will work hard on this project.)
CLAIM
(The group will do well on the class project.)
WARRANT
(Hard work usually results in success.)

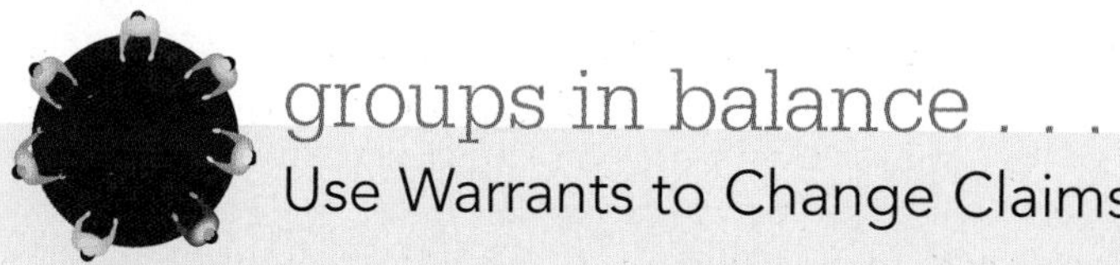

groups in balance . . .
Use Warrants to Change Claims

Warrants are the most difficult of Toulmin's components to understand and appreciate because they may not be expressed aloud. Warrants give you permission to make a claim based on evidence. They change claims in significant ways. In the following two arguments, the evidence is the same. The claims, however, are quite different because the warrants are different.[1]

> Argument 1: The reserves of fossil fuels are limited and will be used up in a few generations. Satisfactory alternative sources of energy are not yet available. Therefore, we must allow industries to continue using our fossil fuel reserves.

> Argument 2: The reserves of fossil fuels are limited and will be used up in a few generations. Satisfactory alternative sources of energy are not yet available. Therefore, we may allow industries to continue using our fossil fuel reserves only if they accept their share of responsibility for developing alternative sources of energy.

Look at the way in which different warrants justify the claims in the two arguments:

> Warrant for Argument 1: Because industry cannot function without fuel and society is dependent on industry, we must let industry go on doing what it has to do in order to keep society functioning.

> Warrant for Argument 2: Because industry and society are jointly involved in a common venture, industry must adapt its activities to the broader needs of society.

[1]Example from Stephen Toulmin, Richard Rieke, and Allan Janik, *An Introduction to Reasoning* (New York: Macmillan, 1979), p. 303.

Backing, Reservation, and Qualifier

Beyond the "basic T," there are three additional components: backing, reservation, and qualifier. The **backing** provides support for the argument's warrant. In the preceding class project example, backing for the warrant might be the fact that the group that worked the hardest on the last assignment received the best grade. If you believe that members may doubt the validity of your evidence, make sure you have backing to support it.

Not all claims are true all the time. The **reservation** component of the Toulmin Model recognizes exceptions to an argument or indicates that a claim may not be true under certain circumstances. At the first meeting, group members said that they would work hard. If, however, some members do not attend the planning meetings, the group is less likely to do well. You now have reason to doubt your claim about group success.

The final component of the model is the qualifier. The **qualifier** states the degree to which the claim appears to be true. Qualifiers are usually words or phrases such as *likely, possibly, certainly, unlikely,* or *probably.* A claim with a qualifier might be "The group will *probably* do well on the class project." Figure 11.2 on page 274 illustrates the entire structure of this argument.

Applying the Toulmin Model

The Toulmin Model lets you diagram and evaluate arguments. In most cases, you don't need to state every component of the argument. However, understanding the model lets you know what questions to ask about your own and other members' arguments. If someone only states an argument's claim, you may ask for evidence to support that

Figure 11.2 The Toulmin Model of an Argument

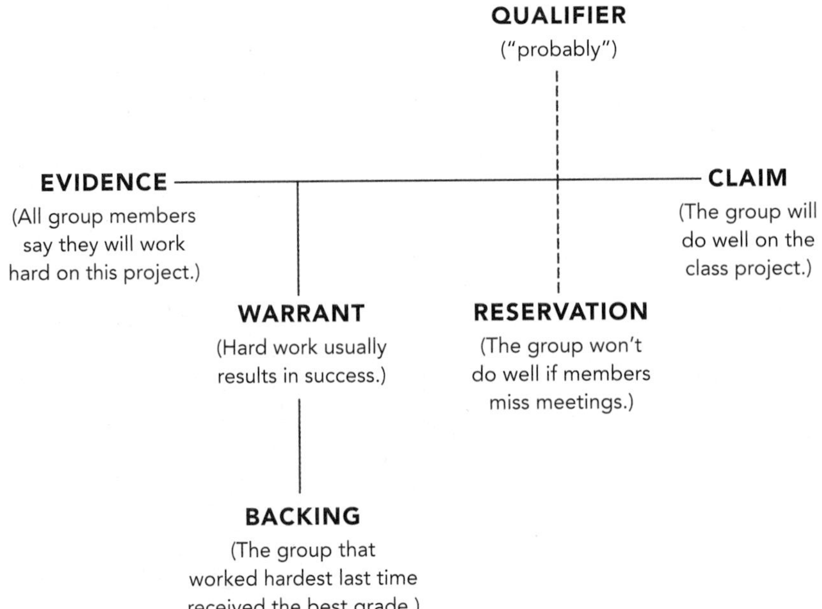
QUALIFIER
("probably")
EVIDENCE
(All group members say they will work hard on this project.)
CLAIM
(The group will do well on the class project.)
WARRANT
(Hard work usually results in success.)
RESERVATION
(The group won't do well if members miss meetings.)
BACKING
(The group that worked hardest last time received the best grade.)

claim. If the warrant is questionable, you may ask for backing to support it. Recognizing that situations may alter the certainty of your claim, you may ask for qualifiers that recognize exceptions. When you develop your own arguments, the Toulmin Model can help you test the strength of every component. When you are analyzing someone else's argument, the model helps reveal the strengths and weaknesses of the claims.

Supporting Arguments

Arguments fall apart if the evidence used to support the claim and back the warrant is insufficient or flawed. All arguments gain strength when you research your position and use appropriate evidence to make your case.

Research is a systematic search or investigation designed to find useful and appropriate evidence. Even if you already know something about the topic area, good research can make you look and sound even better. For example, you may know that Americans watch a lot of television; research lets you know that the average American watches TV more than four hours a day.[15]

A researcher with a good research strategy becomes an effective investigator with a systematic plan for searching sources of information—in the same way a detective searches for clues. The information you need is out there; you just have to find it. You can search different kinds of libraries, do electronic and online research, and interview knowledgeable individuals. As you do your research, make sure you choose appropriate types of evidence and test the validity of your evidence.

Types of Evidence

Toulmin lists evidence as an essential component of his model of an argument. Evidence takes many forms: (1) facts and opinions, (2) definitions and descriptions, (3) examples and illustrations, and (4) statistics.

The Toulmin Model of an Argument lets you diagram and evaluate arguments. It also helps you know what questions to ask about your own and other members' arguments. Do you believe that group members can reach a unanimous decision about an important issue if they engage in effective argumentation? Why or why not?

Facts and Opinions. A **fact** is a verifiable observation, experience, or event, something known to be true. An **opinion** is a personal conclusion regarding the meaning or implications of facts. Here is a fact: In 1876, Colonel Henry M. Robert used the British Parliament's procedures and Thomas Jefferson's code of congressional rules as a basis for *Robert's Rules of Order.* Here are two contrasting opinions:

- *Robert's Rules of Order* is outdated and makes a meeting more complicated than necessary.
- *Robert's Rules of Order* is time tested and ensures fair and objective decision making.

Unlike opinions, facts can usually be proved true or false. Group members should not mistake their opinions for facts.

When used as evidence, opinions usually express an authority's judgment or interpretation of facts. For example, "According to James C. McCroskey and Virginia Richmond, communication apprehension 'may be the single most important factor in predicting communication behavior in a small group.'" Keep in mind that different experts may not reach the same conclusions. Look for a variety of opinions rather than relying on claims that represent only one perspective.

Definitions and Descriptions. A **definition** clarifies the meaning of a word, phrase, or concept. A definition can be as simple as explaining what you mean by a word or as complex as an encyclopedia entry. Here is an example:

> According to Warren Bennis and Bruce Nanus, "There is a profound difference between management and leadership, and both are important. 'To manage' means 'to bring about, to accomplish, to have charge of or responsibility for, to conduct.' 'Leading' is 'influencing, guiding in direction, course, action, opinion.'"[16]

During an initial meeting, a group should define key terms. For example, a group dealing with sexual harassment policies should gather several definitions of sexual

harassment. Groups negotiating legal contracts carefully define their terms before reaching agreement.

Descriptions are more detailed than definitions. Rather than clarifying the meaning of a word or concept, a **description** creates a mental image of a person, event, place, or object. Causes, effects, historical contexts, characteristics, and operations can all be included in a description. Here is a description of *feelers,* one of the Myers-Briggs personality types: "Feelers are people-oriented members who seek group harmony. They want everyone to get along. Feelers will spend time and effort helping other members."

Examples and Illustrations. An **example** refers to a specific case or instance. Examples are usually brief. An **illustration** is a longer, extended example that can take up an entire paragraph or tell a lengthy story. Here's a series of examples from Chapter 1: "Groups communicate in a variety of group settings and circumstances—at school and at work, with family members and with friends, and in highly diverse arenas ranging from sports and science to courtrooms and classrooms." That same chapter opens with two illustrations—one about the 2008 Super Bowl champions; the other about Dr. Peter Agre, winner of the 2003 Nobel Prize for Chemistry.

Statistics. Information presented in a numerical form is the basis for **statistics**. Statistics take various forms, including averages, percentages, rates, rankings, and so on. For example, in this textbook, you have read that according to James McCroskey and Virginia Richmond, "about 20 percent of the general population experiences very high levels of communication apprehension." You've also learned that according to the U.S. Census Bureau, "During the 1990s, the Hispanic population increased 58 percent, and the Asian population increased 48 percent."

Many of us believe statistics, particularly when published by reputable sources. However, you should examine all statistical findings carefully. The source and form of a statistic can result in different interpretations of the same numbers. Misinterpreting statistical information can jeopardize a group's effectiveness and success. For example, in 2005, the number of miles driven by Americans grew by just 1 percent, the smallest increase since the 1991 recession.[17] Here are some interpretations of that statistic: (1) health-conscious Americans were walking more and driving less, (2) Americans concerned about the environmental effects of automobile exhaust decreased their driving, and (3) record-high gas prices encouraged people to cut down on optional trips and use mass transit. Expert analysts identify the third reason as the correct interpretation.

Questions to Test Evidence

Is the Source Identified and Credible?

Is the Source Unbiased?

Is the Information Recent?

Is the Information Consistent?

Are the Statistics Valid?

Tests of Evidence

Evaluate every piece of evidence before using it in an argument or sharing it with group members. Make sure your information is **valid**, that the ideas, opinions, and information you include are accurate, reasonable, and justified.[18]

Is the Source Identified and Credible? How credible are your information sources? Who are the author(s) and publisher? Are they reputable? For example, credible sources such as *The Information Please Almanac* and *The New York Times Almanac* have been in business for many years, and their continued success depends on their ability to collect and publish information that is accurate and up-to-date.

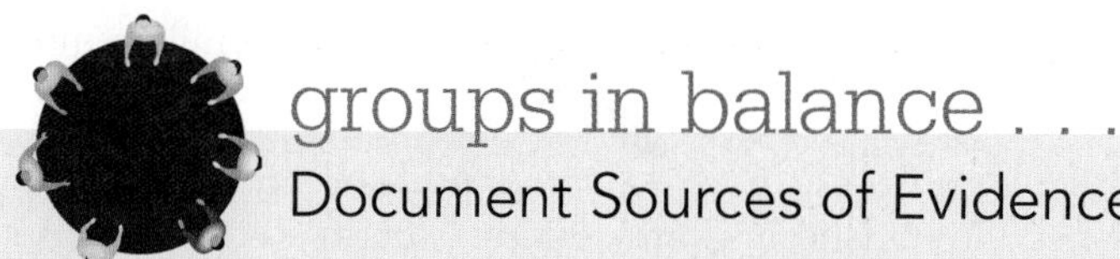

groups in balance . . .

Document Sources of Evidence

Documentation is the practice of citing the sources of evidence. All group members should document their evidence, including information from Internet sources and interviews, in writing and then orally in discussions. Documentation enhances your credibility and the validity of your arguments.

Unlike writers, you will rarely display footnotes during a discussion, unless perhaps a PowerPoint presentation gives you that opportunity. Rather, you provide an **oral citation**, a comment that includes enough information to let members find the original source you're citing. It's a good idea to provide the name of the person (or people) whose work you are using, say a word or two about their credentials, and mention the source (e.g., publication, website, television program) and its date. For example, if you claim that the United States puts a greater proportion of its citizens in jail than any other country, you could say, "According to a 2008 report by the International Center for Prison Studies in England, the United States has 2.3 million criminals behind bars, more than any other nation. Even China, which has four times the population of the United States, is a distant second."[1]

[1] Adam Liptak, "Inmate Count in U.S. Dwarfs Other Nations'," *New York Times*, April 23, 2008, p. A1.

Also evaluate newspapers and online news and information services. Their reputations, too, depend on their ability to publish accurate information. There are, however, big differences among sources. The sensational *National Enquirer* may be fun to read, but the *New York Times* is more likely to contain reliable information. Ask yourself if the source is a recognized expert, a firsthand observer, or a respected journalist.

Is the Source Unbiased? You can identify sources with a **bias** by asking two questions: Do their opinions seem one-sided, self-serving, unreasonable, or unfair? Do they directly and significantly benefit by your agreeing with them? For years, tobacco companies publicly denied that cigarette smoking was harmful, even though their own research told them otherwise. Now we recognize that the tobacco companies' pronouncements were biased and untrue. Even not-for-profit special-interest groups such as the National Rifle Association, pro-choice or pro-life groups, or the American Association of Retired Persons (AARP) have biases. The information they publish may be true, but the conclusions they draw from that information may be skewed toward their own goals.

Is the Information Recent? Always note the date of the information you use as evidence. When was the information collected? When was it published? In this rapidly changing information age, your information can become old in a matter of hours. Books provide a wealth of background information and historical perspectives. For current events or scientific breakthroughs, use recent magazines, journals, newspaper articles, or reliable Web sources.

Is the Information Consistent? Ensure that the information you include reports facts and findings similar to other information on the same subject. Does the information make sense based on what you know about the topic? For example, if most doctors and medical experts agree that penicillin will *not* cure a common viral cold, why believe an obscure source that recommends it as a treatment?

Are the Statistics Valid? Determining the validity of statistics generally requires answering three questions:

1. *What is the source of the statistics?* Knowing who or what organization collected and published the statistical information may alert you to biases. For example, when tobacco company studies found no relationship between cigarette smoking and cancer rates, unbiased scientists greeted their results with great skepticism.
2. *Are the statistics accurate?* Researchers may generate statistics by surveying or observing people. Statistical research that includes too few people or subjects who are not representative of the studied population may be invalid. For example, one study examined the effects of diet on breast cancer by studying only men.[19] Clearly, the exclusion of women from the study makes any results or conclusions suspect if applied to all people.
3. *How are the statistics reported?* The way in which the source reports the statistic can conceal or distort information. For example, if group members hear that customer complaints have increased 100 percent over the past year, they

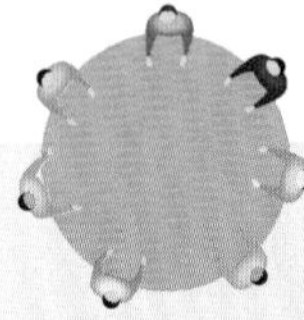

virtual groups

Think Critically about the Internet

Despite the enormous benefits of electronic research, there are significant disadvantages. William Miller, a former president of the Association of College and Research Libraries, notes, "Much of what purports to be serious information [on the Web] is simply junk—neither current, objective, nor trustworthy.[1]

The Internet does not cover all the possible sources of information. What you find can be difficult to test for validity. The most trustworthy websites include information from major newspapers and magazines, professional associations, government agencies, libraries, institutions of higher education, legitimate media outlets, and well-known experts. Unfortunately, Internet sources are often biased and deceptive. Sites that appear legitimate may be fronts for pornography, hate speech, and fraudulent advertising. Because no one can possibly screen everything on the Internet for accuracy, it can be difficult to separate reliable from unreliable sources. Here are four related questions to ask when you find and want to use an Internet source:

Criterion #1: Authority

1. Are the *sponsor's* identity and purpose clear?
2. Are the *author's* identity and qualifications evident?
3. Can you verify the legitimacy of the page's sponsor (e.g., a phone number or postal address to contact for more information)?

Criterion #2: Accuracy

1. Are the sources of information available so you can verify their claims?
2. Has the sponsor provided links you can use to verify claims?
3. Is statistical data well labeled and easy to read?
4. Is the information free of grammatical, spelling, and typographical errors that could indicate a lack of quality control?

Criterion #3: Objectivity

1. Is it evident why the sponsor is providing the information?
2. Is the sponsor's point of view presented clearly with well-supported arguments?
3. Does it account for opposing points of view?

Criterion #4: Currency

1. Is the material recent enough to be accurate and relevant?
2. Are there any indications that the material is revised and kept up-to-date?
3. Do you see statements indicating when data for charts and graphs were gathered?

[1]Quoted from *Chronicle of Higher Education*, August 1, 1997, A44, in Ann Raimes, *Keys for Writers*, 2nd ed. (Boston: Houghton Mifflin, 2000), p. 73.

may believe that they have a serious problem to address. Upon closer examination of the statistic, though, they may discover that last year only two customers complained, and this year there were four complaints. The problem no longer appears to be as serious.

Good statistics can be informative, dramatic, and convincing. Statistics can also mislead, distort, and confuse. Make sure your statistics are valid—that they are legitimate, justified, and accurate—and that you explain them correctly.

Presenting Arguments

If you want your ideas taken seriously by your group, you must present your arguments skillfully.[20] Figure 11.3 shows a four-step process for presenting arguments.

In some cases, you may not need to include every step of the process when you present an argument. If the evidence is strong and clear, you don't need to provide the warrant. If your argument is very brief, a summary may not be necessary. However, you should be prepared to include all the steps if group members want further justification for your arguments.

State Your Claim

The first step in presenting an argument is to state your claim clearly. Chapter 10 identifies four types of discussion questions—fact, conjecture, value, and policy. Discussion questions help groups focus on their goals. Claims for arguments fit into similar categories. However, when presenting arguments, group members rarely state claims in the form of questions. A *claim* is a declarative statement that identifies your position on a particular issue.

- A **claim of fact** attempts to prove that something is true, that an event occurred, or that a cause did have an effect. For example, "Sex education in schools promotes teenage promiscuity" is a claim of fact. Whether this claim is true or not depends on further analysis of the evidence and the warrant.
- A **claim of conjecture** suggests that something will or will not happen. For example, you could say, "Inflation will increase by 5 percent by next year." Although your group cannot predict the future, it can make well-informed decisions based on the best information available.
- A **claim of value** asserts that something is worthwhile—good or bad; right or wrong; best, average, or worst. "My instructor is the best professor at the college" is a claim that places a value on someone. Arguments involving claims of value are often difficult to prove because each group member brings personal opinions and beliefs to the discussion.
- A **claim of policy** recommends a particular course of action. "We should raise tuition by 9 percent next year" is a claim of policy.

Figure 11.3 Procedure for Presenting Arguments

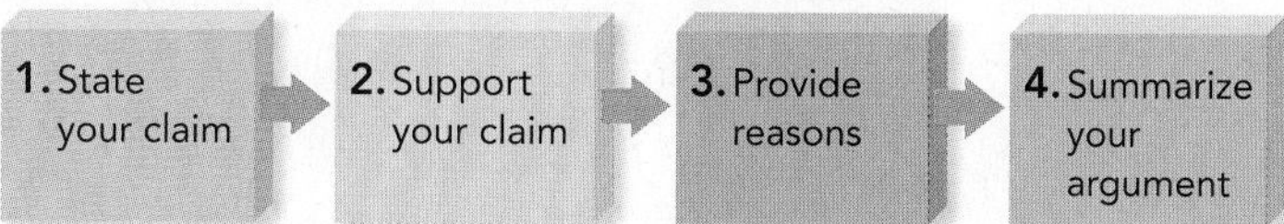

Support Your Claim

The fact that a claim is stated does not mean that it is true. In order to be convincing, you must support your claim with strong and valid evidence. Regardless of whether that evidence takes the form of facts, opinions, definitions, descriptions, examples, illustrations, or statistics, groups should continuously evaluate the quality of any evidence.

Provide Reasons

If it isn't clear to others why a particular piece of evidence proves your claim, demonstrate the link between your evidence and your claim. In the Toulmin Model, this link is the warrant and the backing—statements that explain why the evidence is sufficient to prove the claim.

Suppose a friend tells you that drinking a glass of red wine daily combats heart disease and reduces your chances of a life-threatening heart attack. Your friend cites the conclusions of several scientific studies as evidence. You may wonder: How can this be? Isn't alcohol dangerous—doesn't it do more harm than good? When you question the claim, your friend provides the argument's warrant: The alcohol in a glass of red wine suppresses the accumulation of fatty plaques in the blood vessels, particularly the coronary arteries that supply the heart. Now the argument makes sense because you understand the reason for the claim.[21]

Summarize Your Argument

A good summary restates the original claim and summarizes the supporting evidence. Be brief. Don't repeat all your evidence and reasons. When the presentation of the claim and the evidence has been brief and clear, you can omit the summary. However, lengthy and complicated arguments often need a summary to ensure that all members understand your argument.

Refuting Arguments

Refutation is the process of proving that an argument is false or lacks sufficient support. Refutation can question, minimize, and deny the validity or strength of someone else's argument. Group members should be willing and able to refute claims that are unsupported or untrue. A group unwilling to evaluate arguments risks the perils of groupthink. Figure 11.4 shows six steps that can help you refute another member's argument.

Listen to the Argument

First, listen for comprehension. You must fully understand an argument before you can refute it effectively. Ask questions and take notes. Once you comprehend the

Figure 11.4 Procedure for Refuting Arguments

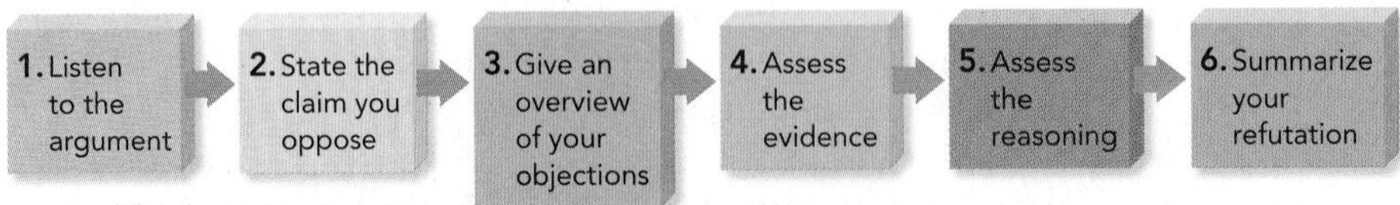

meaning of an argument, you can shift to critical listening. What type of claim is it? Is there evidence to support the claim? How well does the evidence support the claim? What is the implied or stated warrant? Is the claim qualified in any way? Analyzing the argument as you listen will help you formulate an appropriate response.

State the Opposing Claim

Group members may offer several claims during an argumentative discussion. Don't try to respond to all of them at once. When you are ready, state the claim you oppose. Clearly stating the claim gives you the opportunity to make sure that you understand the argument. You may think the claim was "Employees are stealing supplies from the company." Instead, the claim was "The company should identify ways to use supplies more efficiently." If you have misunderstood a claim, other group members can clarify their arguments for you.

Preview Your Objections

Provide a brief overview of your objections or concerns. Let the others know the general direction of your arguments, particularly when your refutation will be lengthy or complicated, such as "I don't believe we should raise funds for a carnival for three reasons: the high cost, the unpredictable weather, and the undesirable location." If they have a general idea of the reasons for your refutation, group members will be better prepared to listen to and understand your objections and concerns.

Assess the Evidence

When refuting a claim, you may be able to show that the evidence supporting the claim is faulty. You can do this by presenting contradictory evidence. For example, if a group member contends that the college's tuition is high, you may present evidence from a survey showing that the college's tuition is one of the lowest in the state. You can also question the quality of evidence. For example, an outdated statistic or a quotation by a discredited source can be reason enough to reject an arguer's evidence—and claim. Proving that the evidence is of poor quality does not mean that the claim is untrue but does highlight potential weaknesses.

Assess the Reasoning

Assess reasoning by identifying fallacies. A **fallacy** is an argument based on false or invalid reasoning. It is not always necessary to identify the fallacy by name, particularly if group members are not familiar with the different types of fallacies. It is much more important to explain why the reasoning in the argument is flawed. Table 11.1 lists and briefly describes some of the most common fallacies of argument.

- ***Ad hominem* attack.** In Latin, this phrase means "to the person." An *ad hominem* argument attacks a person's character rather than responding to the argument. Responding to a claim that children should attend school year-round with "What would you know? You don't have kids" is an attack on the person rather than on the real argument. Unfortunately, negative political campaigns have become little more than a series of *ad hominem* attacks that often prove false when fully investigated.
- **Appeal to authority.** Using the conclusions and opinions of experts can provide strong support for an argument. However, when the supposed expert

Table 11.1 Fallacies of Argument

Fallacy	Description
Ad Hominem Attack	Attacks the person rather than the argument made by that person.
Appeal to Authority	Relies on biased or unqualified expert opinion to support a claim.
Appeal to Popularity	Justifies an action because many others do the same thing or share the same opinion. "Everyone's doing it."
Appeal to Tradition	Resists changes to traditional behavior and opinions. "We have always done it this way."
Faulty Analogy	Compares two items that are not similar or comparable. "Comparing apples and oranges."
Faulty Cause	Claims that an effect is caused by something that has little or no relationship to the effect.
Hasty Generation	Uses isolated or too few examples to draw a conclusion.

has no relevant expertise on the issue, the fallacy of appeal to authority occurs. The argument that "according to a talk show host, most men cheat on their wives" commits this fallacy. Unless the talk show host has expert credentials on issues of fidelity and marriage or quotes recognized experts, the argument is vulnerable.

- **Appeal to popularity.** An argument of this nature claims that an action is acceptable or excusable because many people are doing it. When residents of New Orleans looted stores after Hurricane Katrina, some people defended their actions by saying that everyone else was doing it. Just because many people engage in an action does not make it right. Instead, it may mean that many people are wrong.
- **Appeal to tradition.** Claiming that people should continue a certain course of action because they have always done so in the past is an appeal to tradition, as illustrated in the argument, "The group meets on Monday afternoons because that is when we have always met." Just because a group has been meeting on Mondays for a long period of time does not mean Monday meetings are the best choice.
- **Faulty analogy.** Claiming that two things are similar when they differ on relevant characteristics is a faulty analogy. During Operation Desert Storm (the conflict before the war in Iraq), critics claimed that the United States was involving itself in another Vietnam. However, supporters refuted the argument by pointing out critical differences between these two engagements, particularly the fact that the U.S. military action in Operation Desert Storm had a specific objective and was over in a relatively short time.
- **Faulty cause.** Claiming that a particular event is the cause of another event before ruling out other possible causes is a faulty-cause fallacy. The claim that "increases in tuition caused enrollment to decline" may overlook other explanations, such as the possibility that a decline in enrollment could be a result of fewer eligible high school graduates or a perceived decline in a college's academic quality.

- **Hasty generalization.** An argument flawed by a hasty generalization uses too few examples or experiences to support its conclusion. This fallacy argues that if it is true for some, it must be true for all. "A Volvo is an unreliable car because I once owned one that was always breaking down" is a hasty generalization. The experience of a single car owner does not prove that all cars produced by that manufacturer are unreliable.

Summarize Your Refutation

The final step is to summarize your response. If your refutation has been lengthy or complex, it is helpful to restate the major points of your response. It is not necessary to review all your arguments in detail because doing so wastes valuable group discussion time. If your refutation has been short and to the point, it may not be necessary to summarize your argument.

Adapting to Argumentation Styles

Research suggests that men and women argue differently, as do group members from different cultures. Moreover, members' emotional intelligence also affects how they develop and refute arguments. These differences appear to be a function of how we learn to argue and what values we believe are important. Effective group members recognize and try to adapt to other members' ways of arguing.

Gender Differences

Researchers have found that women and men may argue differently in group decision-making interactions.[22] Men tend to be competitive arguers, whereas women are more likely to seek consensus within a group. Men tend to view issues as only two-sided—for or against, right or wrong. Women are more likely to search out many different perspectives on a subject as well as ask questions.

However, there were *no* differences in men's and women's use of facts, opinions, statistics, or other types of evidence. In addition, men and women were relatively equal in voicing objections to others' statements.

We caution you against stereotyping the way men and women argue. Don't assume that the women in your group are more submissive and the men are more assertive. Instead, we prefer a dialectic approach: Groups benefit when members value *both* competition *and* cooperation. When group members argue, they must balance "the tension between the need to agree and disagree, to challenge and reach convergence, to ask questions and make statements." Although these "tasks may be divided along gender lines . . . there is nothing inherently superior or inferior about either men's or women's communication. They may be different, but they are both necessary and equally important to the group's success in argument."[23]

Cultural Differences

Cultures often dictate who should and should not argue. In some cultures, a young person would not challenge or argue with an older adult. Among several Native American and African cultures, the elderly rightfully claim more wisdom and knowledge than younger members.

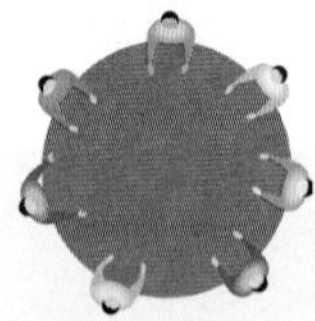

ethics in groups

Ethical Argumentation

Regardless of how persuasively you present an argument, you should also argue ethically. In *Advocacy and Opposition*, Karyn and Donald Rybacki describe four ethical responsibilities in argumentation: research responsibility, common good responsibility, reasoning responsibility, and social code responsibility.[1]

1. *The Research Responsibility.* Group members should be well informed and prepared to discuss the issues. To fulfill this responsibility, follow these guidelines:
   - Do not distort or suppress important information and evidence.
   - Never fabricate or make up information.
   - Reveal the sources of information so others can evaluate them.
2. *The Common Good Responsibility.* Ethical arguers look beyond their own needs and consider the circumstances of others. Group members should be fully committed to achieving the group's goal rather than merely winning an argument as indicated in the following two principles:
   - Consider the interests of those affected by the decision.
   - Promote the group's goal as more important than winning an argument.
3. *The Reasoning Responsibility.* Group members understand the structure of an argument and apply that knowledge to presenting arguments and recognizing fallacies. Ethical members fulfill their reasoning responsibility by applying the following guidelines:
   - Do not misrepresent the views of others.
   - Use sound reasoning supported by evidence.
   - Avoid making or accepting fallacious arguments.
4. *The Social Code Responsibility.* Group members promote an open and supportive climate for argumentation by following several guidelines:
   - Treat other group members as equals.
   - Give everyone, including those who disagree, the opportunity to respond to an argument.
   - Do not insult or attack the character of a group member.
   - Give the group an opportunity to review the evidence.

[1]Karyn Charles Rybacki and Donald Jay Rybacki, *Advocacy and Opposition: An Introduction to Argumentation*, 3rd ed. (Boston: Allyn & Bacon, 1966), pp. 10–13. Subsequent editions of Rybacki and Rybacki do not include these four responsibilities, but do discuss ethical standards for argumentation. See Karyn Charles Rybacki and Donald Jay Rybacki, *Advocacy and Opposition: An Introduction to Argumentation*, 5th ed. (Boston: Allyn & Bacon, 2004), pp. 14–21.

One of the most significant cultural differences in argumentation is the way in which people use evidence to support a claim:

> There are no universally accepted standards about what constitutes evidence. Among many devout Muslims and Christians, for instance, parables or stories—particularly from the Koran or Bible—are a powerful form of evidence. . . . The European American culture prefers physical evidence and eyewitness testimony, and members of that culture see "facts" as the supreme kind of evidence . . . [whereas] in certain portions of Chinese culture . . . physical evidence is discounted because no connection is seen between . . . the physical world and human actions. . . . In certain African cultures, the words of a witness would be discounted and even totally disregarded because the people believe that if you speak up about seeing something, you must have a particular agenda in mind; in other words, no one is regarded as objective.[24]

Given such different perspectives about the value of evidence, the data used to support a claim in one culture may seem irrational in another.

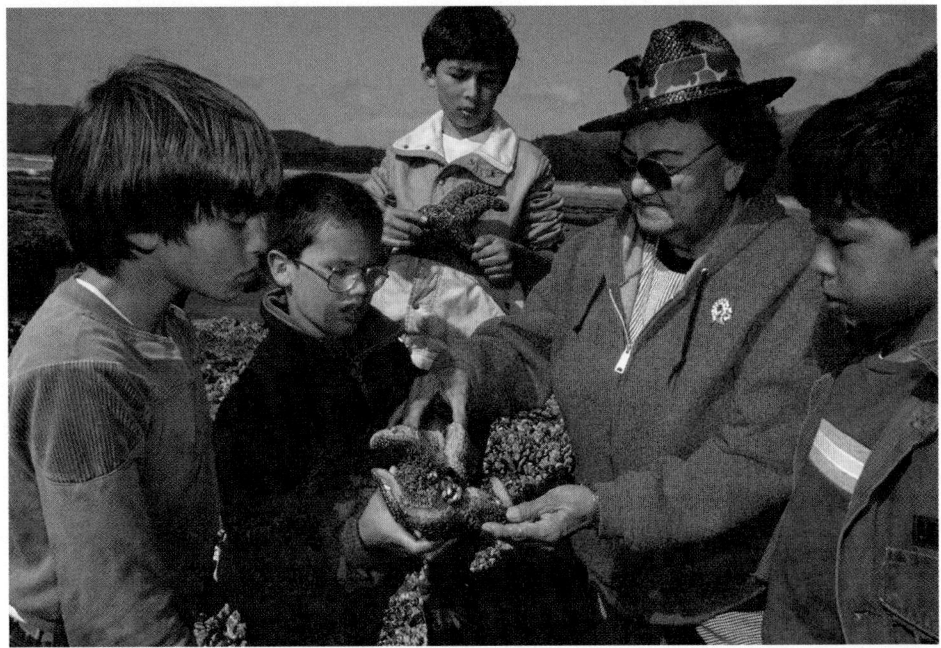

In Neah Bay, Washington, a Makah elder teaches children about a sea star they have found on the beach. In many American Indian and African cultures, young people rarely challenge or argue with an older adult. Do you believe that older people in a community can rightfully claim more wisdom and knowledge than younger members?

Argumentation and Emotional Intelligence

Daniel Goleman, author of *Emotional Intelligence,* defines **emotional intelligence** as the "capacity for recognizing our own feelings and those of others, for motivating ourselves, and for managing emotions well in ourselves and in our relationships."[25] In many ways, emotional intelligence represents a significant aspect of effective group argumentation. The role of emotions in argumentation can take two forms: (1) curbing inappropriate emotions and (2) expressing appropriate emotions. Effective group members understand the need for both and learn how to balance their use.[26]

When group members argue about the wisdom of adopting a controversial proposal, whether to hire an unconventional job applicant, or how to break bad news to colleagues, they may need emotional intelligence to help them achieve their goal. In some cases, members will have to curb their emotions. In other circumstances, they can exert influence by heating up a discussion and/or strong emotions.

If group members become highly emotional or aggressive during a group discussion, you may be able to cool things down by suppressing your own emotions by using the following five tactics that correspond to the characteristics of emotional intelligence:

- *Self-awareness:* Calm down, tune in to your own feelings, and be willing to share those feelings with group members.
- *Self-Regulation:* Handle your emotions responsibly. Delay personal gratification to achieve group goals.
- *Self-confidence:* Show that you are willing to work things out by talking over the issue rather than escalating it.
- *Self-control:* State your own point of view in neutral language rather than using an antagonistic tone or combative words.
- *Empathy:* Look for an equitable way to resolve the dispute by working with those who disagree to find a resolution that both sides can embrace.[27]

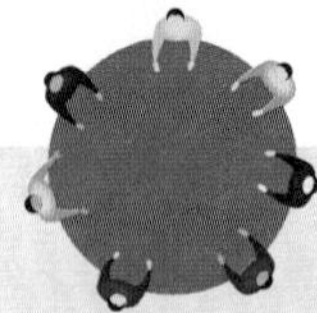

theory in groups
The Origins of Emotional Intelligence

Many people mistakenly believe that Daniel Goleman, author of *Emotional Intelligence,* created the concept of emotional intelligence. Goleman, who has a Ph.D. in psychology and previously reported behavioral and brain science news for the *New York Times,* does not claim this honor for himself:

> A comprehensive theory of emotional intelligence was proposed in 1990 by two psychologists, Peter Salovey and John Mayer. Another pioneering model of emotional intelligence was proposed in the 1980s by Reuven Bar-On, an Israeli psychologist. . . . Salovey and Mayer defined emotional intelligence in terms of being able to monitor and regulate one's own feelings and to use feeling to guide thought and action.[1]

In addition to those whom Goleman credits, we recommend the works of Dr. Antonio Damasio, a neurosurgeon who links emotions to human consciousness and—most important for the study of communication—decision-making ability.[2] Damasio focuses on what happens when people cannot make emotions work for them. He began his investigation by studying patients with damage to the emotional center of their brains. He noted that these patients make terrible decisions even though their IQ scores stay the same. Though they test as "smart," they "make disastrous choices in business and their personal lives, and can even obsess endlessly over a decision so simple as when to make an appointment." Their decision-making skills are poor because they have lost access to their emotions. Damasio concludes that feelings are *indispensable* for rational decision making.[3]

Consider whether you could answer any of these questions without taking emotions into account: "Should I marry?" "What career should I pursue? "Should I buy this house?" Now put these kinds of questions into a group context: "What are the human consequences of our decision or solution?" "Should I let the others in my group know how uncomfortable I am with their proposed actions?" "What should I say to a bereaved colleague?"

[1]Daniel Goleman, *Emotional Intelligence* (New York: Bantam Book, 1995), p. 42.

[2]Goleman, pp. 27–28. Also see Antonio R. Damasio, *Descartes' Error: Emotion, Reason, and the Human Brain* (New York: Quill, 2000).

[3]Goleman, p. 28. See Damasio, *Descartes' Error;* Antonio Damasio, *The Feeling of What Happens: Body and Emotion in the Making of Consciousness* (San Diego: Harvest/Harcourt, 1999).

If you care about your group and its goal, express your emotions openly to intensify what you say. If, for example, your group needs motivation, you may enlist your emotions to express "infectious" enthusiasm and passion. If, however, your group is considering a decision you see as unethical or potentially disastrous, an appropriate display of anger, fear, or sorrow may help to underscore your arguments. Emotions capture attention, and operate as warnings, alarms, and motivators. They generate powerful messages by conveying crucial information without using words.[28]

summary study guide

Critical Thinking and Argumentation

- An argument is more than an opinion. It is a claim supported by evidence and reasons for accepting it.
- Argumentation is the way in which group members use critical thinking to advocate proposals, examine competing ideas, and influence one another.
- Effective argumentation promotes understanding of others' views, promotes critical thinking about ideas, helps avoid groupthink, and improves group decision making.
- Argumentativeness is the willingness to argue controversial issues with others. Individuals vary in how comfortable they feel arguing.

Structuring Arguments

- The Toulmin Model of Argument represents the structure of an argument and a way to evaluate arguments. The components of the model include a claim, evidence, warrant, backing, reservation, and qualifier.
- The claim component of the Toulmin Model of Argument is the conclusion or position you advocate.
- The evidence component of the Toulmin Model of Argument consists of the facts, statistics, opinions, examples, and other materials you use to support a claim.
- The warrant component of the Toulmin Model of Argument refers to the justification for accepting the evidence as support for a particular claim. It answers the question, "How did you get there?"
- The backing component of the Toulmin Model of Argument provides support for the warrant. It explains why the warrant is reasonable or acceptable.
- The reservation component of the Toulmin Model of Argument recognizes and acknowledges exceptions to an argument which would make the claim untrue under certain circumstances.
- The qualifier component of the Toulmin Model of Argument states the degree to which the claim appears to be true using terms such as *likely, possibly, certainly, unlikely,* and/or *probably.*

Supporting Arguments

- A group member's argument falls apart when that member fails to do research to find valid evidence to support a claim and back the warrant.
- Evidence takes many forms including facts, opinions, definitions, descriptions, examples, illustrations, and statistics.
- Valid evidence must meet several criteria. It should come from an identified, credible, unbiased, and recent source, and the information should be consistent with other evidence.
- Determining the validity of statistical evidence requires answering three questions: (1) What is the source of the statistics? (2) Are the statistics accurate? and (3) How are the statistics reported?

Presenting Arguments

- When presenting an argument, state your claim, support your claim, provide reasons, and summarize your argument.
- Argument claims generally fit into four categories—claims of fact, claims of conjecture, claims of value, and claims of policy.

Refuting Arguments

- Refutation is the process of proving that an argument is false or lacks sufficient support. It is used to question, minimize, and deny someone else's argument.
- Six guidelines can help you refute an argument: (1) listen to the argument, (2) state the opposing claim, (3) preview your objections, (4) assess the evidence, (5) assess the reasoning, and (6) summarize your refutation.
- A fallacy is an argument based on false or invalid reasoning. Common fallacies include *ad hominem* attack, appeal to authority, appeal to popularity, appeal to tradition, faulty analogy, faulty cause, and hasty generalization.

Adapting to Argumentation Styles

- Women and men may argue differently. Men tend to be competitive arguers, whereas women prefer to seek consensus. However, there is no significant difference in men's and women's use of evidence.
- Cultures often dictate who should and should not argue. Culture also influences the way in which people use evidence to support a claim.
- Emotional intelligence refers to the capacity to recognize our own and others' feelings and to manage our emotions. The role of emotions in argumentation can take two forms: (1) curbing inappropriate emotions and (2) expressing appropriate emotions.
- Five tactics can help calm a highly emotional or aggressive discussion. Use self-awareness, self-regulation, self-confidence, self-control, and empathy.

key terms

ad hominem attack 281
appeal to authority 281
appeal to popularity 282
appeal to tradition 282
argument 268
argumentation 268
argumentativeness 271
backing 273
bias 277
claim 272
claim of conjecture 279
claim of fact 279
claim of policy 279
claim of value 279
cooperative argumentation 268
critical thinking 268
definition 275
description 276
documentation 277
emotional intelligence 285
evidence 272
example 276
fact 275
fallacy 281
faulty analogy 282
faulty cause 282
hasty generalization 283
illustration 276
opinion 275
oral citation 277
qualifier 273
refutation 280
research 274
reservation 273
statistic 276
Toulmin Model of Argument 272
valid 276
warrant 272

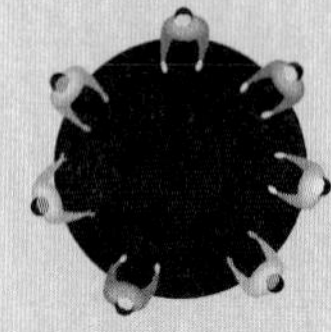

critical thinking about the case study

Slicing the Pie

1. To what extent is the Student Finance Board experiencing the benefits of argumentation such as enhanced understanding, better critical thinking, avoiding groupthink, and improving decision making?
2. What is Patrice's primary claim in her argument? What evidence and warrant support her position?
3. What types of evidence do various Student Finance Board members use to support their positions? Is the evidence valid? Why or why not?
4. Which fallacies of reasoning are evident in some of the board members' arguments?
5. How can the Student Finance Board improve the quality of their arguments in order to reach final budget decisions that are fair and justified?
6. How can board members better adapt to the different argumentation styles among its members?
7. Which dialectic tensions are most evident in this group and what could be done to achieve a *both/and* resolution of the tensions?

group work Got Water?

Directions: Read the passage from "Got Water?" When you finish reading, complete the tasks described after the passage.

> *Got Water?*
>
> In the August 12, 2005, edition of the *New York Times,* Tom Standage writes that Americans squander billions of dollars on bottled water. Americans drink, on average, twenty-four gallons of bottled water a year; among beverages, only soda outsells it. And it's not a bargain. In fact, a gallon of Evian or Poland Spring costs more than a gallon of gasoline—which explains how we're spending $10 billion a year on the stuff. But why do we do it? Not for the taste. In blind tastings between bottled water and tap water from major municipal systems, "most people cannot tell the difference." Tests show that bottled water is just as likely as tap water to contain contaminants, while offering no nutritional advantage. And whereas tap water is nearly free, plentiful, and has no negative impact on the environment, shipping and refrigerating bottled water consumes a lot of energy and creates serious disposal problems.

1. List three of the claims made in Standage's article:

   (a) ____________________

   (b) ____________________

   (c) ____________________

2. Identify three types of evidence Standage uses to support his claims:

   (a) ____________________

   (b) ____________________

   (c) ____________________

3. Identify two stated or implied warrants for Standage's claims:

   (a) ____________________

   (b) ____________________

4. Does Standage provide backing for the warrants, reservations, or qualifiers of his argument? If not, which ones were missing—and were they needed to make his case?

   ____

   ____

   ____

   ____

group assessment Argumentativeness Scale

Directions. This questionnaire contains statements about arguing over controversial issues. Indicate how often each statement is true for you personally by placing the appropriate number in the blank. Use the following ratings to respond to each statement:

1 = almost never true 2 = rarely true 3 = occasionally true 4 = often true 5 = almost always true

_____ 1. While in an argument, I worry that the person I am arguing with will form a negative impression of me.

_____ 2. Arguing over controversial issues improves my intelligence.

_____ 3. I enjoy avoiding arguments.

_____ 4. I am energetic and enthusiastic when I argue.

_____ 5. Once I finish an argument, I promise myself that I will not get into another.

_____ 6. Arguing with a person creates more problems for me than it solves.

_____ 7. I have a pleasant, good feeling when I win a point in an argument.

_____ 8. When I finish arguing with someone, I feel nervous and upset.

_____ 9. I enjoy a good argument over a controversial issue.

_____ 10. I get an unpleasant feeling when I realize I am about to get into an argument.

_____ 11. I enjoy defending my point of view on an issue.

_____ 12. I am happy when I keep an argument from happening.

_____ 13. I do not like to miss the opportunity to argue about a controversial issue.

_____ 14. I prefer being with people who rarely disagree with me.

_____ 15. I consider an argument an exciting intellectual exchange.

_____ 16. I find myself unable to think of effective points during an argument.

_____ 17. I feel refreshed after an argument on a controversial issue.

_____ 18. I have the ability to do well in an argument.

_____ 19. I try to avoid getting into arguments.

_____ 20. I feel excitement when I expect that a conversation I am in is leading to an argument.

Scoring Instructions

1. Add your scores on items 2, 4, 7, 9, 11, 13, 15, 17, 18, and 20.
2. Add 60 to the sum obtained in step 1.
3. Add your scores on items 1, 3, 5, 6, 8, 10, 12, 14, 16, and 19.
4. To compute your argumentativeness score, subtract the total obtained in step 3 from the total obtained in step 2.

Interpretation of Scores

73–100 = high in argumentativeness
56–72 = moderate in argumentativeness
20–55 = low in argumentativeness

Source: Dominic A. Infante and Andrew Rancer, "Argumentativeness Scale," from *The Journal of Personality Assessment*, 1982. Reprinted by permission of Lawrence Erlbaum Associates and the scale authors.

notes

1. David R. Seibold and Renee A. Meyers, "Group Argument: A Structuration Perspective and Research Program," *Small Group Research* 38 (2007), pp. 315, 320.
2. D. Christopher Kayes, "From Climbing Stairs to Riding Waves: Group Critical Thinking and Its Development," *Small Group Research* 36 (2006), p. 615.
3. Seibold and Meyers, p. 320.
4. Josina M. Makau and Debian L. Marty, *Cooperative Argumentation: A Model for Deliberative Community* (Prospect Heights, IL: Waveland, 2001), p. 87.
5. Josina M. Makau, *Reasoning and Communication: Thinking Critically about Arguments* (Belmont, CA: Wadsworth, 1990), p. 54.
6. Seibold and Meyers, p. 320.
7. See Sandra M. Ketrow and Beatrice G. Schultz, "Using Argumentative Functions to Improve Decision Quality in the Small Group," in *Argument and the Postmodern Challenge: Proceedings of the Eighth SCA/AFA Conference on Argumentation,* ed. Raymie E. McKerrow (Annandale, VA: Speech Communication Association, 1993), pp. 218–225.
8. Dominic A. Infante and Andrew S. Rancer, "A Conceptualization and Measure of Argumentativeness," *Journal of Personality Assessment* 46 (1982), pp. 72–80.
9. Dean C. Kazoleas and Bonnie Kay, "Are Argumentatives Really More Argumentative? The Behavior of Argumentatives in Group Deliberations over Controversial Issues" (paper presented at the meeting of the Speech Communication Association, New Orleans, LA, 1994).
10. Stephen Toulmin, *The Uses of Argument* (London: Cambridge University, 1958), p. 94.
11. Toulmin, pp. 97–113.
12. Toulmin, p. 99.
13. *The American Heritage Dictionary of the English Language* (Boston: Houghton Mifflin, 2000), p. 1940.
14. Based on an example in Stephen Toulmin, Richard Rieke, and Allan Janik, *An Introduction to Reasoning* (New York: Macmillan, 1979), p. 45.
15. *New York Times 1999 Almanac* (New York: Penguin, 1998), p. 395.
16. Warren Bennis and Burt Nanus, *Leaders: The Strategies for Taking Charge* (New York: HarperPerennial, 1985), p. 21.
17. *USA Today,* quoted in *The Week,* January 6, 2006, p. 16.
18. See Isa N. Engleberg and Dianna R. Wynn, *The Challenge of Communicating: Guiding Principles and Practices* (Boston: Pearson/Allyn & Bacon, 2008), pp. 340–341.
19. Carol Tavris, *The Mismeasure of Woman* (New York: Simon & Schuster, 1992), p. 94.
20. Dominic A. Infante and Andrew S. Rancer, *Arguing Constructively* (Prospect Heights, IL: Waveland, 1988), p. 57.
21. For articles about the cardiac benefits of red wine, see http://circ.ahajournals.org/cgi/content/full/111/2/e10 from the American Heart Association and http://www.ynhh.org/online/nutrition/advisor/red_wine.html from the Yale-New Haven Hospital. Retrieved May 5, 2008.
22. Renee A. Meyers, Dale Brashers, LaTonia Winston, and Lindsay Grob, "Sex Differences and Group Arguments: A Theoretical Framework and Empirical Investigation," *Communication Studies* 48 (1997), p. 33.
23. Meyers et al., pp. 35–36.
24. Myron W. Lustig and Jolene Koester, *Intercultural Competence: Interpersonal Communication across Cultures,* 5th ed. (Boston: Allyn & Bacon, 2006), p. 241.
25. Daniel Goleman, *Working with Emotional Intelligence* (New York: Bantam, 1998), p. 317.
26. Based on Goleman, p. 318. Also see Henrie Weisinger, *Emotional Intelligence at Work* (San Francisco: Jossey-Bass, 1998), pp. xix–xxii.
27. Goleman, p. 182.
28. Goleman, p. 165.

chapter 12

Planning and Conducting Meetings

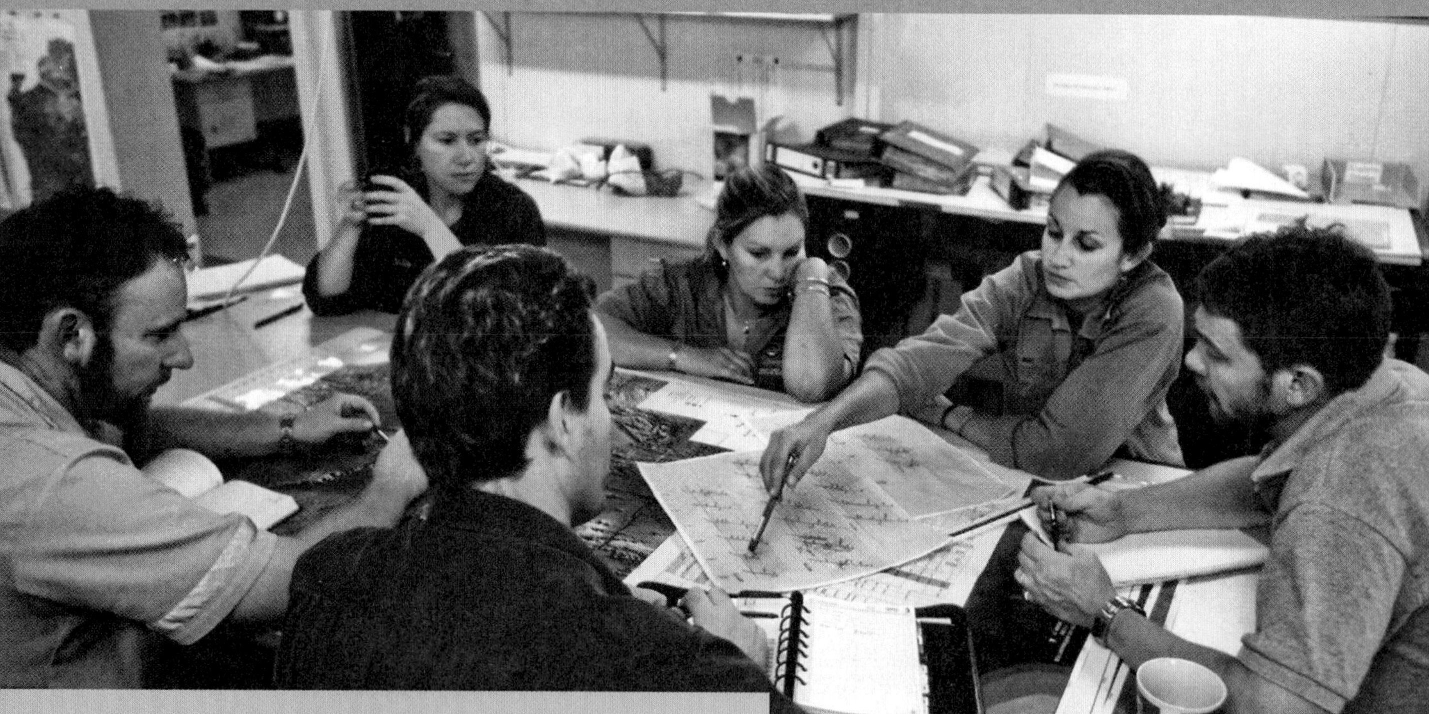

chapter outline

study questions

What are meetings and why do many people dislike attending them?

How should you prepare for a meeting?

How should a group adapt to member differences and minimize disruptive behavior in meetings?

What guidelines should an effective recorder follow when taking minutes in a meeting?

When and how should a group use parliamentary procedure?

What criteria can help you evaluate a meeting's efficiency and effectiveness?

Meetings, Meetings, Meetings

Humorist Dave Barry has nothing nice to say about meetings. He compares them to funerals—people sit around in uncomfortable clothes and would rather be somewhere else. At least, he notes, funerals have a purpose and a definite conclusion. Most meetings don't. Barry continues, "If you have ever seen the movie *The Night of the Living Dead* you have a rough idea of how modern meetings operate, with projects and proposals that everybody thought were killed rising from their graves to stagger back into meetings and eat the brains of the living."[1]

Tyler Cowen, an economist at George Mason University, has a very different opinion of meetings. He preaches "good news for the legions of meeting haters: Most meetings aren't as wasteful as they seem." When meetings are well planned and conducted, they build strong alliances and confer a sense of control. Members have a real voice in decisions that, in turn, boosts their motivation to implement group ideas and actions.[2] We hope that by the conclusion of this chapter you'll side with Tyler Cowen about the value and necessity of effective group meetings.

More than eleven million business meetings take place in the United States every day. The typical employee spends almost fifteen hours a week in meetings and may attend sixty formal or informal meetings a month.[3] Odds are that you've spent your share of time in meetings. Certainly you will attend them in the future. Unfortunately, many of these meetings will not be productive or rewarding group experiences. One study reports, "There is a direct correlation between time spent each week in meetings and an employee's desire to find another job."[4]

Many meetings fail to achieve their goal. Studies and our own observations suggest several explanations for why so many people dread meetings:

- The meeting was unnecessary.
- The meeting was too long and wasted time.
- The meeting's goal was unclear.
- The meeting failed to use or follow an agenda.
- The meeting used an agenda that had too many items on it.
- There was not enough prior notice or time to prepare.
- There were too many people at the meeting.
- The right people did not attend or were not invited.
- The meeting was held at the wrong time or place.
- The chairperson was ineffective.
- There was too much political pressure to conform or take sides.
- The meeting ended without accomplishing anything.

Meetings also fail because we take them for granted. Too often, we resign ourselves to attending unproductive meetings rather than trying to improve them. In one study, workers rated 69 percent of the meetings that they attended as "ineffective."[5]

If people get together in the same room at the same time, you have a meeting, right? Wrong. You merely have a gathering of people in one place. A **meeting** is a scheduled gathering of group members for a structured discussion guided by a designated chairperson.

Let's take a closer look at the three elements in this definition: schedule, structure, and chairperson (see Figure 12.1 on page 294). First, most meetings are scheduled in advance for a particular time and place; a coincidental gathering of group members does not constitute a meeting. Second, meetings can be formal and highly structured or informal and loosely structured. A meeting using parliamentary procedure is an example of a formally structured meeting, whereas an emergency staff meeting relies

Figure 12.1 Three Essential Elements of a Meeting

on an event to structure the discussion. Effective groups balance the amount of *both* structure *and* spontaneity appropriate for the meeting's goal and the group's norms. The third element of a meeting is a designated **chair** or **chairperson**, an appointed or elected member who conducts the meeting.

Planning and Chairing Meetings

The success or failure of a meeting largely depends on good planning. One study found that careful planning can prevent at least twenty minutes of wasted time for each hour of a group's meeting.[6] Planning a meeting is not something you do a few minutes before the meeting takes place. In some cases, a critical meeting requires weeks of preparation and planning to make sure that it achieves its goal.

Meeting Planning Questions

Why Are We Meeting?

Who Should Attend the Meeting?

When Should We Meet?

Where Should We Meet?

What Materials Do We Need?

Questions about Meeting

Of all the reasons so many people criticize and dread meetings, "The meeting was unnecessary" topped the list. Before spending hours preparing for a meeting, make sure your group needs to meet. Use the answers to the following questions to guide the planning process.

Why Are We Meeting? The best way to avoid wasting time or frustrating members is to be sure you need a meeting:

- Is an immediate decision or response needed?
- Are group input and interaction critical?
- Are members prepared to discuss the topic?

In many situations, a memo, fax, email, voice-mail message, or one-to-one conversation may be sufficient. In other situations, a meeting is the most effective and efficient way to inform and interact with a group of people.

The most important step in planning a meeting is defining its goal as clearly as possible. A meeting's goal is not the same as its subject. The subject is the topic of the discussion. The goal identifies the desired outcome. For example, if an executive calls her assistant and says, "Call a staff meeting next Thursday at 2:00 p.m.," the assistant may ask, "What will the meeting be about?" "Employer-provided day care," the executive replies. Has the executive revealed the goal of the meeting? No. We only know that the subject of the meeting is employer-provided day care. If the executive had said, "We need to determine whether our employer-provided day-care system needs expansion," we would know the purpose or goal of the meeting.

case study

Monday Morning Blues

On the second Monday of every month, the full-time staff of the Foxglove Athletic Club attends a meeting from 1:30 to 3:00, a time when there are very few club members in the gym. Four part-time staff members share reception duties and assist members.

At 1:30, seven staff members assemble in the aerobics studio sitting on floor mats or bouncing on the large exercise balls. Darrell, the club director, rushes in at 1:40, looks around, and asks, "Where's Maggie and Guy?" Everyone shrugs; Maggie and Guy are late for everything. Then Darrell addresses Eli, "I think it's your turn to take minutes. Kim did it last month." Eli groans, resigns himself to this bothersome task, leaves to get paper and a pen, and returns a few minutes after the meeting has begun.

Darrell takes his usual seat on a short stool in front of the full-wall mirror. "Okay," he begins, "we have a lot to cover today, but I promise we'll be done by 3:00." Darrell lifts his clipboard on which he's written a list of topics on the back of an exercise workout form. The first two items are announcements about the new treadmills they've ordered and plans to redesign the layout of the small shop in which they sell athletic equipment, athletic wear, energy bars, and fortified beverages.

As Darrell talks, the two aerobics instructors begin a whispered conversation about their aerobics group. Meanwhile, Chris, the shop manager, interrupts Darrell and describes, in detail, how great the redesigned shop will be and how he's ordered some cool designs for athletic wear. Darrell tries to interrupt him, but Chris chatters on and on. It's now 2:00 and in walks Maggie. "Where's Guy?" asks Darrell. "He's busy doing something," answers Maggie. The rest of the group shakes their heads as though they're thinking, "Typical."

Since the meeting began, Rob's been sitting in his usual corner, stewing. Finally he can't stand it anymore. "Hey! I've had enough of this. We've been here for half an hour and accomplished nothing. This is a joke . . . ."

"Robert!" exclaims Darrell in his don't-make-me-mad voice. "I know *you* may not be interested in all this, but others are. Let's give it a rest and jump ahead to the fifth item on my list."

"It's time," announces Darrell, "to decide whether we should expand our aerobics classes to meet the growing demand for more." The preoccupied aerobics instructors look up in confusion, hoping they haven't missed anything important. This discussion drags on . . . 2:30 . . . 2:45 . . . 3:00 . . . 3:15. Finally, Rob breaks in saying that it's almost 3:30 and the gym is beginning to fill up. Darrell looks out the glass door of the aerobics studio to see a line of people on the treadmills. "Well, we didn't get through everything but there's always next month's meeting. So let's get out there with lots of energy, excitement, and enthusiasm!"

When you finish reading this chapter, you should be able to answer the following questions:

1. How well was this meeting planned and structured?
2. Would the meeting have been more productive if everyone had seen Darrell's agenda in advance? Why or why not?
3. To what extent did group members behave productively and responsibly during the meeting?
4. What advice would you give Darrell about running meetings in the future?

Who Should Attend the Meeting? The membership of many groups is predetermined. However, if a task does not require input from everyone or needs the expertise of only certain people, you should select participants who can make a significant contribution and who have a stake in the outcome of the meeting. In addition, choose participants with special expertise, different opinions, and the power to implement decisions. Although you may be tempted to invite only those people with similar points of view, participants who disagree or who represent minority opinions provide a more balanced and realistic discussion of issues.

Make sure that your group is a manageable size. Try to limit meetings to fewer than twelve participants; a group of five to seven members is ideal for problem-solving sessions. In many situations, the size of the group is predetermined. For instance, an organization's bylaws may require that a majority of the board members attend in order to conduct a vote.

When Should We Meet? The next step is deciding what day and time are best for the meeting. Should the meeting be in the morning, in the afternoon, after work hours, or during lunch? Avoid scheduling group meetings near holidays or at the beginning or end of the week when members are not quite ready to work. Determine what time the meeting should begin *and* end.

In general, the optimal meeting length is one hour. If your meeting must run longer, schedule breaks that give members a chance to stretch, get food or drinks, or visit the restroom. When they return, they should be relaxed and ready to work when the meeting reconvenes.[7] For a time-consuming and difficult goal, you may decide to schedule several meetings.

Contact group members to find out when they are available, and schedule the meeting at a time when the most essential and productive participants are free. If only a few can attend, the meeting will not be very productive and will waste the time of those who do show up.

Where Should We Meet? Choose an appropriate location and room size for group meetings. The room should be large enough, clean, well lit, not too hot or cold, and furnished with comfortable chairs. In addition, look for a quiet meeting room where members cannot hear ringing phones and hall conversations. Although you may have little control over such features, do your best to provide a comfortable setting. Working in an attractive meeting room can make a group feel more important and valued.

What Materials Do We Need? The most important item to prepare and distribute to a group prior to a meeting is an agenda, outlining what topics will be discussed and in what order. The chairperson should also distribute essential reading materials to every member and make sure that needed supplies and equipment, such as markers, paper, flip charts, projectors, or computers, are available to the participants.

Preparing the Agenda

An **agenda** is an outline of the items for discussion at a meeting. A well-prepared agenda is an organizational tool—a road map that helps group members focus on a progression of tasks. It helps participants prepare for a meeting by telling them what to expect and even how to prepare. An agenda also provides a sense of continuity for a group—it tracks members' assignments and provides status checks for work in progress. After a meeting, you can use the agenda to assess the meeting's success by looking at how the group addressed each item.

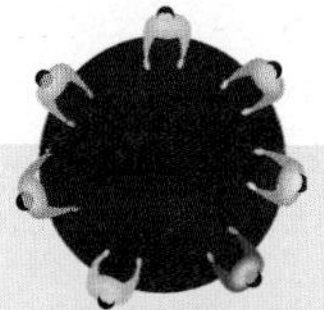

groups in balance . . .
Choose Good Meeting Places

The location and quality of a meeting's setting can mean the difference between comfortable, attentive members who participate fully in a discussion and distracted members who must contend with disruptions or an uncomfortable room. For instance, business meetings typically occur in four types of locations, each with its own advantages and disadvantages.[1]

Business consultants Robert Heller and Tim Hindle point out that "the choice of location is vitally important to the success of a meeting. It is not only a question of comfort; participants must feel that the place is appropriate for the occasion."[2]

Types of Location	Advantages	Disadvantages
Leader's Office	Convenient; access to materials and resources; enhances the meeting's importance	Members may feel like "guests" rather than equals; subject to distractions
Member's Office	Convenient; access to materials and resources; boosts the member's status	Subject to distractions; may be a smaller office with cramped seating
On-site Meeting Room	Avoids distractions of a working office; more spacious and comfortable than an office	Subject to interruptions; distant from materials and resources; may be time limits on use
Off-site Meeting Room	Eliminates most distractions; provides neutral territory; more attractive and comfortable	Costly in terms of room rental and travel time; distant from materials and resources

[1]Robert Heller and Tim Hindle, *Essential Manager's Manual* (New York: DK, 1998), p. 445.

[2]Heller and Hindle, p. 444.

When you are very busy or when a meeting is routine and predictable, preparing an agenda may seem like a waste of time. Just the opposite is true. Failure to plan and prepare an agenda denies a chairperson and a group one of the most powerful tools in meeting management.

Elements of an Agenda. Although the chairperson is responsible for preparing and distributing an agenda in advance of the meeting, member input can ensure that the agenda covers the topics that are important to the entire group. Table 12.1 on page 298 summarizes the elements of a traditional business meeting agenda.

Many meetings do not follow the traditional sequence of business agenda items. The norms of a group and the goals of a meeting should determine the agenda's format. For example, if you schedule a meeting to address or solve a specific issue or problem, the agenda items may be in the form of questions (see Figure 12.2 on page 299) rather than the key word format of a more formal agenda.

Agenda questions should follow the problem-solving method the group decides to use. In addition to identifying the discussion topics, agenda items should include any information that will help group members prepare for the meeting. The following guidelines can improve meeting productivity:

- Note the amount of time it should take to complete a discussion item or action. This will let the group know the relative importance of the item and help to manage the time available for discussion.

Table 12.1 Elements of a Business Agenda

Purpose of the Meeting	A clear statement of the meeting's objective and topic for discussion helps members prepare.
Names of Group Members	A list of all participants lets members know who will be attending.
Date, Time, and Place	The agenda clearly indicates the date, time, duration, and precise location of the meeting.
Call to Order	This is the point at which the chairperson officially begins the meeting.
Approval of the Agenda	This gives members an opportunity to correct or modify the agenda.
Approval of the Minutes	The minutes of the previous meeting are reviewed, revised if necessary, and approved by the group as an accurate representation of the last meeting's discussion.
Reports	Officers, individuals, or subcommittees report on the progress of their activities.
Unfinished Business	The agenda lists topics that require ongoing discussion or issues that the group was unable to resolve during the last meeting.
New Business	New discussion items are outlined and discussed in this section.
Announcements	Any items of information that the group needs to know but that do not require any discussion are announced.
Adjournment	The chairperson officially dismisses the participants and ends the meeting.

- Identify how the group will deal with each item. Will the group share information, discuss an issue, and/or make a decision? Consider putting the phrases For Information, For Discussion, and For Decision next to appropriate agenda items.
- Include the name of members responsible for reporting information on a particular item or facilitating a portion of the discussion. Such assignments remind members to prepare for a specific topic or action item.

Determine the Order of Items. After selecting the agenda items, carefully consider the order for discussing each topic. When a group must discuss several different topics during a single meeting, put them in an order that will maximize productivity and group satisfaction:

- Begin the meeting with simple business items and easy-to-discuss issues.
- Reserve important and difficult items for the middle portion of the meeting.
- Use the last third of the meeting for easy discussion items that do not require difficult decisions.

This sequence provides the group with a sense of accomplishment before it launches into more complex, controversial issues. If a difficult but important decision takes more time than anticipated, the group may be able to deal with the remaining, less important items at the next meeting or via email. For example, when

Figure 12.2 Sample Discussion Meeting Agenda

Recycling Task Force
November 20, 2009, 1:00 P.M. – 3:00 P.M.
Conference Room 352

Purpose: To recommend ways to increase the effectiveness of and participation in the company's recycling program.

I. What is the goal of this meeting? What have we been asked to do?

II. How effective is the company's current recycling effort?

III. Why has the program lacked effectiveness and full participation?

IV. What are the requirements or standards for an ideal program?
  A. Level of Participation
  B. Reasonable Cost
  C. Physical Requirements
  D. Legal Requirements

V. What are the possible ways in which we could improve the recycling program?

VI. What specific methods do we recommend for increasing the recycling program's effectiveness and level of participation?

VII. How should the recommendations be implemented? Who or what groups should be charged with implementation?

preparing an agenda for the monthly School Library Resources Committee meeting, Ron anticipates a lengthy and controversial discussion about purchasing new sex education books. He decides to begin the meeting by reviewing the budget and reporting on the effort to update media technology, then devote a significant amount of meeting time to discussing the sex education books. The last item on the agenda is a discussion of plans to purchase foreign-language books, which the group can address at another meeting if time runs out.

Chairing the Meeting

If you are the chairperson of a meeting, you have tremendous influence over, and responsibility for, the success of the meeting. In addition to conducting the meeting, you also may create the agenda, schedule the meeting, distribute the minutes, and follow up or implement decisions after the meeting is over. Effective chairpersons facilitate productive discussions by making sure that they have fulfilled their responsibilities prior to, during, and after the meeting (see Table 12.2 on page 300).

Table 12.2 Chairperson's Tasks

Pre-Meeting	During Meeting	Post-Meeting
• Notify members • Distribute materials • Remind members • Prepare for discussion	• Begin on time • Delegate minutes • Follow the agenda • Facilitate discussion • Provide closure	• Evaluate the meeting • Distribute minutes • Monitor assigned tasks

Prior to a meeting, the chairperson should notify every group member, preferably in writing. The announcement should include a clear statement of the meeting's goal, a list of pre-meeting responsibilities (such as reading a report in advance or preparing recommendations), and the time, location, and duration of the meeting. In addition, send group members all materials needed for the discussion in advance including a preliminary agenda. Check with all members to confirm they plan to attend and, if necessary, send a brief reminder before the meeting.

During meetings, effective chairpersons "balance strength with sensitivity; they balance knowing where they want the meeting to go with allowing the group to sometimes take it way off course; they balance having something to say with the restraint to say nothing; they assume the role of traffic cop in discussions without coming across with stifling authority."[8]

The agenda will be your guide for conducting the discussion in an orderly manner. Begin on time, distribute an up-to-date agenda, and determine who will record the minutes. Take attendance and make sure the recorder includes the results in the minutes. Ask the group to review the agenda and make any needed revisions. Then take up each of the agenda items in order. Finally, refrain from dominating the meeting. Your first priority is facilitating the group's discussion.

At the end of a meeting, the chairperson should briefly summarize meeting accomplishments, identify items that still need attention and action, and delegate assignments to specific members. If the group plans to schedule another meeting, ask for agenda suggestions and, if possible, set the date, time, and place of the next meeting.

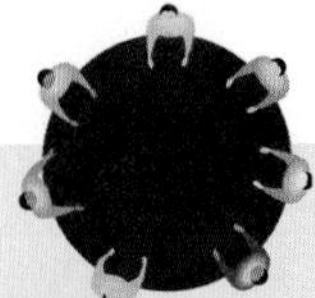

groups in balance . . .
Pace the Meeting

There is nothing worse than sitting through a meeting that moves too slowly, strays from the agenda, or lasts too long. A good chairperson allows enough time for everyone to participate but still ends the meeting on time. The following strategies can help keep your meetings moving at a comfortable pace:[1]

- Start the meeting on time and stick to the agenda.
- Don't waste time reviewing the earlier discussion for latecomers.
- Place a time limit on each agenda item.
- Stay focused on the meeting's goal.
- End the meeting on time or schedule another meeting to discuss unfinished business.

Approximately 75 percent of meeting participants admit they do other work during a meeting. Almost all of us have probably daydreamed during a boring meeting.[2] However, in a well-planned and skillfully chaired meeting, group members are so involved, they focus their attention and energy on the discussion.

[1]Robert Heller and Tim Hindle, *Essential Manager's Manual* (New York: DK, 1998), pp. 470–71.

[2]Jeff Davidson, *The Complete Idiot's Guide to Getting Things Done* (New York: Alpha Books, 2005), p. 232.

The 3M Meeting Management Team describes the critical role of the chairperson as "a delicate balancing act" in which chairpersons must

> . . . influence the group's thinking—not dictate it. They must encourage participation but discourage domination of the discussion by any single member. They must welcome ideas but also question them, challenge them, and insist on evidence to back them up. They must control the meeting but take care not to overcontrol it.[9]

Adapting to Member Behavior

A well-planned meeting, clear agenda, and skilled chairperson are prerequisites for a productive meeting. However, none of these elements prepares a group for the interesting mix of member behaviors. In previous chapters, we address how member needs, personalities, and communication styles affect group interaction. Here, we examine specific behaviors that can distract members, disrupt a meeting, or lead to misunderstandings.

Dealing with Disruptive Behavior

A carefully planned meeting can fail if members' behavior disrupts the group process. Group members should address such behavior rather than assuming that the chairperson can or will resolve the problem. In *How to Make Meetings Work,* Michael Doyle and David Straus write that "dealing with these problem people is like walking a tightrope. You must maintain a delicate balance between protecting the group from the dominance of individual members while protecting individuals from being attacked by the group."[10] Here, we examine a few common types of disruptive behavior.

Nonparticipants. You don't need full participation from all members all the time; the goal is a balanced group discussion over the course of a meeting. However, you should be concerned about the **nonparticipant,** who never or rarely contributes. Take some time to analyze why such members may be reluctant or unable to participate. Are they anxious, unprepared, or uninterested?

Do not force apprehensive or introverted members to contribute before they are ready to do so. At the same time, though, provide opportunities for reluctant members to become involved in the discussion. When nonparticipants do contribute, respond positively to their input to demonstrate that you see the value in their ideas.

Loudmouths. A member who talks more than others is not necessarily a problem. However, when a person talks so much that no one else gets a chance to speak, the group has a **loudmouth** problem and must respond appropriately. At first, allow loudmouths to state their ideas, and acknowledge that you understand their positions. It may be necessary to interrupt them to do so. Then shift your focus to other members or other issues by asking for alternative viewpoints. If a loudmouth continues to dominate, remind this person of the importance of getting input from everyone. The next time the group meets, you may want to assign the loudmouth the task of taking minutes as a way of shifting focus from talking to listening and writing.

Interrupters. Sometimes group members are so preoccupied with their own thoughts and goals that they interrupt others when they have something to say. Although most **interrupters** are not trying to be rude, their impatience and excitement

cause them to speak out while other members are still talking. When a group member continually interrupts others, it is time to interrupt the interrupter. Invite the previous speaker to finish making her or his point. A more aggressive option is to prohibit interruptions—to intervene and say, "Let Mary finish her point first, and then we'll hear other viewpoints."

Whisperers. A **whisperer** carries on confidential conversations with another group member during a meeting. The interference caused by whispering or snickering makes it hard for other members to listen and concentrate. Directing eye contact toward such sideline conversations can make the offenders more aware of their disruptive behavior. If the behavior persists, ask the talkers to share their ideas with the group. This usually stops the behavior or may uncover issues that deserve discussion.

Latecomers and Early Leavers. **Latecomers** and **early leavers** disrupt meetings and annoy group members who have managed their time well enough to arrive on schedule and stay through the entire meeting. If you are the chairperson, start the meeting at the scheduled time. Do not waste meeting time by summarizing meeting business for the benefit of latecomers. Let them sit without participating until they have observed enough to contribute to the discussion. Rather than publicly reprimanding or embarrassing latecomers or early leavers, talk to them after the meeting about the importance of attending the entire meeting.

When you have to confront member disruptions, be sensitive and focus on the behavior rather than making personal attacks. Describe the behavior, suggest alternative behaviors, and indicate the consequences if the behavior continues. Don't overreact; your intervention can be more disruptive than the problem member's behavior. It is best to begin with the least confrontational approach and then work toward more direct methods as necessary.

Adapting to Differences

Very often, group members from different cultural, ethnic, and age groups do not share similar expectations about group roles and individual behavior in meetings. In some cultures, a young group member would never interrupt an older member; a new group member would not challenge a veteran member. In such cases, it is easy to interpret lack of participation as inattention or lack of interest, when, in fact, the group member is demonstrating a high degree of respect for the group and its members.

At one college, the president appointed an advisory council to coordinate activities designed to improve the racial climate on campus. A member of the group reported the following observation:

> One council member was a former diplomat from a West African country. He rarely spoke, but when he did, he always began with a very formal "Madam Chairman." After that, he would deliver a three- to five-minute speech in which he would summarize the discussion and offer his opinion and recommendations. When he was finished, he would thank everyone for listening. At first, we didn't know how to respond. It was so formal, so complex. Eventually we learned to expect at least one "speech" from this member. We learned to listen and respond to a very different style of participation. This member defined his role very formally and acted accordingly. Patience on the part of other participants helped the group accept and adapt to his style of participation.

Group members may represent different ages, genders, educational and work backgrounds, religions, political viewpoints, and cultures. All these elements can

virtual groups
Meeting in Cyberspace

Deborah Duarte and Nancy Snyder point out that "The right technical tools enhance our ability to share concepts, merge ideas, and use synergy to accomplish our group goals." At the same time, "Technology cannot make up for poor planning or ill-conceived meetings. In fact, it can make the situation worse."[1] Fortunately, many of the same principles that apply to planning a productive face-to-face meeting apply equally well to planning virtual meetings. Test your group's readiness to meet in cyberspace by checking off items on the following "to do" list:

_____ 1. Does everyone know the meeting's goal?

_____ 2. Did all members get the agenda in advance, including notes on which discussion items will use any specialized technology?

_____ 3. Are only the members who need to participate invited?

_____ 4. Is the group small enough to allow everyone a chance to contribute actively?

_____ 5. Is the group meeting at the most convenient time for the most members?

_____ 6. Is the group using the most appropriate technology for achieving the meeting's goal?

_____ 7. Does the group have access to the technology or facilities that support audioconferences, videoconferences, and textconferences?

_____ 8. Do all the members have compatible technology?

_____ 9. Are all members trained adequately on the chosen technologies?

_____ 10. Does someone always test the technology prior to the meeting?

[1]Deborah L. Duarte and Nancy Tennant Snyder, *Mastering Virtual Teams: Strategies, Tools, and Techniques That Succeed*, 3rd ed. (San Francisco: Jossey-Bass, 2006), p. 165.

affect how well a meeting accomplishes its goals. Adapting to the diversity of group members involves understanding and accommodating differences while pursuing shared goals.

Preparing the Minutes

The **minutes** of a meeting are the written record of a group's discussion and actions during a meeting. The minutes record a group's discussions and decisions for those who attend a meeting and provide a way to communicate with those who did not attend. By looking through a group's minutes over a period of time, you can learn about the group's activities, measure how productive the group has been, learn about individual members' contributions to the group, and know whether group meetings tend to be formal or informal. Most important, minutes help prevent disagreement over what was decided in a previous meeting and what tasks individual members agreed to do.

Selecting a Recorder

The chairperson is ultimately responsible for the accuracy and distribution of the minutes. However, during the meeting, the chairperson must be free to conduct the meeting. It makes more sense to assign the task of taking minutes to another group

CLOSE TO HOME JOHN McPHERSON

As soon as Mrs. Felster began to read the minutes of the last meeting, the board members knew she was not going to work out as the new secretary.

member. The group may designate a **recorder** or secretary to take minutes at every meeting, or members can take turns. Remember that regardless of who takes the minutes, the chairperson is responsible for checking, editing, and distributing copies to all group members.

Determining What Information to Include

For the most part, the minutes should follow the format of the agenda and include the following:

- name of the group
- date and place of the meeting
- names of those attending
- name of the person who chaired the meeting
- names of absent members
- the exact time the meeting was called to order
- the exact time the meeting was adjourned
- name of the person preparing the minutes
- summary of the group's discussion and decisions, using agenda items as headings
- specific action items

An **action item** is a task assigned to individual members for completion after the meeting. An action item includes the person's name, the assignment, and the deadline. For example, an action item might look like this: "Action: Mark Smith will review and bring samples of good website designs to the next meeting." Underline or italicize action items in the minutes to make it easier to refer back to them when reviewing the group's progress.

Taking Minutes

Well-prepared minutes are brief and accurate. They are not a word-for-word record of everything that every member has said. To be useful, they must briefly summarize the discussion. These guidelines can help you take useful minutes:

- Instead of describing the discussion in detail, write clear statements that summarize the main ideas and actions.
- Make sure to word decisions, motions, action items, and deadlines exactly as the group makes them in order to avoid future disagreements and misunderstandings.
- If you are not sure about what to include in the minutes, ask the group for clarification.
- Obtain a copy of the agenda and any reports that were presented to attach to the final copy of the minutes. These documents become part of the group record along with the minutes.

Immediately after the meeting, prepare the minutes for distribution. The longer you delay, the more difficult it will be to remember the details of the meeting. After preparing the minutes, give them to the chairperson for review. When a group officially approves the minutes, they are final and become the official record of the meeting. Figure 12.3 shows a sample of informal minutes.

Figure 12.3 Sample of Informal Minutes

Domestic Violence Class Discussion Group Meeting
February 10, 2009, in Library Conference Room 215

Present: Gabriella Hernandez (chairperson), Eric Beck, Terri Harrison, Will Mabry, Tracey Tibbs

Absent: Lance Nickens

Meeting began at 2:00 P.M.

Group Topic: The group discussed whether emotional and verbal abuse should be included in the project. Since we don't have much time to do our presentation, we decided to limit the topic to physical abuse only.

Research Assignments: Since the assignment is due in two weeks, we decided to divide the issue into different topics and research them on our own.

Action: Eric will research why people stay in abusive relationships.
Action: Gabriella will research the effects on the children.
Action: Terri will find statistics and examples of the seriousness of the problem.
Action: Will is going to find out why and how the abuse happens.
Action: Tracey will find out what resources are available in the area for victims.

Members will report on their research at the next meeting.

Absent Members: Lance has not been to the last two class meetings. We don't know if he is still going to participate in the group. *Action: Gabriella will call Lance.*

Class Presentation: We need to think of creative ways to make a presentation to the class. The group decided to think about this and discuss it at the next meeting.

Next Meeting: Our next meeting will be at 2:30 on Tuesday, February 14th, in the same place. *Action: Terri will reserve the room.*

The meeting ended at 3:15 P.M.

(Meeting notes taken by Tracey Tibbs)

Using Parliamentary Procedure

Parliamentary procedure is a term that describes a set of formal rules used to determine the will of the majority through fair and orderly discussion and debate. For group members who are new to parliamentary procedure, the process can be confusing and intimidating. Not only are there hundreds of rules, but the language of parliamentary procedure also has a unique vocabulary, including statements such as "Mr. Chairman, I call the previous question" or "Madam President, I rise to a point of order."

Many organizations and associations specify in their constitution or bylaws (rules governing how an organization operates) that parliamentary procedure must be used to conduct meetings. *Robert's Rules of Order*—considered the "parliamentary bible" by many organizations—provides rules that ensure reasonable and civil debate as well as timely group decisions that are accepted by supporters and opponents alike. This

time-honored system ensures that group decisions express the will of the majority while also protecting the rights of minority members.[11]

If you want to learn more about parliamentary procedure, a comprehensive web chapter on when and how to use parliamentary rules is available online at www.pearsonhighered.com.

Before learning the rules of parliamentary procedure, you should understand its guiding principles. In this way, you can appreciate why this procedure continues as "the law of the land" in many meetings.

Robert's Rules of Order, Newly Revised claims that the rules of parliamentary procedure are "constructed upon a careful balance of the rights of persons or subgroups within an organization's . . . total membership."[12] These guiding principles form the basis for all parliamentary rules:

- *Majority Will.* The group accepts the will of the majority. In the case of critical or controversial issues, decisions may require a two-thirds vote rather than a simple majority.
- *Minority Rights.* The group protects the rights of all members by guaranteeing everyone the right to speak. At the same time, parliamentary rules assure that, in the end, the majority prevails.
- *Balanced Discussion.* The group guarantees the rights of all members to speak on different sides of an issue by balancing participation between frequent and infrequent contributors as well as between members who support and those who oppose a proposal.
- *Orderly Progress.* The group follows an approved agenda that promotes orderly business while also allowing flexibility to make decisions.

Many groups do not use formal parliamentary procedure to conduct business or achieve their goals. At the same time, there is great value in borrowing the basic principles of parliamentary procedure to guide the deliberations of a group and balance majority and minority interests. When everyone has an equal opportunity to speak, a sense of fairness is more likely to prevail.

Many organizations and associations specify that parliamentary procedure must be used to conduct meetings. Here, the newly elected mayor of a small city in New York State presides over the organizational meeting for the city council. How does parliamentary procedure help groups make decisions that express the will of the majority while also protecting the rights of minority members?

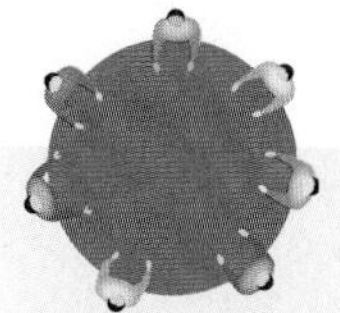

ethics in groups
Use Discretion When Taking Minutes

The person charged with taking minutes has an ethical obligation to exercise good judgment when deciding what to include in the minutes and what to omit. Everything included in the minutes must accurately reflect the discussion of major issues and group decisions. At the same time, a recorder must balance the need for accuracy with discretion.

There are times when a group does not want the details of its discussion recorded in the minutes. For instance, groups discussing sensitive legal or personnel issues often keep information confidential. If the agenda includes confidential items, the chairperson should remind members that some information is not to leave the group and the recorder will not include discussion details in the minutes.[1]

During a meeting, group members may make comments that should not appear in the minutes. For example, a group that vents its frustration with a boss will not want to read in the minutes that "The group agreed that Dan is unreasonable and insensitive." Groups often express complaints in a meeting. Including such comments in the minutes can stifle open communication and is not necessary for making the meeting minutes useful.

These guidelines can help you determine when to include information and when to leave it out:

- Report the facts and all sides of a discussion accurately.
- Never insert your own personal opinions.
- Be discreet. If the group determines that a portion of the discussion should be "off the record," you should honor that decision.
- When in doubt, ask the group if an issue should be included or how to word it for the minutes.
- Always keep in mind that the minutes are often the only record of the meeting and that individuals outside the group may read them.

[1]Robert Heller and Tim Hindle, *Essential Manager's Manual* (New York: DK, 1998), p. 429.

Evaluating the Meeting

To determine the effectiveness of meetings and identify areas for improvement, groups should evaluate their meetings. There are a number of ways to do so:

- Throughout the meeting, the chairperson may ask for comments and suggestions before moving on to the next item. This feedback allows the group to modify its behavior and improve its interaction when discussing the next item.
- At the end of the meeting, the chairperson can briefly summarize his or her perceptions of the meeting and ask for comments and suggestions from the group before adjourning.
- After the meeting, the chairperson should ask members for their comments and suggestions for improving the group's next meeting.
- Before adjourning a meeting, the chairperson may distribute a Post-Meeting Reaction form to all members.

A **Post-Meeting Reaction (PMR) form** is a questionnaire designed to assess the success of a meeting by collecting written reactions from participants. The chairperson should prepare the form in advance of the meeting, distribute it at the end of a meeting, and collect it before participants leave. A PMR form should ask questions about the discussion, the quantity and quality of group interaction, and the effectiveness of meeting procedures. Use group feedback to improve subsequent meetings. The sample PMR form in the assessment section at the end of this chapter contains typical questions for evaluating a meeting.

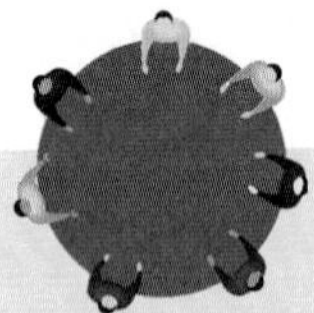

theory in groups

Chaos and Complexity Theories

Group meetings can be boring and/or exciting; simplistic and/or complex; orderly and/or chaotic. Watching a well-planned meeting underscores the role of group dialectics as members strive to find a *both/and* approach to accomplishing a variety of group goals.

Chaos and complexity theories give us valuable scientific tools for analyzing group dynamics, particularly as applied to meetings. **Chaos theory** claims "that although certain behaviors in natural systems are not predictable, there is a pattern to their randomness" that emerges over time.[1] In other words, you can never predict exactly what will happen in a meeting, but you can assume that most meetings will eventually share similar properties and processes.

Complexity theory goes even further than a search for patterns; it examines three characteristics of complex systems—order, complexity, and chaos. Mitchell Waldrop, author of *Complexity: The Emerging Science at the Edge of Order and Chaos*, explains complexity theory with an analogy that contrasts and compares order, complexity, and chaos to different states of water: ice, liquid, and steam. Order is like ice—frozen and solid. Chaos is like steam—in constant motion and insubstantial. Complexity, however, has the properties of liquid—fluid and relatively controllable. Waldrop also uses the example of national economies to illustrate order (economic stagnation), chaos (economic collapse), and a complex economy (strong *and* flexible).[2]

So what, you may ask, does this have to do with planning and conducting meetings? Throughout this textbook and particularly in this chapter, we emphasize the need for groups to balance dialectic tensions such as group goals ↔ individual goals, structure ↔ spontaneity, and conflict ↔ cohesion. Meetings require a judicious mix of such opposites. McClure's analysis of leadership gives us an example of this *both/and* approach: "You can either contain a group or perturb [agitate and arouse] it."[3] Consider what happens in meetings. Group members work best when they have a clear goal for the meeting, but they also need the freedom to change that goal if needed. Group agendas provide a clear structure for group work, but also constrict groups if they prohibit or restrict spontaneity. Genuine cohesiveness relies on conflict to settle differences and find common solutions. The seeming rigidity of parliamentary procedures may obscure rules designed to guarantee minority rights and opinions.

Effective meetings walk a fine line that balances order and chaos. Enlightened group members understand that too much order or too much chaos stifles group progress. A *both/and* approach allows a group to make first-rate decisions and progress toward its common goal.

[1]Bud A. McClure, *Putting a New Spin on Groups: The Science of Chaos* (Mahwah, NJ: Lawrence Erlbaum Associates, 1998), p. 3.

[2]Based on a lecture by M. Mitchell Waldrop, *Complexity: The Emerging Science at the Edge of Order and Chaos* (New York: W. W. Norton, 1989).

[3]McClure, p. 82.

summary study guide

Meetings, Meetings, Meetings

- The primary characteristics of a meeting are a schedule, a structure, and a designated chairperson.
- When meetings are well planned and well conducted, they build strong alliances, confer a sense of control, and give members a real voice in decisions that boosts their motivation to implement group ideas and actions.

Planning and Chairing Meetings

- For an effective meeting, decide who should attend, where and when to meet, and what materials members need in order to be prepared and productive.
- An agenda is an outline of the items to be discussed and the tasks to be accomplished at a meeting.
- The traditional business meeting agenda includes: purpose, names, date, time, place, call to order, approval of agenda and minutes, reports, unfinished business, new business, announcements, and adjournment.
- The chairperson is responsible for planning, preparing for, conducting, and following up a meeting.

Adapting to Member Behavior

- Controlling disruptive behavior should focus on achieving the group's goal and maintaining group morale.

- Common types of disruptive group behavior include member labels such as nonparticipants, loudmouths, interrupters, whisperers, latecomers, and early leavers.
- Meetings should be adapted to the diverse needs and expectations of members.
- Virtual meetings require agendas and minutes as well as special adaptation to group size, member availability, and choice of technology.

Preparing the Minutes

- The minutes of a meeting are the written record of the group's discussion, decisions, and actions.
- Well-prepared minutes are brief, accurate, objective, and appropriately discreet.

Using Parliamentary Procedure

- Groups using parliamentary procedure employ a set of formal rules to determine the will of the majority through fair and orderly discussion and debate.
- The basic principles of parliamentary procedure ensure majority will, minority rights, balanced discussion, and orderly progress.

Evaluating the Meeting

- Groups can learn from experience by evaluating meetings and using such feedback to improve future meetings.
- A Post-Meeting Reaction (PMR) form can help a group analyze the quality of a discussion, the quantity and quality of group interaction, and the effectiveness of meeting procedures.

key terms

action item 304
agenda 296
chair, chairperson 294
chaos theory 308
complexity theory 308
early leaver 302
interrupter 301
latecomer 302
loudmouth 301
meeting 293
minutes 303
nonparticipant 301
parliamentary procedure 305
Post-Meeting Reaction (PMR) form 307
recorder 304
whisperer 302

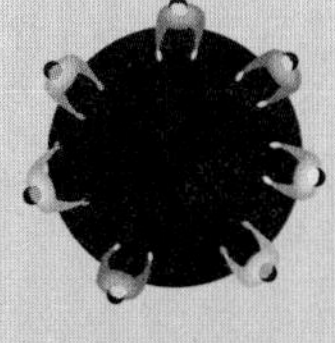

critical thinking about the case study

Monday Morning Blues

1. In what ways did Darrell fail to plan and conduct the staff meeting?
2. To what extent did Foxglove Athletic Club staff members behave responsibly and productively during the meeting?
3. What could the staff have done to improve the ways in which the Monday morning meetings were scheduled, structured, and conducted?
4. Did these staff meetings need someone to take minutes? Why or why not?
5. Of all the guidelines suggested for conducting an effective meeting, which three would significantly improve the staff meetings at the Foxglove Athletic Club? Explain your choices.
6. What labels or descriptions would you give the members who were the least cooperative and productive?
7. Which dialectic tensions were most evident in the way the staff meeting was conducted and its outcome?

group work Disrupting Disruptive Behavior

Directions: Read the following descriptions of meeting behaviors. In the space provided, record two strategies you would use to deal with each behavioral problem before, during, *or* after a meeting.

The Broken Record: Brings up the same point or idea over and over again. Regardless of what other members say, the broken record keeps "singing the same song."

1. ______________________________

2. ______________________________

The Grenade: Sits quietly and rarely participates but becomes more and more annoyed or angry as the meeting continues. Finally, the grenade cannot hold it in anymore and explodes into a tirade of harsh criticism.

1. ______________________________

2. ______________________________

The Know-It-All: Uses age, seniority, credentials, and experience to argue a point. Know-It-Alls declare, "I've been here for twenty years and I know this won't work," or "I'm the only one here with an accounting degree, so you'd better listen to me."

1. ______________________________

2. ______________________________

The Backseat Driver: Keeps telling everyone what they should do or should have done. "If we'd met earlier this week, we could have avoided this problem," or "I would have let everyone read the report rather than summarizing it."

1. ______________________________

2. ______________________________

The Attacker: Launches personal attacks on other group members or the chairperson. Purposely zeros in on and criticizes the ideas and opinions of others.

1. ______________________________

2. ______________________________

group assessment Post-Meeting Reaction (PMR) Form

Directions: After a selected meeting, complete the following PMR form by circling the number that best represents your answer to each question. After compiling the answers from all participants, including the chairperson, use the results as a basis for improving future meetings.

1. How clear was the goal of the meeting?

unclear	1	2	3	4	5	clear

2. How useful was the agenda?

useless	1	2	3	4	5	useful

3. Was the meeting room comfortable?

uncomfortable	1	2	3	4	5	comfortable

4. How prepared were group members for the meeting?

unprepared	1	2	3	4	5	well prepared

5. Did everyone have an equal opportunity to participate in the discussion?

limited opportunity	1	2	3	4	5	ample opportunity

6. Did members listen effectively and consider different points of view?

ineffective listening	1	2	3	4	5	effective listening

7. How would you describe the overall climate of the meeting?

hostile	1	2	3	4	5	friendly

8. Were assignments and deadlines made clear by the end of the meeting?

unclear	1	2	3	4	5	clear

9. Did the meeting begin and end on time? Did the group use its meeting time efficiently?

unproductive	1	2	3	4	5	productive

10. How would you rate this meeting overall?

unsuccessful	1	2	3	4	5	successful

Additional Comments:

notes

1. Quoted in The 3M Meeting Management Team with Jeannine Drew, *Mastering Meetings: Discovering the Hidden Potential of Effective Business Meetings* (New York: McGraw-Hill, 1995), p. 1. From Dave Barry, *Claw Your Way to the Top* (Emmaus, PA; Rodale Press, 1986), p. 25.
2. Tyler Cowen, "On My Mind: In Favor of Face Time," www.members.forbes.com/forbes/2007/1001/030.html (October 1, 2007). Retrieved April 24, 2008.
3. Jeff Davidson, *The Complete Idiot's Guide to Getting Things Done* (New York: Alpha Books, 2005), p. 232.
4. Matthew Gilbert, *Communication Miracles at Work: Effective Tools and Tips for Getting the Most from Your Work Relationships* (Berkeley, CA: Conari Press, 2002), p. 173.
5. *The Week*, April 2, 2005, p. 35. Study reported in CNNMoney .com.
6. Karen Anderson, *Making Meetings Work: How to Plan and Conduct Effective Meetings* (West Des Moines, IA: American Media, 1997), p. 17.
7. Robert Heller and Tim Hindle, *Essential Manager's Manual* (New York: DK, 1998), p. 471.
8. Bobbi Linkemer, *How to Run a Meeting That Works* (New York: American Management Association, 1987), p. 42.
9. 3M Meeting Management Team, with Jeannine Drew, *Mastering Meetings: Discovering the Hidden Potential of Effective Business Meetings* (New York: McGraw-Hill, 1995), p. 78.
10. "How to Be a Good Facilitator," from *How to Make Meetings Work* by Michael Doyle and David Straus, copyright © 1976 by Michael Doyle and David Straus. Used by permission of Berkley Publishing Group, a division of Penguin Group (USA) Inc.
11. Henry M. Robert III, William J. Evans, Daniel H. Honemann, and Thomas J. Balch, *Robert's Rules of Order: Newly Revised*, 10th ed. (New York: HarperCollins, 2000). Also see: O. Garfield Jones, *Parliamentary Procedure at a Glance, New Edition* (New York: Penguin, 1971); Alice Sturgis, *The Standard Code of Parliamentary Procedure*, 3rd ed. (New York: McGraw-Hill, 1988).
12. Robert et al., p. xliv.

chapter 13

Making Presentations in Groups

chapter outline

study questions

- *Under what circumstances do group members make presentations?*
- *What are the key elements and guiding principles of presentation speaking?*
- *How should a group prepare a successful team presentation?*
- *What strategies will help you answer audience questions?*
- *How can you make presentation aids more effective and influential?*

Presentations in Groups

In her book *Keeping the Team Going,* Deborah Harrington-Mackin responds to a frequently asked question by her management clients:

Question: I like the idea of having team members speak on panels and give presentations, but how can I trust that they will give the right answer when under pressure?

Answer: I'm always pleasantly surprised at how competent, composed, and prepared team members are when they sit on panels or give presentations. Remember, they're in the spotlight and want to look and act their best. If you still have doubts, do a practice session with them and see how they do.[1]

We agree with Harrington-Mackin's answer, but we also know there's a lot more involved in an effective presentation than trusting it will turn out fine. This chapter focuses on preparing you for success in three types of group presentations: (1) those you give to group members in the group's meetings, (2) those you give to nongroup audiences on behalf of your group, and (3) those you give with other group members in a panel or team presentation.

The following scenarios illustrate how these types of presentations become part of the group process:

- *Discussing a tuition proposal.* The student government association discusses the college's proposal to increase tuition by 10 percent. In order to ensure that everyone has an equal chance to speak at the meeting, student representatives are limited to three-minute statements.
- *Opposing the tuition proposal.* The student government association selects a spokesperson to make a presentation opposing the proposed tuition increase at the monthly meeting of the college's board of trustees.
- *Appealing for state funding.* The college president asks the student government's spokesperson to participate in a group presentation to the state legislature's appropriations committee in which a team of administrators, faculty, staff, and students has a total of twenty minutes to request increased state funding.

Whether it is within a group, on behalf of a group, or by an entire group, a group **presentation** occurs whenever a member speaks, relatively uninterrupted, to other group members or audience members. Every group member should know how to prepare and give a successful presentation adapted to the needs and characteristics of a group and its goals.

Presentation Guidelines

In this chapter, we offer guiding principles for making intelligent presentation decisions about what to say, giving good reasons for your decisions, and evaluating your decisions by assessing the success of your presentation. The guiding principles will help you make critical decisions about your presentation from the minute you find out you will have to speak to the minute you've said your last word.

We have selected a single word to represent the key element in each guiding principle (see Table 13.1 on page 316). Are the principles represented by these seven words all you need to know about effective speaking? No. Rather, the seven key elements and guiding principles provide a framework for strategic decision making about the complex process of presentation speaking.[2]

case study

Testing the Team

As the final project in their Media and Message Design course, student teams describe a promotional campaign for increasing enrollment in one of the college's academic departments. Each team must submit a written report describing its research, its overall plan, and designs for a poster, a brochure, and Web page for the chosen department. All group members must participate in a thirty-minute team presentation that summarizes their plan and explains their media designs to an audience of class members, three communication professors, and two members from the client department.

Brittany, Simon, Leah, Jose, and Paula enlist the theatre department as the client for their final project. After weeks of research, analysis, and intense discussions, the group drafts a promotional plan. Jose and Paula—two art majors—design a highly creative poster. The poster's design becomes a template for both the brochure and website. Leah writes the brochure's content. Simon and Brittany prepare a model for a website. Now the group faces the task of preparing a well-coordinated and persuasive team presentation.

The group decides that, in addition to the required presentations by every member, Paula should serve as a moderator to help the group move from topic to topic. Jose wants to present the poster by himself, now that Paula has another role. Paula objects, saying that, as moderator, she has to make a presentation too. While Paula and Jose argue, Leah claims the task of explaining the brochure. Simon and Brittany watch Jose and Paula as they vie for the honor of presenting the poster and decide that they want to present the website together.

As the date of the team presentation approaches, the group realizes they are spending most of their time trying to decide who will present each media design rather than focusing on the campaign and presentation as a whole. They declare a moratorium on arguments about media and shift to discussing the overall presentation.

Brittany suggests that they use quotations from famous plays as titles for each part of the presentation. Although everyone likes the idea, no one can think of any lines that work. Simon suggests that they go back to basics and look at the elements they need for an effective team presentation. "Just remember," says Brittany, "our purpose is to get an A!"

"No," says Jose. "Our purpose is to present our brilliant promotional plan and designs to the audience—and if we do it well, we'll earn a good grade too."

Leah asks the group to put aside concerns about grades and look at the presentation in a broader sense. "Aren't we supposed to demonstrate how our promotional plan and designs will help the theatre department attract more majors?" The group agrees.

The group decides to focus on how they should organize the team presentation and in what order they should make their individual presentations. Paula says that as much as she would like to present the poster (and as long as Jose gives her credit as the codesigner), she'll open the presentation by focusing on the research they did—interviews with theatre faculty and students, Web searches of theatre departments at other colleges, and reviews of theatre advertising in newspapers and magazines. Leah interjects that maybe Simon or Brittany should do that section because they did most of the research.

By now the team is becoming anxious. They're still arguing about who does what rather than what to do. "What if," says Jose, "we look at this as members of the theatre department. What would we want to know? Why would we trust the judgment of this team?" Paula adds, "You're right. But we also need to consider, how to 'perform' this presentation in a way that will impress the theatre department *and* our communication instructors." The group looks at Jose and Paula with gratitude. "I guess we're back to square one," says Simon. The group acknowledges and accepts the fact that they need to find an appropriate approach to planning their team presentation.

When you finish reading this chapter, you should be able to answer the following questions.

1 How could this group have gotten off to a better start in planning its team presentation?

2 Which elements of presentation speaking were and were not considered?

3 How can the group enhance its credibility in front of students and faculty members?

4 How should the group use the poster, brochure, and website in the presentation?

Table 13.1 Key Elements and Guiding Principles of Presentation Speaking

Key Element	Guiding Principle
Purpose	Determine your speaking goal.
Audience	Connect with your audience.
Credibility	Enhance your believability.
Logistics	Adapt to the setting and occasion.
Content	Select appropriate ideas and information.
Organization	Strategically organize your content.
Performance	Plan and practice your delivery.

Purpose

The first and most important step in developing a successful presentation is identifying your purpose—much like the need for groups to identify and agree on a common goal. Your purpose is not the same thing as your topic. Your **presentation purpose** is what you want your listeners to know, think, believe, or do as a result of your presentation. For example, a proposed tuition increase is the discussion topic for the student government association. A student speaker's purpose, however, may be to support or oppose the increase. Having a clear purpose does not necessarily mean that you will achieve it. But without a clear purpose, you may not accomplish anything.

Dr. Terry Paulson, psychologist and author of *They Shoot Managers, Don't They?* cautions speakers against making a presentation without a purpose:

> There are so many messages and memos hurled at today's business professionals [that] they are in information overload. It's like sipping through a fire hydrant. Don't unnecessarily add to the stream by including unnecessary fill, fact, and fluff. Volume and graphs will not have a lasting impression: having a focus will. Ask yourself early in the process: What do I want them to remember or do three months from now? If you can't succinctly answer that question, cancel your presentation.[3]

Audience

After determining the purpose of your presentation, turn your attention to analyzing and adapting to your listeners—the members of your group or an outside audience. This process begins by seeking answers to two questions: What are your listeners' characteristics? What are their opinions?

Characteristics. Two types of audience characteristics demand your attention: demographic traits and individual attributes.

- **Demographic traits** include age, gender, race, ethnicity, religion, and marital status. If you have been working in a group for a long time, you can easily catalog the demographic traits of group members. For a presentation to a new or a large audience, however, the task is more difficult. Take a good look at your listeners and note visible demographic traits, such as age, gender, and

race. At the same time, assume that there is more diversity than similarity among your audience members.

- **Individual attributes** take into account the distinctive features of particular group members, such as job title and status, special interests, personality traits, relationships with other members, and length of group membership.

Demographic traits and individual attributes can affect how your listeners react to you and your message. For example, students who support themselves on limited incomes may oppose a tuition increase more strongly than students who can afford the increase.

Opinions. There can be as many opinions in an audience as there are members. Some members will agree with you before you begin your presentation, whereas others will disagree with you no matter what you say. Some will have no opinion about an issue and will be quite willing to accept a reasonable point of view. Effective presenters try to predict who or how many listeners will agree, disagree, or be undecided (see Table 13.2).

If most of your listeners agree with you or are undecided, your presentation should focus on introducing new information or summarizing important ideas and arguments. When people share opinions and goals, you should update listeners who need new information and motivate them to work as a cohesive group. For example, if the members of the student government are universally opposed to a tuition increase, a speaker could focus on motivating the audience to take political action.

If audience members disagree with you, make sure you set realistic goals. Asking students to storm the president's office may get the administration's attention but may be too radical an action for most students to support. A second strategy is to work at getting audience members to listen to you. You can't do that by telling them that you're right and they're wrong. You can't change their minds if they won't listen. Instead, try to find **common ground**. Find a belief or value that you share with those who disagree with you. Emphasizing shared ideas, feelings, history, and hopes can help you overcome resistance. For example, if a student speaker tells the board of trustees that the student government wants to help it find a solution to the financial crisis, the board may be more willing to listen to student concerns about the proposed tuition increase. Finally, when you address a controversial issue, make sure you support your arguments with fair and reasonable evidence. If your arguments and evidence are weak, your opponents are likely to use those weaknesses against you. Chapter 11, Critical Thinking and Argumentation in Groups, discusses methods for developing and presenting valid arguments.

Credibility

In a presentation, your credibility depends on whether the audience believes you. No matter how much you know about the subject or how sincere you are about your

Table 13.2 Adapting to Audience Attitudes

If the Audience Agrees with You, Is Undecided, or Has No Opinion	If the Audience Disagrees with You
• Present new information • Summarize important ideas • Motivate the audience	• Make sure your goals are realistic • Find common ground • Use fair and reasonable evidence

purpose, your audience decides whether you seem competent and trustworthy. Your **credibility** as a speaker represents the extent to which an audience believes you and the things you say.[4] Of the many factors researchers have identified as major components of speaker credibility, three have an especially strong impact on the believability of a speaker: character, competence, and caring.

- **Competence** refers to your expertise and abilities.[5] If you are not a recognized expert on a subject, you must demonstrate that you are well prepared. There is nothing wrong with letting your audience know how much time and effort you have put into researching the topic or with sharing your surprise at discovering new information. In both cases, you are demonstrating that you worked hard to become a qualified and competent speaker.
- **Character** reflects your trustworthiness. Are you honest and sincere? Do you put the group's goal above your own? "Do you make a special effort to be fair in presenting evidence, acknowledging limitations of your data and opinions, and conceding those parts of opposing viewpoints that have validity?"[6] If your audience or the members of your group don't trust you, it won't matter what you say.
- **Caring** refers to whether you have listeners' interests at heart, demonstrate an understanding of others' ideas, and are empathic and responsive to audience responses.[7] Caring speakers let their actions speak louder than their words. Are you merely concerned about the homeless, or do you volunteer your time and energy at a local homeless shelter? Do you complain about higher tuition and cutbacks in student services, or do you write to your college's board of trustees expressing your concerns? By showing that you are active and committed to caring for others, you can better stimulate an audience to join you—and enhance your credibility.

Confident speakers are also more credible presenters. Chapter 3, Group Membership, explains that the majority of speakers experience some level of communication

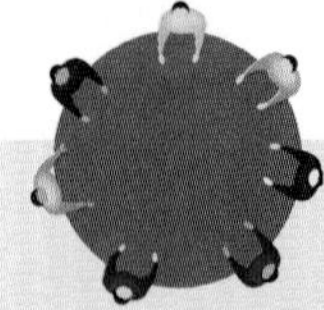

theory in groups
Aristotle's Ethos

The concept of *speaker credibility* is more than two thousand years old. Even in ancient times, speech coaches (yes, speech coaches existed back then, too) recognized that the qualities of a speaker were just as important as the speech. In *Rhetoric*, Aristotle wrote about **ethos**, a Greek word meaning *character:* "The character [ethos] of the speaker is a cause of persuasion when the speech is so uttered as to make him worthy of belief. . . . His character [ethos] is the most potent of all the means to persuasion."[1] Aristotle's concept of *ethos* has evolved into what we now call speaker credibility—the extent to which an audience believes you and the things you say.

Numerous studies back up the importance of speaker credibility. In most of these studies, two different audiences listen to an audiotape or see a live performance of the same presentation. One audience is told that the speaker is a national expert on the topic. The other audience is told that the speaker is a college student. After listening to the presentation, each audience is asked for their reactions. Can you guess the results? The "national expert's" presentation persuaded more audience members to change their minds than the one by the "student"—even though both audiences listened to the same exact presentation. The only difference was the *perceived* credibility of the speaker.

[1]Lane Cooper, *The Rhetoric of Aristotle* (New York: Appleton-Century-Crofts, 1932), pp. 8–9.

apprehension when faced with doing a presentation. Chapter 3 provides several effective strategies for reducing apprehension and building communication confidence.

Logistics

Adapting to the occasion and place where you will be speaking requires critical thinking about logistics. **Logistics** describes the strategic planning, arranging, and use of people, facilities, time, and materials relevant to your presentation. Adapting to the occasion and setting of a presentation requires more than taking a quick look at the seating arrangements for a meeting. Ask questions about *where* and *when* you will be speaking.

Where? Where will you be delivering your presentation—in a large conference room, an auditorium, a classroom, a meeting room? What are the seating arrangements? Are there any distracting sights or sounds? Will you need a microphone? Do you need special equipment to display your presentation aids? Once you have answered such questions, figure out how to adapt to the location. For example, requesting a microphone would be in order if a student government spokesperson learns that several hundred students plan to attend the board of trustees meeting.

When? Will you be speaking in the morning or in the afternoon? Are you scheduled to speak for five minutes, twenty minutes, or an hour? What comes before or after your presentation—other presentations, lunch, a question-and-answer session? The answers to questions about timing may require major adjustments to your presentation. If there is a time limit for the presentation, respect and adhere to that limit. Regardless of whether you have five minutes or one hour for your presentation, never add more than 5 percent to your allotted time. Even better, aim for 5 percent less. Most people lose patience with someone who speaks too long.

Content

As soon as you know you have to make a presentation, start collecting relevant ideas and information. Gathering materials can be as simple as spending a few hours thinking about the purpose of your presentation or as complicated and time-consuming as spending days doing research. In Chapter 11, Critical Thinking and Argumentation in Groups, we devote a significant section to finding and testing various types of evidence. These recommendations also apply to gathering and assessing content for a presentation.

Organization

Most speakers underestimate the importance of a well-organized presentation. Researchers confirm that audiences react positively to well-organized presentations and speakers, and negatively to poorly organized ones.[8]

Planning a presentation requires organizing your ideas and supporting material in a way that helps you achieve your purpose. Ask yourself whether there is a natural structure or framework for your message. What common ideas have appeared in most of your materials? What information seems most interesting, important, and relevant to the purpose of your presentation?

Your ability to organize a presentation also depends on whether you have selected appropriate ideas and information based on your analysis of purpose, audience, and logistics. Without well-thought-out content, you may have nothing substantive to organize.

Organizational Patterns. Even the most experienced speakers sometimes find it difficult to see how their content fits into an organizational pattern. If you're in a similar position, do not despair. Several commonly used organizational patterns can help you clarify your central idea and find an appropriate format for your presentation. Table 13.3 summarizes several common patterns.

Outlining Your Presentation. Presentation outlines begin with a few basic building blocks. Use the following outline as a model for organizing almost any kind of presentation.

I. Introduction
II. Central Idea or Purpose (Preview of Main Points)
III. Body of Presentation
  A. Main Point 1
    1. Supporting Material
    2. Supporting Material
  B. Main Point 2
    1. Supporting Material
    2. Supporting Material
  C. Main Point 3
    1. Supporting Material
    2. Supporting Material
IV. Conclusion

Naturally, every outline will differ, depending on the number of main points you have and the amount and type of supporting material you use. Once you outline your presentation, the major sections should be filled in with more specific ideas and supporting material.

Table 13.3 Organizational Patterns

Organizational Pattern	Example
Reason Giving	Three reasons why we should increase the dues are . . .
Time Arrangement	The college's hiring steps must be complied within the following order . . .
Space Arrangement	The following membership increases occured in the East, South, West, and Central regions . . .
Problem–Solution	This research method avoids the problems we encountered last time . . .
Causes and Effects	Here's what could happen if we fail to increase our dues . . .
Stories and Examples	I've contacted four community associations in this county and here's what I found . . .
Compare–Contrast	Let's take a look at the two research methods we considered . . .

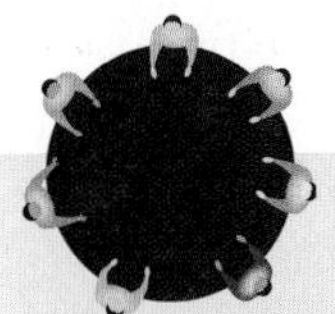

groups in balance . . .
Order the Main Points

In many cases, the organizational pattern you choose will dictate the order of your main points. If, for example, you are using time arrangement, the first step in a procedure should come first. If you are discussing a historical event, you can begin at the beginning and work your way forward to the finish. In other instances, your format may not suggest an order. In these cases, identify your strongest ideas and place them in strategic positions. Do you "put your best foot forward"? Or do you "save the best for last"? Your answer to these questions depends on many factors, such as the audience's attitude toward you, your group, and your message. The following strategies can help you make the right decision:

- *Strength and familiarity.* If one of your ideas is not as strong as the others are, place it in the middle position. This sequence avoids beginning or ending the presentation with a weaker point.
- *Audience.* Consider what you know about your audience and what it expects from the presentation. For example, if your audience is not very interested in your topic, don't begin with detailed technical information. Instead, begin by explaining why the topic is important and appealing.
- *Logistics.* If you are one of a series of speakers, you may end up having less time to speak than you expected. Put your most important points first. That way, if you have to shorten your presentation, your audience will have heard your major points.

There are no absolute rules about ordering your main points. Make sure that you put them in a logical progression that will help your audience members understand and remember them.[1]

[1]From Isa N. Engleberg and John A. Daly, *Presentations in Everyday Life: Strategies for Effective Speaking*, 3rd ed. (Boston: Pearson/Allyn & Bacon, 2008), p. 216.

The introduction of a presentation is critical because, when well crafted, it gains audience attention and interest. An effective beginning should direct the audience's attention toward you and your message. An interesting example, statistic, quotation, or story at the beginning of a presentation can "warm up" your audience and prepare it for your message.

The "central idea or purpose" section of a presentation lets you state your purpose and preview your main points. This section should be brief, no more than a few sentences. The heart of your presentation is the "body" section. Here you add your supporting material to each main point. No matter how many main points there are, each one should be backed up with at least one type of supporting material. If you can use several different types of material, your presentation will be more interesting and impressive.

The end of a presentation should have a strong and well-planned conclusion. An effective conclusion helps listeners remember the most important parts of your message. A quick summary, a brief story, a memorable quotation, or a challenge to the group can leave a strong final impression. Figure 13.1 on page 322 shows one possible organizational structure, including notes, for a presentation by a student spokesperson to a college's board of trustees.

Performance

By the time you ask questions about your delivery, you should know what you want to say and have given a lot of thought to how you want to say it. David Zarefsky writes that "*how* a speaker says something affects *what* is really being said, and it also affects what listeners actually hear and understand."[9]

Figure 13.1 Sample Presentation Outline

OUTLINE

Hold the Line on Tuition

I. Introduction

Story: Student who had to choose between buying shoes for her children and paying tuition for her nursing courses.

II. Central Idea or Purpose

Because a tuition increase will have a devastating effect on many students, we ask you to search for other ways to manage the college's financial crisis.

III. Body of Presentation

A. Another tuition increase will prevent students from continuing or completing their college education on schedule.

1. More students are becoming part-time rather than full-time students. (College statistics)
2. Students are taking longer to complete their college degrees. (College statistics)
3. Students are sacrificing important needs to pay their tuition bills. (Quotations and examples from college newspaper)

B. There are better ways to manage the college's financial crisis.

1. Consolidate areas and reduce the number of administrators and support staff. (Compare to college of same size that has less staff)
2. Seek more state and grant funding. (Statistics from national publication comparing funding levels and grants at similar types of colleges)
3. Re-evaluate cost and need for activities and services such as athletic teams, the off-campus homecoming and scholarship balls, intersession courses, and full staffing during summer sessions. (Examples)

IV. Conclusion

Money is a terrible thing to waste when students' hearts and minds are at stake. Let's work together to guarantee that all of our students become proud and grateful alumni.

Forms of Delivery. In many group and public audience settings, you will speak **impromptu**—a form of delivery without advance preparation or practice. For example, a member of the board of trustees may ask a student spokesperson a question after a presentation. The student responds impromptu.

When you do have advance notice, you will be more effective if you speak extemporaneously. **Extemporaneous speaking**—the most common form of delivery—involves using an outline or notes to guide you through your presentation. Your notes

can be a few key words on a small card or a detailed outline that includes supporting materials. These notes will reflect the decisions you have made during the preparation process, but they will also give you the flexibility to adapt your presentation to the audience and the occasion.[10]

Unless the situation is very formal or your words are intended for publication, avoid reading a manuscript version of your presentation. Even though your manuscript may be well written and well read, this delivery style is too formal for most settings. Moreover, reading from a script prevents you from observing listeners' reactions and modifying your presentation. If you must use a manuscript, write it as though you are speaking; that is, avoid long sentences, complex words, and formal term-paper grammar. Also, do not memorize your manuscript and try to deliver it without any notes. What if you forget or go blank? Unless you have the skills of a professional actor and can memorize a script and make it sound as if you just came up with the wording, forget about memorizing a presentation.

Vocal and Physical Delivery. The key to a successful performance is practice. Once you begin your presentation, it's too late to make many delivery decisions. Moreover, the only way to predict the length of your presentation accurately is to practice it aloud and time it.

You can control, improve, and practice vocal characteristics such as volume, rate, pitch, articulation, and pronunciation. Rehearse your presentation in a strong, loud voice, but without shouting. Even in a small-group setting, a presentation requires more volume than you would use in normal conversation. Also, monitor your speaking rate. Many listeners have difficulty following someone who speaks at a rate that exceeds 180 words per minute. The tolerable, all-purpose rate is 140 to 180 words per minute.[11]

Sometimes speakers are difficult to understand because their articulation is not clear. Poor articulation is often described as sloppy speech or mumbling. Generally, it helps to speak a little more slowly and a little louder and to open your mouth a little wider than usual. Similar problems can occur when words are mispronounced. Because it can be embarrassing to mispronounce a word or a person's name, look up any words you are not sure of in a dictionary or ask someone how to pronounce them correctly.

The single most important physical characteristic in an oral presentation is eye contact. Look directly at individual members of your audience, eye to eye. Even before a large audience, "the only kind of eye contact that successfully establishes the feeling of connection with members of the audience is a reasonably long, in-focus look at specific individuals."[12]

There is more to body movement than thinking about how you sit in a chair or stand before a group. Your gestures, appearance, and actions can add to or detract from your presentation. Your gestures and movements should be natural. At the same time, try to avoid distracting gestures such as pushing up eyeglasses, tapping the table with a pencil, or pulling on a strand of hair. Such movements draw attention away from the content of your presentation.

Group Presentations

The seven key elements and guiding principles—purpose, audience, logistics, content, organization, credibility, and performance—apply to any presentation you might make to your small group or to external audiences. If, however, you make a

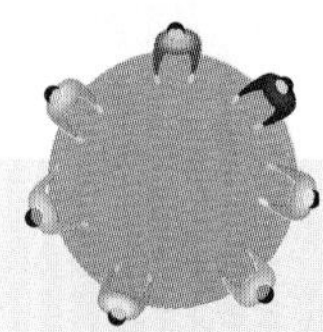

virtual groups
Mediated Presentations

Presentations are no longer the sole domain of people who speak, uninterrupted, to an audience that they can see and hear in real time. Groups use technology to communicate across time, distances, and organizational boundaries. Preparing and delivering effective virtual presentations are essential skills for anyone working in a virtual group.

In audioconferences, you must use your voice to communicate your meaning and emotions. Speak as clearly as you can. Use changes in rate, pitch, and inflection to emphasize particular ideas and to communicate your feelings. When you add video to the virtual mix, your appearance sends a powerful message to those who are watching. Dress appropriately. Avoid busy patterns, noisy jewelry, and stark white or black clothing. If you are talking to an audience at another location, speak directly to the camera as though it were a group member instead of a machine. Try to keep your delivery natural and sincere. This isn't prime-time live; it's a group at work.

If you have to make a "presentation" in a text conference, you have two options: You can write a report and send it to all members, or you can write minipresentations to make your point. Think of your writing as a substitute for speech. Also, remember that the basic requirements of any good presentation still apply—you need a clear purpose, audience analysis, logistical planning, thorough preparation, good organization, personal credibility, and a well-rehearsed delivery.

presentation as a member of a public group or as part of a team presentation, there are additional factors to consider.

Public Group Presentations

Chapter 1 describes four different types of public groups: panel discussions, symposia, forums, and governance groups. In all these settings, group members speak to a public audience. In addition to following the presentation guidelines described in this chapter, make sure you have considered the unique requirements of a presentation by a public group for a public audience. As a member of a public group, you have a responsibility to yourself, your group, and your audience.

When you are participating in a public group, remember that you are "on stage" all the time—even when you are not speaking. If you look bored while another member is speaking, the audience may wonder whether what that speaker is saying is worth sharing. During a presentation by a public group, an attentive audience will notice other group members' "gestures, facial expression, and posture. They deliberately look for unspoken disagreements or conflicts."[13] For example, if a member of the college's board of trustees rolls his eyes every time another board member speaks in support of student concerns, the audience will receive a mixed message about the board's commitment to serving student needs. Look at and support the other members of your group when they speak, and hope that they will do the same for you.

Team Presentations

When, as a solitary group member, you prepare a presentation, you must make dozens of critical decisions. When an entire group prepares a team presentation, the task becomes more complex. A **team presentation** is a well-coordinated, persuasive presentation by a cohesive group of speakers who are trying to influence an audience of key decision makers. For example, team presentations are common in nonprofit agencies and international corporations.

- A professional football team seeking backing for a new stadium brings a well-rehearsed group of executives and players to a public meeting, at which they explain how the stadium will enhance the economic development and prestige of the community without adversely affecting the surrounding neighborhoods.
- Companies making the "short list" of businesses being considered for a lucrative government contract make team presentations to the officials who will award the final contract.
- In a presentation to the state legislature's appropriations committee, a state college's board chairperson, college president, academic vice president, and student representative have a total of twenty minutes to justify their request for more state funding.

A team presentation is not a collection of individual speeches; it is a team product. Team presentations influence decisions about whether the group or represented company is competent enough to perform a task or take on a major responsibility. They make every effort to present a united front when organizations are seeking support. Although a symposium is a coordinated presentation, symposium speakers do not necessarily present a unified front or have a persuasive goal as their purpose. In many ways, the team presentation is the ultimate group challenge because it requires both efficient and effective decision making and a coordinated performance. Groups that work well in the conference room may fall apart in the spotlight of a team presentation. Marjorie Brody, author of *Speaking Your Way to the Top*, writes:

> To be effective, team presentations must be meticulously planned and executed. . . . If a team works like a smooth, well-oiled machine, if one member's presentation flows into the next presentation, and if all members present themselves professionally and intelligently, the impression left is one of confidence and competence.[14]

The presentation guidelines in this chapter direct a group through the critical decision-making steps for developing an effective team presentation. Much like an individual speaker, a team should consider the key elements of presentation speaking:

- *Purpose:* Every group member should understand and support the group's goal.
- *Audience:* Research the listeners' characteristics, needs, attitudes, and values. If possible, spend time with audience members before the presentation and then adjust the presentation to what team members learn.
- *Credibility:* Enhance the team's credibility by demonstrating the team's expertise and trustworthiness. In a team presentation, one weak link can damage the entire team's credibility.
- *Logistics:* Adjust to the time and place of the team presentation. Get there early to make sure the setting and equipment meet the group's needs.
- *Content:* Research and select appropriate and consistent supporting materials for the team presentation. Don't overwhelm listeners with unrelated details.
- *Organization:* Plan the introduction, body, and conclusion for each team member's presentation as well as those for the entire team's presentation. Make sure the session begins with a strong introduction.
- *Performance:* Practice until the team's performance approaches perfection. Each member also should pay attention to audience reactions and to other members' presentation in order to adjust subsequent presentations.

In addition to these guidelines, every group member should know what the team is going to do as well as every detail of the presentation. Make a special effort to link each presentation to the next one with effective transitions. Each member (or a leader)

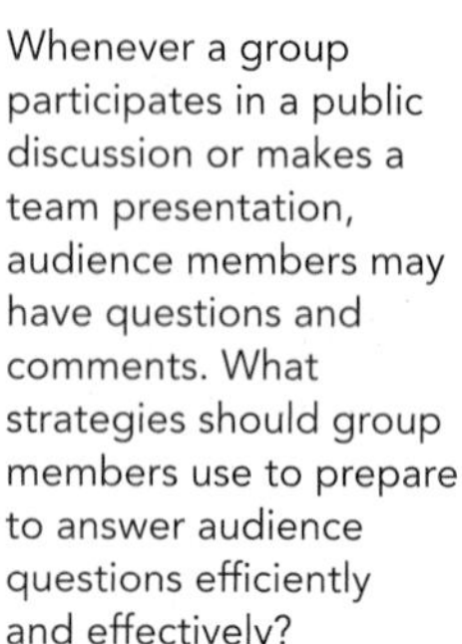

Whenever a group participates in a public discussion or makes a team presentation, audience members may have questions and comments. What strategies should group members use to prepare to answer audience questions efficiently and effectively?

should introduce the next team speaker, preview the importance of the topic, and bolster the speaker's credibility. In addition to describing the member's credentials, a brief story or humor about the person gives the audience another reason to listen.[15]

Rosa Vargas, the human resources manager for the Topps Company in New York City, learned about team presentations in graduate school:

> During my MBA studies, I was part of a team, and our purpose was to launch a new product to market. I feel that preparation and rehearsal are key to a successful team presentation. I was nervous in the beginning of our presentation (we presented to a panel of professors and students), but as the presentation progressed, I relaxed a bit. Our group had practiced, and I know this helped us give a more focused presentation.[16]

Team presentations require a great deal of time, effort, and money to prepare and present. The payoffs, however, are high. For instance, following team presentations by several companies, the Department of Energy awarded a $2.2 billion contract for environmental cleanup to a team headed by Fluor Corporation. Fluor made the best impression. "All the firms had capabilities, but how the team works as a team in the oral presentations is a key determining factor."[17] The awarding of a $2.2 billion contract should convince anyone who doubts the value of effective team presentations.

Questions and Answers

Once you or your team has completed a presentation, group or audience members may have questions or comments. The key to making a question-and-answer session a positive experience for everyone is to be prepared to answer a variety of questions and to know what to do when you don't have an answer.

If there is a single rule, it is this: Answer the question. Practice for a question-and-answer session using these guidelines:

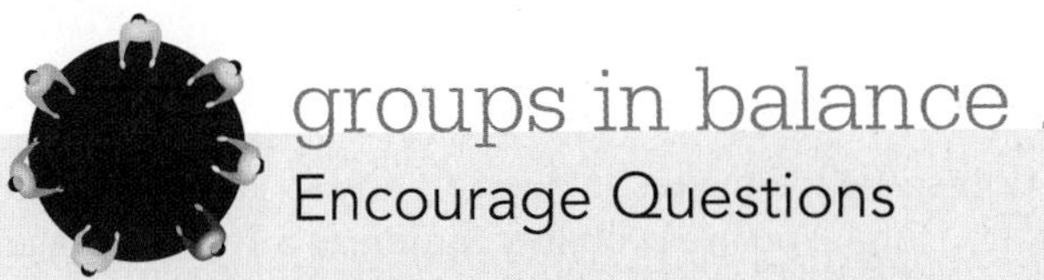

groups in balance . . .

Encourage Questions

Effective presenters use a variety of techniques to encourage audience members to ask questions. Never open a question-and-answer session with "Are there any questions?" If audience members do not have any questions in mind, they may just sit there. Instead, begin by asking a question that assumes that there are questions, such as "What are your questions?" or "Who has the first question?"

If no one answers at this point, pause and wait. Inexperienced presenters often feel uncomfortable waiting the several seconds it takes for audience members to come up with questions. Keep in mind that just as you may need a few seconds to organize your thoughts for an answer, audience members may need time to frame their questions. If you still don't get any questions after a significant pause, be prepared with some of your own. For example, "One of the questions our group often hears after our presentation is . . ." or "If I were in the audience, I'd want to know . . ."

Once an audience member asks the first question, you may find yourself facing the opposite situation: You may get an overwhelming number of questions and not have time to answer them all. As you near the end of your allotted time, or when you determine that the question-and-answer session has gone on long enough, bring the questioning to an end by saying, "I have time for two more questions." Then do just that: Answer two more questions and thank the audience for its participation.[1]

[1]Isa N. Engleberg and John A. Daly, *Presentations in Everyday Life: Strategies for Effective Speaking*, 3rd ed. (Boston: Pearson/Allyn & Bacon, 2008), p. 461.

- *Be brief.* Respond to questions with no more than three sentences.
- *Be honest.* If you don't know the answer to a question, admit it. Don't change the subject. The audience will know if you are avoiding the issue.
- *Be specific.* Provide appropriate information. Have some ready-made remarks, including interesting statistics, stories, examples, and quotations you can use in your answers.

If you run into difficult or hostile questions, remember that just because one listener disagrees with you doesn't mean everyone is against you. Follow the listening guideline "listen before you leap." Take your time before answering, and do not strike back in anger. Try to paraphrase the question to make sure you understand what the person is asking. If you are prepared for questions, you should have little difficulty dealing with the unexpected.

Presentation Aids

Presentation aids are supplementary audio and/or visual materials that help an audience understand and remember the content of a discussion or presentation. Effective presentation aids can make a dull topic interesting, a complex idea understandable, and a long presentation endurable. Studies sponsored by the 3M Corporation found that group "presenters who use visual aids are perceived as better prepared, more professional, more highly credible, and more interesting than those who do not."[18] At first, these findings may be difficult to believe. Can something as simple as an overhead transparency make that much difference? The answer is *yes*—but only if the presentation aid is clear, appropriate, and well designed.

Creating Presentation Aids

The availability of presentation software makes it possible for speakers to create professional-looking presentation aids. You are probably familiar with some presentation software. The most popular is Microsoft's PowerPoint. **Presentation software** allows you to create slides on a computer, for display on an overhead projector or directly from the computer to a screen.

The first question you should ask yourself about presentation aids is whether you need them. Sometimes a message needs nothing more than well-chosen words and effective delivery. Many listeners complain that even the simplest presentations have become dull displays of unnecessary slides that waste everyone's time. Although we cannot provide comprehensive instruction on how to use presentation software, we suggest that you follow the basic principles in Figure 13.2 regardless of what software you use.

Restraint. Presentation software offers such a dazzling array of graphics, fonts, colors, and other visual elements that you may be tempted to use them all. Resist the temptation. More often than not, a simple slide will be much more effective than a complex one.

Two recommendations can help you decide how much is "just right" for a presentation using computer-generated slides: (1) Make only one point on each slide, and (2) follow the six-by-six rule. Each slide should make only one point, and the title of the slide should state that point. Everything else on the slide should support the main point. It takes less time to present two well-structured slides than to load up one slide with a muddled message.[19] In addition, aim for no more than six lines of text with six words per line. This allows your slide to contain the main heading and several bullet points without information overload.[20] These recommendations also apply to other types of presentation aids, including hand-drawn posters and flip charts.

Make slides compact and concise, while using them to add variety and interest. Finding this balance depends on understanding the value of presentation aids and the pitfalls to avoid when adding technical "sizzle" to your presentation.[21]

Type. After deciding what you want to put on a slide, select an appropriate typeface or font. "Users of presentation software have instant access to a veritable candy store of typefaces with tempting names like Arial, Calypso, Gold Rush, and Circus."[21] Again, exercise restraint. Using too many typefaces looks amateurish. As a rule, never use more than two different fonts on a single slide. Avoid the fancy, but difficult-to-

Figure 13.2 Presentation Aid Guidelines

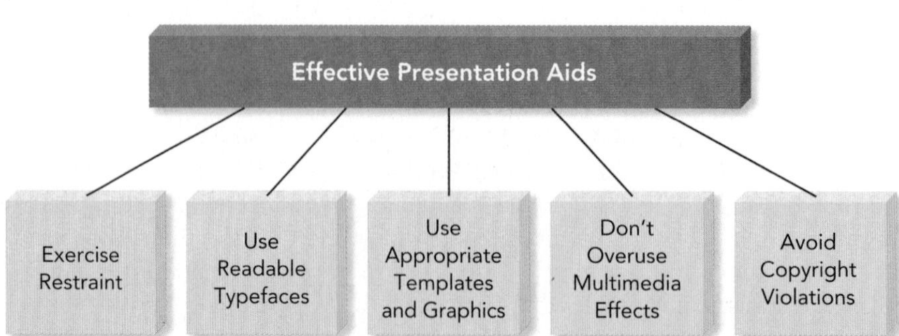

read, fonts. You are better off choosing common typefaces such as Helvetica, Arial, or Times Roman.

Type size is as important as the font. The best way to determine if your type is large enough is to prepare a few sample slides and project them in the room where your group will be meeting. Generally, you should try to avoid type that is smaller than 24 points. If you have more text than will fit on a slide, don't reduce the size of the type. Two clear slides are always better than one cluttered slide.

Templates and Graphics. On a slide-by-slide basis, use a consistent style and background. From within your presentation software, you can select any of several dozen backgrounds or templates. Here, too, exercise restraint. In most cases, it is better to choose a modest background that will spruce up your slide but not compete with your words, charts, or graphics.

When choosing graphics, ask yourself whether group members really need to see the picture you want to use. If, for example, you are making a presentation about a new medical device, it may be useful to show a picture of the device. On the other hand, showing a picture of a doctor would probably not be useful. A picture of a doctor does not help explain the device.

Artwork that doesn't have a specific purpose can get in the way of your presentation. Presentation software often comes with numerous clip-art images, but resist the temptation to use graphic elements just because you can. More often than not, clip-art graphics get in the way of messages when the graphic is not the reason for the slide. See Figure 13.3 for an example of an effective presentation slide.

Figure 13.3 Sample Presentation Slide

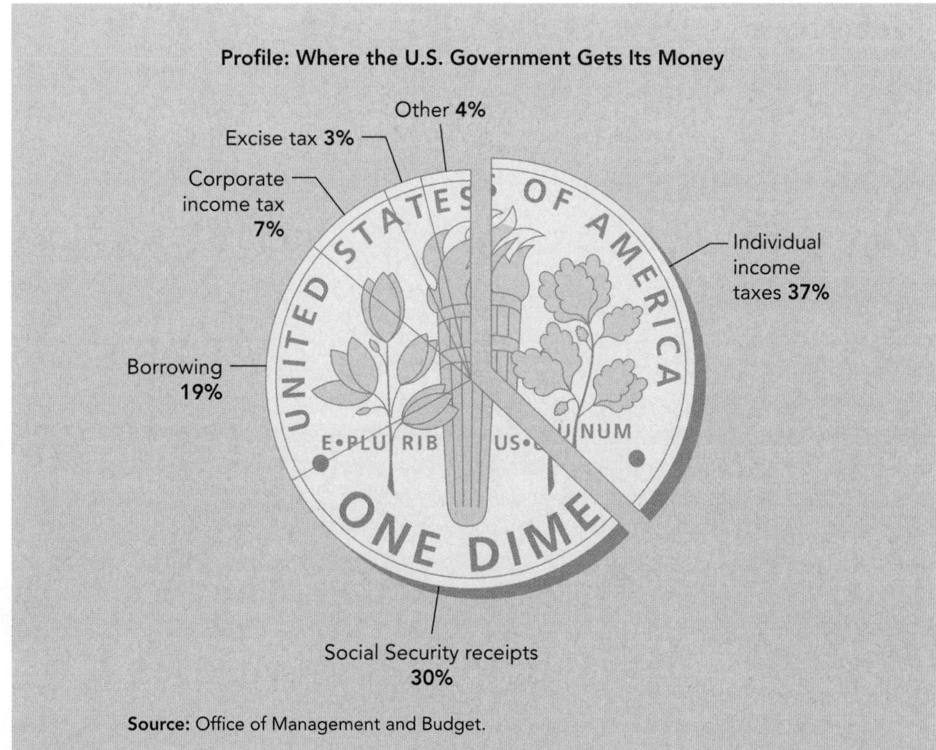

Multimedia. **Multimedia** technology allows you to use words, charts, graphics, sounds, and animation in a single presentation. It is possible to create presentation aids so dazzling that group members remember more about the slide show than about you or your message. Although there are times when animation or sound may enhance understanding, these multimedia components are frequently no more than window dressing that get in the way of the message. The last thing you want is for your audience to leave a presentation wondering how you got the Tyrannosaurus rex to eat the pie chart instead of discussing the data represented in the pie chart. In addition, some effects are so overused that they have become clichés. Beginning a presentation with the theme from *Rocky* or *2001: A Space Odyssey* is not only unnecessary, but old and trite. If you decide to include multimedia effects in a presentation, you should be able to articulate a reason for doing so other than "it's neat."

Pitfalls of PowerPoint

Many presenters use PowerPoint (or other brands of presentation software, such as Lotus Freelance or Corel Presentations) without thoroughly investigating whether it enhances the listeners' comprehension or helps speakers accomplish their purpose. Some corporations have even banned PowerPoint presentations by employees who have not had extensive training in visual design and its relationship to audience comprehension and reasoned analysis. The 3M Corporation discourages the use of PowerPoint because "it removes subtlety and thinking."[23]

Edward Tufte, author of several books on graphic design, notes:

> Presentations largely stand or fall on the quality, relevance, and integrity of the content. . . . If your numbers are boring, then you've got the wrong numbers. If your words or images are not on point, making them dance in color won't make them relevant. Audience boredom is usually a content failure, not a decoration failure. . . . PowerPoint cognitive style routinely disrupts, dominates, and trivializes content. PowerPoint presentations too often resemble a school play: very loud, very slow, and very simple.[24]

A survey of college students concluded that students like technology in the classroom, but some gave professors failing grades when it came to using PowerPoint.

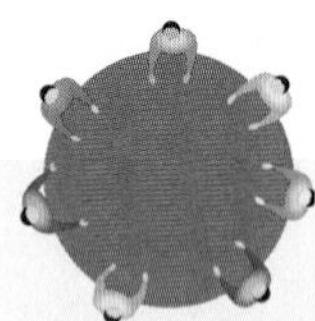

ethics in groups
Respect Copyrights

Technology not only makes it easier to create professional-looking presentation aids, but it also makes it easier to appropriate the creative work of others in a presentation. When the creation of visual or audio images is a person's livelihood, the uncompensated use of such images raises ethical questions. Such unfair use may even be a violation of federal copyright laws. A discussion of whether a particular use of an image is illegal is far beyond the scope of this book; however, you should be aware of the legal and ethical implications of using unlicensed images.

A whole industry has developed to provide clip art and clip audio to computer users. A user who purchases such packages has the right to make copies of the images and use them in presentations. Likewise, the visual and audio images included with presentation software are free. On the other hand, if you create a computer image by scanning an image from another source or if you obtain an image from the Internet, your conscience and your knowledge of copyright law must act as your guide.

They complained that many professors cram slides with text and then recite the text during class, which some students say makes the delivery flatter than if the professor did not use the slides.[25] As one student put it, "The majority are taking their lectures and just putting them on PowerPoint. . . . With a chalkboard, at least the lights were on and you didn't fall asleep." One professor reported a 20 percent drop in attendance when he posted his PowerPoint slides on the Web. Now his slides are "riddled with blanks and missing information, which he fills in aloud during lecture."[26]

In many cases, paper handouts can show text, numbers, data, graphics, and images more effectively than slides can. Images on paper have a higher resolution. Content can include more words and numbers. Thoughtfully planned, well-written handouts tell your audience that you are serious and thorough, that your message has consequences, and that you respect their attention and intelligence.[27]

Using Presentation Aids

Presentation aids can take many forms: handouts, posters, flip charts, overhead transparencies, computer-generated slides, and videos. The following list of dos and don'ts can help you avoid some common pitfalls when using any type of presentation aid.

- *Explain the point.* A presentation aid does not speak for itself. You may need to explain why you have chosen it and what it means.
- *Wait until it's time.* Prepare listeners for a presentation aid so that they will want to see it. Give them enough time to look at it so that they don't mind turning their attention back to you.
- *Don't talk to your aid.* You control the presentation aid; it shouldn't control you. Talk directly to the people in your audience, not to the poster, flip chart, or slide.
- *Be prepared to do without.* Presentation aids can be lost or damaged; equipment can malfunction. Have a backup plan. Be prepared to make your presentation without your aids.

Beyond these dos and don'ts, here is one more piece of advice: practice, practice, practice. Not only can practice improve your overall performance, but it can also alert

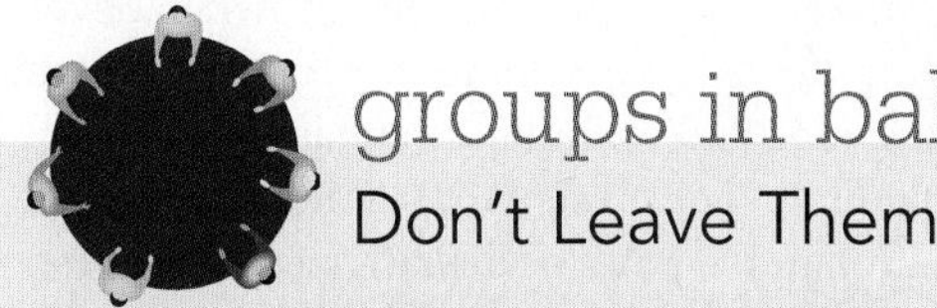

groups in balance . . .

Don't Leave Them in the Dark

Although adjustable lighting has considerable advantages over simple on/off switches, use it carefully. If you are going to display videotapes, overhead transparencies, or computer-generated slides, turn the lights down, but don't leave your audience in the dark. You never want the lights any dimmer than they need to be. If the room is too dark, your audience may drift off to dreamland in the glow of your beautiful slides.

If you intend to turn off your projector when you are not displaying slides, remember that the room will become even darker without that light source. Another problem may occur if you dim the lights sufficiently to let everyone see your slides or overheads: The room may become too dark for you to read your notes.

Find a middle ground. Dimming the lights only partially is one solution. Getting a lectern with a light might be another option. The more you know about the lighting system in a room, the better you can plan how to speak and how to use your presentation aids effectively.

you to problems with your presentation aids. For example, we once watched a consultant put almost everything in her talk on transparencies. As soon as she projected something onto the screen, she would turn around and point out the numbers that she thought were important. Unfortunately, she stood right between the screen and the projector, so that most of the information projected onto her back. If she had practiced in front of others before making the presentation, she could have avoided the problem.

summary study guide

Presentations in Groups

- A group presentation occurs whenever a member speaks, relatively uninterrupted, to other group members or audience members.
- Group members make presentations within a group, on behalf of a group, or as part of a team presentation.

Presentation Guidelines

- The seven critical decision-making guidelines of presentation speaking revolve around the following key elements: (1) purpose (2) audience, (3) credibility, (4) logistics, (5) content, (6) organization, and (7) performance.
- The first and most important step in developing a successful presentation is to determine your purpose—what you want your listeners to know, think, believe, or do as a result of your presentation.
- Three major factors that enhance a speaker's credibility are perceived competence, character, and caring.
- Seek common ground with your audience by analyzing their demographic traits, individual attributes, and opinions.
- An effective presentation should have an interesting introduction, the statement of a central idea, a preview of key points, a well-organized body, and a memorable conclusion.
- Forms of delivery include impromptu, extemporaneous, manuscript, and memorized delivery.

Group Presentations

- When you are the member of a group making a public presentation, remember that you are "on stage" at all times—even when you are not speaking.
- A team presentation is a well-coordinated, persuasive presentation by a cohesive group of speakers who are trying to influence an audience of key decision makers.

Questions and Answers

- You can prepare for and practice responses to potential questions in advance.
- During a question-and-answer session, answer questions directly and as clearly as possible.

Presentation Aids

- Consider the following design elements when developing computer-generated slides: restraint, type, templates, graphics, and multimedia enhancements.
- When planning your presentation aids, make sure you can explain the point of the aid, know when to display it, know where to stand when using the aid, and be prepared to make the presentation without the aid.

key terms

caring 318
character 318
common ground 317
competence 318
credibility 318
demographic trait 316
ethos 318
extemporaneous speaking 322
impromptu 322
individual attribute 317
logistics 319
multimedia 330
presentation 314
presentation aid 327
presentation purpose 316
presentation software 328
team presentation 324

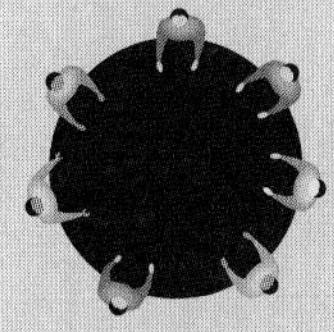

critical thinking about the case study

Testing the Team

1. What "hangups" did the group face as it began planning its team presentation?
2. What, in your opinion, is the team presentation's purpose or purposes?
3. How well did the group consider the needs of its audience—other students, the course instructor, and faculty members from the theatre department?
4. Which key elements/guiding principles of presentation speaking were or were not considered?
5. Which of the group's decisions are likely to improve the probability that their team presentation will succeed?
6. Which dialectic tensions are likely to affect whether the group's team presentation is successful?

group work Reenvision the Visual

Directions: Use the design principles presented in this chapter to redesign one or both of the following slides. Explain why your design decisions produce a better slide than the examples. In addition to changing the design, you may change wording (add, subtract, substitute other words) but not the basic meaning.

Slide #1

Common Cents

Save half a buck a day in loose change	$ 15
Drink 12 fewer cans of soda per month	6
Order 20 regular coffees instead of cappucinos	40
Avoid ATM fees and credit-card late charges	60
Eat out two fewer times a month	30
Borrow, rather than buy, a book or CD	15
TOTAL MONTHLY SAVINGS	$166

Source: America Saves as quoted in *Newsweek*, March 24, 2003, p. 60.

Slide #2

Challenges We Face

We lost 3% of our market share last year

Our stock price is down by 7% from just a year ago

Customer complaints—no matter how silly—are up by 14%

Retention of key people is down by 5%

group assessment Presentation Rating Scale

Directions: Use the following presentation guidelines to assess how well a group member, group spokesperson, or team makes an oral presentation to the group or a public audience. Identify the speaker's strengths and make suggestions for improvement.

PRESENTATION GUIDELINES	SUPERIOR	SATISFACTORY	UNSATISFACTORY
Purpose: Sets clear and reasonable goal			
Audience: Adapts to listeners			
Credibility: Demonstrates competence, character, and caring			
Logistics: Adapts to occasion and setting			
Content: Uses a variety of effective supporting materials to support main points			
Organization: Uses clear organization and an effective introduction and conclusion			
Performance: Uses voice, body, and presentation aids effectively			

Comments

Strengths of Oral Presentation:

Suggestions for Improvement:

notes

1. Deborah Harrington-Mackin, *Keeping the Team Going: A Tool Kit to Renew and Refuel Your Workplace Teams* (New York: AMACOM, 1996), pp. 88–89.
2. Based on Isa N. Engleberg and John A. Daly, *Presentations in Everyday Life: Strategies for Effective Speaking,* 3rd ed. (Boston: Pearson/Allyn & Bacon, 2009), pp. 6–8 and 76–89.
3. Quoted in Lilly Walters, *Secrets of Successful Speakers* (New York: McGraw-Hill, 1993), pp. 3–4.
4. Engleberg and Daly, p. 134.
5. Engleberg and Daly, pp. 135–136.
6. Jo Sprague and Douglas Stuart, *The Speaker's Handbook,* 6th ed. (Belmont, CA: Wadsworth, 2003), p. 255.
7. James C. McCroskey and Jason J. Teven, "Goodwill: A Reexamination of the Construct and its Measurement," *Communication Monographs* 66 (1999), pp. 90–103. McCroskey and Tevan note that Aristotle envisioned ethos as composed of three elements: intelligence, character, and goodwill. The results of McCroskey and Tevan's research establish that goodwill is a primary dimension of the ethos/source credibility construct.
8. Some of the best research on the value of organizing a presentation was done in the 1960s and 1970s. See Ernest C. Thompson, "An Experimental Investigation of the Relative Effectiveness of Organizational Structure in Oral Communication," *The Southern Speech Journal* 26 (1960), pp. 59–69; Ernest C. Thompson, "Some Effects of Message Structure on Listeners' Comprehension," *Speech Monographs* 34 (1967), pp. 51–57; James McCroskey and R. Samuel Mehrley, "The Effects of Disorganization and Nonfluency on Attitude Change and Source Credibility," *Communication Monographs* 36 (1969), pp. 13–21; Arlee Johnson, "A Preliminary Investigation of the Relationship between Organization and Listener Comprehension," *Central States Speech Journal* 21 (1970), pp. 104–107; Christopher Spicer and Ronald E. Bassett, "The Effect of Organization on Learning from an Informative Message," *Southern Speech Communication Journal* 41 (1976), pp. 290–299.
9. David Zarefsky, *Public Speaking: Strategies for Success,* 4th ed. (Boston: Pearson Education, 2005), p. 302.
10. Engleberg and Daly, pp. 314 and 315.
11. Authors of voice and articulation textbooks generally agree that a useful, all-purpose speaking rate is around 145 to 180 words per minute. See Lyle V. Mayer, *Fundamentals of Voice and Articulation,* 13th ed. (Boston: McGraw-Hill, 2004); Jeffrey C. Hahner, Martin A. Sokoloff, and Sandra L. Salisch, *Speaking Clearly: Improving Voice and Diction,* 6th ed. (New York: McGraw-Hill, 2002); Ethel C. Glenn, Phillip J. Glenn, and Sandra Forman, *Your Voice and Articulation,* 4th ed. (Boston: Allyn & Bacon, 1998).
12. Marya W. Holcombe and Judith K. Stein, *Presentations for Decision Makers: Strategies for Structuring and Delivering Your Ideas* (Belmont, CA: Wadsworth, 1983), p. 169.
13. Holcombe and Stein, p. 178.
14. Marjorie Brody, *Speaking Your Way to the Top: Making Powerful Business Presentations* (Boston: Allyn & Bacon, 1998), p. 81.
15. Judith Filek, "Tips for Seamless Team Presentations—A Baker's Dozen," Impact Communications Inc. *Face-to-Face Communications Skills Newsletter,* September 2006, www.impactcommunicationsinc.com/pdf/nwsltr_2006/ICINwsltreff0609.pdf. Retrieved May 17, 2008.
16. Engleberg and Daly, p. 483.
17. Thomas Leech, *How to Prepare, Stage, and Deliver Winning Presentations* (New York: AMACOM, 1993), p. 288.
18. 3M Meeting Management Team, with Jeannine Drew, *Mastering Meetings: Discovering the Hidden Potential of Effective Business Meetings* (New York: McGraw-Hill, 1994), p. 140.
19. RAND, *Guidelines for Preparing Briefings* [online] (1996). Available at www.rand.org/pubs/corporate_pubs/2005/CP269.pdf. Retrieved December 21, 2008.
20. William J. Ringle, *TechEdge: Using Computers to Present and Persuade* (Boston: Allyn & Bacon, 1998), p. 125.
21. Ringle, pp. 125, 135.
22. S. Hinkin, "Designing Standardized Templates: First You Choose It, But How Do You Get Them to Use It?" *Presentations* 8 (August 1994), p. 34.
23. "Microsoft PowerPoint," Wikipedia, http://en.wikipedia.org/wiki/PowerPoint.
24. Edward R. Tufte, *The Cognitive Style of PowerPoint* (Cheshire, CT: Graphics Press, 2003), p. 24.
25. Jeffrey R. Young, "When Good Technology Means Bad Teaching," *Chronicle of Higher Education,* November 12, 2004, pp. A31–32.
26. Young, p. A32.
27. Tufte, p. 24.

chapter 14

Technology and Virtual Groups

chapter outline

study questions

- *How do face-to-face and virtual groups compare in terms of overall effectiveness?*
- *What are the primary advantages of audioconferences, videoconferences, textconferences, and electronic meeting systems?*
- *What are the primary advantages of using email and bulletin boards as media for virtual groups?*
- *How do differences in member abilities and attitudes about technology affect virtual groups?*

The Nature of Virtual Groups

Whether you love it or hate it, you live in a wired world. You can sit at home, at work, or in your favorite Wi-Fi–enabled coffee shop and connect to the world using your cell phone, iPhone, BlackBerry, and laptop computer. You can communicate with friends, family, shopping outlets, and colleagues by text, photo, video, or voice throughout the day—and night. You also can use these same technologies to work in groups.[1] But before we claim bragging rights about the wonders of U.S. technology, let's consider where we stand compared to other countries. South Korea, not the United States, is the most wired country on the planet.[2] The race is on. Groups that can "go virtual" will rightfully claim their status as influential leaders in a wired world.

As we've noted in other chapters, **virtual groups** rely on technology to communicate, often across time, distance, and organizational boundaries. This definition recognizes that thousands of miles and several time zones may separate virtual group members, while others may work in the same room using technology to do group work. Virtual teams are everywhere. More than two-thirds of U.S. workers surveyed engage in virtual work. Nearly half (46%) are involved in virtual group work at least once a week and 14% do so every day.[3] Diverse and geographically distributed teams have become the norm for businesses and governments around the world.[4]

In the preface to *CyberMeeting: How to Link People and Technology in Your Organization,* James Creighton and James Adams emphasize the need to balance the advantages and disadvantages of using technology for working in groups. On the one hand, they note that organizations will spend billions of dollars "connecting their employees through technology that will permit collaboration and electronic participation in meetings." On the other hand, "hundreds of millions of those dollars will be wasted

virtual groups
A Chapter-by-Chapter Review

Every chapter of this textbook includes a Virtual Groups feature. A review of their titles underscores the ways in which virtual groups have become an integral part of group work. As you prepare to work in a virtual group, review the material in the following chapters:

- Chapter 1: From Email to EMS (synchronous and asynchronous communication)
- Chapter 2: Developmental Tasks (planning and technical expertise requirements)
- Chapter 3: Confidence with Technology (computer anxiety and confidence)
- Chapter 4: Cultural Diversity in Cyberspace (adapting to cultural dimensions)
- Chapter 5: Sharing Leadership Functions (leading virtual groups)
- Chapter 6: Mediated Motivation (preparing members for virtual communication)
- Chapter 7: Expressing Emotions Online (using emoticons appropriately)
- Chapter 8: Listening Online (active listening versus faked attention)
- Chapter 9: Conflict in Cyberspace (politeness and civil behavior)
- Chapter 10: Adapting Decision-Making and Problem-Solving Methods (choosing appropriate technologies)
- Chapter 11: Think Critically about the Internet (testing Internet sources)
- Chapter 12: Meeting in Cyberspace (planning and conducting virtual meetings)
- Chapter 13: Mediated Presentations (presenting in audioconferences, teleconferences, and text conferences)

case study

Virtual Misunderstanding

A project manager has organized a conference call with a staff writer and designer to discuss a missed deadline for a sales brochure.[1] Ellen, the staff writer, is listening on speakerphone at her desk. She also has her laptop computer open and is doing other work as she participates in the audioconference. Charlie, the designer, is speaking on a phone line. A partial transcript of the audioconference follows:

Manager: Listen, how're you guys doing?
Ellen: Ah, okay.
Manager: Listen, you guys. We have got to get that brochure finished by next Friday for the sales meeting. I did not get final graphics from you, Charlie, and I did not get the final edited copy from you, Ellen.
Ellen: I have the edited copy. I left you a voice mail that I had it ready. I was waiting to hear from Charlie, so there is nothing I could do.
Manager: Did you contact Charlie?
Ellen: Yes, I left him emails and voice mail—and he never got back to me.
Manager: Charlie?
Charlie: Yeah . . . ah . . . uh . . . no . . . ah, I, uh . . . . What'd you do? Change some more stuff?
Manager: No, Charlie. Did you get the communication from Ellen?
Charlie: No, ah, I'm sorry. I haven't looked at my email. What did you change . . . I thought we were done. I thought we had finished.
Ellen: Why don't you check your email?
Charlie: Because the last email I did check said we were done. You were finishing up the copy that you . . . and the graphics were fine.
Manager: Okay, there must have been a misunderstanding.
Charlie: I guess.
Manager: We had a slight change in direction for the concept for the brochure. We talked about this at our last conference call. I need to go ahead and get the final graphics from you, and I need to get the final copy.
Ellen: I have the final copy.
Charlie: Did you send me the final copy?
Ellen: Yes, I did!
Charlie: Is it more copy than there was before?
Ellen: No, it's the same amount.
Manager: What I need you to do is send off a draft to me by 9 o'clock tomorrow.
Charlie: By 9 a.m. tomorrow.
Manager: Yes.
Charlie: Ah . . . I . . .
Ellen: Don't count on it.
Charlie: I heard that.
(*After listening to more sniping between the writer and designer, the manager interrupts.*)
Manager: We set up this project in this fashion because you guys wanted the flexibility of working from home. This is the concern that we had—that we were going to have communication difficulties. If you guys cannot sort this out, then you're either going to have to come in for a face-to-face or I'm going to have to find another designer and writer—and I don't want to do that because you guys are the best I've got.

(The manager's message gets both Ellen's and Charlie's attention rather quickly. They come up with a plan for getting the design and copy to the manager by 9 a.m. the next day. The audioconference concludes as follows:)

Manager: Do both of you have each other's cell phone numbers, so if there are any questions you can get them resolved?
Ellen: I have Charlie's.
Charlie: Yeah, yeah. I've got hers.
Manager: I expect that brochure tomorrow at 9 o'clock. We'll have a conference call at 9:30 tomorrow morning!
Charlie: Oh? You mean 9 a.m. tomorrow morning? Nah, I'm just kidding you.
Manager: Yeah, that's why we love you. Okay, thanks guys. 'Bye.

When you finish reading this chapter, you should be able to answer the following questions.

(*continued*)

1 How efficient and effective was the audioconference?

2 How does reading a transcript rather than hearing voices or seeing nonverbal behavior affect your perceptions of the meeting?

3 How well did the project manager conduct the meeting? How, if at all, would you have done it differently if you were the manager?

4 Is designing and writing copy for a brochure a task appropriate for virtual groups? Why or why not?

[1]A short video of this group discussion is available through the publisher, Pearson/Allyn & Bacon. Watching the discussion adds important nonverbal perspectives to understanding the advantages and disadvantages of computer-mediated communication in virtual groups.

chasing fads and installing technology that people will use to work the same way they worked before the technology was installed."[5] As important as it is to understand how to use technology in group settings, it is even more important to understand why and when to choose technology as a tool for enhancing group efficiency and effectiveness. In the end, "the real issue is collaboration; technology is simply a valuable tool for helping to bring it about."[6]

In Chapter 2, Group Development, we present the eight characteristics of successful teams identified by Carl Larson and Frank LaFasto (a clear elevated goal, competent team members, etc.).[7] A study by Staples and Webster identifies "best practices" that significantly improve group performance and member satisfaction in virtual groups.[8] The following list summarizes several of these best practices:

Best Practices in Virtual Groups

- We have adequate resources (funding, people, skills, etc.) to achieve our goal.
- We have appropriate and effective information technology and support.
- We have adequate electronic communication skills training.
- We have adequate remote coordination skills training.
- We have members who serve as role models so we can learn from them in day-to-day interactions.

In this chapter, we examine challenges that arise when you work in virtual groups. As you read, keep in mind that the "convenience of electronic communication does not diminish the importance of face-to-face meetings. Relying totally on electronic communication often diminishes the bonding and synergy that happens when team members meet and work face-to-face."[9]

FTF versus CMC

Academic researchers use the acronyms **FTF** and **CMC** as shorthand for describing face-to-face group meetings and groups working in a computer-mediated communication environment. Much of their research examines how efficiently and effectively these two types of groups work to achieve their goals.

Many businesses, government agencies, and organizations embrace CMC groups because they save travel time and money by connecting geographically dispersed

members, from as far away as other continents to as close as networked offices in one building. A study of *Meetings in America* found that "saving time and money" was the number-one reason for supporting virtual work and groups.[10]

Are CMC groups as effective as FTF groups? Here's what some of the research says. When group tasks are complex, face-to-face groups usually perform better than groups using computer-mediated communication. However, when a group task is simple, CMC groups do just as well as FTF groups.[11] Depending on the complexity and nature of the task, CMC groups are less efficient than FTF groups in terms of communication effectiveness. They also use more time than FTF groups to complete their tasks.[12]

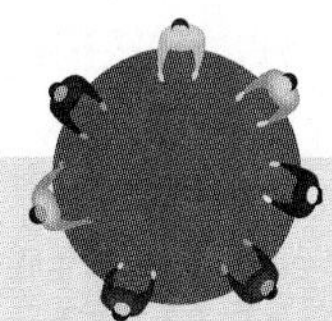

theory in groups

Media Richness and Media Synchronicity Theories

Media Richness Theory helps explain a significant difference between FTF and CMC groups. In today's electronically connected world, group members interact in several ways: face to face, through audioconferences and videoconferences, and by email and text messaging, as well as through bulletin boards, chat rooms, and electronic meeting systems.

Media Richness Theory contends that when you use more communication channels, you will be more successful communicating with others. Thus, face-to-face groups are often more successful because members can (1) see and respond instantly to feedback, (2) use nonverbal communication (body movement, vocal tone, facial expression) to clarify and reinforce messages, (3) use a natural speaking style, and (4) convey personal feelings and emotions to other group members. In contrast, text-based communication channels such as email are quite the opposite.[1] Readers only have printed words and illustrations to interpret someone's meaning.

Face-to-face communication (be it in a group meeting, presentation, or conversation) is the richest communication medium. In addition to your words and your vocal/physical delivery in face-to-face meetings, you can supplement group interactions with audio and visual aids as well as written materials and illustrations. In short, face-to-face communication engages more of our senses and sensibilities than any other form of communication. Thus, if your group interacts primarily in a virtual environment, try to use more media and create a richer communication environment.

A more recent theory expands Media Richness Theory by taking into consideration how group needs, group development, and member characteristics interact with media richness. **Media Synchronicity Theory** claims that "the key to effective use of media is to match the media capabilities to the fundamental communication processes required to perform the task." In other words, just because face-to-face may be the richest medium, it may not be the best way to achieve a group goal given differences in group development and the nature of the task. For example, a group that has worked together and successfully on multiple projects may be more effective and efficient using email than by meeting face to face. However, the members of a newly formed group may need to work in face-to-face settings as they move through forming, storming, and norming before shifting to audioconferences or electronic meeting software to achieve their common goal.[2]

[1]See Richard L. Daft and Robert H. Lengel, "Information Richness: A New Approach to Managerial Behaviour and Organizational Design," in *Research in Organizational Behavior,* ed. Barry M. Staw and Larry L. Cummings (Greenwich, CT: JAI Press, 1984), pp. 355–366; Richard L. Daft, Robert H. Lengel, and Linda K. Trevino, "Message Equivocality, Media Selection, and Manager Performance: Implications for Information Systems," *MIS Quarters* 11 (1987), pp. 355–366; Linda K. Trevino, Robert K. Lengel, and Richard L. Daft, "Media Symbolism, Media Richness, and Media Choice in Organizations," *Communication Research* 14 (1987), pp. 553–574.

[2]Alan R. Dennis and Joseph S. Valacich, "Rethinking Media Richness: Towards a Theory of Media" (proceedings of the 32nd Hawaii International Conference on System Sciences, 1999, p. 9). See also Dorrie De Luca and Joseph S. Valacich, "Virtual Teams In and Out of Synchronicity," *Information Technology and People,* 19 (2006), pp. 323–344.

Synchronous and Asynchronous Communication

As we note in Chapter 1, when group members use technology to interact simultaneously in real time, they engage in **synchronous communication**. Conference calls, videoconferences, and Internet chat rooms are examples of synchronous communication media. Because synchronous communication is spontaneous and dynamic, it can enhance group processes such as brainstorming and problem solving.

Asynchronous communication is the opposite of synchronous communication. Asynchronous communication is linear and not interactive. During asynchronous communication, one person makes a statement and, for example, posts it online for the group to see. Group members, often at their convenience, look at the message and then post responses. Asynchronous communication does not require group members to hold a meeting. Instead, members read and respond to messages as their schedules permit. Email and bulletin boards are examples of asynchronous communication media. Table 14.1 summarizes the advantages and disadvantages of these two types of virtual communication.

Groupware

The term **groupware** refers to computer-mediated methods and tools designed to support group collaboration, even though participants may not be together in either time or space.[13] Groupware combines two basic ideas: *group* + *ware*, or people + technology.[14] Groupware describes an entire category of electronic options available to virtual teams that integrate software and hardware to enable communication and collaborative work.[15]

The most common type of groupware is email. However, more sophisticated types of groupware, such as electronic meeting systems, are becoming more available, affordable, and widely used. For example, specially constructed **telepresence** studios connect a conference table in one studio to a similar conference table in another, identical studio enabling geographically dispersed group members to sit around the same "table" and interact in real time. The environment is so real that at the end of some meetings, a few participants stand up and offer their business cards or handshakes to on-screen participants. The companies that create and sell telepresence systems are a Who's Who in information technology: Cisco, Halo by Hewlett-Packard and Dreamworks, Tandberg, and LifeSize by Polycrom.[16]

Table 14.1 Advantages and Disadvantages of Synchronous and Asynchronous Communication

	Advantages	Disadvantages
Synchronous Communication	• Group cohesion and synergy • Spontaneous and dynamic interaction	• Typing speed is slower than speaking speed • Messages might be received out of order
Asynchronous Communication	• More time to compose responses • Facilitates document review and editing	• Lacks spontaneity • Linear rather than interactive

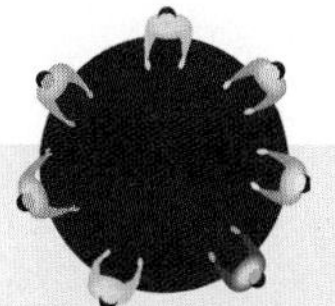

groups in balance . . .
Negotiate the Dialectics of Virtual Groups

Virtual groups experience the same dialectic tensions as face-to-face groups. The nature of virtual groups, however, can intensify dialectic tensions. Here we use two dialectics to illustrate some of the unique tensions in virtual groups: (1) conformity and nonconformity and (2) conflict and cohesion.

Conformity ↔ Nonconformity

Psychologist Patricia Wallace explains that group interaction seems to intensify the viewpoints of individual group members and moves them toward extremes.[1] This tendency—known as **group polarization**—is quite strong in virtual groups because there are fewer nonverbal cues to moderate opinions and behavior. Thus, although the potential for flocking with "birds of a feather" in virtual groups has advantages, it also "can lead to a false sense of security in one's point of view."[2] At the same time, virtual group members may feel more independent when contributing online because they cannot see one another's reactions. Virtual groups in balance understand that some level of group polarization can lead *to both* strong group agreement (conformity) *and* fruitful risk taking (nonconformity).

Conflict ↔ Cohesion

Virtual groups are often more successful in balancing conflict and cohesion because members feel more independent and are physically removed from the "dangers" of face-to-face conflict. Researchers also note that the content of messages in virtual groups tends to be "less controversial than is popularly believed: Conversations are more helpful and social than competitive. Interactive messages seem to be more humorous, contain more self-disclosure, display a higher preference for agreement and contain many more first-person-plural pronouns."[3] In short, virtual groups provide an environment that encourages *both* constructive conflict *and* genuine cohesion while avoiding the perils of false consensus and groupthink.

[1]Patricia Wallace, *The Psychology of the Internet* (Cambridge: Cambridge University Press, 1999), p. 75.

[2]Crispin Thurlow, Laura Lengel, and Alice Tomic, *Computer Mediated Communication: Social Interaction and the Internet* (London: Sage, 2004), p. 63.

[3]Sheizaf Rafaeli and Fay Sudweeks, "Networked Interactivity," *Journal of Computer-Mediated Communication* 2 (1997), available online at www.december.com/cmc/mag/current/toc.html, October 23, 2003, cited in Thurlow, Lengel, and Tomic, p. 67.

Synchronous Groupware

Synchronous groupware ranges from low-tech telephone conferences to high-tech electronic meeting systems. Here we offer guidelines for using voice-, video-, and text-based groupware as well as a meeting technology that combines all three types of virtual communication.

Audioconferences

When virtual groups use voice-only media to communicate, they engage in an **audioconference.** Audioconferences take two forms: conference calls (also known as teleconferences) and computer-based voice links. Conference calls only require a telephone with service that supports conference calling. Almost all business telephone services and some residential phone services have teleconference capabilities.

Guidelines for Audioconferences. Audioconferencing is the easiest type of virtual group interaction to understand because we are familiar with the basic technology—the telephone or computer microphone. However, author and business executive Clyde Burelson offers the following advice: "Do not think of teleconferencing as

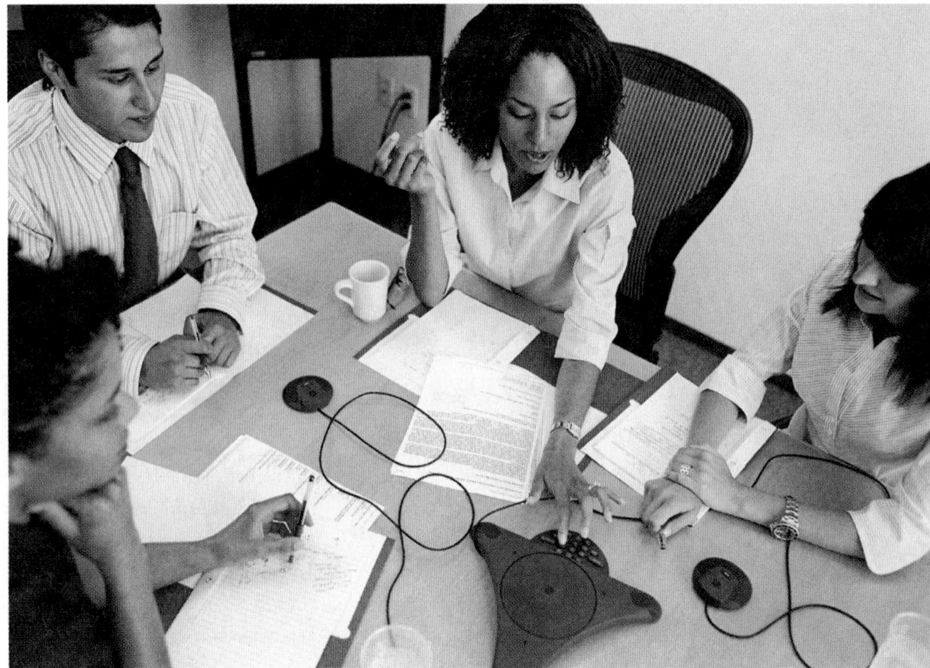

A group should plan for an audioconference just as it would for a face-to-face meeting. This means developing an agenda and making all other preparations appropriate for the meeting. What are some of the advantages and disadvantages of audioconference meetings?

talking on the telephone. This is a meeting."[17] A group should plan for an audioconference just as it would for a face-to-face meeting. This means developing an agenda and making all other preparations appropriate for the meeting. The following guidelines help you conduct and participate in effective audioconferences:

- Limit participation to no more than five active participants.
- Prepare and distribute an agenda and any necessary documents well in advance.
- Take "roll" and make introductions at the beginning of the meeting.
- Identify yourself by name whenever you speak.
- Keep your comments short, clear, and to the point.
- If someone must "sign off" before the end of the meeting, ask that member to inform the group when she or he is leaving.
- At the end of the meeting, summarize the discussion and describe the next step or announce the date and time for a subsequent meeting.
- Distribute the minutes of the meeting as soon as possible.

The most obvious difference between a voice-only conference and a traditional meeting is the fact that the participants cannot see one another. Consequently, it can be difficult to determine who is speaking. Burelson emphasizes that "not knowing who is speaking affects how you perceive the messages. It's like sitting in a regular meeting blindfolded, trying to guess who is making what point. That is bound to impact your judgment."[18] A simple introduction is usually sufficient: "This is Deidre, and I think we should. . . ." As we explain in Chapter 7, Verbal and Nonverbal Communication in Groups, you express a significant portion of your meaning nonverbally during face-to-face communication. For example, you might make a sarcastic remark in a meeting that everyone knows is a joke because you smile when you say it. However, in a voice-only environment, no one can see you smile. Someone might take your joke seriously.

Figure 14.1 Advantages and Disadvantages of Audioconferences

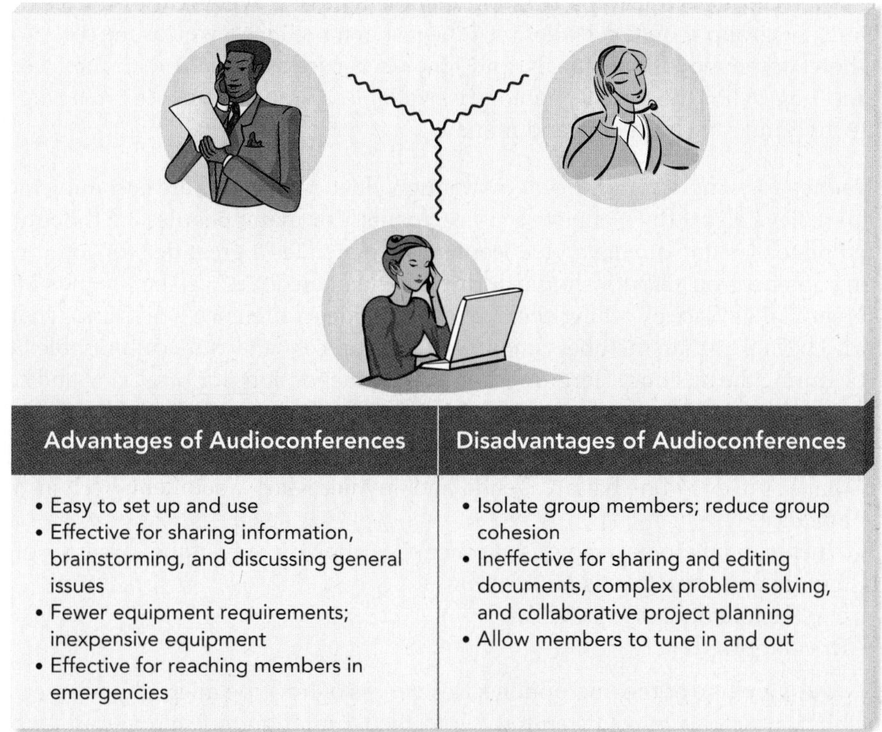

Advantages of Audioconferences	Disadvantages of Audioconferences
• Easy to set up and use • Effective for sharing information, brainstorming, and discussing general issues • Fewer equipment requirements; inexpensive equipment • Effective for reaching members in emergencies	• Isolate group members; reduce group cohesion • Ineffective for sharing and editing documents, complex problem solving, and collaborative project planning • Allow members to tune in and out

Pros and Cons of Audioconferences. The primary advantage of an audioconference is that it is typically quick and easy to set up and use, especially in the case of a conference call. In general, audioconferences are most effective for sharing information. However, if an issue or an emergency arises that requires immediate action, audioconferencing may be the best method for getting a group together. And for virtual groups without immediate access to computers, a conference call may be the only way to communicate and collaborate.

Audioconferencing does have some drawbacks. Because members may feel isolated, the quantity and quality of their participation may suffer. For example, group members who would never think of bringing nongroup work to a face-to-face meeting may be tempted to work on other matters during an audioconference. Group members may feel less a part of the group when they don't meet with one another face to face. Figure 14.1 summarizes the advantages and disadvantages of audioconferences.

Videoconferences

A **videoconference** is much like an audioconference with the addition of a visual component. The visual element of a videoconference eliminates many of the drawbacks associated with audioconferences. However, videoconferences require more sophisticated and expensive equipment than do audioconferences.

The most sophisticated videoconferences take place in specially designed studios equipped with professional lighting, cameras, and a crew. As technology improves, the cost of videoconferencing will continue to drop, the equipment will become easier to use, and the picture quality will improve.

Groups should balance the high technical cost of videoconferencing against the costs of a face-to-face meeting. If group members must travel great distances for a meeting, the group should consider the time lost in traveling as well as the cost of airfare, hotel accommodations, meals, and other expenses associated with the face-to-face meeting. When the right technology is available, a videoconference can be highly productive and save both time and money.

Guidelines for Videoconferences. Although videoconferences are becoming more popular, they can produce anxiety in participants. For many people, the thought of being "on television" during a videoconference generates a great deal of communication apprehension. Groups should address member anxieties well before the videoconference takes place by telling everyone how a videoconference works and what to expect. The more group members know about the process, the more comfortable they will be during the meeting. Here are several recommendations for preparing and conducting a videoconference:

- Brief all members about the operation of the videoconferencing system.
- Make sure everyone has an agenda and any necessary documents well in advance.
- When you talk to participants at other sites, look directly at the camera, not at their images on a television monitor.
- Use the microphone discreetly.
- Dress appropriately.

Always be aware of the microphone. Regardless of how the microphone is set up, remember that it is always listening. Avoid the temptation to lean over and whisper something to the person sitting next to you. Although the people across the room may not be able to hear you, everyone at the other end of the videoconference will.

Figure 14.2 Advantages and Disadvantages of Videoconferences

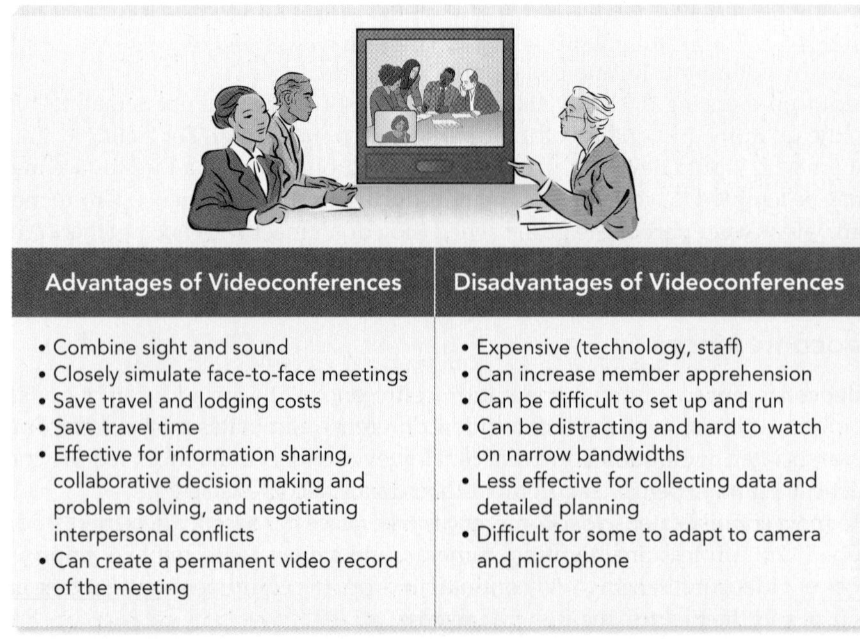

Advantages of Videoconferences	Disadvantages of Videoconferences
• Combine sight and sound • Closely simulate face-to-face meetings • Save travel and lodging costs • Save travel time • Effective for information sharing, collaborative decision making and problem solving, and negotiating interpersonal conflicts • Can create a permanent video record of the meeting	• Expensive (technology, staff) • Can increase member apprehension • Can be difficult to set up and run • Can be distracting and hard to watch on narrow bandwidths • Less effective for collecting data and detailed planning • Difficult for some to adapt to camera and microphone

Consider what you are going to wear to a videoconference. If your clothing is distracting, you will create a barrier to effective communication. Avoid clothes with narrow, contrasting stripes because video monitors can make stripes appear to pulsate. Also avoid wearing shiny or reflective clothing as well as jangling jewelry.

Pros and Cons of Videoconferences. The primary advantage of videoconferencing is that it allows group members to see and hear one another much as they would during a face-to-face discussion. Once participants' apprehension about being on camera passes, a videoconference can operate as efficiently and effectively as a traditional meeting. Videoconferences are well suited for sharing information, collaborative decision making, problem solving, and negotiating technical or interpersonal problems.

Videoconferencing, however, may not be as effective for collecting and sharing data, brainstorming, prioritizing, outlining, or reaching consensus about complicated issues.[19] Compared to audioconferences, videoconferences require much more planning and set-up time as well as more money. Furthermore, if your video equipment lacks sufficient bandwidth, or if you are using video via the Internet or desktop videoconferencing, the visual distortions and poor quality can become very annoying and tiring. Figure 14.2 summarizes the advantages and disadvantages of videoconferencing.

Textconferences

Think of a **textconference** as using a computer keyboard or keypad (and, in some cases, an accompanying voice link) to communicate and collaborate with a group in a synchronous environment. Linked together via local area networks and the Internet, computers provide a "place" for groups to communicate and work together.

Guidelines for Textconferences. Textconferences have many names: chat room, desktop conferencing, real-time computer conferencing, and Internet relay chat (IRC), to name a few. All of these variations occur in real time. The questions, responses, concerns, and comments of all members are visible to all participants.

At first glance, textconference sessions may *look* confusing. Because people read faster than they type, written comments may overlap, be highly repetitive, or seem irrelevant. Yet despite the presence of these multiple messages, participants "seem to be able to keep track of their particular thread in the conversation because of the textual record that is preserved as contribution after contribution is displayed on the screen."[20] Several guidelines can help a virtual group take advantage of the freewheeling nature of textconferences:

- Plan the session carefully. Send participants an agenda and access to relevant information or documents well before the interchange begins.
- Make sure everyone has similar technology and the ability to use that technology.
- Appoint a facilitator or moderator to keep the discussion on track.
- Limit group size to keep the process under control.
- Monitor member participation and deal with nonparticipants and members assuming negative roles.
- Don't become sidetracked by irrelevant threads of conversation.
- Summarize the meeting and distribute the summary to all members.

Pros and Cons of Textconferences. Compared to face-to-face interaction and audioconferencing, textconferences give members more time to prepare their

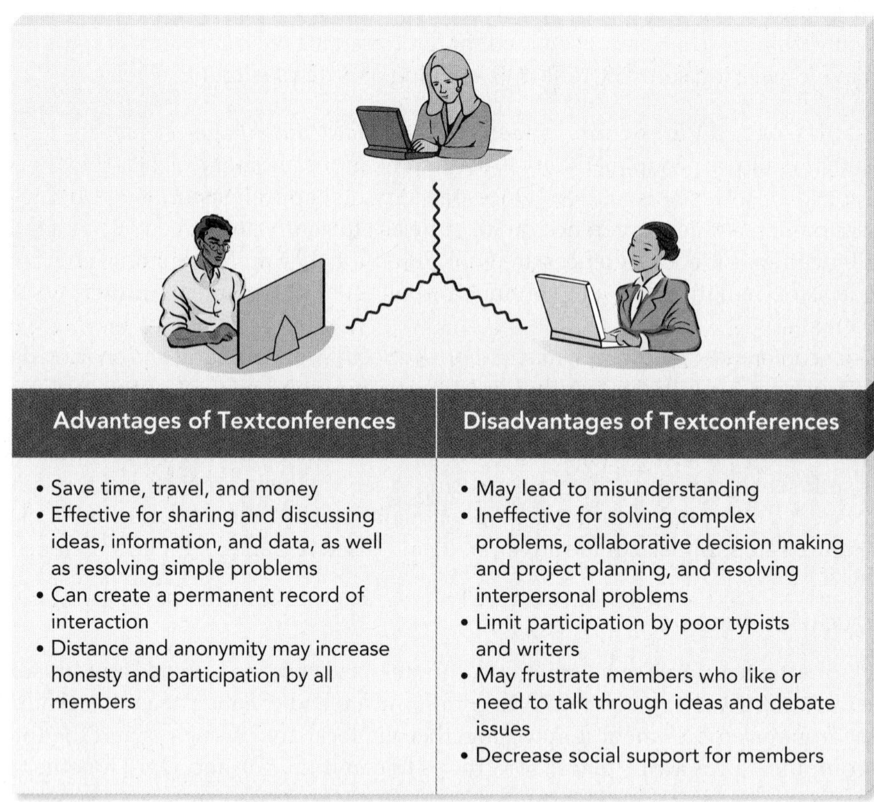

Advantages of Textconferences
• Save time, travel, and money
• Effective for sharing and discussing ideas, information, and data, as well as resolving simple problems
• Can create a permanent record of interaction
• Distance and anonymity may increase honesty and participation by all members
Disadvantages of Textconferences
• May lead to misunderstanding
• Ineffective for solving complex problems, collaborative decision making and project planning, and resolving interpersonal problems
• Limit participation by poor typists and writers
• May frustrate members who like or need to talk through ideas and debate issues
• Decrease social support for members

Figure 14.3 Advantages and Disadvantages of Textconferences

contributions. Of all the media available to virtual groups, textconferences allow members to send messages at any time from any place for future reading. The pervasiveness of email has made textconferencing both easy and available to just about everyone. Also, whereas a domineering member can monopolize other types of meetings, you don't have to wait your turn in order to contribute to a textconference. However, research by K.A. Graetz and his colleagues indicates that group members in text-only environments have more difficulty coordinating input and verifying information, take longer to make decisions, and may experience greater difficulty solving complex problems. As a result, members may find the experience frustrating.[21]

In most cases, there is an informality and an immediacy in textconferencing that separates it from the other kinds of writing that we do. As a result, read your messages carefully before you send them if you think they might be misunderstood. Consider the real-life example of a group that received an important message from a group member with the concluding sentence, "I resent the report." What she meant was that she had *re-sent* the report to someone who hadn't received it the first time. For days, however, committee members assumed that she resented (was offended by) what was written in the report, and no one could figure out why. Figure 14.3 summarizes the advantages and disadvantages of audioconferences.

Electronic Meeting Systems

The **electronic meeting system** (EMS) is the most versatile and powerful of all synchronous meeting technologies. By combining specialized software and hardware,

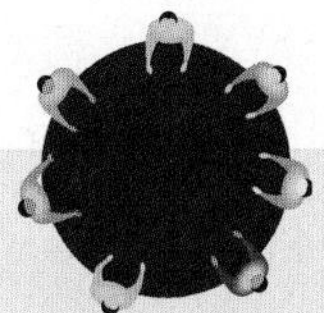

groups in balance . . .
Use Netlingo and Netspeak

David Crystal, who writes about language, believes that "Netspeak is a development of millennial significance. A new medium of linguistic communication does not arrive very often in the history of the [human] race."[1] Savvy Internet users are fluent in netlingo and netspeak. Here we offer a brief description of these languages.[2]

Netlingo refers to a variety of language forms used in Internet communication, such as the familiar FYI (for your information) and FAQ (frequently asked questions):

- *Compounds and blends.* Examples: shareware, netiquette, e- and cyber- anything.
- *Abbreviations and acronyms.* Examples: BTW = by the way; THX = thanks; IRL = in real life; F2F = face to face; IMHO = in my humble opinion; GMTA = great minds think alike; BBL = be back later; WDYT = what do you think?
- *Less use of capitalization, punctuation, and hyphenation.* Examples: Internet and email.
- *Less use of traditional openings and closings.* Examples: *Hi* or *hey* instead of *dear* or using no greeting phrase at all.

Netspeak includes common typographic strategies used to achieve a more sociable, oral, and interactive communication style.

- *Letter homophones.* Examples: RU (are you); OIC (oh, I see); CUL8R (see you later)
- *Capitalization or other symbols used for emphasis.* Examples: YES, * yes *
- *Onomatopoeic and/or stylized spelling.* Examples: coooooool, hahahahahah
- *Keyboard-generated emoticons.* Examples: :-) = smiley; @>—;— = rose; ;-) = winking; ;-o = shocked, uh-oh, oh-no

Be careful when using netlingo and netspeak. Some readers won't "get it" and will become confused or frustrated. Don't load your messages with unnecessary or "show-off" symbols. Too many in one message can make reading difficult and annoying, as well as make you and your writing appear immature.[3]

[1]David Crystal, *Language and the Internet* (Cambridge: Cambridge University Press, 2001), pp. 238–39, cited in Crispin Thurlow, Laura Lengel, and Alice Tomic, *Computer Mediated Communication: Social Interaction and the Internet* (London: Sage, 2004), p. 123.

[2]For definitions as well as several categories and examples of netlingo and netspeak, see Thurlow, Lengel, and Tomic, pp. 124–125.

[3]For additional examples and warnings about overuse of symbols, see Deborah Jude-York, Lauren D. David, and Susan L. Wise, *Virtual Teams: Breaking the Boundaries of Time and Place* (Menlo Park, CA: Crisp Learning, 2000), pp. 91–92.

EMS meeting participants perform many group tasks, such as brainstorming, problem solving, and decision making, at individual workstations.[23] Whether they are in the same room or miles apart, participants using electronic meeting systems can collaborate on a variety of group tasks. Most electronic meeting systems include several capabilities:[23]

- *Generating ideas and brainstorming.* Electronic meeting systems resemble a chat room in which virtual group members present ideas and are able to see the ideas contributed by all other members on their monitors or on a projection screen.
- *Grouping and analyzing issues.* Collectively, group members can move ideas into discrete categories, identify ideas that merit further discussion, outline a plan, and finalize a list of ideas or issues for further development.
- *Creating and editing documents.* Members can write assigned sections of documents and comment on or revise material written by other members.
- *Voting.* Special voting features can assess the degree of consensus on ideas and decisions without pressuring members to make a final decision. EMS software also can display voting results in total, graphic, or tabular form.

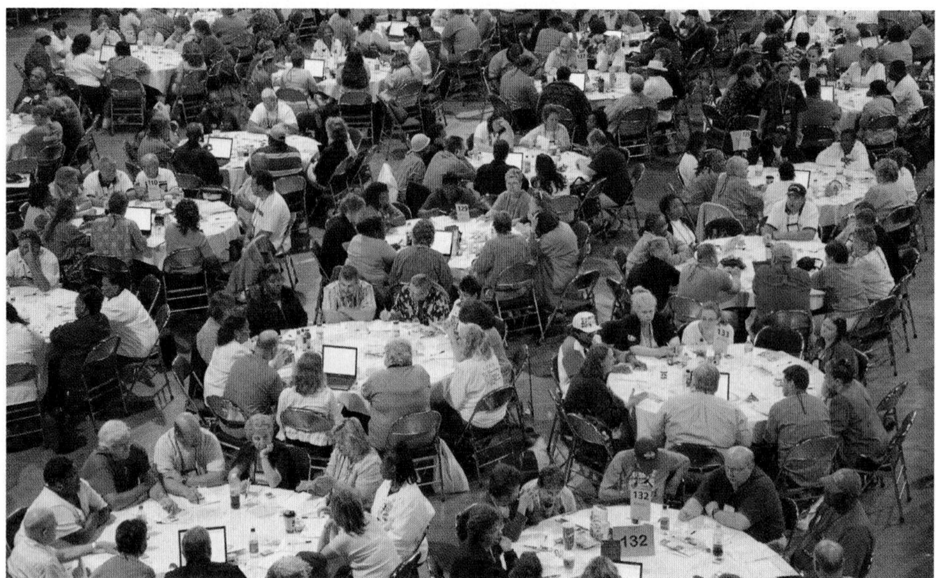

Convention delegates of the public employees union AFSCME participate in an interactive town meeting to discuss union issues. They use small-group discussions in which member viewpoints are tabulated electronically. What are the advantages and disadvantages of using electronic meeting systems?

Consider the following examples of how two very different groups used EMS to make important, far-reaching decisions:

Example 1: Corporate Risk Taking. Nine senior executives of a $2.5 billion transportation leasing company took less than four hours to brainstorm fifty-two risks to the corporation and then to identify the ten that presented the greatest risk to the company's achieving its strategic objectives and the ten that should receive the highest priority for an internal audit. After six months, the results of this four-hour meeting were still guiding the focus of both the senior executives and the internal audit staff.[24]

Example 2: Church Priorities. The members of the congregation filed into the church sanctuary, filling every seat in every pew. The top-ten priorities of each of the five church task forces were projected on five screens along the side wall. The task of the 467 people in the sanctuary was to choose, from among all fifty priorities, the ones on which the church should spend its limited resources. By using 467 keypads (a combination of handheld numeric keypads, computer software, and a projection screen), the members took only three hours to reach agreement on thirteen priorities for the coming year.[25]

Guidelines for Electronic Meeting System Conferences. In addition to the usual requirements for effective participation, electronic meeting systems require specialized software, compatible and specially networked hardware, and computer expertise to make the process work. An EMS meeting usually requires a facilitator to keep the group moving through the process, a coach or trainer to help inexperienced or nonparticipating members, and a technician to solve technical problems. The best advice we can offer to participants in such a complex virtual group is this: Follow instructions and leave the rest to the hardware and software.

Deborah Duarte and Nancy Tennant Snyder, the authors of *Mastering Virtual Teams,* share a set of best practices for making electronic meeting system conferences more effective:[26]

- Make sure that everyone's system is compatible and working properly.
- Make sure that everyone can access the software as well as any shared files.
- Develop and use a clear, focused agenda and set of technical instructions.

Figure 14.4 Advantages and Disadvantages of Electronic Meeting System (EMS) Conferences

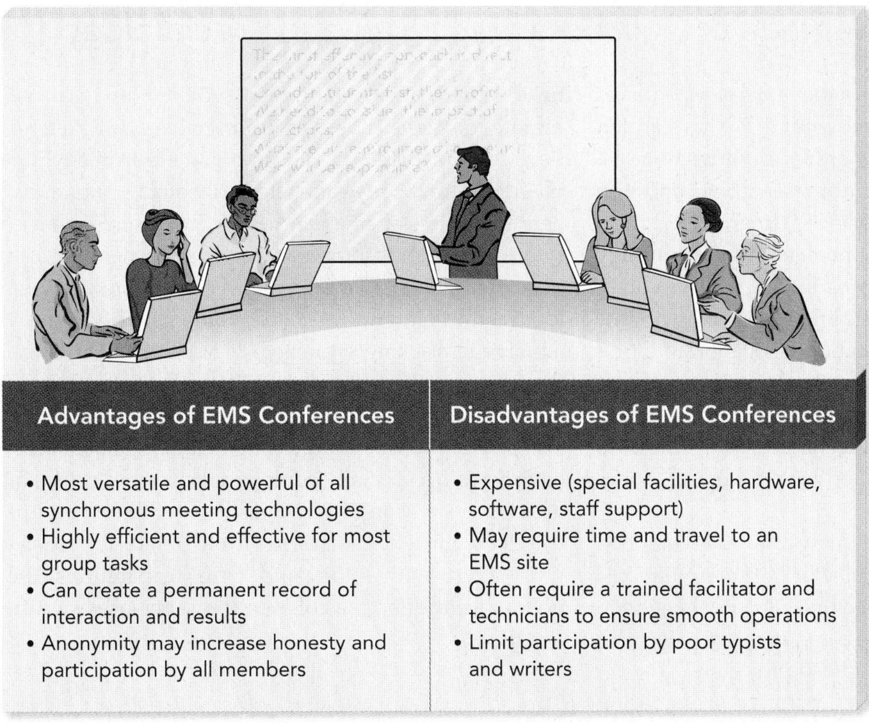

Advantages of EMS Conferences	Disadvantages of EMS Conferences
• Most versatile and powerful of all synchronous meeting technologies • Highly efficient and effective for most group tasks • Can create a permanent record of interaction and results • Anonymity may increase honesty and participation by all members	• Expensive (special facilities, hardware, software, staff support) • May require time and travel to an EMS site • Often require a trained facilitator and technicians to ensure smooth operations • Limit participation by poor typists and writers

- Decide if and when input will be anonymous (e.g., brainstorming, voting).
- Rotate functions, such as sorting information and voting, to avoid fatigue.

Pros and Cons of Electronic Meeting Systems. Depending on the system and a group's technical expertise, members can move back and forth from the EMS to other computer-based applications, such as word processing, spreadsheets, presentation software, and project-management software. The EMS can integrate other systems, such as desktop video, to capture the nonverbal and interpersonal dynamics of a meeting.[27] Projects that would otherwise have taken weeks or months to complete are finished in hours or days. Ideas flow, posted results lead to highly targeted discussions, and the final product can be of high quality.

As much as we wish that every business, professional organization, civic association, and meeting facility had the capacity to use electronic meeting systems, the cost of installing and maintaining such systems is still high. Even renting an EMS facility can be prohibitive for many groups. In addition, a technician is often needed to make the process work. At the very least, a skilled facilitator is necessary to keep the group moving and to ensure that group members are using the software and hardware properly.

Fortunately, EMS services have become available and more affordable via the Web. After downloading a peer-to-peer collaboration platform, groups pay a user fee to establish direct, instant communication and collaboration with other group members. Groove.net, chatspace.com, huddle.com, and cogos.com are just four examples of providers offering this type of electronic collaboration service. Figure 14.4 summarizes the advantages and disadvantages of EMS conferences.

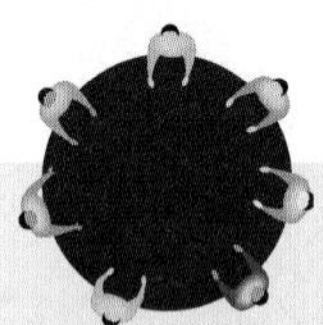

groups in balance . . .

Take Advantage of Collaborative Presentation Technology

When you see the term *presentation technology*, PowerPoint presentations may come to mind. We have added the word *collaborative* to this phrase in order to move beyond individual PowerPoint presentations and into the realm of technology-enhanced, interactive group presentations. **Collaborative presentation technology** projects an idea or graphic onto a screen, wall, or whiteboard so that both face-to-face and virtual participants can interact with the presentation.[1] Collaborative presentation tools make it possible to display information without being physically present with other group members. The use of these technologies also allows members to review, revise, edit, and finalize documents.

Sophisticated meeting rooms now come fully equipped with the tools necessary for collaborative presentations: projection screens, LCD projectors, whiteboards, video cameras and monitors, laptop computers, and even old-fashioned flip charts and overhead projectors.

One of the most useful collaborative presentation technologies is the **electronic whiteboard**. Computer-based electronic whiteboards allow members to work on the same document or drawing simultaneously. Anything written on the whiteboard is instantly digitized, stored, printed, and displayed in both local and remote locations. Thus, group members can sketch a flow chart or display a design on an electronic whiteboard that can be seen and altered by other group members, regardless of whether they are in the same room or located thousands of miles away. Group members can pose ideas, suggest modifications, draw links among ideas, edit text, and format documents. The primary advantage of using whiteboards is that they build on the team members' existing skills and meeting behaviors while also providing some sense of social presence. The primary disadvantage is that team members must have access to specially equipped conference rooms or desktop systems in order to participate.[2] When groups use electronic whiteboards in virtual or face-to-face settings along with audio and video capabilities, the potential for effective collaboration increases significantly.

[1]David Coleman (ed.), *Groupware: Collaborative Strategies for Corporate LANs and Intranets* (Upper Saddle River, NJ: Prentice-Hall, 1992), p. 266.

[2]Deborah L. Duarte and Nancy Tennant Snyder, *Mastering Virtual Teams: Strategies, Tools, and Techniques That Succeed*, 3rd ed. (San Francisco: Jossey-Bass, 2006), pp. 36, 38–39.

Asynchronous Groupware

Although there are numerous advantages to using synchronous groupware, an asynchronous group meeting has a double advantage: It is both less costly and more easily accessed from almost anywhere at any time. At first, you may not think of email and bulletin boards as groupware. They are, however, the first types of groupware available to groups and—despite the advantages of using synchronous groupware—they serve the needs of many groups efficiently and easily.

Email

As a worldwide, text-based, asynchronous medium, **email** lets group members interact from great distances and across time zones. In many corporate and professional settings, group members communicate via email more than they do on the phone or in person. In fact, some group members are able to express themselves better through email than in face-to-face meetings.[28]

One way of reaching every member of a virtual group with email is by using a **listserv**, a program that delivers messages to everyone in the group. You may have

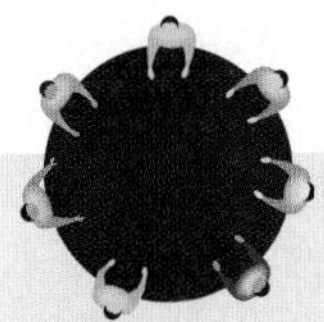

groups in balance . . .

Resist Internet Addiction

The phrase *Internet addiction* is no joke, although it began as one. In 1995, psychiatrist Ivan Goldberg lightheartedly posted a diagnosis for **Internet Addiction Disorder (IAD)**, which he described as "a maladaptive pattern of Internet use, leading to clinically significant impairment or distress."[1] Although Goldberg intended his "diagnosis" as a joke, it quickly became a popular term and a serious topic for study by mental health professionals. Today, researchers shun the word *addiction* and instead use labels such as "problematic" or "pathological" to describe excessive or disturbed patterns of Internet use, with symptoms that include mood alteration, inability to fulfill major role obligations, guilty feelings, and cravings for more.[2] Here are some general symptoms that can help identify group members with problematic Internet use:

- They feel a strong need to use the Internet and spend increasing amounts of time doing so to achieve satisfaction.
- They feel restless, moody, depressed, or irritable when attempting or forced to cut down or stop Internet use.
- They stay online longer than they originally intended.
- They have lied about or concealed the amount of time they spend on the Internet.
- They use the Internet as a way of escaping problems or relieving feelings of anxiety or depression.[3]

Internet behavior can help explain a member's nonproductive or antisocial behavior. For example, are any of these behaviors characteristics of one or more group members?

- They prefer Internet interaction to face-to-face communication.
- They eagerly volunteer to do an Internet search for the group when, in fact, the issue does not require extensive research.
- They are reluctant to leave their computers for a meeting and may even bring a wireless laptop to meetings so that they have access to the Internet.

Groups are often sidetracked by computer-dependent members. The newest version of this addiction is the *crackberry*, a reference to people addicted to their BlackBerries. However, we urge you to be cautious about drawing unwarranted conclusions about problematic Internet use or about discouraging members from using the Internet. Instead, we advocate a balanced approach. As Andrew Goodman put it, "For every story about Internet addiction leading victims to ignore their families and become withdrawn, antisocial, and depressed, there is an [opposite] example of a person who has found a support group, employment prospects, or a community of like-minded topical enthusiasts through the 'net."[4] To that list, we would add group members who use the Internet effectively and responsibly to help a group achieve its common goal.

[1]For a summary discussion of Internet addiction issues, see Crispin Thurlow, Laura Lengel, and Alice Tomic, *Computer Mediated Communication: Social Interaction and the Internet* (London: Sage, 2004), pp. 148–154. Also see the following websites: Anne Federvisch, "Internet Addiction?" *Nurseweek/Healthweek*, www.nurseweek.com/features/97-8/iadct.html; Ivan Goldberg message posted to the *Psychology of the Internet*, available at www.rider.edu/suler/psychberg/psycyber.html; Leonard Holmes, "Internet Addiction—Is It Real?" http://mentalhealth.about.com/cs/sexaddict/a/interaddict.html, March 10, 1997; Leonard Holmes, "What Is 'Normal' Internet Use?" http://mentalhealth.about.com/cs/sexaddict/a/normalinet.htm, March 10, 1997.

[2]Janet Morahan-Martin and Phyllis Schumacher, "Incidence and Correlates of Pathological Internet Use Among College Students," *Computers in Human Behavior* 16 (2000), p. 14.

[3]Kimberly S. Young, "Internet Addiction: The Emergence of a New Disorder," *CyberPsychology and Behavior* 1 (1998), pp. 237–244.

[4]Andrew Goodman, "Online Communities Endure as Platforms Come and Go," www.traffick.com/story/2001-04/online_community.asp, April 28, 2001.

worked on a committee or had a course in which the chairperson or instructor used a listserv to send messages to the entire group.[29]

Guidelines for Email Discussions. Email is asynchronous. You receive a message that may have been sent days, hours, or just seconds ago. You respond to it when you can or by a designated deadline and hope that other members will do the same. If you are going to participate in an email discussion, the following guidelines can help your group achieve its common goal:

- Make sure that all participants know what is expected of them. They should know the group's specific purpose, the deadlines and schedule for returning email, and the amount of time expected for the task.
- Ask for confirmation that group members received your email. In most cases, you can get that information from your software system.
- Develop a common system for editing documents (underlining, strikeovers, colors, or the track changes feature in your software), and make sure that everyone knows how to use these computer features.
- Provide training for members who are unfamiliar with a computer system's email and editing features.
- Contact and encourage members who are not participating. You may have to telephone them or meet with them in person to find out why they are not responding to the group's email messages.
- Observe good grammatical form. Don't abandon the rules of capitalization, spelling, grammar, and formatting. Good grammatical form is more professional and much easier to read.
- Include a context for your reply. A message that says only "I disagree" may leave other members unsure about what you oppose.

Pros and Cons of Email. Email is a terrific way to share ideas and information, and to revise documents. When group participation is active, email can help define and solve problems. Members can take time to reflect and write their responses carefully.

Even though email has become as common as regular mail, telephone conversations, and face-to-face meetings, it still has drawbacks. As was the case in textconferencing, you cannot see or hear other group members. Text-only communication can lead to misunderstandings and decreased member involvement.

Email makes it difficult to debate complex issues and to make critical decisions. And unfortunately, email is easy to ignore. Nonparticipants can be *loafers* (infrequent and detached members), *lurkers* (members who are present but offer no comments or contributions), or *newbies* (inexperienced or apprehensive email users).[30] An effective group will make sure that every member is an active participant. Table 14.2 summarizes the advantages and disadvantages of email discussions.

Table 14.2 Advantages and Disadvantages of Email Discussions

Advantages of Email Discussions	Disadvantages of Email Discussions
• Easy to use, accessible, and inexpensive • May be easier for some members to discuss personal or controversial issues • Effective for sharing information; revising ideas, plans, and documents; defining and analyzing uncomplicated problems • Easy to transmit files • Can include many people	• Content subject to misinterpretation • Easy to ignore messages, fake participation, or avoid difficult conversations and decisions • Ineffective for brainstorming and prioritizing, debating issues, making difficult decisions, and solving complex problems • Too many messages can waste time and discourage use • Not well suited for interpersonal conflict resolution

groups in balance . . .
Use Blogs and Wikis

Virtual groups are beginning to recognize the potential of blogs and wikis for doing research, sharing information, and editing. When we wrote the first edition of this textbook, blogs did not exist. The term *weblog* appeared in 1997. The short form, *blog,* appeared in 1999 when a blogger divided the word *weblog* into the phrase "we blog" as a sidebar on his own weblog. A **blog**—short for *weblog*—is a website on which a person posts text, images, Web links, and other files on a regular basis. Unlike open-ended chat rooms or bulletin boards, only the author or authoring group can create new subjects for discussion on a blog. Blogs can be personal online diaries; political blogs that post personal opinions, essays, and relevant Web links; and topical blogs that focus on narrow topics ranging from community issues to stock market discussions.[1]

Multiuser and group-based blogs—a rapidly growing phenomenon—support group projects by giving all members input into the decision-making process. Group blogs can be used to share information and member input, develop goals and milestones, solve problems, and write collaborative reports. Group blogs are not a simple compilation of individual comments; they are a mesh of ideas that intercept, overlap, and complement one another by encouraging collaborative interaction and inspiration.[2]

A **wiki** is a website that allows users to add and edit content and is particularly well suited for collaborative writing. The WikiWikiWeb was established in 1995 and is based on the Hawaiian word *wiki,* meaning "quick, fast, or to hasten."[3] Wikipedia, a free English-language encyclopedia, is the world's largest wiki. A nonprofit parent company manages Wikipedia but allows anyone to edit its content. An expert-led investigation by the journal *Nature* found Wikipedia's content more current and close to the prestigious *Encyclopedia Britannica* in accuracy.[4] Wikipedia demonstrates the power of groups in that biased, out-of-date, or incorrect information is usually and quickly corrected by participants.[5]

Group wikis have many of the same features as group blogs. Wikis, however, function primarily as sites for editing documents. A group can use a wiki to identify and codify key issues, recommend solutions to problems, or write reports and publishable materials. Much like the track changes feature in word-processing software, a wiki allows group members to edit and change copy over time, while keeping track of all changes so that a page can restore any of its previous states.[6]

[1]Wikipedia, "Blog," http://en.wikipedia.org/wiki/blog. Updated November 14, 2005.

[2]Wikipedia, "Blog."

[3]Wikipedia, "Blog."

[4]Editorial, "Wiki's Wild World," *Nature* 438 (December 2005), pp. 900–01; www.nature.com/nature/journal/v438/n7070/fu8ll/43889a.html. Retrieved July 5, 2008.

[5]George Johnson, "Commentary: The Nitpicking of the Masses vs. the Authority of Experts," *New York Times,* January 3, 2006, p. F2.

[6]Wikipedia, "Wiki" and "Wikipedia."

Bulletin Boards

Like email, a **bulletin board** is an asynchronous, text-based communication medium. What distinguishes bulletin boards from email and synchronous textconferences is the size of the audience they attempt to reach and the manner in which members write and read messages. If you subscribe to a bulletin board, you send your message to a single address. The program or a designated moderator then sends your message to everyone else on the bulletin board. But unlike a real bulletin board, a computer-mediated bulletin board organizes incoming materials and posts subsequent messages as responses to specific issues, one right after the other.[31] This system is called a *thread,* and it can continue and extend for as long as participants send submissions. Thus, a **threaded discussion** occurs when a series of related email messages about a specific issue appears on a bulletin board.

Guidelines for Bulletin Board Discussions. Generally, bulletin boards make fewer demands on participants than email does. Good bulletin boards become a source of

Table 14.3 Advantages and Disadvantages of Bulletin Boards

Advantages of Bulletin Boards	Disadvantages of Bulletin Boards
• Easy to use, accessible, and inexpensive • Provide space for shared messages, display, and documents • Effective for brainstorming; discussing ideas, plans, and documents; collecting and sharing information • Use threaded discussions that allow complex interactions and analysis • Can create synergy and increase collaboration • Effective way to communicate with numerous group members	• Content subject to misinterpretation • Easy to ignore • Difficult to organize • Ineffective for debating, voting, prioritizing, and collaborative decision making and problem solving • High message volume can waste time, discourage users, and result in information overload • Discussions can degenerate into nonproductive personal arguments

information and a means of following the development of an argument, plan, or report. Being a loafer or a lurker on a bulletin board can be perfectly acceptable. If, however, you want to post messages or respond to others, there are several guidelines to follow:

- Determine whether someone will moderate the bulletin board or whether the program will accept and post all messages. If the group uses a moderator, the program should not permit anonymous input, particularly if virtual group members are responsible for the outcome.
- Organize your thoughts before you contribute to a bulletin board. State your point clearly. No one wants to read your ramblings.
- Be careful of being highly critical. Your written comments will become part of a permanent record.
- If you want to pursue an issue with only one or two members, contact them by email. Don't take up bulletin board space with a private conversation.

Pros and Cons of Bulletin Board Discussions. Bulletin boards allow many conversations to occur at once, and, as a result, they are time savers.[32] Bulletin boards allow you to think before sharing your ideas, to evaluate the ideas of others, and to word your response carefully. They support brainstorming as well as generating and commenting on ideas. They provide a useful workspace for collecting information and discussing the implications of that information.

However, participating in a bulletin board can also be a dreadful experience. A bulletin board can become a free-for-all, with participants venting their frustrations and criticizing others. Mean-spirited members can do a lot of damage to a group if they can run wild or express themselves anonymously. Moderated bulletin boards ensure that the comments made are relevant and appropriate. Table 14.3 summarizes the advantages and disadvantages of bulletin board discussions.

Group Diversity and the Digital Divide

In virtual groups, cultural differences combine with technical differences to produce unique challenges. For example, language differences are an obvious, but often overlooked, cultural difference among computer and Internet users. For a group member whose native language is different from that of the majority of the group, communicating online can be difficult and frustrating. Members should "forgive" nonnative

speakers for spelling, pronunciation, or grammar errors and encourage their active communication.[33]

There are also "haves" and "have nots" as well as "know a lots" and "don't know a lots." Those of you who rely on computers and Internet access at home, work, or school for a wide range of tasks may assume that everyone has the same opportunities and skills. Certainly members of virtual groups must have access to compatible technology and possess comparable abilities in order to work efficiently and effectively. Those who "have" and "know a lot" about technology may work in the same group as members who "do not have" and "do not know a lot."

Virtual groups may face the digital divide and its consequences. The phrase **digital divide** refers to inequalities in access to, distribution of, and use of information technology between two or more populations. For example, surveys of Internet use in many countries provide a profile of the typical user as young, urban, male, and relatively well educated. This profile leads to discrepancies in use based on factors such as age, gender, and socioeconomic dimensions.[34]

Age

If you have grown up during the personal computer and Internet age, you are probably relatively comfortable, confident, and competent when using these technologies. Many children know more about computers and the Internet than their parents do. Interestingly, Internet use by "senior surfers" is increasing for those who have the time and money to go online.[35]

In terms of virtual groups, older members vary significantly—from those who have embraced computer technology and excel in its use to those who fear or have avoided learning and using computer technology. However, the same disparities in ability and attitude also affect young group members. Sociologist Eszter Hargittal studies the technological fluency of college freshmen. She has found that many of them lack both skill and an understanding of basic computer functions.[36]

Gender

The digital divide often separates men from women, particularly given that most highly skilled Internet users are well-educated urban males. Only in countries where Internet use is well developed, such as Scandinavia and the United States, has the gender gap begun to close. Even so, a study by the American Association of University Women concludes that

- Girls consistently rate themselves significantly lower on computer ability than boys do, and boys exhibit higher self-confidence and more positive attitudes about computers than girls do.
- Software programs (and gaming) often reinforce gender bias and stereotyped gender roles.
- Girls use computers less often outside of school. Boys enter the classroom with more prior experience with computers and other technology than girls have.[37]

Socioeconomic Factors

Income level is a strong determinant of a person's access to computer technology and the Internet. One government study on Internet use in the United States found that urban households earning incomes more than $75,000 a year are *twenty times* as likely to have home Internet access as rural households at the lowest income levels.[38] The

Pew/Internet and American Life Project found that 15 percent of Americans have neither a cell phone nor Internet access. These Americans tend to be older adults, nearly three-fifths are women, and they have low levels of income and education.[39] Moreover, "two of every three white students—67%—use the Internet, but less than half of blacks and Hispanics do. . . . Some 54% of white students use the Internet at home, compared with 26% of Hispanic and 27% of black youngsters."[40] When asked which demographic groups of college students are less Web-savvy, Eszter Hargittal identifies socioeconomic status and its effects on women, Latin/Hispanic, and African American students whose parents have lower levels of education.[41]

In international terms, nearly 90 percent of all Internet users are in industrialized countries, with the United States and Canada alone accounting for 57 percent of the worldwide total. In contrast, Internet users in Africa and areas of the Middle East together account for only 1 percent of global Internet users.[42]

Think of the practical and technical barriers facing certain populations. People who live in communities that have only sporadic electricity or that have no telephone

ethics in groups

The Ten Commandments for Computer Ethics

Dr. Ramon C. Barquin introduced the following ten commandments of computer ethics in a paper titled "In Pursuit of a 'Ten Commandments' for Computer Ethics."[1] In discussing the need for a set of standards to guide and instruct people in the ethical use of computers, he calls for the use of the following "Ten Commandments for Computer Ethics" by today's computing professionals:

1. Thou shalt not use a computer to harm other people.
2. Thou shalt not interfere with other people's computer work.
3. Thou shalt not snoop around in other people's computer files.
4. Thou shalt not use a computer to steal.
5. Thou shalt not use a computer to bear false witness.
6. Thou shalt not copy or use proprietary software for which you have not paid.
7. Thou shalt not use other people's computer resources without authorization or proper compensation.
8. Thou shalt not appropriate other people's intellectual output.
9. Thou shalt think about the social consequences of the program you are writing or the system you are designing.
10. Thou shalt always use a computer in ways that ensure consideration and respect for your fellow humans.[2]

Barquin's commandments have been widely adopted by the computing industry as a starting point for ethics standards. However, most professionals recognize specific circumstances may present ethical dilemmas.[3] For example, consider the third commandment, "Thou shalt not snoop around in other people's computer files." "What if the 'other people' are using the computer to do harm? Should we still refrain from interfering? Should computer files be private even if they are being used as part of a criminal conspiracy?"[4]

As is the case with many ethical issues, there are no easy answers to the questions that arise from these commandments. At the same time, Barquin's code is widely accepted and forms the basis for developing useful guidelines about the ethical use of computers, whether used by individuals or by virtual groups.

[1]Ramon C. Barquin, "In Pursuit of a 'Ten Commandments' for Computer Ethics," Computer Ethics Institute, 1991.

[2]Copies of the Ten Commandments for Computer Ethics are available from the Brookings Institute at cei@brookings.edu. Also available at www.cpsr.net/oldsite/externalSiteView/program/ethics/cei.html.

[3]Ben N. Fairweather, "Commentary on the 'Ten Commandments' for Computer Ethics," available at www.ccsr.cse.dmu.ac.uk/resources/professionalism/codes/cei_command_com.htm.

[4]Fairweather.

lines or mobile network connections also lack computers and access to the Internet.[43] There are also huge cost factors involved. For example, the national average monthly wage of farm workers in South Africa is less than $50. Most workers earning that wage can't afford transportation into the village to buy groceries, let alone afford to use technology at current prices. While Internet access represents 1.2 percent of the average monthly income in the United States, it would represent 278 percent of the average annual income in Nepal, 614 percent in Madagascar, and 191 percent in Bangladesh.[44]

Implications for Virtual Groups

Effective groups understand, respect, and adapt to the many ways in which group diversity and the digital divide affect groupwork and group success. They also develop strategies for fully integrating all group members into the virtual group environment. Here are several challenges to working in virtual groups that groups should address and resolve:

- diverse technical skills
- diverse writing skills and styles due to differences in languages and education
- diverse abilities and experiences using technology and the Internet
- diverse attitudes toward technology, such as technophobia or online shyness
- diverse hardware, software, and technical support
- diverse languages and computer-related vocabularies.

By their very design and function, virtual groups include people from different locations, organizations, lines of work, ages, genders, socioeconomic backgrounds, and cultures. Although there are challenges, virtual groups can offer a rich diversity of members seeking to achieve a common goal.

summary study guide

The Nature of Virtual Groups

- Technology allows virtual groups to collaborate across space and time.
- Media Richness Theory claims that when you and your group use more communication channels, you will be more successful communicating with others.
- Virtual groups can interact synchronously (simultaneously in real time) or asynchronously (consecutively and uninterruptedly).
- Specially constructed telepresence studios connect a conference table in one studio to a similar conference table in another, identical studio, enabling group members to sit around the same "table" and interact in real time.
- Groupware refers to computer-mediated methods and tools that support group collaboration, even though members may not be together in either time or location.
- Virtual groups may experience more intense dialectic tensions than groups communicating face to face.

Synchronous Groupware

- Audioconferences are coordinated phone calls and computer voice links among three or more group members. In addition to following audioconference guidelines, remember that audioconferences can isolate members, reduce cohesion, allow members to tune in and out, and be less effective for dealing with complex problems and projects.
- Videoconferences can be as effective as face-to-face interaction but may require expensive equipment and technicians to run the meeting. Members may need special training and should be patient with poor-quality visuals.
- Textconferences are very effective for sharing information, data, and resolving simple problems but can

also lead to misunderstanding, frustration, and lack of social support for members.

- Electronic meeting systems are versatile, powerful, efficient, and effective for group work but rely on expensive networked equipment, staff support, and (in some cases) time and money to travel to a fully equipped EMS site.

Asynchronous Groupware

- Email discussions are a highly accessible and inexpensive way for virtual groups to communicate, although written messages may be misinterpreted and members may ignore messages or fake participation. Email discussions are not effective for brainstorming, debating issues, and dealing with complex decisions and problems.
- Bulletin board discussions make fewer demands on members than email and can be highly focused, although written messages may be misinterpreted and ignored. Bulletin board discussions are effective for brainstorming and discussing ideas, but are not effective for debating, voting, and collaborating on complex problems and projects.

Group Diversity and the Digital Divide

- Older group members may be less skilled and less comfortable using communication technology, particularly as an alternative to face-to-face meetings.
- In some cultures, women are less skilled and less comfortable using the Internet and other communication technologies.
- Group members from rural and low-income households or from undeveloped countries may be less skilled and less comfortable using communication technology.
- Ramon Barquin's Ten Commandments of Computer Ethics provide standards to guide and instruct group members on how to use computers to their greatest advantage without harming, interfering, or disrupting others.

key terms

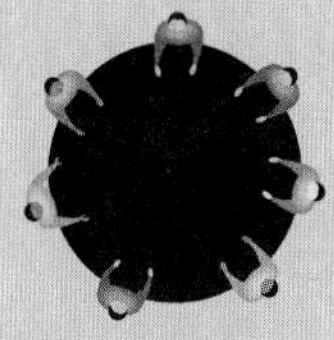

critical thinking about the case study

Virtual Misunderstanding

1. Was it a good idea for the project manager to set up a virtual group to work on the sales brochure? Why or why not?
2. What are the advantages and disadvantages of an audioconference like the one in this case study? How could the group improve the effectiveness of its audioconference?
3. If you could choose another type of groupware for this situation, which one would you choose and why would you choose it?
4. How well did the project manager conduct the meeting and handle the problems she encountered?
5. Which dialectic tensions were most evident in this case study? To what extent did the group resolve these tensions?

group work Match the Medium to the Message

Directions: The left column of the following table lists six types of virtual groups discussed in this chapter. Across the top of the table, we list common group tasks. Rate how well each type of virtual group matches the group tasks using the following scale:

1 = Very effective and useful 2 = Moderately effective and useful 3 = Ineffective

	SHARING AND ANALYZING INFORMATION	GENERAL DISCUSSIONS AND BRAINSTORMING	COLLABORATIVE DECISION MAKING AND PROBLEM SOLVING	HANDLING INTERPERSONAL PROBLEMS AND CONFLICT
Audioconferences				
Videoconferences				
Textconferences				
Electronic Meeting Systems (EMS)				
Email				
Bulletin Boards				

Source: The categories are adapted from a more extensive analysis of strengths and weaknesses for several types of groupware in Deborah L. Duarte and Nancy Tennant Snyder, *Mastering Virtual Teams: Strategies, Tools, and Techniques That Succeed,* 3rd ed. (San Francisco: Jossey-Bass, 2006), pp. 30–48. Duarte and Snyder's recommended ratings are in the *Instructor's Manual* accompanying this textbook.

group assessment Virtual Meeting Evaluation

Directions: When you participate in an audioconference, videoconference, or textconference, use the following criteria to evaluate the success of your virtual meeting. Circle the number that best represents your assessment of each statement.

Audioconference

1. An audioconference was appropriate for this meeting.
   Disagree 1 2 3 4 5 6 7 Agree
2. The sound quality was satisfactory.
   Disagree 1 2 3 4 5 6 7 Agree
3. Members received and followed a meeting agenda.
   Disagree 1 2 3 4 5 6 7 Agree
4. Members introduced themselves before speaking.
   Disagree 1 2 3 4 5 6 7 Agree
5. Members adapted to the oral-only medium.
   Disagree 1 2 3 4 5 6 7 Agree

Videoconference

1. A videoconference was appropriate for this meeting.
   Disagree 1 2 3 4 5 6 7 Agree
2. Members received and followed a meeting agenda.
   Disagree 1 2 3 4 5 6 7 Agree
3. The video quality was satisfactory.
   Disagree 1 2 3 4 5 6 7 Agree
4. Members used the microphones effectively.
   Disagree 1 2 3 4 5 6 7 Agree
5. Members dressed appropriately.
   Disagree 1 2 3 4 5 6 7 Agree

Textconference

1. A textconference was appropriate for this meeting.
   Disagree 1 2 3 4 5 6 7 Agree
2. Members received and followed a meeting agenda.
   Disagree 1 2 3 4 5 6 7 Agree
3. Members typed clear and succinct messages.
   Disagree 1 2 3 4 5 6 7 Agree
4. Members interacted frequently and met deadlines.
   Disagree 1 2 3 4 5 6 7 Agree
5. Delays between messages were reasonable.
   Disagree 1 2 3 4 5 6 7 Agree

Comments:

notes

1. "Nomads at Last," *The Economist,* online, April 10, 2008, www.economist.com/surveys/displaystory.cfm?story_id=10950394. Retrieved May 19, 2008.
2. Birgitta Forsbert, "The Future is South Korea," *San Francisco Chronicle,* online, March 13, 2005, www.sfgate.com/cgi-bin/article.cgi?f=/c/a/2005/03/13/BROADBAND.TMP. Retrieved May 19, 2008.
3. Modalis Research Technologies, *Meetings in America III: A Study of the Virtual Workforce in 2001,* from http://e-meetings.mci.com/meetingsinamerica/pdf/MIA3.pdf. Retrieved May 7, 2008.
4. Stacey L. Connaughton and Marissa Shuffler, "Multinational and Multicultural Distributed Teams: A Review and Future Agenda," *Small Group Research* 38 (2007), pp. 387, 388. Connaughton and Shuffler cite a variety of research findings in the introduction to their article.
5. James Creighton and James W. R. Adams, *Cyber Meeting: How to Link People and Technology in Your Organization* (New York: AMACOM, 1998), p. ix.
6. Creighton and Adams, p. 225.
7. Mark L. Knapp, "Introduction," to Carl E. Larson and Frank M. J. LaFasto, *TeamWork: What Must Go Right/What Can Go Wrong* (Thousand Oaks, CA: Sage, 1989), pp. 7–8.
8. D. Sandy Staples and Jane Webster, "Exploring Traditional and Virtual Team Members' 'Best Practices,'" *Small Group Research* 38 (February 2007), pp. 90, 91.
9. Fran Rees, *How to Lead Work Teams* (San Francisco: Jossey-Bass/Pfeiffer, 2001), pp. 114–115.
10. Modalis Research Technologies, p. 16.
11. Shu-Chu Sarrina Li, "Computer-Mediated Communication and Group Decision Making," *Small Group Research* 38 (2007), pp. 596–597.
12. Li, p. 609. See also Jamonn Campbell and Garold Stasser, "The Influence of Time and Task Demonstrability on Decision-Making in Computer-Mediated and Face-to-Face Groups," *Small Group Research* 37 (2006), pp. 271–294.
13. For a brief history and explanation of the term *groupware,* see David Coleman (ed.), *Groupware: Collaborative Strategies for Corporate LANs and Intranets* (Upper Saddle River, NJ: Prentice-Hall, 1997), pp. 1–2.
14. Gerald O'Dwyer, Art Giser, and Ed Lovett, "Groupware and Reengineering: The Human Side of Change," in *Groupware: Collaborative Strategies for Corporate LANs and Intranets,* ed. David Coleman (Upper Saddle River, NJ: Prentice-Hall, 1997), p. 566.
15. Deborah L. Duarte and Nancy Tennant Snyder, *Mastering Virtual Teams: Strategies, Tools, and Techniques That Succeed,* 3rd ed. (San Francisco: Jossey-Bass, 2006), p. 30. Throughout this chapter we rely on Duarte and Snyder's categorization, explanations, and analysis of groupware.
16. See Dawn Bushaus, "Telepresence: Ready for Its Close-Up," *TelephonyOnline,* http://telephonyonline.com/broadband/new/telecom_ready_closeup_2/index1.html .March 17, 2008; Linda Tucci, "Videoconferencing Systems Ready for Their Close-Up," http://searchcio.techtarget.com/tip/o,289483,sid182_gci1308909,00.html. Both retrieved May 11, 2008.
17. Clyde Burelson, *Effective Meetings: The Complete Guide* (New York: Wiley, 1990), p. 168.
18. Burelson, p. 171.
19. Duarte and Snyder, pp. 41, 71.
20. Andrew F. Wood and Matthew J. Smith, *Online Communication: Linking Technology, Identity, and Culture* (Mahwah, NJ: Erlbaum, 2001), p. 13.
21. K. A. Graetz, "Information Sharing in Face-to-Face, Teleconferencing, and Electronic Chat Groups," *Small Group Research* 29 (1998), pp. 714–743.
22. Creighton and Adams, p. 86.
23. Duarte and Snyder, pp. 37, 71.
24. W. A. Flexner and Kimbal Wheatley, in *Groupware: Collaborative Strategies for Corporate LANs and Intranets,* ed. David Coleman (Upper Saddle River, NJ: Prentice-Hall, 1997), p. 193.
25. Flexner and Wheatley in Coleman, p. 194.
26. Duarte and Snyder, p. 185.
27. Duarte and Snyder, pp. 36–37.
28. Wood and Smith, p. 80.
29. Wood and Smith, p. 12.
30. Michael F. Hauben, "The Netizens and Community Networks," *CMC Magazine,* February 1997. Available at www.december.com/cmc/mag/1997/feb/hauben.html. We have substituted the term *loafers* for the term *surfers,* which was originally used in this 1997 article.
31. Wood and Smith, p. 11.
32. Duarte and Snyder, pp. 44–45, 71.
33. Deborah Jude-York, Lauren D. Davis, and Susan L. Wise, *Virtual Teaming: Breaking the Boundaries of Time and Place* (Menlo Park, CA: Crisp Learning, 2000), p. 50.
34. Wikipedia, "Digital Divide," available at http://wiki.media-culture.org.au/index.php/DigitalDivide. Major revisions by Adam Margerison, October 28, 2005.
35. Crispin Thurlow, Laura Lengel, and Alice Tomic, *Computer Media Communication: Social Interaction and the Internet* (London: Sage, 2004), pp. 216–217.
36. Eszter Hargittal, "Linked in with . . . ." *The Chronicle of Higher Education,* May 2, 2008, p. A13.
37. Cynthia Lanius, "Girls and Technology," available at http://math.rice.edu/~lanius/pres/cwac99.html, April 24, 1999.
38. "'Digital Divide' Widening at Lower Income Levels." Available at www.clickz.com/stats/sectors/geographics/article.php/5911_569351. Retrieved May 12, 2008.
39. John B. Horrigan, "A Typology of Information and Communication Technology Users," *Pew/Internet and American Life Project,* May 2007, p. vi.
40. Ben Feller, "Digital Divide Still Separates White and Minority Students," *USA Today/Associated Press,* www.usatoday.com/tech/news/2006-09-05-digital-divide_x.htm. Retrieved May 12, 2008.
41. Hargittal.
42. "Digital Divide Widening."
43. Thurlow et al., p. 83.
44. Thurlow et al, p. 83. Also see Bridges.org, "Spanning the Digital Divide: Understanding and Tackling the Issues," available at http://bridges.org/spanning/summary.html, March 28, 2003.

Glossary

abdicrat A group member whose need for control is not met; an abdicrat is submissive and avoids responsibility.

abstract word A word that refers to an idea or concept that cannot be perceived by your five senses.

accent The sound of one language imposed on another language.

Accommodation Conflict Style An approach to conflict in which a person gives in to other group members, even at the expense of his or her own goals.

achievement norm A norm that determines the quality and quantity of work expected from group members.

action item An item in the written minutes of a meeting that identifies the member responsible for an assigned task.

***ad hoc* committee** A committee that is formed for a specific purpose and disbands once it has completed its assignment or task.

***ad hominem* attack** The fallacy of making an irrelevant attack against a person's character rather than a substantive response to an issue or argument.

adjourning stage The group development phase in which a group has achieved its common goal and begins to disengage or disband.

A-E-I-O-U Model A conflict resolution model with five steps: *A*ssume that other members mean well; *E*xpress your feelings; *I*dentify your goal; clarify expected *O*utcomes; and achieve mutual *U*nderstanding.

affection need The need to express and receive warmth or to be liked.

affective conflict A type of conflict that reflects the emotions stirred by interpersonal disagreements, differences in personalities and communication styles, and conflicting core values and beliefs.

agenda An outline of the items to be discussed and the tasks to be accomplished at a meeting.

agreeableness trait A Big Five Personality Theory trait that describes a cooperative, friendly, flexible, trusting, and tolerant personality.

aggressiveness Critical, insensitive, combative, or abusive behavior that is motivated by self-interest at the expense of others.

aggressor A group member who puts down other members to get what she or he wants (a self-centered role).

analysis paralysis A situation in which group members become so fixated on seeking more information and on analyzing an issue or problem that they are reluctant or unable to make a decision.

analytical listening A type of listening that focuses on evaluating and forming opinions about a message.

antecedent phase The first phase of new member socialization in which the newcomer's beliefs and attitudes, culture, traits, and prior experiences are identified.

anticipatory phase The second phase of new member socialization in which group members determine if a newcomer meets the group's expectations in terms of characteristics and motives.

apathy The indifference that occurs when members do not consider the group or its goal to be important, interesting, or inspiring.

appeal to authority The fallacy of using the opinions of a supposed expert when in fact the person has no particular expertise in the area under consideration.

appeal to popularity The fallacy of claiming that an action or belief is acceptable because many people do it or believe it.

appeal to tradition The fallacy of claiming that people should continue a certain course of action because that is the way it has always been done.

appreciative listening A type of listening that focuses on valuing or enjoying how an idea, opinion, or act is expressed.

arbitration A conflict resolution method that involves a third party who, after considering all sides in a dispute, decides how to resolve the conflict.

argument A claim supported by evidence and reasons for accepting it.

argumentation The use of critical thinking to advocate a position, examine competing ideas, and influence others.

argumentativeness The willingness to argue with others and take public positions on controversial issues.

assertiveness Speaking up and acting in your own best interests without denying the rights and interests of others.

assessment A mechanism for monitoring group progress and determining whether a group has achieved its goals.

assimilation phase The fourth phase of new member socialization in which a newcomer becomes fully integrated into the group and works toward the common group goal.

asynchronous communication Electronic communication that does not occur simultaneously or in real time; communication that is linear and not interactive.

Attribution Theory A theory that claims we make judgments about people's motives and characteristics that go beyond what we see and hear.

audioconference A voice-only communication medium that usually takes one of two forms: a teleconference or a computer-based voice link.

authority rule A situation in which a leader or an authority outside a group makes final decisions for the group.

autocrat A group member whose need for control is not met; an autocrat tries to dominate and control the group.

autocratic leader A leader who uses power and authority to strictly control the direction and outcome of group work.

avoidance conflict style A passive and nonconfrontational approach to conflict.

avoidant decision maker A person who feels uncomfortable and shuns making decisions.

backing The component of the Toulmin Model of Argument that provides support for an argument's warrant.

belongingness need The need for friendship and love within Maslow's Hierarchy of Needs.

bias A source of evidence that is one-sided, self-serving, unreasonable, or subjectively unfair.

Big Five Personality Traits A theory that describes five factors (extraversion, agreeableness, conscientiousness, emotional stability, and openness to experience) that, taken together, describe a personality.

blocker A group member who stands in the way of progress and uses delaying tactics to derail an idea or proposal (a self-centered role).

blog A website on which text, images, Web links, and other files are posted on a regular basis by an individual or organized group.

brainstorming A technique that encourages group members to generate as many ideas as possible in a nonevaluative atmosphere.

bulletin board An asynchronous, text-based communication technology in which group members read one another's messages and that can be organized in a threaded discussion.

bypassing A form of miscommunication that occurs when people have different meanings for the same words or phrases and miss each other with their meanings.

caring A major factor in determining credibility that relies on listeners' perceptions of a speaker as willing and able to demonstrate understanding, concern, and empathy for others.

certainty Behavior that may contribute to a defensive communication climate in which members act as though only their ideas and opinions are absolutely correct and therefore refuse to consider or support other members' ideas and opinions.

chair or **chairperson** A person who has been appointed or elected to conduct a group meeting.

channel The media (hearing, seeing, touching, smelling, and/or tasting) through which group members share messages.

Chaos Theory A theory that claims that although certain behaviors in natural systems are not predictable, there is a pattern to their randomness.

character A major factor in determining credibility based on listeners' perceptions of a speaker as trustworthy and honest.

charismatic power A type of personal power that relies on a leader's character, competence, and vitality.

civic group A group dedicated to worthy causes that help people within the group.

claim The component of the Toulmin Model of Argument that states the proposition or conclusion of an argument.

claim of conjecture An argument suggesting that something will or will not happen.

claim of fact An argument stating that something is true or false or that something did or did not occur.

claim of policy An argument advocating a specific course of action.

claim of value An argument evaluating whether something is good or bad, right or wrong, worthwhile or worthless.

clarifier-summarizer A group member who explains ideas, reduces confusion, and sums up group progress and conclusions (a task role).

climate The group atmosphere, characterized by the degree to which members feel comfortable interacting.

clown A group member who injects inappropriate humor into the discussion and seems more interested in goofing off than in working (a self-centered role).

CMC An acronym for computer-mediated communication.

co-culture A group of people who coexist within the mainstream society, yet remain connected to one another through their cultural heritage.

codeswitching The ability to change from the language or dialect of your own culture and adopt the language or dialect of another cultural group.

coercive power A type of position power with the ability or authority to pressure or punish group members if they do not follow orders and directions.

cognitive restructuring A technique for reducing communication apprehension that analyzes worrisome, irrational, and nonproductive assumptions about speaking to and with others (cognitions) and seeks to modify those thoughts (restructuring).

cohesion The mutual attraction that holds the members of a group together.

Collaboration Conflict Style An approach to conflict emphasizing the search for solutions that satisfy all group members and that also achieve the group's common goal.

collaborative presentation technology Technology that enhances interactive group presentations by allowing members to project ideas or graphics onto a screen, wall, or whiteboard.

collectivism A cultural value or belief in interdependence that places greater emphasis on the views, needs, and goals of the group than on the views, needs, and goals of individuals.

committee A group given a specific assignment by a larger group or by a person in a position of authority.

common ground An identifiable belief, value, experience, or point of view shared by all group members.

communication apprehension An individual's level of fear or anxiety associated with either real or anticipated communication with another person or persons.

competence A major factor in determining credibility based on listeners' perceptions about a speaker's expertise and abilities.

Competition Conflict Style An approach to conflict that is focused on achieving a person's own goals rather than the group's goals, even if this upsets the group and its members.

completer/finisher A group member who emphasizes schedules, deadlines, and task completion and searches for errors.

Complexity Theory A theory that seeks patterns in complex systems by examining states of order, complexity, and chaos.

comprehensive listening A type of listening that focuses on accurately understanding the meaning of spoken and nonverbal messages.

Compromise Conflict Style An approach to conflict that involves the concession of some goals in order to achieve others.

compromiser A group member who helps minimize differences among group members and helps the group reach consensus (a maintenance role).

concrete word A word that refers to something that can be perceived by the senses.

confessor A group member who inappropriately reveals personal feelings and problems and constantly seeks emotional support rather than promoting the group's goal (a self-centered role).

conflict The disagreement and disharmony that occurs in groups when differences regarding group goals, member ideas, behavior, and roles, or group procedures and norms.

conflict ↔ cohesion A group dialectic in which the value of constructive conflict is balanced with the need for unity and cohesiveness.

conforming ↔ nonconforming A group dialectic in which a commitment to group norms and standards is balanced with a willingness to accept differences and change.

conformity The choice of behavior that is socially acceptable and favored by a majority of group members.

connotation The personal feelings connected to the meaning of a word.

conscientiousness trait A Big Five Personality Theory trait that describes a self-disciplined, organized, responsible, achievement-oriented personality.

consensus A situation in which all group members accept and are willing to support a group decision.

constructive conflict An approach to disagreement in which group members express differences in a way that values everyone's contributions and promotes the group's goal.

constructive nonconformity The act of resisting conformity to group norms and expectations while still working to achieve the group's goal.

context The physical and psychological environment in which group communication takes place.

Contingency Model of Leadership Effectiveness A leadership theory claiming that effective leadership depends upon an ideal match between the leader's style and the group's work situation.

control Member behavior that may contribute to a defensive communication climate by imposing personal ideas, preferences, and solutions on others.

control need The need to feel competent, confident, and free to make your own choices.

controlling feedback Positive or negative feedback used to influence member behavior by telling them what to do.

cooperative argumentation A process of reasoned interaction intended to help members make the best assessments or decisions in a given situation.

coordinator-chairperson A group member who clarifies group goals, helps allocate roles and duties, and articulates group conclusions (a task role).

creativity The nonjudgmental process and outcome of searching for, separating, and connecting thoughts to form new ideas.

credibility The extent to which others believe you and your messages.

critical thinking The kind of thinking used when analyzing something read, seen, or heard in order to arrive at a justified conclusion or decision.

culture The learned set of shared expectations about beliefs, values, and norms that affect the behaviors of a relatively large group of people.

decision making The act of reaching a conclusion; a group selects an option from among possible alternatives.

Decreasing Options Technique (DOT) A procedure for reducing and refining a large number of ideas or suggestions into more manageable categories.

defensive climate A communication situation that triggers group members' instincts to protect themselves when physically or verbally attacked by someone.

definition A statement that clarifies the meaning of a word, phrase, or concept.

democratic leader A leader who practices social equality and shares the decision-making process with group members.

democratic member A group member whose need for control is met and who has no problems dealing with power in groups.

demographic traits An audience trait such as age, gender, race, ethnicity, religion, and marital status.

denotation The objective, dictionary-based meaning of a word.

dependent decision maker A person who seeks the advice and opinions of others before making a decision.

description 1. Member behavior that contributes to a supportive communication climate by making understanding and helpful statements and using *I* and *we* language. 2. A type of evidence that creates a mental image of a person, event, place, or object.

deserter A group member who seems bored or annoyed with the discussion and stops contributing (a self-centered role).

designated leader A leader selected by a group or an outside authority.

destructive conflict Disagreement expressed through behaviors that create hostility and prevent achievement of the group's goal.

destructive nonconformity Resistance to conforming to group norms and expectations without regard for the best interests of the group and its goal.

dialect The distinct regional and cultural variations in vocabulary, pronunciation, syntax, and style that distinguish speakers from different ethnic groups, geographic areas, and social classes.

dialectics Two seemingly opposing ideas or tensions in a relationship or group that can be resolved with a both/and approach.

digital divide Inequalities in access to, distribution of, and use of information technology among different groups or populations.

discrimination Acting out and expressing prejudice by excluding groups of people from the opportunities and rights granted to others.

discriminative listening The ability to distinguish auditory and/or visual stimuli.

documentation The practice of citing sources of evidence.

dominator A group member who tries to assert authority and prevents others from participating (a self-centered role).

early leaver A person who disrupts a meeting or annoys others by leaving before a group meeting is over.

Electronic Meeting System (EMS) A synchronous meeting technology that combines specialized software and hardware to allow group members to perform group tasks such as brainstorming, problem solving, and decision making,

electronic whiteboard A writing board fully linked to a computer system that allows information written on the board to be stored, printed, and displayed.

email A worldwide, text-based, asynchronous technology that allows group members to interact from great distances.

emergent leader A person who gradually achieves leadership status by interacting with group members and contributing to the achievement of the group's common goal.

emoticon Typographical characters used to express emotion when communicating via computer.

emotional intelligence The capacity for recognizing your own feelings and those of others, for motivating yourself, and for managing emotions in yourself and in various interpersonal relationships.

emotional stability trait A Big Five Personality Theory trait that, when positive, depicts a calm, poised, and secure personality.

empathic listening A type of listening that focuses on understanding a person's feelings, motives, and situation.

empathy Member behavior that contributes to a supportive communication climate by expressing acceptance, caring, and understanding of others and their feelings.

encounter phase The third phase of new member socialization in which a newcomer tries to fit in and adjust to the group.

encourager-supporter A group member who praises and agrees with others, provides recognition, and listens empathically (a maintenance role).

energizer A group member who motivates others and helps create enthusiasm for the task (a task role).

engaged ↔ disengaged A group dialectic in which members' loyalty and labor are balanced with the group's need for rest and renewal.

equality Member behaviors that contribute to a supportive communication climate by respecting everyone's ability to make useful contributions.

esteem need The need for respect and admiration within Maslow's Hierarchy of Needs.

ethics An understanding of whether group members' communication behaviors meet agreed-upon standards of right and wrong.

ethnocentrism A mistaken belief that your culture is a superior culture with special rights and privileges that are or should be denied to others.

ethos A Greek word meaning character that has evolved into the concept of credibility.

evaluation Member behavior that may contribute to a defensive communication climate by making judgmental and disparaging statements about other group members.

evaluator-critic A group member who assesses ideas and diagnoses problems (a task role).

evidence The component of the Toulmin Model of Argument that provides facts, statistics, opinions, examples, or other material to support a claim.

example A type of evidence that refers to a specific case or instance.

exit phase The final phase of new member socialization in which a newcomer may leave an established group.

Expectancy-Value Theory A theory that motivation results from a combination of individual needs and the value of the goals available in the environment.

expert power A type of personal power with the ability to motivate and persuade others by demonstrating special expertise or knowledge.

explicit norm A norm that is written or stated verbally.

extemporaneous speaking A form of presentation delivery in which the speaker has done prior preparation but uses limited notes.

extrinsic rewards Rewards that come from the external environment, such as money, benefits, and job perks.

extraversion trait A Big Five Personality Theory trait that describes an outgoing, talkative, sociable, assertive, and active person.

extrovert A Myers-Briggs personality type who is outgoing, usually talks more than others, and is often enthusiastic and animated during a discussion.

face The positive image that a person tries to create or preserve that is also appropriate to a particular culture.

fact A verifiable observation, experience, or event; something that is known to be true.

fallacy An argument based on false or invalid reasoning.

false consensus A situation in which members succumb to group pressure and accept a decision that they do not like or support.

faulty analogy The fallacy of claiming that two things are similar when they actually differ with regard to relevant characteristics.

faulty cause The fallacy of identifying the cause of an event before ruling out other possible causes.

feedback The verbal or nonverbal response or reaction to a message.

feeler A Myers-Briggs personality type who wants everyone to get along and who will spend time with other group members to achieve harmony.

feminine society A culture in which gender roles overlap: Both men and women are supposed to be modest, tender, and concerned with the quality of life.

5M Model of Leadership Effectiveness An approach to leadership that divides leadership tasks into five interdependent functions: (1) *M*odeling leadership behavior, (2) *M*otivating members, (3) *M*anaging the group process, (4) *M*aking decisions, and (5) *M*entoring members.

forming stage The group development phase in which member and group goals are explored and interpersonal relationships are tested.

forum A meeting in which audience members express their concerns and ask questions, often to public officials and experts.

4Rs method A method of analyzing conflict before selecting a conflict resolution method by examining (1) *r*easons, (2) *r*eactions, (3) *r*esults, and (4) *r*esolutions.

FTF An acronym for face-to-face communication.

Functional Leadership Theory An approach to leadership that claims that any capable group member can assume leadership functions when necessary.

functional perspective A problem-solving theory claiming that a set of preparation, competence, and critical thinking/communication functions can explain and predict how well a group will solve problems.

Fundamental Interpersonal Relationship Orientation (FIRO) William Schutz's theory that examines the extent to which the satisfaction of inclusion, control, and affection needs affects why people join groups and how well group members communicate and behave toward one another.

gatekeeper A group member who monitors participation and tries to regulate the flow of communication in a discussion (a maintenance role).

goal The purpose or objective toward which a group's efforts are directed.

Goal Theory A theory that examines the value of and techniques for setting group goals and the methods needed to accomplish those goals.

Golden Listening Rule The principle that you should listen to others as you would have them listen to you.

governance group A group that makes public policy decisions in public settings such as a state legislature, city or county council, or the governing board of a public agency or educational institution.

group communication The interaction of three or more interdependent members working to achieve a common goal.

group dialectics The contradictory tensions groups experience as they work toward a common goal.

group motivation The inspiration, incentives, or reasons that move group members to work together in order to achieve a common goal.

group polarization A tendency for group members (and especially virtual groups in which there are no visible nonverbal cues) to express more extreme opinions and take more extreme actions.

groupthink The deterioration of group effectiveness and moral judgment that can result from in-group pressure.

groupware Computer-mediated methods and tools that are designed to support group collaboration.

harmonizer A group member who helps resolve conflicts and promotes teamwork (a maintenance role).

hasty generalization The fallacy of using too few examples or experiences to support a conclusion.

heterogeneous group A group composed of members who are different from one another.

hidden agenda An individual member's private motives and goals that differ from a group's common goal.

high-context culture A culture in which very little meaning is expressed through words; gestures, silence, facial expression, and relationships among communicators are more reliable indicators of meaning.

high power distance A cultural norm of accepting major differences in power; assuming that all people are *not* created equal.

high uncertainty avoidance A cultural characteristic of members who feel a need for predictability and are threatened by uncertain or unknown situations.

homogeneous group A group composed of members who are all the same or very similar to one another.

homogeneous ↔ heterogeneous A group dialectic in which member similarities are balanced with member differences in skills, roles, personal characteristics, and cultural perspectives.

hyperpersonal communication An increase in confidence and decrease in communication apprehension that occur in computer-mediated rather than face-to-face communication.

illustration An extended or detailed example.

implementer-completer A group member who transforms ideas into action and develops action plans for members (a task role).

implicit norm A norm that is rarely discussed or openly communicated.

impromptu A form of presentation delivery in which a person speaks without prior preparation or practice.

inclusion need The need to be accepted and affiliated with a group; the need to belong or be involved.

individual attributes Distinctive features of particular group members, such as personality traits, job titles, status, special interests, relationships with other members, and length of membership.

individual goals ↔ group goals A group dialectic in which members' personal goals are balanced with the group's common goal.

individualism A cultural value or belief that the individual is important, that independence is worth pursuing, that personal achievement should be rewarded, and that individual uniqueness is an important value.

information giver A group member who provides and organizes relevant information (a task role).

information seeker A group member who asks for needed information, requests explanations and clarifications, and makes the group aware of information gaps (a task role).

informational feedback Feedback that provides a group with an assessment of its performance and the extent to which a goal is being achieved.

informational power A type of position power with the ability to control and transmit information and sources.

initiator A group member who proposes ideas and suggestions, provides direction for the group, and gets the group started (a task role).

innovator A group member who advances proposals, offers ideas, and provides insights on courses of action.

interaction Communication among group members who use verbal and nonverbal messages to generate meaning and establish relationships.

interaction norm A norm that determines how group members communicate with one another.

intercultural dimension An aspect of a culture that can be measured relative to other cultures.

interdependence The extent to which group members are affected and influenced by the actions of other members.

Internet Addiction Disorder (IAD) A maladaptive pattern of Internet use that results in clinically significant impairment or distress.

interpersonal space The psychological space surrounding each person that expands and contracts in different contexts.

interrupter A person who speaks out during a meeting while other members are still talking.

intimate distance Interpersonal space ranging from zero to eighteen inches, typically reserved for close friends, family, and lovers.

intrinsic rewards Rewards that are satisfying and energizing in themselves.

introvert A Myers-Briggs personality type who needs time to think before speaking and who may prefer to work alone rather than in a group.

intuitive A Myers-Briggs personality type who likes to make connections and formulate big ideas but who may become bored with details.

intuitive decision maker A person who makes decisions based on instincts and feelings.

jargon The specialized or technical language of a profession.

judger A Myers-Briggs personality type who is highly structured and likes to plan ahead.

kinesics The study of body movement and physical expression.

laissez-faire leader A leader who lets the group take charge of all decisions and actions.

latecomer A group member who disrupts a meeting by arriving late.

leader–member relations A situational leadership factor that assesses how well a leader gets along with group members.

leadership The ability to make strategic decisions and use communication to mobilize a group toward achieving a common goal.

leadership ↔ followership A group dialectic in which effective and ethical leadership is balanced with loyal and responsible followership.

learning group A group that helps its members acquire knowledge and develop skills by sharing information and experience.

legitimate power A type of position power that resides in a job or position.

listening The ability to understand, analyze, respect, and appropriately respond to spoken and/or nonverbal messages.

listserv An email option that delivers messages to everyone in a group.

logistics The strategic planning, arranging, and use of people, facilities, time, and materials.

loudmouth A person who talks so much that no one else gets a chance to speak during a group meeting.

low-context culture A culture in which meaning is expressed primarily through language; people from a low-context culture tend to speak more, speak louder, and speak more rapidly than people from a high-context culture.

low power distance A cultural perspective in which power distinctions are minimized.

low uncertainty avoidance A cultural characteristic of members who accept change, tolerate nonconformity, take risks, and view rules and regulations as restricting and counterproductive.

maintenance role A positive role that affects how group members get along with one another while pursuing a common goal.

majority vote The results of a vote in which more than half the members vote in favor of a proposal.

masculine society A culture in which men are supposed to be assertive, tough, and focused on material success, whereas women are supposed to be more modest, tender, and concerned with the quality of life.

Maslow's Hierarchy of Needs A specific sequence of needs (physiological, safety, belongingness, esteem, and self-actualization) that can explain why people are attracted to particular groups.

Media Richness Theory A theory that contends that communication will be more successful when more communication channels are used.

Media Synchronicity Theory A theory that extends Media Richness Theory by matching media capabilities to the fundamental communication processes required to perform a group task.

mediation A facilitated negotiation that employs the services of an impartial third party for the purpose of guiding, coaching, and encouraging disputants to a successful resolution and an agreement.

meeting A scheduled gathering of group members for a structured discussion guided by a designated chairperson.

member Any individual whom other members recognize as belonging to the group.

member readiness The extent to which a member is willing and able to contribute to achieving the group's goal.

message An idea, information, opinion, and/or feeling that generates meaning.

method A strategy, guideline, procedure, or technique for dealing with the issues and problems that arise in groups.

minutes The written record of a group's discussion and activities during a meeting.

monitor/evaluator A group member who analyzes problems, monitors progress, assesses others' contributions, and explores options.

Monochronic Time (M Time) An approach to time that favors clear deadlines and the scheduling of one thing at a time.

motivators Extrinsic and intrinsic factors, such as fulfillment of belongingness, esteem, and self-actualization needs, that encourage and inspire group members to work together to achieve a common goal.

multimedia Technology that enables you to combine words, charts, graphics, sounds, and animation in a single presentation.

Muted Group Theory A theory that claims that power imbalances inhibit some female and minority group members from expressing themselves assertively and impede their ability to participate effectively in group work.

Myers-Briggs Type Indicator (MBTI) A widely used inventory that identifies specific personality types based on the ways in which people perceive the world around them and make judgments.

negotiation A process of bargaining for the purpose of settling differences or reaching solutions.

netlingo Language forms common to communication via the Internet, such as abbreviations, acronyms, and less use of punctuation.

netspeak Typographical strategies common to communication via the Internet that are used to achieve a more sociable and interactive style.

neutrality Member behavior that may contribute to a defensive communication climate when members appear withdrawn, detached, and indifferent.

noise Anything that interferes with or inhibits communication.

Nominal Group Technique (NGT) A procedure in which members write and report suggested ideas, after which discussion and multiple votes are used to decide the priority or value of the listed suggestions.

nonconformity A member's behavior that does not meet the norms or expectations of the group.

nonparticpant A person who never or rarely contributes during a group meeting.

nonverbal communication The behavioral elements of messages other than the actual words spoken.

nonverbal immediacy Behaviors that communicate greater physical closeness to or liking of others.

norm An expectation held by group members concerning what kinds of behavior or opinions are acceptable or unacceptable.

norming stage The group development stage in which members resolve conflicts and work as a cohesive team to develop methods for achieving the group's goal.

observer-interpreter A group member who monitors other members' feelings and behaviors and who paraphrases others' ideas, opinions, and emotions (a maintenance role).

offensive language Terminology that demeans, inappropriately excludes, or stereotypes people.

openness to experience trait A Big Five Personality Theory trait that describes an imaginative, curious, broadminded, and artistically sensitive personality.

open system ↔ closed system A group dialectic in which external support and recognition are balanced with internal group solidarity and rewards.

opinion A personal conclusion regarding the meaning or implications of facts.

opinion giver A group member who states personal beliefs and interpretations and offers analysis and arguments (a task role).

opinion seeker A group member who asks for others' opinions (a task role).

optimal group experience An experience in which all group members are caught up in the group's work and are performing at a high level of achievement.

oral citation A comment that includes enough information to allow others to find the original source of any evidence.

overpersonal member A group member whose affection needs are not met and who is too talkative and overly personal.

oversocial member A group member whose inclusion needs are not met and who seeks attention as a way of compensating for feelings of inadequacy.

panel discussion A group discussion in which participants interact with one another on a common topic for the benefit of an audience.

paraphrasing A form of feedback that uses different words to restate what a person has said as a way of indicating that the listener has understood what the speaker means and feels.

parliamentary procedure A systematic method and set of formal rules used to determine the will of the majority through fair and orderly discussion and debate.

passive-aggressive Uncooperative and obstructive behavior that appears to be cooperative.

passivity Nonassertive behavior characterized by a lack of confidence and a reluctance to communicate.

perceiver A Myers-Briggs personality type who is less rigid about deadlines and time constraints and who is flexible and willing to try new options.

performing stage The group development stage in which group members focus their energy on doing the work needed to achieve group goals.

personal distance Interpersonal space ranging from eighteen inches to four feet, typically used for friends and acquaintances.

personal member A group member whose affection needs are met and who is comfortable interacting with group members.

personal power Power that stems from a member's individual characteristics.

persuasive power A type of personal power that relies on effective communication skills.

physiological need The most fundamental need for the basics of survival, such as water, food, and shelter, in Maslow's Hierarchy of Needs.

Polychronic Time (P Time) An approach to time that allows many things to be done at once; schedules are flexible, and deadlines may be missed.

position power Power that depends on a member's job or status within an organization.

Post-Meeting Reaction (PMR) Form A questionnaire designed to assess the success of a meeting by collecting written reactions from participants.

power The ability or authority to influence and motivate others.

power distance A cultural dimension that reflects the physical and psychological distance between those of different status.

prejudices A negative attitude about other people that is based on faulty and inflexible stereotypes.

presentation A relatively uninterrupted talk or speech to a group of people.

presentation aid Supplementary audio and/or visual material used in a discussion or oral presentation.

presentation purpose What a speaker wants listeners to know, think, believe, or do as a result of a presentation.

presentation software Computer programs used to design presentation slides.

primary group A group of family members or friends who provide affection, support, and a sense of belonging.

primary tension The social unease and inhibitions experienced by group members during the getting-acquainted phase of a group's development.

principled negotiation A process of resolving conflict that involves respecting people, focusing on interests, generating solutions for mutual gain, and using fair criteria.

problem orientation Member behavior that contributes to a supportive communication climate by focusing on solving a problem collaboratively rather than imposing a personal preference.

problem solving A complex process in which groups analyze a problem and develop a plan for solving it or reducing the harmful effects of the problem.

procedural conflict A disagreement over what method or process a group should follow to accomplish its goal.

procedural norm A norm that dictates how a group will operate.

procedural technician A group member who assists with preparations for meetings, including suggesting agenda items, making room arrangements, and providing needed materials and equipment (a task role).

provisionalism Member behavior that contributes to a supportive communication climate by being open-minded and accepting, offering tentative suggestions, and avoiding unyielding claims.

proxemics The study of how people perceive and use personal space and distance.

public distance Interpersonal space beyond eight feet, typically reserved for large audiences.

public group A group that discusses issues or makes presentations in front of or for the benefit of a public audience or key decision makers.

punishment A penalty or negative consequences for a group or group member.

qualifier The component of the Toulmin Model of Argument that states the degree to which a claim is thought to be true.

question of conjecture A decision-making question that asks whether something will or will not happen.

question of fact A decision-making question that asks whether something is true or false, or whether something did or did not occur.

question of policy A decision-making question that asks whether and how a specific course of action should be taken to solve a problem.

question of value A decision-making question that asks the group to decide whether something is good or bad, right or wrong, or worthwhile or worthless.

rational decision maker A person who carefully weighs information and options before making a decision.

recognition seeker A group member who boasts about her or his accomplishments and tries to become the group's center of attention (a self-centered role).

recorder-secretary A group member who keeps and provides accurate written records of a group's major ideas, suggestions, and decisions (a task role).

referent power A type of personal power held by a person who is admired and respected.

reflective thinking process A set of practical steps that a rational person should follow when solving a problem.

refutation The process of proving that an argument is false and/or lacks sufficient support.

Relational Dialectics Theory A theory that claims that relationships are characterized by ongoing, dialectic tensions between the multiple contradictions, complexities, and changes in human experiences.

relationship-motivated leader A leader who tends to establish close personal relations with group members.

religious literacy The ability to understand and use the religious terms, symbols, images, beliefs, practices, scripture, heroes, themes, and stories that are employed within a culture.

reprimand A form of feedback that identifies and discusses a person's work-related problems or deficiencies.

research A systematic search or investigation designed to find useful and appropriate evidence.

reservation The component of the Toulmin Model of Argument that recognizes the conditions under which a claim would not necessarily be true.

resource investigator A group member who explores opportunities, makes contacts, shares external information, and negotiates with outsiders.

reward Something that is given or received for excellent service, outstanding achievement, or worthy behavior.

reward power A type of position power that comes from the authority to give group members something that they value.

role A group member's unique set of skills or behavioral patterns that serve specific functions within the group.

safety need The need for security and protection in Maslow's Hierarchy of Needs.

satisfiers Actions or compensations that meet group members' basic deficiency needs—money for food and shelter, job security, insurance—but do not necessarily motivate members to work harder or better.

secondary tension The frustrations and personality conflicts experienced by group members as they compete with one another for acceptance and achievement.

self-actualization need The need to fulfill one's own human potential; the personal reward of becoming the best that is possible.

self-centered role A negative role in which individual needs are put ahead of the group's goal and other members' needs.

self-help group A group that offers support and encouragement to members who want or need help with personal problems.

sense of choice The shared feeling that the group has the power and ability to make decisions about how to organize and do its job.

sense of competence The shared feeling that the group is doing good, high-quality work.

sense of meaningfulness The shared feeling that the group is pursuing a worthy task.

sense of progress The shared feeling that the group is accomplishing something.

sensor A Myers-Briggs personality type who focuses on details and prefers to concentrate on one task at a time.

service group A group dedicated to worthy causes that help people outside the group.

shaper A group member who seeks patterns in the group's work and pushes the group toward agreement and decisions.

short-term memory The content a person remembers immediately after listening to a series of numbers, words, sentences, or paragraphs.

single question format A problem-solving procedure that focuses group analysis on answering a single agreed-upon question in order to arrive at a solution.

Situational Leadership Model Hersey and Blanchard's approach to leadership that links leadership style to the readiness of group members to achieve a common goal.

Situational Leadership Theory An approach to leadership that helps leaders improve their skills by carefully analyzing their attitudes, their group, and the circumstances in which they must lead.

social dimension A group's focus on the interpersonal relationships among group members.

social distance Interpersonal space ranging from four to eight feet, typically reserved for new acquaintances and strangers.

social group A group in which members share common interests in a friendly setting or participate in common leisure activities.

social member A person whose inclusion needs are met and who enjoys working with other people but is comfortable working alone.

solution criteria The standards that a group establishes for the ideal resolution of a problem to meet.

special interest pleader A group member who tries to influence others to support nongroup interests (a self-centered role).

specialist A group member who is single-minded, dedicated, and provides unique expertise and skills.

spontaneity Member behavior that contributes to a supportive communication climate by being straightforward, appreciative, direct, open, encouraging, and honest.

spontaneous decision maker A person who is impulsive and makes quick decisions on the spur of the moment.

standard agenda A procedure that guides a group through problem solving by using the following steps: task clarification, problem identification, fact finding, solution criteria, solution suggestions, solution evaluation and selection, and solution implementation.

standing committee A committee that remains active in order to accomplish an ongoing task.

statistics Information presented in a numerical form.

status norm A norm that identifies levels of influence among group members.

stereotype A generalization about a group of people that oversimplifies their characteristics and results in erroneous judgment about the entire group of people.

storming stage The group development stage in which members compete with one another to determine individual status and to establish group goals.

strategy Member behavior that may contribute to a defensive communication climate by manipulating and controlling others as well as furthering the goals of hidden agendas.

structure ↔ spontaneity A group dialectic in which the need for structured procedures is balanced with the need for innovative and creative thinking.

Styles Leadership Theory An approach to leadership that identifies specific behaviors or styles that can be learned; these can be put into three categories: autocratic, democratic, or laissez-faire leadership.

substantive conflict A disagreement over ideas, issues, decisions, actions, or goals.

superiority Member behavior that may contribute to a defensive communication climate by implying that you and your ideas and opinions are better than others.

supportive climate A communication context in which members feel free to share their opinions and feelings.

symposium A group presentation in which participants give short, uninterrupted speeches on different aspects of a topic for the benefit of an audience.

synchronous communication Communication that occurs simultaneously and in real time, either face to face or electronically.

synergy The cooperative interaction of several factors that results in a combined effect that is greater than the sum of individual contributions.

system A collection of interacting, interdependent elements working together to form a complex whole that adapts to a changing environment.

Systems Theory A group of theories that examine how interdependent factors affect one another.

task dimension A group's focus on achieving its goal.

task dimension ↔ social dimension A group dialectic in which the responsibility and motivation to complete tasks are balanced with promoting relationships among members.

task force A type of committee appointed to gather information and make recommendations regarding a specific issue or problem.

task-motivated leader A leader whose major satisfaction comes from successfully completing the group task rather than from promoting positive interpersonal relationships with group members.

task role A positive role that affects a group's ability to do the work needed to achieve its goals.

task structure A situational leadership factor that assesses how a group must organize or plan a specific task.

team presentation A coordinated presentation by a group of speakers who are trying to influence an audience of decision makers.

Team-Role Theory R. Meredith Belbin's theory that claims group members will seek out and perform roles that are compatible with their personal characteristics and skills.

team talk Anne Donnellon's term to describe the nature of the language that group members use as they work together.

teamworker-follower A group member who provides personal support, resolves conflict, and serves as an in-group diplomat (a maintenance role).

telepresence A specially constructed studio in which a conference table in one location is identical to one in another location so that members in two locations appear to be seated around the same table during a videoconference.

tension releaser A group member who alleviates tension with friendly humor and tries to relax other group members (a maintenance role).

territoriality The sense of personal ownership attached to a particular space.

textconference A conference in which group members use their computer keyboards to communicate and collaborate with one another.

theory A principle that tries to explain or predict events and behavior.

thinker A Myers-Briggs personality type who takes pride in thinking objectively and making difficult decisions.

third-party intervention The use of an impartial outsider to analyze and resolve conflict.

thought speed The speed (in words per minute) at which most people can think compared to the slower speed at which most people speak.

threaded discussion A series of email messages about a specific issue posted on an electronic bulletin board.

tool A resource or skill that helps a group carry out or achieve its common goal.

Toulmin Model of Argument A model developed by Stephen Toulmin that represents the structure of an argument.

Trait Leadership Theory An approach to leadership that tries to identify common characteristics and behaviors of effective leaders.

Transformational Leadership Theory An approach to leadership that examines the ways in which leaders inspire followers to move beyond self-interest and become a unified group.

Tuckman's Group Development Stages A model of group development that identifies five stages in the life cycle of groups—forming, storming, norming, performing, and adjourning.

two-thirds vote The results of a vote in which at least twice as many group members vote in favor of a proposal as oppose it.

uncertainty avoidance A cultural dimension that reflects the extent to which people within a culture are uncomfortable in unstructured, unclear, or unpredictable situations.

underpersonal member A group member whose affection needs are not met and who has only superficial relationships with other group members.

undersocial member A group member whose inclusion needs are not met and who may withdraw from the group or feel unworthy.

valid Accurate, reasonable, and justifiable; refers to evidence that is considered reliable.

verbal communication The use of words and language to generate meaning.

videoconference A form of communication that combines audio and video media to provide both voice communication and video images.

virtual group A group that relies on technology to communicate synchronously and/or asynchronously, often across time, distance, and organizational boundaries.

visualization A technique for reducing communication apprehension that encourages positive thinking about communicating in groups by relaxing and imagining yourself succeeding.

warrant The component of the Toulmin Model of Argument that provides the justification for how the evidence supports a particular claim.

whisperer A person who carries on confidential conversations with another group member during a meeting.

Wiki A website that allows users to add and edit content.

word stress The degree of vocal prominence given to a syllable within a word or to a word within a phrase or sentence.

work group A group responsible for achieving specific tasks or performing routine duties on behalf of a company, organization, association, agency, or institution.

work team A group given full responsibility and resources for achieving a goal.

working memory The memory subsystem used when we try to understand information, remember it, or use it to solve a problem or communicate to someone.

Working Memory Theory A listening theory that claims that listening involves not just short-term memory but also engages your working memory.

Index

Page numbers followed by a *t* or *f* indicate a table or figure. Page numbers followed by a *w* indicate a page in the web chapter.

Credits

Chapter 1: p. 1: Darius Koehli/SuperStock; p. 2: Scott Boehm/Getty Images; p. 6: Richard Lord/The Image Works; p. 18: Bob Daemmrich/The Image Works. **Chapter 2:** p. 28: Ingram Publishing/SuperStock Royalty Free; p. 36: Greg Epperson/age fotostock/SuperStock; p. 41: Solus-Veer/Corbis. **Chapter 3:** p. 51: Jim West/The Image Works; p. 57: FogStock LLC/Index Open; p. 63: Reza Estakhrian/Riser/Getty Images **Chapter 4:** p. 76: Jeff Greenberg/PhotoEdit, Inc.; p. 89: Fujifotos/The Image Works; p. 96: © Jim West/The Image Works. **Chapter 5:** p. 107: Bob Daemmrich/PhotoEdit, Inc.; p. 114: Image Source Black/Alamy Royalty Free; p. 123: Purestock/SuperStock Royalty Free; p. 129: Charlie Schuck/wink/Jupiter Images. **Chapter 6:** p. 137: Paul Burns/Photodisc/Getty Images Royalty Free; p. 146: Sonda Dawes/The Image Works; p. 151: Monika Graff/The Image Works; p. 152: Steve Warmowski/The Image Works; p. 154: Jeff Greenberg/PhotoEdit, Inc. **Chapter 7:** p. 162: Juice Images/Corbis Royalty Free; p. 169: Jonathan Ross/Blend Images/Jupiter Images Royalty Free; p. 177: Masterfile. **Chapter 8:** p. 186: image 100/Corbis Royalty Free; p. 189: Bob Daemmrich/The Image Works. **Chapter 9:** p. 210: Golden Pixels/Index Open; p. 217: Mitch Wojnarowicz/The Image Works; p. 226: Steve Warmowski/The Image Works. **Chapter 10:** p. 235: Jeff Greenberg/PhotoEdit, Inc.; p. 246: Elizabeth Crews/The Image Works; p. 255: Blend Images/Alamy Royalty Free. **Chapter 11:** p. 267: David Bacon/The Image Works; p. 275: David Young-Wolff /Riser/Getty Images; p. 285: Richard A. Cooke/Corbis. **Chapter 12:** p. 292: Bill Bachman/Alamy; p. 304: CLOSE TO HOME ©1994 John McPherson/Dist by UNIVERSAL PRESS SYNDICATE. Reprinted with permission. All rights reserved. p. 306: Mitch Wojnarowicz/Amsterdam Recorder/The Image Works. **Chapter 13:** p. 313: Bob Daemmrich/The Image Works; p. 326: Syracuse Newspapers/Michelle Gabel/The Image Works. **Chapter 14:** p. 337: Comstock/SuperStock Royalty Free; p. 344: Jim West/The Image Works; p. 350: BananaStock/SuperStock Royalty Free. Web Chapter: p. 1: CORBIS ROYALTY FREE